# TAMMANY
## The Evolution of a
## Political Machine
## 1789–1865

A NEW YORK STATE STUDY

# TAMMANY

## The Evolution of a
## Political Machine
## 1789-1865

# JEROME MUSHKAT

SYRACUSE UNIVERSITY PRESS

**To Bobbie**

# FOREWORD

THE TAMMANY HALL of political mythology was a wild and disreputable political operation, which gained strength through exploitation. The organization contributed nothing to the science of governing American cities, but did provide lessons in venality, graft, and open dishonesty. Its one purpose was to marshal voters, march them off to the polls in well-disciplined ranks, and win elections. Once in power, spoils—the "loaves and fishes" of job-hungry hacks—absorbed the machine's total interest. By making Tammany the instrument for specific material gains, politicians debased the system of government into a never-ending scramble for office, with spoilsmongering as the only rationale for politicking.

Since Tammany has existed in one form or another since 1787, considerable evidence strengthens these assumptions. As early as 1809, the Federalist *New York Evening Post* charged Tammany with corruption in the erection of a memorial dedicated to American prisoners of war who had died during the Revolution. For the next three-quarters of a century, the scandalous behavior of such Tammanyites as Samuel Swartwout, who bilked the federal government out of $1,250,000, and William "Boss" Tweed, whose political machinations became legend, added credence to charges of corruption.

The machine's severest and most articulate critics emerged in the late 1880s, and made the Hall the symbolic whipping-boy for the nation's inability to create efficient municipal government. As the Progressive movement gained momentum, crusading newspapermen, muckrakers, and sincere political reformers used the term "Tammany Hall" as a code to denote a self-serving urban political machine.

Another line of attack against Tammany, particularly aimed at its close association with Irish Catholics, reflected a harsh and intolerant nationalism. During the latter two decades of the nineteenth century, Grover Cleveland and William Jennings Bryan each constructed national alliances of Southern and Western Democrats that had programs and styles heavily anti-Tammany. In the 1920s, misguided men, partly out of patriotism, partly out of partisanship, tied the Hall to a sinister plot designed to subvert traditional American democratic values. Hence, the presidential candidacy of Al Smith, an Irishman, a New Yorker, and a Tammanyite evoked fear and suspicion. To his detractors in both political parties—men such as William H. White, who in 1928 wrote *Al Smith's Tammany Hall*—the New Yorker's close association with Tammany made him unfit for high office. By far the deepest decline in Tammany's reputation occurred in the backlash of Judge Samuel Seabury's investigation of James J. Walker's administration and, subsequently, Fiorello H. La Guardia's rise to power.

Tammany's apologists tried to respond to these attacks but without much success. William Gover's *The Tammany Hall Democracy of the City of New York* (1875), Mrs. Euphemia Vale Blake's *History of the Tammany Society from Its Organization to the Present Time, 1901*, and Edwin Kilroe's *Tammany, a Patriotic History* (1924), all stumbled over the same hurdle: the tendency to whitewash the Hall while ignoring its strengths and evading its all-too-human weaknesses.

Gustavus Myers, a reformer by temperament, wrote the first judicious examination of Tammany. First published in 1901 and last revised in 1917, his *The History of Tammany Hall* was a ground-breaking study on which all subsequent students have relied. However, Myers sometimes rewrote the past to serve his purposes, and he often ran the risk of being misread as a partisan rather than a neutral observer. Edwin Kilroe's *Saint Tammany and the Origins of the Society of Tammany or Columbian Order in the City of New York*, a Columbia University dissertation, published in 1913, was an excellent study but only covered the Tammany Society's activities from 1787 to 1795. Morris Werner's *Tammany Hall* (1928) improved on the two earlier works, but he leaned heavily on stereotyped ideas and seemed more interested in sensationalism than analysis. The latest study of Tammany by Alfred Connable and Edward Silberfarb, *Tigers of Tammany: Nine Men Who Ran New York* (1967), updates Myers and Werner and extends coverage to the post-1920 period. Two other excellent works that are both scholarly and authoritative, Seymour Mandelbaum's *Boss Tweed's New York* (1965) and Alexander Callow's *The Tweed Ring* (1967) describe how the mature machine functioned or, in some cases, malfunctioned.

Political scientists, sociologists, and contemporary politicians have used a different perspective to judge Tammany Hall. Moisei Ostrogorski's *Democracy and the Organization of Political Parties* (1902) and Robert Merton's *Social Theory and Social Structure* (1957) presented a functional theory of machine politics that other commentators such as Edward N. Costikyan, in his *Behind Closed Doors: Politics in the Public Interest* (1966), find agreeable.

They felt that for the Tammany machine to survive it had to do more than control votes and grant favors—it had to serve larger human needs. According to this reasoning, the Hall's pursuit of power was not inherently evil. Aware that public stability depended upon the government's ability to institutionalize dissent and prevent the polarization of latent social conflict, Tammany acted as a broker between competing interest groups. The Hall's handling of the thorny immigrant problem vividly emphasized the point. Immigrants were usually faced with open affronts, but Tammany realistically lent them a helping hand, thus not only serving as a buffer against a formal power structure that disdained them but also unclogging the channels for upward mobility. By stifling potential class conflict, the braves facilitated the evolution of an open society based on talents and achievements, not accidents of birth, heritage, race, or religious ties.

Although all of these studies are worthwhile and in some cases have revealed hidden facets of Tammany's operation, several gaps still remain in the story of the Hall's pre-1865 history. In order to fill these gaps, I have posed several key questions. How did the machine evolve and what role did the Tammany Society play in the process? Were Tammanyites aware of their own development and did they consciously control the direction of this growth? What did Tammanyites believe and were their ideas ever formulated? Or, were they primarily men of action; men who were politicians before anything else—trimmers, fixers, intriguers—men who were nothing but opportunists on a grand scale, working within the loose framework, as one of their editors put it, that "anything in politics is fair"? It is also interesting to note that all of the Hall's opponents—Federalists, Clintonians, National Republicans, Whigs, Know-Nothings, Republicans, internal Democratic splinter groups, disgruntled reformers—copied the braves' political blueprint, but why were they not as successful as Tammany?

In examining these questions I have used manuscript materials and contemporary newspapers that other historians have slighted. I have also consulted with care the great amount of secondary works and articles that various writers have published about the Hall in an effort to correct stale and inaccurate myths while analyzing Tammany's formation and growth.

As a result of my research, I feel that Tammany Hall, far from being unique or reprehensible, was eminently a product of American civilization. The evolution of the Tammany Society and its political arm, Tammany Hall, into a political machine presents in microcosm a study of how this nation, and particularly New York City, adjusted to the major social, economic, and political changes that transformed the United States in the nineteenth century and how it carried out the everyday conduct of its political affairs.

In my reexamination of the growth of the pre-1865 Tammany Hall political machine, I have addressed myself to seven major questions.

First, I have asked what issues produced Tammany Hall, how these issues affected its growth, and how these fit into an over-all political philosophy. Immediately, these questions raised a host of lesser ones. Did Tammany indeed have a consistent political philosophy? If so, how did it differ from that of its opponents? How did the Hall handle key issues that seemed to clash with its stated beliefs; that is, how did Tammanyites distinguish between expediency, techniques, and principles?

Second, I have questioned Tammany Hall's evolution as an organized political movement. How did it originate? Did its political structure change as conditions and issues themselves changed? What role did the Tammany Society play in its growth? How did the machine evolve, and, above all, how did the concept of a single "Boss" come to dominate its table of organization?

Third, because Tammany was linked closely with immigrants, I have asked how consistently the organization defended the rights and interests of the so-called "adopted citizens." As I quickly discovered, a vast gap existed between what Tammanyites professed and how they acted. Nativism proved to be a recurring theme in the Hall's history. Ultimately, then, I faced two major questions on this topic. What techniques did Tammany use to court and cater to immigrants? When and how did the organization finally make peace with its own nativism?

Fourth, I focused my attention on the impact that the city's rapid urban growth had on traditional political norms. As New York multiplied into a complex few men understood, how did Tammany react? Since the rapidly increasing population and the difficulties it created were the major realities of city life, Tammany somehow had to surmount and master those realities or die.

Fifth, I have examined the question of the Hall's class composition. Who were the Tammanyites? How closely did they represent a cross section of city life? How did their class perceptions affect their political lives? What were the differences in class structure between the Tammany Society and Tammany Hall? If any existed, what forms did they take in terms of occupation, recruitment, and political activity?

Sixth, I have explored the organization in terms of men. Because Tammany Hall was an intensely human organization, its leaders stamped their image on the apparatus, and it in turn molded the type of men it needed. But who were these men? What did they believe? What did they expect from a political career? Why did so few of them rise to prominence outside of the city?

Finally, I have questioned Tammany's place in the sweep of state and national developments. That is, how did local politics fit into the larger mass movements of the day, movements such as the formation of the first and second political party systems, economic policies, increased democratization, antiextensionism of slavery, and the problems inherent in the expanding cities?

In answering these questions, I have advanced four major themes: the growth of New York City's Republican, then Democratic party, popularly called Tammany Hall; the machine's evolution; the role that the Tammany Society played in this process; and the Hall's operational political philosophy. In the first two chapters, I have emphasized themes one and three, not only because they are interrelated, but also to underscore the idea that without the Tammany Society, Tammany Hall could not have developed in the manner that it did, nor could Boss Tweed have gained power. The key that unlocks the history of Tammany Hall, as I see it, lies in the exact nature of the Society—both as a fraternal order and a political institution.

# ACKNOWLEDGMENTS

I WISH TO THANK the staffs of the New York Public Library, the New-York Historical Society, the New York State Library, the Albany Institute, the Library of Congress, the New York Municipal Archives, the Massachusetts Historical Society, the Historical Society of Pennsylvania, the Rush Rhees Library of the University of Rochester, the Special Collections section of Columbia University for permission to use the DeWitt Clinton, Thomas Olcott, Azariah Flagg, and John Dix Papers, the Clements Library of the University of Michigan, Syracuse University Library, Cornell University Library, the University of Chicago Library for the Stephen Douglas Papers, and the inter-loan division of the University of Akron. I owe special gratitude to the Association for the Study of State and Local History for a grant, and the generous help afforded to me by several grants from the University of Akron's faculty research fund. Without compromising them, I am indebted to Dr. James Richardson, Dr. Warren Kuehl, Dr. George Knepper, and Dr. John Lindquist for their thoughtful help and advice. My greatest scholarly obligation is to Dr. Robert Rayback of the History Department at Syracuse University whose inspiration and valuable judgments first made me realize what the craft of history really meant. Above all, I thank my wife Barbara and my children Linda and Steven for their help and understanding.

*Cuyahoga Falls, Ohio*                                                          J. M.
*Spring, 1970*

# CONTENTS

Foreword    vii

Acknowledgments    xii

Introduction    1

1. The Early Tammany Society    8

2. The Birth of Tammany Hall    32

3. The Spirit of Tammanyism    56

4. The Challenge of Jacksonian Democracy    75

5. Tammany and the New Politics    102

6. The Bank War    128

7. The Loco Foco Revolt    158

8. The Pivotal Years: Tammany, Nativism, and
    the School Crisis    185

9. The Politics of Flux    208

10. Division, Reunion, and the Tammany Society    242

11. Political Chaos and the Tammany Society    267

12. The Tammany Society and Mozart Hall    300

13. The Civil War, the Tammany Society, and
    Tweed's Consolidation    326

14. Epilogue: Tammanyism    364

Abbreviations    381

Bibliographical Essay    383

Notes to Chapters    409

Index    463

# TAMMANY

**The Evolution of a**
**Political Machine**
**1789–1865**

# Introduction

ANY DISCUSSION of Tammany must begin with the clarification of two points. First, because the terms are confused, there must be a definition of the differences between the Tammany Society and Tammany Hall. Second, because urban growth made the conditions of machine politics possible, there must be a general description of these factors.

Originally, the Tammany Society was a nonpolitical, fraternal order; part of a national patriotic network that sprouted throughout the early United States. By mid-nineteenth century, however, the national movement lost its thrust and quietly died of neglect. In its strictest sense, the name Tammany Hall referred to the executive arm of the Democratic Republican General Committee that ran the Republican, later the Democratic party, in New York County.

At the same time that the national Tammany Society movement faltered, the chapter in New York City grew in strength. In 1809 it became the vehicle for a Burrite minority group, led by Matthew L. Davis, Aaron Burr's lieutenant, in its war against the DeWitt Clinton Republicans who dominated the local party. Three years later, again under Burrite leadership, the Society built a permanent home, the Wigwam, popularly called Tammany Hall.

Part of the resultant confusion in terms came from the fact that several organizations, each pursuing different goals and having different functions, bore similar names. Since the Democratic Republican General Committee met in the building owned by the Tammany Society, people gradually came to use the terms "General Committee" and "Tammany Hall" synonymously. The terms became even more confused when the Tammany Society, run by its steering committee, the Council of Sachems, used its ownership of the building to determine which competing faction could hold meetings in its main assembly hall,

1

the Long Room. Over a period of time, people used the names General Committee, Tammany Hall, and Tammany Society interchangeably. They were incorrect. The General Committee was a political organization, Tammany Hall a building, and the Tammany Society a fraternal order.

The Society, however, was also political in a limited but critical sense. For ambitious Democratic politicos on the make, membership in the Society was prized highly because many party leaders were Tammany braves. But not every brother was a politician, a member of the party's hierarchy, nor even a Democrat. As late as 1858, Whigs, Republicans, and Know-Nothings enjoyed the Society's fellowship. As a result, the Society often did not share Tammany Hall's aims or preoccupations.

On the surface, the Tammany Society seemingly mirrored its self-image: purely a social and patriotic organization with only an incidental political association. Such a case was only true when the regular General Committee lacked rivals. On five occasions before the Civil War, however, the Council judged party legitimacy when several dissident Committees, each purporting to represent the party, demanded the Wigwam's exclusive use. Because of tradition or "party usages," the rank and file considered the group that met in the Long Room as the party's authentic ruling body; all others were impostors. In the 1850s the Council appropriated another equally vital function: the right under special conditions to set party policy. By virtue of these circumstances, the Society had vast political potentialities that were essentially dormant during periods of intraparty peace but became critical when factionalism erupted.


Nineteenth-century American urbanism refashioned the pattern of national growth, and Tammany Hall's evolution as a political machine was part of this process. Moreover, the growth of "Boss" rule grew naturally as the city itself grew.

The changing sociopolitical structure of society was the first factor that created the conditions for machine politics. Independence from Great Britain gave New Yorkers the opportunity to change many local institutions according to their own values. In particular, they no longer paid deference to the few great families—the Livingstons, the Schuylers, and the Clintons—which had dominated the state on and off since the colonial period. But while social mobility became more pronounced, political habits were not so easily broken. Because of such outstanding leaders as George and DeWitt Clinton, Robert R Livingston and his brother Edward, and Philip Schuyler along with his son-in-law Alexander Hamilton, family politics still controlled the state long after its social importance had diminished.

During this interval, Tammanyites favored the creation of an open society and led the movement to democratize the political process. But not until 1822, when a new state constitution granting almost total white manhood suffrage was passed, did political mobility match social mobility. Old-style politics was dead, and a great upheaval took place in political techniques. Candidates now ran for office, sought wide-ranging mass support, and cynically manipulated the electorate by evoking popular symbols.

The first stirrings of the industrial revolution further accelerated these changes. In New York City, a major trade center even before the Erie Canal's success, a new breed of entrepreneur competed with the old merchant-capitalists for dominance. But while Tammany was often a step ahead in the process of social and political change, it was frequently unaware of the meaning of these new developments. By the 1830s the Hall had made an alliance with a new aristocracy, one based on wealth and political connections with Martin Van Buren's Albany Regency. Not all Tammanyites, however, were pleased with the situation. The city's lower classes—men who were free laborers, apprentices, and immigrants—rebelled against the Democratic party's elite and demanded that Tammany should fulfill its libertarian and egalitarian commitments.

Perhaps politicians would have preferred to ignore these pleas, but the weight of numbers bore them down. In 1790, New York City had a population of 33,131. In thirty years it increased to 123,806, and by 1855 the population had swollen in size to 629,810, half of whom were immigrants. Thus, the leaders of Tammany Hall faced a critical decision. Should they gear their emerging machine, they wondered, to the needs of a powerful but narrow elite or cater to the worries, expectations, and fears of the masses? By the 1840s, the Hall made its choice and cast its lot on the side of the more populous group. As a result, Tammany gave itself the vital edge to dominate the local urban scene for almost the next century.

The consequences of this municipal explosion brought into focus the second factor that stimulated machine politics: the bewildering impact of urbanism on a people unprepared for its consequences. The city lacked adequate sewerage facilities; street cleaning was practically unknown. Until the formation of the New York Metropolitan Board of

Health in 1866, pigs still served as perambulating garbage disposals, much as had been the practice in colonial New York, and periodic epidemics cut a cruel swath through the population. Aaron Burr's Manhattan Company and the Croton Water Works, opened in 1842, barely supplied the city's inexhaustible thirst for fresh, potable water.

Violent crimes and other antisocial behavior were commonplace. In 1845, the Common Council substituted professional police for the older system of night watchmen, political hacks, and well-meaning volunteers. Twelve years later, the Republican-controlled legislature formulated the Metropolitan Police Law. But neither change provided the city's police agencies with either the resources or the public backing necessary for honest crime-fighting. Moreover, politicians, no matter if they were Tammanyites, Whigs, Republicans, Know-Nothings, or sincere reformers, viewed the police department as a political annex and made the problem of law and order a partisan issue. The fire department was equally impotent. City dwellers, often living in substandard wooden buildings or cellars, were particularly vulnerable to fires, but the city placed its reliance on volunteer fire companies rather than paid professionals. In times of need, they proved to be pathetic jokes.

Tenement life and slums were wretched. In the older, lower wards along the river and below Canal Street, poor people of all descriptions and nationalities huddled in squalor. Worse, gangs of rootless youths, such as the Bowery Boys and the Dead Rabbits, terrorized citizens and made life miserable for the police. Other groups—the Spartan Club, led by a colorful professional Irishman, Mike Walsh, and the Empire Club, the plaything of Isaiah Rynders, a mean-tempered brawler—disrupted politics and threatened to turn the government into the rule of the strong-arm tough.

The mass arrival of the immigrants compounded these evils. Pauperism, disease, crime, intemperance, and urban congestion presented many political problems, but the system seemed unable or unwilling to respond. Both upstate and in the city, politicians operated as if the need for enlightened government was irrelevant to their own personal gains.

At first, even though Tammany Hall had decided to help the urban masses, it lacked any idea of what remedies might work. As a result, the political process, instead of formulating long-range solutions to pressing local problems, initially abdicated responsibility and made the situation worse. Politics was still based on patronage, special favors to key interest groups, payoffs between city officials and voters, and, worst of all, found itself continually manipulated by upstate agrarian legislators.

Prior to 1822, the state constitution placed the city in an anomalous position. With simple finality, the framers denied local self-rule by not allowing city voters to select municipal executive officers: the mayor, recorder, Common Council clerk, and coroner. Property qualifications similarly lowered political involvement. In charter elections to name the city's legislature, the Common Council or Corporation, only freemen and freeholders of property worth in excess of £20 could vote for aldermen, assistant aldermen, collectors, and assessors. Until 1804, two anachronistic provisions in the 1732 Montgomerie Charter, under which the municipality still operated, further stifled mass participation. A freeholder could cast multiple ballots in as many wards as he or his wife owned property or held tenements worth more than £20. Equally undemocratic, voice voting, not the secret ballot, was the rule.

City residents particularly resented the fact that they could not elect the mayor, who had the power to fill over 1,100 city jobs ranging from high constable to manure collector. Until 1813, moreover, the mayor drew no salary but could make a handsome income from fees collected on his judicial and administrative rights. Even if he were as incorruptible as DeWitt Clinton, the mayor could still earn upwards of $15,000 a year. It also irritated city residents to observe that even though he had to meet residency requirements the mayor often represented the interests that controlled the legislature, not the city.

The Common Council lacked many of the mayor's prerogatives, but had its own measure of power in the issuance of ordinances and the sale or disposal of city property. Here the aldermen could and did enrich themselves. In 1806, for example, some butchers who sold meat in public stalls erected by the city revealed that they had bribed certain aldermen for prime locations. Other officials became wealthy by using inside contacts to ferret out information about real estate values.

In the decade of the 1820s, two constitutional changes altered the city's government but not necessarily its methods. The new state constitution of 1822, besides increasing the number of eligible voters, gave New Yorkers the right to elect all their public officials except the mayor, whom the Common Council still chose for the next twelve years. In 1829, a special municipal convention thoroughly scrapped the Montgomerie Charter, but the new framework of government, which began operating the next year, proved almost as unworkable. Although the charter established a bicameral legislature based on the principle of separation of power, the aldermen and assistant aldermen worked in collusion and reduced the mayor to a figurehead, not a chief executive. Even more self-defeating, the Council used standing committees as administrative agencies, and failed to develop a bureaucracy of responsible civil servants for continuity when a change in government occurred. Without an orderly passage of authority, the voters lacked a means to establish a systematic accounting of public duty.

Conditions in New York City deteriorated to such an extent during the 1850s that the state legislature, partly due to partisanship, partly due to honest reformism, amended the city charter on three separate occasions. But instead of placing responsibility for city government in the hands of appropriate officials, the legislature further decentralized the municipality's power structure. The upshot was that by the time of the Civil War, New York City was little more than an overgrown town in its governmental organization.

Throughout much of this period, the Democratic party controlled the state and the city, but Van Buren's Albany Regency did not address itself to urban problems. For years, Tammanyites split into three groups, one in favor of working with the Regency because of a lust for office, a second which disliked the upstaters' insensitive attitude toward local needs, and a third which supported Van Buren out of ideological considerations.

Superficially, the Regency's callous treatment of downstaters symbolized the state's classic urban-rural split. Yet, in a larger sense, the situation was not so simple. The commercial farmers of upstate New York and Long Island held divergent social, economic, and, eventually, political interests from their fellows in New York City. Adding to the confusion, such urban centers as Buffalo, Rochester, and Syracuse operated with a different pattern of commercialism than downstate. Then, too, as life in the city became more and more impersonal, moral codes cracked, local traditions lost meaning, and a new way of life evolved in a manner few agrarians understood. As the *Democratic Review* noted in 1838, urbanism forced men to lose their individuality, and created a fresh political climate at sharp variance with normative theories of majoritarian rule. In many ways, this new society was depersonalized, confused, and, above all, ready for a firm hand that would guarantee it stability, order, and leadership.

Although the conditions for machine politics reached maturity in the mid-1850s, one final factor both stimulated and retarded its growth. New York City lacked any authority to coordinate municipal rule. The chief characteristics of its government were diffusion of power, instability, lack of responsibility, and honest or dishonest graft. Periodic reform movements sprang up to correct these abuses, dedicated public-minded citizens, with the somewhat cynical help of upstate Republican legislators, tinkered with the governmental machinery, politicians moved into power by promising reforms, but none really exerted the far-reaching leadership the community needed, or crystallized and harmonized the city's heterogeneity.

As things worked out, local Democrats realized that in order to cope with the difficulties of urban life, they would have to work around the system, not through it. Improvising as they moved along, these Tammanyites used their organization as a conduit to humanize and personalize the city government so that they gave bewildered citizens ready access to a power structure that might ameliorate their problems. For a price that many New Yorkers thought negligible—their votes— Tammany paved the streets, made building codes, improved sanitation, cleaned the litter, dug the sewers, supplied the water, provided the fire and police departments, and tried to ease problems that few men understood and even fewer men would cope with.

Yet Tammany's evolution as a political machine did not come cheap. By reacting to events rather than anticipating and mastering them, Tammany was not geared to exercise responsible leadership. Unable to face and surmount reality, the Hall's leaders often faked issues and made personality the *sine qua non* of politics. At least until Boss Tweed, Tammany Hall was an inefficient machine, driven to win elections, not govern. Its political life span was chaotic simply because it failed the ultimate test of truth: the art of managing the city in a constructive manner.

The Hall's instability, its administrative bankruptcy, then, were Tammany's real capstones. In the resultant maze of conflicting self-interests, personal ambitions, and divergent translations of party principles, compromise, accommodation, adaption, and conciliation were the only sensible tools for intelligent politicking. But the Hall was not omnipotent; it could not please everyone. Yet because Tammany, even with its structural weaknesses, was the city's majority party, many would-be strongmen—men such as Daniel Sickles, Fernando Wood, Elijah Purdy, Lorenzo Shepard, and William Tweed—recognized the Hall as the instrument with which to attempt Boss rule. Through all this pulling and hauling, however, one institutionalized party pattern held the final key to regularity, stability, and victory: the Tammany Society. For whatever group dominated the Council of Sachems dominated the Society, and through it, the Democratic party of New York County.

The history of Tammany Hall and its evolution as a political machine, then, must begin in 1787 with the formation of the Tammany Society.

# ⤙ 1 ⤚

# The Early Tammany Society

THE NEW YORK TAMMANY SOCIETY began operations in 1787 as purely a fraternal order. As early as 1771, Pennsylvanians had celebrated "St. Tammany Day" in honor of the legendary Indian, Tamanend, or Tammany in its Anglicized version, a person who had supposedly paved the way for a peaceful settlement of the American colonies. The Tammany Society movement, however, did not spread until after the Revolution when many nationalists, eager to overthrow all vestiges of British rule, substituted St. Tammany as their titular Saint in St. George's place. The gesture caught popular imagination, and in the next few years clubs were established throughout the United States.[1]

The local Tammany Society's fraternalism reveled in the mystical mumbo jumbo so dear to the youthful in spirit: secret handshakes, outlandish costumes, and grandiloquent titles. The rigmarole carried over into the organizational structure. The brothers or "braves" elected the officers: thirteen "sachems," who acted as a board of directors; a secretary or "scribe"; a treasurer; a "sagamore" or protocol chief; and a "wiskinsky," who acted more as a glorified bouncer than as a doorkeeper or master at arms. The sachems met separately in the Grand Council of Sachems, elected one of their number as Grand Sachem, the Society's nominal head, and named some prominent brave as Father of the Council to act as a master of ceremony. Further, Tammany subdivided itself into thirteen tribes, each with a semiautonomous organization and chaired by its own sachem, appointed by the Grand Council. Adding to the plethora of titles, each tribe had an "okemaw" or warrior, a tribal hunter called "machawalaw," and an "alank" or clerk.

The entire Society met once a month for an evening of comradeship and frivolity. Usually, the main order of business centered directly on holiday planning. That done, the members adjourned into the Com-

**8**

mittee of Amusement. Here, conviviality reigned. It was a time for toasts, formal debates, tall stories, and patriotic songs. Occasionally, members staged a lively debate on some current problem.[2]

Tammanyites counted their proudest moments when they went on parade. With tremendous zest and enthusiasm, they costumed themselves on any excuse: off went coats and knee breeches; on went Indian regalia complete with paint, feathers, and bucktails. Exhibitionism and display were the orders of the day. The Society marched on Washington's birthday (at least until 1795), Founders' Day in May, Independence Day, Columbus Day, Evacuation Day (the anniversary of the British evacuation of New York), and, after 1815, January 8, the anniversary of Andrew Jackson's victory at New Orleans.

The procedures involved in holiday celebrations generally followed a set pattern. The Society assembled at its headquarters and then marched off in a colorful procession to church. After services, an orator delivered an address or ode composed especially for the festival. Then a sachem took up a collection, which was followed by another parade, sometimes in company with other societies, to an elegant dinner where prominent politicians often graced the table. After the meal, the sachems proposed thirteen toasts, usually prepared in advance, and then other braves offered their own. By late afternoon the weary braves were ready to go home; happy, well fed, slightly tipsy—but ready and eager for the next time.[3]

Many non-Tammanyites questioned the Society's childish pageantry. Lingering hatred against things Indian had carried over from the Revolution, and some New Yorkers saw nothing romantic in warpaint and feathers. Though criticism mounted in volume, the Society refused to change. The price tag attached to its stubborness grew too expensive, however, during the War of 1812. Bowing before the public's anti-Indian animus, Tammany reluctantly stored its costumes for the duration, and exchanged such high-flying titles as grand sachem and wiskinski for such mundane ones as president and doorkeeper. But when peace arrived, the Society went back to its traditional ways.[4]

As a patriotic order, Tammany's Americanism had an ugly side. Its fraternalism was provincial, exclusive, narrow, and inclined toward clannishness. Furthermore, New Yorkers distrusted foreigners, and the Society shunned them as members. At first, Tammany was merely anti-British, but in the early 1790s it extended its antipathy toward the newly arrived Germans and Irish. Article 2 in the Society's first constitution bore the hallmark of prejudice: Tammany "shall connect in the indissoluble bonds of patriotic Friendship, American Brethren, of known attachment to the Political Rights of human nature, and the Liberties of this Country." Some brothers, however, rejected the Society's nativism and suggested that Tammany could not restrict freedom and liberty to American-born citizens. By the first decade of the nineteenth century the Society stilled its denunciations of foreigners, yet its nativism lingered on as a recurring symptom. Here, the Order showed its hypocrisy by verbalizing egalitarianism while tacitly advocating social restrictiveness. The dichotomy was to prove embarrassing in the future.[5]

Its antiforeignism aside, Tammany had a liberal veneer. Beginning with the premise that it was "founded on true principles of patriotism, and has as its motives charity and brotherly love," the braves saw their welfare as linked with that of the country and were soon discussing questions of civic and moral improvement. The Society favored ending imprisonment for debt, a more just penal code, abolition of human slavery, and discarding property qualifications as the basis for voting. Furthermore, during Tammany's festivals a special committee solicited voluntary contributions to aid the poor. In 1804 the Society institutionalized its philanthropy in a formal Committee on Charity, financed through an increasing fund. In time, Tammany expanded its altruism into a wide-ranging welfare system with vast political meaning.[6]

In their own nation, the braves prided themselves as being the watchdogs of freedom. "May the sons of Tammany," a toast ran, "ever esteem it their greatest glory to keep alive the sacred flame of liberty." This was the intent of John Pintard, one of the Society's earliest members and the man most responsible for its growth, when, in 1790, he called Tammany "a political institution" with a strong "republican basis" whose "democratic principles" would check the local aristocracy. His idea was not offered in a narrow partisan sense because Pintard was a Federalist, but rather as a form of government where the people exercised sovereignty through their chosen representatives. Tammany reaffirmed his meaning in its 1801 bylaws. A member's sponsor swore that his protégé firmly supported the Constitution, believed in the rights of man, and held "in utter abhorrence, every species of monarchial and illegitimate authority." [7]

The Tammany Society had a vision of a better world. To the fearful, it promised security; to the dispirited, it promised in-group fraternalism; to the alienated, it promised regard for their well-being and ethical growth; to the uncertain, it promised a Lockean myth of human freedom to validate a belief that the events of the past twenty years had followed a course of moral good that would eventually make the United States the finest nation in the world's history. Traditional American values, Tammany emphasized, were not outdated. The nation faced a genuine opportunity for greatness; the people only needed vocal and active reassurances. Within the Society's warm bonds—united by a mystical "chain of union"—patriotism, fraternalism, nativism, nationalism, and Lockean idealism highlighted Tammany's perception of Americanism. When the braves thought of their nation's future, they visualized it in terms of a Fourth-of-July emotional reflex: a messianic promise that would destroy absolutism and monarchy throughout the civilized world. For example, when news of the French Revolution reached the city, brother Thomas Greenleaf, the editor of the *New York Journal*, trumpeted the millennium's arrival while the Society asserted that a new empire of worldwide liberty was at hand.[8]

In order to ensure that their own nation was secure, Tammanyites cooperated with other national organizations. The Society of the Cincinnati was one of its most unusual partners. Founded at the end of the Revolution as a bridge to link the Continental Army's officer class with its French comrades in arms, and as a charitable and fraternal order to support indigent brother officers, their families and dependents, the Cincinnati was actually an elitist organization with a closed membership policy. Given Tammany's primordial Americanism, the two Societies should have been enemies. The reverse took place. In the five years between 1789 and 1794, both shared similar objectives. Each in its peculiar way romanticized the past, only differing in value structures, and as long as they mouthed generalities they avoided open clashes over specifics. As one sachem toasted at a 1792 Tammany festival: "To the Cincinnati and those heroes who fell in defense of the liberties of our country." On proper holidays the Societies held separate dinners but generally met afterward for a round of mutual toasts. Yet their fellowship could not last. By 1795, because of differing interpretations of the meaning of the French Revolution, the two drifted apart and open animus replaced fellowship.[9]

Meantime, the Tammany Society had attracted an increasing number of new members. Although it grew slowly until the spring of 1789, two men—John Pintard and upholsterer William Mooney—reorganized the Society and tailored it to local needs. In the first full year under their direction, Tammany initiated 252 dues-paying members and found itself in the pleasant dilemma of having outgrown every meeting hall in the community. By 1795, with almost 500 members on the books, the Society ended its first growth phase.[10]

In terms of membership, the Tammany Society was basically a middle-class, open-ended organization. As Grand Sachem Dr. William Pitt Smith remarked with pride, Tammany united "in one patriotic band the opulent and the industrious—the learned and the unlearned, the dignified servants of the people and the respectable plebeian, however distinguished by name, or sentiment, or by occupation." Most eligible New Yorkers could afford the Society's nominal charges. Initiation fees ranged from $2 to $8, and active members paid quarterly dues of 24 cents. A select committee screened prospective candidates proposed by members in good standing. Brothers from other chapters could transfer, but again they needed a local sponsor.[11]

Under these equitable conditions, the Society's kinetic fraternalism should have attracted a growing membership list. This condition was true in the period from 1789 to 1794; Tammany initiated 498 braves. But from the end of 1794 to June of 1797 the Society did not enroll a single member. Just as strange, only 112 men joined in the following four-year period, supposedly the time that marked Tammany's emergence as the leading political engine in New York City. Something had indeed halted the Tammany Society's growth pattern. That something was politics.[12]

More than anything else, the state constitution of 1777 set the substance of local politics. A remarkable document, considering its wartime birth, it proved to be a carefully balanced blend of political compromises and sound colonial precedents. Yet, as it turned out, the framers could not resolve two problems, political suffrage and executive leadership, that haunted politicians for almost the next half-century.

Colonial experience had taught New Yorkers to distrust centralized power. As a result, they diffused authority wherever possible. The people now selected the governor but, because of property qualifications, only freeholders worth £100 or more and tenants on life leases with the same value could vote. The governor lacked two vital prerogatives: the sole right to veto bills and appoint lesser officials. At each annual legislative session, the assembly named one senator from each great district, the western, middle, southern, and eastern, to form the Council of Appointment. Charged with naming all nonelective state officials, the Council rapidly became the focal point for an embryonic spoils system. The governor, who chaired the Council, initially had the sole nominating power. But in 1801, after six years of Federalist control, the Republicans added an amendment through a special convention which gave each member the same prerogative. The Council of Revision, consisting of the governor, the chancellor, and state supreme court judges, likewise shackled the executive. It reviewed all legislation and could veto any bill it deemed unconstitutional, subject to overrule by a two-thirds vote in both legislative houses.

In theory, the senate, chosen by the same suffrage requirements as the governor, and the assembly, elected by all £20-freeholders or renters of tenements worth forty shillings a year, plus freemen of Albany and New York, operated on the principle of the separation of power. As events developed, however, the governor's paucity of patronage and privileges made him seek allies from among the legislators, thus creating the cement for factional arrangements.

Politically, then, the state constitution stimulated the very thing it meant to prevent. Since New Yorkers left suffrage requirements unchanged until 1822, highly personal factions, unchecked by mass public opinion, had the means to centralize power in themselves. Furthermore, the Council of Appointment, which by 1821 controlled over 14,000 civil and military jobs, conditioned New Yorkers to view politics as a system of dispensation where they earned or lost favors based on real or imaginary services. Once this attitude hardened; once the people were ready to barter their votes for favors; political machines—which were really based on elitism, favors, and patronage, though marked by different methods—were only a step away.[13]


During the period of the Confederacy, the Clintonian faction, led by Governor George Clinton, had dominated the state by shrewdly playing divide-and-conquer politics among its foes, keying its program toward "the middling classes," and putting local needs before national interests. But the struggle over ratifying the United States Constitution changed all the political ground rules. Dubbed the "Antifederalists," the Clintonians fought a bitter, last-ditch battle against the Constitution. The Livingston-Schuyler group, the Federalists, led by Alexander Hamilton, brushed the Antis aside, and plunged ahead to win mass support. By late 1788 the Federalists held the upper hand. As the party of progress and prosperity, with the august George Washington's charismatic figure as their symbol, the Federalists cut deeply into Governor Clinton's normal constituency. They did so by playing toward the grandstand of public opinion, muting their class prejudices while portraying themselves as sincere democrats, and arguing that the Constitution would benefit the entire state. On an organizational level, they formed a thorough network of local committees with nationwide ties, while the frustated Antis remained provincial and disoriented.[14]

When Clinton ran for reelection in 1789, he failed to carry New York City and won by a narrow margin. In the 1790 spring elections city voters again stamped their approval on the Federalists. Although the Clintonians headed by merchant David Gelston sought to "confer with the Mechanics in order to obtain a coalition of parties" in the assembly election, they failed to dent the opposition. The story was much the same the next year. The Clintonians called themselves the "Mechanics' ticket," and nominated a split assembly slate: three Tammany moderates, two Tammany Federalists, and two regular Federalists. The "Merchants" ticket scorned any camouflage, headed their ballot with Alexander Macomb, a well-known speculator tied in with the Bank of New York, and won again.[15]

The Clinton-Livingston-Burr alliance, the Republican-Interest, ran into similar problems within the Tammany Society. Largely composed of men from the city's middle class, the Society generally favored the Federalists' program. Hoping to win some influential friends by becoming braves, more and more Interest politicos joined the Society. Some Clintonians—Thomas Greenleaf and John Stagg, the president of the General Society of Mechanics and Tradesmen, for example—were charter members. But now others such as Walter Bowne, Benjamin Romaine, Simeon DeWitt, and DeWitt Clinton were initiated. For the Burrites, merchant Melancton Smith and Tunis Wortman, the future head of the New York Democratic Society, joined. Brockholst, Peter, and Edward Livingston represented their clan. But while the Tammany Society and the Republican-Interest shared many values in common, much still kept them apart. The Council of Sachems, led by Josiah Ogden Hoffman, remained Federalist, the majority of Tammanyites supported Hamilton, but the Society remained generally nonpolitical.[16]

Confusion and indecision, then, marked Clintonian strategy in New York City. During Washington's first presidential term, the city remained a Federalist stronghold. The party's alliance with the mercantile community, artisans, and "middling class" held firm, for in the first Congress the Administration lived up to its promises. It pushed through moderate tariff protection as city workmen requested, kept other goods free for the merchants, and, most important, laid the groundwork for fiscal stability. Furthermore, Alexander Hamilton's program of forced savings through his financial plans, though it stirred up opposition among states' rights Antifederalists, barely disrupted local political lines. As the *New York Journal* matter-of-factly reported, "it is expected the BANK BILL will receive but little opposition." [17]

The short-lived but sharp depression of 1792 was the first indication of growing Republican-Interest strength in the city and deeply reduced Tammany's confidence in Federalist leadership. Beginning in July 1791, when the Bank of the United States began to sell subscriptions, "stock jobbers" and "speculators" had a field day. In the city, Greenleaf noted, "the scrip mania continues to prevail." Then, in January of 1792, several different groups began to petition the legislature to incorporate new banks in the city. One combine proposed a "Merchants Bank," a second, sponsored by the Livingstons, was capitalized at $1,000,000, and the third originated with the Tammany Society.[18]

Tammany's interest in banking was purely speculative. Because of its burgeoning growth, the Society needed a meeting hall large enough to house its monthly meetings, its reading rooms, and Pintard's American Museum. Like other men in the financial swirl, the sachems, led by Pintard and Melancton Smith, organized a tontine for building such a hall, and quietly added a seemingly innocuous provision that the directors—six Interest politicians and nine Federalists—could apply the fund "to the best of their judgment for the advantages of those concerned." By the terms of the organization, the directors sold 4,000 shares at $16 each with only $4 down. During the first thirty days of sale, the tontine limited purchases to Tammanyites; after this, the shares went on the open market. According to its constitution, the Tammany Tontine would be in force twenty-eight years; the surviving members would divide the property and profits between them.[19]

In the scramble for bank charters, Tammany's proposal excited little comment. But the tontine had a second side that struck some New Yorkers with deep misgivings. They noted that the Society also proposed to build a waterworks to supply the city with fresh water, and "that the emoluments (provided they do not exceed twelve and one-half per cent per annum) are to be employed by the society as a compensation for the use of its money." Such a project, Tammany's critics complained, through its self-perpetuating membership, was monopolistic and clearly wrong.[20]

Before these cries grew strident, the tontine ran into unexpected difficulty. By late January the three groups merged under the name

"State Bank," and petitioned the legislature for a charter. Despite strong evidence that the bank promoters came from both sides of the political fence, Hamilton and Schuyler feared its long-range effects might impinge on Federalism's banking preserve. In April the legislature followed their bidding, and killed the bill. At the same time, William Duer, the celebrated prince of speculators and Hamilton's close friend, went into bankruptcy and ruined many small investors who had naively backed his plans. When that happened, the market dipped into a breathtaking decline; creditors called in loans; real estate values depreciated; business ground slowly to a halt; and a full-dress panic began. As for the Tammany Tontine, its shares went begging on the market.

The bull market's collapse and the rapid panic that followed had serious political overtones for the Federalists because most of the public's vocal discontent centered on Duer's close association with Hamilton. Even Tammany Society braves began to have second thoughts about supporting the Federalists.[21]

Despite sizable gains at the Federalists' expense, the Republican-Interest squandered its advantages during the 1792 gubernatorial election. From the outset, the campaign was a tasteless affair, conducted on the lowest political levels by both sides. The "Jayites" pictured Clinton as a venal old man, intent on amassing a huge fortune in the illicit disposal of western New York public land. In reply, the Interest accused Jay of being an aristocrat with deep Tory leanings, hypocritically parading as a democrat. Clinton won reelection, but his victory was suspect. The official Committee of Canvassers—a joint legislative body of twelve members—invalidated the returns of three counties on technicalities, and gave Clinton the edge he needed for victory. Although the Federalists were infuriated, Jay counseled restraint, and urged his followers to await the next election.[22]

As for the Republican-Interest, the campaign and the struggle over Clinton's tainted election made them a political party rather than a faction. Because of a series of anonymous articles written by Chancellor Robert R Livingston under the name of "Cato" and Edward Livingston's actions in the "stolen" election, their clan cut their last remaining ties with Federalism. Even maverick Aaron Burr forfeited his precious independence when he was forced to defend Clinton. Adversity, then, created party union. As Federalist Senator Rufus King noted: "The opposition, that now exists, arises from other principles than those which produced an opposition to the Constitution, and proceeds from the Rivalry, which always has & will prevail in a free Country."[23]

Even so, the Interest had lost almost as much as it had gained. Many of Clinton's most loyal followers backed away from him in disgust, and the lord of Clermont, Robert R Livingston, felt dispirited and betrayed. In Virginia, Thomas Jefferson felt that Clinton had discredited the entire effort to build a national party. In the city, things were equally difficult. Although Clinton improved on his previous totals, the Interest had obscured the banking problem and lost its chance to make its democratic pretensions credible because of Jay's charges against the governor's land dealings.[24]

The Interest lost similar ground among Tammanyites. Although both sides courted the braves—particularly Clinton's friends, who wrote a series of articles in the *Journal* under the name "Tammany" calling for his reelection—the Society played a passive role in the contest. Of the twenty-nine members on the Interest's New York City correspondence committee, a mere six were Tammanyites. And out of these six, only one, Ephraim Brazier, had been a sachem. On the other side, of twenty-seven Jayite committeemen, seven were braves. Among the seven were four current sachems including Grand Sachem Josiah O. Hoffman. The reason for Tammany's lack of involvement was simple. It remained a fraternal order, only individually political.[25]

The governor's controversial victory, however, turned the Society against him. As a matter of common courtesy at its Independence Day festival, Tammany traditionally toasted the state's leading officeholders. Toasts four and five, the *Journal* reported, nonetheless, "were not drank [sic] by the whole society." Both praised Clinton: "The State of New York and all of its officers, civil and military," and "George Clinton, the Governor of the State of New York." Sachem William Pitt Smith, attempting to heal the damage, led a debate which concluded that the people should accept the verdict, and patiently await the next election if they disagreed. If anything, however, these problems indicated that the Federalists still retained a firm hold over the Society.[26]

At this point the uprising in France, the capture of the Bastille, and the subsequent unfolding of the French Revolution slowly polarized public opinion in the United States and made foreign policy the chief political topic of the day. It was this issue that saved the Republican-Interest, helped it to become a true national party, and ultimately transformed the Tammany Society.

In the French Revolution's earliest stages, Americans took a paternal pride in its activities and, with some variations, followed its course with sympathy. Such an attitude was especially true in the city, where Greenleaf heralded the movement as the end of "despotism, and its concomitant national evils—ignorance, superstitution, and barbarity." Within the Tammany Society, the Revolution brewed a headier brand of Gallomania. Exhilarated by the Revolution's libertarianism, Tammany whipped up popular support for the French, dispensed propaganda, and did missionary work to arouse an American protest against other reactionary European nations. By instinct, Tammany was Anglophobic; by emotion, prorevolutionary; and by extension, anti-Hamilton. But politically, the Society did not as yet forfeit its nonpartisanship. So far, the Revolution was essentially a mystical and romantic concept, not a divisive political question. That problem lay in the future.[27]

The three years from 1790 to 1793 marked the peak of the Society's almost universal affinity for the French. At its festivals, Tammany made the same point with almost metronomic regularity. "Lewis [sic] the sixteenth," one sachem proposed "and all our Gallic brethren—may the glorious empire of reason and liberty they have reared, attain that summit of excellence which its auspicious establishment predicts." The Society assumed that the American and French revolutions shared a common parentage and a common upbringing. On almost every official and unofficial occasion, Tammanyites cheered the Revolution's progress from weak infancy to bellicose adolescence. On Bastille Day, July 14, 1792, Federalist Grand Sachem Benjamin Strong dedicated a special festival in France's honor. In addition to their normal costumes, the braves wore French national cockades as a mark of respect and empathy. After a long dinner, Sachem Strong toasted, "the empire of reason—and the downfall of monarchy." [28]

As a further indication of its sympathy, Tammany held another festival in December 1792, to celebrate a French military victory. An awed Thomas Greenleaf reported: "It would be impossible to describe the rapturous enthusiasm felt at this meeting. It could not have been greater in the victorious army of Dumourier, or in the bosom of the patriotic Jacobin Club. It was felt as the common cause of humanity, and none, but who love the Rights of Man, who hate oppression in all its forms, however flattering, can imagine or participate in its enjoyment.[29]

By early 1793, two separate but related events in France shook Tammany's emotional adulation of all things French. The Reign of Terror condemned Louis XVI to the guillotine, and the Anglo-French War began in earnest. The King's death at once began to polarize opinion among Tammanyites. Pro-French braves rationalized that the deed was sound since it proved that "kings are like other men"

in that they were subordinate to just laws. On the other hand, Federalist Tammanyites viewed the beheading as the first step toward anarchy, and slowly began to question the Society's unreasoning Gallomania.[30]

President Washington, fearing any direct involvement in the war, issued his Proclamation of Neutrality, and cautioned his fellow citizens not to take any sides in the growing hostilities. But, as one sneering Federalist put it, "the sage and venerable Order of St. Tammany and the Sans Culottes" had already settled the question. With important Federalist defections, the braves spoiled for a fight, or least an emotional outlet for their feelings. The Society got its opportunity when word reached the city that a French frigate, which had just captured a British prize, had arrived in Philadelphia. As Edward Livingston told his brother, "some hundreds of Republicans" toasted the French and "a Cap of Liberty was put over the Bar and several Enormous Bowls of Punch drank to its support." [31]

In June, the arrival of the French man-of-war *L'Embuscade* gave the Society another excuse to show its pro-French spirit. Tammany honored the ship's commander, several seamen, and Citizens Hauterive and DePine, the French consuls in New York and Boston. At the height of fellowship, Grand Sachem William Pitt Smith told the guests, "you behold a society, who, in their temple have erected a temple to freedom, and hold themselves bound to preserve upon it a bright and unextinguishable flame." [32]

Despite Tammany's flamboyant Gallomania, the Republican-Interest failed to realize that the Society had modified its being. All along, Burrite, Federalist, Clintonian, and Livingstonian braves had voluntarily mouthed the same democratic clichés during Tammany festivals. Each agreed on fundamental universals: the American Revolution's high-minded idealism, the people's right to govern themselves, the power of public opinion, the glory of fighting to make men free, the blessings of liberty. These were nonpartisan ideals and, if anything, the Federalist party—a least in the public mind—stood closer to them than the Interest. But the French Revolution changed the picture. In a metamorphosis few braves yet understood, many Federalists became inactive brothers, and the Society was evolving into a crypto-Republican-Interest pressure group with vast political potentials. Yet the Interest initially failed to grasp the point that Tammanyism and Federalism were now at odds. Misled by the Society's adamant statements that it was a purely fraternal order, the Interest simply overlooked the fact that Tammany now had a partisan objective which eclipsed its original purpose.

In July and early August of 1793, the Tammany Society's Francophilia reached fever pitch. Not content with its accustomed fanfare, Tammany linked Independence Day and Bastille Day into huge love feasts. On August 3, the French repaid Tammany's fellowship. A few days before, outside New York City harbor, *L'Embuscade* fought the British frigate *Boston*. When the French ship docked, thousands of admirers gawked and cheered when her commander presented the Society with his flag as a token of respect "from their republican brethren in France." [33]

Against this backdrop, Citizen Edmond Genêt arrived in the city. For Tammany, Genêt represented the quintessence of the French Revolution. Yet, in a larger sense, Genêt was a disaster for the Interest. Totally mistaking emotional public ovations for real disapproval of Washington's neutrality policy, Genêt quickly alienated many of his wellwishers and handed the Federalists a potent weapon for declaring the Interest disloyal, not only to the nation but the President himself. "I am persuaded Genet's intemperance has served the federal interest," Schuyler told Hamilton, "instead of Injuring it." [34]

While the Federalists were congratulating themselves, the Genêt affair precipitated Tammany's moment of truth. As American foreign policy increasingly became a political rather than a patriotic question, Tammanyites could no longer hide behind the fraternal mask. It was all well and good to raise huzzas for the French; it was even more fun to drink endless rounds of porter to Fraternity and Liberty; but the sweeping changes on the political compass made life more complex. All men faced a time of testing. The Tammany Society could not hold back.

Meantime a new phenomenon, the New York City Democratic Society, entered the story. Formed in early 1794 and modeled on clubs in Philadelphia and upstate New York, the new Society, which extolled pure democratic idealism, enabled the Interest to extend its power base at Federalist expense. All right rested with the people, the Democratic Society emphasized, and government existed for man's happiness. Representatives were accountable to their constituents and were public servants. Since men operated with an unqualified freedom of conscience, all class distinctions, inherited aristocratic barriers, and self-perpetuating government elites nullified the social-contract theory. If natural law was to prevail, the government had to guarantee the electorate its share in freedom. In membership, the Democratic Society welcomed all classes. But while many Tammanyites joined, not all Democratic Society members were Tammanyites. Moreover, the

Democrats recruited Anglophobes from the middle class and mercantile community who resented the Administration's soft approach toward Great Britain. As for leaders, the ranking Democrats came from two areas: long-time Interest politicians, and young, idealistic men receiving their political baptism. Beyond all else, the Democratic Society resurrected the "Spirit of '76"—the battle between tyranny and republicanism—and studded its platform with libertarian ideals that stirred the imagination of a new political generation.[35]

On another level, the Democratic Society rebelled against the slow-moving Republican-Interest, the wavering Tammany Society, and the pro-British Federalists. Not a political party in any sense, the Democrats acted as a pressure group that pushed the Interest into a mainstream of public opinion by channeling Anglophobia into a definite partisan direction. In doing so, the Democrats experimented with a variety of techniques the Interest politicians had absorbed from Federalism. They held meetings, directly involved the rank and file in decision-making, manipulated public celebrations as excuses for propaganda, and coordinated action with other clubs outside the city. In sum, the Democrats operated at the highest stratum of practical politicking.[36]

The Tammany Society gave its new neighbor a chilly reception. Despite similarities in background and pro-French feelings, obvious differences existed between them. Tammany espoused fraternalism—the Democrats were one-dimensional; Tammany was essentially passive—the Democrats fought to turn participation into power. Then, too, the Federalists retained a working majority in the Council of Sachems and resisted all efforts by Interest members toward a closer agreement with the Democrats. Twice in 1794 the Federalists sachems passed up opportunities on Founders' Day and Independence Day to stamp approval on the Democrats. Yet the Federalist structure was not as sound as events seemed to indicate. Within the organization and unappreciated by the general public, Republican-Interest and Federalist Tammanyites were locked in an intricate, behind-the-scenes power struggle. For the moment, neither had the upper hand.[37]

Tempers in Congress grew sharp over Great Britain's disregard for neutral rights by the spring of 1794, and Americans waited tensely for Washington to act. The President realized that diplomatic negotiations were necessary lest inaction anger the public and sent John Jay to London. By the time he left, the Tammany Society found it increasingly difficult to reconcile its coolness toward the Democratic Society

with its pro-French sympathizers. The celebration that marked the
French recapture of Toulon revealed Tammany's inner torment. It held
a special meeting, replete with liberty caps, and wildly toasted French
armed might. "Perdition and Contempt to the Tongue of Calumny and
Malice," Grand Sachem William Pitt Smith offered, "that would divide
at this period the friends of Liberty and Equal Rights of Men." But the
friends of liberty were divided. Federalist Tammanyites boycotted the
rally, and the Democratic Society, holding a separate meeting, slighted
Tammany at toasting time.[38]

As the Interest's political stock climbed, the Tammany Society's
painful indecision continued. Within the Council of Sachems angry,
bickering voices drowned out all efforts at harmony. Founders' Day
bore witness to Tammany's problems. Along with the Reverend John
B. Johnson's patriotic call to fortify the city's harbor, the usual pro-
French toasts clashed with several that favored Jay's mission. Even more
disconcerting, some Federalist Tammanyites invited Hamiltonian
Mayor Richard Varick as a special guest, while several Democratic
braves asked the French consul. Despite these signs, however, most
middle-of-the-road brothers still had no wish to sacrifice Tammany's
fraternalism. So Tammany's confusion multiplied. When Jay left for
London, he carried with him the braves' good wishes. Independence
Day followed the same inconsistent pattern. In its parade, Tammanyites
marched "with the flags of America and France entwined, and the *cap
of liberty*." Yet at its formal dinner, the brothers once more offered a
bumper to Jay's success and completely ignored the Democratic
Society.[39]

While the argument raged, the Federalists added a new dimension
to the controversy. The origin of the problem lay in western Pennsylvania when a group of farmers rose in armed rebellion against federal
marshals who attempted to collect excise taxes. Although the government crushed this "Whiskey Rebellion," the Administration was convinced that a sinister pro-French international conspiracy—personalized
in the United States by the Democratic Society movement—had fomented the uprising, and President Washington angrily urged all
Americans to help crush all such "self-created societies."

City Federalists quickly responded. Using guilt by association, they
linked Tammany to the purported "Jacobin" conspiracy and demanded
that the braves either dissociate themselves from the Francophiles and
denounce the Democrats or completely dissolve. Shortly after issuing
the threat, Tammany Federalists took action. Due to the inclement
weather, few brothers showed up at the regularly scheduled meeting in

January of 1795. When the Federalists realized their opportunity, Grand Sachem Jonathan Little, a merchant by trade, hastily appointed a special committee to draft and publish an address that would explain the organization's true purpose. Before he finished, the few Interest braves objected and argued that Little had breached the Society's rules. A committee, they pointed out, could not issue a report in Tammany's name unless a quorum of the full membership agreed. Their objection failed by a vote of 31 to 15.

On January 21, 1795, the committee issued its report in both Federalist and Interest newspapers. Beginning with the premise that the President's denunciation of "self-created" societies was correct, the report assailed the Democrats as troublemakers and charged that they were interfering with the "constituted authorities of the Country." Furthermore, the report suggested that if Tammany did not reform itself, the Federalist braves had no option but to resign.

Although many Democrats were indifferent to Tammany's fate, they realized the danger implicit in the Federalist stand. Above all else they wanted Tammany to remain politically neutral, because if Federalism destroyed that brotherhood over the self-created society issue, then they also were clearly vulnerable.

The Interest and the Democrats, then, had to defend Tammany. As Matthew L. Davis, the editor of the short-lived *Evening Post* saw it, the Federalists had packed the original meeting and issued a false report. To preserve Tammany's honor, Davis, who was not yet a brave, demanded a second meeting.

When the Society again met, Interest Tammanyites were prepared. Before Grand Sachem Little could interfere, a resolution to disapprove the address was moved and passed by a vote of 100 to 65. The Federalists were infuriated, and they stormed from the meeting followed by hisses and catcalls. In this highly charged atmosphere, Little closed old business—but not before the remaining braves called for yet a third meeting.[40]

Now certain that their suspicions were correct, Federalist braves responded with a burst of activity. "A Calm Observer" in their *Daily Advertiser* set the party line. He charged that Tammany was indeed a self-created society cast in the Democrats' mold, disloyal to President Washington and everything good he represented. Under such conditions, the "Observer" maintained, all true Federalists should immediately resign. Federalist lawyer William Willcocks, who had become a brave in 1793, was far more violent. Wielder of a pen dipped in vitriol, he loathed the Interest, hated the Democrats, and, by extension, Tammany. In a series of bitter tirades, he lumped both societies together as un-

American, and warned any hesitant Tammany Federalists that if they did not resign, "such will be the Catastrophe, at some future period, as certainly as ever an effect proceeded from a cause." His words settled the matter. Taking a cue from Little, who canceled his membership, Federalist braves followed suit and left Interest brothers in command.[41]

Matthew Davis once more came to Tammany's aid. Writing as "A Shade of Tammany" in the *Journal*, he pitched his appeal toward the moderates, and soothingly assured them that Tammany was still based on sociability and benevolence; its aims were charity, patriotism, and Americanism. In no sense was it political. The trouble with Willcocks and "The Calm Observer," Davis maintained, was their inability to "think proper to draw a line between principles on which a society is established, and the principles of its individual members." In contrast to Federalist notions, Tammany had every right to stay alive and vital.[42]

The third Tammany meeting closely followed Davis' approach. With Grand Sachem pro tem Coertland Van Beuren in the chair a select committee resolved that, "this society neither acknowledges political principles for its establishment, nor political objects for its purpose; but it is solely designed to 'connect American Brethren in the indissoluble bonds of partiotic friendship.'" The Federalists, however, refused to allow the Van Beuren braves an easy escape. "What! no political principles," the *Advertiser* hooted, "when there has been scarce a public day for this three or four years back but your sentiments, your toasts, your principles, and your objects have been in the most formal manner obtruded upon the public?" [43]

The moderates, however, agreed with the Van Beuren braves and kept Tammany alive as purely a fraternal order. But the price the organization paid for its survival left it destitute for the next fourteen years. After the ugly confrontation with the Federalists, the Society lived a twilight existence as a struggling fraternal order that occasionally functioned as a minor cog in the Interest's political machinery. Tammany stood between two worlds, the social and political, but never made peace with either.

After the Federalist walkout, the braves dutifully celebrated George Washington's birthday for the last time and kept up their pro-French pronouncements. But much of the old spirit was dead or dying. During the next two years the Society did not initiate a single member, attendance at meetings ebbed to a new low, and fewer and fewer New Yorkers paid it more than passing attention.

Even so, the Tammany Society had a singular importance in the development of the city Republican party. While it was quite true that the controversies over John Jay's peace treaty and the Keteltas Affair —a partisan disagreement over the legality of the whipping system, which the Federalists favored and the Republicans did not—became the catalysts for transforming the local Interest into both part of a true national party and the representative of the downtrodden, the Tammany Society played a vital role in transferring to the Republicans the democratic *mystique* that Federalism had once claimed. Quite simply, Tammanyism gave local Interest politicians a credible vehicle for posing as patriotic, nationalistic democrats, devoted to constitutional principles and Lockean idealism. In this sense, Tammany helped the Republicans to gain the American Revolution's Whiggish aura. Nevertheless, the Tammany Society still lacked a consistent self-image.[44]

In terms of membership, by 1800 the Society became more Republican. But fewer merchants joined in the first growth stage, and Tammany still remained elitist, middle-class, and clannish. Despite its class and occupational exclusiveness, some prominent Republicans did become braves. Philip Freneau, editor of the new *Time Piece*, joined in 1797, the same year as his co-editor, Matthew Davis. George Clinton, Jr., the governor's nephew, joined his brother DeWitt in the lodge. Moreover, both James Cheetham, editor of the new Republican *American Citizen*, and his partner David Denniston, became braves. On the other hand, no more Livingstonians appeared on the membership lists. The Tammany Society failed to match the Republican party's vitality, however, and newly initiated braves did not even represent a true cross-section of the organization's growing preoccupation with the submerged classes.

OCCUPATIONAL STATUS, NEW MEMBERS OF
TAMMANY SOCIETY, 1797–1801 [45]

| Occupation | Number |
|---|---|
| Artisans | 57 |
| Taverns, hotels | 10 |
| Lawyers | 7 |
| Cartmen | 7 |
| Printers | 6 |
| Merchants | 4 |
| Miscellaneous | 3 |
| Doctors | 2 |
| Government officials | 2 |
| Unknown | 14 |
| | 112 |

By 1800, in fraternal terms—excluding Clintonian Samuel Osgood and Burrites Marinus Willett, David Gelston, John Nicholson, and Aaron Burr—all the important city Republican leaders were Tammany-ites. Politically, no one could question the Society's devotion to the party line. On July 4, 1799, the sachems toasted Thomas Jefferson, proposed confusion to President Adams, his undeclared naval war against France, and the Alien and Sedition Acts; then on Evacuation Day added freedom of the press, the ending of taxation for war purposes, and Burr's strategy in getting the Bank of the Manhattan Company through the Federalist legislature to the Republican litany. George Washington's death temporarily sobered Tammany's partisanship; for three months all the braves wore black crepe armbands, but its political ideals remained intact.[46]

In the 1800 electoral campaign, the Tammany Society was strongly pro-Jefferson and pushed George Clinton, not Aaron Burr, for the vice-presidency. Despite the popular mythology shrouding Tammany's place in the election, it was not the sinister, awesome machine that "used every influence, social and political, to carry the city for Jefferson." Nor did Aaron Burr or Matthew Davis succeed in tooling it into a personal vehicle. Rather, Tammany stood in the same relative position it occupied in the backlash of the Federalist exodus: a small, struggling fraternal order that was also a Republican pressure group, useful for pronouncing party principles and issuing policy statements, but hardly the city organization's nucleus. Even more, the majority of sachems were Clintonian, not Burrite, in sympathy. As an indication of its stand, when the House of Representatives finally elected Jefferson over Burr, the braves illuminated their temporary wigwam, the *American Citizen* reported, by placing sixteen lights at each window, emblematic of the states of the Union. Then the Society began its toasts and cheers: sixteen for Jefferson; nine for George Clinton; nine for Burr—in that order. Finally, at Tammany's three major 1800 festivals, the sachems convivially toasted Jefferson and George Clinton as the co-leaders of Republicanism. Significantly, none of the toasts mentioned Burr or noted his candidacy. In the same year, moderating the slight somewhat, Matthew Davis delivered the Long Talk on Independence Day; but Clintonian Grand Sachem William Boyd selected DeWitt Clinton for the position at the next celebration.[47]

The controversial 1801 Common Council election provided another

index of the Tammany Society's political unimportance. In November and December of 1801, the Republicans organized a tontine to enfranchise freehold voters in two city wards. The enraged Federalists protested the "faggot" scheme, which their rural brethren had used for years, and the Corporation's business ground to a halt. The issue of whether or not these voters were legal dragged on unresolved until August 1802, when the Republicans tacitly admitted defeat and sought to widen the electorate through legislative remedies.[48]

Historical opinion credited Burr with devising the tontine strategem, and his followers purportedly implemented the plan through Tammany. A close inspection of tontine membership lists suggests another theory. Of the thirty-nine men in the Fourth Ward, six were active anti-Burrites, five followed the Vice President's "Little Band." In the Fifth Ward, out of seventy-four men the anti-Burrites had ten, the Burrites six. More to the point, prominent local political leaders from both sides joined the tontine. True, the remaining men were generally poor mechanics and students who swung the election for the Republicans. But it was sheer overstatement to credit the Burrites with leading the movement. Rather, the tontine was a bifactional idea, neither fully Burrite nor Clintonian-Livingstonian.

Again, historical analysis cites the tontine as an example of Tammany's partisanship. The reverse was true. Out of a total of 113 men, only 32 were braves. Of the remainder, only 17 later joined the Society —but even so, this was hardly a feather in Tammany's political headdress.

Up to 1804, a freeholder could vote in all wards in which he or his wife owned property. Since the Tammany Society was basically a middle-class organization, most braves could vote in Corporation elections and some cast multiple ballots. Thus, that a small number of Tammanyites appeared in the tontine suggests two assumptions: either the braves financed the poorer tontine members, or, more likely, the Society was politically inert. The latter idea is correct. From 1801 to 1804, eighty-four men served as sachems. Of these, twenty were anti-Burrites, five Burrites, the rest apolitical. The entire tontine episode, then, revealed Tammany's miniscule position within the Republican party.[49]

In May 1802, an intraparty uproar raised in the wake of several toasts at the Founders' Day celebration further compromises the theory of Tammany's political importance and Burr's mastery over the organization. After the usual fulsome praise for Jefferson, one of the sachems, probably Burrite William Mooney, offered a bumper to the Vice President. Ordinarily, the courtesy should not have caused any friction. But Clintonian editor James Cheetham, the leader of the local anti-Burrites, whose *American Citizen* was the only paper authorized by the party as an official organ, doctored the toast to give it a meaning the Burrites never had intended. Originally, the toast ran: "Aaron Burr: Father of the Columbian Council: He has deserved well of his country." Cheetham, however, punctuated two key words to give the toast an entirely different meaning. By underscoring "has" and "well," the toast now implied that Tammany censured Burr and was in league with his foes.

The irate Little Band demanded a retraction, and Davis, using the name "A Son of Tammany" in the Federalist *Evening Post*—edited by Hamiltonian William Coleman, who nonetheless admired Burr—cautioned that "The Tammany Society is a respectable institution and I sincerely hope its members will keep it so by holding to truth and honor." In defense, Cheetham explained how the toast originated, and by doing so incidentally revealed the Society's lack of partisan importance. At the regular monthly meeting where the members drafted resolutions, he explained, an unusually large number of braves—fifteen, "of whom a majority was the little band"—drew up the toast. Cheetham further claimed that Tammany had over 150 dues-paying members, and the Little Band, "which cannot boast of more than a dozen or fourteen persons in the whole, are members of the society." Given the editor's understandable need for political understatement, the Burrites were not using Tammany as a partisan engine, nor did they dominate its membership. Moreover, as Davis revealed offhandedly, the Society had nothing to do with politics or political factionalism. Tammany, he wrote, was a fraternal order, and it was indefensible for any of its "patriotic sons" to pervert "any of the anniversary toasts." [50]

In short, Tammany had few political assets. It still performed a valuable function as a sounding board for Republican principles, and strove to catch the party's patriotic, pro-Jefferson sentiments. If anything, the Clintonian-Livingstonian alliance against Burr dominated the Society, but even they felt Tammany lacked any partisan importance. In 1803, at the height of intraparty feuding, Tammany stood foursquare in the allies' camp. Ignoring Burr, the sachems toasted Governor George Clinton, "may the gratitude of his fellow-citizens never cease," and

Thomas Jefferson, "our present Great Grand Sachem . . . his wisdom, prudence, & love of peace we approve & admire." The following year, when Burr hesitated before approving the Louisiana Purchase, Tammany indirectly censured him. In an overblown eulogy of Jefferson, the Society urged all the braves to hail the sale as "resulting from the wisdom, uprightness, and Resolution OF THE MAN CHOSEN BY THE PEOPLE to administer their Government." [51]

But in the hotly contested 1804 gubernatorial election between Aaron Burr and Livingstonian Morgan Lewis, Tammany's lack of partisan importance still held true. Out of 114 city freeholders who acted as Burr's central committee, only 23 were braves. The same low ratio held true for the allies: a mere 25 Tammanyites out of 64 men served as ward representatives. The Council of Sachems' political affiliations further documented the Society position; 9 backed Lewis, 2 were for Burr, while 8 claimed neutrality. [52]

After the election, Tammany went on proclaiming its faith in Jefferson, again damning Burr. "All future candidates for office," one toast went, "let them henceforth learn the salutary lesson, to respect the majesty of the people." By 1805, the Society settled back even more comfortably into its normal fraternalistic rut. On Independence Day it invoked the names of Jefferson and George Clinton, the Army, the Navy, the fair ladies, and diplomats, such as James Monroe and Robert R Livingston, who opposed Great Britain. Despite Tammany's Republican pugnacity, the reporter who covered the festivities for the *American Citizen* inadvertently hit on the reason for the Society's lack of influence in party affairs. "Nearly *one hundred* sat down to dinner— The day was spent with uncommon hilarity; friendship and harmony was the order of the day." Here in a capsule was the real Tammany Society: small, patriotic, fraternal; hardly the motive force that carried on the party's electioneering and guided the Republican apparatus. [53]

From 1801 to mid-1806, local issues dominated city politics. In 1803, the second round of the Anglo-French war barely disturbed New York's parochialism beyond periodic Federalist requests for better port fortifications. During the next two years, city merchants enjoyed an enormously lucrative trade with the belligerents, and business profits filtered through to every segment in the community. In 1805 the situation began to change when the warring nations, unable to strike at each other directly, began to pass restrictions against American shipping.

Meantime, the Tammany Society stayed on its well-worn fraternal path. In 1805 the legislature had reinforced Tammany's original intentions when it granted the Society a charter that officially incorporated it as a benevolent and charitable institution, clearly not political in either ideals or programs. Yet, starting in March 1807, the Society abruptly began a vigorous recruitment program that lasted four years, a program that drastically reshaped Tammany's entire purpose. In this period the Society initiated 1,502 braves. Equally significant, the Council of Sachems' composition changed. Stalwart Clintonians, men such as Samuel Cowdry and Benjamin Romaine, gave way to a new breed of Tammanyite who had little faith or sympathy with the older leadership elite. [54]

Ironically, the partisan nature of American foreign policy, which almost destroyed Tammany in the 1790s, helped transform it a decade later. In June 1807, the friction that had been building between the United States and Great Britain reached a critical point because of the *Chesapeake-Leopard* affair. While patriotic New Yorkers howled for war, President Jefferson sought honorable peace. In the next few months until Congress met, the Administration delayed action, and mulled over what options it could use to protect legitimate American rights.[55]

By contrast, the spirit of jingoism gripped the city. The Republican party's central steering council, the General Committee, with De-Witt Clinton serving as chairman, joined the Federalists in denouncing British aggression, and passed resolutions that called on the Administration to fight back. During the following weeks, however, the Clintonians' war fever abated. They backed the President's search for a peaceful formula, cautiously deprecated the war spirit, and picked up the preparedness issue. All might have gone well for them except for two things. In the midst of demonstrating their loyalty to the Administration, the Clintonians underestimated both the city's honest indignation at Great Britain's insult to the American flag, and the ferment brewing in the Tammany Society.[56]

Part of the reason for Tammany's rapid rebirth lay in its patriotism and Americanism. The British attack on the *Chesapeake* stirred the Society into a frenzy of flag-waving and Anglophobia. On Independence Day the grand sachem called for "unceasing and undivided" vigilance to protect liberty and freedom from foreign incursions. When the General Committee, meeting at Abraham Martling's tavern, which served as the party's headquarters, called on the citizenry to form corps of infantry and artillery as a home guard, Tammanyites responded quickly. They arranged their active membership into war bands, "the main body to consist of 234 warriors and hunters, exclusive of officers, viz. 156 warriors, 73 hunters, which by subdividing into 13 war parties, give 12 warriors and six hunters to each." A sachem and three sub-alterns commanded each company, and the grand sachem headed the entire organization.[57]

Without exaggerating its importance at this point—Tammany was still relatively small in terms of active members—the Society had reached a turning point in New York City's political history. As it spurted ahead in membership, as it evolved into the city's staunchest defender of Jefferson's, then Madison's diplomacy, Tammany by necessity lost its exclusive fraternal character and became political as foreign policy differences became the paramount issues of the day.

Yet there was nothing inevitable about the Tammany Society's transformation. It could have remained a fraternal order and pro-Administration without forfeiting its original characteristics. That is, it could have if the Burrites had not been behind Tammany's new thrust. Hidden from most viewers—including the Clintonians—the Burrite Little Band, led by Matthew Davis, was cleverly playing on Tammany's patriotic reputation to advance its own stock. The Society, therefore, began the process that would make it the mainspring in city politics because the Burrites had entrenched themselves in the Order, using it as a respectable power base and saving themselves from political extinction just at a time when their chief was making his name synonymous with quasi-treason.

# ⌐ 2 ⌐

# The Birth of Tammany Hall

FOR THE CLINTONIANS, the essence of local politics lay not in patriotism and aggressive calls for war but in protecting New York's agrarian interests and in promoting Vice President George Clinton's belated ambition to become Thomas Jefferson's successor. In order to do so, the Clintonians had to tighten control over the party because of their recent falling-out with the Morgan Lewis Livingstonians. As their first move, the Clintonians decided to purge editor James Cheetham, a man George Clinton considered "impudent" and a liability to the "Cause he wishes to promote." Yet, by a grotesque irony, just as they were ready to make their move, Cheetham went off on an independent rampage against Jefferson's foreign policy and the public assumed that DeWitt Clinton had masterminded the attack.[1]

During the period when the Administration sought to form its new foreign policy, the city's Chamber of Commerce, which was generally Federalist, had joined with the *American Citizen* in pleading with Jefferson for an approach that would not harm business. But Cheetham, with an instinct for the jugular vein, damaged his own argument. Beginning with the premise that France, not Great Britain, was the real enemy, he charged that the Administration's Embargo Act on American shipping was actually a pro-Napoleonic measure, implanted in Jefferson's unsuspecting mind by a sinister "French Influence" in his cabinet —personified by Secretary of State James Madison. By criticizing Madison, Jefferson's heir apparent, the editor accomplished three things. He reassured agrarian New York interests that the Clintonians championed them, maintained George Clinton's independence as a potential presidential candidate, and hopefully drew a line between disloyalty toward Jefferson and legitimate dissent.[2]

Once his ratiocinations were public, Cheetham expected support from a variety of sources. That the Embargo hurt the city, few Republicans denied. Thousands of men were unemployed, and in their distress hunted for a scapegoat. Even more, Morgan Lewis told Madison, the Clintonians were using their opposition to the Embargo as a means to cement an alliance with the Federalists in preparation for George Clinton's presidential bid.[3]

Despite these signs of unrest, the local party rallied around Jefferson. Postmaster General Gideon Granger, who was in the city, reported that the Administration's supporters "loudly & strongly censured" Cheetham, and he would now either "change his ground or be given up by our friends. The Republicans here will give support & countenance to the measures of the Government." Ironies abounded. The Republicans Granger referred to were the Burrites and Livingstonians, who had replaced the Clintonians as Jefferson's chief supporters within the local party. As the crowning irony, the argument forced DeWitt Clinton to save himself by defending a man he personally despised—James Cheetham. First, the *American Citizen*, under strong Clintonian goading, now lamely supported the Embargo as a "weapon of negotiations against Great Britain." Next, Clinton called the General Committee into special session, and helped draft resolutions that called the "French Influence" charge "base and infamous calumnies" but straddled an all-out Embargo endorsement.[4]

Yet the two Clintons had not really made peace with the Administration. Defying the tradition that once a Congressional Caucus had made its decision the loser had to support the ticket or risk expulsion, George Clinton charged that James Madison, who had won, had rigged the meeting. Once home, the aged Clinton forced the legislature to nominate him for the presidency. But his bid was doomed from the start. James Monroe, the other candidate who rejected the Caucus decision, also ran as an independent, and scorned the New Yorker. Even worse, the Federalists, whom the Clintonians were wooing, nominated their own ticket and dismissed the proposed coalition as "All Fudge." As a result, Jefferson concluded that "DeWitt Clinton sinks with his tool Cheetham." In state after state, local organizations confirmed the President's judgment. As Senator William Plumer of New Hampshire put it, "when the political pot boils, the *scum* will rise." [5]

The reaction that counted, however, was not among national leaders or politicians in other states but in the local party. Upstate, Chancellor Livingston urged all his connections to back Madison, while in the city the Burrites and Livingstonians—or the "Madisonians," as the press called them—did their best to isolate the Clintonians. To do

so, the Madisons made the election a test of loyalty toward the administration, demanded that the party expel Cheetham, blamed DeWitt
Clinton for masterminding the insurgency, and sought to leave his followers little room to maneuver.[6]

The controversies shaking the local party had another effect that
the Clintonians had not anticipated. In a direct line of development,
these two problems split the party, shifted power to the Burrite-
Livingstonian coalition, made the Tammany Society the key force in
local politics, and helped create Tammany Hall.

By August of 1808 the Madisonians felt confident enough to challenge the Clintonians for the control of the party, and they forced the
General Committee into holding a special session at Martling's Tavern.
After a hasty search for dependable men, a group of raucous Clintonians moved toward the barroom, but were temporarily blocked when
Abraham Martling refused to open the door. Pounding on the walls
and threatening to wreck the tavern, the irate Clintonians forced their
hard-pressed host to yield. The sight that greeted them was hardly
reassuring. The Madisonians had arrived early and packed the room.
When the newcomers burst in, shouts of "Hustle him—Hustle him—
He is a Clintonian," rocked their composure. Instantly, men on both
sides began shouting and jeering. Somehow in all the hubbub, the
Madisonians managed to adopt a series of resolutions proposed by Tunis
Wortman which criticized the Clintonians, and won control over the
General Committee.[7]

As the happy Madisonians left the tavern, they had no way of knowing that they had just added the new words "Martlingism," or "Martling-Men," to the lexicon of American politics. More to the point, they
had parlayed their assets into a promising political revolution that heralded a new partisan alignment. For the Burrites, the change meant
spoils and respectability; for the Livingstonians, revenge against the
Clintonians. Yet, in a different sense, some things had not really
changed. DeWitt Clinton still ran the party outside New York City,
and he had demonstrated his survival power on more than one occasion. While his foes now dominated the General Committee, they
had no guarantee that the local party would remain in command. Despite these fears, however, city Madisonians had one great advantage
that Clinton did not appreciate—the Tammany Society's political coming of age.

In February 1808, as a patriotic gesture, the Society had sponsored
a proposal to dedicate a cemetery in the Wallabout district of the

waterfront in memory of American prisoners of war who had died on the ships' hulks used by the British as prisons during the American Revolution. In the 1790s, Matthew Davis, then working on the *Columbian Gazetteer*, had made the same suggestion, but now the proposal fitted the city's patriotic mood. The ever suspicious Federalist *Evening Post*, nonetheless, saw a sinister plot at work. Because of men like Davis, editor William Coleman claimed, the Tammany Society had become a purely political organization: "The truth is, and it ought to be known— *The politics of this city are now governed by a* JACOBIN CLUB—an organised JACOBIN CLUB which holds its nightly orgies at a certain public house, and there dictates to those of its party in power, and controuls their conduct at its pleasure." As for the Wallabout idea, the *Post* dismissed it as a crude attempt to "further the political views of party." Both Cheetham and Davis hotly denied the accusations. Tammany, they argued was not a Jacobin Club; it was not political, nor were its motives partisan.[8]

Although Coleman's criticism marked the first time since 1795 that anyone had suggested that Tammany was political, he was correct. The year 1808 was the critical year in its history. Superficially, Tammany's fraternalism ran as strong as ever, counterpointed, as it were, by the braves' growing preoccupation with foreign policy matters. But on an organizational level, things were much different. Eight prominent Clintonian sachems, including Grand Sachem Benjamin Romaine, who held various jobs at Mayor DeWitt Clinton's behest, were deeply involved in municipal graft. When their activities became public, all eight resigned their jobs and temporarily suspended activity in the Society. Significantly, Burrites took their slots on the Council of Sachems, and, most important, Matthew Davis became Tammany's secretary in charge of recruitment and the chairman of the sachems' Committee on Organization, which ran the Society on a day-to-day basis.

Again DeWitt Clinton and James Cheetham overlooked the importance of these moves. Both had grown immune to Coleman's constant faultfinding; his insistence that any club containing Republicans, like the Deistical Society, the Uranian Society, the Illuminati, or the Hibernian Provident Society, were based on the defunct Democratic Society's partisan mold. Although the Federalists, under young Gulian Verplanck's lead, were on the verge of forming the Washington Club movement to counter these real or imagined threats, Clinton still considered Tammany totally nonpartisan. And when the Society invited him to deliver the chief remarks at the Wallabout dedication, he would have needed superhuman powers to suspect anything was amiss.[9]

From March to August of 1808, the Society did remain politically inert. It scorned a stand on the presidential question beyond a pious wish that the "friends of the American Cause" remain united. To those who disliked the Embargo, Tammany patriotically recommended an alternative economic system based on domestic manufacturing. But in September, when Martlingism took shape, Tammany threw off its disguise and revealed its true identity. Davis, writing as "Tammany" in the Madisonian *Public Advertiser,* firmly endorsed the national ticket, and placed the Society's reputation against Clintonian "apostasy and faction." The upshot was that under Davis' guidance Tammany merged with Martlingism, and almost immediately Martlingism became synonymous with the Tammany Society.

At the same time, then, that Aaron Burr's name became a curse to his countrymen, his Little Band became the driving force in city politics. Yet although the Burrites controlled the Tammany Society, most new braves failed to see Burr's image imprinted on the organization. Instead, the bulk of these acolytes, Jeffersonian to the core, responded to Tammany's measured patriotic drum beat and felt that the Society was a legitimate vehicle through which to express their pro-Administration sentiments. The reason for this attitude lay in Matthew Davis' practicality. To William P. Van Ness, who as "Aristides" had written a violent attack on both Jefferson and the Clintonians, Davis explained: "I think [we] have learned sufficiently to know the folly of connecting our political destiny with that of any Individual; and more especially when the wishes and conduct of that Individual is not in unison with the wishes and expectations of the party." [10]

Davis, the true founder of Tammany Hall, also epitomized the archetypal Tammany politician of the future: the faceless, ambitious, opportunistic, self-seeking man, more interested in imagery than substance, guiding policy by public opinion, while constantly maintaining that he believed in the Jeffersonian slogan of "measures not men." By using Davis' calculated approach, stretching in a firm line toward the days of Boss Tweed, Tammany Hall would ultimately dominate New York City.

Meantime, the presidential race in New York wound down. The party united behind Madison, an Albany politician informed Jefferson, because it had full confidence in his "talents and patriotism" and a feeling "that the republican party will be fostered by him or under his administration." When the legislature met to name electors, it ignored Cheetham's last-ditch appeal for state pride and gave Madison a thumping majority.[11]

Once the election ended, however, many upstate Madisonians feared that the rejuvenated Federalist party (which had made impressive gains in the fall elections) might have emerged as the real victor and urged the Republicans to reunite. Different forces were at work in New York City. The Martling-Men were aware of the growing movement in favor of an accommodation, but demanded that the party sacrifice DeWitt Clinton as their price for an agreement.[12]

Yet Clinton, sensitive as always to any shift in the political weather, had already begun to take the initiative away from his foes. In the city Cheetham pleaded for reconciliation and harmony, while in the legislature Clinton introduced a series of resolutions that approved the Embargo and pledged support to the President-elect. Then, to burn his bridges behind him completely, he made an elaborate attack on the Federalists, whom he traduced as men who would rather "reign in Hell than serve in Heaven." [13]

As the pressure mounted in the city to forget the past, Martlingism fought back. "If we are to unite," one letter to the *Advertiser* suggested, "let those yield unconditionally who disunited us." Again, Clinton had his own answer. To counter the Tammany Society's patriotic allure, a group of former Clintonian Tammanyites, led by Sachem Samuel Cowdry, organized the Whig Club of the City of New York along Tammany's model and daubed itself with the red, white, and blue of primordial Americanism. Even the name "Whig Club" was an artful dodge to establish a link with the Revolutionary Whigs who had led the American fight for independence. Next, Clinton flexed his economic muscles, and had Tunis Wortman committed to Debtor's Prison for failing to pay back some money he had borrowed from George Clinton, Jr. Finally, in a move to show that he still controlled the legislature, DeWitt Clinton replaced United States Senator Samuel L. Mitchill with Obediah German.

The Martling-Men struck back by using Cheetham as their symbol of defiance and chose Tammany as their instrument of power. At the Society's regular March meeting, they introduced a list of charges against him, Cheetham angrily reported, and "moved its adoption, and after being opposed by gentlemen who were fraternally *hissed* by the *Brothers*, it was carried." The bill of particulars blasted Cheetham as a political traitor and hired editorial assassin, and demanded that the Society expel him because he was unworthy of being "hereafter acknowledged as a brother." [14]

Cheetham denied the censure and claimed that Tammany lacked any means to oust him. The legislature, he argued, had chartered Tammany for charitable purposes, not for being "perverted to the worst purposes of faction." Yet, to his total astonishment, the Whig Club congratulated Tammany on its move, and not one Clintonian hustled to his defense. Although disappointed when its move drew little blood, the *Advertiser* took advantage of Cheetham's difficulty by having Tammany and the General Committee petition the legislature to switch the state's printing patronage from the *Citizen* to itself.

Thwarted by Clintonian willingness to sacrifice Cheetham, the Martling-Men attempted next to destroy the Whig Club movement. Some Madisonians, who had secretly joined the Club, now seceded and formed a second group, the Harmony Whig Club. It, too, pledged allegiance to orthodox Republican and American ideals, and joined the hue and cry against Cheetham. Taken by surprise, the parent organization sent out peace feelers which its offshoot accepted. The two clubs met on March 28, but the Clintonians were outnumbered. The Martling-Men had packed the hall, and under their direction a third organization emerged, the United Whig Club, whose tenets were loyalty to the Administration and subservience to no individual.[15]

DeWitt Clinton's transparent regard for his own skin made Cheetham's position intolerable. But the editor was a fighter, and did not intend to bow his head meekly in surrender. During the spring election, he called in all the political debts party workers owed him for years of hard service, and demanded that they boycott the canvass to discipline Martlingism and rebuke the Burrites who now controlled the Tammany Society. "As [the] Tammany Society, like the tail of a ship," he growled "govern the party, Mr. Davis actually dictated the ticket." [16]

The most striking aspect of the election, however, was not Cheetham's interference but the voters' growing disenchantment with Madison's foreign policy. Even though the Martling ticket carried the city, the party's over-all margin of victory fell to its lowest point since Alexander Hamilton's heyday. Adding to the perplexity, the Federalists finally put the Washington Society into shape as a charitable and benevolent institution, whose real design, the *Advertiser* noted, was to be "an efficient political engine." [17]

The Republican setback jolted the Martling-Men's assumption that they could purge Clinton and Cheetham and carry the city at the same time. In reassessing its prospects, the General Committee organized a special unit headed by Wortman, who was now free, to investigate the reasons behind Federalist resurgence. The report confirmed the wisdom of some factional accommodation. Thus armed, the Martling-Men made a complete turnabout, and arranged a secret meeting with the Clintonians to explore the possibility of a compromise.[18]

At the resultant meeting, few of the politicians worried about consistency. After Chairman Marinus Willett, a former Burrite, called for order, Matthew Davis spoke for the Martling-Men and the Tammany Society and offered the terms for an agreement. Turning first to Willett, he said: "As an old associate of mine, when the unfortunate Burr was our chief, I rejoice in the opportunity of once more offering myself to your attention. Yes, Sir, I was the friend of Mr. Burr, the advocate of Mr. Lewis, and don't blush to say so, but, sir, although I always was opposed to the Clintonians, is not an union of all parties at present expedient? . . . if, sir, the chiefs unite, our experience tells us that we can lead the way."

The reasons behind such an extraordinary merger, he continued, were purely selfish and practical because without such a coalition the Federalists would win and take over Republican spoils. Having made his point, Davis then listed his specific terms: all newspapers would drop factional labels and merge under the Republican rubric; furthermore, the three Whig clubs would disband while their members joined Tammany. If, however, the Clintonians thought it more "advisable to put down the society altogether," a new Republican club should take Tammany's place. On this last point, Davis clearly favored maintaining Tammany in its current form.[19]

During the next few weeks, leaders of both factions tacitly implemented the compromise. The Martlingism-controlled General Committee welcomed a few new Clintonian ward delegates, the Whig clubs slowly shut down operations, and Tammany began a wholesale initiation spree. Even so, an uneasy calm gripped the party. Despite the lack of a public uproar matching that of the Dyde affair—an abortive coalition in 1806 between the Burrites and Clintonians—neither faction trusted the other. As their final fusion move, the Martling-Men and Clintonians framed a common letter to both Jefferson and Madison that praised the Administration's foreign policy. Both men sent back flattering answers, carefully neutral but full of praise for the New York City's Republican party's confidence.[20]

Just as everything was moving along so smoothly, Clinton upset the agreement when he finally dismissed Cheetham, hired Charles Holt to edit a new journal, the *New York Columbian*, and thus incurred the *Public Advertiser's* wrath since it hoped to keep the state's printing patronage. As a result of these moves, the now heartened Federalists gained control over the Corporation, and threatened to undo all Republicans.[21]

Matthew Davis' secret machinations were typical of the problems the New York City party faced. During the legislative session, the Federalists named two of their men for the Council of Appointment, but because they lacked any senators from the southern and middle districts it seemed that the Republicans could again control patronage. But one of the senators the Republicans had chosen, Robert Williams, was a political turncoat, and helped Federalism gain sway over the Council.

Davis was elated because Williams was an old friend, and among the Council's first moves was its dismissal of Clinton from the mayoralty. But when the greedy Federalists lost perspective and removed Republicans of all factional stripes, the Clintonian-Martling compromise reached full maturity. Both honestly cooperated in the 1810 spring gubernatorial election, though Federalist Jonas Platt carried the city with 53 percent of the vote. Incumbent Governor Daniel Tompkins, who was nominally a Clintonian, ran well upstate, however, and won handily. Equally satisfying, the Republicans regained the legislature and the Council of Appointment. As Madison joyfully observed, "in N.Y. every branch of the Govt. is again sound." [22]

On the surface, local politics remained calm. Each side publicly kept up its end of the bargain. Although the Tammany Society again dominated the General Committee, Holt refused to cross editorial swords with the quarrelsome *Advertiser*, and DeWitt Clinton remained active as a brave by buying forty shares in the hall Tammany planned as its permanent headquarters. Even so, the Republicans could not escape Madison's unpopularity and fumbling diplomacy. In the fall Corporation election, the Federalists retained their position.[23]

The Martling-Men's flush of triumph at taking over the Tammany Society and the General Committee turned to apprehension as few leaders outside of New York City made any effort to help them. President Madison, despite mounting evidence that local Clintonian federal officials were working against his Administration, refused to make any removals because most of them had been Jefferson's appointees. Governor Tompkins, who was slowly becoming disenchanted with the Clintonians, was equally evasive and refused to commit himself until Martlingism proved a winner. Next, Davis needed a bank to counter the Clintonian-dominated Bank of the Manhattan Company's economic powers. But the legislature was reluctant to grant new charters, even though it allowed the Manhattan to establish branches upstate. Finally, DeWitt Clinton doggedly maintained his regularity and lectured the party that any new internal rift would mean more damage at the polls.[24]

In the midst of such gloom, however, the Martling-Men found their reprieve when Congress failed to recharter the Bank of the United States. When that happened, New York City interests flooded the legislature with memorials for new charters. "The rage for Banks is beyond your conception," one upstater wrote William Edgar, a Clintonian Manhattan Company director. One proposal from city Federalists was particularly impressive. Organized by stockholders in the defunct Bank, it set up a huge promotion, capitalized at $6,000,000. Still another came from the Martling-Men. Then, too, a group of upstaters, headed by Clinton's friend, Solomon Southwick, the editor of the powerful *Albany Register,* pressed its demands for a mechanics' and farmers' institution.[25]

Few skilled guides existed who could move through this morass where politics and business overlapped. The Martling-Men hurt their own cause when they stressed that a new charter "was the only means of uniting the Republican party in New York," and that DeWitt Clinton opposed it as part of a deal to win Federalist support. Unsure of what to do, the legislators tabled all the city memorials but did charter the Albany bank. At the session's end, Clinton was in an awkward position. Although most economic barometers indicated that the city needed more banking facilities, he had steadfastly impeded the move while helping his Albany connections. More damaging, Martling charges of Federalist collusion aroused considerable animosity among city Republicans. "It may be proper to inform you," Clinton self-righteously wrote Edgar, "that none of the applications rejected have received any encouragement or countenance from me." [26]

Mere words were not enough. The city's money market was depressed, every war rumor contracted credit, and business plummeted into a downward spiral. Even so, the question was political, not economic. Without the Bank of the United States' countervailing power, the Martling-Men warned, the Clintonians would use the Manhattan's power to coalesce with the city Federalists' mercantile interests. "We

must have an establishment founded on principle," Davis noted
brusquely. "One that will unite our republican friends; and concentrate all their energies at this interesting crisis." [27]

The banking question, however, was of secondary concern to
Clinton. Late in 1810, Lieutenant Governor John Broome died, and the
legislature called a special session to name his successor. Clinton wanted
the job. As lieutenant governor, he could avoid the senate's bickering
debate while subtly directing its policy decisions. Too, he was fasci-
nated with a proposed canal from Albany to the Great Lakes, and the
state office would allow him leisure time to lobby among hesitant
voters.

The Martling-Men wanted no part of him. Although they had lost
ground when the Council of Appointment again named Clinton as
mayor, they made a partial comeback by nominating Tammany brave
Nathan Sanford for the state senate over strong Clintonian objections.
The situation became critical, however, when the legislative caucus
named Clinton for lieutenant governor. "Thus you perceive that the
People of the State are uncontaminated by the Martling spirit, & are
determined to uphold Mr. Clinton against the unjust violence of those
deluded men," his brother-in-law Judge Ambrose Spencer gloated. The
reverse was true. The Martling-Men held another nominating convention, defied the state party by nominating Marinus Willett for the
same office, and, with Davis calling the shots, began a statewide effort
to defeat Clinton.[28]

Caught unprepared by Willett's insurgency, the Clintonians fought
back. Above all, they wanted both unity at home and a whopping
majority in the city to prove that Clinton was still the master of the
New York Republican party. To do so, his local followers soft-pedaled
the factional split by endorsing Sanford on their ticket. But their next
move was far less successful. Clinton made the monumental blunder of
renewing his courtship of the Federalists.[29]

The mayor's mistake encouraged the Martling-Men. Speakers
roamed through the wards accosting hesitant voters and warning them
that Clinton was a power-hungry egomaniac who had secretly converted to Federalism. Furthermore, the *Advertiser* argued that while
Clinton publicly bid for the Tammany Society's support, he privately
called the braves "Savages, Indians, Madmen, etc." Holt denied that his
chief ever straddled the question. The mayor, the *Columbian* editorialized, scorned the Federalists, still retained his membership in the So-

ciety, paid his annual dues, and subscribed to Tammany's building fund.[30]

When the city polls closed, neither the Clintonians nor the Martling-Men had any cause for jubilation. Nicholas Fish, the Federalist candidate, swept easily to victory, and his party beat the Martling assembly ticket by an average 1,400-vote margin. When the legislature received all the votes, the situation reversed itself with Clinton the winner. Even so, his victory raised serious questions about the future. In the city, compromise between Clintonianism and Martlingism was an obvious nullity. Upstate, Clinton ran extremely well in traditionally Federalist bastions. If anything, these votes elected him. Well pleased with such an idea, Morgan Lewis insidiously informed Madison that the Federalists would "support the Devil, were he hostile to your Administration." [31]

In New York City, the canvass indicated Clinton's faltering hold on the party. Nonetheless, he made no move to strengthen his position until the following fall. The reason for his delaying tactics lay in another matter. As one of the commissioners for the proposed canal, he and Federalist Gouverneur Morris threw themselves unsparingly into the work. As expected, the Martling-Men, past masters of suspicion, called the canal a hoax and suggested that Clinton only intended it as a catalyst for a new coalition with the Federalist party. In December 1811, when both men visited Washington to lobby for a government subsidy, the *Advertiser* grew even more peevish. Predictably, Congress proved unsympathetic. The Madisonian Republicans, with little ready cash at hand, also interpreted Clinton's activities as a political ruse and sent the New Yorkers home emptyhanded.[32]

Meantime, the Martling-Men sensed that the tide of public opinion had swung in their favor. There were several sound reasons for their optimism. First, the Tammany Society had prospered far beyond John Pintard's wildest dreams. It had over 1,500 dues-paying members, and its new Wigwam neared completion. In politics, the Society presented a solid Madisonian phalanx and headed local Administration forces. Next, Madison began to cultivate Governor Daniel Tompkins as a counterweight to the Clintonians. On a trip to Washington, Davis noted the change. "Tompkins stands well with the Executive; and a friend of the administration [probably Secretary of the Treasury Albert Gallatin] pointed out to me the instances in which his recommendations had decisive weight." The Clintonians themselves supplied the final ingredient when editor Holt at last declared war against the Martling-Men and berated them as "the tail-piece of a contemptible faction, the gag-end of quiddism, the outcasts of republicans and federalists, as insignificant as venomous, as powerless as malignant, as destitute of credit as veracity, and worthy only of silent hate and scorn of society." [33]

In October 1811, the Clintonians made their break official by electing antiorganizational ward representatives and forming an insurgent General Committee. In the Corporation election, two rival Republican tickets, each claiming party regularity, vied for votes. Although Federalism emerged victorious, Martlingism gained immense prestige. By creating an independent Committee and challenging their older rival's authority, the Clintonians symbolically made their spiritual break with the Administration, thus confirming the Martling-Men's claim that they were the only true local standard-bearers of Jeffersonian-Madisonian Republicanism.[34]

While the Martling-Men picked up local political chips, Madison's failing diplomacy threatened to make their triumph a hollow victory. Throughout the nation, the martial spirit grew in direct proportion to the President's inability to make both France and Great Britain respect American rights. The situation was equally bad in the city. As Holt put it, New York "wishes either for war or peace, and is disgusted with a state which is *both and neither*—which is despised abroad and ridiculed at home, and is ruining the country, while it disgraces the administration of its government." [35]

In the first weeks of 1812, politicians confused subjective motives with objective facts. Momentarily uncertain, the *Advertiser* snapped that although it favored peace, the nation should not forfeit its freedom and independence. Even the Tammany Society was perplexed. Firmly Madisonian, it backed the President's program, but as a patriotic organization, its Council of Sachems instructed Congressman Samuel Mitchill that war was just and necessary unless Great Britain mended her ways. Making the situation more complex, DeWitt Clinton blurred his position and opportunistically capitalized on Republican discontent to boom either himself or his uncle for the coming presidential election. "The Clinton party are hostile & active," General Henry Dearborn cautioned Jefferson, "and no measures are, or will be omitted for rendering the measures of the President unpopular, or his reelection doubtful." [36]

In the midst of such uncertainty, the Tammany Society prepared to move into its new Wigwam, at the corner of Nassau and Frankfort streets. The Society had built its new home, at a cost of $55,000, with two purposes in mind. As a hotel, it leased the establishment to David Barnum, a former Philadelphia innkeeper, who boasted that his establishment was the finest in the city and had the best liquors money could procure. Above the "lodging rooms" was a spacious meeting hall, the "Long Room," 57 feet long and 53 feet wide, capable of accommodating meetings of upward of 2,000 braves. Here the Society would hold its gatherings, dances, and festivals.

At the same time, the Tammany Society's alter ego, Martlingism—or, more formally, the Regular General Republican Democratic Committee—held its rallies in the new Wigwam, promptly dubbed "Tammany Hall" by the public. By 1812, then, as the Madisonian Republicans moved out of Abraham Martling's tavern and into their gleaming, fresh headquarters, the public began to use the term Martlingism interchangeably with a new label—"Tammany-Men," or more simply, "Tammany Hall."

Inadvertently, Matthew Davis also helped define a new power equation in city politics. In the coming years, the Long Room, one party chieftain later pointed out, was to become "the place of concentrated opinion and action, and a rallying point of the democracy of the city." As the General Committee merged its identity with the Tammany Society, then, the Wigwam gained tremendous prestige as the tabernacle of party regularity. Under such conditions, future city Republicans, and later the Democrats, could not fully dominate the local organization unless they controlled four critical variables: the voters, the municipal government, the General Committee, and the Tammany Society.[37]


All this lay in the future. Before the Madisonians could think of dominating local politics, they had to remove Clinton from the scene. But as events soon proved, this effort was neither simple or easy.

Before the 1812 legislature began its session, the banking mania of the year before continued unabated. Only one factor changed. Matthew Davis still pressed for a Republican institution, but his greed betrayed his political instincts. Unknown to his fellow Tammanyites, Davis had agreed with another group headed by his political foe, Clintonian Theodorus Bailey, to drop his efforts in exchange for a promised job as cashier in the new bank. Before Davis' friends learned of his chicanery, Governor Tompkins abruptly changed the picture. In his annual legislative address, he came out against charters for all new banks and charged that only speculators and cheap-money men favored an expansion of the credit system.[38]

Davis was hardly pleased with Tompkins' stand but could not oppose him. The reason lay with DeWitt Clinton and his continued flirtation with Federalist banking interests, whose proposed Bank of America offered the state a huge series of bonuses for incorporation—including one to finance internal improvements such as the canal. In the past, Clinton had been hostile toward banks in general, the Manhattan Company excepted, and most of his followers felt he would so continue. But Clinton confounded them. In a low-keyed way, the Bank of America promotion fitted his political needs because many of its sponsors were Republicans as well as Federalists. The upshot was, Davis noted, that "Clinton, I understand, is opposed to all Banks, but will not interfere to any extent." [39]

But Clinton's trimming did not suit several of his associates, particularly Ambrose Spencer and Judge John Taylor, president of the Albany State Bank. Both men had substantial interests in the status quo and saw no reason to incorporate new banks. When Clinton publicly continued to straddle the issue, even though he privately assured them he still opposed granting fresh charters, both men sought new allies.

In direct proportion, Governor Tompkins' prestige increased. The banking mania and its attendant taint of a "monied aristocracy" repelled some men, and others deprecated the legislature's moral decline when rumors of bribery became common knowledge, while still others such as Spencer and Taylor saw in the governor a practical brake on credit expansion. But outside of the extreme step of proroguing the legislature, the lobbyists seemed effectively to have limited his options.[40]

At the end of March, amid mounting evidence of graft, the Bank of America bill passed the assembly and moved to the senate. Before debate began, however, the governor lost his patience and prorogued the legislature for sixty days. Intent on conciliation, some upstate politicians hoped to use the move as a means to reunite the party. But in the city, Tammany's General Committee had other ideas. Seizing on the opportunity to brand Clinton as a traitor, it called a special pro-Tompkins meeting, barred any of the mayor's supporters from attending, and, according to Davis, drew the biggest crowd "we have witnessed for many years." A much smaller group of Clintonians, no more than eighty at best, held a similar rally, and also vociferously backed the governor. But to an ebullient Robert Macomb, one of Tompkins' staunchest supporters, "the republicans, called Martling-Men, merit eternal honor for their conduct on this occasion." [41]

Upstate, Clinton lost more support. When Solomon Southwick charged that Tompkins had acted only to curry favor with Madison by preventing the legislature from nominating Clinton for president before the Congressional Caucus met, Ambrose Spencer drew back in anger. "If Mr. C[linton] countenances such fellows he need not expect my co-operation," he wrote John Armstrong. After a few months of reflection, Spencer sponsored a new Albany newspaper, the *Republican*, which at first merely backed Tompkins but later in the summer became harshly anti-Clintonian.[42]

"We live in a Strange time," Matthias Tallmadge, George Clinton's brother-in-law sniffed. "Our Governor has prorogued our Assembly. Farmer's boys are as apt to use power when in power as perhaps Gentlemen's sons." Despite Tallmadge's disdain, the bank struggle defined an emerging political realignment within the local party. Although Tompkins welcomed Spencer's aid, he knew the wily judge was actually grooming Senator John Armstrong for the presidency when Madison retired in 1816. Above that, the Livingstonians were too unpredictable. As Martin Van Buren noted some years later, they were the type of friends one had in profusion when they were not needed, "but apt to be very scarce under different circumstances." Tammany, in contrast, gave the governor a dependable power base, and the prorogation became the catalyst for the coalition. It had little political impact, then, when the legislature reconvened and passed the Bank of America bill. Of far more importance, Tammany had helped create a lasting statewide alliance, capable of destroying Clinton and dominating the state Republican party.[43]

For all of Tammany's success with the banking issue, the question of war or peace prevented any undue optimism. In the city, the Society backed the Administration yet felt the nation was militarily unprepared for war. The Clintonians also deprecated war, but for other reasons. From purely a practical standpoint, DeWitt Clinton's anti-Administration position became a rallying point for dissident Republicans throughout the nation. Moreover, his latent candidacy carried its own potent internal logic. As the spokesman for the North's agrarian and commercial interests, he honestly felt that Madison had forfeited the Republican party's basic ideals. The so-called Virginia Dynasty, Clinton believed, was merely concerned with self-aggrandizement and the promotion of Southern interests. As a matter of expediency and principle, then, Clinton prepared his race for the presidency.[44]

On the other hand, he labored under some severe handicaps. His uncle hovered near death, the Council of Appointment was hostile,

and Tammany gave him little respite. The prorogation was the next
blow because it barred an independent nomination until after the Congressional Caucus would name Madison.

Clinton's position became intolerable in the spring election. In order
to validate his claims of innocence in the Bank of America scandal,
Clinton coveted Tompkins' aid, as did Tammany. "The governor,"
the *Post* wryly noted, "has somehow got astride the fence, as they say."
The reverse was true. Tompkins now wanted to cast off his dependence
on the Clintonians and establish his independence by a clear-cut Tammany victory. The issue of party versus emotional loyalty became
even more difficult for Clinton when his uncle died on election eve
and the *Advertiser* accused him of cynically using the legitimate grief
of many New Yorkers to advance his political prospects.[45]

The election proved a Federalist victory. In the city, they defeated
both incumbent Tammany congressmen and the entire legislative slate.
Upstate, it was much the same story as the Federalists elected enough
men to control the lower house, although the disunited Republicans
retained the senate. At last, the bitter Clinton faced political reality.
Rejected by Tammany, scorned by Tompkins, deserted by the city
organization, Clinton now made a fateful decision. Positive that he
could tap a vein of deep frustration and resentment over the way
Madison was running the country, Clinton became a formal presidential
candidate.[46]

By comparison, to Washington politicians and President Madison
in particular, the threat of war made New York politics and Clinton's
insurgency seem both remote and unimportant. Tammany's failure to
make Madison choose sides over the appointment of a new federal
district judge symbolized its frustration. During early May, Albert
Gallatin asked Tompkins for recommendations, and the governor submitted a long list. Tammanyites, however, thrust the question into a
larger perspective. Using lame-duck Congressman Samuel Mitchill as
their intermediary, Sachems Adrian Hegeman, John Haff, Peter
Schenck, and John Bingham bombarded the President with unsolicited
advice. All stressed the idea that removing the Clintonian collector,
district judge, marshal, and surveyor of the port was absolutely vital.
"We must build up the party," Hegeman pleaded, "or forfeit everything." After reading the letters, Mitchill tied them in a bundle and
penned a short facing note to Hegeman's outburst: "Read it, admirable

and excellent Sir, read it." But like Jefferson before him, Madison would not interfere directly in local politics.[47]

In May, the Clintonian-dominated legislative caucus added a note of urgency to Tammany's efforts when it nominated DeWitt Clinton for the presidency. Although they realized that they were defying the Congressional Caucus' authority, the Clintonians rationalized their move by stressing the idea that Clinton would rally disgruntled Republicans in other states and save New York's agrarian interests from Madison's callous indifference. Strangely, few of Clinton's city foes were alarmed. As Tammany brave Maturin Livingston put it, "as a friend to the state and the republican cause I regret the occurrence, but as a political opponent of Mr. Clinton I rejoice in it. It is not possible he can succeed, and I think the measure must prostrate him, as well in this State as in the union." [48]

While this maneuvering preoccupied local politicians, the nation drifted inexorably into war. On June 1, Madison sent Congress a special message that recommended war, and for the next three weeks Federalists joined dissident Republicans in bitter tirades against the request. In the final showdown, despite an overwhelmingly negative New York vote, Congress backed the President and the nation faced an uncertain future.

In the city, the decision for war set the substance of partisanship for the next three years. The Federalists objected violently and called on the people to use all constitutional means to avert "this dreadful calamity, by a change of men, that there may be a change of measures." The Clintonians were equally opposed, but skirted the line that separated disloyalty from dissent. Holt recommended a united effort in terms of defense, but added that a "blind devotion to men and slavish subserviency to party" was unthinkable. Tammany made the conflict a test of party regularity. Despite the hopes of some upstate leaders that the war would stifle "party spirit," the Hall systematically barred Clintonians from all organizational affairs, and scorned the Federalists as traitors.[49]

Even so, the Administration's clumsy efforts at waging war had severe repercussions in Tammany Hall. New York was not at all prepared for the conflict, and unscrupulous merchants (including Matthew Davis), scenting huge profits, jacked up commodity prices of goods needed by the militia. Then, too, the War Hawks' dreams of an easy Canadian conquest ended in bitter nightmares. As it became increasingly apparent that jingoistic gasconades could not win battles, Madison's popularity plummeted, and in the city Holt seemed plausible when he argued that only DeWitt Clinton could save the country from the President's monumental inefficiency. The Federalist *Post* agreed. A change of men, it predicted, would give the nation "new energies and resources" to end the war.[50]

Although public criticism harassed Madison, Clinton did not automatically pick up significant nationwide Republican support. With party officeholders fearful of losing their jobs through picking the wrong side, Clinton's only chance for winning hung on Federalist willingness to back his candidacy.

In September, after much soul-searching, the Federalists decided to back Clinton and not make an independent nomination. Their move, however, proved a mixed blessing. One group led by Rufus King rejected Clinton outright, and tacitly helped Tammany gather votes for Madison. The Federalists in New England carried their area for Clinton, but even then the move backfired. Many Republicans who had long feuded with Madison, like William Duane of the *Philadelphia Aurora*, felt that Clinton could not win. It was not the President's popularity or his program that saved him, Duane wrote, but "the apprehension of the return of federal rule." [51]

For all these cheerful signs, the New York City Madisonians were in deep trouble. The President's policy of soft-pedaling Clinton's apostasy strengthened the belief, Senator John Smith of Long Island complained, that local party workers could work against the national ticket with impunity. Well aware of such an attitude, Tammany Hall and the *Advertiser* maximized Clinton's alliance with the Federalists to caution voters that he would sell out Republican principles for "personal influence."

In November, when the legislature met to select electors, both sides marshaled their lobbyists for a last massive effort. But the Madisonians found themselves outgeneraled. Following a devious plan that stressed the need for party unity outlined by young State Senator Martin Van Buren, the combined vote gave Clinton a majority. But New York and New England did not represent the United States, and Madison won reelection. No sooner had the outcome become known than the Clintonians sought to scramble back into the party's good graces. Tammany and Ambrose Spencer, however, had other ideas.[52]

Before Tammany could savor the fruits of victory it had to settle some of its own internal problems. Grand Sachem Matthew Davis, who remained a wheelhorse in the Society until 1826, suddenly found business profits more desirable than continued revenge against Clinton and left a power vacuum in the Hall. In his place, a fresh group of Tammanyites he had helped recruit—men like sailmaker Stephen Allen, silversmith John Targee, old Liberty Boy Benjamin Bailey, and lawyer John Ferguson, along with former Burrites William and Peter Irving and the Swartwout brothers—gradually grasped the reins of power. In a secondary sense, Davis' shift toward the business world heralded a process that countless other local politicos would repeat. Politics to them was less the art of government than an avenue for immediate personal gain. Until Boss Tweed's time, fluctuating leadership cliques— some from the Tammany Society, some from Tammany Hall—fought for power and often limited the organization's influence in state and national councils.[53]

By 1813 the Administration began to put something in the local party's grab bag for everyone except the Clintonians. When the *Advertiser*'s new editor, George White, proved an indifferent propagandist, Albert Gallatin helped recruit Henry Wheaton, a brilliant Rhode Island lawyer and newspaperman, for Tammany's new journal, the *National Advocate*. Above that, Madison's reelection had melted his political frigidity, and he finally built up Tammany as a buffer against Clintonianism. Removing the incumbents, the President appointed John Smith federal marshal, Sachem John Haff surveyor of the port, Sachem John Ferguson naval officer, and William P. Van Ness as federal district judge. Governor Tompkins, Ambrose Spencer, and Samuel Mitchill demanded an even more ruthless housecleaning. Tompkins was most outspoken. Clearly his own man, he angrily warned Postmaster General Return J. Meigs to cease appointing the "Schismatics denominated Clintonians." Thus, by 1817, Tammany had muted to a whisper DeWitt Clinton's once powerful voice over federal patronage.[54]

Madison's belated show of strength created a new sense of urgency among the Clintonians. Under these conditions, Clinton could not afford the loss of a single state office, and he desperately wanted the party's renomination for lieutenant governor. At the same time, he needed to keep his channels to the Federalists unclogged because his tenure as mayor depended upon their good will in the Council of Appointment. In short, his fate had become an emotional, almost traumatic, issue for everybody concerned.

Blithely ignoring his insurgency, Clinton demanded that the Republican legislators issue a call for an immediate nominating caucus, confident that he still controlled the party's machinery. Tammany anticipated the move, and offered a substitute plan for a popularly elected, representative state convention. But state Republicans who had just fought a bitter battle in defense of party "usages" feared innovations at this point and voted the move down. Even so, the Hall had no intention of backing Clinton if he won. "Thee may be assured that the Republicans of this quarter," a city merchant wrote Davis, "will not support DeWitt merely because he may again receive a Legislative nomination." The problem, however, quickly became moot. Just before the caucus, Martin Van Buren became convinced that Clinton had deceived his party over the question of naming a new United States Senator and swung over to John Taylor, who now gained the coveted nomination.[55]

Meantime, Holt braced the entire party for an inevitable Federalist purge and freely predicted a massive slaughter. But when the Council met, it made the editor regret his words. Swayed by Jonas Platt's arguments that the Federalists, for consistency's sake, could hardly remove Clinton as mayor after they had supported him for president, the Council made a reappointment. The Federalists' hands-off policy, however, did not include Clinton's followers or Tammanyites. As a result, Clinton's stay of execution proved a mixed blessing. On one hand, Tammany claimed he had sold out his principles for continued power, while on the other, his henchmen felt he had abandoned them. With the ground slipping from beneath him, Clinton faced two hard choices. He could either confirm Tammany's verdict by becoming a full-fledged Federalist, or remain within the Republican party and fight back. He chose the latter.

Clinton's rejection of Federalism, nonetheless, proved easier than moving back into the Republican party's good graces. At the Tammany Society's huge inaugural ball to celebrate Madison's victory, John Swartwout assailed the mayor, and promised full aid to win the war. When a few Clintonian loyalists tried to crash the party, Tammany toughs pushed them down the Wigwam's spiral staircase and out the front door. The General Committee made a similar move during the gubernatorial campaign when it rejected any Clintonian participation. Even efforts from Clinton's own political backyard hurt him. In answer to the *Columbian*'s call for party unity to support the "country's cause," the *Evening Post* sneered that the only thing consistent among the Clintonians was their inconsistency.[56]

In the 1813 elections, although Tammany beat the drum for "Union, Sailor's Rights and Free Trade," city voters ignored the tune. Tompkins gained only 44 percent of the total ballot, while the Federalists, or "Peace Ticket" as they styled themselves, again won the assembly ticket. Ultimately, upstate voters saved Tompkins, but not before Federalism increased its margins in both legislative houses. Caught in the cross fire of peace advocates, Clintonians, and Federalists, Tammanyites nevertheless did not waver, and refused to buckle despite the organization's massive losses. And as for Clinton, the Hall fully agreed with Ambrose Spencer: "I cannot but pity him. He is a victim of ambition, treachery & rage; but he must never be forgiven." [57]

By 1814 the question of war or peace, then, had smashed New York City's already badly splintered Republican party into impotency and widened the cracks between Clinton and his followers. Feeding on such discontent, Federalism made the city its private preserve. It controlled the Corporation, held a majority in the city's legislative delegation, and gave no indication of faltering. Yet Tammany did recover. But its climb back into local dominance lay more in a combination of luck and chance than any particular skill on its part.

Governor Tompkins led the way. His heroic efforts as a war leader, his calm in the face of military disasters, his willingness to incur huge private debts in order to buy military equipment when the Federalist legislature refused to appropriate war funds, his loyalty to Madison, sharply counterpointed Clinton's defection and John Armstrong's spectacular failure in defending Washington from British attack. Tompkins was now a national figure, a possible presidential candidate, and the Hall rode to glory on his coattails.

Nationally, General Andrew Jackson's victory at New Orleans reassured many New Yorkers that Tammany's patriotic incantations were real. All but forgotten were the earlier frustrations as Americans convinced themselves that they had indeed gloriously won the war. The feeling even infected the Federalists. One wrote: "While our rulers have disgraced themselves, and brought the nation to death's door, Jackson at New Orleans has given a noble finish to our part of the fighting, and helped to give us a national character." [58]

Above all, Tammany's greatest reprieve came from Federalist blunders. First, the party erred in not removing Clinton as mayor and gaining full control over his vast prerogatives. Moreover, Clinton proved an effective champion of local preparedness despite Tammany's interference, and made the Federalists seem selfish in contrast. Next, a

group of men led by Gulian Verplanck, an aspiring author and a
founder of the Washington Club movement, who wrote a pro-
Tammany pamphlet under the name "Abimelech Coody," broke with
the party because of its antiwar position and Clintonian flirtation. Finally, the Federalists proved masters at criticism, but novices in constructive remedies. Meeting at the ill-fated Hartford Convention, they
skirted near treason, and gave their foes enough partisan ammunition
to grind the party into oblivion. By the end of the war, Federalism had
essentially committed political suicide. The best it could now hope for
was to again play broker politics among the constantly feuding Republicans.[59]

In the 1815 spring legislative session, the Republicans with "Coody"
aid controlled the new Council of Appointment. Immediately, Tammany demanded that it replace Clinton as mayor. The Council deadlocked, 2–2, however, and Tompkins, who had the deciding vote, held
back. As Ambrose Spencer mused, "the Governor is everyman's friend
& he is so ardent in his pursuit of popularity, that he will not venture
to lose an atom of it, by approving the preconceived idea of any man,
however flexible he may be." Moreover, Tompkins, no matter his personal distaste for Clinton, felt that a new round of intraparty brawling
might compromise his own presidential ambitions. The Hall was adamant. "Our friends in this City are in a compleat uproar respecting the
Mayoralty," a suddenly aroused Matthew Davis wrote. "They are
fearful DeWitt will not be removed. Such an event renders the city
Federal, to a certainty." Tompkins drew back. His rule over the party
was firm but not absolute, and he could ill afford the Hall's mounting
displeasure. Unwilling to forfeit his hard-won laurels, then, Tompkins
pressed Clinton's two Council supporters to reverse their stand, and, by
early March, the Council named John Ferguson, the Tammany Society's grand sachem, as the new mayor.[60]

Clinton's removal created a storm of protest. The New York Irish,
led by Thomas Addis Emmett, shouted his praises and stressed their
loyalty to him rather than the Republican party. Even the Federalist-
dominated Common Council joined in and lauded Clinton for his outstanding contributions as mayor. Yet, while the Hall bent to these
winds, it steadily tightened its grip over the local party, and Ferguson
replaced Clintonian job-holders with loyal ward workers.

By early summer, as the cries of distress became muted, the Hall's
triumph seemed secure. The Tammany Society dominated the city

through Ferguson, the Clintonians were out of power, rumors circulated through the city that Clinton was drowning his problems in alcohol, and the Federalists were in disgrace. But DeWitt Clinton was a political creature, and his retirement was more of a strategic retreat than a withdrawal. Once more, he was ready to start a new chapter in the story of Tammany Hall.[61]

# ～⁄ 3 ⁄～

# The Spirit of Tammanyism

THROUGHOUT HIS CAREER, DeWitt Clinton had exhibited the knack of turning political adversity into personal advancement. In late 1815 and early 1816, he again showed such skill by reviving the idea of building a canal across upper New York State. In order to gain legislative approval, he drafted a model memorial which other canal boosters copied, downplayed the project's partisan dimensions, and emphasized that its construction would benefit the entire state, not merely one section or interest.

But Clinton could not escape his past. In the city, unforgiving Tammanyites scoffed at his sudden altruism. By the strict rule of local partisanship, the canal became a political issue because of its sponsor. Clinton, too, his disclaimer to the contrary, viewed the project as a political lifesaver. With it, he intended to rescue the career that Tammany had almost destroyed.[1]

Meantime, the Congressional Caucus nominated Governor Tompkins for vice president. Since the local Republicans knew that the national election was hardly more than a formality, Tompkins' imminent removal from the state set the stage for a massive power struggle. In one camp Judge Ambrose Spencer, furious because Martin Van Buren had managed to gain control over the Council of Appointment, made a spectacular shift and sought an accommodation with DeWitt Clinton. By mid-April of 1816, the two erstwhile enemies were the best of friends and, after ironing out minor differences, joined against Van Buren and Tammany Hall.

Although Tompkins was certain of being elected vice president, he wanted to hold the party together for as long as possible and again ran for governor. For the moment, Spencer and Clinton backed the move, but planned a new canvass once Tompkins resigned because no precedent existed for the lieutenant governor to inherit the job. "There can be no wavering with me, Clinton must be pushed, & he will succeed," Spencer wrote John Armstrong. "He has a greater value for my opinions now than he ever had, & my friends are his, if they choose to be so." [2]

Through all of these maneuverings, Martin Van Buren's strategy was simple, however complicated his tactics might become. Clinton, he felt, had enough natural enemies within the party to make a full comeback impossible. Although he miscalculated on the Spencer-Clinton alliance, Van Buren still thought his tactics were correct. Then, too, he supported Tompkins' reelection, assuming that the governor would hold both offices and not resign. At the same time, Van Buren realized the Erie Canal's full political potential, and sought to neutralize Clinton's identification with it. Moreover, Van Buren felt the canal would aid upstate grain growers and raw wool interests he was wooing. Even so, he could not convince Tammany Hall to accept his logic. In senate debate, then, Van Buren proposed a compromise. Against Clintonian wishes for immediate construction, he suggested that the canal commissioners restudy their financial needs and report back the following year. Eventually, the bill passed with his amendment.[3]

With Clinton preoccupied, Tammany Hall consolidated its position. In the spring election, the Hall pushed its entire congressional and legislative slates to victory, while carrying Tompkins to a handsome margin in the gubernatorial race. But the Hall's success made it politically imperative for Clinton to make sure the rank and file understood that only he had the necessary vision to carry the plan through. In a broad-ranging attack during the summer, Spencer and Clinton charged that Van Buren had secretly opposed the bill, only voting for it "lest it might harm" his faction's "popularity at the approaching election." [4]

Tammany's reply to these charges was marked by stubbornness and invective. Rather than debate the canal's merits, the Hall besmirched Clinton's motives, and tongue-lashed him for making the project his private political engine. In a typical thrust, Charles Ferris, the main speaker on Independence Day, shouted that the electorate should trust patriotic men bound by integrity and love of country rather "than a blind devotedness to any particular Individual." [5]

But neither Tammany's opposition nor Van Buren's guile could halt Clinton's momentum. In the next several months, the legislature called for a special election after Tompkins became Vice President, the Clintonians won control over the Council of Appointment, and Spencer seized upon Tammany's earlier idea for a statewide representative convention to name the new gubernatorial candidate. By March 1817, Clinton had come full circle. As he read the signs of the times, Enos Throop, a Van Burenite from western New York, noted that certain areas once hostile to Clinton—particularly those which would profit from the canal—were now his staunchest followers.[6]

The canal, then, placed a major stumbling block in Van Buren's drive for power. He had no alternative but to place the project above party and the political fortunes of one individual or one group of politicians, while coercing Tammany into backing the measure. But the Hall, surrounded by a tightening chain of Clintonian hostility, ignored his wishes.

Much of Tammany's stubbornness stemmed from Mordecai Noah, the *National Advocate*'s new editor. An intense, articulate, idealistic bundle of contradictions, Noah at one moment could play the fawning courtier, the next a pugnacious individualist. After a riotous career in the diplomatic service, he settled in the city where his polemic skills created numerous uproars for the next three decades. Never fully trusting Van Buren, Noah was a constant thorn in the side of upstate Republicans who gradually came to view him "literally with abhorence." Too, few Tammanyites yet recognized Van Buren's skill in party management. Van Buren's Albany Regency, that well-drilled disciplined corps of politicians that would later awe his contemporaries and dominate the state until the 1840s, was still to come. Tammany, then, followed its own provincial needs and hatreds in rejecting the new canal bill. But by April 1817, the Hall's obstructionist tactics failed to halt the project's passage and it became law.[7]

For an organization that prided itself on its political acumen, Tammany had instead displayed remarkable ineptness. Because of its refusal to accommodate itself with the Erie Canal, Clinton had successfully capitalized on the measure to reestablish his political career. On the night of April 24, 1817, the problem's full magnitude startled the Tammany chieftains. That night about two hundred Irishmen rioted at the Wigwam, destroyed most of the furniture in the Long Room, and sent several Tammanyites to the hospital before the arrival of the mayor and police ended the brawl. All this was seemingly due to the General Committee's refusal to nominate Thomas Addis Emmett for the assembly. Yet in a larger and more critical sense, the uproar focused attention on a major problem that perplexed Tammany for the next four years— how to discredit Clinton and transfer the canal's popularity to itself.

In practical terms, the Hall had to steal the issue from the governor and somehow adopt it as pure Tammany doctrine.[8]

All immigrants, particularly the Irish, played a vital role in city politics. Both DeWitt Clinton and Tammany catered to these "adopted citizens" and sought their voting allegiances, either before or after naturalization. Yet the Tammany Society did not initiate these men as braves until they gained respectability, affluence, and middle-class status. The upshot was that while the Hill politically stressed its egalitarianism, its elite arm practiced discrimination and nativism.

Aware of the dichotomy, the Irish gave Clinton their primary loyalty. Tammany drew only their secondary support. Because the Irish valued the canal as a potential job market even more, Clinton's political stock had increased while the Hall's plummeted correspondingly. Fortunately for Tammany, however, Clinton was unable to transfer this devotion to his party. As one Irishman, Dr. William Mac-Neven complained, "we Clintonians have not had any regular plan or System, at least I know of none, while it is obvious that our adversaries [Tammany] have all their measures predetermined & arranged." [9]

Beginning in February 1817, the Clintonians sought to change this situation by launching a full-scale movement to alienate the Irish permanently from the Hall. The *Columbian* and *The Exile*, another pro-Clinton propaganda sheet, both charged that the Tammany Society had amended its secret constitution to exclude all adopted citizens, and told the Irish that they would serve their interests best by boycotting the Hall in the upcoming gubernatorial election. In the same spirit, several exhilarated Clintonians made violent anti-Tammany toasts at the Hibernian Provident Society's annual Saint Patrick's Day dinner.[10]

For the next few weeks the Hall ignored these storm warnings, refused to placate the Irish by placing Emmett on its ticket, and went its own way until the riot changed the ground rules. Yet as provocative as the Irish mutiny was, it more than anything else forced the organization to reassess the attitude towards the Erie Canal, the one key issue that held the Irish to Clintonianism. But while opposition was now a luxury the Hall could no longer afford, party chieftains could see no easy way to identify Tammany with the waterway without increasing Clinton's stature.

The spring election underscored the fact that Clinton could not transfer immigrant loyalty to his party. Tammany gained all the local and state offices except the governorship. According to Henry Meigs, one of the Tammanyites elected to the assembly, the results proved that "our majority is formed of independent voters, not managed or directed, not given to please any Individual." As for Peter Porter, the Hall's gubernatorial candidate, few sober-minded politicos expected him to win. Even so, the Hall could not forget that the threat of insurgency still existed, a threat Holt made more explicit when he reminded the Irish, "*we have deserved success*, if we have not obtained it." [11]

Having decided to woo, rather than scorn Irish voters, Tammany floundered over the techniques of seduction. Noah, who concealed a deep streak of nativism in his heart, failed to help when he growled that "we are not to be frightened by snarling asses, nor their keepers." But the General Committee's determination for a rapprochment dampened his fiery spirit. Under pressure, Noah relented. First, he carefully outlined Tammany's position on the canal. The Hall, he wrote, had not opposed the project because of "personal motives or individual hostility," but on the impracticality of "a young and rising state, yet in its infancy, to complete a canal of *360* miles in length." If, on the basis of wealth, the state could not afford the effort, the editor continued, why had the legislature authorized it? Why had the canal commissioners, led blindly by DeWitt Clinton, proposed such a massive undertaking without first deciding how the state could honestly finance construction? In answering himself, Noah hung the burden of guilt squarely upon Clinton. The governor had used the canal, Noah insinuated, solely for self-advancement. In contrast, he ended his argument, Tammany stood for fiscal sobriety, not public plunder.[12]

At its Independence Day celebration, Tammany continued to refine its technique. Deserting his desk at the *Advocate*, Noah made the principal address. All the Tammany Society required from immigrants, he explained, was devotion to the United States, "an abandonment of foreign prejudices, a peaceful demeanor, and loyalty towards the Constitution." When the festival reached its toasting stage, however, a more partisan feeling emerged. To "the City of New York," shouted one party worker. "Her late triumph over a *drilled mob* is the triumph of national feelings and national principles." Appalled at such blatant xenophobia, Sachem Benjamin Romaine, who had rejoined the Society after his disgrace eight years before, sought to make the point that immigrants could not trust an aristocrat like Clinton. "He that builds his greatness on *personal influence* aims a blow at the root of the tree of liberty. He is not a republican, whatever his profession might be." [13]

In August, Noah completely abandoned his earlier nativism. He began a series of dialect articles, purportedly written by one of Clinton's Irish "bully boys," which satirically made the point that anyone aiding Clinton only ended by hurting themselves and alienating the bulk of society. The series further suggested that a few malcontent Irishmen were bringing all New York immigrants into disrepute. Despite the paper's soft sell, the Irish held aloof. They wanted deeds, not sophistry.[14]

Clinton, too, knew that tangible results counted. With this in mind, he planned to operate his administration on three assumptions. First, he intended to place the canal above the "ephermeral [sic] political questions of the day." Next, he would only seek allies from among the "most virtuous and capable persons." Finally, in order to sooth the lingering tensions Tammany and Van Buren had created, the governor sought to control both federal and state patronage. His expectations, however, were short-lived. Although President James Monroe continued Jefferson's aim of amalgamating all political factions into one great party, Secretary of the Treasury William Crawford had other plans. He assumed that Vice President Tompkins was a cipher and that Clinton was again eyeing the presidency. As a result, Crawford, who hoped to succeed Monroe, used spoils to form a working agreement with Martin Van Buren. A similar story occurred in the state when Van Buren gained the upper hand in the new Council of Appointment. Even so, the governor was a highly resourceful man. Displaying a knack for rebuilding old political fences, he once more began to sound out some former Federalist allies about a fresh alliance.[15]

Impressed by Van Buren's efforts, Tammany finally succumbed to his leadership. But its attitude was based more on selfish motives than deep and abiding loyalty. To Walter Bowne, John Targee, and Benjamin Romaine—who saw politics as a means of honest graft—Van Buren offered patronage; to ambitious men-on-the-make, such as Noah and John Irving, Van Buren promised respectability; and to those neo-Jeffersonians like Stephen Allen and Michael Ulshoeffer, Van Buren stood well within the mainstream of legitimate Republicanism. But more to the immediate point, Van Buren led Tammany out of the Clintonian thicket.

Meantime, Tammany continued to woo the Irish. Eldad Holmes, a prominent banker and sachem, gave a toast at the St. Patrick's Day dinner held by the Hibernian Provident Society, a Clintonian hotbed, that echoed Noah's mature approach: "The Adopted Citizens—May they always be a link in the chain of Union." The toast caught the mystic phrase, "chain of union"—an integral part of the Society's ritual—and implied that Tammany would welcome large numbers of Irish as braves. The revolution in the Hall's tactics was progressing.[16]

Despite Tammany's new attitude, the 1818 spring elections ended as a draw rather than as an indication of a definable trend. Politically, the *Advocate* continued to print its pro-Irish editorials, the General Committee nominated a Sixth Ward immigrant for the Corporation, and Noah accused the Clintonians of being secret aristocrats because one of their candidates favored the whipping penalty for minor crimes. But in the end it was Clinton's first blunder in his canal policy that saved Tammany.

Politically, the first spadefull of earth dug on the project also dug the Hall's partisan grave. For if the Erie showed the slightest profit, or even hinted at partial success, much of Noah's specious economic opposition would backfire. Less dangerous but still hazardous, Clinton promised the Shamrock Friendly Association that jobs awaited all Irish immigrants.[17]

At this point, Clinton made a mistake. He and his fellow canal commissioners fell into a violent disagreement about which section of the canal—the western, middle, or eastern—should be dug first. Eagerly, the Hall exploited the dispute. "The project has already answered all the *political* consequences contemplated," Noah lashed out, "and . . . [Clinton] wishes it stopped; but, above all, is desirous that the republicans, or, as he calls them, the Tammanymen, shall stop it." In plain words, Tammany openly served notice that it was willing to embrace the canal—if conditions were right.[18]

When the legislature convened, the Hall drew the circle of opposition tighter around the harassed governor. Although he made a strategic retreat in his annual message and recommended full construction, the *Advocate*'s reaction was quite mild. Surprisingly, Noah wrote that "the legislature will be the proper judge, having more correct information on the subject than we have." Yet only the most unsophisticated politico could mistake Tammany's intent: it was laying a trap to ensnare Clinton.[19]

For all his other failings, Clinton was a political realist, and he immediately suspected the Hall's sudden moderation. "The enemies of these great improvements," he cautioned a friend, "have abandoned the field of direct opposition, but their enmity is no less envenomed on account of its insidious character." So, when the commissioners presented their full report, the Governor's hand was apparent in the unanimous suggestion that full construction should begin as soon as the ground softened.[20]

If trimming a political question was one attribute of a politician, then Clinton was a success; if trimming a political question alienated important sections of his party, then Clinton was a failure. The latter was true. Senate Clintonians, led by William Ross and Jabez Hammond, the future state historian, balked, and demanded that the western sections be completed before work commenced on the eastern. Grasping again on the quarrel, all but two Van Burenites (or "Bucktails," as the public now called them after Tammany's symbol), reversed their earlier position by voting for the commissioner's report. While this turnabout did not personally harm Clinton, it seriously split his party. Moreover, many ardent canal advocates now began to think that it was so well established that its success or failure no longer depended on the governor's political fortunes.

During the summer, the Bucktails added to Clinton's unease. Joseph Ellicott, one of the canal commissioners, resigned because of ill health, and Clinton, who as governor had the power to name an interim commissioner until the next legislative session, appointed Ephraim Hart, a man with many enemies in the Federalist party. At once a controversy flared. Since taking office, Clinton had steadily courted the Federalists and appointed them to key positions. In return, they had supported his program, often supplying the critical difference between victory and defeat. But now, snapping with irritation, they demanded that Clinton drop Hart as a sign of good will and the price of future cooperation. At this point, Van Buren injected himself into the controversy, and capitalized on the governor's unusual lack of political finesse.[21]

Van Buren realized that the Federalists were hungry for spoils and public recognition. But because of the Hartford Convention, they could not campaign as an independent party. As a result, they worked with whatever group would promise them more. Since Clinton was in such a position, they had apparently coalesced with him. Yet a young group of pragmatic Federalists, led by Rufus King, distrusted the governor and were ready to desert him at the right opportunity.[22]

When the 1819 legislative session began, Henry Meigs noted that King Federalists immediately tested their standing with Clinton. "They mean to have certain important offices filled by men of their own party," Meigs wrote. But when the governor made no concessions, the disgusted King-men realized that the Clintonian party was the creature of one man's will and would only bend at his word. Sensing the opportunity, Van Buren approached Kings' supporters with a deal that was as simple as it was breathtaking. In exchange for Bucktail support of King's reelection to the United States Senate, his followers would vote for a Van Burenite as canal commissioner.[23]

Van Buren's strategy was not popular in Tammany Hall, however, and Noah refused to abet the scheme. "It is palpably false that the republicans," he wrote, "or Tammanymen, have made any advances towards the Federalists." From Washington, Van Buren's close friend, Secretary of the Navy Smith Thompson, further warned that the Bucktails would forfeit massive prestige, as had Clinton, by such an alliance. In the face of these difficulties, the Clintonians, who had an idea of what was taking place, organized the Council of Appointment with Federalist aid and discounted the menace of any defections from their ranks. Then, to make Van Buren's chances even dimmer, the legislative Bucktails ignored his wishes, ran an opposition candidate against King, and forced the legislature to postpone action until the next legislative session.[24]

Luckily for Van Buren, the General Committee, led by State Senator Walter Bowne, had no intention of allowing Noah to set party policy, and forced him to join the *Albany Argus*, Van Buren's official state paper, on King's behalf. In the spring elections, Tammany further signaled this new spirit by nominating James Hamilton, Alexander's son, on its assembly ticket. The uncomprehending Clintonians harshly upbraided the young man as a traitor to his friends, his party, and his heritage—but Tammany's deeper motives escaped them.

Reacting instinctively to the Clintonian chorus of censure, the Federalist *Evening Post* cogently explained the arrangement. Since Clinton's ambitions far outweighed his cooperativeness, Coleman expounded, the Federalists had a right, even a duty, to strike out in a fresh direction. Upon principle, not expediency, he continued, it became imperative to find men of similar high-minded ideals. Tammany Hall furnished such men.[25]

These maneuverings reached a head in the legislature. When neither house agreed on a common candidate for canal commissioner, the King Federalists voted with the Bucktails on the joint ballot and narrowly elected Henry Seymour, one of Van Buren's more pliable lieutenants, a man Noah called friendly "to the project, but politically opposed to Mr. Clinton." With Seymour on the canal board, the Bucktails now held a working majority on the commission, and, of more importance, all its patronage. Anyone who sought a contract to supply goods or even work on the Erie thus needed Van Buren's aid rather than Clinton's. Years later, Van Buren noted that the Bucktails gained more political leverage from the project than the governor did from the Council of Appointment.[26]

Blithely ignoring the fact that it had opposed the canal for over four years, Tammany now boldly claimed credit for the waterway's success. The Hall and the Erie were synonymous, Noah proudly trumpeted. But the General Committee realized that so blatant a policy shift needed firm justification. The *Advocate* explained:

> After an experiment of nearly two years, it has been ascertained that the operations of the Canal have been such, as to satisfy those who doubted, that the project was within the resources and capabilities of the state, and from the late measures adopted by the legislature, it appears, that the people, who, alone should have the power deciding upon a question for which they are to pay, have agreed to authorize the completion both of the western and northern canals, and accordingly, these projects have been authorized. Opposition, therefore, should cease because it is the spontaneous will of the people, freely expressed; and, moreover, it has ceased to be a *political* project, pretended to depend on the will and capabilities of one man.[27]

Once the General Committee spoke through Noah, the ward organizations swung into action and each endorsed the new policy. That done, the General Committee held a mass meeting to reemphasize the fresh party line. After passing resolutions in favor of Van Buren, the Hall made a mockery of consistency by sanctimoniously approving the entire concept of internal improvements and announced that "the character of such measures [is] too sacred to be perverted to the purpose of faction." [28]

While the Hall did its best to convey the idea that it controlled the canal's destiny, the Irish seemed unimpressed. As a result, Tammany became more aggressive. Paradoxically, Noah accused the Clintonian-dominated Shamrock Aid Association and the Hibernian Provident Society of being "political machines instead of charitable institutions," which followed the "tenets of a demagogue, instead of the practice and the principles of the gospel." Even Van Buren, who professed a personal admiration for the governor, belittled his intellectual and political pretensions. Additionally, Tammanyites scurried through the wards to recruit as many Irish as possible. By word and deed, the Hall increasingly criticized the notion that Clinton was the adopted citizen's best friend. It was Tammany, the *Advocate* insisted, which provided the bulwark of freedom, while Clinton was merely a charlatan. No more would the downtrodden, Noah forecast, need "be indebted for exclusive kindness to a solitary individual." [29]

By the fall of 1819, Tammany recovered its local primacy. The Irish-Clintonian alliance appeared shattered, at least on the surface, as more and more Irishmen voted the Hall's ticket. Even more, the Society inducted a few token adopted citizens. Yet in a larger sense, Tammany's nativism, its dislike of parvenu "foreigners," became a recurring theme in its later history. When the old stream of Protestant Irish dried up, replaced by a Catholic-Irish deluge, the Hall's xenophobia again flowed. In sum, Tammany had not yet come to terms with the immigrant problem; it had merely formed a temporary accommodation.

Whatever else he might have been, Clinton was not a quitter. More concerned with his own salvation than any philosophic acceptance of defeat, he used sarcasm as a weapon to exploit the monumental inconsistencies in Tammany's new Erie policy. In collaboration with Pierre Van Wyck, Clinton wrote a series of anonymous articles in the *Columbian*, later published as *Martling Men*, and scornfully ridiculed men like Noah who believed that "everything is fair in politics." Furthermore, Clinton pictured Tammany as shot full of Federalists, a situation impossible in George Clinton's lifetime. Worse, Noah drilled home the horrible untruth that "Mr. [DeWitt] Clinton was not the real projector of the [Erie Canal], and . . . his merit [lay] only in borrowing the thoughts of other people." How, then, the anonymously sneering authors asked, could honest men vote for Tammany when its leaders stole an issue they once opposed—and then turned that very issue against its originator "to ruin his popularity." [30]

In a large way, the pamphlet revealed more about Clinton than it did about his enemies. He still wanted to live with a political situation that no longer existed: the intimate, elitist, family-controlled politics in which he had grown to political maturity. A new era was dawning in New York politics, and he was sadly unaware of the fact.

Although Henry Meigs, still a Tammany assemblyman, personally disliked the fondness which his associates now showed toward the Erie, nonetheless he epitomized the transitional politician caught between old-style elitism and the cynical manipulation of public opinion that typified the substance of partisanship in the coming generation. As a loyal party man, Meigs hesitated to challenge the General Committee, but he frequently unburdened his conscience when he wrote his father. To the older man, Meigs explained apologetically that because the people wanted the canal, the Hall had to satisfy their demands. The premise Tammany followed was simple: "Sit still, say the People to the Government, see *which way* we wish to proceed and direct us otherwise at your peril." [31]

Whether he realized it or not, Meigs expressed the real spirit of Tammanyism. A party's ultimate success or failure rested on its ability to maximize popular issues while, at the same time, neutralizing its opponents' abilities to use the same issue against it. Consistency meant nothing in this regard, as long as Tammanyites could rationalize the question to fit within the organization's Jeffersonian framework. The public enthusiasm for the canal, coupled with the Irish mutiny, were two of these issues, and Tammany used both in its drive for victory. It was as simple as that.

In the fall of 1819, Tammany's chances for upsetting Clinton in the next gubernatorial election gained impetus when the Federalist party split. One group, generally older men from the moribund Schuyler-Hamilton nexus and called the "Swiss" Federalists because of their purported willingness to sell their services, supported the governor, convinced that his "liberality" and "firmness" gave the state a "distinctively favorable character." It was to counter these men as well as Clinton that Charles and John King, Rufus' able sons, along with Johnston Verplanck, Gulian's half-brother, founded the *New York American*.[32]

As the paper joined the *Advocate* in heightening the volume of abuse against the Clintonians, Gulian Verplanck joined the fray. Using the talents of two gifted fellow King Federalists, John Duer and Rudolph Bunner, Verplanck wrote a series of satiric verses, "The Bucktail Bards," for the paper, which he later collected, published, and sent to various national political leaders. As the lampoons' popularity spread, Clinton became progressively more embarrassed, and answered them in kind. But as Johnston Verplanck gloated to Van Buren, "we have got the good humor of the public, and I have little doubt we shall get their votes." [33]

Such high hopes spurred the Bucktails' search for a suitable gubernatorial candidate. Their choice settled on Vice President Tompkins who, eager to leave Washington, accepted their overtures. Nevertheless, the situation was fraught with difficulty. Tompkins' personal war accounts were in an unsettled state and soon became a highly charged partisan issue. Worse, he was in a very emotional frame of mind, perhaps due to a weakness for alcohol, and seemed incapable of defending himself. At any rate, Van Buren helped rearrange his ledgers, Noah published a tract which downplayed his shortcomings as an accountant while emphasizing his war record, and a party caucus nominated him.[34]

Tammany was elated. At Evacuation Day celebrations, one sachem proposed that "his fellow citizens are his shield, while the Hydra of the state shall sink remorseless at his feet." Despite such sentiment, Van Buren was obsessed not so much with the Hall's protestations of loyalty as with Noah's unwillingness to absorb the King Federalists. Again and again Van Buren warned Tammanyites that they were "committed to his support—it is both wise & honest & we must have no fluttering in our course." Then, to make the pressure more intense, Van Buren, in collaboration with young William Marcy (soon to be major figure in his own right), wrote and circulated a pro-King pamphlet among Bucktail legislators.[35]

Although some Tammanyites continued to grumble about the move, it was not Noah's attitude but the question of admitting Missouri to the Union that almost upset Van Buren's calculations. As debate reached a critical stage in the Senate, Rufus King became the spokesman for the antiextensionism forces and laid himself open to the charge that he had instigated the dispute to split the Republican party and form a new Northern alliance based on a Federalist-Clintonian axis.

Van Buren perceived the subtle but potent danger here, and quickly moved to counter the charge. But once again Noah proved troublesome. Raised in Charleston, South Carolina, and sympathetic toward Southern interests, he already distrusted King and suspected the worst. At this point, Clinton added some real rather than imagined dimensions to the conspiracy charge when he recommended that the legislature debate the Missouri question and issue a policy statement. His next move cast a pall of mistrust over the entire episode, for he backtracked on King's reelection bid and now endorsed him.

Despite this rapid and bewildering turn of events, local politics, not massive collusion, prompted Clinton's actions. Quite simply, the Swiss and King Federalists had totally severed relations and their party was no longer united in any real sense. Furthermore, Assemblyman John King suggested that his father's followers should align with the Bucktails. If a plot existed, then, it was one-sided—if indeed it existed at all. Clinton, in his usual calculating way, utilized the Missouri crisis to serve his own ends and quash the proposed King–Van Buren alliance.[36]

During these developments, Noah had not been silent. Determined to assert his independence from upstate interests, he added a freewheeling note to the controversy. In a series of articles the editor deplored the institution of slavery, but denied that Congress had the constitutional right to interfere with the "municipal affairs" of any state, nor possessed the power to prescribe "terms and conditions to the admission of any state." Had Noah rested his argument here, his legalism would not have upset Van Buren. But in a gratuitous slap at King, the editor went on to say that the "noisy and clamorous" Northerners who favored restrictions were "perfectly unworthy of confidence" because they had been the ones who deserted their country in "the darkest moment." [37]

Luckily for Van Buren, the King Federalists did not take offense at Noah. Despite Rufus King's adamant refusal to endorse Tompkins, then, Van Buren's efforts began to jell. Just before the election, forty-nine prominent Federalists, some bearing the most distinguished names on their party's rolls, bitterly attacked Clinton and asserted that their party was dead. By attaching themselves "unequivocally and without reservation" to the Bucktails, these "High-Minded Federalists" created a political sensation, but did not materially aid Tompkins. As Van Buren recalled, these men made few converts among the Swiss Federalists, and "their success was not equal to their expectations." [38]

This situation was particularly true in the city where the Tammany Society held the High-Minders in low esteem. While five of them were old braves, men who had been initiated before Davis' heyday, just three of the remainder joined the Society. Tammany Hall, on the other hand, welcomed them on an individual basis, and over a period of time these talented men moved into the Hall's power structure.

The Hall, although convinced "principle will triumph," braced for trouble in the election. After a bitter fight centered mainly on Tompkins' public honesty and morality, the Hall carried the city for him with 59 percent of the total vote and elected its entire senate and assembly slates. Upstate, however, Tompkins did not fare as well, and lost the race by 1,457 votes. Although the Bucktails now controlled both legislative houses and the new Council of Appointment, Van Buren found little solace in victory. "We have scotched the snake," he penned, "but not killed it." [39]

Triumphantly, Clintonian Representative John W. Taylor, soon to become Speaker of the House, wrote a friend that the Bucktails were crushed and bewildered, their days of influence numbered. What

Taylor did not appreciate was that Tammany Hall had a natural resiliency in the face of disaster and it refused to accept the finality of Clinton's reelection. Instead, the defeat gave Noah and the Hall an opportunity to share Bucktail leadership with the upstaters like Van Buren who were attempting to control the local party. To do so, Tammany captured another popular issue favored by public opinion—the movement to amend the state constitution.

Over the years, various people had objected to some inequalities perpetuated by the constitution. The 1819 depression quickened the reform movement. Finding themselves without direct access to the legislature, debtors and needy people, who were almost all disenfranchised by property qualifications, demanded a change. Gradually, all the resentment brought on by the legislature's refusal to grant relief burst into an open attack on four anachronistic constitutional provisions: suffrage requirements, the Council of Revision, the Council of Appointment, and the judiciary.[40]

Because of these inequities, Bucktails and Clintonians sought to remedy the situation, but neither group agreed on what to revise or even the method for revision. In the city, Tammany Hall at first lacked firm guidelines. On one hand, many committeemen feared that liberalizing suffrage might work to DeWitt Clinton's benefit, much in the way he had gained immigrant loyalty. Others, led by Michael Ulshoeffer and Sachems Ogden Edwards and Stephen Allen, scoffed at their fears. With intelligent politicking, they felt that Tammany could alter the document to serve the organization's ends. Clinton's victory settled the matter.[41]

In July 1820, Noah began a series that called for immediate reform. Aiming his barbs at the landed aristocracy and the Clintonians, he wrote: "We must eradicate from the Constitution, all seeds of discord between the Rich and the Poor." But just as everything moved smoothly, Noah staggered the Hall by reviving the accusation that Rufus King plotted *"the erection of a northern party, the triumph of federalism, or the separation of the nation."* Tammanyites were appalled at Noah's lack of discretion, and the General Committee threatened to fire him unless he desisted. Here was language the reckless editor understood, and he dropped his crusade. With that problem solved, the Committee, under Stephen Allen's direction, whipped up a show of unity, and prepared a memorial calling on the legislature to authorize a new constitutional convention.[42]

Even though he was forewarned of Tammany's intention, the governor knew he could not back reform if the Hall gained credit for any benefits a revision brought. As the fierce political infighting continued in the November special session called by the Bucktails, Clinton growled: "The Tammany Horse rides through the Legislature like a wild ass's colt." But he could not control the reins. Michael Ulshoeffer reported a bill that echoed the General Committee's memorial but added two ingeniously devised items. The convention, he proposed, should have unlimited powers, and the voters must accept or reject the finished product *in toto*. Clinton and his Swiss allies derided the bill out of hand and called it a political gimmick, not serious reform. Their efforts failed. With only cursory debate, Ulshoeffer's bill passed and moved into the Council of Revision where it faced an uncertain future.[43]

Governor Clinton now stood at the crossroads of his political career: to approve the bill would be partisan suicide; to disapprove it would be equally hazardous. As his way out, he hoped that the Council of Revision would settle the issue, thus relieving him from having to take a public stand. Unfortunately for his future, this did not happen. When the Council deadlocked, 2–2, he had to cast the deciding vote and, after an agonizing delay, voted against the bill.[44]

Clinton based his decision on the ground that before the bill became law, the voters should first decide whether they really wanted a convention. Unaware of the magnitude of the governor's blunder, however cogent his line of reasoning, his supporters felt the opinion would "have weight with the people & cannot be ridiculed as puerile & frivolous, with any chance of success." But the howls of outrage that swept over the state quickly sobered the governor's friends: "It seems to me that Mr. Clinton's rejection of your convention bill," a jubilant Henry Meigs congratulated Van Buren, "was an instance in which his usual political discernment deserted him. I trust we shall reap the benefit of his folly." [45]

The General Committee did just that. In meeting after meeting, Tammany and the *Advocate* accentuated their role as the defenders of the downtrodden, the champions of human rights over property rights. Clinton, Noah wrote in a typical thrust, had insulted a free people, destroyed confidence in his administration, and made suspect the "good faith of his future executive professions and recommendations." [46]

By the time the legislature convened, Clinton sought to salvage a modicum of his lost prestige by joining the call for a convention. Noah did not relent. "To the republican party may be ascribed the benefits of radical reform. Men and measures must be changed." In the election campaign to decide if the people indeed wanted the convention, held

to satisfy the Council of Revision's preconditions, Tammany continued
to flay Clinton and refused to give him any credit for his tardy move.
"The History of the Convention is a brief one. It originated with the
republican party, and must be carried through by that party," Noah
admonished. The electorate agreed. In the city, 82 percent of the
voters cast "yes" ballots, while the proposition ran equally well upstate. In June, when the people named convention delegates, the Clintonians once more tasted defeat. Out of 126 men chosen, the Bucktails
had 110 and the old-line Federalists 13, while only 3 were Clintonians.[47]

Now that the Bucktails had secured the convention, party chieftains
refused to allow idealism to interfere with self-interest. It was Van
Buren, more than any other man, who called the tune. "Although I
have not taken a lead in this business," he confided to Rufus King,
"being some what timid in all matters of innovation, still I am thoroughly convinced that temperate reform & that only is the motive of
those of our friends who urge it most strenuously." Not too surprisingly, Tammany Hall agreed. It had sponsored the issue out of political
gamesmanship and backed reform because of public opinion, not to
shake society or put some abstract principles into operation. Prudence
and moderation were Tammany's passwords. Noah wrote that it would
be injudicious for the delegates to dump the entire constitution. Rather,
he lectured, they should "only amend those parts that experience has
shown to be wrong." [48]

But neither Van Buren, Tammany, or other moderate leaders could
stay the fresh innovative spirit that they helped conjure. The Council
of Revision died relatively peacefully; the governor now held an executive veto, which the legislature could override by a simple majority.
The delegates then limited the governor's term to two years, and, more
important for Tammany's immediate needs, called for a fresh gubernatorial election after the voters adopted the constitution. On the suffrage question, the moderates prevailed. They retained some property
qualifications by limiting the franchise to every white male over
twenty-one who had lived in his district six months, and who had
either paid taxes, served in the militia, or worked on public roads. The
only freehold requirements left were for free Negroes, who generally
voted Federalist.[49]

These reforms pleased Van Buren and moderate Tammanyites because the new constitution promised to bring about a massive shift of
political power. Inadvertently, however, Van Buren alienated the Hall

when his committee spelled out its report on the Council of Appointment. Basically, he and Tammany agreed that the Council was an anachronism, but parted company on whether or not some offices should remain appointive. The committee recommended that the legislature should select some high state officers—the comptroller, treasurer, secretary of state, surveyor general, and commissary general—while the governor, with senate approval, would name the bulk of the state's judicial and law enforcement officers. Justices of the peace, however, would be elective. As for New York City, the Common Council, not the voters, would choose the mayor. "I do not like your report," Tammanyite Michael Ulshoeffer angrily wrote Van Buren, "neither as it respects the state or the city." As it turned out, Van Buren also disagreed with the report, but only on the question of justices of the peace. After a long, heated debate his will prevailed, and the office of justice of the peace, a tremendous lever for enforcing party discipline and unity, was made appointive. But as part of the deal, to keep the Erastus Root–radicals happy, Van Buren agreed to make sheriffs' offices elective.[50]

Tammany went home with mixed feelings. Many of its more radical delegates resented Van Buren's agrarian fears that his successful methods of party management would not sway urban masses. Others grumbled over his refusal to help the city gain full autonomy so that the Corporation could handle local matters without worrying about upstate, agrarian interference. But the moderates realized that the Hall could live with these disappointments and still prosper. Most Tammanyites swallowed their unhappiness, rationalized that the party would now dominate city politics for the next generation, and capped their efforts by plotting the governor's imminent partisan demise.[51]

The Hall had sound reasons for focusing its attention on politics rather than complaining about unfulfilled reforms. Before the convention, the Clintonians had hoped to decoy public opinion by copying their foes' tactics. Ambrose Spencer explained, "we must be democratic, we must be on the side of the people. . . . If the real republicans of our party would make half the noise about their republicanism that the Bucktails do, we should be safe." Despite these intentions, the Clintonian position became untenable during the convention. In failing to capitalize on the cleavages among the Van Burenites, the governor's supporters often found themselves forced to defend unpopular issues. To the dismayed John Pintard, who admired the governor above all men,

his "political foes, & deadly they are, exult that he is completely pros-
trated, nor shall I wonder if he be obliged to retire from public life."
By the time the convention adjourned, then, Clinton's entire political
future was in doubt.[52]

Once again, Tammany exploited the situation. Since the voters had
to approve the constitution, some Clintonians hoped that a small turnout would symbolize the public's unhappiness with the document.
Others, however, conceded defeat without a struggle. That attitude left
the field open for Tammany. The General Committee organized the
voters, precinct workers held rallies and parades, and the *Advocate*
demanded a strong showing to rebuke the governor. In the special
election, party lines tended to disappear as the Hall had hoped, and
city voters and upstaters gave the constitution an impressive endorsement.[53]

Since 1822 was an election year, DeWitt Clinton had the dubious
choice of either running for reelection and probably losing, or retiring
gracefully. Some friends, such as former Postmaster General Gideon
Granger, who now lived in Canandaigua near Rochester, pleaded with
him to fall "with every wound in front" and seek vindication at the
polls. But Clinton faced the problem realistically, even if his supporters
did not, and decided grudgingly to retire rather than risk defeat. The
Hall's revolution was now complete.[54]

# 4

# The Challenge of
# Jacksonian Democracy

IN THE SPAN OF little more than the three decades from the formation of the local Republican organization to Tammany's absorption of the constitutional reform issue, the whole function and nature of party had undergone drastic alterations. In the 1790s, the city apparatus had been elitist and highly concerned with ideology, and operated with limited electioneering committees that appeared only weeks before the actual voting. By the 1820s, Tammany Hall had evolved into a highly structured, open-ended party, more interested in power than consistency. It functioned on two levels, the practical and the moral. On the one, its approach lay in tactics and strategy; on the other, by its democratic, Jeffersonian orientation.

As practical politicians, Tammanyites developed a style designed both to predict behavior and force the electorate to identify its best interests with the party's continued success. To do so, the Hall swayed voters through imagery, symbolism, and emotional appeals. The Tammany Society, with its ritualistic links to traditional American values, was irreplaceable in the effort. Both organizations used parades, rallies, processions, patriotic songs, and official party newspapers to spread the gospel. Editors such as Thomas Greenleaf, Matthew Davis, James Cheetham, James Main, and Mordecai Noah adopted simple, direct styles, characterized by invective, one-sided partisanship, emotionalism, and manipulation of popular symbols.

Tammany's party machinery completed the effort. Operating under centralized control and a formal table of organization, the Hall felt that party discipline, or "usages," was the only sensible method to structure a community so polyglot as New York City. Each fall, party workers

75

elected a three-man ward committee which in turn supposedly represented the voters. These committees formed the General Committee headed by a chairman chosen from within its ranks. Functionally, the General Committee served as a clearinghouse for problems that arose in the wards, mapped out campaign techniques, and directed strategy for turning out the voters.

As political moralists, Tammanyites had a credo they derived from the ideological questions the Federalists and Republicans had raised in the 1790s. Both the Hall and the Society stressed Lockean idealism, symbolized in the party's Jeffersonianism, and insisted that they believed in democracy as a way of life. By adopting the slogan of "measures not men," Tammany further argued that political leaders had to be constantly ready to change their opinions in light of new facts or circumstances. The Hall, in short, explained to the public that it acted as a sounding board to express the popular will, or, at times, popular whims, and thus incarnated the electorate's value structure. As a result, Tammany rationalized that while its techniques were based on expediency, the principles based on the popular will and Lockean idealism limited what the organization could or could not do.

Despite these words, a powerful irony limited Tammany's effectiveness. By 1822 the Hall stood in the vanguard of two great innovations in American life: increased democratization of the political process, and the development of modern party organizations. But paradoxically, the Hall did not understand the implications of these changes and underestimated their motive power. Worse, once the Bucktails changed the rules of the political game with the 1822 constitution, the biggest imponderable politicians faced was the extent to which the city's fast-changing social, economic, and political structure would affect traditional voting patterns. For all its vaunted flexibility, then, the Hall was not prescient. It did not at first appreciate the forces the constitution set free, and fumbled with some antiquated techniques of party management before finding the keys that unlocked the future. Instead of immediately catering to the expanded electorate's needs and expectations in trade for political support, the Hall had simply become too conservative and too institutionalized.

Specifically, Tammany's strategy went astray when it modernized its caucus system, which the General Committee personified in closed nominations, rather than abandoning the device for the tactics of mass appeal. Normally, each ward committee elected delegates to a city-wide "primary" meeting, which usually named a preselected ticket. Then the entire party met to ratify the slate. In 1822 the Hall sought to absorb the newly enfranchised voters by a shift in management. First, it increased the General Committee's size to create the impression of wider voter participation in decision-making. But, at the same time, it stressed that the essence of party loyalty lay in "regular nominations" and "traditional usages," for "without such a system and a permanent adherence to it, there can be no security and no permanency to the party." [1]

Tammany's attempt to equate party discipline with the caucus, even in a modified form, antagonized several Republican interest groups. Yet in a large way, such a confrontation was inevitable. Although the Hall seemingly rejected President Monroe's amalgamation policies and sneered at his "Era of Good Feelings" in politics, the organization welcomed many diverse men in its mania to defeat Governor DeWitt Clinton. By 1822, because of partisan necessity, the Hall had become essentially what the Great Virginians had envisioned: a large, loose-knit collection of interest groups, nominally Republican, but amorphous in policy. Among these men was William Coleman, the editor of the influential *Evening Post*, whom Tammany had inherited along with other High-Minded Federalists. And it was Coleman who first grumbled that the Hall's closed nomination system was a "slavish" plot aimed at transferring "the general right of suffrage from the many to the few." [2] Others would soon add more substance.

The ferment brewing within Tammany Hall had a counterpart in the Tammany Society. As the Hall became increasingly a haven for political chieftains, the Society became less partisan and reverted to its earlier ideals. Except for Mordecai Noah, grand sachem in 1823 and 1826, the leaders of Tammany Hall were not the leaders of the Tammany Society. Partly due to scandal, partly due to the wear and tear of time, the type of men Matthew Davis had recruited retired from politics and a new generation of freewheeling politicos took their slots in Tammany Hall, but the Society held aloof and welcomed few of them. In the decade from 1819 to 1829, the Society only initiated 128 new members, the bulk of whom were either lawyers, skilled artisans, or merchants. As the base of suffrage expanded, then, the Tammany Society once again became the symbol of middle-class respectability, and generally remained politically inert.

Even so, the Society's Wigwam physically epitomized traditional Republicanism and party regularity. Matthew Davis' political equation was still valid: The Council of Sachems leased the Long Room to the General Committee, which in turn held its meetings in the Wigwam. But unwittingly, the Council gained the power to make or break any party faction by simply allowing or refusing it the Long Room's use. As long as the party remained united, however, the sachems were politically unimportant. But when Tammany Hall fragmented in the presidential elections of 1824 and 1828, the Council became the most vital element in the local Republican organization. For whatever faction controlled the Council of Sachems ultimately controlled Tammany Hall.[3]

Tammany Hall's fragmentation, which was really only a matter of time, actually grew out of Senator Martin Van Buren's determination to play presidential kingmaker for William Crawford and end the Republican party's drift into "Monroe's heresy." The move at first proved popular among the Hall's power elite. Both Noah and Henry Meigs admired the Secretary of the Treasury, and felt "his friends among us are numerous & increasing." Nonetheless, the effort brought into the open the dormant question of how the shapeless Republican party would nominate its candidate. Van Buren had an answer. The party would summon the Congressional Caucus, it would make Crawford the official choice, and all others would have to run as apostates—Clinton's fate in 1812.[4]

As far as it went, the plan was brilliant—but flawed. The caucus idea, both on the state and national levels, had outlived its usefulness and Crawford's foes would not obey it under any circumstances. As the course of events unfolded, Van Buren stood on the brink of making a fatal error. By relying on a system the voters scorned, his organization was forced to defend an unpopular anachronism. There were other hazards the usually astute Van Buren overlooked. Inadvertently, he based his political power on the exact thing he meant to destroy. Just like Tammany Hall, the state Bucktail party, because of local needs—not Monroe's fusion program—was almost a perfect duplication of his ideas. Moreover, since there was no second national party, Republican insurgents had no recourse except to factionalize within the existing framework. Thus, Van Buren, whether he realized it or not, was about to engage in a self-destructive controversy which, by its very nature, he could not win.[5]

Locally, the national election of 1824 therefore became a screen behind which the real battle took place. For Tammanyites, the canvass did not mean which contender or what state or national groupings controlled the presidency, but which faction within the Hall would dominate the organization.

Initially, Tammany's Van Burenites, the "Regulars"—led by Churchill C. Cambreleng, Michael Ulshoeffer, and Mordecai Noah—began the struggle with several advantages: Van Buren's prestige, the alliance with the just-evolving Albany Regency, and control over the party's organizational machinery. But even with such leverage, the Regulars operated against great odds. Despite optimism about Crawford's local popularity, he had few supporters in the city because he courted the party's establishment and seemed indifferent to ordinary voters. Even worse, when he suffered a paralytic stroke in 1823 and refused to withdraw, his stature plummeted to a new low. Finally, his reliance on the Congressional Caucus made him appear antidemocratic.

Van Buren's foes realized these problems, capitalized on the anti-caucus feeling, and mounted a strong attack against the Regulars' "aristocratic" stance. Following Coleman's lead, the *American*, heretofore a Regular organ, broke away, endorsed John Quincy Adams for president, and demanded the formation of a fresh "uncontaminated" party which would have "its weight in the community," not in a political machine run "by hypocrisy or intrigue." [6]

Mordecai Noah's headstrong efforts at self-promotion further eroded Republican discipline. In the old constitution's waning days, the Council of Appointment had named him sheriff of New York County and, in the first election to the office by popular vote, Noah expected Tammany's nomination. Moreover, he insisted to the Regency that the *Advocate*, which was losing money, share the state's printing patronage with the *Albany Argus*.

When the Regency, which was having financial problems of its own with the *Argus*, turned him down, Noah refused to accept the rebuff. Unable to vent his spleen at Van Buren, Noah blamed three prominent committeemen—John Stagg, Michael Ulshoeffer, and Benjamin Sharpe —for his problems. Feeling the attack unjust, the three retaliated by running a separate candidate for sheriff, Peter Wendover, a long-time anti-Clintonian, despite the fact that the primary meeting had already nominated Noah.

In reply, Noah stressed the legitimacy of his position. Again and again he emphasized that Wendover was a turncoat who scorned all party traditions. The *Post* and *American* gleefully accentuated Noah's embarrassment when they backed his opponent. As a last resort, Noah identified his candidacy with Tammany's best interests. "The character of the State, the tranquility of the party," he claimed, "and the ascendancy of republicans in this city are to be tested by this election." In this sense Noah was correct, for he emphasized the main problem:

party organization, not his ambition, was at stake. Rufus King agreed. To Van Buren he wrote: "Noah I conjecture will fail unless the Reluctance to vote ag[ainst] the regular nomination saves him." [7]

Wendover won, but the consequences were far-reaching. Victorious, he proved a major point that Tammany would have preferred remain unnoticed: its unequivocal endorsement of a candidate was not necessary to ensure success. In the future, then, city Republicans had a convenient excuse to explain their defiance of the General Committee. Equally logical, the Congressional Caucus' formidable character had diminished. Even more, the squabble blunted Noah's authority, and gave other newspapers some justification to challenge the *Advocate* as Tammany's only valid spokesman. Perhaps Noah had these in mind when he reported to Van Buren: "We are in a tolerable confusion and have the prospect of a Grand Split in the fall." [8]

Other factional elements in Tammany Hall proved the wisdom of the editor's prediction. Encouraged by the Regulars' floundering tactics, the followers of John Quincy Adams wasted little time in establishing an independent position. Despite his penchant for self-depreciation and his campaign's low-keyed tempo, Adams commanded the respect, one admirer wrote, of "the old Jeffersonians, the middle class of the republicans & the yeomanry." Aware of this, Noah attempted to deflate Adams' presidential balloon by adopting the strategy of damning him with faint praise for his "unimpeachable character" and "willingness to throw away his early anti-republican principles" when he had deserted his father's Federalism during the Embargo argument. But by 1823 the Regulars' insidious whispering campaign gave no indication of working. Instead, the Adamsites totally ignored Noah, played on local grievances against the caucus system, and carefully laid the groundwork for a massive attack on local "party usages." [9]

City followers of Secretary of War John C. Calhoun followed the Adamsites' lead. Because the *Advocate*'s decaying prestige lent momentum to the establishment of rival Republican newspapers, Calhoun secretly subsidized his own propaganda sheet, the *New York Patriot*. The unsuspecting Regulars, assuming the paper had no ulterior aims, sanctioned it as an official party organ. Once it gained legitimacy, however, the *Patriot*'s editors—Henry Wheaton, Selleck Osborn, and Charles Gardiner—dropped their deception.

They confronted the already vexed Regulars with a novel idea by demanding that the legislature junk its caucus for naming presidential electors and replace it with a convention of popularly chosen electors. As for Tammany, they denounced the General Committee and called on the Council of Sachems for aid. Noah saw scant good in either proposal, and refused to discuss them. Nevertheless, the *Advocate*'s position gave the *Patriot* further ammunition to hurl at local Crawford supporters and made Calhoun appear a true "democrat." [10]

These developments elated Henry Clay's followers. Although he grossly overestimated his strength, especially in the city where Matthew Davis was the only prominent politician to back him, Clay hoped to pick up support as the other contenders faltered. Upstate, he laid similar tactics. But he misread the political currents. As a result, his faction was a partisan nightmare: poorly organized and financed, tactically unsound, too inflexible to barter for support. [11]

Three uncommitted groups stood on the periphery of the battle. All had powerful anti-Regular credentials; and, by coincidence, shared an aversion against the caucus system.

The first group initially lacked the cohesion and leadership that distinguished the other two. Composed at first of men with little in common beyond a mutual thirst for victory and spoils, they lacked a presidential candidate around whom to rally. Past loyalties, John King warned Van Buren, would mean little when this group determined its allegiance:

> Since the war a race of men have grown up, animated with love of country unaccustomed to party discipline, and uninterested in those questions which have in an eminent degree sustained and nourished it. They constitute the active and most efficient body of voters and will not fail to give an impulse to public opinion in reference to the Presidential question. [12]

The constitution had thus liberated a new type of voter, nationalistic and egalitarian by nature. No one, including themselves, knew what presidential candidate they favored. Under these conditions, they were an army in search of a general.

Second were the Federalists, half-scorned, half-wooed by all Republican factions. On the basis of political kinship, many of Adams' contemporaries expected that a massive outpouring of Federalist aid would flow naturally into his camp. The reverse was actually true. Because of his defection over the Embargo, "the Old Feds. regard him as an apostate," an upstater confided to Clay. Equally long on memory, William Coleman rejected John Quincy Adams as being his father's son, a man no true Hamiltonian could support. Such narrow horizons did not hinder many of the High-Minders. But here, too, Adams stood on treacherous ground. Just having won Bucktail aid, Rufus King cautioned the impetuous *American* editors that they might forfeit their hard-won spoils by prematurely backing the wrong man. Strangely, Adams showed little interest in conciliating the Federalists. Afraid of compromising his Republican credentials by an open flirtation, he decided to accept Federalist support if freely given, but held aloof from striking any bargains. The other candidates found themselves in a similar dilemma. Although the Calhounites were willing to meet the Federalists more than halfway, they—as well as the Clay and Crawford supporters—could not do so without alienating large segments of the local party.[13]

The Clintonians were also looking for a rallying point. In January 1823, shortly after his unwilling retirement from the governorship, Clinton reconnoitered the corridors of power and came away encouraged. The Bucktails, he felt, were fragmenting over the caucus question and Van Buren had "lost almost all his influence and is daily losing power." In this optimistic view, Clinton felt that his foes' internal problems would obscure his fumbling the question of constitutional reform. But first he needed to support a suitable presidential candidate.[14]

In checking the pluses and minuses of each contender, Clinton rejected Crawford, and passed over Calhoun and Clay because both eyed him with intense suspicion. Clinton considered the idea of backing Adams, but the New Englander proved too remote. Yet beyond these judgments, Clinton saw no great advantage in taking sides with a front-runner. It would be more politic to find a candidate who needed his support. With this in mind, he turned to General Andrew Jackson.

By orthodox standards, Jackson was not a serious candidate and he even depreciated his own chances. Most professional politicians dismissed him as a lightweight—a popular hero, true, but nonetheless a man temperamentally and emotionally unsuited for the presidency. "It would indeed be a serious day for this Country," Noah wrote, "when General Jackson should be its Chief Magistrate." [15]

But Jackson's local appeal did not rest with party leaders. The uncommitted voters about whom John King cautioned Van Buren made the general the incarnation of all their aspirations. Partly out of admiration, partly out of necessity, they backed him—the only candidate without a formal organization or newspaper in the city. The same pattern, with some deviations, held true for Clinton. By using his earlier friendship with Jackson as a stratagem, Clinton avoided the danger of surrendering his identity to a well-established front-runner and gained tremendous leverage as an "original Jacksonian."

The general's posture grew more imposing with Calhoun's aid. Altruism aside, the latter's supporters cynically assumed that the expected deflation of Jackson's boom would enhance Calhoun's prospects. Even so, he was wary of Clinton, and shrewdly warned his local campaign manager, General Joseph Swift, not to bow to political pressure by overplaying the former governor's role.[16]

Surprisingly, many anti-Adams Federalists viewed the general's emergence with ill-concealed joy. Hardly believing that Jackson was a stalking-horse for either Calhoun or Clinton, they saw in Jackson, the national hero, a second chance to regain favorable public esteem. Just as dazzling, Jackson was a political independent; a man who lacked both a well-oiled local machine or a firm patronage policy. They prudently bided their time, waiting for the general's grassroots support to show further signs of life.[17]

Despite his latter-day image as the candidate of the "Common Man," Andrew Jackson's earliest New York City supporters were Clintonians, Swiss Federalists, most newly enfranchised voters, and other political outs. Although the general represented many different things to these people, all shared one common denominator: he opened an avenue for advancement the other candidates blocked. As for the Van Buren Tammanyites, they simply did not play any positive role in the initial surge that later formed Jacksonian Democracy.

The campaign conformed to few traditional political rules. Despite the Regulars' bland assumption that the party backed Crawford and Van Buren, the surge of popular indignation against the caucus issue gave the other contenders an excuse to forget their own rivalries and temporarily coalesce against the Albany Regency. As a way to halt them, Noah stressed the need for party discipline above all other considerations, and darkly predicted that the destruction of the caucus device would, in the end, destroy "the union of the party, the influence of the state, and the safety of the nation." On a more practical front, the General Committee suggested that Congress settle the matter by passing a constitutional amendment giving the voters the right to name their own electors—in the future. This eleventh-hour stab at conciliation could not save the Regulars, nor would words and resolutions restore party harmony. The initiative had passed into the anti-Crawfordites' hands, and they were ready to peel away the Regulars' hard-core support.[18]

On October 3, 1823, each Tammany ward committee, using the Hall's traditional system, met to elect representatives to the nominating convention, scheduled for the last Thursday in the month. But their opponents capitalized on the swelling demand for electoral reforms and won the overwhelming support of the party's rank and file. Out of the seventy-two ward representatives elected, thirty-nine were anticaucus men, twenty-two claimed neutrality, while a mere eleven were Regulars.

Next, the anti-Crawfordites formalized their insurgency by creating a new organization, the People's party, and made opposition to the caucus their keystone. The play on words was hardly subtle. Quite simply, the People damned the Regulars as aristocrats and made the campaign a question between democrats and power-hungry demagogues.[19]

The first goal of the People's Party was to consolidate fully their control over Tammany's party machinery by stopping the Regulars from getting their legislative slate approved at the Wigwam. This time the Crawford supporters prepared for trouble. In the Long Room, ward heelers packed the floor, and because of sheer physical numbers kept the People from entering. During the ensuing confusion the Regulars organized the meeting, named a chairman and secretary, and adopted the ticket. They concluded none too soon, for the People drowned out any further action and took over the platform. Adamsite John King, after stinging the Van Burenites for their highhanded ways, rhetorically asked the cheering, whistling People: "Will you consent to trust men, who have refused to trust you?" Obviously, trust of the Regulars was not included in the People's platform, and they named an independent ticket.[20]

The fact that both the Crawfordites and the People's party had nominated their tickets on hallowed Republican soil left the voters without a clear understanding as to who really controlled Tammany Hall and with it, party regularity. Lacking any precedent to follow, the rank and file found party discipline meaningless. As a result, Tammany Hall crumbled into a factional mess, only important as a prize of battle, control of which would legitimize the victors' power grab and identify them with traditional Republicanism.

Even though the People's party encompassed groups with little in common beyond the caucus issue, it soundly thrashed the Regulars in the fall canvass. The People won control over the Corporation, sent one senator and seven out of ten assemblymen to Albany, and outpolled the Regulars by strong margins.

By any reasonable standard, the People's party had totally captured public opinion and created a viable movement. The reasons behind this surge, a Tammanyite explained to John Quincy Adams, were not hard to find. Many voters had grown tired of Noah's incessant carping, "and would right or wrong oppose anything he is for." Propaganda from a battery of clever anticaucus writers also hit the mark: "A large majority of the republicans have hitherto considered themselves bound to support such men as might be nominated, in this way, whether they approved of them individually or not. But this mode has by degree been growing unpopular, & the great noise made about it by the American and the Patriot papers has determined many to oppose it." Thus, few politicians in the city took issue with the *Patriot* when it exulted: "The *People* have now come out and are determined to manage their own concerns." [21]

As one disaster piled on another with disheartening regularity, few realistic city leaders optimistically embraced Crawford's prospects or expected the Van Burenites to keep their hegemony over Tammany Hall. Everything seemed to be going badly for them: President Monroe refused any commitment despite urgent pleas from Noah, Daniel Tompkins stayed aloof, and Van Buren's leadership limped. Quite openly, Noah showed his torment. The election, he felt, was both "mortifying" and "unexpected." The only way to save the party was for the General Committee to purge the insurgents, "draw the line of separation," and reorganize.[22]

But in a larger sense, the local People's phenomenon marked the transition from an informal anticaucus attitude into an institutionalized effort in the legislature to settle the entire question by giving the voters the immediate right to select presidential electors. But the question was not as settled as some voters assumed. Governor Joseph Yates attempted to straddle the issue, and the Van Burenites used parliamentary skulduggery to bury the People's elector bill in committee. Then, in February, when the Congressional Caucus named William Crawford, the Regulars' comeback seemed secure.[23]

Appearances, however, were highly deceptive. In the city, the People organized a mass pro-elector bill rally in the Wigwam and, despite the Regulars' interference, passed resolutions "remonstrating with the Legislature against any further withholding from the People the choice of presidential electors." Furthermore, although Stephen Allen, a firm Regular and long-time party stalwart, reminded the Hall's congressional delegation to "attend the Caucus to a man," few were present. As a result, the very limitations of the meeting hurt its authority because

Crawford's foes used it as evidence of the unpopularity and antidemocratic tendencies of the entire procedure. At this point, the People's bill wiggled its way out of committee, passed the assembly, and presented the Regulars with a fresh hazard.[24]

In the senate, the Van Burenites tried every trick in their book to avoid a showdown vote. As debate went on, the tide of public opinion flowed against the Regulars. But they refused to pay heed, and used their majority, 17–14, to halt further action. The votes of the "immortal seventeen" ended the question for the moment.

The Regulars may have won in the legislature but they lost in the public forum. "A great revolution has taken place in public opinion," DeWitt Clinton noted. "The rejection of the Elector Bill will certainly excite firm fervor." Clinton was correct. By any measurement, when the "seventeen" killed the bill, the Regulars totally misjudged the rising spirit of reform. The issue agitating New Yorkers had thus matured in a disagreeable way for the Van Burenites: would the voters be given their "rights" as free citizens, or would they be "slaves?" [25]

Politicians so obviously oblivious to the nature of the problems they had created could hardly avoid making other mistakes. Since 1824 was a gubernatorial year, Mordecai Noah and State Senator John Craemer formed an elaborate scheme to replace Governor Yates with Samuel Young, a well-known anti-Clintonian, whom the People were also considering. The move was totally unwise. It antagonized the governor, who soon called for a special legislative session to reconsider the entire electoral question, and split the Regulars. Moreover, the People's party ignored the opportunity to endorse Young, and exploited the situation for its own ends. "I consider this a very important event," Henry Wheaton exulted. "The faction is now broken into two factions, and we shall perservere in our determination of appealing back to the *People in Convention*." As things worked out, then, the anti-Crawfordites had gained another chance to pose as the apostles of popular liberties.[26]

So far, the Regulars had shown a singular lack of finesse, but their next move capped their stupidity. Without Van Buren's knowledge— partly for revenge, partly to ensnare the People—a group of Regency leaders decided to remove DeWitt Clinton from his last public office as canal commissioner. These men felt that Clinton was such a political liability that a party made up of Republicans, even malcontents, could not afford to cooperate with him. Yet if they could trick the People into supporting him, it would actually appear that he was a member of their party. Both, therefore, would be discredited. But when Senator Bowman from Monroe County, one of the "immortal seventeen," introduced the motion to drop Clinton, the People's party avoided the snare and they too voted for his ouster.[27]

For once, the public viewed political sophistry as political cupidity. Even the normally anti-Clintonian *Evening Post* protested that the firing had to "cause the cheek of every honorable man who calls himself an inhabitant of New York, to glow with shame." By now, the Regulars saw they had miscalculated the weight of one variable: many voters separated the "political Clinton" from the "canal Clinton." But it was too late to correct the blunder because Clinton jumped at the chance to play the innocent martyr. Gradually, many voters, who were normally apathetic, howled that Clinton deserved redemption—and only the People's party could accomplish this by running him for governor. But the People had no intention of directing the mounting indignation, and refused to become an instrument of revenge. As Rufus King saw it, "the public feeling everywhere condemns the removal of Mr. Clinton, and will I fear have the effect of destroying the discrimination between the friends and enemies of the electoral law." [28]

Less noticeable but potentially more dangerous, the city Jacksonians gathered momentum at Calhoun's expense. As the general's bandwagon picked up more and more converts, the secretary of war bowed gracefully out of the race and became the only vice-presidential candidate. Here was the signal the local Jacksonians awaited. On April 9, they held a meeting at the Wigwam and endorsed the general for the presidency. One week later, the *Patriot* began a short-lived existence as Jackson's official campaign newspaper.[29]

Until May, despite fervor and democratic rhetoric, Jackson's candidacy seemed to have developed too late in the election. Then, with stunning impact, Pennsylvania and Washington Crawfordites made a fatal error in publishing a series of letters that Jackson and President Monroe had exchanged eight years earlier, in which the general supported Monroe's fusion policies. For many Federalists, such sentiments cleared away all their inhibitions. They could now fully back Jackson, confident he would give them a just share of the "loaves and fishes." On the other hand, local Adamsites viewed the Jackson-Monroe letters with ill-concealed joy. "It operates to clear you from the *odium* of Federalism & Clintonianism," one New Yorker told Adams, "which the Van Buren junto have so sedulously contrived to throw around your prospects in this State." The Clay supporters agreed, but for a different reason. William Rochester predicted that despite the former governor's help, the "Old Hero" would not gain New York's vote because "the story has become quite current that Mr. Clinton is to be

*Prime Minister* to President Jackson." These sentiments did apply to some Republicans, it was true, but the general's powerful credentials outweighed Clinton's liabilities. Even so staunch a Regular as Mordecai Noah now had second thoughts about continuing to boom Crawford.[30]

Meantime, the city Regulars' position deteriorated rapidly. The People's party captured control of the General Committee: William Todd, a Calhounite merchant turned Jacksonian, became the new chairman; and Adamsite Henry Wheaton became secretary. In effect, the People now ruled Tammany Hall; however, the distinction was meaningless—there was no Tammany Hall as such but rather two squabbling General Committees, each claiming regularity.[31]

The Regulars had anticipated such a contingency and played their trump card by pressing the Tammany Society into the game. Up to this point, the Society had avoided any presidential commitment and minimized its partisan involvement. But Sachem Mordecai Noah changed its routine. In April, the Council of Sachems appeared to have made an outrageously self-serving deal with Federal District Judge William Van Ness, Burr's old defender, when it rented the Long Room for use as a courtroom for a $1,500 yearly fee. There was more to the arrangement than met the eye. According to the lease, while Van Ness and Supreme Court Justice Smith Thompson were in session, "no public meetings are to be allowed there [Wigwam] while it is occupied as a court room." With one lethal blow, then, the Regulars had denied the insurgents the symbol of full legitimacy—the right to meet in the party tabernacle. But the Regulars still retained their rights. By the Council's contract with Van Ness, "the tenant promises and engages that no committee or Body of Men shall be permitted to meet, for political purposes, or as a political association, in any room or apartment at present rented to said Tenant excepting only, the Committee or Committee of the Democratic party known to be and designated, as the *Committee Friendly to Regular Nominations*." [32]

The infuriated leaders of the People's party and the Jacksonians tried to break the deal; first by charging that a court of justice should not function in a tavern; then by pressuring Smith Thompson, who had recently broken with Van Buren, to hold court elsewhere. Finally, in October, the Common Council, dominated by the People's party, offered the judges a room in City Hall (where they had always met before) and Van Ness gave up the fight. Yet, for the moment, the Regulars had won their gamble and retained their symbolic link with traditional Republicanism. Even the Tammany Society felt satisfied; in effect, it had not made a decision about regularity. But what was disquieting for the future was that the Council of Sachems had flexed its potent, if unused, powers. Henceforth, whenever factional warfare erupted, politicians now realized that the quickest means to establish legitimacy lay in dominating the Council of Sachems, and, through it, Tammany Hall.[33]

During this jockeying, the Regulars' sluggish campaign showed signs of reviving. In July they had used a technicality of the law to force the special legislative session to adjourn without altering the elector law. Equally encouraging, Clinton had plunged into politics, made his candidacy for governor synonymous with Jackson's, and thus threatened to rupture the People's party. Despite the Adamsites' hopes that the party could hold together, Clinton's abrasive reputation rubbed against their grain. Cautious James Tallmadge, Clinton's Hamlet-like chief opponent for the nomination, spoke for many of them when he wrote Adams that "the course of principle, connected with this electoral question is to be converted into a personal party—or to be broken down by this interference." Then, too, the backbone of the party, the *Evening Post* and the *American*, scorned Clinton's candidacy, while the *Post* hinted it might support Crawford if the People did not name Tallmadge. Nothing daunted, Clinton pressed forward. Above all else, the People's party gave him an opportunity to capture a fully functioning political vehicle with cogs in every segment of society.[34]

But before the Regulars could capitalize on these developments, Mordecai Noah again demonstrated his unique ability to upset the political balance. An inveterate theatergoer and would-be playwright, Noah's romantic nature rebelled against compromising his conscience for the sake of political advantage. Worse, the *Advocate*, which lacked a Regency subsidy, faced a serious financial problem. Circulation was down; many Tammanyites bought either the *American* or the *Post*, and merchants took their advertisements elsewhere. Seeking help, Noah asked several local Republicans for contributions. Merchant Henry Eckford and Judge William P. Van Ness were agreeable, in the expectation that Noah would stand his ground for Crawford. But when the editor began tortuously shifting toward the Jacksonians, Eckford and his cronies demanded possession of the paper. Noah refused and charged that Eckford, whom the paper had not supported in a previous bid for the House of Representatives, wanted the *Advocate* for revenge rather than any financial or political reasons. Bickering continued when Noah threatened to start a fresh newspaper with the same name. By now neither side was willing to compromise and, on September 6, the Regular General Committee fired Noah for insubordination. It explained that "the press over which he has the control, so far as it respects *men* or *measures*, belongs not to him, but to the party of which he is the organ." This falling-out amused the Adamsites, who felt that Noah's dismissal would "have a powerful influence upon the November elections, and [help] defeat . . . the Crawford party." While Noah subsequently regained his job before eventually starting his own newspaper, the *New York National Advocate,* and sullenly paid Crawford lip service, the entire controversy symbolized Tammany's failure to cope with reality.[35]

By September it became obvious to most practical Tammanyites, no matter what their factional labels, that they had demanded too much of their organization and, since they had asked the electorate to do contradictory things, that anarchy had replaced purpose. Now these men began to question themselves. Had they gone too far? Had they really destroyed Tammany Hall in their efforts to control it? The answer lay with their fellow Tammanyites within the People's party, just beginning their convention in Utica.

As the delegates took their seats, all signs indicated that most of those from the city would not accept Clinton. But when upstate groups ignored these storm warnings and did nominate him, the entire New York City delegation walked out, led by Henry Wheaton. As he left, Wheaton warned that "no consistent Republican could support DeWitt Clinton." Aghast, the remaining delegates belatedly sought to placate the irate New Yorkers by naming James Tallmadge for lieutenant governor.[36]

But as far as local Adamsites were concerned, the damage was irreparable. The *American* protested that Clinton had undermined the People and pledged not to "take part in the struggle." Yet to keep the Regulars from misinterpreting the decision, the paper made it clear that it still battled "against caucus dictation" and the "hungry office holders constituting the Albany Regency." Tallmadge was just as eager to dissociate himself from Clinton. The nomination, he wrote Adams, was "not my act, or my wish." For once, Secretary of State Adams helped himself. Drawing a distinction between Clinton's candidacy and the larger issue New Yorkers faced, he pleaded with Tallmadge that old wounds be "mutually forgotten and forgiven." Adams' politicking, however, worked no wonders. Just as the People had hoped to capture Tammany Hall, so had DeWitt Clinton captured them.[37]

While Clinton's candidacy cut a deep swath through the ranks of the People's party and almost guaranteed a reconciliation among Tammanyites, a score of short-term commitments blocked them from healing differences until after the election. Both the Regulars and the People ran separate slates, heckled each other at every opportunity, and spared no pains to get out the vote.

Superficially, Clinton and the People crushed the Van Burenites. Once again, the People won the Common Council and elected seven out of ten assemblymen. But on the other side, all the Regulars' congressional candidates won. As a result, while the Regulars were beaten, they were not destroyed. Above that, their organization was still intact, and they wielded tremendous potential simply by controlling the Tammany Society. The Van Burenites' real disaster was in the gubernatorial contest where Clinton carried six out of ten wards and gained 58.3 percent of the total votes cast.[38]

Even though the presidential succession drew the most attention, Clinton's dramatic reemergence radically altered the local political picture. No longer could the bits and pieces of Tammany Hall luxuriate in their fraternal warfare, confident that somehow, someway, the party could coalesce when a new man gained the White House. Based on past evidence, Clinton as governor would build a party in his own image and seize power over the state. As things stood, then, Tammanyites—excluding the Rufus King Federalists—were under no illusions that they could survive politically without a party reunion.

For the moment, the unsettled presidential question delayed the momentous shift in city politics. In Albany, intrigue became the order of the day. "Great confusion prevails," one Adamsite reported, "meeting after meeting has been held but it is impossible yet to say what will be the result." Gradually, a pattern emerged. Van Buren's hold on his home state was slipping, Crawford's candidacy was hopeless, Adams and Clay delegates were seeking some sort of bargain among themselves, while the Jacksonians deemed "it of great importance to gain time." When the long, drawn-out voting ended, Thurlow Weed, a young, conniving and astute student of the political scene on his way to prominence, outmaneuvered the supposedly flexible Van Burenites, and helped Adams gain 25 votes, against 7 for Clay and 4 for Crawford. "The dissapointment [sic] on the part of our opponents is quite unaffected," Henry Wheaton gloated. "They had kept this [legislature] even so long in training under the Caucus discipline, with all its slavish habits, that they had what they declared, sufficient reasons for implicit confidence." [39]

The fabric of this parliamentary wheeling and dealing was extremely flimsy. Without party discipline to hold the electors in line, the tempo of trade-and-barter politicking increased. This was particularly true among the Jacksonians, warned Joseph Blunt, Adams' local campaign manager, who were still trying to seduce New York electors. The Jacksonians' efforts failed. When the contest reached the House of Representatives, the Adamsites fused with Clay and, under what many men considered shady circumstances, elected the secretary of state as the new President. In this bitter no man's land, the Regulars supported Crawford to the predictable end. Political necessity, not personal loyalty, determined their unwavering policy. "The party had to stand together & back Crawford," James Hamilton explained aptly, "not only because he was their Candidate, but also this way they show their stand for party & their principles & practices." [40]

While Senator Van Buren played out his role in Washington, his local henchmen began to analyze the roots of their defeat in hope of laying a solid foundation to rebuild their shattered party apparatus. The prospect was none too reassuring. Repudiated by the voters, infused with unrealistic ideas, living vicariously on past victories, the Regulars seemed destroyed by friends and foes alike. But the situation, they realized, was far from hopeless. Their major fault lay in not realizing that they could not reshape outmoded political techniques to conform with new realities. Thus, the caucus, instead of being the instrument of popular participation in government and the means to enforce party discipline, could only work with a limited electorate that accepted elitism in all its forms. Then, too, the Regulars understood that the success of the People's party lay in their astute handling of public opinion, not their inherent political strength.

From the moment Clinton gained the People's nomination, the Regulars demonstrated their ability to survive under unique conditions. Clinton, they felt, had enough natural enemies in the state to make his position impossible. By defusing the caucus question and not openly criticizing President-elect Adams, then, the Van Burenites could gain precious time to heal wounds left over from the bruising electoral campaign, isolate Clinton, and give the Regular General Committee the opportunity to stimulate the electorate's party loyalty.

In short, the People's party, largely formed by rebel Tammanyites, became the connecting link between the past and the future. Moreover, the General Committee's earlier stab at running the party through popularly elected ward nominating conventions pointed the way out of the caucus tangle. By so doing, the Regulars could retain the caucus' basic idea—that party discipline was not only the determinant of individual behavior but also the means of enforcing majority rule—yet in a democratic disguise. The political situation in the city was remarkable in another sense. In the absence of a second national party, the Hall's main organization, which the Regulars controlled through the Tammany Society, still survived because the voters had nowhere else to go. As a result, the Regulars could still maintain their identity, absorb the insurgents who hated the governor, and ostracize the Clintonians without surrendering any of their political prerogatives.[41]

Beginning in March 1825, the Regulars put their strategy into operation as soon as copies of Adams' inaugural address reached the city. Despite a marked aversion to many of his domestic recommendations, city editors promised Adams "an open field and a fair trail." In a typical reaction, James Snowden, the *National Advocate*'s new operator, promised to give the President "fair support, such as becomes democrats—to approve the right, to oppose the wrong." But in local politics, Snowden continued, the Regulars would only support measures "best calculated to promote the interests of the people, and to reunite the republican party in its former vigor and purity." These ideas reflected Van Buren's long-term reasoning: silence on national affairs; noncommittalism on Jackson's future candidacy; and a militant grassroots effort on the local scene.[42]

In addition, the Regulars made a subtle play on words when they called their remodeled organization the Democratic party, as distinguished from the Adams-Clay National Republicans. During its battles with DeWitt Clinton during the preceeding decade, the Hall had at times adopted the term "democrats" to set itself apart from the upstate Bucktails, but both still pledged loyalty to the Republican party of Jefferson, Madison, and Monroe. In overthrowing the fusion policies so dear to these men, however, the Regulars had no intention of forfeiting the traditional symbols of party loyalty. Their new party label by implication, they announced, extended Jeffersonian principles so that the Democratic party was the spiritual, if not physical, embodiment of the "Spirit of '98," the battle between the people and the aristocrats. Thus, the Democrats posed as the spokesmen for the majority will, and their officeholders became the people's tribunes.[43]

All of the Regulars' plans hinged on whether or not President Adams intended to be both the leader of his nation and the leader of the national party. Local politicians did not have long to wait. Bitterly disappointed over his tainted election, Adams continued Monroe's amalgamation policy even to the extreme of offering to retain William Crawford in the cabinet. In trying to appease all factions, however, the President shortsightedly alienated his friends, gave his enemies privileged sanctuary, and misjudged the public's mounting annoyance with the politics of consensus.[44]

Adams blundered particularly badly in New York. Although he had no qualms about using patronage to placate DeWitt Clinton, offering him the prestigious post of ambassador to Great Britain, Adams held aloof from Van Buren because he was "too much warped by party spirit." Although Clinton politely declined and Adams subsequently appointed Rufus King, the episode was of special importance. The Clintonians interpreted the move as a sign of weakness—the Regulars, as a declaration of war; while the Adamsites privately stormed that they could not easily oppose the governor without making their leader seem a fool.[45]

The Adamsites became more discouraged when they discovered the full extent of the President's intentions. Party workers expected patronage in proportion to their efforts during the campaign. Instead, Adams only removed incumbents for incompetency, rewarded ability rather than partisanship, and never became the spoils-monger his more outspoken friends wished. In vain did men such as Thurlow Weed, Albert Tracy, Joseph Blunt, James Tallmadge, and Charles King await a call that did not materialize. Worse, many of the undisturbed officeholders used their positions in Andrew Jackson's behalf.[46]

The Adamsites, aware of their problems in New York City, warned the President through Joseph Blunt that he had to help his supporters or forfeit their aid. To clear the now badly clouded political atmosphere, Adams should have taken Blunt's advice, but instead muddied the situation even more. In mid-August of 1825, Rodger Skinner (the Federal Judge for the Northern District of New York) died, and the Adamsites expected an appointment from within their ranks. Again the President disappointed them, for however well-intentioned his consensus policy might have been, it lacked thought of consequences. As a result, when he neglected eminent lawyers from within his own faction and selected Alfred Conklin, a Clintonian, local Adamsites sputtered with rage. As one anonymous intemperate from Albany expressed it, "the friends of Mr. Adams in this section of the State of New York, who had staked their political reputation on his success are distressed at this appointment of a known political opponent to a Judicial station of no inconsiderable importance and influence." A tired, disappointed, and frustrated James Tallmadge was even more angry. "Those Repub-

licans who seceded from the Party—& won the Electors in this State,"
he cried, "now find themselves opposed by the Clintonians—unsup-
ported by the Crawford men & unacknowledged by the Genl. Administration." The President was not sympathetic. "If there are those
whose disposition lead them to take more thought of the morrow, than
the public good requires," he wrote with magnificent detachment,
"they will perhaps when the morrow comes, be looking still for the
day after. The morrow will take care of itself." [47]

Heartened by the Adamsites' drive toward self-destruction, Regular
Tammanyites continued to mend their political fences. In the winter
legislative session, led by Van Buren's agents, they helped introduce a
bill to decide in which one of three ways presidential electors should
be chosen: by district, by a plurality on a general ticket, or by a simple
majority on the general ticket. This calculated effort to prevent the
caucus issue from ever again exploding had far-reaching consequences.
The Regulars rallied moderate opinion, accommodating themselves to
the new democratic spirit of the electorate, and widened the factional
lesions among their foes. To evoke further symbols, the Regency then
proposed constitutional amendments for the popular election of justices
of the peace and the elimination of remaining white suffrage requirements.[48]

By the summer, once Congress adjourned, Van Buren took to the
stump. In touring the state, speaking at ward meetings, courthouses,
and on dusty side roads, he stressed the same theme to country leaders
and voters alike: Republicans had to revive orthodox party loyalties,
accommodate to public opinion, and strengthen the local power base.
His therapeutic affect on the faithful was soon apparent. One Tammanyite happily reported to Azariah Flagg, a Regency leader: "Our
friends in New York, tho much divided on minor subjects, all agree in
saying that we shall carry the next election in New York, and throughout the first district." [49]

For all his surefooted efforts upstate, however, Van Buren slipped
in dealing with Mordecai Noah and the Tammany maverick spirit he
personified. After losing the *National Advocate*, Noah continued his
peculiar brand of independence in his own newspaper, and before the
year was out made it a vigorous competitor for its older rivals. In
March 1825, although fully acquainted with Van Buren's plans, Noah
went his own way and zestfully attacked President Adams both on
policy matters and the purported "corrupt bargain" with Henry Clay.
Adams' continuation of Monroe's fusion policy was stupid, Noah
fumed, because political parties were indispensable for governing the

nation and guaranteeing popular rule. As a cryptic hint to Van Buren, Noah moreover urged, "let us concentrate our force, and unite on the man who stands the best chance of being elected by the people." [50]

Noah's carping marked a new turn in city politics. Locally, during late 1824 and early 1825, the Jacksonian movement began to excite real enthusiasm and rapidly picked up converts. But the general's party was an unorganized, decentralized, anomalous faction—"joined by a rope of sand," John Spencer sneered—that lacked a permanent local committee to supervise its campaign between elections. Noah, the Tammany Society, and the Regular General Committee—moving faster than the Albany Regency—wanted to carry the Old Hero's burden. To Andrew Jackson, a sachem proposed on Independence Day, "his vigilance, faithfulness and bravery secures him the nation's gratitude and the *people*'s love." [51]

Although Jackson fulfilled the political requirements of the era in general and of the Regular Tammanyites in particular, they could not immediately back him without cooperating with DeWitt Clinton. In their dilemma, Noah and his friends halfheartedly continued to harass the governor, but it was evident that they were fighting strictly on memory. In order to put Jackson over, they had to forge an accommodation with Clinton: even for flexible political trimmers such a dazzling switch took time. These problems, according to one of Adams' delighted partisans, made the likelihood of a firm city Jacksonian movement very questionable. "The *nucleus* . . . will never be able to collect anything very formidable about it, altho' it may boast of a republican core." [52]

Regardless of the hazards involved, however, Noah and the Regulars were determined to capture the local Jacksonian movement. They began their efforts in March when a group of city merchants, headed by Calhoun's associate, Surveyor of the Port Joseph Swift, held a public dinner dedicated to Pan-American friendship. As was the custom, Swift sent invitations to prominent national leaders, not in expectation of their physical presence but of letters sympathetic to the meeting's spirit. In a slapstick series of blunders, Swift was late in mailing an invitation to Adams, who therefore did not answer in time, and the dinner went on with a well-publicized silence from the White House. Although the festival was ostensibly nonpartisan, Samuel Swartwout, an original Jacksonian, disconcerted the Adamsites even more when he proposed: "Andrew Jackson—Education and habit may make a diplomat, or a Cabinet minister; but God alone can make an honest man and a hero." [53]

While the dinner marked the first step in an emerging coalition of Calhounites, Regulars, Clintonians, and Federalists into a firm local Jacksonian movement, nothing more could be accomplished until Tammany Hall came to terms with the rising spirit of democracy and thus eliminated the People's party. On the elector question, despite a momentary squabble over the merits of the district versus the general ticket plan, the Hall announced that it would follow whatever direction "a majority of the Republican party" indicated "to be best for the democratic interests" of the city. In late September, Benjamin Bailey, the old, battle-scarred chairman of the General Committee, made Tammany's final peace with the caucus question by calling for open ward elections to select delegates for the Hall's city-wide convention. For the next few weeks, committeemen circulated through the wards, consulted the rank and file, and left the impression among ordinary citizens that the organization both respected and followed their wishes. That done in late October, the convention formed a ticket dedicated to the *"Great Cause* of the *People's Rights."* [54]

Since Tammany had reappropriated reformism, the Adamsites could not run on a dead issue. They hoped, and the *American* expected, that the Hall would follow the President's consensus policy by nominating some of their men. When Tammany refused, the Adamsites had no recourse but to fall back on the shopworn People's party, once again assuming that the Clintonians would follow suit. The Adamsites miscalculated. The Clintonians kept outwardly neutral, the Hall made itself synonymous with "democracy," and the People absorbed a crushing defeat. Hardly containing his jubilation, Noah crowed that "reason and reflection" had reestablished "the fact that the democratic party of the old school" was now fully united.[55]


The highly successful fall elections, both in the city and upstate, whittled away much of New York politicians' initial restraint on the presidential question, and both the Clintonians and the Van Burenites engaged in some serious reflection. Some men, such as blunt Silas Wright, one of the Regency's most outstanding leaders, wanted to take on the governor in a final knockdown fight, preliminary to backing Jackson. But Van Buren wanted to avoid such a showdown. Up for reelection in 1827, he had no wish to compromise his political ambitions by engaging in an open quarrel with Clinton. In fact, Van Buren was deftly moving toward a conciliation with him. To weave such a fabric took time, and the Regency waited until early 1827 before openly declaring for Jackson. As for the governor, caution became his watchword. To an Ohio admirer, Caleb Atwater, he confided that a premature pledge for Jackson made no sense. "Men change," he wrote. "Circumstances vary." [56]

Meantime, Van Buren used stealth and cunning to make his peace with the Jacksonians. Nationally, the furor over the Panama Conference provided him with an opportunity to narrow the gap between the Regulars and the general's followers. Locally, he suggested to some intimate advisers that the Albany Regency not oppose Clinton's reelection as a sign of concord with the emerging coalition. Upstate, the Regency recoiled with alarm at the suggestion. According to Silas Wright, such a move would split the party because most loyalists "cannot under any terms be brought to join Mr. Clinton." [57]

Tammanyites were more flexible. Convinced by Van Buren's hints that the party would not make a nomination, the *New York National Advocate* began to praise the governor. By making a neat distinction between Clinton and the Clintonians, Noah claimed that the governor was the captive, not the master, of his faction, and was willing to restore the state government to legitimate Democratic forces with the proper encouragement.

For the moment, however, the gubernatorial question hung in suspension. The Regency, in deference to the democratic impulses sweeping the nation, scheduled a popularly elected convention for the following September in Herkimer. At the same time, Clinton tested his standing with the Administration. Through John Taylor he learned that Adams would not interfere in local politics and indicated that his local supporters would not run an opposition candidate.[58]

Only Noah took direct action. Van Buren's agreement to hold a convention, which implied that the Democrats would run a candidate, disconcerted Noah because he had practically endorsed Clinton's reelection. Too much his own man, Noah still strove hard for fusion. In June, he attempted with the governor's covert aid to flush Van Buren into the open. Taking a steamboat outing, ostensibly at Mrs. Clinton's request, Noah and the governor consulted on the terms for a factional compromise. After dropping a veiled hint of neutrality toward Van Buren's Senate bid, Clinton praised his ability and implied a willingness to forget old battles.[59]

On hearing the news, Van Buren expressed his gratification but again kept his own counsel. Yet Noah was too fidgety to sit still and pen a party line he felt was wrong. In July he scuttled the *New York National Advocate*, took the paper's advertisers with him, and formed a new journal, the *New York Enquirer*. Once settled, he plunged head-long into the preconvention maneuverings. The question before Tammanyites, he emphasized, was irrelevant to Clinton's candidacy. It was "whether the Democratic party in the state of New York is to be sustained in its power, system and usages. *We say it must be sustained.* If we surrender or break down in this state, what section of the Union will be the rallying point?" [60]

In sum, this editorial summarized not only Noah's position, but that of Tammanyites in general. In 1824 they had to bear their humiliation and disappointment in public when their work for Crawford failed. Now, they did not relish being wrong a second time. Positively convinced that Jackson was a winner, Noah and his fellow braves wanted to jump on the bandwagon as it began rolling, earn the general's gratitude, and secure a lock on the new Administration's public plunder. Noah's support of the governor was the means to an end; the same end Van Buren sought through other means.

In September, Van Buren's strategy became clear. After the Clintonians renominated their chief with a minimum of fuss, Van Buren surprisingly hand-picked William B. Rochester, an upstate Clayite and known Administration supporter, as the party's candidate. It was a masterly stroke. Because the Albany Regency was not committed to Jackson, Van Buren reasoned that many Adamsites would vote for Rochester out of loyalty; Clinton would then suspect that the nomination originated in Washington and would assail the President for his duplicity. As a result, Van Buren schemed, the Regency would have severed "the frail cord" binding the Clintonians and the Adamsites, forcing the governor (if he should win) into the Jacksonian camp not as the leader but a cog in the New York Democratic party.[61]

Upstate, the plot worked perfectly. Most loyal Regulars supported Rochester, the Adamsites temporarily joined them, and Clinton won— but by a paper-thin margin. Then, as Van Buren anticipated, the infuriated Clinton turned on the President. Yet, the Regency had the last word. "Whether Rochester succeeds or not," an upstater noted during the campaign, "I think Clinton is used up." [62]

In the city, however, the story was far different. The local party split into three warring camps that threatened to undo all of Van Buren's high-level scheming. Stunned by the Regency's tactics and infuriated at Van Buren's refusal to take him into confidence, Noah was unenthusiastic over supporting Rochester as party discipline dictated and sat the contest out. Angrily, the *National Advocate*, still a Regular organ, leveled a stinging attack on Noah's indifference. Equally alarming, the *Evening Post* unexpectedly backed Clinton, and the city Adamsites capitalized on the situation by running an independent ticket in the charter election.[63]

So matters rested until the campaign ended. But once the returns were in, the *Advocate* demanded that the General Committee discipline Noah and oust the *Enquirer* as an official party newspaper. "It ought to be one of our *first principles*," the *Advocate* flared, "to be united at home. Mr. Noah sails under the Regency banner, but fights under his own device." [64]

As the bickering mounted in volume, the *Albany Argus*, edited by Noah's long-time rival, Edwin Croswell, added its voice. Instead of fuzzing over Tammany's internal divisions, Croswell bluntly called Noah a professional liar, secretly on DeWitt Clinton's payroll. Sputtering with rage, Noah hunched over his desk and prepared a massive barrage of his own until Van Buren brought him up short. The wounded editor now publicly recanted, and ended the crisis he had fomented by simply keeping quiet. Yet his defiant humility did not come close to satisfying the powers in Albany. Van Buren's subsurface coolness and loss of respect for Noah rapidly turned into a deep chill which boded ill for the future.[65]

By 1827, the Regular Tammanyites in the city and the Albany Regency upstate had made their peace with the Jacksonians. Nationally, Van Buren became the general's unofficial campaign manager, and was instrumental in resurrecting the old New York–Virginia axis for him which since the days of the old Republican-Interest had proven indispensable for victory. Locally, Van Buren's politicking toward DeWitt Clinton bore impressive dividends. Clintonians and Regular Tammanyites, bitter foes since Burrism's day, a vindicated Noah wrote, "unite in supporting Jackson, thus consolidating the power of the two parties, and securing every district, and consequently every electoral ticket." The *Advocate* agreed. Regular Tammanyites, it admonished, "must soften old animosities, to restore tranquility, and to talk discreetly to their political friends on the present conditions and future prospects of this state." [66]

In pursuit of such a policy, the local Jacksonians continued to refine their techniques. By invoking the spirit of democratic idealism that was sweeping the nation and making Andrew Jackson the partisan legatee of the late Thomas Jefferson, Tammanyites helped to give their candidate additional massive credentials. The Sage of Monticello, the Hall's propagandists emphasized, had spent his life seeking to prove man's capacity to achieve beneficent social change through the popular will. Andrew Jackson shared the same commitment. But in contrast, President Adams was intent on setting up an aristocratic, monarchistic system of government, a reversion to his father's earlier beliefs and policies. Only by a restoration of the "Spirit of '98," only by adherence "to the established usages" of Jeffersonian traditionalism, could city voters guarantee that Thomas Jefferson had not lived his life in vain. As far as most Tammanyites were concerned, the campaign of 1828 was more than a personality struggle. It was a battle between two divergent sets of political principles with the nation's very future at stake.

In coming to terms with the spirit of Jacksonian Democracy, Tammany Hall embarked on a new political era. But before it could ponder the significance of its transformation, the Hall had to solve two remaining problems: the election of Jackson to the presidency, and how to apply the concept of democratic participation in politics to sound party decision-making without disrupting the rules, standards, and expectations of its ruling factional elites. Neither answer, as it turned out, was either simple or predictable.

# ⌇ 5 ⌇

# Tammany and the New Politics

IN CONTRAST TO the emerging Democrats, the Adamsites had squandered most of their advantages but yet retained impressive leverage. Adams was still Chief Executive, a legitimate Jeffersonian in the tradition of a two-term presidency, and, most critical of all, the possessor of immense patronage. Taking a hard look at his prospects, Adams' local advisers concluded that he could win reelection if he acted more as a party chieftain and less as a statesman. Joseph Blunt insisted that the President's first obligation was to take care of his friends because "party men & party machinery may decide the question. These men . . . are activated by interest, or hopes of preferment, & their present coldness has been caused by a belief, that you had determined on a course incompatible with patronising your friends." [1]

But again the President proved obdurate. On the positive side, he did appoint Tammany Adamsite Peter Stagg as surveyor of the port in place of Joseph Swift, who had run afoul of the law. Yet in 1826, when William P. Van Ness died, Adams ignored his local supporters who boosted Henry Wheaton for the job and named Samuel Betts, a Jacksonian—an appointment which editor Charles King of the *American* felt "a deep personal humiliation and wrong." Further shattering any hope for aid from outside the state, Adams rebuffed Blunt's suggestion. "I write no letters upon what is called politics—that is electioneering," he lectured. "But I listen with interest to whatever my friends say upon topics of public concern." [2]

Shackled by the President's poor judgment, the discouraged city Adamsites hunted for a political issue with mass appeal that might save them. In terms of zeal and numbers they found their answer in the Anti-Masonry hysteria spreading in western New York counties. But the Adamsites found it difficult to capture the movement. Thurlow

Weed, who was manipulating the crusade for his own ends, hesitated to unite with the Adamsites because of rumors that the President was a Mason. Then, too, the movement was largely a rural phenomenon, and became political mostly because of the political vacuum created through Adams' abdication of party leadership.

Anti-Masonry, in short, could only spread to the city because of Democratic mistakes. For a time, it seemed Noah might help. The Antis, he scoffed, were as ridiculous as they were dangerous, and "ought to be put down" before they disrupted "the whole frame of society in the west." Noah's unabashed hostility flabbergasted Van Buren. Privately, he agreed that Anti-Masonry was an absurd crusade. But he also realized that no sane politician would dignify the movement by attempting to refute its charges of a public conspiracy. More of Noah's commotion, he pointed out, would only rub the infected areas in their sore spots and increase the Antis' political following. For all of Van Buren's sensible advice, however, he could not cool Weed's manipulation and the new party daily gained converts. Even so, New York City remained immune.[3]

Regretfully, the local Adamsites turned to other issues. Their patience suddenly seemed rewarded by the emergence of a fresh controversy the Democrats could not handle—the passage of a protective tariff. In the city, the question had severe political repercussions. Old-line Federalist merchants, auctioneers, mercantile and states' rights Tammanyites—along with dogmatic followers of economic natural law such as William Coleman of the *Post*—were free traders. Tammany Adamsites, Tammany Society nationalists, and enterprising local industrialists felt that protectionism was both a curative and a panacea. Somewhere between these two wings, moderate Tammanyites struck an ambivalent stance. As patriotic nationalists, they believed in America first; as Jeffersonians, they traditionally favored low-scheduled tariffs that were foreign policy instruments rather than bounties for domestic manufacturers; and as Jacksonians, aware that the general was straddling the issue by favoring a "judicious" tariff, they feared that the Adamsites were manipulating the issue for their own advantage.

Beginning in February 1827, when Congress began debate on a new tariff bill, the issue became a rich source of public controversy. William Coleman, whose support the Regency coveted, opposed the bill on states' rights grounds, and only proved willing to protect legitimate agrarian interests such as New York raw wool raisers whom Van Buren also wished to aid. Charles King, the Administration's most articulate spokesman, favored across-the-board increases in order to protect American industry from the British practice of dumping goods on American shores.

During these initial skirmishes, the moderate *Enquirer* and *National Advocate* adopted a middle-of-the-road course. Both called for "some judicious law on the subject of the woolens trade," but scorned full-scale protectionism as an Adamsite device for political profit. Two events during the summer forced Tammany to make its position clearer. In Albany, Van Buren addressed a protectionist meeting and left the impression that he favored some general increases, particularly for agrarians. As a result of Van Buren's studied prudence, Noah now suggested that the Jacksonians wanted an open and impartial review of the entire question, free from "personal fealty in return for high dividends." But the Harrisburg Convention, sponsored by the Pennsylvania Society for the Promotion of Manufacturing and the Mechanical Arts, proved harder to handle. Since many of these ironmongers were Jacksonians, the Regency had to modify its stand. Its immediate aims, then, included friendship toward upstate woolgrowers and Pennsylvania iron interests, moderation on the free trade question, silence on explicit principles, and political unity at home. Once Croswell made this pronouncement, Tammany Hall followed the party line. But swift-breaking events in the city dramatized that neither the Adamsites nor the tariff question would be conquered without a stiff fight.[4]

Adams' political stock had slipped so badly by mid-1827 that many of his friends despaired of his reelection. Nonetheless, his inner circle of advisers felt they could rekindle interest by the formation of a coordinated newspaper network. In May, after Charles King refused to sell his interest in the *American*, they turned their attention to the struggling *National Advocate*. Owner and publisher James Snowden was interested. His subscriptions were falling, advertisers were hard to find, and he resented Noah's prominence. Like so many hacks before him, Snowden sold out to the highest bidder. On May 10, he secretly transferred the paper to the Adamsites, and became a co-editor with New Englander Samuel Conant. For the next few weeks, the paper followed its usual course but it then slowly began to carp against the Albany Regency and the General Committee. On June 18, the *Advocate* dropped all pretenses and declared that the "republican family" of New York "was decidedly friendly to the national government."[5]

At the same time, Tammany Society Adamsites launched a bold bid to capture the organization and all its trappings of regularity. During

1825 and 1826, the pro-Adams braves absented themselves from all Society functions and created the impression that the Jacksonians could have the Order by default. But as the political tempo increased, so did the Society's internal discords. In May 1827, the Adamsites elected ten sachems to the Council, but remained a slight minority. At Tammany's Independence Day celebration, however, they chipped away at the Society's Jacksonian base when Sachem Joseph Blunt endorsed the tariff and the entire protectionist concept.

The next sign of trouble erupted in August during a General Committee meeting. Because the Democrats had an elemental instinct for organization, the Committee, under Benjamin Bailey's chairmanship, by a vote of 18 to 8, repudiated the *Advocate* as an official party newspaper. Yet the Tammany Society did not follow suit. Instead of following traditional "usages," Scribe Richard Grant disregarded the Committee, normally the party's governing board, and continued to place the Society's official notices in the *Advocate*'s columns.

In September, the matter reached a crisis. At the General Committee's monthly meeting, the delegates beat back an Adamsite attempt to restore the *Advocate*'s regularity, and dogmatically warned the ward subcommittees that the party could no longer tolerate any deviation from the Jacksonian line. At once, twelve Adamsite committeemen, led by Surveyor Stagg and former Clintonians Benjamin Romaine and James Fairlie, stormed from the room, shouting that they would not "consent to be driven like a flock of sheep into Van Buren's fold, for Clintonian slaughter." Instead, they challenged the Jacksonians for ward nomination delegates and attempted to capture Tammany Hall from the inside.[6]

The Adamsites mounted a formidable assault on the party simply because all city voters still considered themselves lineal descendants, whatever factional guise they assumed, of Thomas Jefferson's Republican party. The Adamsites had not withdrawn from this party, nor had the Jacksonians expelled them. In fact, the President's consensus policy made it even harder for his foes to claim he was a traitor to traditional "usages." Tammany's convention election, then, subjected the party to severe psychological strain. Each side bribed voters, used strong-arm tactics, and escorted unnaturalized voters to the polls. But in the end, the Adams faction made a sorry showing. The Jacksonians elected a clear majority, and they dominated the convention.

The Adamsites had prepared for such a contingency. Political power, they reasoned, rested on five variables: the electorate, the nominating convention, the General Committee or Tammany Hall, the

Corporation, and the Council of Sachems. Control over the Council was the key to control over the first four, yet the Jacksonians had foolishly not reorganized the sachems since the May elections. The Adamsites made the most of the oversight and used it to gain control of the local apparatus. Secretly, they began to negotiate with the ten Adamsite sachems for the sale of the Wigwam.[7]

On October 6, oblivious to any trouble, the Council of Sachems held its regular monthly meeting. The Adamsites had carefully planned in advance and took advantage of the absence of fifteen Jacksonian sachems to buy the building's lease from their fellow conspirators. "The General Committee, which has assumed so much," the *Advocate* chortled, "has but an ephemeral existence, just chosen yearly for especial purposes. In the Council of Sachems is found the pure gold of the party."[8]

Initially taken aback by this staggering stratagem, the Jacksonians regrouped for a counterattack. On first impulse, they offered to buy the lease back, but the Adamsites claimed the contract was binding. Shifting ground, the Jacksonians waged their own psychological warfare by keeping the trappings of tradition. They held their nominating convention in the building's basement, derisively known as the "coal hole." Then the Jacksonian Council majority called the entire Society's membership together to discuss the problem. About 600 braves responded on October 15, and adopted resolutions that censured "the *minority* of the Council of Sachems for having illegally altered the lease of said Hall, in such a manner as to permit the enemies of the republican party to hold their meetings there."[9]

For the remainder of the campaign, both Tammany factions gathered almost nightly in the Wigwam, each stressing party legitimacy. On October 29, the Adamsites held a grand rally, attended by over 1,000 enthusiastic men, and challenged the Jacksonians to match them. Three nights later the Jacksonians answered, when over 6,000 of them pushed and shoved their way into the Long Room and forced chairman Charles Livingston to adjourn to City Park. Once there, the aroused partisans denounced the tariff, Adams, Clay, the Council minority, and the corrupt bargain with scornful impartiality.

Upstate, Van Buren read the news from the city with mounting alarm. At the end of October, he chaired a meeting of the Andrew Jackson's Young Men's Committee in the Wigwam and came away impressed. Even so, he cautioned Churchill Cambreleng, his right-hand man among the Tammanyites, "the only hope of the administration is to bring about a re-action in the state by their success in the City, and you must therefore exert every care."[10]

The campaign was such a one as the city had not witnessed for years. Amid mutual accusations of fraud, nativism, bribery, and intimidation, the electorate announced its feelings in no uncertain terms. "New York is for Jackson," Noah thundered; for once, the facts bore him out. The Democrats elected their full assembly slate by over 5,000 votes, hardened control over the Corporation, 9–5, and sent both city senators back to Albany.[11]

Within the Tammany Society, the Jacksonians' activities were equally intense and rewarding. Reestablishing full grasp over the errant Council of Sachems, the Jacksonians held a boisterous victory rally in the Long Room and physically barred the Adamsites from using any of the building's facilities. Fully alive to the symbolic power inherent in the Society, moreover, the Jacksonians placed further temptation beyond Adamsite reach. The Council restored the lease to Lovejoy and Howard, its original lessees, but reserved to itself the sole "right to decide on all questions of doubt, arising out of the rooms being occupied or otherwise for political purposes." [12]

The upshot of these developments was that the Tammany Jacksonians killed all Tammany Adamsite hopes of forming a viable party within traditional forms. Unlike the People's party episode three years earlier, the Jacksonians had reasserted their authority over the old symbols of Republicanism by their domination of the Tammany Society, and forced the Adamsites to establish a new organization that bore little family resemblance to former factional alignments. In terms of outmoded labels, the Jacksonian Democratic party consisted of Crawford Regulars (even though Crawford favored Adams), Clintonians, Swiss Federalists, the majority of the Burrites, and anti-Adams High-Minders. On the President's side were upstate Clayites, a smattering of unreliable Anti-Masons, the Rufus King High-Minders, some Burrites led by Matthew Davis, nationalists, anti–Van Buren Republicans, and a few Clintonians who could not abide any cooperation with the Albany Regency.

Psychologically, the city election and their failure to capture the Tammany Society had lasting results on the Adamsites. Without much enthusiasm, they mechanically formed a separate General Committee, organized branches in every ward, and set up a statewide network of John Quincy Adams' Young Men's Republican Clubs. Yet for all their efforts, the Adamsites never recovered their momentum in the city. Instead, as Joseph Blunt saw the situation, their main chance lay in the state "& with proper organisation [we] can make it manifest." At this point, however, the Jacksonians really did not control the city. With a proper effort, the Adamsites might have fought back. But because the President would not confuse private feelings with what he conceived to be his public duties, the result was almost predictable. Yet in concentrating their efforts upstate, the Adamsites committed a gross error.[13]

The Adamsites's blunder in New York City came into focus during the next few months as the tariff question again became the center of controversy. In December 1827, a group of New Yorkers—led first by James Tallmadge, then by Morgan Lewis—formed the American Institute, osentensibly as a nonpartisan pressure group to support measures "favorable to domestic industry" and to oppose legislation it deemed detrimental to the national interest. At first, the Tammany Society badly mistook the Institute's real purpose and allowed it free run of the Long Room. In April 1828, however, the Institute emerged as the spokesman for the city protectionists.

In pushing for higher rates the Institute attacked the local auction system, a vestige of the free trade era, and unexpectedly created a sensation. After the War of 1812 the United States had allowed the British to dump goods in American ports, thus undercutting domestic manufacturers. In New York, the commodities were sold by auctioneers—appointed by the governor—and the state, which taxed the sale, valued the system as a political as well as a financial device. Its opponents were less complimentary. They argued that the auction system was an immoral monopoly that harmed the general welfare, caused fluctuating prices, and, worst of all, was un-American because it aided British manufacturers.[14]

Since the financial interests of many city merchants, mechanics, and tradesmen were involved, the auction system had as many enemies as it had friends. But until 1828 neither party made it an important political question. Yet as the American Institute kept up a steady barrage of criticism, the Adamsites, led by Joseph Blunt, discovered that popular indignation against auctioneering cut across party lines and held immense value as a Jacksonian counterweight. To capitalize on this attitude, the Institute held a mass anti-auction rally and drew up a memorial which it forwarded to Congressman Gulian Verplanck for action. Meantime, the General Committee, which did recognize some injustice in the system, sought to bury the question. Noah contended that the memorial had arrived too late for congressional action and proposed that the question be settled some time in the future, "beginning at the root, and following it up in a business-like mode, apart from all *political views.*" [15]

Granting the logic in the editor's words, the Adamsites had touched on an emotional campaign issue that had vast potential. But incredibly, they made no further move to mesh the anti-auctioneers with the President's late-blooming reelection efforts. As a result, the issue remained dormant until October when it regained life.

An air of unreality now surrounded Adamsite politicking. When the tariff finally passed Congress, city Jacksonians were generally distressed, yet as Noah put it, "the tariff may be bad but we can easily live through it." Upstate, the Adamsites suffered a similar reversal when the Anti-Masons held aloof from a formal alliance, and both parties ran separate candidates. In contrast, nothing seemed likely to prevent Jackson and the Democrats from carrying the state. [16]

Yet the Jacksonians did encounter difficult problems and, as so many times in the past, DeWitt Clinton complicated Van Burenite plans. In late 1827 the governor unequivocally endorsed Jackson for the presidency. The Adamsite press, which had up to this point treated Clinton with elaborate if cynical deference, now peppered him with sarcasm. In a typical editorial, the *Advocate* growled: "he is the apostate politician,—the ungrateful friend, and the syncophantic hypocrite, whom federalism had twice spewed out upon democrats; and whom democrats have twice vomited back upon federalism."

For most Tammanyites, whatever sort of advantage they gained by cooperating with the governor remained problematical. Since both Clinton and Van Buren pictured themselves as kingmakers, many New Yorkers honestly questioned if the party was big enough to absorb their conflicting ambitions. Then, too, the state's patronage picture would be clouded if Jackson won. In the inevitable scramble for spoils, the DeWitt Clinton–Regency dogfight might duplicate the Clintonian-Burrite-Livingston brouhaha.

Despite these qualms, the majority of Tammanyites never lost sight of their major goal and worked with Clinton until his sudden death in February of 1828. In all sections of the state people paused momentarily and paid tribute to a great man; then they began to weigh the political dimensions inherent in his passing. Most out-of-staters assumed that Adams would now pick up the Clintonians because they had "merely adopted Jackson, to advance Clinton." Even Daniel Webster felt that the state would fall by default to Adams. [17]

In contrast, local Adamsites were not so confident that the Clintonians had been captives of their departed leader's ambition and would now silently desert the general. During the next few months, various signs indicated that Clinton's party, which had depended so heavily upon his personality in life, still retained some cohesion in death and would not fuse with the National Republicans. As one anonymous Clintonian succinctly wrote: "There is nothing in the Adams party which is in unison with our feelings or principles." In the final reckoning, some Clintonians did support the President; others, like John Pintard, remained aloof, not even bothering to vote; but still others, such as Caleb Atwater, an Ohio Clintonian, pumped hard for Jackson, not so much for possible spoils as for personal fulfillment and vindication. As Noah wisely summarized, many Clintonians simply admired the general's "character, and they will continue to do so from the same motives." [18]

As for Tammany, despite the many rationales pouring from the Jacksonian press, the General Committee had felt uncomfortable with Clinton—as if opportunism had run amuck. His death changed the picture. Tammanyites could now fully support the general without worrying that Clinton might reap the reward of their exertions. Ironically, in the city, Clinton dead played a bigger role in winning the state for Jackson than Clinton alive could have done.[19]

Organizationally, the Jacksonian campaign, as directed by Van Buren, was marked by flexibility, imagination, cunning, and symbolic appeals based on raw emotionalism. In the city, as in other areas, the Jacksonians added several clever innovations to the old game of mass manipulation. Two of their favorite devices were elaborate dinners to commemorate the battle of New Orleans and the symbolic planting of hickory trees. For example, the Tammany Society drew over 1,600 people in the Long Room at its New Orleans celebration, while similar dinners in the wards did equally well. "The greatest humbug that has been got up for a long time is the scheme of the Jackson dinners," the *Advocate* complained. But the success of these Jacksonian efforts was quickly apparent. "The more he is known," the *Post* concluded, "the less and less the charges against him seem to be true." Tammany's planting of hickory trees followed the same technique of mass appeal. With grandiose ceremony, Hickory Clubs in each ward planted trees, then retired to a local barroom to toast the general's health. Mordecai Noah approved. "There is nothing that shakes the nerves of the Adams' gentry, so much as the planting of hickory trees." [20]

While the Democrats successfully enshrined Andrew Jackson as the symbol of the "Common Man," many party leaders wondered if Tammany Hall could absorb Federalism without fragmenting. During the campaign, both the Jacksonians and National Republicans were hyper-sensitive about open Federalist support, and bitterly attacked each other for consorting with traitors. To the Adamsites, "The course adopted by Mr. Jackson is food and raiment for the federalists and the no-party men." To this charge, the Democrats answered that Jackson "ever since the formation of the party [had been] a *uniform republican*" who scorned any trimming. Nevertheless, both sides did covet Federalist aid and welcomed any converts.[21]

Tammanyite reaction against the Jacksonian flirtation with Federalism was negligible. Determined to win, the Hall accepted all comers, regardless of party labels and heedless of Van Burenite propaganda that the campaign was based on old party grounds, and practiced the politics of conclusion and inclusion. As a result, many Federalists joined the local apparatus, campaigned vigorously, and labored with an eye focused on the future. Their real problem would come when Jackson initiated his spoils policy.[22]

Until the summer, the Tammany Adamsites continued to sleepwalk through the campaign. In June the *Advocate* complained: "We want in such a crisis as this, a bold, active and energetic General Committee. Why do they not come to work and do the duty expected of them?" Stirred by the censure, the Adamsites momentarily shed their defeatism. Once again they tried to disrupt the Democrats by meeting in the Wigwam. But this time the sachems were prepared. The Council barred the National Republicans from the building (even though many of them were brothers in good standing), locked and bolted all the doors, and jeered their subsequent humiliating exodus to Shakespeare's Hotel, an undistinguished hangout without any political significance. With heavy-handed sarcasm, Noah reported: "We learn that the Adams men have been locked out from Tammany Hall, bag and baggage—they now hold the candle and drink their beer in the Shakespeare. In fact, the increase of Jacksonism of late at Tammany Hall and the neighborhood has been so great, that the Adams men saw it with grief and fled." [23]

By mid-September the Tammany Adamsites resigned themselves again to defeat. Their spirits rallied temporarily at the death of city Postmaster Theodorus Bailey, a holdover from James Madison's Administration. But once more the President plunged them into despair by appointing James Monroe's son-in-law, Samuel Gouverneur, a one-time Adamsite now turned Jacksonian. Completely embarrassed, Charles

King strove to place the situation in the best light. "The patronage of the general government is not employed to support the measures or to promote the re-election of Mr. Adams," he wrote, "and this is the first time since the establishment of this government that its patronage has not been so employed." King's rationalization might have been good moral tonic for sick spirits, but it was hardly the medicine to cure apathetic party workers.[24]

As September waned, it was remarkable that the President still had any active partisans in the city. Federal patronage brought Tammany Adamsites little if any satisfaction; the General Committee and ward clubs deteriorated with disuse and neglect, while the national leadership concentrated on unclogging channels toward Anti-Masonry. Then, by one of those sudden quirks of fate that can dramatically shift the political balance overnight, the local Adamsites stumbled upon a potentially explosive issue with vast popular dimensions that could obscure all their shortcomings.

In October the auction question surfaced again. Beginning as a mood rather than as a formal organization, the anti-auctioneers represented a wide range of normally Democratic local interest groups. Two weeks before the election, these men held an impromtu rally, blasted Jacksonian Tammanyite Congressmen Verplanck, Cambreleng, and Jeronomus Johnson for their refusal to co-sponsor the May memorial, and then nominated an independent congressional slate of three new candidates, bankers Walter Bowne and Campbell P. White, and merchant David Ogden, all of whom were also Jacksonian Tammanyites.

Noah and Coleman rejected the ticket on the basis of its irregularity. "It is reserved to the Nominating Committee to make such recommendations as shall best comport with the wishes, the interests, the character, and the permanent establishment of the republican party," Noah chided. Bowne and White agreed, and struck their names off the ticket because they were not chosen "in the usual and regular manner." Completing the circle, the Jacksonians dropped Johnson, who wanted to retire, and nominated Cambreleng, Verplanck, and White. The embarrassed mutineers had now lost direction and again called for another meeting to reassess their location on the political map. Once more bitterly taking Verplanck and Cambreleng to task, the insurgents reendorsed White and Ogden and added Adamsite Thomas C. Thomas to the ticket. Nonetheless, the anti-auctioneers emphasized that their rebellion stood apart from party: "It has nothing to do, directly or indirectly, with the local politics of this country, and particularly with the great contest to be decided in November."[25]

Although the Jacksonian anti-auctioneers had been more than generous in handing the National Republicans an issue that might have swung the election, they failed to manipulate it correctly. Instead of wooing dissident Democrats, especially the workingmen, the Adamsites concentrated on the less numerous merchants. Indeed, the Adamsites compounded their blunder when neither the *American* nor *Advocate* took serious offense at Coleman's false statement that "the cause of our mechanics cannot be identified with that of manufacturers." Moreover, the Adamsites did not show the insurgents the illogical inconsistency in their position: that the issue *was* synonymous with protectionism and that the President, not the equivocal Jackson, represented their best interests. To cap their series of misunderstandings, the Adamsites did not even counter the anti-auctioneers' unsophisticated stand that the issue was purely local. For all practical purposes, then, the movement never reached full maturity. In failing to capitalize on the discontent in Jacksonian ranks, the Adamsites were the real architects of their ultimate defeat.[26]

As the city election neared its predictable climax, Tammanyites still encountered a few anxious moments. Ever since 1822, when he had become the object of party contempt, Noah had lusted for office, partly out of ambition, partly for vindication. In spite of continued rebuffs, he finally wangled the nomination for sheriff. But at the ratification meeting, a group of men led by James Watson Webb vehemently objected. A quick-tempered, haughty martinet, Webb had recently joined the struggling Jacksonian *New York Courier,* and under his forcible, if somewhat indiscreet editorship, the paper soon challenged the *Enquirer*'s self-appointed role as party spokesman. Too self-willed and arrogant to be able to bear seeing Noah in such a lucrative office, Webb mounted a chair during the meeting, demanded that the party select a more deserving man than Noah, and asked for a show of hands to back his stand. On the question, should "the whole Ticket pass as nominated," the delegates out-voted Webb, 53–12, with 33 abstentions. Barely controlling his fury, Webb called for another poll and charged that the delegates were Noah's paid stooges. At this point, a few of Noah's equally short-fused friends called a recess, and began a rowdy shoving match that ended when they pushed Webb and his allies "out of the Hall, without ceremony." [27]

The farce did not end on such a ludicrous note. Despite a hastily formed ward resolution that called on the Democrats to support only those "regularly nominated at Tammany Hall, for Congress, Senate, Assembly, and County offices," Webb advised the rank and file to elect Noah's opponent, Adamsite James Shaw. So far as Noah was concerned, the critical moment had passed. But Webb's outburst left an unhealed lesion in the organization that later required careful doctoring.[28]

"I advise the family to prepare for defeat," an unusually gloomy Charles Francis Adams wrote his mother. In marked contrast, gubernatorial candidate Martin Van Buren expected an easy victory for all Democratic aspirants. Despite young Adams' pessimism and Van Buren's optimism, the city election was actually much closer than anyone, including the President's most hopeful followers, had anticipated. Both sides fought with never-say-die fury. "Houses were hired, bars opened, victualling stands engaged, the best electioneers secured, carriages hired, young, active men employed, illegal votes brought up and votes purchased"—this is Noah's description of Adamsite tactics. The Jacksonians had equally dirty hands. In the end, however, organization counted, and the Democrats (except for Noah) swept all the offices and gave Jackson a 5,789-vote plurality. Upstate, Adams and Jackson ran evenly, and the President lost New York by merely 5,350 votes out of a total of 276,176 cast. Even Van Buren ran a poor statewide race. If the total vote of his two gubernatorial opponents, Smith Thompson and Francis Granger, were added together, he would not have been elected governor.[29]

In retrospect, for all of Adams' faults as a politician, and they were undoubtedly many, he lost the election through his own ineptitude, not because of Jackson's appeal or the Hall's and Van Buren's painstaking organizational spadework. It was New York City that gave Jackson and Van Buren sufficient votes to win—and it was in New York City where the Adamsites made no real effort, after their debacle in the Tammany Society, to form a viable party movement that could save the President. If New York City, then, proved the key to Jackson's victory in the state, then the Tammany Society provided the main thrust behind that victory. For if the Jacksonians had failed in their efforts to regain the party tabernacle, the Adamsites might have been able to tarnish the general's transformation into the hero of the common man, the legitimate inheritor of the party's Jeffersonian tradition.

Such reflections did not bother Jacksonian Tammanyites. Elated by success despite Noah's embarrassing but not unexpected loss, their grip over the Common Council, mayoralty, and legislature tightened, the Democrats faced the future with anticipation and, for the moment, reveled in the heady intoxication of victory.

As for the opposition, confusion reigned. President Adams retired into sullen despair, his local followers lacked any rallying point as Henry Clay became their national leader by default, and Governor Van Buren used his patronage powers to sow confusion among the Anti-Masons. Bereft of issues, lacking any cooperation, the anti-Jacksonians were immobilized and could now only hope to galvanize public opinion through Democratic mistakes.[30]

Intent on patronage, Tammanyites awaited some sign that the President-elect meant to pay loyal party workers the dividends they had earned. But much sophistry clouded Jackson's forthcoming spoils policy. As a candidate, his artful hedging perplexed friends and foes alike. Even so astute an operator as Van Buren feared that Jackson might continue Monroe's fusion program. Only in March when he became a cabinet member did the New Yorker learn that the Old Hero endorsed the rotation-in-office doctrine and would reward or punish on the basis of services rendered.[31]

In the meantime, Tammanyites fretted with uncertainty as the days passed without some inkling of Jackson's intentions. In particular they eyed the lucrative collector's slot in the Custom House and bombarded Van Buren with demands that he co-sponsor Jonathan Coddington, an organization man who had done yeoman work in the wards, for the job. In order to foster Coddington's aspirations, the General Committee made two more strategic moves. First, it cautioned Jackson's original Federalist supporters that staunch Tammanyites deserved the bulk of local spoils. Then, to keep the workingmen in line and preserve peace at home, the Committee memorialized the legislature to modernize the auction system.[32]

Despite these tactics, Jackson refused any commitment. In general, most Tammanyites applauded his choice of Van Buren as secretary of state even though they felt his successor, Lieutenant Governor Enos Throop, was a political lightweight. But the patronage crisis grew in intensity when rumors circulated through the city that the President intended to make his long-time friend and former Burrite, Samuel Swartwout (a notorious party maverick), the collector. Tammanyites immediately wrote Van Buren strongly worded protest letters. Back came his reply. Threats and demands would not shake Jackson and might have the reverse effect of making him more obstinate. Rather, Van Buren suggested that Cambreleng, Mayor Bowne, and other party chieftains write the President a "courteous & just letter" that detailed the Hall's objections. Meantime, Van Buren personally interceded with

Jackson. Naming Swartwout over Tammany's demurrers, the Secretary cautioned, "would not be in accordance with public sentiment, the interests of the Country, or the credit of the administration." [33]

Swartwout was equally busy on the hustings. He attempted to soothe Tammany's feelings by assuring the General Committee that if appointed he meant to purge all National Republicans from federal jobs, and would replace them with loyal Tammanyites. His words converted few doubters. In a showdown, the Hall preferred one of its own over a man whose clouded career smacked more of unlimited opportunism than any willingness to follow the General Committee's dictates on patronage.

By the end of April, Jackson settled the question in his own way. He did select Swartwout, but attempted to appease the Hall by naming Noah as surveyor. Despite the fact that the editor had as many enemies outside the party as in it, Tammanyites publicly accepted the President's will. Privately, however, they raged against Jackson's disregard of the local party's wishes. Cambreleng was especially bitter. To Van Buren he predicted that the new collector would covertly attempt to finesse the Regency by pushing Calhoun as Jackson's successor. Worse, Cambreleng feared that Swartwout was corrupt, and forecast that he might become a "defaulter in four years." On organizational matters, Cambreleng was equally blunt. Because of Jackson's intemperate move, he ended, "we have driven from our ward meetings a body of strong republicans who for 20 or 30 years have been the back-bone of our party." [34]

Yet in a way that he did not yet understand, Cambreleng's emotional outburst presaged a new era in local politics. Unlike any of his predecessors since Jefferson, Andrew Jackson was slated to dominate his times and set the style and substance for all political activity. Headstrong, impatient, dictatorial, Jackson was uniquely his own man. Tammany Hall had helped elect an unknown quantity who was now quietly preparing a thrust destined to disrupt city politics for the next decade and reshape the Hall's image. Yet, for the moment, all these changes lay in the uncharted future.

In the forty-three days that he served as governor, Martin Van Buren laid plans for an administration that would move as smoothly as possible and compare favorably with DeWitt Clinton's tenure in office. Buried deep within his legislative message Van Buren offered a vague suggestion, made with a minimum of consideration, that the legislators devise a plan to stabilize the state banking system. If any doubters questioned the move, he reminded them that thirty-one out of forty state bank charters were up for renewal. In the busy weeks that followed, Van Buren consulted a long list of advisers. Out of their deliberations emerged the Safety Fund System, a plan designed to create a statewide insurance fund for insolvent banks.[35]

Actually, the proposal had its roots in the bickerings and jealousies of a few thwarted canal boomers. The year before, two members of the assembly's Committee on Internal Improvements, Anti-Mason Francis Granger and Jacksonian Abijah Mann, disagreed violently on authorization of the Chenango Canal feeder into the Erie. As matters stood, Granger realized that he lacked enough votes for passage, and scanned the legislative agenda for possible logrolling. He found allies among the bankers who were lobbying for immediate recharters. In exchange for their aid, Granger agreed to swing the Anti-Masons behind the bank bill. The deal seemed secure until Mann learned of the bargain, and introduced a bill to make all banks individually liable for their debts. His ingenuity forced the bank interests to drop Granger, and the legislature adjourned without acting on either measure.[36]

When politics regained equilibrium after the fall elections, the bankers decided to reconcile sound fiscal policies with partisan reality. To do so, they used Van Buren as a cats-paw. Economically naive about high finance, his was a mind that held strong agrarian prejudices against all banks, particularly in respect to their abuse of corporate privileges. On the other hand, he pragmatically recognized their necessity. Since part of his secret for success rested on giving various influential interest groups what they evidently wanted, he looked after their desires and threw the problem unto the laps of his trusted advisers, particularly Comptroller Silas Wright, Thomas Olcott, cashier of the Albany Farmers' and Mechanics' Bank, and Benjamin Knower, its principal stockholder.[37]

As a result, the Safety Fund bore his imprimatur but lacked his full sympathy. The bill raised interest rates from 6 percent to 7 percent. Each member bank annually contributed one-half of 1 percent until the fund reached 3 percent of the total bank capital in the state. The other one-half of 1 percent was clear profit for the individual banks. The bill also provided for a board of commissioners who oversaw, inspected, and regulated all member banks. In addition, these men had the power to levy *pro rata* contributions from each participating institution to maintain the fund. Moreover, if any bank violated its trust, the commissioners, acting with the attorney general, could suspend operations until the offender mended its ways.[38]

Although the bill passed, it encountered heavy opposition from city bank interests and Tammany Hall legislators. Local financiers, confident of their own stability, felt the plan penalized them and unnecessarily favored upstate interests, particularly Olcott's Farmers' and Mechanics' Bank where the commissioners intended to deposit the bulk of the Safety Fund moneys. In order to bolster their opposition, city bankers, after threatening to give up their charters and relocate in New Jersey, curtailed loans, and constricted the money market. As interest rates climbed, trade plummeted, and business slowed to a crawl.[39]

Efforts from Tammany's power structure, which was heavily dominated by bank interests, were equally intense. The General Committee sent lobbyists to Albany, headed by Walter Bowne; the *Evening Post* harassed Governor Throop; and Tammany legislators protested against Olcott's influence among Regency leaders.

In this welter of confusion, defiance, and acrimony, all eyes turned toward Nicholas Biddle and his Bank of the United States. On principle, Biddle rejected the Safety Fund concept because it protected bad management, hindered sound practices, and put an unreasonable burden on responsible bankers. But he had no intention of meddling directly with the question as long as it was political. When the crisis disrupted economic stability, however, he dropped his detached air. To one city branch Bank director he wrote that we must "occupy the ground from which the City Banks choose to recede." To another, he went on to state that the branch should lend its "facilities to the trading community wherever it can be done safely." The branch Bank carried out the directives at once. It pumped money into the sagging loan market, publicly announced its willingness to take up the slack, and generally followed an easy-money policy. By June 1829, the lending market had recovered momentum and the immediate crisis ended.[40]

The reaction of city bankers toward Biddle ranged from shocked disbelief to livid rage. For some time, they had considered the Bank of the United States a check on the upstate financiers headed by Knower and Olcott. Now, city interests oscillated between momentary fury and the realization that they needed Biddle's institution to ward off further upstate raids. In another sense, Biddle's action had a deep psychological impact on local politicians, particularly dogmatic agrarians and states' rights advocates, who now began to reflect upon the continued need for a quasi-federal instrument of government, politically unresponsive to public control. But like the local bankers, most Tammanyites could see no alternatives. In contrast, upstate Regency bankers made no effort to conceal their elation at the city's chagrin, and lauded Biddle's impartial financial leadership.[41]

For all his skill as a central banker, Biddle recognized that the Bank owed its continued existence to a favorable partisan climate. Despite his claims of political noninvolvement, he was very much engaged in city politics. In January 1829, when rumors reached his office that Tammanyite Churchill Cambreleng was agitating against the Bank, Biddle hired him as a special agent to investigate a site for a new branch in western New York. Later, learning that Congressman Gulian Verplanck had applied for a loan without sufficient collateral, Biddle reminded his local directors that when an opportunity arose "to convert enemies into friends, we owe it to ourselves and the Stockholders not to omit that occasion." [42]

Above that, Biddle maintained an elaborate information-gathering network. As might be expected, the branch directors often fed him rumors instead of facts. But between April of 1829 and mid-1834, he found a much more useful source. James Gordon Bennett, a grasping, ambitious, devious man, who had been an editor of the *National Advocate* and was now Noah's Albany and Washington correspondent, supplied Biddle, for a fee, with a secret window into the Democracy's innermost operations. As to other agents—bustling, egotistical, city merchant Silas Burrows for one—Biddle was less fortunate. [43]

During late 1829 and early 1830, Biddle continued to weld prominent Tammanyites into his net of politics, banking, and self-interest. After he had antagonized some powerful upstate Regency bankers by selecting Buffalo as the new branch site, he attempted to repair any remaining tension in the city by suggesting to his local directors that they name some prominent Jacksonians to the next board. After a few weeks, the directors submitted a long list of names including those of Tammanyite bankers Campbell White, Walter Bowne, and Saul Alley. After pondering the alternatives, Biddle named all three. When Bowne declined because of his mayoralty duties and recommended his son-in-law, John W. Lawrence, Biddle readily accepted. Not all the directors approved such tactics. "A *large* portion of the present Board," one objected, "are decided Administration men." Nonetheless, Biddle took pride in his political acumen and never hesitated to use his Tammany contacts to further Bank interests. [44]

Meantime, a sense of routine settled over Tammany Hall. After the pangs of the banker-induced recession wore off, the party showed great skill in handling two problems that caused temporary concern.

The General Committee first settled the rivalry that existed between

Noah's *Enquirer* and Webb's *Courier*. With both sheets losing money, the Committee saw little sense in condoning the struggle. On May 25, 1829, it acted as midwife for the birth of a new consolidated city paper, the *Courier and Enquirer*. Under the agreement's terms, Webb and his business partner, Daniel Tylee, cashier of the Savings Bank of New York, bought out Noah for $35,000, although he remained as an associate editor. Noah further bound himself in a $20,000 rider that he would not start another city paper for eight years. The General Committee exacted one concession from the new owners. In order to keep Tammany's patronage and general advertising, Webb and Tylee agreed that the Committee could name the paper's political editor. After some indecision, Chairman Benjamin Bailey named James Gordon Bennett.[45]

The other problem was far more serious. For years, city residents had felt that the 1731 Montgomerie Charter was obsolete, but were unable to decide if it should be thoroughly modernized or completely scrapped. In 1824, and again in 1828, the legislature had proposed the former course at the Common Council's behest, but in both instances the voters had rejected the proposed amendments. By 1829, however, the clamor for a new charter reached a pitch that Tammany could not safely ignore.

Propelled by this thrust, a group of public-spirited citizens, with the Common Council's blessing, called for and received authorization for a special convention to draw up a new charter. Meeting from June to September of 1829, the delegates drew up the document, which the voters approved in November and which became law the following year when ratified by the legislature.[46]

The new Common Council consisted of two houses, the Board of Aldermen and the Board of Assistant Aldermen, each chosen for one-year terms at the same election. The mayor, still named by the Corporation, lost his seat on the Council but gained veto power over all its ordinances, resolutions, and laws. Although the charter intended to invest the mayor with broad administrative prerogatives through the creation of executive departments, the Council still conducted business in the old unstructured manner. In theory, the charter's bicameralism combined legislative action with popular rule in order to make the Corporation more responsible. In practice, the reverse occurred. Through collusion and downright bribery, both Boards cooperated through their standing committees as the functional branch of government. In the long run, then, Tammanyites rapidly adjusted to the new charter, and almost effortlessly molded the Common Council into the Hall's image.[47]

To the extent that Tammany reflected public opinion, then, all surface indications pointed toward its uninterrupted domination of city politics. Above that, the anti-Jacksonians lacked any local organization, and wide differences of opinion existed among them over what techniques could excite the public. Merchant William B. Lawrence wrote Henry Clay that his New York City followers had decided "to avail themselves of some local question" such as the Safety Fund "instead of meeting the whole force of the Jackson party." But, he ended pessimistically, "whether this is attempted or not the present year must depend on the development of public opinion during the next few weeks." [48]

Things did work out as the Clayites anticipated—but in a different way. Far below the passive surface of city politics, a movement of far-reaching consequences was just beginning to rumble among dissatisfied city workingmen. It was from this force, not the Safety Fund, that the Clayites launched their counterattack.

For some time, many skilled city artisans had realized that they were living in a time of flux and were not sharing in the prospect of future advances. As the fights over the tariff and the auction system so vividly demonstrated, the political system minimized such changes. After Jackson's election, these men turned toward Tammany for relief but met a cool response. While the Hall indeed courted labor's support and pretended to be its champion, banking and corporate interests dominated the party's power structure and left a deep imprint on its programs. By not making a distinction between the needs of "the producing class" and the special interests that dominated the General Committee, by assuming continued blind loyalty, Tammany created a sense of urgency, of unity, among the "workies" that held grave political warnings.

On a second but related level, the workies resented the fact that although Tammany had seemingly come to terms with the spirit of Jacksonian Democracy, it actually did not implement its democratic slogans. The Hall, in short, operated as if the popular will set party policy while in reality the organization did little more than follow the wishes of a small, wealthy clique.[49]

The Safety Fund argument precipitated the workies' fury at the Hall's vested interests. In April 1829, reacting against rumors that employers planned to lengthen the normal ten-hour day as a means of recouping losses incurred during the recession, a group of workingmen held a protest meeting and appointed a Committee of Fifty to present their grievances.

The Committee was silent until the following October. But during the interval, it fell under the influence of three colorful but erratic leaders, Thomas Skidmore, Robert Dale Owen, and Fanny Wright. An imperious man with a low tolerance for the opinions of others, Skidmore's *The Right of Man to Property!* advocated a utopian plan designed to end private land ownership and eliminate inherited wealth. As substitutes, he proposed "equal rights" based on a redistribution of land and other discriminatory practices against the rich. A machinist by trade and an Adamsite in politics, Skidmore dominated the Committee. Robert Dale Owen, a humanitarian reformer whose father's communitarian experiment in New Harmony, Indiana, had just failed, was a newcomer to the city. Along with the fascinating Fanny Wright, an emancipated woman who delighted in smashing society's shibboleths, Owen established the radical *Free Enquirer* and urged free, universal education as labor's panacea.

The Committee of Fifty's report, the upshot of this unstable alliance, presented a strange combination of radicalism and moral-political outrage. To answer labor's most immediate problems, the document condemned the auction system, imprisonment for debt, chartered monopolies, banking privileges, the failure to tax church-owned property, and the lack of a mechanics' lien law. On a more nihilist tack, the Committee also substantially endorsed Skidmore's confiscatory notions and the Owen-Wright educational scheme.[50]

If the workies had stopped there, Tammany might have dismissed them as eccentrics. But they had just started. Just before the fall election, they nominated an assembly slate on which two Adamsites and one Anti-Mason ran with eight other bona fide Jacksonians. By now, the Hall realized that other leaders besides Skidmore, Owen, and Wright—particularly Matthew Davis—were obsessed not so much with the workies' frustration as with an attempt to manipulate the rebellion on behalf of the displaced National Republicans. For the moment, however, the anti-Jacksonians wavered over which issue could engender the most support—the Safety Fund or the workie movement. The *Evening Journal*, a newly formed Clayite newspaper, wooed the workies and sought to make Tammany's closed nomination system the contest's key issue. At the same time, the *Morning Herald*, an Adamsite paper formed when the *National Advocate* fused with the Clintonian *Statesman*, played on the banking community's hostility toward the Safety Fund, and instigated a Tammany splinter group, the Pewter

Mug Democracy, to drop three men on the regular ticket and substitute their own.

The strategy split among its foes gave Tammany time to regroup. As a way of neutralizing the Pewter Mug rebels, the Hall reminded the electorate that party irregulars, just as in 1824, meant to destroy the organization for their own purposes. As for the workies, the General Committee belittled them as social, political, and economic deviates whom "all sober, respectable mechanics of New York" ought to shun. Any people like Skidmore, Owen, and Wright, the *Post* jeered, "who scoff at morality and propose a system of public robbery" deserved nothing short of complete ostracism.[51]

Tammany could not dismiss its opponents with words. Even though eight regulars won, the Pewter Mug ticket carried two seats, and one workie gained victory. Moreover, two other workies, Skidmore and Alexander Ming, Sr., a Revolutionary War veteran and Tammany Society brave, lost by a wafer-thin margin of 60 votes. To put the Hall's troubles in a different light, the total workie ticket polled over 6,000 ballots to Tammany's winning but unimpressive 11,000.[52]

After the contest, the workingmen adopted all the paraphernalia of a mature political party. Under the able direction of George Evans, an agnostic British expatriate, their new party organ, the *Working Man's Advocate*, began a war of words with Tammany's press. At the end of December they formed a General Committee based on a loosely structured ward network, which Skidmore opposed, to challenge the Hall in its own backyard.[53]

After the movement adopted a permanent organization, an inevitable shift took place as the older humanitarian cure-alls lost their luster and political considerations replaced them. As the new year began, the workies coalesced around four factions: the *Evening Journal* Clayites, soon joined by the Adamsites—who now saw greater gains in this movement than banking—led by commissary agent Noah Cook and stoneware manufacturer Clarkson Crolius, Jr., who meant to transform the party into a frankly anti-Jackson vehicle; the radical levelers of the Thomas Skidmore type; the Owen-Wright-Evans reformers; and the bulk of the workingmen, pragmatic to the core, more interested in practical results than any starry-eyed nostrums.

Under such grinding pressure the party fragmented, with the Cook wing and the Owenites temporarily in command. Convinced that Skidmore would repel more voters than he could reasonably draw, the two allies drummed him out of the party while Evans vilified him in print. With Skidmore dismissed, the victors themselves split. The Owenites, who abhored political action, felt that they could achieve their ends through persuasion and friendly discussion. Cook's supporters had other objectives. As Peter Porter told Clay, the Workingmen's party "will embrace most of the friends of the late administration, & particularly your friends, and will form a rendevous [sic] for all those who detest and despise Jacksonianism & Antimasonry. It promises well." On May 19, the fragmentation became complete. In a Committee meeting, the Cook group adopted a series of resolutions that criticized the Owenites. One week later the Owenites adopted counter-resolutions and firmly held their ground.[54]

Through a process of self-distillation, the workies had thus resolved their ambiguities in a way none of their original leaders had anticipated. As Evans now realized, the Clay National Republicans, who were in search of a general issue that promised broad-based appeal to unite all the scattered anti-Jacksonians in the state, had first infiltrated, then subverted the movement. The faction opposing the Owenites, Evans complained, had "for its sole object THE ELECTION OF HENRY CLAY AS OUR NEXT PRESIDENT." [55]

Forewarned of Clayite strategy, Tammany Hall once again began to accommodate itself to changing public opinion. Aware that the workies indeed had some solid grievances, Tammanyite Assemblyman Silas Stilwell, a crony of Campbell White and Walter Bowne, sponsored and helped pass a mechanics' lien law. And city Jacksonian bankers liberalized their tight-money policy and made borrowing easier for the workies. Yet the Hall's major asset was that the pragmatic, moderate workie centrists, who had revolted because of Tammany's indifference, were more interested in practical results than in radical idealism or Clay's presidential ambition. All that remained, as Evans ruefully conceded, was a sign of Tammany's sincerity—real or artificial, it mattered not.[56]

Even so, the Hall's efforts to placate the workies did not succeed overnight. In January 1830, fourteen aldermen and assistant aldermen, some workie sympathizers, others against the Safety Fund, jarred the Hall by refusing to support Mayor Bowne's reelection bid. In the resultant impasse when a tie occurred, Bowne took the unprecedented step of voting for himself and emerged the winner. The episode had harsh repercussions for Tammany because the workies charged that the episode proved that the Hall's vested interests, particularly bankers such as Bowne, were politically irresponsible. Only by making public opinion the test of men and measures, they asserted, could good government survive. In July, further trouble awaited the Hall. In a special Fifth Ward aldermanic election, Cook's followers elected General Anthony Lamb, a former Clintonian-Adamsite, over the Hall's Myndert Van Schaick, a wealthy merchant, and Owenite William Leavens.[57]

Yet despite these signs, the shifting political alignments within the Workingmen's party accrued to the Hall's eventual benefit. Basically, Clay's natural local supporters, "the men of property and education," failed to understand that Davis and men of his ilk were cynically using the workies as a stalking horse. In their fear of radicalism, these upper-class interests paid far too much attention to Skidmore's rhetoric, overlooking the Cookite's machinations. Then, too, the schism between the Owenites and the Cookites widened into an unbridgeable gap. In the fall, the Cookites gained control through trickery over their gubernatorial nominations and headed their ticket with quondam Van Burenite Erastus Root. The Owenites then selected their own slate, headed by leather manufacturer Ezekiel Williams for governor. When Root declined the nomination, the mortified Clayites had no recourse but to drop out and throw their support behind Francis Granger, the Anti-Masons' gubernatorial candidate. A similar disintegrative process occurred in the city. The Owenites, Skidmore radicals, and the Cook-men ran independent tickets and sniped at each other constantly.[58]

Meantime, Tammany found the formula for victory and avoided damaging mistakes. At the state convention, all went smoothly. With almost no opposition, the delegates nominated Governor Throop for a full term, lauded Jackson's conduct of the presidency, and passed resolutions "approving the safety-fund & discountenancing all attempts to embarrass it."[59]

In the city, the *Evening Post* lost little opportunity to point out how the Cookites had perverted workie deals. The paper pictured them as ruffle-shirted lawyers and "milkwhite diplomatists" who, holding their noses, cynically caressed "the hard palm of the bricklayer" and flattered the credulous artisan. The antithesis of such deceit lay in Tammany's ticket where "the merchant, the seaman, the tradesman, the mechanic, and the professional man, have all their especial representatives in our delegation to the legislature."[60]

Other indicators, however, sobered the Hall. As many Tammanyites had feared, Collector Swartwout ignored the organization and secretly worked against the ticket. Then, again, up to the very moment of actual polling, an outside chance always existed that the anti-Jacksonians might coalesce. But events took their predictable course. The fastidious gentry refused to support either the Anti-Masons or the Cookites. The workies' pragmatic center, unable to see a significant difference between the Owenites and Tammany, fell in with the Hall's propaganda and generally supported its ticket. The upshot was a smashing Tammany victory. It easily carried the city for Throop and elected full senatorial and assembly slates. The Hall immediately pressed its advantage. The General Committee sponsored a meeting of workingmen and, with Noah in the chair, adopted a memorial, which the busy Stilwell later introduced in the legislature, that called for the total abolishment of the state's debtor laws.[61]

"I fear that both of the other parties have come out of the election stronger, and we weaker than before," an abnormally pessimistic Clay wrote Porter. Jabez Hammond drew a similar conclusion. "Nearly one half of the State are firmly united & constitute a valid disciplined Phalanx who will support the re-election of General Jackson or any other man Mr. Van Buren may indicate," he wrote John Taylor. But other observers were not ready to write Clay's political obituary. James Gordon Bennett, for one, felt the anti-Jacksonians were lively cadavers. Writing to Biddle, he pointed out that the total vote against Tammany had risen by nearly 5,000 in one year. Moreover, many city bankers had still not forgiven the Safety Fund proponents and the Regency. If the National Republicans should play on local grievances such as banking, Tammany might yet prove vulnerable.[62]

In sum, the local anti-Jacksonians were not in as bad a position as Clay and Hammond assumed. William B. Lawrence, an activist among the Cookites, held glowing hopes for the future—provided the pro-Clay forces frankly copied the Hall's formula for success. To do so, he wrote Clay, his local followers should "go on the broad ground of opposition to the existing powers without putting on evidence any principles that may distract those, who might otherwise be made cordially to cooperate." The difficulty lay in finding a suitable issue as a catalyst, because the Anti-Masons were not impressed with the tariff or internal improvement controversies currently raging in Congress. "We have, therefore, determined to avoid, as far as possible, all debatable ground & rest on the faults of the present Administration," he continued. Only one minor irritant—Matthew Davis—Lawrence ended, could cause trouble. Davis, he warned, "is not entitled to confidence, & that, though possessed of considerable experience & sagacity, his connection with any political party is calculated to do it material injury in the estimation of our fellow-citizens." [63]

In January 1831, the Cookites followed Lawrence's suggestions and merged identities with the freshly revived National Republicans. Taking a leaf from the Hall's political handbook, they formed a General Committee, subdivided on a ward basis; coordinated efforts with a central planning board located temporarily in Albany; and downplayed their own deficiencies while emphasizing the Regency's faults. Yet defeat still hounded them. They shrugged off serious losses in the city's spring municipal elections as temporary setbacks, and later blamed bad roads for their sparsely attended state convention. But the more they pushed, the more Clay looked like a permanent loser. As things stood, the National Republicans had stalled for want of a suitable issue to activate Clay's potential supporters. Whether or not he succeeded depended on finding that issue.[64]

In the interim, the Working Men's party quietly evaporated. In face of the Hall's massive courting, coupled with the poor showing that the Owen and Skidmore candidates made at the polls, the majority of workingmen backed into Tammany's welcoming embrace. Yet by eliminating the workies' options and leaving them no room to bargain, the Hall's success obscured the main point—it had still not really come to terms with the motive force implicit in Jacksonian Democracy. Quite simply, the ease with which the General Committee handled the insurgents made it difficult for party leaders to believe that anything was amiss. It was almost inevitable, then, that the workies' deep-seated unrest would presently surface in a fresh movement that would create a far more sophisticated force to challenge the Hall's complacent hierarchy.[65]

# ⌐ 6 ⌐

# The Bank War

IT WAS President Andrew Jackson, that stubborn, blunt man in the White House, who gave Henry Clay and his local followers the issue they so desperately sought. And it was Jackson's initially solitary crusade against the Second Bank of the United States that dramatically shattered Tammany Hall and restructured the substance of New York City politics.

Unknown to most politicians who had clambered onto Jackson's bandwagon, the general distrusted all banks in general, Biddle's in particular. In December 1829, the President's attitude became public knowledge. Despite the opposition of nearly all his intimate advisers, including Martin Van Buren, Jackson used his first annual message to criticize the Bank in forceful generalities, only becoming specific when he questioned its constitutionality and failure to establish a "sound and uniform currency." More to the point, he suggested that Congress investigate the matter and ascertain if a new institution, constitutionally sound, could better secure the advantages "that were expected to result from the present bank." [1]

Before the message appeared, Amos Kendall, the man most responsible for helping Jackson formulate the attack, sent Mordecai Noah and James Gordon Bennett the gist of the President's feelings on the subject. On November 30, 1829, with Webb out of town on business, the *Courier and Enquirer*, under Noah's and Bennett's direction, assailed the Bank as unsound, unconstitutional, and an unsafe place as a Federal repository; then, like the President, they awaited some signs of public support. If at this point Jackson represented a widely shared point of view, then Tammany, by all the rules of politics, should have supported him. This did not happen. The moderate *Evening Post*—now edited by William Cullen Bryant, the poet and part-time polemicist, assisted

**128**

by William Leggett, an abrasive, strong-willed writer—ignored the *Courier and Enquirer*'s stand. Instead, Bryant and Leggett mildly suggested that the whole question lacked relevance because the Bank's charter ran for six more years. The President had merely placed Biddle on notice, nothing else. Party chieftains such as Tammanyite Congressman Campbell were even less enthused. "It was very unexpected to me the paragraph in the Message relative to the Bank," he wrote Biddle, "as I had previously supposed the President was favorably disposed to it." More followed in the same vein at the Society's Founders' Day celebration. One toast praised Congressman George McDuffie of South Carolina, whose House Ways and Means Committee had just rejected both of Jackson's anti-Bank criticisms.[2]

Martin Van Buren's actions, or rather lack of action, provided a further index of party sentiment. Van Buren, who valued the Bank's aid in disciplining unruly New York City financiers who still fought a holding action against the Safety Fund, did not initially back Jackson. While the political risks inherent in such a stand were enormous, especially if the President took it as an insult, Van Buren could do so reasonably safely because the question was not yet a party issue. As late as May 1830, Biddle assured Walter Bowne: "I am satisfied that Mr. Van Buren was neither the instigator nor the advisor of the President's remarks on the Bank & I believe that any agency which he may have used on that occasion was rather to discourage than to promote them."[3]

In New York City, by every criterion that politicians used to test public opinion—save Noah's editorials—Jackson's anti-Bank stand gathered no party support. Tammanyites were far more concerned with the Maysville Veto, the titillating Peggy O'Neale affair, the city bankers' petition to modify the Safety Fund, and the continuing tariff struggle and the resultant nullification threat, to indulge themselves in a seemingly quixotic crusade against an institution that protected local interests from upstate financial predators. In fact, as William Rochester, the president of the Buffalo Branch Bank, happily told Biddle, the message had apparently backfired because Jackson had actually forced men to appreciate the Bank's pivotal role in maintaining economic stability.[4]

If Biddle had allowed matters to resolve themselves, he might have avoided a political showdown with Jackson. But unwilling to do nothing, Biddle accepted the responsibility for educating the American people as to the Bank's irreplaceable role in maintaining economic stability. What he wanted was a thumping vote of confidence, a public mandate to continue his policies, so that Jackson would back off.

In the city, Biddle sought support among newspapermen, particularly the *Courier and Enquirer*'s editors. Taking advantage of Bennett's position, Biddle flattered and cajoled him in an effort to moderate the paper's attitude. Bennett dashed his hopes. Whatever influence he had, Bennett claimed, rested on his "competence and knowledge in newspaper management," not political management. Yet, Bennett did have some useful information. Daniel Tylee, Webb's business partner, wanted to sell out his half-interest and Bennett suggested that the Bank lend him the necessary capital. Biddle was aware of the situation, however. Earlier, Webb had made the same request for himself. But unlike Bennett, Webb had substantial collateral, including western real estate. For the moment, Biddle did not commit himself, and played one man off against the other. As a result, each thought the banker might make a loan and separately supplied him with added information about local politics.[5]

By the end of 1830, Biddle appeared to be in firm command. Nationally, Jackson's assault against the Bank had lost some of its drive. In his annual message, he again expressed grave reservations about the institution but damned it now with faint praise. In New York, Biddle seemed equally secure. He had flooded the legislature with pro-Bank literature, dispatched Silas Burrows—an erratic merchant who claimed to have influence among Democratic party leaders—as a lobbyist to Albany, and cultivated leads in the Anti-Masonic party. In short, Biddle prided himself on being a hardheaded realist who could put professional politicos in their places. "In respect to Gen. Jackson and Mr. Van Buren," he told a Bank director, "I have not the slightest fear of either of them, or both of them." [6]

Yet Biddle's efforts in New York to save the Bank were more heavyhanded than he realized. His self-delusion began to end in February 1831, when the legislature debated a resolution that the Bank's charter "ought not to be renewed." He now committed the first in tragic series of blunders. Convinced that the Administration, in league with Van Buren, had ordered the move, Biddle erroneously assumed that a monolithic conspiracy menaced the Bank. In the process, he completely misread several important facts reported by his informants: the bill lacked the Regency's backing; its sponsor was Lot Clark, an experienced Albany lobbyist and the agent of Olcott's Farmers' and Mechanics' Bank; Thomas Morehead, the man who introduced the resolution and a minor Oswego politician, was not within the Regency's inner circle; and the majority of Tammany's delegation, led by Assemblymen Charles Livingston and Silas Stilwell were seeking to bury the resolution in committee. Yet, even possessing all this information, Biddle assumed that Tammany Hall and city bankers were part of a Wall Street plot to make it, not Philadelphia, the nation's financial center.[7]

With all his suspicions aroused, Biddle felt that the Bank was fighting for its very survival. Out went the word from Philadelphia—the resolution must not pass. In order to accomplish the move, Biddle sent Tammanyite Bank director Saul Alley to aid Burrows as a means of refuting the charge that the institution was a Clayite crypto-political adjunct, and encouraged newspapers to oppose the resolution openly. Biddle's efforts were more than rewarded when the *Courier and Enquirer* came out on the Bank's side. Congressman Gulian Verplanck proved another useful Tammany ally. He uncovered an 1823 legislative report, written by a special committee that had been chaired by Silas Wright, Van Buren's chief lieutenant, that called the Bank both constitutional and necessary. The local directors passed the item on to Charles King, who immediately reprinted the entire report in the *American*.[8]

Despite all these efforts, Biddle did his cause more harm than good. He certainly did not help the Bank when, on the one hand, he posed as a nonpartisan central banker, but on the other, took part in the game of political maneuvering. Above all, his failure to appreciate the split in Democratic ranks paradoxically contributed to the Morehead Resolution's final passage.

In the first round of legislative debate, the Democrats floundered in uncertainty. Some Van Burenites agreed with Webb's recently printed editorial which suggested that because the Jacksonian-controlled Pennsylvania legislature had passed a pro-Bank memorial, New York should follow suit. Others waited for direction from the Regency. The pro-Bank Jacksonians split. One group led by Charles Livingston sought a compromise and suggested a resolution to recharter the Bank but with some modification. A second group, following Tammanyite Dudley Selden, a city bank director, opposed the Morehead Resolution and sought to postpone debate.

But while party lines evaporated in this initial phase, Biddle's activities gradually restored a semblance of order among the Democrats. Some Jacksonians felt that he had bribed Webb and lavished Bank funds to stifle dissent. Silas Burrows' aggressive lobbying lent substance to these assumptions. John Mumford, the editor of the anti-Bank New York City *Standard* charged, with some justification, that Burrows had offered him a $500 bribe to alter the paper's policy. Using this as an excuse, state bank interests demanded that the Jacksonians stand firm. Forced to make a choice between loyalty toward Jackson or friendship for the "corrupt" Bank, hesitant legislators fell into line. On the final vote, the assembly passed the Morehead Resolution, 73–35, and the senate concurred, 17–13.[9]

The voting pattern of Tammany's legislative delegates epitomized the agony Jackson's anti-Bank policy caused among party loyalists. On the postponement question, eight Tammanyites voted in its favor, while only one, John Bogert, who had no connection with local bank interests, cast a negative vote. Two others, Gideon Ostrander and Sachem Mordecai Myers, were conveniently absent. Bending to immense political pressure on the Morehead Resolution, three men—Bogert, Ostrander, and Myers—voted yes, while four others—Abraham Cargill, Stilwell, Livingston, and Selden—were pro-Bank. The remainder who had voted for postponement—Dennis McCarthy, John Morgan, and city bank directors Isaac Varian and Nathaniel Jarvis—stayed at home. In the upper house, both Tammany senators, Stephen Allen and Alpheus Sherman, voted against the Resolution.[10]

Surprisingly, despite the great pressure that anti-Bank forces were exerting in Albany, Tammany Hall took no official position on the Morehead Resolution. The Bank question did not play any role in the spring aldermanic elections won by the Hall, the General Committee kept aloof, and the Tammany Society debated other problems such as the nullification threat, states' rights, and the increasing role that former Federalists played in party affairs. Beyond that, while the *Working Man's Advocate* scorned all banks, some individual workies felt that Biddle's institution shielded them from local and state financiers. So the Hall saw no sense in alienating its reconverted allies for a cause in which the organization lacked any material involvement.[11]

Tammany's indifferent attitude, however, was soon to end. And it was Nicholas Biddle, not Andrew Jackson, who forced the organization to take a stand. The Hall's moment of truth on the banking question began with the business association of Silas Burrows and James Watson Webb.

By 1831, Daniel Tylee had grown more desperate than ever to liquidate his partnership, but Webb lacked the capital to purchase his holdings. In vain, Webb pleaded with Van Buren for aid, complaining that the paper fought hard for the party yet gained little material help in return. Other factors also irked Webb. Personally pro-Bank, he could take no stand without the General Committee's approval. Frustrated and powerless to act, he grew progressively more unhappy as his paper became the spearhead of the anti-Bank forces and he was powerless to blunt the attack. But the Regency was unsympathetic. As Bennett noted on a tour of upstate New York, Van Buren despised Noah so much that the powers in Albany would make no move to aid any paper which he edited.

As the *Courier and Enquirer*'s problems mounted, Webb and Noah sought money from outside the party hierarchy. Their search stopped at Burrows, a man they considered a sound Jacksonian with unlimited personal funds. A born conspirator, Burrows agreed to lend Noah $15,000 to buy out Tylee, claiming that his father had advanced the funds. Webb and Noah certainly thought so. It was not true. Unknown to both men, Biddle was their financial angel.

In March, Burrows had visited Biddle and suggested that if the Bank made the loan, Webb and Noah would change the paper's editorial policy. Such a transaction was sound from a financial point of view, and Burrows' assurances elated the banker. With the approval of the Bank's Exchange Committee, he lent Burrows the money. He, in turn, kept the $15,000 and gave Noah his father's notes for the same amount. Biddle then made a grave mistake. Knowing that a public loan coming at this acute juncture would be highly impolitic, he ignored normal procedures and waited nine months before entering the transaction in the Bank's ledgers.[12]

Momentarily, the loan seemed a brilliant stroke when the paper indeed broke with its earlier stand and endorsed the Bank. But in mid-April, when Biddle's implicit trust in Burrows' honesty was shattered by John Mumford's bribery charge coupled with Gulian Verplanck's assertion that Burrows was "a wholly unsafe advisor or agent," the situation began to deteriorate. Visibly shaken, Biddle tactfully asked Burrows to make a public disclaimer of his connection with the Bank. Burrows retreated into silence, only occasionally sending Biddle un-solicited advice, and did not follow the banker's wishes. Here matters rested until early fall, when the effect of Burrows' deception reached a critical stage. Webb and Noah again needed more operating funds—and applied for a Bank loan. Astonished, Biddle now learned that neither man knew of the earlier deal. Worse, Webb had grown to dislike Burrows, and announced his intention to denounce him in print. Hearing the news from a friend, Burrows bristled with anger. He argued to Biddle that he had gone into debt for the Bank's sake, and hinted at blackmail if scorned. Taken aback, Biddle placated him, exacted a pledge of secrecy, and did not inform the editors of the mechanics of the first loan. Instead, Biddle used normal procedures to advance Webb $35,000 in two separate transactions.[13]

Yet Biddle was trapped whether he realized it or not. Politics, especially New York politics, was a game for professionals, not amateurs. By meddling where he should have remained aloof, Biddle the politician blundered into snares that Biddle the central banker would have avoided. Thus, in his manipulation of public opinion, innocent as it may have been, Biddle lost his way. Up to this point, the half-myths surrounding the Bank's purported subversion of the free press lacked substance, and, in the absence of direct proof, he easily refuted the rumormongers. But Biddle could not hide the first Burrows loan indefinitely. It would be a supreme humiliation for all four men involved if the public ever received reasonable evidence to suspect that the *Courier and Enquirer* had changed its editorial policy because of crass bribery, not high-minded principles.

An even more acute danger haunted Biddle, Webb, and Noah. The editors personally were no better than paid editorial assassins—men whom the public had long grown to tolerate but not to respect or trust. But in a larger sense, Webb and Noah symbolized a major unresolved dilemma among Tammany Jacksonians—the problem of how to support the Second Bank of the United States while still being loyal to the President. Until the question became a test of party regularity, both they and Tammany Hall were safe. But this situation could only remain so if the Burrows loan had never been transacted.

1832 began auspiciously for Biddle. From all sides, the Bank apparently moved toward checkmating the President. In Washington, Secretary of the Treasury Louis McLane favored recharter, as did such influential New Yorkers as Samuel Swartwout and Dudley Selden. Furthermore, the President backed down from his earlier stands in his annual message, and suggested that the "enlightened people and their representatives" should settle the matter—at some future date. The shape of things in New York seemed equally sound. In the city, several Tammany Jacksonians were on the new Board, while upstate the Regency had failed to prevent Charles Livingston's election as assembly speaker.

By mid-January, after sounding out his congressional contacts, Biddle felt that he commanded enough votes to pass a recharter bill. Webb and Verplanck objected. Both felt that a delay made political sense because Jackson would veto the bill to prove his courage. Biddle scoffed at their fears. He explained that all the stockholders agreed that if Congress and the President willfully rejected recharter, "the sooner the country and the Bank know it, the better for both." As for the forthcoming presidential race, he suggested that the bill was purely an economic issue devoid of any partisan overtones.[14]

Once committed, Biddle worked through his local directors, and sought in every possible way to couple the Bank's security with the national interest. Above all, he wanted memorials to show the institution's popularity: memorials from merchants, from ordinary citizens, from state banks, from legislatures. His principal object was to demonstrate that the Bank had nothing to do with politics but everything to do with the business of maintaining national economic stability.[15]

Biddle had impressive support in New York City. On the debit side, city banks, as institutions, refused to sign memorials because of Biddle's role in the Safety Fund crisis. But as individuals, city bankers rallied around. Among them were such influential Jacksonians as Walter Bowne, Saul Alley, Gideon Lee, Silas Stilwell, Myndert Van Schaick, Campbell White, and Dudley Selden. City merchants, led by John J. Astor, and western businessmen, appreciative of William Rochester's management of the Buffalo Branch, added other memorials.

Nor was this all. Many elements in Tammany Hall rejected the anti-Bank campaign. Even Bryant's rabidly pro-Jackson *Evening Post* regarded the Albany "money-changers"—headed by Olcott and Knower, who had just introduced a legislative bill to charter a $35,000,000 institution on Wall Street once recharter failed—as selfish fools out to destroy the party. By pushing against recharter, the paper warned, the local Democracy endangered Jackson's reelection and moved counter to public opinion. The *Post*'s view, shared by many pro-Jackson, pro-Bank Tammanyites, was that the recharter bill, "ill-advised and impolitic" as it might be, should be buried in committee until after the presidential election.[16]

Webb's *Courier and Enquirer* disagreed. Congress, he stressed, should recharter the Bank with modifications if no other reason than to rebuke Albany's selfish money manipulators and "stock jobbers." Webb reserved his greatest contempt for Olcott and the Safety Fund. Pointing out that Olcott had the major voice in picking bank commissioners, Webb claimed that state money "which is supposed to be invested, is left in Albany banks at low rates of interest, and in some cases, at no interest at all." For all his words, however, Webb feared that the Clayton Committee's investigation of the Bank's financial operations might turn up the embarrassing fact that the paper had borrowed $35,000 in the fall of 1831. Perhaps, he suggested to Biddle, "we might shew that the whole was but an ordinary business transaction—that it offered security at the time." But realistically he added, "as you know, this would not prevent the transaction being distorted into an open case of Bribery." [17]

Webb's letter worried Biddle. With everything going so well, he wanted to avoid any new element that might touch off a fresh wave of speculations and rumors. In January, he had finally recorded the first $15,000 *Courier and Enquirer* loan in the Bank's books, but Noah and Webb were still uninformed. In this fluid situation, Biddle summoned Burrows to his office and lent him money through the New York Branch, payable in ninety days, in exchange for Burrows' settling of Noah's original notes. Once back in the city, Burrows openly boasted of his sudden wealth. Webb now learned the truth, and immediately attempted to repair the damage. After assuring Biddle that the paper would have come out for the Bank even without the loans, Webb hurriedly raised $15,000 as part payment. "I wanted no inducement to support the Bank," he explained, "but jumped at the movement of the Jackson party in Pennsylvania to do what I had always desired—and to get rid of a course which had its origin in Washington and with which I had nothing to do." [18]

Meantime, the recharter bill carved deep cleavages in the local Democratic party. Just as with the caucus issue, party discipline was meaningless. Instead, the Democracy forgot partisan lines and split into four groups. One, composed mostly of western New Yorkers, resented Olcott's dictatorial use of credit and felt the Bank protected them against Albany business interests. In direct opposition, the second group, drawing support from Albany and New York City, demanded the Bank's immediate destruction and replacement with a new monster state institution located on Wall Street. In between was a third faction, whose members placed Van Buren's career and Jackson's reelection above all other considerations. But within this section, wide differences existed on how to handle the thorny Bank question. Some, like Webb and Noah, favored recharter with modifications; the *Evening Post* group favored delay; while others, the General Committee and certain Regency leaders such as Silas Wright, awaited some sign of Van Buren's wishes. Making the situation more complex, city bankers nursed deep grudges against Olcott and the Safety Fund, but could not bring themselves to make any formal commitments. Then, too, many states' rights Tammanyites had not forgiven Biddle for interfering in the fight against the Safety Fund. On purely constitutional grounds, these men questioned the Bank's legality.[19]

Worst of all, the workies who formed the fourth group adopted a more radical anti-Bank position than most uncertain Tammany leaders appreciated. As early as 1830, the *Working Man's Advocate* had denounced legislative monopolies and demanded the total elimination of all banks in favor of a purely metallic currency. In political terms, the workies offered their collective conscience as the guide for the party's anti-Bank activities. But they found themselves well ahead of public opinion. The upshot was that editor Evans and the men he represented lost faith in both Tammany and President Jackson. During the city elections in November 1831, the paper decried Tammany's silence on the banking issue, and the next month scoffed at Jackson's willingness to compromise. The workies' feeling was that the proposed Wall Street Bank was a fitting climax to the party's hypocrisy. Biddle's institution, the paper concluded, was bad enough in its monopolistic "exchange of property." But a new bank, or worse a series of new banks, "might enable a few to draw from the labor of many enough to support them in idleness." [20]

As their remedy, they suggested that the party nominate for president a true Jeffersonian opposed to all banks. In Kentuckian Richard Johnson, sponsor of a national law to end imprisonment for debt, they found their man. Yet political reality made it clear that they could not unseat the incumbent Jackson. So, they praised President Jackson faintly and boomed Johnson for the vice-presidency. Van Buren they felt totally unfit for high office. Even when the party did nominate him as Jackson's running mate, the workies kept up their flow of objections. Saner heads ultimately prevailed. Given the choice between two evils, the Bank's "green rag aristocracy" and the Regency's "timidity," the workies accepted the latter. But in backing the national ticket, the workies firmly resolved to reform the party from within, purge Tammany's vested interests, and use the organization to eliminate all banks, not merely Biddle's.[21]

With the Bank issue so imprecisely defined, each Democratic faction made its own decisions and evoked widespread confusion. At one level, the *Argus, Evening Post*, and *Courier and Enquirer* disagreed violently over the next gubernatorial candidate, while in Albany the same lack of discipline bedeviled the party's legislative chieftains. In February, the anti-Bank forces introduced a resolution in the legislature that would instruct the state's congressional delegation to reject the recharter bill. Although the resolution easily passed (20–10 in the senate, 75–37 in the assembly), important politicians defected. Tammany Hall caused the most concern. Both its senators voted against the resolution, and five assemblymen—Van Schaick, Stilwell, Livingston, Judah Hammond, and John Morgan—joined them in opposition. To make matters worse, Jacksonian Benjamin Bailey died, and the General Committee's new chairman, lawyer Robert Morris, lacked Bailey's steadying influence. The workies' indiscretion in booming Johnson capped the Regency's humiliation. If it could not trust Tammany Hall to do the correct thing, then Van Buren's entire career hung in jeopardy.[22]

The Clayton Committee's investigation ended the local Democracy's disoriented policy drift. Beginning its inquiry in March, the Jacksonian-controlled committee immediately issued subpoenas for Burrows, Webb, Biddle, Noah, and the Bank's records. The struggle began at once, but nothing these men said could erase the committee majority's prejudgment that bribery was the root cause of the paper's editorial switch.

The beleagured witnesses fought back. Webb testified that because city financiers refused to lend him money for being pro-Bank, his only alternative was to seek operating funds from Biddle. As evidence of his innocence, Webb pointed out that Tammany committeeman, Sachem Walter Bowne, had endorsed his request. Noah wrote directly to Clayton, and explained the original loan's mechanics. Above all, Noah stressed Burrows' duplicity and need for self-aggrandizement. Biddle did his best to aid the hard-pressed editors. Through Seaton's and Gales' *National Intelligencer* he published a list of all the newspapermen, from both parties, who had borrowed Bank money. Even Burrows lent a hand. Before appearing at the investigation, he had a private meeting with Jackson, and disarmingly assured him that "I entered into [the transaction] on his account and for the benefit of the party." [23]

Despite these efforts, the Jacksonian committee members—Clayton, Cambreleng, Richard Johnson, and Francis Thomas—sifted the evidence to suit their own purposes, and used their report to sway public opinion, not only in Congress but in the nation at large. Over the violent objections of the pro-Bank minority members led by John Quincy Adams, the Jacksonians used innuendo and frank distortions of fact to link Biddle to a monstrous plot aimed at destroying a free American press.[24]

Public response in New York City was electrifying as the *Evening Post* and *Albany Argus* made Webb and Noah the scapegoats for party reunion. The *Courier and Enquirer,* William Leggett taunted in one of his milder epithets, was "a piece of the most palpable, barefaced, downright corruption." As for the Bank, it was morally, if not politically, bankrupt. In its place, he suggested a fresh institution, strictly regulated, located in New York City, "the commercial metropolis of the nation." [25]

The reactions of the General Committee and the Tammany Society followed the same strident line. Both issued powerful endorsements of Jackson, boomed Van Buren for the presidency, and for the first time adopted militant anti-Bank resolutions. Equally predictable, they used Webb as the catalyst to forge a united anti-Biddle front. At the Founders' Day celebration, in an oblique reference to Webb, Sachem John Mills sneered: "Palsied be the tongue of him who forfeits his obligation to the Tammany Society." To make its meaning even clearer, the Society blackballed the *Courier and Enquirer* as an official party organ by not sending Webb its proceedings, as in the past, for public printing. The General Committee concurred. Under Morris' direction, it denounced Webb and Noah as traitors, and called on all party loyalists to cancel their subscriptions.[26]

Webb's position epitomized the dilemma of many pro-Bank Jacksonians. Desperately trying to remain a loyal Democrat, he still supported the party's national ticket, endorsed William Marcy for governor, and took Jackson's last annual message literally by presenting a strong case for modifying but retaining the Bank. Since the recharter bill had not yet passed Congress, Webb's formula retained a degree of legitimacy. Until the President took a definite stand, then, Webb like so many pro-Jackson, pro-Bank Tammanyites resisted all organization efforts to identify the party as anti-Biddle. Moreover, Webb defended himself by patiently documenting the paper's financial plight and asserted that he and Noah had borrowed the money to keep the journal out of Clayite hands. Finally, Webb took uncharitable delight in pointing out that Cambreleng, at the same time that he had attacked Biddle, was on the Bank's payroll as a special agent.[27]

Despite Webb's efforts, it was apparent that the pro-Bank Tammanyites had forfeited their legitimacy because of the Burrows loan. In the next few months, until the recharter bill passed Congress and Jackson used his veto, Webb and his sympathizers struggled under the weight of public opinion that was running against them. The pressure became more intense because of the way President Jackson treated the Bank in his veto message. Scorning any compromise, he forced the party to choose between himself or Biddle, regardless of the Bank's utility. As a sign of things ahead, the General Committee firmly seconded the veto, and held an enormous rally to dramatize its allegiance. Moreover, the Hall's Young Men's General Committee, the proving ground for future party leaders, agreed that the message was "sound and conclusive," and called on all loyal Tammanyites to oppose "a monied aristocracy, which has already subsidized the press and threatens to influence our elections, and thus to control the political destinies of our country." [28]

As Tammanyites began to line up behind the President, Webb refused to play the scapegoat's role the General Committee had written for him and attempted to form an independent position within the Democratic party. First, in order to establish a firm economic base, he borrowed $20,000 (secured by his western land) from Rosewell Colt, a Baltimore financier and Biddle's close personal friend. Once secure, Webb dropped Noah and Bennett from the paper, and promised Biddle "a judicious movement in favor of the great interest of the country." [29]

The paper's new editorial policy exceeded Biddle's fondest wishes. On August 23, Webb began a threefold attack. As his primary step, he struck the names of Jackson, Van Buren, and Marcy from the paper's masthead and replaced them with the Jeffersonian slogan, "Measures not Men." Second, in a wordy manifesto that he later circulated throughout the nation, Webb claimed that the "toils, cares and anxieties of an active life" had robbed the President of his former keen judgment. Treating him as a superannuated cipher manipulated by the party's "political gamblers, money changers, [and] time-serving politicians," Webb insisted that the nation was receiving erratic leadership from a President who "no longer possesses his former energy of character or independence of mind." Finally, Webb solicited, received, and published statements from his editorial co-workers, Bennett and Noah, that he had always favored the Bank and the Burrows affair was purely irrelevant.[30]

For all his words, Webb knew that political muscle won elections. What he needed were some practical steps to counter Tammany's hold over the voters. At the outset, in a calculated effort to cut off the Hall's supply of foreign auxiliaries—particularly the Irish, who lacked an alternative to Tammany since Clinton's death—Webb portrayed Francis Granger, the Antis' gubernatorial candidate, as Clinton's spiritual heir. When the Hall blocked the move by choosing several Irish delegates to the state convention, the resourceful Webb turned to Biddle for aid. "Success in politics as in war frequently depends upon the moral energy requisite for great efforts," he lectured the banker. Biddle could aid them in the city "by directing the Branch to use the utmost possible liberality possible to our local Banks & merchants until after the election." [31]

Biddle had come to the same conclusion, but for different reasons. Reacting to earlier pleas, such as the one from Tammanyite merchant Cornelius Lawrence, he did loosen credit—but for economic, not political motives. Even so, the Bank did not go far enough. Fighting for survival, Biddle did not materially aid local Clayite elements, and conducted the Bank's normal functions as if the election was an irrelevancy. [32]

Although Webb worked hard against the national ticket, he remained a party traditionalist by not carrying his insurgency to its logical conclusion and backing Clay for the presidency. During the remainder of the campaign, Webb was anti-Jackson, not pro-Clay. Quite simply, Webb again symbolized the dilemma of many pro-Bank Tammanyites who assailed the President for going astray but still considered themselves party loyalists. Hoping for Jackson's defeat, these men planned that once the Democracy lost the election over the Bank issue, they would pick up the pieces and put the party together on their own terms.

Tammany Hall had its own plan. To "curtail expenses," the General Committee withdrew public printing contracts from the paper, and dropped it from the list of official party organs. That done, ward committeemen obtained lists of Webb's subscribers and intimidated over 450 of them into canceling their subscriptions. Determined to prevent further squabbling, the Democrats organized for the fall election with elaborate care. After the state convention had dropped Governor Throop in favor of William Marcy, the Regency's strongest vote-getter, Tammany Hall purged Congressman Gulian Verplanck, who had voted for recharter, and replaced him, oddly enough, with Dudley Selden, a local bank director who also favored recharter. *Evening Post* editor William Cullen Bryant saw no logic in the move. It was a crime, the paper editorialized, to winnow such "a steadfast party man as Verplanck, with the only excuse that he voted against Andrew Jackson on the Bank." Promptly, some hotheads on the General Committee initiated a move to censure the *Post*, but cooler tempers on all sides prevailed. Verplanck refused a Clayite congressional nomination (though some friends ran him as an independent), the General Committee tabled the censure resolution, and Bryant supported party usages, he lamely explained, not out of coercion but "because they are right." [33]

Tammany's reason for dropping Verplanck perplexed other men than Bryant. Yet the Hall's ratiocinations were apparent. As part of its over-all strategy, Tammany wanted to placate city banks and win their financial support, particularly if the Bank, as Marcy feared, used its vast resources to buy votes. In playing down the onerous Safety Fund system, nominating the pro-Jackson Selden and Cornelius Lawrence for Congress, and putting Charles Livingston, Isaac Varian, Mordecai Myers, and Silas Stilwell on the legislative ticket, the Hall's power-brokers made a conscious bid for local bank support. Seen in the proper light, Tammany sacrificed Verplanck for a higher good. As an indication of this attitude, State Senator Stephen Allen, who had voted against the Morehead Resolution, chaired the Hall's ratification meeting and gave the keynote address. "As becomes all good men and true," he said, "resolve to support the ticket, the whole ticket, and nothing but the ticket." [34]

Tammany also stirred up class animosities as a conscious political strategy. The election, the General Committee suggested, was a struggle between the people and a "monied aristocracy" which had "coerced the *merchants*, harassed the *farmer*, purchased the *press*, and influenced the legislature of our Country." For proof, the Hall had to point no further than Webb, Burrows, and Noah.[35]

In the final sense, what the Democrats did was less important than what the anti-Jacksonians could not do. Clay and the Anti-Masons, despite heroic efforts made by Thurlow Weed and Matthew Davis, never formed a coordinated local party. In addition, Clay's managers simply could not win any respect from pro-Bank Tammanyites such as Webb and Verplanck. Essentially, Clay's problem lay in not finding a broad-based issue that would crystallize public opinion in his behalf. In fact, the veto had the reverse effect of solidifying Tammany's ranks. No matter how the pro-Bank interests structured the situation, the problems facing the electorate were too complex, too controversial, for easy answers. Instead, the voters took the easy way out and personalized the contest as a battle between the people's champion—Jackson—against the pawn of special interests—Clay. In this sense, the voters trusted the President to do the correct thing, and the city gave him 59 percent of the total vote cast. Tammany did equally well, and elected its full congressional and state tickets.[36]

The election of 1832 decided two major questions: locally, which party would rule New York; nationally, who would be president. Since the Democrats won both, Andrew Jackson interpreted the victories as votes of confidence and mandates to destroy the Bank. The voters, however, left one other major question unanswered: did they really support the anti-Bank movement, or did they merely support Andrew Jackson? The answer lay in the near future.

During the next few weeks, as city politicians eagerly awaited the President's annual message, conditions changed rapidly. On the newspaper front, Matthew Davis began a political column in the *Courier and Enquirer* under the pen name, "A Spy in Washington." Rivaling James Cheetham in his prime, Davis unleashed a splenetic attack on the Albany Regency that left the Van Burenites gasping. Under the Hall's pressure, Noah resigned as surveyor. But with funds supplied by pro-Bank interests, he secured Webb's permission to establish a semi-weekly newspaper, the *Evening Star*. In a staggering *volte-face*, Noah now severed his long, intimate association with Tammany Hall, and used his formidable editorial prowess for the Bank. On the economic front, city bankers still throbbed with a fiscal headache left by the depressed money market created by Jackson's veto. Worse, when Biddle postponed the payment of foreign-held debts, the market shuddered again.[37]

These shifts, however, paled in comparison with a major reversal of thinking among greedy Tammany Hall politicos, now called the Bank Democrats or conservatives. Convinced that the Second Bank of the United States was moribund, opportunistic Tammanyites saw a golden chance to translate political power into economic advantage. Party chieftains subtly muted their objections against the Safety Fund, and now began what their enemies had erroneously charged them with during the campaign: a calculated effort to destroy Biddle's institution and to replace it with local banks, having their charters awarded as political plums, unfettered by any outside control.

Stephen Allen's amazing transformation typified Tammany's new stance. A self-made man and former mayor, Allen was a party wheel-horse, high in Van Buren's esteem. Yet in the state senate, Allen had been pro-Bank until the veto. As a loyal Tammanyite, Allen had then shifted position, stumped the wards for the ticket, and taken his turn as a poll-watcher. Once the election ended, he helped crystallize the Hall's new idea that the legislature should reward deserving Democrats with bank charters. The Tammany Society, he told Jesse Hoyt, Van Buren's confidant, had earned the spoils:

My opinion you no doubt know is in opposition to an increase
of these Banking Monopolies in the city—but the Legislature will
make them—and therefore if we must have them there cannot be
a more legitimate object to be effected both in a party point of
view, as well as the charitable attributes of the Society, than the
one alluded to.[38]

Although the Regency did not act on Allen's proposal, an astound-
ing number of party stalwarts shared his views. In January, when the
legislators arrived for the winter session, more than forty new banking
memorials greeted them. As Allen had pointed out, faithful party workers considered the issuance of fresh banking charters a fitting political
payoff for services rendered.

President Jackson's annual message whetted their avarice. Implying
strongly that the Bank was not doing its proper job, he requested that
Congress investigate whether the institution was a "safe depository of
the money of the people." Few local politicians misread Jackson's intent. The Old Hero, Tammanyites reasoned, was in no mood for a
compromise and would remove public deposits from the Bank no
matter what Congress or his cabinet thought. In fact, Tammanyites
were wagering when—not if—the President would begin his new policy
and deposit government money elsewhere.[39]

What was permissible for Tammanyites, however, was another
matter for Jackson. During the next four months, the Bank problem
receded in comparison to the nullification crisis. Tammany Hall reacted
with mixed feelings. One section, the Van Buren states' righters, admired nullification on principle but abhorred John C. Calhoun, the
doctrine's mentor. The second, the free traders, rejected protectionism
but feared outright presidential compulsion might infuse the executive
branch with too much authority. The workies, doggedly against all
"exclusive legislation," rejected the Hall's nationalistic assumptions, repudiated compromise, and demanded a completely free trade system.
Tariffs, they felt, were sham devices that aided the rich and penalized
the poor. If anything, the workies resented the Hall's ties to the city's
business interests, condemned the Regency for sponsoring even limited
tariffs, and agreed with Calhoun that the central government was too
activistic.[40]

Unable to harmonize the three views, the General Committee called
for moderation on all sides. It professed sympathy "with our southern
brethren in the grievances of which they complain," but firmly backed
Jackson's constitutional duty "to enforce the laws while they exist, and
to preserve the Union, the whole Union, full and entire, unmaimed

and unmutilated, at every sacrifice and at every hazard." The ward committees endorsed the policy statement and held pro-Union rallies to line up public support. Then, when a compromise bill (first introduced by Verplanck and later modified by Clay and Calhoun) passed Congress and gained the President's approval, the Hall claimed that only Jackson's firm hand had ended the crisis. Tammany's assessment was correct. In the end, the public credited Jackson, not Clay, for maintaining the Union. Moreover, nullification had an unforseen side effect. Jackson now used his newly won prestige as a safety valve to take the pressure from his hotly debated decision to deposit government money in institutions other than the Second Bank of the United States.[41]

Despite the President's veto message, he lacked a long-range banking program. Essentially, he knew what he did *not* want, but only had a vague idea of what to do next. At a cabinet meeting in March 1833, he made his first concrete proposal by suggesting that Congress form a new federally chartered bank of deposit, located in the District of Columbia, and subject to presidential and congressional supervision. But before making the plan public, he further suggested to his cabinet that the government try to "carry on the fiscal affairs of the nation" without "a national bank of any description." The crucible for such an experiment was the state bank system.[42]

Jackson met stiff resistance. The majority of his cabinet proved unsympathetic; Congress was also hostile and, after a full debate on the deposit question, easily passed a resolution which stressed that the public's money was safe in Biddle's hands. Clay, mulling these facts of political life, concluded: "I can hardly think it possible that this Administration, daring and unprincipled as it has been, will now venture upon such a measure as that of a transfer of the deposits." [43]

Clay misjudged his man. During May and June, Jackson toured the Northeastern states, partly as a gesture of national unity, partly to test his popularity. The results were gratifying on both scores. Huge, enthusiastic crowds turned out to cheer at every stop, and the public's spontaneous show of affection stiffened his resolve. The city's reception was particularly exhilarating. After the Common Council's welcoming ceremonies, the President visited the Wigwam and attended a special Society meeting held in his honor. The braves became almost rapturous when he "expressed great satisfaction in having an opportunity to visit that association whose exertions had so long and so faithfully been devoted to the establishment and maintenance of Democratic principles." After sampling public opinion and finding it heady, Jackson returned to Washington, reshuffled his cabinet, and selected Amos

Kendall as a special agent to decide which state banks should receive the deposits.[44]

Jackson left New York City with rumors and speculation in his wake. Some politicians assumed that the Bank was indeed dead and stepped up their demands for more state charters; others waited to see if the President would authorize the new District depository; while still others favored delay until he made a definite move. It soon became clear, however, that restraint was a thing of the past. Despite Van Buren's silence, the Regency responded to party pressure and joined the speculative mania.[45]

In the city, many business-minded Tammanyites promoted grandiose bank projects. During the legislative session, the Hall's entire assembly delegation, including Livingston, Stilwell, Myers, Morris, and Varian, signed a resolution that praised the Safety Fund as the best means "to supply the wants of a thriving and growing community without endangering the safety or exciting the alarm of our citizens." Others wrote to Van Buren, joined in lauding the system, and predicted that local banks could meet any contingency if the Second Bank of the United States disappeared.[46]

City speculators had a field day. In February, several prominent braves organized a public meeting to establish a quasi-public $35,000,000 Wall Street bank. The Seventh Ward Bank, capitalized for $500,000, was equally spectacular. Passing the legislature under highly dubious circumstances, the bank's charter required its board to sell a majority of its stock to ward residents. But when public sale began, only a fraction was available. At a protest meeting, the directors were forced to reveal the names of the stockholders who had purchased shares before public sale opened. The disclosure showed an embarrassing list of prominent politicians from all three parties, including their friends and relatives. On the list were eight Tammany assemblymen, Mayor Gideon Lee, eight Jacksonian members of the Common Council, and a host of minor city functionaries. To make the deal even more shady, rumors spread through the state that the bank's Albany lobbyists had bribed Thurlow Weed to purchase his connivance.[47]

The prevailing Tammany attitude that public office was synonymous with private gain was a sad commentary on the state of political morality. The Seventh Ward scandal was not atypical. Prominent Tammanyites were on the boards of directors of several other new banks. Stilwell, Varian, and Lee headed the Greenwich Savings Bank. Ward committeemen Daniel Jackson and Preserved Fish were the main movers behind the Wall Street promotion. Walter Bowne was president of the Seventh Ward Bank; Gideon Ostrander, Saul Alley, Stephen

Allen, Assemblyman Benjamin Ringgold, and former Governor Throop (now naval officer) were all directors.

On the removal question, Tammany Jacksonians backed the President for a variety of reasons. The "utterly corrupt and profligate" Bank of the United States, the *Post* wrote, "can not be trusted a single day." Thus, "we are for an immediate removal of General despositories— either deposit here—or six or seven banks in the interior." Kendall's fact-finding inspection accelerated the mood. The day he arrived in the city, 1,400 shares of Bank stock changed hands despite editor Bryant's assurances that Kendall planned no mischief. As conditions grew worse, Biddle's supporters publicly warned speculators against attempting to corner the market. Privately, they told themselves that the President would not dare remove the deposits, and, if by any wild chance he did, the state bank system would not be able to meet its new obligations.[48]

In September, when the President finally made his move, the Bank Democrats who controlled Tammany's organizational apparatus greeted it with thunderous approval. "We consider the Bank of the United States too powerful in its machinery," an Eighth Ward resolution read, "and too profligate in its management, to deserve the support of a virtuous and free people." Jackson's list of city deposit banks was equally satisfying: the Mechanics' Bank, founded by the Society of Mechanics and Tradesmen; the Bank of the Manhattan Company, run by Robert H. White, Campbell's brother; and George Newbold's Bank of America. Kendall's selection of Newbold was a surprise because he had earlier supported Biddle. But in his interview with Kendall, Newbold pledged future cooperation. Then, too, Congressman Cornelius Lawrence was on the board. Upstate, Kendall's failure to include Olcott's Mechanics' and Farmers' Bank was most unexpected. But again, few Tammanyites shed tears over the omission.[49]

Faced with this intolerable situation, Biddle and his directors turned the pressure on Jackson in the only way left to them—loan curtailments. Beginning at first with a general reduction of money loaned at discount, Biddle further squeezed the market by restricting the receipts of state bank loans, demanding the collection of balances against state banks in specie, constricting the amount of Bank bills in circulation, and, finally, making all western branches pay bills of exchange only in eastern offices.[50]

Biddle's contraction solved no problems. He merely defined them. He intended to prove to the people that the nation could not prosper under the Administration's fiscal policy. Matthew Davis nodded in approval. "The impression has been made upon Congress, that the Bank of the U.S. is *powerless*," he wrote Rosewell Colt, "and if not *powerless*, that its directors are *nerveless*, which terminates in the same result. It is a deplorable state of things, but it is nevertheless the truth, that unless the Bank can feel itself justified in putting forth its strength, there is no hope that it will ever receive common justice at the hands of the present Congress." [51]

Having exposed himself to the President's anger, Biddle stepped up efforts in the city to divide and conquer the Jacksonians. Deeply aware that many pro-Bank Democrats like Verplanck, Stilwell, and Selden were suffering all the pangs of conflicting loyalites, Biddle sought to deepen their dilemmas by winning over Collector Swartwout, already a local Bank director. But while Swartwout claimed he was "friendly to the Bank so far as he dared act," he could not disown the President without severe repercussions. The Collector assured Biddle of his continued personal regard, but argued that "want of time" precluded his continuance on the board. At the same time, he offered Biddle a bit of unsolicited advice: "Instead of quarrelling with the Government, do good to the people, and they will remember it." [52]

Biddle ignored him. The bulk of his mail praised curtailment. As the demand for specie increased and credit fell sharply, a deflationary spiral plunged New York's financial community into gloom. "The storm has reached the City," a friend noted, "and many of those who *could not*, or *would* not see the effect of the removal of the deposits have been made to feel its pernicious consequences." James A. Hamilton read the same economic indicators but felt no elation. He wrote Van Buren: "The many dealers & merchants in this city are really in great distress nay even to the verge of general bankruptcy." [53]

As the gulf of miscalculation, or perhaps personal animosity, widened between Jackson and Biddle, Tammany Hall still dominated New York City. By April of 1833, National Republican popularity had fallen to such a low ebb that Leggett observed: "The party has fallen in pieces, its leaders are at issue among themselves, and their adherents are in perplexity whose guidance to follow." [54]

Seemingly, Leggett's apt review was valid. After the election, Webb strove to remain within the Democracy and hoped to broaden the pro-Bank Tammanyite base by using local issues to win support. The Common Council provided his first target. The aldermen, he charged, were extravagant in city expenditures, and often awarded lucrative contracts without competitive bidding. Further, monopolistic influences dominated the Corporation, particularly when it granted the Harlem Rail Road Company exclusive rights to build a line along part of Broadway. Turning to Tammany, Webb charged that the organization snubbed the workies, immigrants, and former Clintonians by giving the old Federalists the bulk of party patronage. The Hall wasted little time in countering these charges. The General Committee also criticized the Harlem Rail Road grant, ran several Irishmen for aldermen, and echoed Webb's shopworn, meaningless attacks on Federalism. Above that, Webb hurt his own cause by railing against the *American* for flirting with nativism, and added a ludicrous note to his frustration by involving himself in a street brawl with William Leggett.

The fracas immobilized the aldermanic election campaign for days while New Yorkers argued over which pugnacious editor had won. The upshot was that the demoralized anti-Jacksonians lacked any sense of unity and watched in mounting anguish as the Hall soared to victory. An index of opportunities lost and time wasted is the fact that these men even failed to capitalize on internal schisms in several wards when the Hall snubbed a few incumbents for not vociferously backing Jackson.[55]

Despite Tammany's easy victory, future signs of trouble abounded. During the legislative session, the Bank Democrats' role in shaping party policy rekindled the workies' dormant spirit of rebellion. Essentially, they could not see how ending one monopoly justified the formation of another. Too, the workies resented the Hall's increasing tendency to again take them for granted and longed to reassert their independence. Richard Johnson's muted but lively campaign for the presidency gave them such a chance.

Aware of the problem, the General Committee placated the workies by holding a public dinner in Johnson's honor, and the Tammany Society made him an honorary brave. For the moment, such flattery achieved its desired effect. But while the Hall had brought the workies' unhappiness under temporary control, much remained to be done to insure future security. In its largest sense, the boom for Johnson really masked the workies' growing disenchantment with all things Tammany. A definite split was now just a matter of time and circumstance.[56]


While the Hall concentrated on its family quarrel with the workies, the recession that Biddle's contraction had induced plagued the city. For the first time, local voters had to face the problem that they had hoped would not appear: the problem of the consequences implicit in

Jackson's "pet bank" policy. It was from this questioning that the local anti-Jacksonians found the cement with which to construct a viable city party.

In early October, as the almost moribund National Republicans prepared for the fall elections, men such as Noah, Webb, and Hiram Ketchum (a successful lawyer who had been one of Clay's most effective liaison agents to the Anti-Masons) felt they could achieve their goals more readily by going outside the old organization to form a new apparatus free from prior connections with repudiated issues. All three men knew that many otherwise loyal Democrats disliked Jackson's dictatorial qualities, and feared that the pet bank system with its easy credit was directly responsible for the nation's growing hard times.

Yet Webb was too shrewd to attack the President directly, since his prestige was still enormous. Rather, in a skillful display of political sophistry, Webb again picked up his earlier argument that "we are in fact all *Jacksonmen*, so far as his acts and proceedings are justified by the laws and constitution." After paying the devil his due, Webb continued that "this therefore, is peculiarily our time for regenerating our State and City, by putting into office men of intelligence, of reputation, of known honesty and tried principles." Then he made a subtle shift in emphasis. Attempting to win popular backing by wooing legitimate business interests who were hunting for a scapegoat, he charged that the Albany Regency—in league with upstate's "Central Monied Power" —had taken advantage of the President's faltering judgment and fomented the entire crisis. As Webb phrased the options, then, in order to save the Union voters could still remain pro-Jackson Democrats; they merely had to oppose the Regency and Tammany.[57]

Webb's strategy worked. During the Hall's primary convention elections, the National Republicans dropped all previous appellations, dubbed themselves the anti-Regency party or Independent Democrats, and ran rival Tammany slates in each ward. Encouraged by their success, they scored their first breakthrough at the nominating convention when they forced Charles Livingston's selection for the state senate on the regular ticket.

Momentarily, Jacksonian Tammanyites underestimated the factors that had steadily built up sentiment against them. Their rivals took advantage of the Hall's failure. Since many of their converts were Tammany Society members, including Noah and Matthew Davis, the Independent Democrats met freely in the Long Room and nominated a full assembly ticket headed by Verplanck and Stilwell. Such a "perversion" of their sanctuary galvanized the Jacksonians. Wielding the massive power of "party usages," the Hall filled its pro-Administration slate with several bank directors, dually endorsed Livingston's candidacy, warned the rank and file that the Independents were National Republicans in disguise, and used the Council of Sachems to bar all opposition groups from the Wigwam.

Ordinarily, Tammany would have expected to quash the Independent Democrats by exploiting their Clayite tinge. But these were not ordinary times. Although the Hall again ran on local issues and played down the city's financial difficulties, it miscalculated on the emotionalism that sparked the Independents' fledgling apparatus. By judiciously mixing the city's fear of a major recession with pure opportunism, they forced many ordinary voters to part company with both the "Albany Junto" and President Jackson.[58]

No knowledgeable politician expected the Independents to defeat the entrenched Tammany organization—except the Independents themselves. On October 31, when the Hall held its customary preelection rally, about 500 Independents, wearing bucktails in their hats to symbolize republican purity, marched to the Long Room and created pandemonium. They drove chairman Walter Bowne from the rostrum, ratified their ticket, and passed anti–pet bank resolutions. Flushed by the triumph, Charles Davis, a local Bank director who wrote satiric political observations under the name of "Jack Downing," exulted to Biddle: "The great Tammany party (a low Van Buren party) got a terrible shaking here the night before last resulting from a split among them. This w'd have occurred long since had the National Republican party done as they now do—abstaining from opposition openly by holding themselves ready to jump on either side of the beam as best suited—for in these splittings a good ticket as in this case is got up— Such as may be approv'd and advocat'd." [59]

The election results somewhat deflated Davis. Since the voters' habits were too ingrained for a sudden shift in allegiance, Tammany won all state offices. But the Independents' tactics were not in vain. For the first time since DeWitt Clinton's time, an opposition party actually out-polled the Hall in several previously safe wards, and generally reduced Tammany's winning margins. All these results counterpointed the realities of a dawning political era. Racked with dissension over Jackson's fiscal wisdom, unable to cope with the stresses and strains wrought by Biddle's curtailment, many hitherto firm Democrats, both in New York and other states, broke with the Administration.[60]

Locally, the Independents lacked a permanent structure. Without even a rudimentary ward network, they were essentially leeches on Tammany's body politic. If they remained in this position, the Hall would inevitably destroy them. But in other ways, the Independents had powerful credentials that the Hall could not so easily liquidate. By pitching their appeal toward Tammany's normal constituency, they linked the depression to the city's traditional suspicion of upstate political interests. Then, too, Jackson's financial policies hurt the party's "bone and strength"—the workingmen—in their pocketbooks, and had serious repercussions among all classes.

By the end of the year, the Independent Democrats perfected their organization by frankly copying Tammany's structural framework. Setting up "Committees of Safety" in each ward as their party nucleus, they coordinated activity through a series of meetings that culminated with a general rally in City Park. Above all, they assiduously cultivated disgruntled interest groups that formed the Hall's backbone. Almost nightly, adopted citizens, workies, clerks, mechanics, and artisans voiced disapproval of Tammany and blamed the Regency for their unemployment. To further broaden the scope of their appeal, the Independents once again changed their party label. Now they called themselves "Whigs," to symbolize their battle against aristocracy and tyranny. Meantime, as a similar political reorganization occurred throughout the nation, the anti-Jacksonians found a new basis for party structure, and solved the problems left over by the Great Virginians' fusion policies.[61]

"The times are dreadfully hard," merchant Philip Hone wrote in his diary as 1834 began. Others shared his gloom. "The pressure is great, and it creates great distress and many are obliged to make great sacrifices," city Bank director Robert Lenox told Biddle. The times *were* bad. Unwilling to compromise, both Biddle and Jackson intensified the crisis. All these troubles, however, were pure political gold to Charles Davis. Keep it up, he pleaded with Biddle, for "it drags heavily & will result in showing a total prostration of the [Tammany] party." [62]

Political events proved Davis' forecast correct. The Hall was thoroughly confused. At the Society's New Orleans Ball, the revelers made light of the city's fiscal predicament. But serious-minded politicians, with deep stakes in financial stability, held grave reservations about Jackson's moves. "I am apprehensive our political friends made a mistake in going too far against a Nat. Bank," Cornelius Lawrence complained. Other Bank Democrats—Jesse Hoyt, Gideon Lee, James Hamilton, and Myndert Van Schaick—agreed that the President's experiment with local depository banks had proven a costly failure, and pressed for the formation of a fresh, modified national institution. Yet other Bank Democrats, particularly upstaters, disagreed, favored the pet bank system, and called for more state charters.[63]

The Whigs compounded Tammany's woes by aggressively following up their advantage. Since the Regency-controlled legislature had
just passed resolutions that favored removals, the Whigs sought to mold
public opinion by holding mass meetings and circulating memorials
that called on Congress to reverse the pet bank system. Their efforts
proved successful. In the city, the memorials were signed by over 3,000
men from all walks of life and both parties. Given such momentum,
the Whigs chose a special committee, headed by James King and Jacksonian James Hamilton, to present the memorial in Washington and
plead with Van Buren, the President, and Senator Silas Wright for aid.
Even so, the New Yorkers met a cool reception. Neither Van Buren
nor Wright paid attention to their complaints, and Jackson blamed
Biddle for creating the entire mess.[64]

In the city, Tammany fought its own war of petitions. First, the
General Committee held separate rallies in each ward, followed by a
meeting in the Long Room attended by over 2,500 of the party faithful.
That done, Tammany designated a second Washington committee to
present its side of the story, and passed resolutions that praised Jackson,
excoriated the Bank, and vilified Biddle. Nonetheless, the depression's
persistence weakened the Hall's position. Naval Officer Enos Throop
warned Van Buren that Tammany, for all its strong words, was beginning to fragment between the people who felt "that there should be no
national bank" and a few greedy men intent on impressing "upon the
administration an opinion of its necessity." [65]

Up to this point, Van Buren had exhibited little real leadership,
content to ride with events rather than attempting to control them.
His silence, the Whigs charged, proved that Jackson was his tool in an
elaborate plot to charter "an enormous substitute for Biddle's bank"
located on Wall Street, "and there, through its branches control the
politics of every state in the Union." Even loyal Democrats, such as
Van Buren's close associate, Attorney General Benjamin Butler, were
uncertain of Regency policy, and assumed the nation could not survive
without some type of national bank.[66]

The Albany Regency, as well as Tammany Hall, rejected the idea.
Both Van Buren and Wright were agrarians in temperament and outlook; each in his own way could sympathize with land speculators, but
not with money or credit plungers. As for Tammany, most Bank
Democrats wanted to widen opportunities, not constrict them by having one huge bank blanket the field. All the mail piling on his desk in
favor of a new institution, coupled with the Wall Street conspiracy
charge, forced Van Buren to publicly state his position at last. Writing
to upstate promoters, to his son John, who was deeply involved in

stock manipulation, and to Olcott through Benjamin Butler, Van Buren stressed one theme. Nationally, he pointed out, Jackson would only accept one federal bank, located in the District of Columbia—but only if all other options failed. Locally, the party could not charter any Wall Street bank because the move would play into Biddle's hands and dignify the innuendoes that the Jacksonians had been "influenced in their opposition by selfish reasons." Then, in March, the Regency took some positive steps to cut the effects of the depression. Governor Marcy requested and received from the legislature a $6,000,000 bond issue to stabilize local banks. If nothing else, the move dramatized Van Buren's determination to sink or swim with the pet bank system.[67]

Despite these efforts, the Democracy made little headway in restoring economic stability. In February, the Albany Farmers' and Mechanics' Bank, which had been living for months beyond its means, neared failure. Only a reorganization of its board of directors, coupled with a transfer of funds from the city by the Safety Fund, prevented bankruptcy. Yet in bailing Knower and Olcott out of their troubles, the Fund commissioners increased the hostility of many city business interests toward both the Regency and Tammany because the move again depressed the money market.[68]

On February 11, amidst the growing crisis, the King Committee reported its failure at yet another pro-Bank rally. But rather than meekly submitting, a group of bankers and merchants, under the direction of Albert Gallatin and Phillip Hone, took the President's advice and formed a Union Committee to seek direct aid from Biddle. The Committee's mission, however, worried many local Whigs because it lessened their plausibility in charging that Tammany and the Regency were responsible for the recession. As Silas Stilwell (now a staunch Whig) cautioned Biddle, *"Much is expected in Wall Street from this mission."* [69]


In all this confused welter of charge and counter-charge, pro-Bank and anti-Bank committees, greed, misunderstanding, and misery, the Whigs had steadily fabricated a powerful indictment against the state's political establishment and set the stage for the city's first popularly elected mayoralty contest. Moreover, Whig image-builders portrayed themselves as the party of the people, the true descendants of Lockean idealism. For these reasons, they nominated Gulian Verplanck for mayor.[70]

Reacting to these developments, Tammany made a few necessary changes in its well-tried routines. Deploying orators in each ward, the Hall pictured itself as the "comman man's best friend," and emphasized that the new party, "The Aristocrats, alias National Republicans; alias Independent [Democrats]; alias Whigs; alias anything else that will answer the purposes of deception," could not be trusted. In order to avoid further factionalism, Tammany nominated Cornelius Lawrence, who quickly assured workie editor George Henry Evans that the Hall, after all, favored his ideas and would work for their passage. On a more practical level, the General Committee pleaded with the workies to prove "that freemen are neither to be bought and sold—nor are yet to be ruled and ruined." Further, by invoking Jackson's magic name, the Hall sought to make the contest one between "the Bankites" and the people. As Evans put it, "let the cry of the useful classes be 'Hickory, Homespun, and Hard Money.' " [71]

If the election had taken place in early March, the Whigs would have won. But reviving business conditions restored a semblance of order. The Safety Fund transferred part of the canal payments from Albany, Governor Marcy's loan created some stability, and confidence slowly returned. On top of these developments, the Union Committeemen, on impeccable economic but poor political grounds, persuaded Biddle that abandoning curtailment would gain the electorate's gratitude. On March 11, Biddle announced a halt until May. When this happened, author James Kirk Pauling told Van Buren, the panic was finished and had actually helped Tammany because only the "debilitated, infested & corrupt portion of the Community" had been ruined, thus leaving "it in a more healthy & vigorous state hereafter." James Gordon Bennett was far less optimistic. "As far as I can judge from present appearances," he wrote Biddle, "the results of the next week's election will be a sort of a *drawn battle*." [72]

Few overconfident Whigs shared Bennett's pessimism. Yet their mistakes played into Tammany's hand. Just before the canvass, they foolishly drove many rebellious workies back to the Hall when they encouraged Whig employers to threaten employees with dismissal if they voted Democrat. Above that, Tammany's campaign to identify Lawrence with the common man bore handsome returns. Not by even the wildest stretch of the imagination was Lawrence sympathetic with the radical workies. But in the heat of battle, Evans—now editing the anti-Bank, Democratic newspaper, *The Man*—blindly followed the Hall's banner.[73]

As polling neared its end, a crescendo of accusations and counter-accusations filled the air. In this situation, one spark could cause a riot.

Unfortunately, the three-day election period provided the incubator. On the third day, a riot began in the Irish Sixth Ward, traditionally Tammany's stronghold, and the resultant orgy of looting, crime, and arson which spread through the city cast a pall of fear over the election. Only the arrival of the state militia prevented mass corruption of the ballot boxes.[74]

In the freewheeling excitement, Lawrence's paper-thin victory by 171 votes goaded the Whigs into fury, even though they had won control over the Corporation. Wildly charging that the workies and the Irish had stolen the election for Tammany, Whig editors struck out in all directions. In abandoning their earlier geniality, Webb, Noah, King, and William Stone of the *Commercial Advertiser* disenchanted many pro-Bank Tammanyites who had crossed party lines for Verplanck. Caught up in nativism and labor-baiting, the Whigs lost their aplomb, and gave the Hall precious time to repair its shattered organization.[75]

For Tammany's future peace of mind, however, Lawrence's election was incidental to a larger problem. The jails were full of unhappy workies and adopted citizens, some innocent, some not, clamoring for freedom. Furious, *The Man* and the *Working Man's Advocate* charged that Tammany's captive constabulary had goaded the workies into breaking the law, and then had arrested them without any regard for their civil rights. As the controversy waxed more strident, both papers further interpreted the victory as a mandate to destroy all banks. When the Hall, controlled by the Bank Democrats, rejected the idea and avoided using influence to free the arrested rioters, Evans and his sympathizers began to wonder if the party had duped them.[76]

Beyond these problems, Tammany faced other imponderables. The election had cast doubt on its ability to hold its shaky coalition together, and the Whig party's emergence presaged a new two-party era. Moreover, the Democracy as a whole had not yet formed a cogent economic policy that could satisfy both its radical and conservative wings. The situation became more urgent because, under the terms of the 1804 Restraining Law, the legislature chartered all new banks, and the Bank Democrats planned to expand the system in their favor.

The roots of Tammany's greatest problem actually lay buried in an interconnected series of bewildering changes that few men understood. Paradoxically, Tammanyites, by adopting Jacksonianism, had stirred the electorate's expectations without fulfilling them. In discussing the dynamics of self-rule, party orators uncovered a growing gap between the Hall's professed ideals and its partisan reality. Tammany's traditional leaders were unsympathetic to many of the changes around them, men such as Evans and Leggett believed, and were more intent on preserving everything anachronistic in the city's life while enriching themselves and serving a small segment of society than in honest civic stewardship. If government of the people made any sense, internal Tammany reformers felt, the party could not tolerate laws or customs that institutionalized archaic privileges.

Here, then, rested the real internal discords that marred the Hall's harmony. Tammany's success had become self-defeating, the reformers swore. In developing a life of its own, the organization had become too bureaucratic, too hidebound, and had lost its Lockean idealism. What the reformers wanted was a redistribution of political power coupled with Tammany's reassertion of its political principles, particularly the idea of "equal rights" for all. But if the Hall's Lockean spirit was just a memory, the reformers proposed a much more revolutionary step: complete divorce and formation of a "purified Democracy" wrought through a radical, even a violent catharsis. As a result, the banking question, with all its hidden layers of privilege and indifference to public opinion, became the symbol, not the cause, of party factionalism.[77]

# ᵥ 7 ᵥ

# The Loco Foco Revolt

As THE Whigs continued to redraw New York's political lines by fusing with the Anti-Masons, Tammany Hall prepared for the fall election by forming an encouraging agreement with the workies that promised to smooth over party fissures.

To appease Leggett, Evans, and the "bone and muscle of society," the Hall adopted three of their main points: opposition to all banks and monopolies; termination of imprisonment for debt; and prohibition of the issuance of paper bank notes under twenty dollars, sometimes also called the "small bills idea." Reciprocating, Evans dropped his objections to Van Buren's run for the presidency and agreed to back Governor Marcy's reelection bid. In return, the Hall nominated four members of the Democratic Working Men's Committee (an internal Democratic reform group) for the legislature, as well as Ely Moore, of the New York General Trades Union, for Congress. Once the ticket became public, the *Working Man's Advocate* exulted that "the whole proceedings, in short, were all that they could be, and effected all that they could effect." [1]

To symbolize Tammany's revitalization, the General Committee held a "great Democratic festival." From all parts of the Union, including the White House, came letters that praised the Hall's new era of harmony. Even Governor Marcy, who was slowly drifting into the conservatives' orbit, placated the workies. When a few vociferous die-hards led by John Windt, Evans' editorial assistant, demanded from him a statement of principles, Marcy assured them that he too felt the legislature should limit the "unwise increase of banking institutions with exclusive privileges," reform the paper currency system, and be guided by "a special regard to the equal rights of all classes of citizens." [2]

As a consensus party, Tammany geared itself to accommodating

**158**

differences, not exacerbating them. The General Committee had thus bowed to the workies' demands, not because it believed in them but for sound political reasons. These concessions, plus a recurrence of good times, worked political wonders. In their exuberance, the Whigs misread the city's partisan barometers. "Our wards are organised better than they have ever been," one wrote Biddle, "& our inspectors . . . are determined to keep out illegal voters if possible. Our opponents are depressed. Their ticket is a poor one & they are somewhat divided." The reverse was true. Despite Webb's renewed courtship of adopted citizens and workies, the electorate gave Marcy an impressively large majority and chose Tammany's full assembly slate.[3]

In contrast to the spring election, the results crushed Whig optimism. Merchant Richard Blatchford called the result "a complete rout," and an equally depressed Webb called on Biddle to "immediately commence curtailment." Among all these mutterings of doom, however, Charles Davis was serene. The Hall's unity, he felt, could not last because its political order was unstable. The Whig party's best policy was to await Tammany's inevitable fragmentation.[4]

Davis pinpointed the Democratic soft spot. Although Leggett and Evans had reached the pinnacle of their influence by forcing Tammany to accept radical doctrines, the Bank Democrats had no intention of implementing any such notions. As Davis predicted, a crisis in the Democracy erupted when the workies tested the Hall's antimonopoly stand. But instead of assuaging them, the conservative *New-York Times* ridiculed Leggett's ideas, and provoked a bitter war of words. With no end in sight, the Bank Democrats tried to win Van Buren's support. They were quite willing, they assured him, to concede the workies a role in party affairs. But it was William Leggett, they claimed, who aggravated the situation. Just as adamant, Theodore Sedgwick, Jr., Leggett's editorial assistant, gave a different diagnosis. Simple explanations could not account for Tammany's problems; nor could they be attributed to one man, he wrote Van Buren. "I incline to believe," he aptly explained, "that this anti-monopoly warfare will expand—& if it do [sic] expand I cannot imagine that there can be a doubt of the issue in favor of those who contend for an overthrow of the present system of corporations." [5]

To the disappointment of both sides, Van Buren, after weighing the opposing views carefully, avoided any binding commitment and sought some middle course. But the Bank Democrats were convinced that they could move ahead without his approval because the Albany Regency was "so much entangled in the net of Speculators that [it] could be drawn in." Therefore, when the legislature met, the Bank Democrats issued a number of new charters, and distributed the stock of these banks among loyal party members. The workies were infuriated. The *Man* wrote: "We have been deceived, damnably deceived. The pretended Democrats have come out in favor of monopolies; they have set to nought the principles advocated prior to the last election; they have shown themselves slaves, base niggardly slaves of aristocratic masters." [6]

The radicals became even more unhappy when the national Democratic convention selected Van Buren as their presidential candidate and named Richard Johnson as his running mate. The choice left them with scarcely an alternative. To oppose Van Buren, as some wished, would defeat the only man they deemed worthy of high office. Avoiding any overt stand, therefore, they copied Van Buren's noncommittal attitude until he should reveal himself on a number of topics dear to their hearts.[7]

Since Van Buren's nomination promised a continuation of existing policies, the Bank Democrats were exultant. Convinced that great profits existed in speculation for any one who had the cash, many men who ordinarily would never have ventured on such a dangerous course saw no end of opportunity in sight. Real estate values climbed, especially on Long Island, brokers underwrote securities as their purchase price rose in a dazzling sweep, and unprecedented prosperity bolstered general confidence. As much as he despised this mania, Van Buren was powerless to stop it. Through Butler he did manage to brake the Bank Democrats' drive for a third national bank, but not their reckless disregard for fiscal sobriety.[8]

Although the workies also lacked the means to halt the speculators, they vented their anger on the enemy at hand—Tammany Hall. In particular, they attacked the Corporation's exclusive right, which Tammany generally controlled, to license a wide variety of local business enterprises ranging from butchers' stalls to transportation facilities. Here, the radicals, now calling themselves the "friends of Equal Rights," called a halt. Presenting a long list of demands that questioned the fundamental nature of equality of opportunity, they settled on the Council's ferry monopoly as the symbol of "exclusive privileges."

The radicals' belligerent tones aroused answering echoes among some Bank Democrats. But unlike the banking monopoly issue, the Equal Righters had wisely selected an issue that split the conservatives' unity. Some of them had speculated in the expanding uptown real estate market and wanted to establish new ferry lines and terminals near their lots in order to increase the value of their holdings. Other conservatives, who owned land in the older wards downtown, wanted to perpetuate the traditional licensing system and limit the number of new ferry lines and terminals as a safeguard against the decline of their own property values.

Encouraged by the controversy they were creating, the Equal Righters next attacked Tammany's closed primary system. The Hall misruled the party, they claimed, because the General Committee no longer reflected public opinion. Only if the people could nominate worthwhile candidates, "a right next in proportion to that of the election franchise itself," could honest men reform "the dominant corrupt party." In the spring election, then, the radicals meant "not merely to elect our *men*, but to advance our *principles*." [9]

Unlike the licensing issue, however, the radicals' attack on "party usages" created a common purpose among the feuding Bank Democrats. The General Committee, which they dominated, immediately took some practical steps to keep the radicals in line. It agreed that the licensing system was wrong, named several workies to the aldermanic ticket, and promised to consider complaints against the nominating convention.

Although the radicals did not trust the Hall, they decided to back the regular ticket as their last-ditch effort at internal party reform. The unfeasibility of insurgency also held them back at this point, because the dispirited Whigs were more interested in business profits than politicking and hardly bothered to field a slate. The contest, then, gave the voters a chance the radicals hardly appreciated. Neither men nor principles were at stake, but continued prosperity. Under these conditions, Tammany regained the Corporation and swept local Whigs out of office.[10]

After six years of violent struggling to establish a viable party movement, not all city Whigs were ready to surrender themselves in the mad drive for business profits. Since the recharter question was dead for the moment, party leaders searched for some alternative issue. After some indecision, their survey came to rest with the city's xenophobic preoccupation, or more simply, its nativism.

Confused and apprehensive after Verplanck's highly questionable defeat, many Whigs viewed the increasing waves of immigrants arriving each year as a challenge to old, established political and social mores. To some brooding minds, this situation proved that a conspiracy to subvert American democracy was afoot. As their vague uneasiness grew, many sincere but bemused men who had never lost their traditional suspicions of "Papists" and, in the city, particularly of Irish Catholics, were ready to switch political affiliations to a party that promised to deprive these newcomers of their political rights. This nativism, then, was a potent weapon for a religious bigot—or a political opportunist.[11]

Events in early 1835 aggravated the tension. During March, a group of Irishmen had rioted in the city, and many Whigs felt that without some restraining force a lawless mob might again disrupt the aldermanic elections. But when the Whig Common Council drafted a municipal registry bill designed to prevent fraud, Mayor Lawrence vetoed it. Then, when the Hall regained control over the Corporation, Whig nativists feared the Democrats might embark on a wholesale naturalization program of persons not yet eligible for citizenship.

In early May, Tammany Hall unwittingly supplied the opening wedge in Whig strategy and, ironically, former Tammanyite Mordecai Noah channeled this nativism into political action. As a matter of course, the new Council cleaned house, and swept two elderly Revolutionary War veterans out of office in favor of minor party functionaries. Noah exploited the move for his own purposes. Claiming that the Hall discriminated against deserving native-born Americans in favor of "foreigners," he called for drastic changes in the naturalization laws and stiffened voting requirements.

By late May the movement was still an amorphous affair, but within days it assumed a definite form and life of its own. The xenophobes created a Native American Democratic Association in each ward, held city-wide meetings, established an official newspaper, *The Spirit of '76*, and sought converts from both established parties. That done, Webb joined the movement. "Our distinctive national character is already being lost by the influx of foreigners who exercise a controlling influence in our relations," he asserted, "and if we do not remedy the evil while it is yet in our power to do so, then time will scarcely elapse before we shall cease to be a Republic." [12]

In acting as nativism's sponsors, Webb and Noah did their demagogic best to link Tammany's success to "depraved foreigners" who depended "upon a blind and passive obedience to an ambitious *Priesthood*." When Catholic Bishop John Hughes objected, Webb retorted that "the church is partial and must meet its fate." Based on its European history, Noah added, "*Popery* and Despotism are synonymous." [13]

By early September, however, the Native Americans split because of Noah's open attempt to make the party the vehicle for the state's pro-Bank forces. One faction made up of Whig nativists formed a fresh newspaper, the *Native American Independent Press,* and followed Noah's suggestion. A second, generally made up of Democratic nativists, gained control over the *Spirit of '76,* printed Van Buren's name on its masthead in support of his candidacy, and vigorously assailed Noah. Still, the Whigs were convinced that for all of nativism's internal schisms and antagonisms, it represented their best chance for the future. For the fall election, Webb advised against a separate Whig ticket and told his readers "that the leading principles of the American Party, are in fact Whig principles, and to such as go to the Polls we should recommend this ticket as being the one most entitled to their suffrages." [14]

Tammany Hall treated the nativist problem with circumspection. Despite some indications that the conservatives secretly favored the Association, both the *New-York Times* and the *Evening Post* condemned the movement. But while the Hall relished the idea of recreating the "Spirit of '98,"—the Jeffersonian battle against the Alien and Sedition Acts—another vexatious problem, abolitionism, limited efforts to relive party history.

At the same time that the nativist cauldron bubbled over, a few wealthy city philanthropists, led by Arthur and Lewis Tappan, defied massive public obloquy by pouring their money and energy into a drive to blanket the South with abolitionist literature. Tammany Hall greeted their efforts with unconcealed hostility. In July, it held a public antiabolitionist meeting in cooperation with such Whigs as James Watson Webb, and resolved that slavery, whether it was an "evil or not," was purely a local question that belonged solely "to the States in which it is tolerated." [15]

William Leggett, who now edited the *Evening Post* because of William Cullen Bryant's illness, was appalled. In particular, he resented the fact that while the workies were intent on liberating themselves from the city's vested interests, they often defended the "Peculiar Institution," lauded its chief defender, John C. Calhoun, and viewed free blacks as potential economic competitors. Then, too, Leggett admired the Tappans' courage in fighting public opinion without any political backing. In August, his silent respect became common knowledge when news reached the city that a Charleston, South Carolina, mob had invaded the post office, burned abolitionist literature, and hung effigies of the Tappans and William Lloyd Garrison. Force could not defeat fanaticism, Leggett warned. If the abolitionists were wrong, the people "must make the final decision." In the meantime, he suggested that it was the Administration's duty to protect the Tappans' right of "free discussion," and punish the agitators responsible for destroying federal mail. Jackson and Postmaster General Amos Kendall disagreed. They ignored the insult to federal property, and encouraged city Postmaster Samuel Gouverneur to bar abolitionist tracts from the mail.[16]

Leggett refused to heed the President's directives. Drawing a distinction between Jackson and Kendall, Leggett charged that Kendall had "truckled" to the slaveowners, and allowed "every two-penny postmaster through the country" to judge what the people could or could not read. But in defending the abolitionists against public censorship, Leggett had few allies. Van Buren, Cambreleng, and the *Albany Argus* backed Kendall, Tammany rejected the *Post*'s moralism, and even the Equal Righters wallowed in silence. To further rebuke the editor, the Hall held another bipartisan rally, and defended the South's constitutional right to settle its own domestic affairs without any outside interference.[17]

As the overwhelming weight of public contempt bore him down, Leggett strove to alleviate the dark passions agitating the city. Agreeing with the idea that the slavery problem was a local, not national affair, he nonetheless condemned both the Administration and Southerners in general for condoning mob violence. As for the Peculiar Institution, Leggett, convinced that it was a dying evil, added that the South, paradoxically, by its "hot, imperious, lawless, and unjustifiable course" did more "to spread abolitionist doctrines, than the preachers of those doctrines . . . could have accomplished in years and years." [18]

Tammany's growing impatience with Leggett smothered all hopes for moderation. In September, Gouverneur withdrew post office advertisements from the *Post*, and Francis Blair, the editor of the Administration's quasi-official mouthpiece, the *Washington Globe*, demanded that the Hall excommunicate Leggett because of his tendency to "fly off from the Democratic party, by running into extremes." By October, Tammany closed the circle of opposition when the General Committee stopped printing its official notices in the *Evening Post*. On October 10, the Hall made the break complete. It formally banished Leggett from the party for "continuing to discuss the Abolitionist question" against the "expressed opinion and views of this Committee." Leggett retorted with more logic than passion that the Hall had proscribed him "not for having deserted democratic principles," nor President Jackson, but "for perservering in the right of *free* discussion." At last, the Equal

Righters awoke. The General Committee's sinister object, one anonymous writer cried, was "to drive the only true democratic journal in this city from the party, that certain objects may be carried on without rebuke." [19]

He was correct. In reality, Leggett's refusal to follow the party line handed the Bank Democrats a safe excuse to cripple the entire Equal Rights movement. The *New-York Times* thus announced that in the past it had made concessions "with professed friends who have demanded terms," but would do so no longer because those men were traitors. The ward committees capped the Bank Democrats' triumph when they too agreed against the "propriety of exacting pledges in any shape." [20]

A cloud of gloom now hung over the radicals. All portents and signs indicated that no matter how hard they tried to reform Tammany from the inside, they could never loosen the Bank Democrats' grasp over party machinery. The situation became even more explosive when the Bank Democrats rejected the advice of Churchill Cambreleng, Van Buren's local spokesman, that the party had to fulfill its pledges regardless of Leggett. Convinced that they could flaunt the reformers because the abolitionist fiction had discredited Leggett, and assuming the party would not split in order to protect adopted citizens, the conservatives ended any chance for compromise. They totally ignored the potentially dangerous character of the Equal Rights Democracy and named a closed ticket for Congress, headed by banker Gideon Lee. Ironically, abolitionism, the one issue on which the reformers and Bank Democrats fully agreed, triggered a full-scale party revolt.[21]

The radicals had one option left. Since the rank and file had not yet confirmed the ticket, they could still gain control over the General Meeting, which would endorse it, scuttle the Bank Democrat's slate, and substitute one of their own. The conservatives, however, were prepared for trouble. As an old but effective dodge, they arrived at the Wigwam early in the evening, packing the Long Room with their henchmen while the overflow filled the corridors. Relentlessly pushing their advantage, they organized the meeting and adopted the ticket before the radicals could interfere. At this point a pushing, turbulent group of Equal Righters gained the rostrum. They quickly reorganized the meeting. But just before Alexander Ming, Jr., the son of a longtime Tammany committeeman, began to harangue the crowd, the conservatives turned off the illuminating gas and plunged the Room into darkness. "We were prepared for this villainy," the *Working Man's Advocate* reported. "We had a corps of loco foco match and wax candle men, and in an instant there were fifty wax candles burning."

The flickering, sputtering candles fired the birth of a new movement. The radicals, dubbing themselves the "Jeffersonian Anti-Monopoly Democrats," formed a composite slate of four regulars and eight rebels. But they still stopped short of forming an independent third party.[22]

"There is not much excitement in the election because there is as yet no efficient opposition," the usually astute Cambreleng mistakenly wrote Van Buren. Cambreleng missed the point. In one week, the "Loco Focos," as the Bank Democrats derisively called them, mobilized a force that radically altered the fabric of local politics.

The *New-York Times* pictured the struggle in terms of principle and tradition, and opined that these "*must* triumph so long as we adhere to them strictly and to our time-honored usages." Even James Gordon Bennett, owner of the newly established *New York Herald*, joined the conservative camp, and warned that if Loco congressional candidate Charles Ferris won, the result would throw the nation into a land of "tumult, disorder, blood, and disunion." [23]

The radicals' fortunes did not depend on having a friendly press, or strangely, even on winning the election. They felt that their cause would grow and prosper if the ticket gained a creditable amount of support. It was therefore incidental that the Bank Democrats eked out a narrow victory over the nativists. Of more importance, Charles Ferris (although he lost) attracted 15.3 percent of the total votes cast for the congressional seat.[24]

Much encouraged by this turn of events, the Equal Righters moved toward their final break with Tammany. They held meetings almost every night, ward committees ran membership drives that cut deeply into the Hall's constituency, and they attacked privilege wherever it existed. The Locos even made their peace with the abolitionist issue. Leggett, the *Working Man's Advocate* claimed, had nothing to apologize for; his was the "force of moral power" involved in a "good and just cause," one that he had "not attempted to advance by any but Constitutional means." [25]

Then, with little advanced warning, the Locos lost their most effective podium. Because of deep emotional distress, Leggett resigned as *Evening Post* editor, but not before imploring the radicals to abandon their insurgency since the "avowed aristocracy" would capitalize on the split to vault into power. When Bryant returned home from abroad, he echoed Leggett's words, and pleaded with the Locos to reform Tammany from the inside. The Locos, however, had gone too far to renege. Although Leggett remained one of their patron saints and the *Post* a valuable friend, in February they formally announced their independence by establishing the Equal Rights party.[26]

Analysts have treated the Equal Rights Democracy in a variety of ways, ranging from neo-Marxian, on one side, to an apology for entrepreneurial capitalism on the other, with a wide divergence of opinion in between. But the Loco Focos did leave a clear self-image of themselves in their statements of principles. What becomes unclear is the interpretation subsequent analysts have made.

Primarily, the Equal Rights party conceived of itself as an agent of reform with a political mission to "show the difference between Jeffersonian Democracy and its counterfeit of the 'monopoly aristocrats.'" The Locos felt especially dismayed by the lack of quality in both parties. The only distinction between "the bank men of whiggery and the banks-men of Tammany" was the one between "ins and outs." No differences "as to political principles" existed among them, and both operated with "scant respect for public opinion." [27]

Much of what ailed Jeffersonian principles lay in Tammany's policy of "sustaining monopolies." Beyond this vague catch-all phrase was a distinct strain of individual self-determination. The Locos contemptuously rejected the Hall's policy of rewarding one vested interest group, the Bank Democrats, while neglecting others. The Hall's choice created an unequal economic, social, and political situation. One of the Loco's cardinal tenets, expressed in their Declaration of Principles, called for the elimination of all laws that aided a small if vocal minority while actually hurting the "rights . . . of the majority." Extending the argument, they wanted to democratize the political process by doing away with all behind-the-scenes maneuverings and giving the voters the right to select their own candidates. As the spiritual descendants of the People's party and the embodiment of the real spirit of Jacksonian Democracy, the Locos revived the caucus question, and charged that Tammany circumvented true democracy.

In analyzing the Equal Righters' rhetoric of protest—their repetitious insistence that they wanted to purify the Hall and eliminate its traditional "usages"—the Locos gouged beneath the party's glittering generalities to lay bare Tammany's hypocrisy. Agreeing with the Jacksonian idea that all government was restraint, the Locos nevertheless felt that "the rightful power of all legislation is to declare and enforce only our *natural rights and duties,* and to take none of them from us." Far from being romantics whose political theories bordered on philosophic anarchism, the Locos firmly believed in democracy, freedom, and an activist government working as an impartial umpire, to guarantee all citizens their "equal rights." [28]

As the main point in their political platform, the Locos hammered away at the point that they were true Jeffersonians who only wanted to reform Tammany "by reviving the landmarks and principles of true Democracy." Instead of being mindless, simplistic destroyers, they sincerely assumed that Tammany Hall and the Tammany Society, the influence "behind the throne, greater than the sovereignty itself," had both strayed from the path of Lockean principles that sustained and constructed the party in the past.

> The Tammany party began in purity: their object was the preservation of equal rights—and their early members, men of principle: the only principle now of those who direct them (for a small faction directs the whole,) is to get into place, and keep in place; either for profit or power; and each ward has its *few* dictators. . . . Tammany under such influence, resolved upon ruling, became *all things* to all men, as circumstances changed; and when sore pressed by the opposing faction, they adopted sound principles for victory, not public good; and when less pressed, reverted to the principles of monopoly for the private benefit of the leaders.[29]

The Equal Rights party, in sum, philosophically moved far beyond its initial workie base. Not a party of radical levelers or class-conscious agitators, the Locos were generally self-employed entrepreneurs, full of exciting schemes, eager for material advancement, Jeffersonian in beliefs; men whom Tammany had depended on for support since at least Matthew Davis' day. A highly mobile lot, the Locos drew support from a power base as varied as the city itself—the artisan and the small businessman, the printer and the public employee, the dreamer and the rationalist, the professional politician and the ordinary citizen—a kaleidoscope of people whose common bond was Jeffersonian. Even in terms of practical politicking, the movement was far more important than its leaders. As a result, the Equal Rights party posed to Tammany —and by extension to the national Democracy—a question that was as simple as it was direct: they demanded to know whether the Hall's stated principles, particularly its Jeffersonian-Jacksonian orientation, were true party guides—or so much campaign flummery. At long last, then, Tammany Hall had to come to terms with the real spirit of Jacksonian Democracy or perish with its evasion.[30]

Events in late 1835 and early 1836 indicated that the Bank Democrats welcomed the Loco's insurgency—and had no intention of paying them any heed. In December, after a rash of flash fires, a dreadful conflagration razed several blocks along the eastern waterfront, resulting in losses worth $20,000,000. Both the Common Council and the legislature authorized loans to relieve the resultant pressure on insurance companies and banks, but did little for the individual sufferers who had lost everything. Even Congress returned to merchants some duties on goods destroyed by the fire. Equally distressing to the Locos, the Bank Democrats in the legislature answered their demands with unbashed greed. "With 7 millions of Bank Capital, and 6 millions of the people's credit pending," Azariah Flagg muttered, "the corruption of a Senator . . . appeared a harmless matter. We [the Regency] have barely escaped the pollution." [31]

In the city, political patterns were the same. The Equal Rights party at first attempted to work as a third force in local partisanship, negotiated with individual candidates of both parties, and proposed to support any man who pledged allegiance to their principles. Neither the Hall nor the Whigs paid them any attention. Tammany assumed that the Locos would repel more voters than they could attract; while the Whigs unsuccessfully tried to reheat the nativist cauldron. When the move failed, the Whigs fielded a separate ticket. Rebuffed by both sides, barred from meeting in the Long Room by the Council of Sachems, the Loco Focos had no alternative left but to nominate their own slate.

Four men ran for mayor: incumbent Lawrence; Whig Seth Greer; Ming, the Equal Righter; and Samuel Morse for the nativist Association. Lawrence won easily, receiving 60.2 percent of the total votes cast, to Greer's 23.5 percent, Ming's 10.4 percent, and Morse's 5.9 percent. The results were far different in the aldermanic contests where the Whigs, with nativist aid, deadlocked the Common Council. Under these conditions, the Locos were slowly making their point—they controlled the critical difference between victory and defeat in city politics.[32]

The Whigs were the first to react. Scenting an opening to play the Hall's internal interest groups off against each other and thus take advantage of the Locos' revolt, the Whigs asked the Equal Righters' cooperation in an effort to repeal the 1804 Restraining Act. Since the offer was consistent with their idea of eliminating legislative privileges, the Loco Focos welcomed such an alliance. But before committing themselves, they asked Tammany where it stood on the issue of free banking. The Bank Democrats still controlled the Hall, however, and they cherished the Restraining Law because it gave them a virtual stranglehold over the issuance of new charters. When this attitude became clear, the Locos openly cooperated with Whiggery. In their efforts to reform Tammany, the radicals had traveled a long and strange road.

Meantime, the conservatives stepped up their efforts to win Van Buren's full endorsement. But, as a worried Cambreleng pointed out, the Equal Rights party's doctrines were much closer to the Regency's basic Jeffersonianism than the Bank Democrats' naked opportunism. John Dix, another able Van Burenite, spotted the same danger. The Bank Democrats, he wrote, had betrayed the party because of their "inordinate spirit of speculation." Their conduct, he felt, lay more with "pecuniary considerations than motives of a higher origin & character." Yet the conservatives, instead of being contrite, wanted more. They demanded that Van Buren polarize the party and purge anyone who stood in their way.[33]

Van Buren felt the moment was hardly propitious for such action. With the presidency almost in his grasp, he had made peace with the antiabolitionists and won over some wavering upstate former Clintonians. In the city, the Bank Democrats numbered among them some of his staunchest followers; on the other hand, the radicals had not yet committed themselves on his candidacy. But when the Equal Righters sent him their Declaration of Principles and asked him for his comments, Van Buren could no longer evade the question.

No matter what position he took, Van Buren inevitably had to insult either the radicals or the Bank Democrats. Under such uncomfortable conditions, he followed the course of least resistance and sought to confuse the radicals with generalities. The stunned and disappointed Locos, however, called his answers "evasive, unsatisfactory and unworthy of a great statesman." Now it was their turn to waver uneasily: if they did not support Van Buren, Richard Johnson would fall with him. Too confused to make a choice, the Locos decided not to make any endorsement and, as a party, told each voter to make up his own mind. Unofficially, nevertheless, they made it clear that they considered all the presidential candidates "second-rate men." [34]

Van Buren's pragmatic political strategy increased the Bank Democrats' position within Tammany Hall. Hastily written letters of reassurance piled on his desk. Richard Riker, long a warhorse in Tammany's stable, for example, optimistically predicted that the Loco's lack of open support "will be of service to you." Unfortunately, Van

Buren let matters rest at this point. He did nothing more to assuage the radicals and gave the impression that the Bank Democrats had captured the Regency.[35]

So far, the Loco Focos had proven far better at criticism than constructive politicking. But when signs of an imminent crisis multiplied after Van Buren's reply, they turned factional improvisation into a united statewide party movement that drew sympathetic responses throughout the nation. Meeting at Utica, they totally forgot past loyalties, nominated a full slate "separate and distinct from all existing parties or factions," and constructed a platform that called for the defeat of aristocrats—of very political persuasion.[36]

With the Loco Focos' defection and the Bank Democrats' intransigence threatening to destroy the party, the Hall's moderates, led by Jesse Hoyt, Stephen Allen, and Churchill Cambreleng, joined by a few pragmatic conservatives like Samuel Swartwout, tried to act as Tammany's peacemakers. At the General Committee's September meeting they rammed through a series of resolutions that called for a "modification of the restraining law" in order to "produce wholesale competition among money-lenders, and essentially benefit the interests of trade and commerce, by promoting the introduction and free use of capital." The Locos had heard the Hall's siren song before, and answered by nominating an independent city ticket.[37]

The Whigs waged an unusual campaign in the presidential election. Unsure of their national strength, they ran three regional candidates against Van Buren in the hope of forcing the contest into the House of Representatives. In New York, they named General William Henry Harrison and selected Francis Granger as his running mate. Frankly borrowing Democratic techniques, they molded Harrison into a latter-day Andrew Jackson, "a tried Republican of the old school," who insisted that Whiggery was the "party of the poor against the vested interests." Locally, the Whigs wooed the discontented, the men who felt that Tammany had neglected or oppressed them. Webb renewed his courtship of the Irish vote; Noah called for an alliance of "Merchants, Mechanics and Traders"; James Brooks' *Daily Express* demanded "Reform, and the Rights of the People"; the nominating convention ran Chief Fire Engineer James Gulick, whom Tammany had assailed for ineptness in the great fire, for registrar; and all criticized the Restraining Law and Tammany's monopoly over banking and insurance companies.[38]

With its once invincible bastions crumbling, Tammany sought to rebuild confidence by shopworn cries of "party usages" and loyalty to President Jackson. But the political situation was fluid. Former Tammanyites mingled with Whigs, tenuously linked together by mutual hatreds. Defections were common. Ambitious Locos such as Edward Curtis and Frederick Tallmadge deserted the radicals and ran on the Whig ticket. The *Evening Post,* long an apostle of reform, backed the Bank Conservative ticket, and protested that a radical victory would merely complicate political lines. Somehow, however, the Loco Foco–Whig alliance held firm. Although Van Buren carried the city on his way to the White House, Loco Foco support again proved the key to local victory. They helped send one Whig and two moderate Tammanyites to Congress, defeating the hated Gideon Lee in the process; four Whigs and six moderate Tammanyites to the legislature; and added to their laurels by electing three radicals to the assembly.[39]

Despite their ticket's poor showing in the gubernatorial race, the Loco Focos could now set their own price for future cooperation with either party. Above and beyond all other considerations, they openly held the balance of power between Tammany and the Whigs. On the face of the returns, furthermore, when given a choice among a Whig, moderate Tammanyite, Loco Foco, or conservative, the Equal Righters voted first, to punish the Hall; second, to reward a friend such as Congressman Cambreleng, whom they helped reelect; third, for their own man if they thought he could win; fourth, for a Whig if they felt they could trust him; fifth, for a total boycott of all Bank Democrats.

Exulting over these returns, Horace Greeley, just beginning an illustrious career, seriously proposed a permanent Whig alliance with the Locos. The sneering *Democrat,* the voice of the Equal Rights party, firmly rejected the offer: "The stupid Whigs think, and boast they have beaten the [Tammany] party. What conceit! Why did they not elect the Harrison ticket? The truth is, the people were resolved to humble Tammany Hall, and therefore they voted for a portion of the Whig Assembly and Congressional tickets." When the Hall also suggested a merger, the paper's editors grew more hostile. Full of disdain, they ridiculed "mother Tammany" as an "old harlot eager to embrace any new movement in order to win elections," and cried out "look at the treachery in the leering eyes of the old hag! . . . Beware." [40]

The city Democracy's chances for amalgamating were not as farfetched as the Locos pretended. Already, the uncommitted moderates sought some binding middle-of-the-road policy and were prepared to sacrifice the Restraining Act for that end. Speaking for these men,

Cambreleng consequently saw some good in the Hall's latest setback. "I hope we shall profit by the lesson we have received," he wrote Flagg, "and that the two extremes will leave the main body of the party hereafter to manage their own concerns and to make nominations of men who shall have no private objects in view—such nominations would never be objected to at Tammany Hall or any where else." [41]

Clearly, Cambreleng and his moderate friends understood that a minority—particularly a progressive, articulate minority—could respond to changing times far better than an institutionalized majority, grown fat and complacent. The Equal Rights party was such a minority. The moderates' highest partisan good, therefore, was no longer the quest for spoils; it was the quest for reunion. They only lacked an issue.

Meantime, the seeds Jackson planted in his hybrid fiscal policy sprouted into wild clusters of inflation and speculation. Ordinarily, Biddle's Bank could have stunted these economic irregularities. But the Bank was finished. While hard-money men suggested that some remedial action was needed, the President's constitutional scruples prevented him from regulating the easy-money state banks that had lost all restraint when he destroyed Biddle. To partially stem speculation, Jackson issued the Specie Circular which directed that public lands henceforth must be paid for either in specie or specie-redeemable bank notes. The Circular, however, was a miserable failure. Early in 1837, a financial crisis in Great Britain sparked a series of bankruptcies in the United States. The Panic of 1837 had begun.

In the city, as the financial crisis deepened and unemployment became a fact of life, the public hunted for a scapegoat. The workingmen ignored the Panic's baffling economic dimensions, blamed the paper money system as the root cause of the hard times, and in a senseless act of destruction attacked the offices of three leading flour merchants whom they accused of artificially forcing upward the price of bread. With equal simplicity, the Bank Democrats snarled that the Loco Focos were behind the flour riot, and petitioned Van Buren to increase fiscal liquidity by repealing the Specie Circular. [42]

Yet, in reading his mail, Van Buren looked for sensible advice, not nostrums. Representative Abijah Mann, an upstate congressman soon to move to the city, struck this responsive chord. "The Government should most regard the producing interest," he wrote, "since it must rely upon that interest for strength and support." While Mann's influence on the Administration's policy-making was difficult to guage, the

Regency basically concurred. It was only a matter of time, then, before the Bank Democrats' reign over Tammany Hall would end.[43]

Even so, the President teetered on a delicate political balance. By inheriting all of Jackson's political assets, Van Buren also inherited all of the Old Hero's economic liabilities. This was especially true in the city, where the party hesitated between adopting Loco Focoism on principle or maintaining conservative fiscal ideas on the basis of inertia. The result, Silas Wright observed, was that the local Democracy was splitting into two camps: "the friends of Log-rolling legislation, stock gambling, & the like," and "the friends of the old republican custom of equal rights and privileges & of using public office for the public service, not private gain." Former Governor Enos Throop, now a Tammanyite in good standing, drew a similar conclusion, and insinuated that Governor Marcy, who favored the Bank Democrats, was intent on making "personal adherents" at the party's expense.[44]

Throop's judgment was unfair because Marcy's support of conservative ideals went deeper than individual ambition. Representing a party tradition equally as valid as the Locos' Jeffersonian idealism, he believed that society rewarded people on the basis of merit. Although Marcy owned stock in various businesses, he honestly assumed that the innovations the Locos proposed would destroy fiscal enterprises, harm the party, and reward misfits. He was therefore quite willing to use executive powers to separate speculators from honest businessmen, but would go no further. As he told his friend, Tammanyite Bank Democrat Prosper Wetmore, the Administration must "take care not to kill their best friends." [45]

While President Van Buren formulated his tactics, local Bank Democrats dropped their open hostility toward the Locos and bid for radical support with unmistakable signals. "The principles of Tammany are based on a rock," the New-York Times announced. "They come from and belong to the people." If self-seeking men abused the nominating process, it mildly added, the trouble arose from "the inattention of the people at their ward meetings, if they remain there." The Equal Righters, however, were in a fighting mood. Without firm pledges, they scorned compromise—at least on the conservatives' terms. By the time the mayoralty contest began, the depression's impact had completely disrupted the Democracy, and Tammany Hall paid the bill. Riding the crest of the Hall's bitter, internal warfare, Whig nativist Aaron Clark, "king of the lotteries," glided to victory.[46]

Each party newspaper responded to this political revolution in its own way. The Times blamed the commercial crisis, the Panic, and the

Hall's poor tactics. To win in the future, it concluded, "we must organise. We must restore our discipline, and go for our nominations." The *Post* interpreted the loss as a mandate for party reunion so that the Democracy would not be "soundly and thoroughly beaten by a minority." The radical *New Era* drew a different conclusion. The Loco Focos, it announced, "as a party, were too young to hope for victory over two matured and powerful opponents, and a great majority of them resolved to conquer one at a time by uniting their forces with the other." On the other hand, Horace Greeley's *New Yorker* professed amusement at Tammany's soul-searching because the Whig party had come of age, with or without Loco support. Matthew Davis had the last word. On the basis of Van Buren's losing the citadel of his state power, Davis predicted that the Whigs would thrash the Regency in the fall elections and carry New York for Henry Clay in 1840.[47]

For the moderates, however, the Democracy's defeat increased their determination to promote fusion by catering to the "producing classes." In the following weeks they did their work well. Cambreleng told his chief that the Bank Democrats did not represent the party's main body; thus, Van Buren could safely ignore their agitation for the Specie Circular's abrogation. "They will, with accustomed wisdom, mistake the opinion of stock holders and speculators for public sentiment," Cambreleng wrote, "and think that they are going to carry everything before them." From Albany, Azariah Flagg also sent reassuring words: "The Specie Circular did not cause the disease & its repeal cannot cure it." Responding to these ideas, Van Buren aptly characterized the situation in a letter to Jackson as particularly delicate and difficult, but promised all would "go well in the end." [48]

In New York City, the Bank Democrats unintentionally helped the moderates' efforts with a show of contempt for the Administration's fiscal policies. Holding a series of ward anti–Specie Circular meetings, the conservatives blamed all their problems on "the errors of our Rulers." The moderates immediately pounced upon such criticism and informed the President that the meetings were Whig-sponsored to meet the "view of Mr. Biddle." Just as important, the Locos hinted that they approved of the Circular, and particularly of Van Buren's hard-money inclination. In Washington, Van Buren heard both sides of the question and gave the same answer to the questions thrown at him: a congressional special session, to meet in September, would solve the economic downswing. Nonetheless, Governor Marcy felt uneasy. To Wetmore he confided, "I fear that there is not a sound state of things at Washington." [49]

On May 10, the economic turmoil reached a staggering level when city banks suspended specie payments. Once this blow fell, the Bank Democrats lost their perspective. Some hurled abuse at former President Jackson, others damned Van Buren, and still others felt confused and overwhelmed by the impersonal forces that were carrying them into bankruptcy. The moderates remained calm. As a sign of things ahead, the General Committee rejected a conservative proposal that Tammany Hall petition Van Buren for a third national bank.[50]

Van Buren was too good a politician to ignore the role that politics, interlocked with business, played in the Panic's birth. Well aware that the Whigs were using him as a scapegoat, his first consideration, nonetheless, was to guarantee party solidarity without antagonizing sizable portions of the Democratic coalition. With these considerations in mind, he rejected both the idea of forming a new national bank and strengthening the state bank system. Instead, consistent with his often understated political principles, he reemphasized his Jeffersonian orientation by deciding to urge Congress to separate state and bank. Before making his move, Van Buren needed to consider other local variables: what would be the reactions of Tammany Hall moderates and conservatives, the Equal Rights party, and the Regency? For the Loco Focos, Assistant Postmaster Barnabas Bates, a former Tammanyite who easily bent with each shift in the political winds, had the answer. Drawing a distinction between the Locos' self-seeking leaders and the party's rank and file, Bates forecast that "the great mass of that party is honest & ready to do what is right & if proper measures are proposed. I have no doubt they may [be] brought into good fellowship with the democratic party." Cambreleng seconded Bates' opinion. Speaking both for Tammany moderates and the Regency, Cambreleng reasoned: "You cannot make a democrat out of a bank director or any man who is overwhelmed with speculation." Clearly, the conservatives were in the minority; they were expendable.[51]

By June 1837, the moderates put their program into action in order to polarize the party and purge the Bank Democrats in the process. To do so, Leggett (who had recently started the *Plaindealer*) and Bryant's *Evening Post* helped Tammany's Young Men's General Committee— led by Fernando Wood, an ambitious merchant and bartender soon to become a political stormy petrel—to begin the complex nuts-and-bolts job of repairing the organization's machinery. As a start, the Committee resolved that all "special banking corporations" went against the "spirit of universal rights," and were a "hindrance to the accumulation of property by honest industry." Gratifyingly, the Locos responded. They applauded the Administration's hard-money policy and Van Buren's pledge that he rejected "paper money as a circulating medium." [52]

The moderates' efforts aroused fierce opposition. Upstate, Senator Nathaniel Tallmadge, the state Bank Democrats' most outspoken leader, joined Edwin Croswell in warning Van Buren to avoid the "ultraism of the day" that the radicals aimed against "the great and paramount interests of the country." Within the Hall, conservative tacticians Gideon Lee, George Strong, Preserved Fish, and Daniel Jackson, angrily sniped back at the moderates. Lee, in particular, used his friendship with the President to lecture him on economics. The ruling passions of the American people, he expounded, were money, profit, and prosperity. Only "a great moneyed power" could restore good times. As for the Locos, their slogans were "but a cuckoo song." [53]

Yet the old guard these men represented was fighting a losing battle; it had lost the President's trust. Instead, Van Buren turned toward Cambreleng for advice; advice which reassured him that the Bank Democrats had "forever lost all influence with the party." The time was ripe, he continued, "to form a pure, sound, democratic and victorious party." After taking soundings of the political currents in Tammany Hall and Washington, Cambreleng further warned that Lee's pontification did not represent true party sentiment. Public opinion, Cambreleng noted, was "decidedly anti-bank as well as national and any effort to run counter to that sentiment will be worse than abortive." [54]

During this transitional period, the Locos lost the initiative. Rather than commit the party to an untenable position, they deferred action until Van Buren's message appeared. In the meantime, however, they did announce their terms of union with the moderates: acceptance of the equal rights concept and the separation of state and bank. That done, they muted their vocabulary of anti-Tammany epithets. In this vein, the Sixth Ward Loco committee announced: "we pledge our united support to the present Administration in maintaining the policy and measures of Andrew Jackson." [55]

The President's carefully worded charge to the special session was magnificent in its timing. Basically, his proposal, the Independent Treasury Plan, dovetailed with Jackson's latter-day policy of divorcing state and bank. Van Buren's plan might have been a backward step on economic grounds, but it was politically impeccable. While Governor Marcy complained that "none but a mad loco foco would think of such folly," Silas Wright happily wrote: "The strong and true men of all sections are in good spirits, and the 'conservatives' look like a collapse of cholera." [56]

For their parts, the Equal Righters enthusiastically endorsed Van Buren's statement. Hard on the heels of his message, both the Locos' General Committee and Tammany's Young Men's General Committee held separate meetings but issued identical policy statements that called for a joint rally to discuss terms of fusion. The President thus had opened the door for reunion—and the Tammany moderates and the Equal Rights Democracy quickly accepted his invitation.[57]

Through habit and instinct, the Bank Democrats had ruled Tammany Hall far too long to allow Loco Foco ideas a free run within the organization. But the more the conservatives criticized the President, the more Tammany moderates made them appear to be party traitors. Equally important, the struggle crystallized a significant but hidden fact: a young, ambitious group of Tammanyites was using the Independent Treasury Plan as a lever to oust the Hall's old guard, not to revive the party but for its own self-interest. The question, then, was of naked politics, based on two divergent interpretations of party principles, with the winner guaranteed control over the apparatus. Clearly, in this context, Loco Focoism was both an ideological issue and a magnificent political expedient.[58]

On September 21, the moderates and the Loco Focos held their first joint meeting. Speaker after speaker mounted the platform to roast the Bank Democrats and endorse the Divorce Bill. Strange allies appeared. Locos such as Alexander Ming, Charles Ferris, and Levi Slamm, who had not been welcome in the Wigwam for two years, now shared the seats of honor with Cambreleng, Stephen Allen, and District Attorney William Price, the three men most responsible for fusion.[59]

The Bank Democrats most emphatically did not agree. Despite Enos Throop's assurances that the conservatives would not oppose the Divorce Bill if they believed it might "prejudice" Van Buren personally or increase the Whig party's strength, long-time Tammany committeeman Myndert Van Schaick was closer to the truth when he told the President that "I shall go with any portion small or large of the democratic party in favour of a National Bank." Four days later, waving the banners of revolt, the Old Men's General Committee, which the conservatives had just formed, held a counter-rally in the Long Room.

The moderates met them head-on. As soon as Judah Hammond started to speak, a jeering, groaning mass of toughs forced its way into the room. Both groups shouted through resolutions, but the moderates forced their foes to retreat. In no uncertain terms, they had demonstrated that they now ruled Tammany Hall.[60]

The conservatives suffered their final debacle when the local ward committees held primary elections. The moderates generally nominated their candidates and held a working majority in the forthcoming city convention. Under these circumstances, reconciliation was inevitable, Tammanyite John McClure forecast, because the Hall had finally purged the men who had "for the last three years kept thousands away from us." [61]

Some self-seeking Loco Foco political fortune hunters, following the example of Fitzwilliam Byrdsall, the future historian of their movement, would not surrender without a struggle. Like the Bank Democrats, they scorned fusion because it meant giving up their partisan importance. Pointing out that the Locos' original purpose had been to reform the Hall, these men charged that the old power-brokers might renege after the election. "Propositions of this kind," Byrdsall wrote Congressman Edward Curtis, "have already had an effect, for a night or two ago, at a Loco-Foco meeting, a motion was made & seconded by a strong [number] to postpone pledging the candidates already nominated." The delaying tactics worked temporarily. The Equal Rights party, after declaring that it was not fully satisfied with the moderates' honesty, named a separate ticket and promised to aid Van Buren but not Tammany. Yet despite such charges of bad faith, the Locos, regardless of Byrdsall, still sought the best deal they could wheedle from the moderates. Barnabas Bates' dictum remained relevant: the main radical group would rejoin the Hall if pragmatic political leaders could arrange suitable terms based on Jeffersonian-Jacksonian ideals.[62]

Below the surface, a silent power struggle gripped Tammany as the moderates created a new coalition. The reshuffling of interest groups was a complicated process, as Webb noted, because the Hall contained extremes of "wealth and pauperism" tenuously linked together by the "immenence of . . . exciting questions." The conservatives wanted Tammany to remain as it was "and to avoid new experiments and untried expedients." But as Stephen Allen put it, the moderates now believed that "the true foundation of liberty is equal rights for all." Out of this flux, a remolded Tammany Hall emerged, a Tammany Hall at peace with Jacksonian Democracy.[63]

Meantime, the Loco Focos agonized over an equally complicated reappraisal. On October 2, the party failed for a second time to form a joint ballot with the moderates. During the next two weeks, a fierce internal struggle ripped the Equal Righters into squabbling factions, each intent on their own ends. Step by step, the party became demoralized. Finally, on October 24, it formed a five-man conference committee to negotiate binding terms with the moderates.

The end was now in sight. In an unruly meeting, the General Committee accepted the radicals' Declaration of Rights and agreed that all monopolies "violated the equal rights of the people." The Locos could no longer equivocate. In a fateful rally, their General Committee, by a vote of 71 to 22, agreed to fuse with Tammany Hall. The decision sealed the Equal Rights party's end.[64]

The next few days left New York City in a confused state. Major political changes were erupting, and no one clearly knew what would happen next. The ultra-radicals, the Byrdsall group, scorned the moderates and formed a splinter ticket. The Judah Hammond-led conservatives, scandalized by "the infusion of *slam bangism*" into Tammany, silently turned toward the Whigs. As the voters went to the polls, three new groups vied for support: moderates reenforced by the majority of Locos, Whigs aided by Bank Democrats, and the "uncontaminated radicals" who refused cooperation with either of the others. The answer to the question of which of these groups had the largest vote-pulling appeal came quickly. The Whig–Bank Democrat slate routed both opponents.[65]

Unaccustomed to defeat, some stunned but still loyal Marcy Democrats hoped Van Buren would write off the merger once the election ended. From Albany, Marcyite Parke Wendell pleaded with him for a thorough policy review. Yet in taking Van Buren and Tammany to task for purportingly running the party "by the Democracy of Numbers," Wendell uncovered the weakness of the politics of expediency. If a party followed public opinion that lacked relevance to principles, then that party was a potential instrument of demagogic men as well as a failure in the process of transforming popular consent into acceptable public policy. If any lunatic fringe, the Marcyites protested, could set party programs at the expense "of thousands of honest Democrats throughout the state," anarchy, not stability, would result.[66]

Heedless of such carping, Van Buren, his chief political advisers, Tammany moderates, and staunch Jacksonians throughout the nation felt that the Bank Democrats and businessmen like the Marcyites erred in not understanding that the Democratic party could not survive without a basic restatement of its political identity. Far too many conservatives, Judge Aaron Vanderpoel, John Van Buren's uncle by marriage, told the President, "fancy that they see a most frightful spook in loco-focoism" without understanding that the apparition had substance based on sound principles.[67]

Yet in a larger sense, the party's real confusion lay in interpreting Jeffersonianism in two separate but legitimate ways. One group, the Bank Democrats and Marcyites who had vociferously backed Jackson's slaughter of Biddle, viewed the government as a positive force that would promote and regulate economic growth, expand the credit system, defend state banking, and, as the spiritual if not material descendants of DeWitt Clinton, extend the canal network. Later, they would add the championship of slavery extensionism. The second, the moderates plus the reformers, distrusted unlimited power in the hands of basically selfish men. Insisting that the older brand of politics stifled individualism and inexorably created distinct layers of privilege, they favored restricting banks, deflationary credit policies, limiting canal extension to a pay-as-you-go scheme, opposition to monopolies of all sorts, and government based on equal rights libertarianism. (A few years later, they made "free soil" another battle cry.) Both groups confidently clung to the ideas that while the government should not hinder private citizens' lives, it was still an instrument of popular opinion, responsive to change. The main difficulty, then, hinged on exactly what public opinion really wanted. But the party's Jeffersonian formula provided no answers—only ambiguity. In such a case, both sides fought for conflicting issues, certain that traditional party dogma justified each stand.[68]

For the moment, Van Buren's control over federal and state patronage stymied the depressed Marcyites, and their habit of following the President's wishes would continue so long as he could reasonably guarantee victory and spoils. But Tammany Hall ultraconservatives still hoped to influence party policy by convincing the Democracy that coexisting with Loco Focoism would cost more votes than it gained. Certain that the Marcyites would join them, the ultras initially concentrated on such hoary shibboleths as party usages and sound banking practices. At first, the new coalition downgraded the ultras' efforts. Congressman Preston King, representing the Regency's radical upstate wing, felt that the party's recent defeat proved "Hell is to pay," but assumed the organization was better served without the ultras. City Locos were satisfied, no matter what the conservatives bleated. The

*New Era* wrote: "Democracy has had a foul load upon its stomach; it has vomited, and is better." [69]

In any case, the ultras were not completely frustrated. In a flash of inspiration, Judah Hammond suggested the trick the Adamsites had used in 1827 and 1828. Why not, he suggested, force the Tammany Society—through its lessees, Howard and Lovejoy—to judge party regularity by having the Council of Sachems bar the Hall's regular General Committee from using the Wigwam and grant the Old Men's Committee exclusive rights to use the Long Room? That done, he reasoned that the Bank Democrats would control Tammany Hall and thus persuade the Marcyites that party traditions favored conservatism and force them to dump the coalition.

Hammond's idea electrified the ultras. By December, they had held public meetings in each ward, formed a General Committee chaired by Samuel Swartwout, and petitioned the Council of Sachems to prohibit the regulars from holding sessions in the Long Room. But this time the Council hoped to find some means to keep from being drawn into the contest. Instead, the sachems felt the Hall's only chance for future victory lay in bifactional conciliation. As its first response, the Council directed its lessees to close the doors to both groups and urged the rival Committees to compromise their differences. The ultras' stubbornness, however, thwarted the sachems' moderation. Styling themselves the Democrats "friendly to the credit system and OPPOSED to the Sub-Treasury," the conservatives scheduled a public rally in City Park to dramatize their strength. They failed miserably. Just as Charles O'Conor, a highly successful lawyer, began to speak, the *Herald* reported, coalition bully boys shouted him down "and in five seconds not a conservative was left in the field." [70]

There was now no question where the sachems stood. In overplaying their hand and directly criticizing the President, the ultras only succeeded in further isolating themselves. On January 9 the Council, through Howard and Lovejoy, recognized the regular General Committee as the Hall's only legitimate voice. The following day, the coalition increased the pressure. In an open meeting, they firmly backed the Administration, called for a free banking system to end the Restraining Act, and thoroughly sacrificed the ultras on the altar of Loco Focoism. For their part, the Marcyites were now sure that the regulars expressed the party's temper while the ultras increasingly did not. Instead of following Swartwout, Hammond, and Gideon Lee into Whiggery, the Hall's Marcyites accepted the situation, refused to be panicked, and resolved to fight for their principles through normal

party channels. Just as significant as the Marcyites' pragmatic acceptance of radicalism was the Tammany Society's critical role in party
development: its latent power to judge regularity. Here again lay a
lesson for the future.[71]

In the months between the Council's action and the spring municipal
elections, both political parties were intent on seeking a public mandate
for their own particular political programs. Neither position admitted
the need for moderation. Both expected victory.

The Whigs, following Henry Clay's advice, campaigned on Democratic mistakes, and retooled their party into a vehicle for the discontented. For the Bank Democrats, they opposed the Sub-Treasury bill;
for those who feared a social revolution, they linked Tammany with
nihilists such as Fanny Wright; for the former Clintonians, they called
for canal extension; for the Marcyites, they suggested a third national
bank; for the nativists, a registry bill; for baffled businessmen and
artisans, plunging deeper into the depression, they charged that the
Administration had failed miserably to cope with relief.[72]

Tammany's approach equally lacked subtlety. It campaigned on its
Lockean credo and accused Whig incumbent Mayor Clark of gross
private and public dishonesty. With even greater contempt, the Hall
censured the Whig Common Council as a nest of irresponsible plun-
derers which spent its time intimidating poor laborers, cheating Almshouse parishioners, and generally turning the city government into an
open farce. To further stiffen the Hall's marrow, Van Buren dismissed
Swartwout and replaced him with Tammanyite Jesse Hoyt, who immediately used the vast patronage of the Custom House on behalf of
the organization.[73]

The ultras made a feeble bid for support. To that end, the Old
Men's Committee, prodded by Gideon Lee and Swartwout, nominated
former Clintonian Richard Riker for mayor. Privately, some Tammanyites feared "Old Dick has picked our pocket of at least a thousand
[voters]," but the *Evening Post* professed amusement, not alarm.[74]

The Marcyites exhibited considerable self-restraint. On the one
hand, they rejected Riker's argument that his candidacy would not
disrupt the party but actually strengthen it by giving the electorate a
choice between two conflicting Democratic theories of government.
On the other, Governor Marcy refused all Whig overtures. If the
people wanted any relief, he told Wetmore, they would find the
"*Gov*[ernor] & his political friends true to them & their interests." As
for the ultras, Marcy sadly felt they had foolishly landed "where I
anticipated they would—in the foul embrace of the Whigs." [75]

The mayoralty election results showed how well the coalition had worked in restoring the party. While Mayor Clark won reelection by slightly over 500 votes out of 39,341 cast, Riker trailed badly with only 393 bitter-end ultra ballots. On a more impressive level, Tammany made strong gains in the wards and captured control over the Common Council.

Interpreting the returns to their own satisfaction, the Democrats considered their comeback a major triumph. Former President Jackson praised the city's "laboring classes" for having done "their *duty well*," thus proving that they would "never surrender their liberty to the money king." Upstate, Edwin Croswell congratulated Van Buren on the "manifest improvement in the confidence of our friends," and predicted that he would carry the state on his way to reelection.[76]

There was another side to the story that the Democrats chose to ignore. The Whigs had obviously formed a political machine that promised to gain even greater momentum. Although Tammany moderates had shown great skill in integrating the Locos and keeping the Marcyites in line, the Hall really had scant reason for premature cheering. Whiggery's foundation stones were no longer shaky; the Democracy could not reasonably expect that the party simply would disintegrate with time.

Sketch from the *Illustrated London News* of a torchlight procession past Tammany Hall, showing pro-Texas sentiment in 1844. (Historical Pictures Service, Chicago)

Matthew L. Davis, the political founder of Tammany Hall. (Courtesy of the New-York Historical Society)

Walter Bowne, banker and politician. (From the *National Cyclopedia of Biography*)

Stephen Allen, a self-made man, philanthropist, and politician (Courtesy of the Kilroe Collection, Columbia University)

Mordecai Noah, newspaperman, political editor, and dreamer. (Courtesy of the Kilroe Collection, Columbia University)

An encounter between a Swell and a "Bowery B'hoy." Five Points in 1827. A reconstruction by Daniel Beard, 1895. (Historical Pictures Service, Chicago)

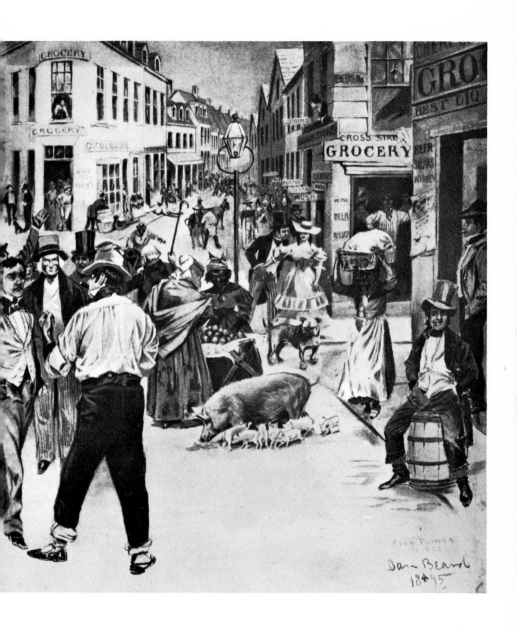

Daniel Sickles, Tammany stalwart, Union Army general, and the "Yankee King of Spain." (Courtesy of the New York Public Library)

Lorenzo Shepard, the "Young Lion" cut down in his prime. (From the *National Cyclopedia of Biography*)

Fernando Wood, the "Model Mayor." (Courtesy of the Kilroe Collection, Columbia University)

William Marcy Tweed, the first Tammany Boss. (From the *National Cyclopedia of Biography*)

The Election of Mr. Horatio Seymour, Governor of the State of New York: Democratic Procession Passing the New York Hotel. Sketch from the *Illustrated London News*, 1862. (Historical Pictures Service, Chicago)

# ～ 8 ～

# The Pivotal Years: Tammany, Nativism, and the School Crisis

In November 1837, Whig tactician Thurlow Weed gloated to a friend that "[Silas] Wright, who has gone through here, says the Loco Focoism of the Administration will be reasserted. If so, we can . . . carry the *next* election." [1]

The discerning Weed read the political signs correctly. For Tammany and the Regency, 1838 was a year of conciliation, consolidation, and further losses. Very simply, the Democratic party, caught in an untenable situation between an unpopular President who was pursuing uncertain fiscal programs on one side, and the opportunistic Whigs using local discontent to gain converts on the other, slid to defeat. As the depression sounded its depths, even the *Daily Express*' argument that the Whigs, not the Jacksonians, truly represented the "common man" seemed plausible. "Whiggism is conservative Democracy," the paper claimed. "On the contrary, Loco Focoism is a barbaric principle, and so is despotic Demonocracy." [2]

Yet for all its fine prospects, the Whig party bungled its opportunities for local dominance by its fatal involvement with nativism. Almost as soon as he took his oath of office, Mayor Aaron Clark adopted the Native American Association's program in the spirit, if not the letter, of its xenophobia. The Whig Common Council in 1837 had raised the commutation fee all immigrants paid on landing, harassed legitimate naturalized voters, and dismissed "foreigners" wherever possible from city jobs. The following year, the *Daily Express* praised the Association's efforts to draft a legislative memorial for a registry bill and urged all patriotic Whigs to endorse the move. As the spring municipal election neared, Whig papers circulated lurid stories about Tammany's

**185**

naturalization mills. Over 2,500 of these fraudulent voters, Horace
Greeley claimed, bore witness to the Hall's chicanery. In the fall, Noah
again sought to balloon the party's nativism into a popular crusade.
Collector Hoyt, the editor maintained, discriminated against native
Americans by appointing "thousands of foreigners" to government
jobs. "Therefore," Noah asked, "what hopes are there of a Native
American being provided for?" [3]

The Whigs faced a critical choice by the end of 1838. Should they
follow their natural inclinations and make nativism a campaign issue,
party leaders wondered, or move along more predictable ground as the
vehicle of protest? They chose the latter course. In a typical thrust,
the *Daily Express* charged that the Democracy meant to centralize
government authority and set class against class. Whig creed, by contrast, editor James Brooks explained, was "the restoration of power to
the people." Webb followed a similar line of attack and hurled abuse
at Democratic mistakes. When the Whigs held their state convention
in September, they nominated William Seward, Weed's protégé who
had lost to Marcy two years before, on a platform that carefully
avoided nativism and concentrated on Van Buren's fiscal failures.[4]

The Democrats began the campaign with high hopes. Both Tammany and the Regency were no less willing than the Whigs to use the
depression as a political instrument. But the Democracy, of course,
began with different working conditions and different goals in mind.
Deluding themselves that the party was "in high tone & spirit," the
Administration's forces generally stopped bickering and attempted to
close ranks, treating the coming election as if it were a normal question
of Democrats against Whigs.[5]

But conditions were not normal. Unlike the past, when party discipline held firm, many local Democrats expressed their frustration at
the depression with a hostile barrage of criticism aimed at Van Buren.
Equally dampening, some anti-Marcy Locos attempted to block his
renomination despite the *New Era*'s warning that the old Equal Righters now owed it to themselves "to vote all fair and regular nominations
made by the party." The ultraconservatives were just as hard to handle.
Under the leadership of Gideon Lee, Judah Hammond, and Richard
Riker, the self-styled "Unchangeable Democratic Republican Committee," held a rump convention in Syracuse and endorsed Seward. To
cap the Democracy's misery, Marcy disdained any association with free
banking, the Independent Treasury bill, and the small bills controversy
as unneeded capitulations to radicalism and stolidly prepared for the
worst.[6]

Once the party nominated Marcy, Tammany prepared for a massive effort. The General Committee held ward rallies, naturalized immigrants, and, like its opponent, imported illegal voters from neighboring states. Even the Hall's ticket was a masterly stroke of political accommodation. For Congress, it named Marcyite Isaac Varian; workie Ely Moore; John McKeon, an Irish favorite; and moderate Van Burenite Churchill Cambreleng, who commanded across-the-board support. The Hall applied the same art to its assembly ticket. Collector Hoyt wrote Van Buren, "I have been at Tammany Hall all the morning, & our people are in good spirits & we shall go at the fight confident of success." [7]

The Whigs were far better organized than ever before. In the critical area of recruiting illegal voters, where they had been vulnerable in the past, they copied the Hall's tactics and added a few new wrinkles by hiring Pennsylvania Whigs as "ghost voters," temporarily freed prisoners for a day at the polls, and bribed Almshouse parishioners. But they failed miserably with potential immigrant voters. Uncertain if they should woo or scorn adopted citizens, the Whigs played a dangerous double game. On one hand, Webb told immigrants to vote their economic interests; on the other, Brooks' nativism was unmistakable when he lauded Maryland Whigs for enacting a registry law. "Let this be borne in mind," he hinted. On election eve, Mayor Clark dropped any pretense of catering to foreign-born voters when he hired a special corps of mounted police to maintain order. His move honed the temper of naturalized citizens to a fine edge. "We have seen Irishmen treated by the [Whigs] with more cruelty and contempt than a humane man would exercise towards a brute," the Irish-Democratic *Truth Teller* snapped, "and yet these men have the hardihood to ask for our vote." Go to the polls, the paper instructed, "and answer with your votes. . . . 'New York is Democratic to the core!' " [8]

New York City was not Democratic. In a stunning reversal, the Whigs won all thirteen assembly seats, the entire senatorial ticket, and all four congressional slots, and carried the city for Seward by 817 votes. "Was ever a triumph more complete?" Thurlow Weed gloated. "Was ever a strong party so utterly overwhelmed in a single contest, except at Waterloo?" He had good cause for jubilation. The young Whig party had at least broken the Regency's decade-long stranglehold over the state, Tammany appeared moribund, and, above all, Van Buren's home state had repudiated his policies. Surely, Whigs beamed, the presidency was within their grasp.[9]

Tammanyites did not surrender to gloom. Within the General Committee, most ward representatives realized that while the election had made a shambles of the ticket, the party was sound because Whiggery's chief gains were most outstanding where economic misery and unemployment were deepest. A return of good times, the committeemen reasoned, would sober the people and restore political stability. Moreover, the remarkable thing about the defeat was the lack of recrimination against Loco Focoism. What Marcy's loss proved, Cambreleng and John Dix explained to Van Buren, was not that the party could not cope with Whiggery, but that electoral fraud, the "corrupt use of money," and false conservative allies, "using all their influence against us in secret," contributed to Whig victory. In December, positive then that a natural gravitation of disgruntled Democrats back into the party was only a matter of time, the General Committee beat back an ultraconservative power grab and Loco Focoism emerged unscathed as Tammany's political rationale.[10]

Before the Hall could launch its counterattack, however, a disastrous problem erupted in the form of two gigantic public defalcations. District Attorney William Price, a prominent Tammany "spouter" who had helped mastermind the moderate-Loco alliance, stood accused of swindling the government out of $70,000. His crime was piddling when compared to former Collector Samuel Swartwout's breathtaking pillage, however. Deeply involved in Texas land speculations, the latter had systematically bilked the Treasury Department of over $1,250,000!

Both political parties were equally nonplussed. The Whigs, who were eager for any opening to reap more political gains out of Tammany's miscues, realized that Swartwout's switch in allegiance generally absolved the Hall. Above that, several prominent city Whigs, including Noah and Webb, were deeply involved in Texas speculation. More than one party stalwart feared an impartial investigation might indicate that some greedy Whigs shared Swartwout's guilt. The Democrats were in a similar dilemma, but as Cambreleng told Van Buren, the party could save face by selecting certain facts to prove that Swartwout was more a Whig than a Tammanyite. Furthermore, Cambreleng pointed out, the Administration through sheer chance had an escape hatch. The year before, Van Buren had proposed some federal bookkeeping reforms; reforms the Whigs had helped defeat. As Cambreleng saw it, "some of this money would have been saved if the Treasury bill had been passed and if the opposition had not sacrificed the public interest to the miserable purpose of party."

The report issued by a special congressional committee generally resembled Cambreleng's views. The system was lax, the man corruptible, and few government auditors raised questions because of Swartwout's political connections, the committee concluded. The same reasoning applied to Price. On this mild note, the episode ended.[11]

With these problems settled, all eyes turned to the approaching spring elections. Confident of victory, Brooks wrote that "New York is now a Whig city, set on a hill, and we must keep it in the proud position where it is." The truth of the matter, however, ran counter to such boasting. During most of the late winter, Brooks and Webb indulged in a violent quarrel over Mayor Clark's bid for a third term. Part of their disagreement centered on personal jealousy, part on Webb's anger at Clark for not gaining a public printing monopoly for the *Courier and Enquirer*. The climax of the affair came when the Whigs did renominate Clark, and Webb warned that the choice was "not palatable to thousands of our most active politicians." [12]

With Whig unity dissolving, Tammany's position improved. In addition, general economic statistics confirmed that the worst of the depression was over. When that happened, the Whigs lost much of their protest vote. Spurred on by such gains, the Hall campaigned on local issues, particularly Whig mismanagement in municipal affairs. Clark, party orators swore, was corrupt; his administration reeked of high taxes, blatant favoritism in granting relief, inefficiency in running the Almshouse, and an "extraordinary waste of public monies." [13]

Above all, the Hall underscored the Mayor's mean-spirited baiting of adopted citizens. It was Clark, Bryant contended, who had instigated a recent investigation of the 1834 mayoralty riot to gratify his anti-foreign phobias and called immigrants the scum of Europe. In contrast, Democratic party propagandists claimed, the Hall's friendship had never wavered. Tammany reached across the abyss of xenophobia, Elijah Purdy, the General Committee's chairman said grandiloquently, to frustrate Whig intolerance. Even President Van Buren's handling of the thorny Maine-Canada border dispute aided the Hall. Twisting the lion's tail for all it was worth, Tammany upbraided the Whigs as mincing Anglophiles who would destroy the nation in a foppish imitation of all things British. All true Americans, on the other hand, were hard-fisted Democrats.

It was a bitter campaign, but the end was never in doubt. Among scenes of almost unbelievable electoral fraud on both sides, the Hall retired Clark to his lottery business, replaced him with "Rag Baron" Varian as mayor, and solidified control over the Corporation, 24–10.[14]

As soon as the returns were in, all sides agreed that the loosely drawn electoral laws were the city's greatest source of political corruption. The contest was "a complete overthrow of our civil institutions," Noah wailed. "The city has been full of outrages," Brooks agreed. Even Webb, after reminding his fellow Whigs that he had been correct about Clark, bellowed "we must have a free poll." Speaking for outraged Tammanyites, Benjamin Butler chided party leaders for adopting "the corrupt examples of the Whigs—the most profligate party that ever existed in our country," and proposed a vague electoral law so "as to ensure hereafter a sounder exercise of the right of suffrage." [15]

While both parties deprecated the same basic flaws, their definitions of *who* was morally at fault diverged when discussing remedies. The Whigs, ignoring their own guilt, blamed corruption solely on Tammany's manipulation of adopted citizens, and agreed with Governor Seward that immediate changes were in order. Moving a step beyond the governor's pious platitudes, however, Webb, Noah, and Brooks clamored for a registry law, applicable only in the city and theoretically designed to hinder all illegal voters. Tammany, while agreeing that reforms were necessary, branded the Whig plan as unconstitutional as it was immoral. Equally as shortsighted as his Whig counterparts, Bryant favored a single day of balloting, plus a division of the wards into smaller electoral districts where the inspectors could keep a closer watch on things. Azariah Flagg, currently the Albany postmaster, refined the *Evening Post*'s suggestions. First, he proposed that each inspector have the legal power to put the voter under oath "as to the location of his actual residence." Second, the inspector would prepare a memorandum based on this list, which official canvassers could later cross-check for fraud. In such a manner, Whig-imported "voters from other states" would find "it hard" to corrupt the ballot box.[16]

City Whigs saw little good in Flagg's plan. They wanted a registry bill; nothing more, nothing less. When the discussion moved into the legislative process, however, a bill closely resembling Flagg's ideas emerged and ultimately gained Seward's approval. The new law imposed stringent penalties on all those who procured, aided, assisted, counseled, or advised fraudulent voters. As Flagg submitted, the inspectors wrote down the names of all legal voters, who, if challenged by poll watchers, were required to take an oath as to their residence and qualifications. But the law, while "preserving the purity of elections," stopped short of Whig nativist expectations. It said nothing about illegal naturalization, nor did it tarnish the Hall's image as the defender of the downtrodden.[17]

During the summer, the state Democracy, buoyed up by slowly returning prosperity, began to prepare for the next year's presidential election. Upstate, Van Buren made another of his celebrated tours and left the impression that the people indeed participated in national decision-making. In the city, party strategists explained the election law and insisted that the Whigs hoped to use it in order to thwart representative government for the sake of partisanship. Finally, Flagg prepared a circular for mass distribution which gave the electorate a rather biased interpretation of the suffrage question in the United States. Ever since the Founding Fathers formed the nation, Flagg claimed, the Democratic party had favored the extension of "the elective franchise to every freeman, whether native or naturalized." In contrast, the Whigs, the lineal descendants of Federalism, had never accepted mass suffrage, and wanted "to embarrass our adopted citizens" by reverting to the days of the Alien and Sedition laws.

At the same time, city Whigs lost their momentum. Brooks announced that the party had never been more healthy, but in the same breath scolded party workers for being lazy and relying on Tammany mavericks for aid. Only self-help and organization, he admonished, could save the day.[18]

The fall elections culminated in the Democracy's comeback. The party, which had fragmented with such explosive force four years before, now combined with the same powerful thrust. Two methods triggered the Hall's fusion. First, because the Common Council named the three election inspectors for each ward, Tammany aldermen appointed only trustworthy individuals. Second, the Hall made its consistency clear on Loco Focoism. It demanded and received a pledge from all candidates that they favored the Sub-Treasury bill, agreed with the small bills proposal, would not vote to charter any new banks or extend present ones, and opposed the use of state credit for internal improvements. Again, while the Marcyites substantially disagreed, party discipline and the lure of public plunder held them firm.[19]

In the city, Tammany outdid itself in piling up big Democratic margins. Upstate however, the party made slight gains, but not enough to offset Whig control of the legislature. As a result of these returns, Tammanyites felt that the worst of the political crisis that had plagued the party was now over. The Whigs sharply dissented. Even before the polls had closed, they were already crying fraud. The difficulty was that they had operated on the assumption that they could pick up support because of the depression, and cope with Tammany by restricting its immigrant base. Upstate, the returns made Whiggery's hypothesis seem partially valid, but the Hall's success threatened to undo all gains. There was nothing contrived about the issues the Whigs raised. With a presidential election at stake, they could no longer enjoy the

luxury of ineffective caterwauling. "Among the first of Whig reforms
when the legislature meets," the *Daily Express* grimly predicted, "will
be a Registry Act for the City of New York." [20]

Governor William Seward called the plan sheer nonsense. His vengeful colleagues, Seward felt, were being shortsighted because any such
bill would further alienate immigrants and drive them deeper into Tammany's embrace. If anything, Tammany's victory convinced him that
Whiggery had to broaden its appeal by frankly imitating Jacksonian
libertarianism. With this in mind, he began to search for some means of
detaching the immigrant vote from Tammany. In his first annual message, he suggested that the immigrants should not deliver their votes in
a block at the Hall's command. The Whig party, he emphasized, also
believed in justice—but, unlike the Democrats, it was sincere. Yet the
more the city Whigs and their upstate allies pushed for a registry bill,
the less Seward seemed credible. What he needed at this point was some
means to win over the naturalized vote while persuading his fellow
Whigs that the move made sense.[21]

Seward found his opening in the city's education system. For many
years he had felt that existing conditions denied children the opportunity to become intelligent citizens. In particular, he directed his wrath
against the city's Public School Society. Begun in 1805 by a group of
civic-minded men, the Society was a benevolent agency charged with
educating children financially unable to attend private or religious
schools. In 1813, the state legislature authorized the Common Council
to use money from the state's Common School Fund to run local
schools. Since many aldermen and Tammany sachems such as Stephen
Allen belonged to the Society, the Corporation allocated most of the
funds to it and ignored the needs of other educational agencies. As
governor, Seward disliked the idea that the Society, a private organization partially financed by the state, held a virtual monopoly over the
city's system. Moreover, he was distressed that Protestant elements controlled the Society, even though it was supposedly nonsectarian, and
encouraged an elementary form of religious instruction.[22]

Several religious denominations shared Seward's unhappiness. Bap-
tists and Methodists criticized the Society because it denied them
School Fund moneys to maintain their own orphan and charity institutions. Catholics also objected to the Society's religious instruction and
ultimately formed separate parochial schools. Bickering between the
Catholics and the Society increased in 1839, when it appointed a special

committee to study the question of finding suitable textbooks that set forth "the fundamental truths of Christian religion free from . . . bias." Catholics were scandalized. Angrily, they reasoned that the committee's real purpose was not education but nativism.[23]

Tammany Hall played no part in the growing argument. In contrast, the discord gave the governor the means to forge an alliance between Irish-Catholic immigrants and his own party. In his 1840 annual message, then, Seward suggested that the city's public educational system lagged because of "prejudices arising from differences of language and religion." As his remedy, he proposed to establish separate schools with state money, instructed "by teachers speaking the same language" as the immigrants "and professing the same faith." Circumstances had thus played into Seward's hands. Posing as a humanitarian and couching his phrases in the best democratic jargon, he seemed a statesman who had the adopted citizens' best interests at heart. But on a more self-serving level, he was a masterful politician striving to turn the Society's intolerance to Whig ends. Luckily for him, the move was a happy marriage of proclivity and politicking.[24]

Tammany Hall at first commented favorably on the proposal but then ignored the question for over a month. Upstate, the *Albany Argus* neglected the topic for almost three weeks. Behind the scenes, however, the Democrats took a reading of public opinion. Of political necessity, they had to oppose whatever Seward proposed, but they could not base their disagreement on frivolous reasons. By the end of January, certain that the proposal was not popular with many people, the Democrats finally spoke out. From Albany, the pacemaking *Argus* quibbled that the plan violated the principle of separating church and state. The *Evening Post* took a more partisan, outspoken stance. Bryant claimed that Seward's only motive was to please the Catholics and thus gain their votes. The Irish-Catholic *Truth Teller* capped the attack. Democratic editor William Denman, who felt that religious instruction belonged in the home, cried: "No, let us have no legislation on the religious character of the schools and teachers. We desire no discriminating acts of legislation, even though they assume the air of toleration." [25]

Unfortunately for him, Seward could not control his party. City nativistic Whigs and their upstate legislative allies snubbed him and pushed the registry bill. At first glance, the bill seemed to meet reformist ends. It changed the span of elections from three days to one, and proposed a general poll list designed to prevent the Hall from using unnaturalized or premature voters. The Whigs then divided the city into electoral districts, containing roughly 5,000 voters, who registered with the Board of Aldermen one month before each election. Once prepared, the Board published the list, and only those registered could vote. Moreover, the Board appointed Inspectors of Elections whose duties were to compare the names of legal voters against the list, maintain order, and guard the ballot boxes from thieves.[26]

Although the proposed bill introduced necessary reforms, Tammany Hall immediately stigmatized it as nativism in disguise. As the Tenth Ward Democratic Committee put it, "resolved, that between natives and adopted citizens we know no distinction except that arising from merit." As a secondary strategem, the Hall hurled abuse at the bill's basic flaw—its discrimination against city voters—emphasizing the idea that upstate interests were intent on depriving the municipality of home rule. In a typical jab, banker Elijah Purdy, a cunning, hard-driving man just beginning an illustrious career, told a party rally that elections must "manifest the wishes of the whole people," or democracy would fail. By the end of March, certain that they had fully educated the public, Tammanyites settled back in pleased comfort.[27]

Governor Seward had his own problems because the Registry bill was about to pass the legislature. To veto it would alienate many of his fellow Whigs; to sign it would disenchant city Irish Catholics. The governor's correspondence on this difficult problem bore mute testimony to the conflicting pressures he faced. James Kelley, a prominent member of various Irish fraternal orders and currently representing the Erin Conservation Association, told Seward that if he signed the bill the Irish would "give it their support . . . only because of their ardent sympathy to [you] personally, not the party." Philip Hone, a nativist in temper, cautioned that a veto would "ruin the Whig party," and prevent William Henry Harrison from winning the state's presidential vote. Conversely, merchant Richard Blatchford, one of Seward's closest city advisers, counseled: "Do I pray you, Veto it if you can find a hook to hang a Veto on." Not to do so, he continued, would "be very disastrous I fear and injurious not only to the party but you personally." After consulting Thurlow Weed, however, Seward decided his best course was to sign the bill, and the Registry Law went into operation for the fall presidential election.[28]

On the surface, it seemed that the governor and Weed had made a gross miscalculation. Even as Seward pondered his move, the *Evening Post* predicted that the Whigs "have given into our hands a weapon with which, if we do not impudently cast it from us, we may beat them to the earth." But Tammany found Seward far less easy to handle.

As Kelley pointed out, the immigrants' fury fell on the Whig party, not its nominal leader. Even better for Seward, if the school proposal passed, he could create a personal coalition, and, like DeWitt Clinton, might be able to loom above both parties by standing on the Irish Catholics' broad shoulders. Just as promising, Seward also realized that nativism was not merely a Whig phenomenon and might disrupt Tammany Hall's homogeneity.[29]

Seward's tactics proved successful at first. Using the power of the spoils system, he cut into the Hall's ward organizations by appointing qualified Catholics to important state posts. To make his outlook even brighter, the normally hostile *Evening Post* and *New York Herald*, while they deplored his politics, agreed that the Public School Society stood sadly in need of reform.

Soon after it became obvious that the Registry bill would become law, however, the school issue became a hotly divisive partisan question. Part of this inevitable development resulted from the covert agreement the governor's friends made with Reverend John Power, co-vicar general of the New York diocese. They agreed that the Catholics would make the initial step for reform by appealing directly to the Common Council for a share of the School Fund.[30]

Although the Regency, through Azariah Flagg, pounced on Power's meddling in politics and used it against Seward, the deal was less firm than the Democrats believed. Despite Richard Blatchford's suggestion to Power that he wield "the just and deserved influence you enjoy" on the governor's behalf, most Catholics felt the move premature. Worse, many alarmed city Whigs refused to pin their faith on his scheme. As an indication of trouble ahead, one of them, Harmon Westervelt, pleaded with him to drop Power because the alliance might destroy Whig "interests and be fatal to our prospects as a party." Seward realized that Westervelt's criticism in itself lacked authority. But as a reflection of Whig thinking, he could not be ignored. Seward therefore took pains to write a long, cogent defense of his position; perhaps making it suitable for future publications. But while he emphasized that the Whig party had to enunciate its humanitarian preoccupations and reject nativism, his city critics remained unconvinced.[31]

By the spring of 1840, then, four fairly definable groups in the city had crystallized their stands on the school question. Tammany Hall used the Seward-Power agreement as an excuse to oppose reform. Other Democrats, generally involved in the Protestant-run House of Refuge and the Public School Society, resented the attacks on their prerogatives and felt their religious scruples were under unwarranted scrutiny.

Basically, they were Tammanyite nativists. Two groups surfaced among Whigs. Seward's personal followers pushed his plan and, at the same time, sought to balance themselves between the Irish Catholics and city Protestants. The nativists refused any cooperation. They felt that the Registry Law, with much less friction and more equanimity, would serve the same end as school reform—Tammany's ultimate defeat.[32]

The spring election tested the school issue's political fall-out. Rather than directly attacking the governor, diligent Tammanyites pointed to his party's obviously inconsistent position as proof of his hypocritical attitudes, and reinforced old fears of nativism. Above that, the plodding city Whigs played into the Hall's hands by their own indecision. While Blatchford and his cronies predicted that upward of 2,000 Irish would desert Tammany, the rest of the party remained irresolute. Finally, as a crowning blow, the Democratically controlled Marine Court naturalized as many aliens as possible in time for the election.

The Whigs could not win. Voters gave the Hall a ringing endorsement by reelecting Varian and returning a Democratic Corporation. Worst of all for Seward's hopes, Varian's strongest showing came in predominantly Irish wards. As a reflex, the stunned Whigs used nativism as the explanation for their defeat and called for tighter controls over naturalization. To Tammany and the Regency, such words were pure political gold. Once again, the Hall reacted with all the vilification it could muster; and, ever so gently, painted the governor with the same brush of defamation that it vigorously applied to his party.[33]

Then, just as it seemed that Tammany had everything well in hand, the situation altered with stunning swiftness. The Catholic petition for a share of the School Fund reached the Common Council and opened the floodgates of sectarian hatreds. To the Democratic Council, beset on one side by political considerations and on the other by Catholic impatience, courage and common sense were needed to keep tempers in check. Instead, cupidity and cunning marred the Corporation's course. Rather than alienate any of the vested interests involved, the Council rejected the petition on the flimsy ground that it lacked proper jurisdiction. The issue, it suggested, was church-state relations, not education as such, and the matter belonged to other agencies. On the subject of which agencies, however, the Council remained strategically silent.

For the unhappy Catholics, the blow transferred the problem to the winter session of the legislature. Psychologically, though, Seward's stature among them grew proportionally with their ill will toward Tammany. "The Catholics you have now with you," one city adviser wrote Seward, "& you can keep them without coming out in their favor any more—Do this and avoid a course that will alienate from you a powerful Protestant support." [34]

As the presidential election approached, Tammany Hall conducted a search for some new issues to take the Irish Catholics' minds off the raging school controversy. Luckily, one materialized when the Hall proved that Whig contractors and merchants had hired illegal Pennsylvania voters to help elect William Henry Harrison. To make the disclosures more damning, particularly in light of the Registry Law, Tammany showed that the governor had awarded some of these dishonest recruiters by appointing them to important state jobs.

Unfortunately for the Democrats, this "Glentworth Affair" could not rescue Van Buren. As expected, he did carry the city with 51.9 percent of the total votes cast. But the Whig-run log-cabin campaign caught popular imagination, carried the state, and swept Harrison into the presidency. Once the Regency regained its normal level of self-esteem, Van Buren's post mortems convinced him, if he needed any convincing at all, that the Whigs had cheated him and grossly tricked the American people. He looked to 1844, not only for vindication, but to reestablish the principles of true Jacksonian Democracy.[35]

Seward faced his own crisis in the fall election. Many city Whigs, despite Harrison's call for party unity, scorned the governor's reelection bid. Ordinarily, such a turn of events should have elated Tammany, but the tall, austere figure of Bishop John Hughes, the spiritual leader of the city Catholics, damped its excitement. During the spring election, the Bishop had been overseas. Once home, he criticized Tammany for tacitly approving the Public School Society and endorsed Seward's efforts, yet stood above active politicking. Under the stress of defeating Seward, however, the Hall made the Bishop a campaign issue by charging that he favored "our natural enemies, the Whigs, at the coming election." In return, Bishop Hughes vigorously defended both the governor and himself, thereby forcibly adding a new dimension to the rapidly expanding controversy.[36]

Some things had not changed. In order to counter fraudulent Whig voters, Tammany quickened the pace of its naturalization program. Interestingly, the Whigs, despite their protestations to the contrary, were also busy along the same lines. "We are doing well here," Horace Greeley informed Seward, "except in the naturalization of persons not entitled, and there they [the Tammanyites] are beating us as badly as ever." [37]

The election's final returns shocked Seward. In spite of Whig gains throughout the state, he ran well behind both the national and state tickets. Studiously reappraising his own political future, he now realized that the issue that he had created to further his ambitions had backfired and threatened to drag him to political destruction. To save himself, he had to make peace with the nativists while at the same time expanding his base among the immigrants. As time soon proved, such tactics were burdened with difficulty.[38]

The crossfire of Seward's needs trapped him. In his annual legislative message, he conjured up a weak solution to the school dilemma. To assuage the nativists, he denied that public school moneys, at least on his part, were ever intended for religious schools. As for the immigrants, he reassured them that he still favored a school system where their children would be instructed by men sympathetic to their particular circumstances.

Predictably, public reaction fell along party lines. Speaking for New York City Whigs, Christopher Morgan wrote: "The school question in the opinion of our friends, is happily disposed of, while you have the credit of firmness in reiterating your views upon that subject." To Tammanyites, the governor's profound ambiguity proved that he was more interested in winning immigrant votes than in honest reforms. As the *Evening Post* noted, his caution made his moral courage suspect and alienated his few Irish friends.[39]

Even so, the Common Council's second refusal to hear the Catholics' petition refurbished Seward's tarnished image. Obviously, the Catholics' only recourse lay with the legislature. But the Regency, using Edwin Croswell as a sounding board, sought to stem Bishop Hughes' reliance on the Whigs. Beginning with a series of articles that reviewed the Society's past history, the *Argus* suggested that the state's independent county school boards, the unit for determining self-rule upstate, be extended to New York County.[40]

Legislative Democrats held back from implementing these suggestions, however, regardless of their semiofficial point of origin. On March 15, the brilliant but erratic John L. O'Sullivan, a Protestant Tammany assemblyman, introduced a bill that substantially incorporated Croswell's suggestions. At the same time, O'Sullivan added his own twist by suggesting that because the school question was purely a local matter, it concerned only the city delegation. His ploy met a great deal of resistance. Cornelius Bryson and William Maclay, two leading Tammanyite assemblymen, wanted to test the electorate's political attitudes before acting, and decided to table the bill until the session after the fall elections by referring the bill to committee. After a period of intense haggling, the assembly managed a compromise. To please O'Sullivan, it created a special investigative committee, but scheduled its report for the coming legislative session.[41]

While the Democrats fumbled for an intermediate position, the governor's friends planned their own strategy. Legislative machinery transferred many Catholic petitions to John Spencer, the Whig secretary of state and ex-officio superintendent of the common schools. Since the assembly would not act on the question, he suggested that the senate debate a plan, as Croswell suggested, to extend the school district system to the city. Thus the schools would be autonomous, and if the majority in a district wanted to change the course or content of instruction it would have every right to do so. Under Spencer's plan, both Catholic and Protestant schools could function and the course of instruction would offend neither religious group. Except for one radical difference, Spencer's plan duplicated O'Sullivan's in that the latter was not willing to use public school moneys for sectarian schools.

As soon as Spencer's plan became public, several lobbyists from the Public School Society hurried to Albany and pressed the senate for delay. Their persuasion made sense to many senators who were uncertain of the electorate's mood. Rather than take a stand that they might regret, then, they laid aside Spencer's report as well, postponing both until the next legislative session.[42]

Meantime, Bishop John Hughes' patience with the Democrats snapped. Although he had previously not known Seward personally, the school issue sparked a correspondence that led to mutual respect and, ultimately, a deep and abiding friendship. As a natural consequence, since the issue had become less humanitarian and more political, the Bishop gradually adopted an anti-Tammany stance. No matter if Seward planned it or not, Bishop Hughes became his colleague in detaching Irish Catholics from the Democracy.

Early in May 1841, the bishop wrote Seward that the time was ripe for reform. The mass of people, he felt, was still indifferent but the Whigs could capitalize on the Society's intolerant position. After the legislature adjourned, he further recommended that Spencer's plan should become their rallying point. A gratified Seward quickly responded, and pledged full support of any move that Hughes might undertake. Then, to ease the bishop's conscience, Seward reassured him that he had no political interests in the school issue. Rather, Seward stressed, humanitarianism guided his policy.[43]

Bishop Hughes' unusual candor bettered Seward's position with the Irish Catholics. But the governor lost an equal amount of support among the Protestants. An abortive judge's appointment ushered in Seward's trouble. In early 1841 he had nominated Clayite Hiram Ketchum as a judge on the state's circuit court in accordance with the wishes of several prominent city Whig attorneys. But when Ketchum began lobbying for the Public School Society, the governor withdrew the nomination. Tammany used the episode to charge that Seward was playing with dangerous religious emotions for his own mean ends. Extending the argument, the *Post* concluded that "it is as a demagogue and not as the statesman, as a miserable and truckling tool, and not as a high-minded man, that he has manifested any interest in this great question of school reform." [44]

New York City Sewardites immediately suggested to the governor that he must mobilize the bishop's influence in order to neutralize Ketchum. Only positive political results, Benjamin Birdsall and Gulian Verplanck counseled, would ease the nativists' qualms. But Jacob Harvey, another Sewardite, warned that time was running short. Since "the Catholic vote is sufficiently [*sic*] to kick the beam on either side," he cautioned, "one party or the other will soon find it necessary to conciliate this empire." [45]

Harvey was correct. But it was Tammany Hall that began to take vigorous steps to manage the school issue and weld the Catholics back into a firm coalition. After defeating a Sewardite attempt to purchase the *Truth Teller*, the Hall sought to persuade suspicious Catholics that they could trust the organization to act in the common interest. But Bishop Hughes remained unimpressed. As a countermeasure, the Hall now attacked him directly. Aware that he was moving over treacherous ground, editor Bryant drew a careful distinction between the bishop as a religious leader and as a political partisan. For the next month a lively dialogue between Catholics and Protestants filled the *Post*'s columns. Finally, the *New Era* timed itself to have the last word and summarized Tammany's position. Seward, the paper chided, intended "to make political capital" by flattering "citizens of foreign-birth." But the Whig party's well-known nativism doomed his efforts. "It would be passing strange, therefore, that William H. Seward, and his party, who have uniformly abused our adopted citizens, should all at once become the champions of their rights." [46]

Despite the Hall's effort to concentrate on the political aspects of school reform, the specter of religious bigotry complicated its program. Deep emotions, stirred by half-remembered hatreds slowly poisoned the good will among New Yorkers. To make the problem more explosive, several Democratic interest groups agreed secretly with the Whig nativists that Catholics menaced American institutions. The more Bishop Hughes and Governor Seward pursued their plans, then, the more they stimulated the nativism that many Tammanyites passively shared.

The problem became acute in the 1841 fall legislative election. The hopelessly nativistic city Whigs refused to abet the governor's plan and defiantly nominated an anti-Catholic ticket. Reacting immediately, Bishop Hughes, who was a highly practical man, realized that the Irish would not yet vote Whig and began to press Tammany to adopt a more friendly position. Other Sewardites, however, were more interested in embarrassing Tammany than in aiding the bishop. David Nagle, a politically ambitious clerk in the Whig-controlled Custom House who was wagering his future on the governor's friendship, helped hatch a plot to undermine the Hall's following among the Irish. Conditions were perfect, he told Seward, "to kindle a flame in order to excite the Catholics against the Tammany Hall clique. We must keep up the excitement which is now at its highest pitch." [47]

Events proved Nagle correct. Tammany's first impulse was to reconcile the bishop, but his outspoken demands, coupled with his obvious Whig leanings, raised the hackles of many nativistic Tammanyites. Despite the efforts of rowdies led by Irish Mike Walsh, the leader of the anti-Tammany Spartan Club, the Hall formed a ticket without any reference to the school question.

Tammany's stand infuriated Hughes. According to his reasoning, the Hall owed Irish Catholics a moral debt for their support, and he meant to see that Tammany paid the price. Moreover, on the basis of Whig action, he felt that if the demoralized Catholics did not assert themselves the school reform question might die of neglect. Essentially, he had to transform Catholic impatience into political action even if it meant the formation of a third party.

Four days before the election, the frustrated bishop presided at a protest meeting held at Carroll Hall. Tammany's equivocation on reform, he shouted, had narrowed down Catholic alternatives. Put the

Democracy to the test, and the only thing the Catholics could expect was hollow words. It was high time, he ended, for the Irish to reward their friends and punish their enemies. In the hectic aftermath of his stirring speech, the enthused Catholics formed an independent slate. Of the thirteen men they named, ten were already on Tammany's ticket but the remaining three belonged to the "Carroll Hall" movement. Spencer's plan, not O'Sullivan's, proved the critical difference: the acceptable Tammanyites had endorsed the secretary's plan; the others had not.[48]

Politically and psychologically, the bishop's move jolted the Hall's complacent idea that the docile adopted citizens were Democratic captives, now and forever. The General Committee clearly saw that although Bishop Hughes' action was one of desperation and intended to mobilize public pressure, Tammany had to reconcile the Irish. Beyond this realization, the Hall also knew that if it gave in on this issue the organization might become dependent upon the strengths or whims of any irate interest group. Before the Hall could form an accommodation with the Irish, therefore, it had to destroy the Carroll Hall insurgency. Then, and only then, as generous humanitarians, not supplicants, would the Hall make its peace with the disgruntled Catholics.

On the other hand, the anti-Seward Whigs failed miserably in understanding the dynamics of city politics. In gambling on the situation as it existed, they did not consider where competitive politics would lead them in the future. As immigration began accelerating at an amazing rate in the years ahead, the Whigs' nativism placed them on the wrong side of the city's burgeoning population growth. Without appreciating the immensity of their stupidity, these local Whigs, by making their party synonymous with antiforeignism, gratuitously guaranteed Tammany's emerging machine more than enough fuel to make it, with occasional time out for reforms, the masters of New York City for almost the next century. In terms of the Hall's future local dominance, then, Bishop Hughes and Governor Seward unwittingly became the pivotal influences behind Tammany's amazing political successes.

It would be far too simplistic, however, to suggest that all Tammanyites were not xenophobes and that immigrants were predestined to find a haven within the apparatus. But in a way, party traditions had limited the Hall's choice. Ever since 1817, Tammanyites had sought to transcend their latent bigotry and reconcile it with their primordial Americanism and desire for office. Then, too, the Loco Focos' doctrine of equal rights meant nothing if the Hall barred certain groups solely on a religious basis. In the future, nativism was destined to disrupt politics on two major but separate instances, and some Tammanyites were more than tempted to follow their prejudices. But as a whole, while individuals wavered, the Hall stifled such attitudes and protected immigrants. By doing so, Tammany strengthened the moral and political propositions that gave it life and meaning.

All of these developments lay in the future, however. For the moment, the Hall had to show its power. Necessarily, each of the ten regular candidates disclaimed any desire to use the School Fund for "sectarian purposes" and rejected "all sectarian nominations." As for the Carroll Hall movement, Bryant rudely scolded the bishop. "Nothing can be imagined more fatal to the demands of the Catholics, than this bringing the Catholic hierarchy to contend for it in the battlefields of politics." [49]

Tammany's efforts contrasted with Whig elation. Ignoring the reasons behind the bishop's moves, city Whigs such as Horace Greeley felt that "everything looks well with us to-day, though every engine is in motion to contravene us. . . . I think the whole ticket is pretty sure." Fawning David Nagle also spread the glad tidings: "Victory has perschased [sic] on our Banner. We will certainly elect our regular nominated Whig ticket by a majority of at least one thousand." Yet these optimistic sentiments did not take Whig nativists into account. Under no circumstances would these men support the Carroll Hall movement, or by extension, the governor. [50]

The election results proved that the Irish now held the balance of power in New York City politics. The ten dually endorsed Tammanyites won, but the other three met with resounding defeats. For further proof, Carrollite Mike Walsh gathered just enough votes to allow a Whig to slip past his Tammany opponent in the congressional race.

Both parties immediately claimed victory. Speaking for Tammany, the *Evening Post* insisted that city Catholics had rejected the bishop's partisanship. After all, Bryant rationalized, the Hall did elect ten out of thirteen candidates. Undaunted by the puny size of their vote, the Whigs cautiously thanked the bishop for his firm stand. Yet, they still refused to adopt the governor's position. [51]

Meantime, the task of turning Catholic unhappiness against Tammany taxed Hughes' ingenuity. For a time, the Carroll Hall movement's momentum carried him along. But he quickly discovered that tongue-lashing Tammany Hall, while it might please the soul, could not match Tammany's organizational techniques. As meeting dragged into meeting, even the hopeful Nagle saw only frustration ahead. Basically, the Bishop's forces were shattering because the Irish Catholics had no place to go outside of Tammany Hall. If the city Whigs were not ready to welcome the Catholics as equals, Nagle warned Seward, the Hall's ability to compromise would swallow the revolt. But Seward again could not deliver his party. The rest of the battle, at least for him, was anticlimactic.[52]

In contrast, Tammany Hall understood that keeping pressure on its foes was the prime requisite of winning politics. In order to do so, the General Committee first disapprovingly told Bishop Hughes that his partisanship compromised the Catholics' future status in the United States. That done, the Hall softened its approach by proposing that O'Sullivan's plan form the basis for a school settlement. "In the disposition of the School Fund," the *Post* announced, "we would have no religious denominations preferred, or opposed, or even recognized." [53]

Tammany placed the bishop in a difficult spot by its willingness to abolish the Public School Society and widen the opportunities for an expanded educational system. If he did accept the Hall's offer, all of Seward's efforts would go unrewarded. Yet if he refused and stuck with the governor, he would compromise his pastoral obligations. Cautiously feeling his way, then, the bishop attempted an impossible double game. He tried to cooperate with Tammany, while at the same time he sought to credit Seward for the Democracy's change of heart.

Despite the bishop's salvage efforts, Tammany would not budge until it had removed Sewardism's taint from the school issue. Belatedly, the Regency followed suit when it endorsed the O'Sullivan plan. Now, with the Democracy's full force behind it, the Hall increased its pressure. In a series of well-orchestrated ward rallies, the General Committee warned Democratic natives that "in union there is strength," thus the party had to "preserve unanimity in the Democratic brotherhood." [54]

By January 1842, Seward's position had so deteriorated that he could no longer even count on being renominated in the fall. But he still hoped to keep his approaches to the Irish open. In his annual address, he again called for the Society's dissolution and recommended that the legislature adopt Spencer's plan. Unfortunately, neither the Democrats nor the Whigs expressed any satisfaction. Worse, nativists howled that the governor had sold them out. Even Bishop Hughes' soothing assurances to Seward that the Catholics throughout the United States held him in veneration failed to alleviate the governor's situation. Conversely, the practical Horace Greeley urged him to use all means to delay the passage of any school bill until after the spring elections. "The School Question *must* go right," he advised Seward. "You see how quiet our press is upon it. Tammany must give up this point or be used by it. If the bill be not passed before April, we must carry the City." [55]

Tammany would not wait. When the legislature convened, the party leadership referred the problem to a special committee chaired by William Maclay, one of the ten Tammanyites whom the Carroll Hall ticket had supported. Maclay was deeply conscious of his responsibilities and wanted to report a bill that would please all concerned. As a result, his committees studied the situation carefully and, despite religious and political pressures for speed, delayed its report for over a month.[56]

In these uncertain conditions, the city's partisan cauldron continued to boil. While some pragmatic Tammanyites pushed the issue by memorializing the legislature for a change, their nativistic brethren were more intent on preserving the Society. To make the Hall's situation more perilous, the Sewardites used the Maclay Committee's slow pace as an excuse to revive the Carroll Hall insurgency and sought to mold it into a permanent third city party. By early February they seemed on the verge of success. Six of the Hall's most reliable wards, generally Irish-Catholic in character, contained full-scale anti-Tammany clubs; a negative school bill would push these wards into revolt. If such conditions persisted, the *Herald* observed, "the chances are that the Whigs . . . will be able to recover their lost ground, and regain the corporation." [57]

Maclay was well aware of the danger. After consulting with Bishop Hughes, Governor Seward, Thurlow Weed, and Regency leaders, Maclay finally reported a bill that closely resembled Spencer's report. The *New York Observer*, the self-appointed conscience of Protestant America, immediately bristled with objections. If the state destroyed the Society, it argued, the open floodgates of Catholicism would soon engulf national freedoms. The Public Society adopted the same line. At a hastily called rally, it roared that Maclay's bill would subvert not only the school system but also the country's religious orientation. In reply, the *Albany Argus* showed how far it was willing to go to end the agitation. "If this be the subversion of Protestantism," Croswell editorialized, "it has been long since overthrown or subverted in this state." [58]

In the assembly, Maclay took personal charge. After some dilatory debate, his efforts succeeded when the lower house passed the bill by a vote of 64 to 16, with over 40 absentions. A far different situation developed in the senate. George Scott and Isaac Varian, two pro-Society Tammanyites, bucked party leadership and threatened to throw their support against reform. They based their objections on the ground that Catholics under Maclay's plan could use state money for their schools, and demanded that the clause be omitted—or they would work to see that the bill would never pass. Bursting with rekindled hope, the Society held another mass meeting to strengthen its Albany champions. At this point, all signs indicated an impasse.

Tammany brooked no nonsense; the bill had to become law. First, Maclay acknowledged that the senators' objections held some merit, and cleared himself of any suspicion of collusion with Bishop Hughes. Then, working with Senator Henry Foster, the Democratic chairman of the senate's school committee, Maclay agreed to drop the provision that provided funds for religious schools. Yet even after the recalcitrant Scott and Varian agreed to co-sponsor the bill on their own terms, various senators, especially Whigs, tried to drag out debate until after the city's municipal elections. Four days before the canvass, however, the bill passed a joint assembly-senate conference committee and, with Governor Seward's approval, became law.

The bill's ultimate shape, for all practical purposes, extended the state's educational system to the city. Each ward elected commissioners who supervised local schools and, with other ward representatives, formed a city-wide board of education. Legally, the main innovation was that Protestants no longer controlled the course of education.[59]

Catholic expectations, however, proved short-lived. Contrary to their hopes, the bill placed the entire system under the state supervisor of education, the well-known nativist and vehement anti–Van Burenite, William L. Stone, who encouraged daily Bible readings. Worse, even though the law forbade any sectarian instruction in schools that shared in Common School Fund moneys, in practice Catholics could only halt such teachings in the Fourth Ward.

In spite of their crumbling enthusiasm, many of Bishop Hughes' flock still hoped to control education when the city held its first election for ward school commissioners. Few nativists were in a cooperative mood. Anti-Seward Whigs joined pro-Society Democratic xenophobes in a coalition that swept the canvass and gave them complete hegemony over the city board of education. In despair, the bishop fell back on his parochial schools, and city Catholics gained little from their efforts.[60]

Politically, the school controversy and its resolution stimulated a renewed nativist outburst. In a mood of open defiance, the Whig

General Committee condemned both Seward and the Maclay law. Worse, the action of an angry mob (made up of both Democrats and Whigs) which stoned Bishop Hughes' home the night that the bill passed, heralded even deeper trouble.

Even so, Tammany consolidated its position. During the senate debate, remnants of the Carroll Hall movement nominated an independent municipal slate. But once the conference committee acted, the Catholics ended their rebellion and resumed their traditional Democratic allegiances. On the surface, then, the Hall had reason to gloat. It had neutralized Seward and Bishop Hughes, absorbed the school issue, and ended Catholic attempts to barter their votes for political favors. But Tammany had not ended the city's nativism. Essentially, what had begun as a difference over school policy soon flared into a vicious crusade against all Catholics and their political appeasers.[61]

# 9

# The Politics of Flux

DURING the two decades before the American Civil War, the nation confronted bewildering, constant change. Problems foreign to Jeffersonian-Jacksonian America—immigration, nativism, temperance, slavery, urbanism, territorialism, expansionism, economic policy—were now everyday concerns, and conjured up new political slogans and images.

In New York City, Tammany Hall faced similar problems brought on by the conditions of urban growth. Because the Common Council operated under complicated and poorly designed charters, the city's staggering population increase emphasized problems that the Hall had heretofore ignored. These developments touched on almost every aspect of municipal life—education, housing, garbage collection, street cleaning, fire protection, mass transportation, crime, prostitution, and disease. Equally frightening, gangs of rootless youths, such as the Bowery Boys and Dead Rabbits, terrorized citizens and made life miserable for the police. As conditions grew worse and no central agency evolved to coordinate the city's efforts to control the situation, many men formed groups outside existing legal structures. Some of them—the Spartan Club, led by professional Irishman Mike Walsh, and the Empire Club, the creation of Isaiah Rynders, a mean-tempered brawler, for example—disrupted politics and threatened to turn the art of government into the rule of the strong-arm tough. Reformers had their own answers. When conditions grew so alarming that urgently concerned city dwellers demanded immediate action, these people formed independent parties and sought to make the government responsible for its citizens' well-being. But most reformers lacked staying power. Essentially businessmen whose interests were temporarily threatened, their public spirit waned as they realized that the problems called for more than part-time efforts. New York City was not governed; it existed.

Under these conditions, the only effective reformers were professional politicians; men who had both the will and executive ability to exert authority over the fragmented, disorganized community. Furthermore, because of its successful resolution of the school crisis, Tammany Hall was now the municipality's majority party with the responsibility for dealing with these urban problems. But the inherent difficulties were many. Throughout all of Tammany's past growth, small, revolving cliques had dominated the General Committee. Moreover, because the Hall was fundamentally a collection of many diverse interest groups where each checked the other, the result was a high degree of inconsistency in terms of long-range policy planning. Thus, Tammany's basic structural weakness, plus its time-tested ability to turn out the vote, encouraged several men to seek power by somehow establishing firm control over the Hall's organizational table while at the same time keeping party loyalists happy with a steady promise of patronage, favors, privilege, and prosperity. Through all this pulling and hauling, however, one institutionalized party pattern held the final key for any consolidation of power and stability—the Tammany Society. For the next two decades, then, until Boss Tweed's political maturity, the Hall's internal power struggles ebbed and flowed around whichever group, or which men, dominated the Council of Sachems, and through it, the Democratic party of New York City.

The Democracy's problems began after William C. Bouck became the new governor. The Albany Regency interpreted his victory as a mandate for the continuation of existing policies, and assumed that the party would back Van Buren's campaign for a third presidential nomination. But as with everything else, conditions had changed, and the Van Burenites had actually lost their grip over the state's political realities. The immediate problem centered on canal expansion. The Regency, led by Azariah Flagg, Michael Hoffman, and Samuel Young, passed the "stop and tax" law of 1842, which suspended further construction, set up a property tax system, and used part of the canal revenue as a reserve to reduce the state's bonded indebtedness. Flagg and company, now dubbed the Radicals or Barnburners, stoked an already hot political furnace. Their intraparty rivals, the Conservatives, sometimes called the Hunkers—men such as Edwin Croswell, former Governor William Marcy, Daniel Dickinson, a young, high-strung Binghamton lawyer, and current Governor William Bouck—agreed that the state's credit did indeed need safeguards, but abhorred what they considered the Radicals' penny-pinching lack of economic foresight.[1]

Despite the indication of bad feelings, the Democracy as a whole was not yet prepared for an open split. For as long as Martin Van Buren had a chance to regain the presidency, most party workers refused to be stampeded into any irrevocable act. Yet these same men realized that such an event was only a matter of time—the Albany Regency had outlived its usefulness. Without patronage to hold the party's centrifugal tendencies in check, Van Buren understood that all of the unhappiness over the canal was nothing more than the preliminary sparring before the main event—the battle to control the state party. Only by becoming the next president could he delay open warfare.

Disunity also seeped through Tammany Hall. Early in 1843 a group of anti–Van Buren Democrats, eager to unseat the old power structure, coalesced behind John C. Calhoun's bid for the presidency. At first, their efforts won widespread approval. Dogmatic free traders and states' righters joined them; men such as Joseph A. Scoville, the future chronicler of the city's business community, and Emmanuel Hart, a bitter foe of the Regency's agrarian protectionism. Calhoun's part-Irish ancestry also appealed to the pride of many adopted citizens like the flamboyant but unreliable Mike Walsh, who delighted in slashing away at all things Tammany. Other converts such as John Commerford and Fitzwilliam Byrdsall came from the ultra-Locos because they viewed Calhoun's aggressive defense of slavery as a bulwark for urban workingmen against the exploitation of Northern capitalists and competition from free Negroes. Rounding off the Calhounite group were the few remaining members of Tammany's Old Men's General Committee, who saw the South Carolinian as their instrument of revenge against Van Buren.[2]

The situation became more complex when the personally ambitious President John Tyler attempted to win reelection by courting disgruntled anti–Van Buren Tammanyites and by forming a working alliance with the Calhounites. But because these men had to work around Tammany, not through it, the Hall thwarted their plans. In the party's election for state delegates of August 1843, Van Buren's friends, using divide-and-conquer tactics, easily selected their slate.

At the Syracuse Convention, everything went mechanically for the Regency. The Radicals conciliated the Conservatives by selecting Marcy as the presiding officer, and even backed a resolution that praised Bouck's conduct in office. Then the delegates gave Van Buren a decisive mark of approval by warmly endorsing his candidacy. In fact, the only jarring note in this superficial display of party harmony occurred when the Conservatives made an abortive move to commit the organization for Bouck's second term.[3]

When news of the convention reached the city, the Calhounites and Tyler-men held a protest meeting. Outside of a few curiosity-seekers, the affair was a dismal failure. "They have now made their last hurrah," one Tammanyite wrote Van Buren, "and with it quietly rests the prospects of John C. Calhoun in this city for the next presidency." To complete the triumph, the Hall formed "Van Buren Associations" in each ward, augmented by a central clearing house with links to each state.[4]

By the end of the year, Van Buren's steamroller appeared to be in high gear. The Democracy, beyond the city, rolled up impressive victories, and its control over the state reached epic proportions. In Tammany, young Samuel Tilden, a brilliant Radical lawyer, headed the Young Men's General Committee, while General Committee Chairman Abraham Hatfield, a rather unreliable man, professed his loyalty. From Washington, Silas Wright assured his chief that all was well; the Speaker of the House and most congressmen felt that renomination was an accomplished fact.[5]

Van Buren's campaign came to grief in Washington and Texas, not Albany or New York City. Up to this point he had been lucky, as any winning politician must be. Every problem that might have hindered him had either vanished, changed, or faded into insignificance through his use of Jacksonian formulas and slogans. The question of annexing Texas, however, defied such incantations. At first he did nothing, perhaps in the hope that the question would disappear. Such silence was self-defeating. "What course will Mr. V.B. and his friends take upon the question of the annexation of Texas? Does he encounter Sentiment of the North by opposing—or the Sentiment of the South by disapproving?" John Spencer asked Thomas Olcott. "He will not be permitted to remain neutral." [6]

As Van Buren's quiescence became more ominous, the mail at Kinderhook became a steady flow. Letter after letter had a common cry: "What are your feelings on Texas?" In the past, Van Buren had proven himself a master of political evasion. Such an approach would no longer work because Texas, as Silas Wright suggested, involved more than his personal destiny—it was a question of statesmanship. At the end of April, Van Buren made his feelings public. Instead of the expected ambivalence, he argued with rare courage that while he was not totally opposed to annexation, it was now being discussed by the wrong people, at the wrong time, using wrong motives. Granting that if elected he would bow to Congress' will, he nevertheless argued that annexation would probably "draw after it a war with Mexico." Under these conditions, he maintained, annexation was a nullity unless Mexico agreed.[7]

Predictably, Van Buren's words went against public opinion. Despite his friends' accolades, he had forfeited his freedom of action; the initiative had passed on to his intraparty rivals. Even so firm a Van Burenite as Preston King now worried that even if his chief won the nomination at Baltimore the voters might reject him in the fall.[8]

In the city, Van Buren's stand had severe repercussions. Expansionism was popular, particularly among land speculators. Others, including many Tammanyites, favored the move out of patriotism. As a result, the General Committee came out for annexation prior to Van Buren's pronouncement. Editor Levi Slamm, the former Loco Foco who now ran the Hall's *New York Plebeian*, speaking for what he claimed represented the majority view, wrote dogmatically that *"Texas should be an integral part of our Republic."* After Van Buren's sentiments appeared, however, Slamm retreated and briefly paid half-hearted lip service to the new party line. Yet, on reflection, the Conservatives realized that annexation gave them a psychological wedge with which to split the Radicals from the national party and justify a movement to dump Van Buren. In this new fighting mood, the *Plebeian* editorialized: "The proposed object of the Democratic party, is now, and ever has been, the ascendancy of their principles; men are of secondary importance." Tilden, sensing the shift in public opinion, worriedly cautioned Van Buren that "the disaffected of all sorts and shades are emboldened to speak their real sentiments, and our people here are as panic stricken as in Washington." [9]

One by one, Van Buren's national supporters fell away. With so much against him, his managers hoped for a quick nomination before his foes coalesced. Their plans failed. The pro-Texas, anti–Van Buren forces used the party's unique two-thirds rule, denied the New Yorker his vengeance, and ultimately selected annexationist James K. Polk, the "Young Hickory" of Tennessee. Then, as a reconciliation gesture, the convention named Silas Wright for vice president. But Wright, who desired to remain a senator, declined.[10]

Temporarily, gloom settled over Tammany Hall. The General Committee and the Van Buren Association packed away their useless banners, and sign painters worked late into the night to prepare new ones. Yet the Conservatives wasted little time and took full advantage of the situation. They rallied behind Polk and forced the Committee to sponsor an elaborate ratification meeting, while Gansevoort Melville, a young party orator much in demand, sent Van Buren a tactless letter urging his attendance.

Van Buren knew the rules of the game dictated that he act like a good loser. His answer to Melville, however, was more of a challenge than an endorsement. The ticket, he wrote, was sound because the candidates were men of correct "political principles," but he hardly mentioned the party's expansionist platform. In the euphoria of the moment, his readers jubilantly applauded his letter and completely overlooked the implication.[11]

Once the meeting ended, politicians rushed for pen and ink. "It was truly a gratifying sight," gushed Conservative John McKeon. "All sections of the party were present. Our personal preferences were all postponed & there was a perfect union of sentiment." Another excited observer scribbled to Polk, "the party is united, and I predict your triumphant success." [12]

Despite the outward appearance of harmony, however, upstate Conservatives interpreted Polk's nomination as an open declaration of war against the Regency. Governor Bouck suggested that Wright's withdrawal smacked of treachery. "Some speak of it with severity," the governor wrote. Others (Croswell, for example) hinted that Polk could not carry the state unless he purged the Van Burenites.[13]

Polk was no fool. His attitude toward the New York Democracy was neither idealistic nor sinister. On the one hand, he knew that the sullen Van Burenites needed special coddling; on the other, it was apparent that Conservative demands were as premature as they were impolitic. Under these conditions, Polk assured Wright that the nomination "was wholly unexpected by me," and demanded strict unity from the Hunkers.[14]

The Barnburners scorned Polk's olive branch, but kept a tight grip on their tempers. As a result, Van Buren advised his distraught friends to adopt the external trappings of regularity. As Slamm unhappily put it, "no man desires the election of James K. Polk more than Mr. Van Buren." To his close aides, the Sage of Lindenwald was far more bitter and honest. "The proceedings at Baltimore have indeed afforded melancholy proof that the profligacy of the Whig canvass in 1840 has not been without its deleterious effect upon our party," he complained. The trickery over Texas "was dismaying," and the whole party stood dishonored.[15]

Meantime, Tammany Hall faced a sharp challenge from new local forces that broke the pattern of normal city politicking. The Democratic Common Council, elected in the spring of 1843 and pledged to reform city-wide abuses, had proved a miserable failure. Using the banners of reform as a cover, the Council merely shifted chairs with Whig politicians and studiously ignored campaign promises. Tammany-ite Mayor Robert Morris took his responsibilities more seriously. In August 1843, he issued a special message that proposed to revamp the municipal government by thoroughly modernizing the city charter. His recommendations shocked the Council, and angry murmurs of disapproval broke out among party regulars. The Mayor, they cried, had gone too far. Time, not tinkering, was the necessary cure-all.

While the Democracy groped for a reformist policy, many civic-minded New Yorkers felt that the urgency for action could not be wished away. Even more, they believed that the pathetically bewildered immigrants who aggravated the city's urban ills were the cause, not the manifestation, of the trouble. Inevitably, as conditions worsened, these men decided to blend both ideas into one course of action. Posing as disinterested reformers out to check rapacious politicians, they used nativism as their vehicle to bring about much-needed improvements.[16]

Organized in the late summer of 1843, the new American Republican party rushed into the political vacuum the Whigs and Democrats had created. In their platform, the American Republicans advocated repeal of the School Law, ostracism of any politician who accepted adopted-citizen support, a freeze of all elective offices and governmental patronage to native-born citizens, and a change in the naturalization law that would lengthen the process to twenty-one years. Such blind xenophobia was not new. But on the reform question, the American Republicans took a clear-cut, unique position that drew impressive bipartisan support. Immigrants, the party charged, were responsible for all the city's troubles. Traditional elective officers were of no use because they shirked their duties by kowtowing for the foreign vote. The only way to cleanse the Corporation was through public-minded, reformist nativism.

Although the American Republicans' analysis was faulty, their obvious concern for good government won many converts. Above that, their strictures rang true in light of Tammany's activities during the school crisis. By running an independent ticket purely on local issues in the fall election, the American Republicans made impressive gains and raised doubts about Tammany's future.[17]

By the next spring, the new party had made a determined drive for control over the municipal government. Organizers perfected grassroots ward support; money flowed into the party's General Committee from a variety of wealthy merchants; and the nominating convention selected publisher James Harper, a Protestant philanthropist, for mayor. On national issues, the American Republicans refused to support any other political group. Nevertheless, because dissident Whigs formed the party's nucleus, it could not remain passive on the presidential question. For the moment, however, local Whigs—according to Thomas Mc-Elrath, Horace Greeley's partner—promised secretly to support Harper in exchange for nativist support in the fall campaign. As a smoke screen, the Whigs therefore ran a minor political hack, Morris Franklin, for mayor, but gave him only perfunctory support.[18]

In contrast, Tammany briefly lost its sense of direction. But by March the General Committee grasped the reins of leadership, framed its platform around Morris' special message, and, in a display of new-found morality, endorsed a legislative bill that proposed fundamental changes in the police force. The Hall's over-all strategy followed traditional lines. Calling on all Democrats to stand for their principles, Slamm ridiculed the American Republicans as sham reformers who were really professional bigots in disguise: "Hatred to foreigners is a foreign principle, not American. *Nativism* does not grow, and cannot live in the heart of an American. It is an exotic plant, not indigenous to a free soil." Then, as a unification move, Morris, who was a Conservative, sponsored Van Burenite Jonathan Coddington as his replacement.[19]

Through the remainder of the campaign, Tammany ran foursquare on reform, religious freedom, the Declaration of Independence, and whatever other slogans seemed handy. Few skeptical New Yorkers were fooled. When all the votes were in, the American Republicans administered a severe drubbing to both older parties by winning twelve out of seventeen seats on the Board of Aldermen and eleven out of seventeen on the Board of Assistant Aldermen. Tammany's greatest loss occurred in the mayoralty, where Harper easily defeated both his opponents.

DIFFERENCES IN PERCENTAGE OF VOTE FOR MAYOR IN
NEW YORK CITY, 1843 AND 1844 [20]

| Year | % Democratic | % Whig | % American Republican |
|---|---|---|---|
| 1843 | 56.3 | 43.7 | 0 |
| 1844 | 40.0 | 11.4 | 48.6 |
| % Difference | −16.3 | −32.3 | +48.6 |

If anything, these returns revealed the vast changes that were taking place in New York City politics. Cutting across party lines, the Americans proved that there were great political profits in both reformism and nativism. If they could fulfill their promises, they could create a formidable third party that might rule the city for years.

The task before the Hall, then, was to show its powers of self-renewal by absorbing reform. But before Tammany could begin, it had to reappraise its situation in respect to the Albany Regency. As the upstate political movements of the day transmuted the Democracy's factionalism into open warfare, the General Committee stood in a difficult position. Many anti–Van Buren Tammanyites, like their colleagues upstate, badly wanted a showdown. Joining them were the Calhounites and Tyler followers who were seeking a political home. Others soon followed. Eager, ambitious, unprincipled men like Fernando Wood, resentful of the power structure, capitalized on the situation as a steppingstone to personal power and urged the Hall to throw its full prestige against the Barnburners. Yet most Tammany leaders urged caution for they were too bound, emotionally and traditionally, to break ingrained habits of a lifetime as easily as these insurgents. On top of that, the Barnburners were still committed to Loco Foco egalitarianism, and many moderate Tammanyites feared that the business-minded Hunkers would reduce them to second-class status. But above all other considerations, the General Committee could not select sides until it had disposed of the nativist menace. In a way that they had never intended, then, the American Republicans did the one thing they had never thought possible and prevented a Tammany split. For the next three years, therefore, the factionalism destined to split the Democracy was basically an upstate phenomenon.

Throughout the remainder of 1844, the General Committee labored unremittingly to close party ranks. Luckily, Harper helped the Hall. Elected on a specific platform, the American Republicans acted less like reformers than as job-hungry "outs." Once his administration began, Harper further demonstrated imaginative bankruptcy and a singular lack of sound executive skill. In a way, though, his failure was predetermined because nativism was hardly the common denominator with which to solve the city's problems. The Democrats used this disillusionment to advantage. Then, too, many nativistic Tammanyites, who feared that a repetition of Philadelphia's recent antiforeign riots might also turn their city into a blood bath, rose above their prejudices and indicated a desire to support the Democratic ticket. Above that, the Hall would not equivocate with the Catholics; the school crisis had eliminated that temptation. In its final form, then, Tammany's program regarding the Hunker-Barnburner split and nativism revolved around "union, harmony, and concert of action." As Elijah Purdy explained to Polk, Tammany "must get all the voters we can without any abandonment of our principles. . . . We mean to succeed if prudent and conciliatory measures will affect an object so desirable." [21]

The Hall implemented Purdy's blueprint by bitterly attacking the Whig party's notorious anti-foreign bias while remaining mute about its own. Moreover, the General Committee received unexpected aid from President Tyler who, after declining an independent nomination, backed the Democracy and appointed Cornelius Van Ness as head of the New York Custom House. At once, Van Ness, working closely with General Committee Chairman Abraham Hatfield, put the great bulk of the port's patronage under Tammany's control.[22]

Organizationally, the Hall used Andrew Jackson's tremendous prestige as Polk's major asset. Almost overnight, a Young Men's Hickory Club sprouted in each ward; a central committee coordinated activity under the leadership of John T. Brady, a successful lawyer who claimed that he had never lost a capital case; and Tammany revived the public tree-planting ceremonies. Equally helpful, the General Committee established a reading room with a large file of propagandist newspapers, printed in both German and English.[23]

The search for an effective party organ was Tammany's remaining task. Before Polk's nomination, the Barnburners had planned a new journal but nothing materialized. When the campaign began, the local Democratic papers lacked both vigor and harmony. In early July, Samuel Tilden and John L. O'Sullivan agreed to remedy the situation by forming a new sheet, the *New York Morning News*. On August 22, the first edition was on the streets. Financially strong and brilliantly edited, the paper welded the local Democracy into a firm front, although in the long run it fomented divisions its Hunker backers had not anticipated.[24]

Despite their yeoman work in the city, many Tammanyites feared that Polk could not carry the state unless "[Silas] Wright can be prevailed on to run for Gov[ernor]." But although under deep pressure to run, Wright shied away. To John Dix he confided: "I do not think that I could be nominated without much trouble, as I am unwilling to believe that the rotten men [Hunkers] have become friends." Yet in the end, Wright's sense of duty prevailed, coupled with Barnburner fears of trying to control the state with an unknown quantity in the White House, and the party subsequently nominated him. Judge Addison Gardiner, Tyler's brother-in-law, became his running mate.[25]

Most Democratic politicians voiced their approval. Marcyite Albert

Gallup, a long-time anti–Van Burenite, told Polk that while most Hunkers regretted repudiating Bouck, party victory was more important than personal ambition. Ely Moore was more excited. To Polk he gushed that the Democrats would now carry the state by over 10,000 votes. From all indicators, Moore's prediction seemed far too conservative. On hearing the news, Tammany staged an "impromtu" rally that drew over 2,000 men; its formal ratification meeting was attended by nearly 15,000.[26]

Despite these signs, party unity was a mirage. Although Bouck philosophically accepted his fate, the Hunkers, even with Wright's assurances of good will, placed Polk on notice that they meant to keep up the fight once the campaign ended. In the city, a far more dangerous problem developed when a group of Van Burenites found it impossible to reconcile private convictions with the party's expansionist commitments. Determined not to straddle the issue for expediency's sake, William Cullen Bryant circulated a confidential letter to a number of like-minded men. In it he proposed that they publish a joint statement which, while backing Polk, should reject Texas' annexation and push in "promoting and supporting at the next election the nomination for Congress of such persons as concur in these opinions." [27]

Few things in politics remained secret. Levi Slamm, who still hoped to split the Barnburners from the party, demanded that the *Evening Post* issue a forthright policy declaration backing the Baltimore Platform. Foolishly, Bryant took the bait. If we make the annexation of Texas Democratic writ, he maintained, "we are broken up and defeated without remedy." At this point, the Hunkers acquired a copy of Bryant's letter, presented Polk with the evidence, and demanded that he rid the party of traitors. Meantime, Slamm published a doctored version of the letter and Bryant, in self-defense, gave out a corrected one. Most pragmatic Democrats, however, felt it more important "to keep out of view just now every question on which our friends differ." In the end, Wright's friend and future biographer, Ransom Gillet, told Polk that the controversy "does not appear to be doing us any mischief, & is mostly to be regretted on account of the authors who are really good fellows." [28]

With this issue momentarily settled, the Democrats fully exhibited, both upstate and in the city, their peculiar genius for coalescing around the party standard. Yet, in the city, Tammany faced a critical unknown over what position the American Republicans would take on the presidential question. On the basis of their covert deal in the spring, Henry Clay's managers expected that the nativists would reciprocate in the fall. Clay also assumed that Whig abolitionists would support him rather than throw away their votes on James Birney, the Liberty party's candidate, who stood no chance of winning.[29]

To hold the line for Polk, Tammany assailed Clay as a secret abolitionist, and warned the Democratic nativists that they were acting as Whig dupes. Slowly, the Hall's strategy began to succeed. And again, nativist blunders aided the Democracy. In return for a fusion Whig–American Republican ticket for the state legislature and Congress, the city nativists agreed to back Clay and Millard Fillmore, the Whig gubernatorial nominee. The bargain disgusted many Democratic nativists who could not stomach the Kentuckian under any circumstances. On October 29, they published a hardhitting manifesto, Gansevoort Melville gloated to Polk, "in which they avow they will come back to the old Tammany wigwam and family, and vote to a man for Polk and Dallas." [30]

In the few days before the election, Tammany redoubled its efforts. It held two massive parades, highlighted by bands and fireworks, to celebrate the end of the Democratic nativists' insurgency and give party workers an emotional outlet for their hard work. Even Martin Van Buren helped. Through the *Morning News*, he pleaded with local Barnburners to support the national ticket. But Tammany's masterly touch in handling the immigrant and alien vote was easily the campaign's most important facet. For the first, but hardly the last time, the Hall's absorption of the school issue paid massive dividends. As Gansevoort Melville described it, "the political head quarters of the different parties thronged. Tammany Hall a perfect jam from 8 a. m. till after midnight. Naturalization going on among our friends to an immense extent. On Saturday, 200—all Democrats rec'd their papers." [31]

Fraud, intimidation, illegal voting, stealing of ballot boxes—here was the order of the day. Taking careful notes for the future, Fernando Wood described the scene for Polk: "Our election has closed, and we have had the severest struggle ever witnessed in this city. Every means of the most disreputable and corrupt character has been resorted to by our opponents. Money has been lavished upon the dissolute and indigent without stint, and where intrigue, gold and calumny could not effect the object, *threats* have been resorted to, but without avail." Wood's account applied equally to Tammany Hall.[32]

When all the hubbub ended, the Democracy had scored an uneven victory. The local elections went disastrously for Tammany. Still having the momentum, the American Republicans elected two state senators and thirteen assemblymen. Of the four Congressmen, only one,

William Maclay, was not a nativist. Democratic sweeps in the presidential and gubernatorial elections, however, eased the party's losses. Yet even there major trouble loomed, because Silas Wright out-polled Polk both in the city and upstate.[33]

The debate over why Wright had fared so well was short but violent. The Hunkers deluged Polk with insinuations that the Barnburners "who voted Wright would not vote our electoral ticket." In reply, a visibly agitated Benjamin Butler told Polk that "nothing can be more unfounded or unjust." Wright was on the ticket to strengthen it, the *Morning News* chimed in, and logically his coattails carried Polk to success. As for Barnburner treachery, the paper argued, the Van Burenites worked doubly hard to prove "their magnanimity, their honor, their disinterestedness, and devoted Democracy." Polk accepted the Barnburners' explanations at face value. Intent on preserving party peace, he soothingly answered Butler: "I fully concur with you in opinion if they [the Barnburners] had withheld their zealous and cordial support,—the Democratic party in New York must have been defeated by a large majority." [34]

While it was thus evident that Polk clearly favored conciliation, New York Democrats, outside of Tammany Hall, could boast no such unanimity. As practical politicians, both sides realized that patronage, not diplomatic gestures, would determine the outcome of their power struggle. The most essential consideration, then, lay in winning exclusive access to Polk's spoils. Perhaps the somewhat sardonic Croswell had this in mind when he told him: "It will not be an easy task to meet the expectations of all sections, or the wishes of all aspirants." [35]

As things stood, the state Democracy teetered on the threshold of an era of violent factionalism, and, for the first time since John Quincy Adams' Administration, local chieftains looked primarily to Washington, not Albany or New York City, for support. Within Tammany, prospects looked equally hazardous. Although nativism prevented the organization from fragmenting, most practical leaders knew that because the Barnburners and Hunkers had about equal strength upstate their relative success or failure largely depended upon Tammany's balance—which could tip in either direction. Nonetheless, Polk's forthcoming spoils policy was bound to be a powerful stimulant. Politically, most uncommitted Tammanyites understood that the sure goad of patronage would ultimately force their hands. Yet, until events took shape, the General Committee steered a steady course between the extremes. But Tammany could not control its destiny. In underestimating the forces eroding the state party, the Hall soon found itself faced by problems it could not master.

As a general rule, President Polk, as his secretary of the treasury notified Elijah Purdy, aimed his patronage policy at doing "equal and exact justice to every portion of the Republican party." In order to do so, the President intended not to adhere "to any particular division or local designation of the said . . . party." [36]

In New York, Polk was anxious to establish good relations with the Barnburners without alienating the Conservatives. The badgered President-elect had made a wise choice, but his methods aggravated rather than soothed, the open discontent in the state Democracy. Despite his intentions, after a comic-opera series of inept acts, Polk found himself in the embarrassing position of having named almost a full cabinet without including one New Yorker. By and large, the fault lay with Van Buren. Silas Wright was the logical choice for secretary of state, but he declined Polk's offer in order to devote himself to local party needs. The remaining men Van Buren recommended for other cabinet posts were all admirable, yet none possessed a national following. Finally, disgusted with Van Buren and determined to have a New Yorker in his cabinet, Polk took matters into his own hands and nominated Hunker William Marcy for secretary of war. [37]

The Barnburners erupted in anger. In a private interview with the President, Van Buren's impetuous son, Smith Thompson, set a pattern for future dealings by giving Polk a tongue-lashing and warning him that the Barnburners intended to "call men & things by their right names." Despite the New Yorker's bad manners and lack of tact, the unhappy President still wished to placate Van Buren. Admitting that he might have commited an "unintentional" error, Polk pleaded for understanding and even went so far to promise that Wright, not Marcy, would be the Administration's chief state patronage officer. [38]

Polk's obvious concern for conciliation, however, failed to appease the Barnburners' anger. Radicals in both Tammany Hall and Albany reproached the President, and even Van Buren lost his normal aplomb. "If you or Mr. Flagg had been appointed Sec'y of the Treasury," he told Benjamin Butler, "we should not have any third party in this State, at least not that which is known as Conservative." [39]

In contrast, the Hunkers scarcely hid their jubilation. Croswell gave the cabinet his "warm approval," and promised the Administration full allegiance. Nonetheless, Marcy feared that the Hunkers might alienate the President by pressing their demands too vigorously. If our friends "at home" be "cautious & wary," Marcy advised an Albany business associate, the Barnburners would isolate themselves." [40]

Marcy's shrewd observations prevented the Hunkers from making a fatal error because Polk continued his equal distribution of state patronage. In fact, perhaps to ease the Barnburners' carping, he gave them the most desirable local federal jobs. He offered Benjamin Butler the post of federal district attorney, Tammanyite Elijah Purdy the surveyorship of the port, Michael Hoffman (the flaming voice of Radicalism) the naval office, and Azariah Flagg the collectorship. All accepted except Flagg, who pleaded that his state duties were too pressing. Subsequent events were to prove his refusal an egregious blunder. Even after the President's obvious conciliatory moves, the Barnburners remained bitter.[41]

While the Hunkers were equally unhappy with Polk's patronage policy, they still planned open warfare against the Barnburners. The swelling demand for the annexation of Texas, which President Tyler pushed as his apologia, gave them such an opportunity.

In New York, as in Washington, the Texas problem became the sole barometer of party loyalty. The Conservatives had no problem in choosing sides, and vocally backed the President. The Van Burenites, particularly in Tammany Hall, faced a more demanding decision. One Barnburner group, led by Bryant, sought to persuade the voters that the expansionists were fighting not so much for new territory as against the future of free labor in the United States. Another, following the O'Sullivan *Morning News* clique, waved the banners of Manifest Destiny and looked at annexation as a peculiar expression of patriotic Americanism.[42]

Encouraged by the split, the Hunkers demanded that Elijah Purdy, the new Van Burenite General Committee chairman, authorize a pro-Texas rally. Purdy immediately found himself trapped between the need to placate "the mass of our party" who favored annexation, and the need to follow the Hall's traditional Van Burenism. As he hesitated, the Hunkers took direct action and pushed through a call for a special Texas meeting. Since the weather was cold and blustery, they also routinely asked the Council of Sachems' permission to use the Long Room.[43]

The nonplussed sachems were taken off guard. Since the Adamsite challenge in 1827, the Society had been generally politically quiescent, only using its power to judge regularity three times in the next eighteen years. Even the Society's fraternalism had slowed down. It no longer celebrated Evacuation Day or George Washington's birthday. Founder's Day festivities were merely pallid echoes of past gasconades, soon to disappear, and even the florid Independence Day celebration had lost meaning. Instead, the Society made the anniversary of the Battle of New Orleans the highlight of its fraternalism. As a further index of its passive behavior, the Society had only initiated thirty-six new braves in the period from 1840 to 1845. Moreover, many former Tammanyites who had become Whigs—men such as Dudley Selden, Matthew Davis, Mordecai Noah, and Robert Swartwout—were still brothers in good standing. "The Society itself is superannuated and useless," one brave told Polk, "and very few members attend its meetings. I have known a Council of Sachems elected by 8 members." [44]

For all its lassitude, however, the Society was still a major factor in party affairs. To underscore the point, the Van Burenite Council rejected the Hunkers' application. Now, it was their turn for astonishment. Defeated for the moment, the Hunkers rescheduled their meeting for City Park despite the threatening weather. But the Society's political renaissance was a factor both sides needed to consider as each plotted future strategy.[45]

Meantime, Purdy feared that the moderates and Barnburners might isolate themselves if they misjudged the Texas fever, and he pragmatically co-sponsored the meeting. The rally was a qualified success. With Lorenzo Shepard, a young, articulate protégé of William Marcy, in the chair, Tammanyites passed resolutions calling on Congress for immediate annexation. In a separate minority report, the Barnburners accepted the party's commitment towards expansionism. But they qualified their stand by adding that the United States should only annex Texas if Mexico approved. In the uproar that followed Texas' final admission to the Union, the public momentarily lost sight of the Radicals' strategic retreat. But for the future, the Barnburners had created problems for themselves that they had scarcely anticipated.[46]

Unhappy that the Barnburners had foiled their attempt to make annexation the litmus test of loyalty to Polk, the Hunkers looked for new opportunities. Through Collector Cornelius Van Ness they found one. Van Ness, who wanted desperately to retain his job, made a deal with the Hunkers—in return for their support, he would remove Barnburners in the Custom House.

The bargain added a new dimension to local politics in the next few months. Realizing that his main problem was not so much his connection with the former Tyler Administration as the lack of organizational support, Van Ness attempted to gain leverage both through the Tammany Society and by electing his own men to the Hall's spring nominating convention. Many Tammanyites balked at both moves. Out of spite they gave the Barnburners a working majority of delegates, who in turn selected William Havemeyer, a wealthy, respectable Van Burenite sugar merchant, for mayor.[47]

Van Ness took the rebuff in stride and made the most of an admittedly poor situation. He ordered all Custom House employees to vote for Havemeyer, and levied an across-the-board assessment against them. Once he gathered the tribute, Van Ness offered to finance selected aldermanic candidates who disliked Purdy's moderation. Before the day ended, the General Committee framed an answer. It barred all of Van Ness' henchmen from the Wigwam, and instructed Alexander Vaché, the party's treasurer, not to act as an intermediary.[48]

The Whigs and their American Republican allies had their own problems. Despite some vociferous protests, the Whigs fielded an independent mayoralty ticket and adamantly opposed Harper's reelection. Given this state of uncertainty, all sides anticipated a close contest. But the canvass demonstrated Tammany's survival power. Havemeyer won easily; most of the Democratic nativists supported him. The Hall found the results for the Common Council equally encouraging. Tammany gained all but four out of thirty-four aldermanic seats; the American Republicans, none. Nativism, the *Morning News* gloated, "can never acquire more than a transitory predominance in this city, if indeed, in any part of our country." [49]

In a limited sense, O'Sullivan was correct. With their reform banners drooping, the American Republicans made one more futile bid for power, but lapsed into silence in 1847. The city's xenophobia was destined to reappear, however, and the reform question lingered on. Tammany had not solved any problems. It merely adjusted to them.[50]


As expected, Tammany's success aggravated the party's dissension. With the Barnburners in control over the mayoralty and Common Council, the Hunkers redoubled their efforts to keep Van Ness in office. Equally determined, the Van Burenites urged his immediate removal. But troubled developed when the Barnburners could not agree on who the new collector should be. Purdy, who considered himself the logical choice, ignored the Regency, armed himself with letters of recommendation from every level of municipal government, and saw Polk in person. Other Barnburners were more discreet but just as clamorous, and pushed Jonathan Coddington, a faithful ward worker, who had run for mayor the year before.

Getting rid of Van Ness proved no simple matter. The Hunkers portrayed him as a man of principle, devoted to the Baltimore Platform, efficient in operating the Custom House, and, above all, one who would not knuckle under to the power-hungry Radicals. Fernando Wood wrote Polk: "I hope you will not allow yourself to be deceived by the artificial excitement adverse to him [Van Ness] which a few, a *very* few interested men are endeavoring to create. Those who ask the change are entirely made up of 'the outs' and the bitter, malignant followers of one man." [51]

The resentful Purdy was equally busy. Hampered by the Barnburners' selection of Coddington but dependent on their continued good will, Purdy sought fresh supporters overlooked by his rivals. He found the Tammany Society. At the Council's regular monthly meeting, his backers capitalized on the absence of eleven Hunker sachems, and drew up an unprecedented recommendation that called on Polk to appoint Purdy. The eleven sachems angrily struck back. At the Council's next meeting, they passed a minority report urging the President to retain Van Ness. [52]

The Conservatives were infuriated. The Society, they howled to Polk, had no right to interfere in an intraparty patronage squabble. But far-sighted power brokers like Purdy saw the Society in a very different light. They granted that whenever the sachems had acted, the Council played the role of a stern but just defender of the party's Jeffersonian-Jacksonian covenant with the rank and file, the symbol of unity that served all honest Democrats in the same impartial manner. Outlining this attitude for Polk, Richard Lester, the Society's long-time secretary, noted that "in my recollections" nothing resembling Purdy's action had ever happened before. Thus, by keeping above the ordinary cut and thrust of day-to-day politicking, Grand Sachem James Connor added, the Society had unwittingly gained tremendous prestige because "the Society . . . seeks to avoid making public political expressions, and in any way interfering with the action of the party." As a result, except for special circumstances when it judged internal regularity, the Tammany Society merely verbalized party morality, not party policy. [53]

Purdy, in contrast, felt the Council's political potential had other possibilities. He realized that in the future the Hall's problem would be instability, not continuity. In the inevitable battle, he assumed that the Society would again serve as the link connecting the rank and file to the symbols of traditional authority. With this in mind, Purdy and men

who agreed with him added a fresh corollary to Matthew Davis' equation. The Society, above and beyond its power to determine party
unity and maintain stability, under the proper conditions could now
become the agency for transcending intraparty feuds by authoritatively
setting organizational policy.

Nevertheless, neither the Hunkers nor the Barnburners immediately
attempted to gain control over the Council of Sachems. When all the
tumult quieted over the collectorship—Cornelius Lawrence got the job
—most Democrats dismissed the Society's brief partisanship as a momentary aberration. Yet as the Society subsided into political apathy
and pursued its old fraternalism, Purdy quietly laid the groundwork
for the future.[54]

The news of Lawrence's appointment filled the Barnburners with
gloomy forebodings, as President Polk had anticipated. They welcomed
Van Ness' removal but saw little good in his successor. Yet, as Polk
had also surmised, local Radicals muted their criticism out of self-
interest until they saw the drift of Lawrence's patronage policy.[55] By
contrast, the Hunkers were elated and welcomed the new collector as
their deliverer. Again, the President had anticipated their attitude. Not
wishing to alienate upstate Barnburners, he defended his choice in a
long letter to Governor Wright. But while Wright appreciated Polk's
thoughtfulness, he retorted that the appointment would nurture the
conflict, not solve it. Patiently, the President held his temper in check
and replied that the Barnburners were spoiling for a fight where none
existed. "In your local policy I ought not & cannot do more than
express an opinion," he ended.[56]

Despite all the uproar concerning Polk's spoils policy, the patronage
question was the symbol, not the cause of Democratic factionalism.
The conditions that had brewed the difficulty had been imminent since
the Bank War. But what had begun as a legitimate dialogue over fiscal
policy now picked up additional and often extraneous factors, and
evolved into a vicious, expedient battle for raw political power. Inevitably, the unqualified possession of this power became more important than party principles. Only when Tammany could develop men,
or a man, who could get things done by somehow smothering the
causes of these problems, particularly the reformist impulse, would the
organization again achieve political stability.

For the next year, both the Hunkers and Barnburners shadow-boxed
with each other as they tried to measure what strength they still had in
the party. Essentially, the test ended in a draw. Nonetheless, the Barnburners held one major advantage. As William Marcy complained to

his close friend Horatio Seymour, who was just beginning his notable political career, "the dictators intend to fight the battle under the banner of Gov. Wright and I discover no indication on his part to dissent to their use of his name." [57]

Wright, however, suffered a paralysis of will at the moment his friends needed him the most. Perhaps it was because of his distaste for the office, or perhaps because for the first time he had to formulate policy, not implement it, that he miserably failed the test of political leadership. As a result, his prestige suffered, particularly due to his handling of the anti-rent rebellion that agitated counties along the Hudson River.[58]

At this juncture, the danger of war with Mexico flared. Although the Barnburners took pride in Van Buren's prediction of trouble if the United States annexed Mexico, they did not flaunt their prescience. When angry words erupted between the two nations, Tammany Radicals pleaded for "moderation and forebearance," and suggested that Polk "seek the mediation of some third party." Backing the President to the hilt, the militant Hunkers welcomed the conflict. The *Argus* bellowed that if Mexico "has the temerity or the folly to venture upon a declaration of war, it will be prosecuted on our part with the utmost vigor and all the means within our reach." [59]

Against this background of controversy, Tammany prepared for the fall election. While the debate between the Hunkers and Barnburners tended to obscure fears of a nativist resurgence, the moderate-dominated General Committee fought to downplay all factional differences and campaign on traditional Democratic values. The Committee found the effort painful, however. The *Morning News* did not care for the ticket, and the Hunkers led by John McKeon sought to isolate the Barnburners by suggesting that they were traitors to the President's foreign policy. But in the end, the moderates had their way.[60]

With this deceptive air of harmony, the united Democrats scored an impressive victory. They gained all thirteen assembly seats and swamped the opposition's municipal ticket. Equally important, the Barnburner-sponsored bill to modernize the state constitution passed. Now, as the principle architects of the stop-and-tax law, they planned to write its provisions into the state's basic fabric. But the Hunkers saw little good in winning. "Another such victory, and we will be defeated," Conservative banker Campbell White groaned.[61]

The election therefore settled nothing. Most uncommitted Tammany chieftains realized that their neutrality was nothing more than a holding action against inevitable polarization. But since public opinion had not yet jelled over the unseemly Conservative-Radical quarrel, they saw no sense in any premature move. But events were already conspiring against the moderates. Tammanyite Barnburners were booming Wright as Polk's successor, a move the Hunkers deplored. Above that, the question of war with Mexico made the situation more frantic.[62]

Even so, the majority of Tammanyites still strove for party peace. In order to do so, the General Committee passed a series of resolutions that it hoped would mollify both sides. To please the Hunkers, it praised Polk's foreign policy; for the Barnburners, it supported "Constitutional Reform of the state debt and 'the Policy of '42' " Tammany's Young Men's General Committee summed up these efforts. "In this city we are united and strong," it claimed. The only "effectual course" to end the "evils of dissension, is to abstain from political fellowship with those who cause the dissension, and are diligent in fanning the embers of discord in a party generally united on leading principles of harmony within itself." [63]

Mere words could not solve the Democracy's problems. But for the moment, bickering stopped while the party concentrated on the question of reform. By 1846 most practical New Yorkers realized that the 1822 constitution was an anomaly. Through inclination, or possibly educated guessing, the Barnburners captured the reform movement at the outset and carried Loco Foco egalitarianism to its logical conclusion. The *Morning News* explained that the Radicals meant "to remove as far as possible the evils of government without impairing its efficiency"; to arouse the many against the special benefits of the few; "to abolish monopolies and exclusive privileges—and to secure equal rights and exact justice to all men." In general, the Hunkers also favored modernization; they merely joined in too late to claim credit.[64]

In New York City, the nativist thrust also made reform an imperative. Again, the Barnburners and moderates struck first. By a vote of 23 to 9, the General Committee suggested some changes in the city charter designed to correct some of its obvious defects. But the Hall would not allow the reformist spirit to enter its own house. Despite mounting evidence that its primary system was a haven for criminal elements who bullied their way into power, Tammany resisted all efforts to change traditional "party usages." The General Committee's interest in reform therefore did not altogether ring true. As the anti-Tammany *Young America* noted, "previous to every election for the [past] ten years we have had municipal reform talked of in Tammany Hall, and are much further from it than at first." [65]

Paradoxically, the Constitution of 1846 marked the zenith of Barn-burner influence over the state's Democratic party. Faced with increasing Hunker resistance at every point on the political compass, the Van Burenites won temporary leverage by being the party of the people, espousing popular causes at the right time. In the city, Radical Tammanyites rode a similar crest of esteem when they limited some of the Common Council's prerogatives. But the outbreak of the Mexican War changed the game, and with it the Barnburners' rapport with the electorate.[66]

Once military action began, patriotism became compulsory. City Hunkers immediately maximized the issue for their own ends, blamed the Mexicans for provoking justified American retaliation, rallied the party around Polk's standard, and force-fed an illusion of unity. At a mass prowar rally, the *News* reported: "Democrats and Conservatives, Whigs and Natives, seemed to vie with each other in the enthusiasm of the occasion." [67]

Inevitably, Tammany's internal unity faded as the city's patriotic euphoria wore off. Goaded by the anti-Administration *New York Tribune*, the Barnburners made their positions clear. After Van Buren's Texas pronouncement, coupled with the Tammany Radicals' stand on annexation, the image they projected, even though they were not abolitionists, was that of anti–slavery extensionists. In order to maintain their political integrity and Jeffersonian principles, therefore, the *Evening Post* and *Morning News* disagreed on the need for and justice of the conflict, but closed ranks on the major issue of war aims. Bryant castigated the appeal to arms as a slaveowners' plot aimed at subverting the free states. The more low-keyed *News* concurred. While the paper called the war constitutional, proper, moral, and fought for Manifest Destiny, it nonetheless advised the Administration to exclude slave labor from all conquered territory.[68]

No such qualms bothered the Hunkers. By the internal logic of their position they backed Polk and became by association, no matter how imperfect, pro–slavery extensionists. President Polk abhorred these labels. Both sides, he confided to his diary, used extensionism as a hobby horse to get elected. As long as they did so, his Administration would play no favorites. The President's well-reasoned words aside, the New York Democrats continued to fling taunts and recriminations at each other on this basis.[69]

By the summer of 1846, the Barnburners' prestige was desperately low. As President Polk fulfilled his domestic campaign promises, his popularity increased among most New York Democrats. In the city, Tammany Hall, the Young Men's General Committee, and even the

Council of Sachems outdid each other in praising Polk's devotion to party ideals. Under these conditions, it was totally unthinkable for the Van Burenites to attack him.

Impelled to agree publicly with an Administration and war they privately despised, the Radicals made Governor Silas Wright the incarnation of their aspirations and seriously began to boom him for the presidency. This strategy had one flaw: Wright first had to win re-election. But the Hunkers wanted no part of him. On hearing that some Conservatives might support Wright because of "party usages," Edwin Croswell warned: "I take it for granted our friends will find themselves overreached." [70]

Tammany Hall mirrored the Barnburners' malaise. On the one hand, the Radicals narrowly controlled the General Committee, Mayor Andrew Mickle ostensibly favored them, and all signs indicated Governor Wright's undiminished popularity. Obscuring these advantages, however, were the Hunkers' wealth and political connections with the Administration. As an indication of such leverage, their refusal to aid in Wright's campaign all but precluded the Hall's ability to turn out the voters. Moreover, when several prominent Hunkers refused to subsidize the faltering *Morning News,* the paper lapsed into bankruptcy. Worse, the governor's enigmatic stand on the war disappointed many patriotic Tammanyites. Clearly, with November approaching, the Democracy had lost its vitality. [71]

President Polk learned of the Hunkers' attitude toward Wright just before the election, and arranged a top-level party conference to aid the New York party. But nothing could save the governor. He did carry the city with 51 percent of the votes cast, but his plurality fell far short of expectations. Worse, his running mate, Addison Gardiner, actually out-polled him.

Both factions interpreted the defeat in terms of their own prejudices. The Hunkers quickly absolved themselves of blame. They placed the onus for the debacle on the "unholy alliance between the Whigs & Anti-Renters," the lack of party harmony "arising from the proscriptive course pursued by our leading friends at Albany," and the "unreasonableness of the leadership press," and implied that Wright's loss actually strengthened the Administration's policy. The Barnburners were furious. Despite Wright's relief, his friends reasoned that a crisis was at hand—a crisis nurtured by Polk's patronage policy. "Thus you see, Gov. Wright had indeed ingloriously fallen," one upstater angrily wrote Polk, "not for any thing he has done, but from circumstances over which he had no control." Equally incensed, another party worker cried: "The General Government made its appointments & in almost every instance, men were taken, designedly to oppose Silas Wright. Consequently what was called *Hunkerism* became a *faction*." [72]

Many orthodox Tammanyites, regardless of factional ties, also anguished over Wright's failure—but for very different reasons. The Hall's first rule of politics was organizational regularity; once a duly authorized convention nominated a candidate, traditional party rules demanded strict compliance and fidelity. Bicker in private, Tammanyites agreed, but close ranks in public. When the Hunkers deserted Wright, they legitimatized insubordination and diminished the General Committee's authority. This situation, Tammany chieftains felt, boded no good for the future.

Wright's loss diminished the Barnburners' hesitancy to attack Polk directly. Positive that he had masterminded the defeat, they sought some legitimate means to criticize the Administration, some issue to rally all anti-Polk Democrats. Luckily, the issues were at hand: extensionism, the Mexican War, and the slaveocracy's purported sinister designs on western lands.[73]

Professional cynics of American political life had a field day scoffing at the Barnburners' sudden solicitude for antisouthernism. Be it for revenge, punishing the Hunkers, or laying the groundwork for Martin Van Buren's next try for the presidency, these scoffers postulated only naked, ugly expediency in the Radicals' attitude.

Tammany Hall's callous treatment of free blacks in New York City added credence to such an attitude. But while it was true that the Hall exemplified the prejudices of its day, strong political realities underlay its refusal to champion the cause of the American Negro, both in the North and in the South. On constitutional grounds, many states' rights Tammanyites assumed that the federal government lacked the power to interfere with the domestic institutions of any Southern state. On business grounds, New York City commercial and maritime interests did not wish to incur Southern wrath by criticizing slavery, forfeiting in the process the city's booming credit and trade arrangements with proslavery customers.

As for local free blacks, even Tammany's most outspoken Negrophobes granted that these people lived under deplorable conditions, enjoyed few civil rights, and lacked opportunities for social advancement. But unlike Irish or German immigrants, who often shared the same initial disadvantages as the blacks, Tammany did not cater to them in order to win their votes.

The factors that buttressed the Hall's approach lay less in prejudice than in political realism, however. The state constitution of 1846, like its predecessor, did not lift property qualifications from free blacks. As a result, in 1845 only 255 Negroes were qualified to vote out of total population of 12,913. Ten years later, the black population declined to 11,840, only 100 of whom could vote. If anything, such a falling rate of population, coupled with the white public's apathy toward blacks, convinced Tammany that white supremacy, not abolitionism, was the wave of the future.

Not all Democrats accepted such negativism. Some Tammanyites argued that if the blacks had the same political rights as whites, they might vote as the Hall determined. In answer, other Tammanyites pointed out that most free blacks were either Whigs or belonged to the Liberty party. Even if the Hall helped to lift the bonds of discrimination, these Democrats countered, little evidence existed that the blacks would shift their loyalty to Tammany Hall. Rather than try to change the situation, then, Tammany followed the course of least resistance, ignored its moral obligations, and gave the blacks little sympathy for their peculiar problems.[74]

Free-soil barnburnerism, however, based itself not on political expediency, antisouthernism, or abolitionism as its detractors assumed. Instead, its approach was deeply rooted in the Democratic party's tradition. As practicing Jeffersonians, the Van Burenites felt the nation's destiny lay in the hands of rugged, incorruptible, white yeoman farmers. Let slavery continue where it exists, the Barnburners insisted. Like most men of their generation, they accepted the notion that blacks could not coexist with free labor. On the extensionism question, the Van Burenites were consistent, despite what their enemies cared to believe. In the past, the Albany Regency had based its national alliance on the New York–Virginia axis and worked in tandem with the Southern Democrats. But the Regency had not supported slavery extension, although it necessarily had hedged its opposition with political obfuscations. Prior to the annexation of Texas and the Mexican War, such tactics had worked simply because extensionism was largely an academic question. Events now made such a policy obsolete. The critical difference, as Silas Wright explained to John Dix, was that in the past most Americans, including slaveowners, considered slavery an evil, "an inheritance from their colonial ancestors" forced upon them by Great Britain's "wicked colonial policy." The Barnburners therefore respected the South's dilemma, and "insisted upon their full and quiet enjoyment of their Constitutional right in regard to such property." This, he continued, the Northern Democracy would always do, "if the South does not ask them to go beyond this point; but it is manifest as the light of day that no part, and no party, of the free states will consent that territory be purchased, or conquered, to extend this institution to countries where it does not, and cannot, now Constitutionally exist." Here was the heart of free-soil barnburnerism.[75]

By February 1847, gathering storm warnings on the political horizon compromised Tammany's policy of restraint. In Washington, Congressman Preston King tied the Wilmot Proviso—which proposed that any territory that the United States might acquire from Mexico should forever be closed to slavery—to an Administration appropriation bill. In the city, the Hunkers relentlessly pressed their advantage and sparked a series of prowar meetings in each ward. Using patriotism as a catchall theme, the Hunkers demanded that Tammany Hall unequivocally endorse the war and publicly condemn the Proviso.

The General Committee, particularly the Radical committeemen, faced a difficult choice. By Hunker standards, to be prowar, pro-Polk, and anti-Proviso was synonymous with patriotism; only traitors took other stands. "Notwithstanding the disputes of the politicians," Addison Gardiner noted, "there is a strong . . . feeling in favor of a vigorous prosecution of the war." As public opinion swung away from them, Tammany Barnburners became more and more convinced that the only way in which they could maintain their position was to back the war but persuade the General Committee to endorse the Proviso. The Hunkers refused the compromise. Mordecai Noah, now back in their good graces, editorialized in his struggling *Sunday Times and Noah's Weekly Messenger* that "such collateral issues should be scouted by every true-hearted American. Put your shoulders to the wheel, conquer a peace, and then talk of the past or the future." Moreover, the Tammany Society dropped its neutrality and agreed with the Hunkers: "Resolved, that the actions of the President merits, and receives, the confidence of the members of this Society, as evincing a due regard to the national Interest and honor." [76]

Over the Barnburners' objections, then, the Hunkers forced the General Committee to approve of the war without mentioning the Proviso. Meeting separately, the recalcitrant Radicals tried to recover some lost ground by endorsing the Committee's stand, while at the same time emphasizing the Proviso—all to no avail. Clearly, Tammany moderates and the majority of sachems would not condemn a Democratic war waged by a Democratic Administration.

The approaching municipal election did little to reverse the Hall's drift into Hunkerism. At the convention they nominated J. Sherman

Brownell, a well-known Marcyite businessman, for mayor. The Barnburners now faced a distasteful situation. Deeply repelled by the
Hunker ticket, many impetuous Van Burenites advocated a third, independent slate. Such a course was unthinkable, however, in light of their
recent oratory about the sacredness of party usages. Instead, they decided to give Brownell cursory support and contest the Hunkers in
the aldermanic contests. Thus, if Brownell lost, the Hunkers would lose
tremendous prestige, while if the Radicals won in the wards, they could
dominate the Corporation. But once the Barnburners' plot took shape,
they lost control. Ten rival Tammany tickets blossomed in the eighteen
wards, with no less than twenty-six men running for office. The upshot
was that the Whigs easily won the mayoralty and gained working control over the Common Council.[77]

Wild recriminations filled the air in Tammany Hall. The *Evening
Post*, now the Barnburners' only voice in the city, openly threatened
insurgency. "If the nominations are not reformed, the party in this city
will be dissolved," editor Bryant snapped. Let the malcontents leave,
the Hunkers taunted. Tammany would be well off without them. From
the sidelines, the independent *New York Herald*, although generally
sympathetic towards Hunkerism, disagreed with both Democratic factions, and claimed that the Whigs won because of the voters' unhappiness with "the enormous increase of our city taxes, together with the
filthy conditions of the streets during the year past." [78]

When all the tumult ended, most Tammanyites realized the hard
fact that the organization could not pick sides without further col-
lapsing party lines. Above that, with the Whigs in power, the General
Committee dared not risk any fragmentation. As things stood, the Hall,
whether it wanted to or not, lacked any option but to again work for
party peace.

The organization's practical decision did not satisfy militants in
either camp. During the summer, therefore, both factions hoped for
some breakthrough that would eliminate the other. But, again, a stalemate developed. As a result, the fall state convention became a critical
testing ground.

The Barnburners prepared a three-pronged attack. First, they continued to boom Silas Wright, both as a man and as a symbol, for the
presidency. Next, Bryant sought to reduce all distinctions between
the Barnburners, Hunkers, and Whigs to one common denominator:
slavery extensionism. Loudly calling on all honest men to take a stand,
he forecast that the issue was "one in which the members will not vote
according to any present association." Finally, John Van Buren, who
was rapidly moving to the forefront of his faction, intended to form "a

sound radical" ticket, "headed at all hazards & by all means by Mr. Flagg." [79]

Beyond all other considerations, Wright's candidacy would be the foundation for all Barnburner hopes. But Wright was a shell of his former greatness. Retired from office, he had gone home to Canton, back to the soil. Tired, spent, drained of ambition, he hoped to stay away from politics for the rest of his life. But this could not be—his party needed him. On August 27, nature intervened. He suffered a fatal heart attack, and the Barnburners' hopes plummeted.

The first shattering days after his death united all the discordant elements within the Democracy in silent communion. But the accord could not last. The Barnburners blamed Wright's death on the Hunkers and demanded that the state convention purge his crypto-assassins. Hunker editor Croswell viewed the former governor's demise with mixed feelings. Sad at losing an old friend, he nevertheless felt that "it prostrates the hopes of the Wilmot Proviso faction; & much as the event is to be deplored, must paralyze its kindred faction here." [80]

As the lack of agreement among party leaders widened, Tammany-ites struggled to define some trends in public opinion. They found none. Sharply divided in policy and mentality, the Hall could not even agree on which men to send to the convention. Though the Radicals made a dogged effort to control the delegation, the Hunkers held the majority, ten to six, with three contested seats open.

The 1847 Syracuse Convention set a pattern that persisted for the next seventeen years. The delegates fought over which Tammany dele-gates were legitimate representatives, clashed over candidates, disagreed on policy, and refused all compromises. At another level, all Barnburner efforts came to naught. The Hunkers halted their efforts to trigger the natural sympathy over the fallen Wright, the delegates approved the Administration's war policy, shouted down the Wilmot Proviso, and drew up a state ticket without naming Azariah Flagg for comptroller. These moves forced the Barnburners into apostasy. Shattering party usages, they held an independent convention, framed a platform around the Proviso, and decided to send a complete delegation to the national party convention in order to force it to decide which faction repre-sented the New York Democracy.[81]

Now that the party had formally split, the major uncertainty in Democratic politics rested on what action Tammany's temporarily quiescent rank and file would take. Both groups prepared with elaborate care. Each sent orators into the wards in order to explain the situation; each held city-wide rallies to garner mass popular support. But the Hunkers held one high card the Barnburners lacked: the insurgent

Radicals had directly challenged the party's durability and tight-knit discipline by running a third ticket. Noah wrote: "A house divided against itself must fall; and if the ticket is to be defeated, it would have been more generous, more in consonance with sound principles and established usages, and political systems, to have allowed it to be defeated *sub silento*, than for the *leaders* of the party—those who have lived on regular nominations all their lives to have strangled those nominations openly." [82]

In the end, the Hunkers tapped a vast party reservoir of sympathy for their position. What bothered many Tammanyites, as Noah anticipated, was the Barnburners' callousness toward party usages: a principle that the Hall cherished as an article of faith. The upshot of this feeling was that both the Tammany Society and the General Committee scorned the Radicals and lent the Hunkers their services. Castigated as traitors and severely outmaneuvred in the wards, the Barnburners had failed to capture the masses' imagination and were losing precious momentum. [83]

The election results failed to dim the Barnburners' revolt. They had gone too far and said too much for a graceful retreat, even if they wanted one, which they did not. In those wards where the Van Burenites directly challenged the Hunkers, the Whigs managed to slip ahead of both. Upstate, the same situation occurred. For the exuberant Bryant, then, the returns proved that the Barnburners held the balance of power. Moreover, part of their over-all goal—punishment of the Hunkers at the polls—had been achieved.

Everything now depended on what actions the national party would take on the New York situation. The Barnburners rested their case on antiextensionism. Flagg reasoned that the defeat of the Hunker ticket proved "that a dough-face [a proslavery Northerner] cannot get the vote of this State for President in 1848. And no one can get it who is not for free elections." [84]

The Hunkers were just as busy on the hustings. Following the State Central Committee's call for a convention to select national convention delegates, they rejected any notion of a compromise. Croswell felt that they had "the right & strength of position," and saw no sense in yielding "for the purpose of enabling the . . . disorganisers to escape from a position which they had found intolerable." [85]


At the beginning of 1848, the drift of city politics was as unclear as ever. The Barnburners briefly gained an advantage when Van Burenite Robert Maclay was named chairman by the ward committeemen. But in a series of meetings scattered throughout January, the Hall's various subcommittees continually bickered over the war, the Proviso, which state delegation the rank and file favored, and anything else that came to mind. As an indication of how this chorus of invective and abuse distorted the organization's stability, both sides held simultaneous rallies at the Wigwam despite warnings from the Council of Sachems. When both meetings ended, a large group of boisterous men retired to the taproom on the building's first floor. Amid the usual conviviality, an undercurrent of violence flowed. Suddenly, a few Hunkers began shouting that the "d——d traitors" should be bounced out of the room. The alert *Herald* reported, "a general outbreak was momentarily expected, which, however, did not take place" because of the arrival of the police.[86]

All these developments placed the Tammany Society in an uncomfortable position. As it became increasingly clear that the Council of Sachems would again have to judge regularity, individual sachems tried to come to terms with the party's changing realities. On the face of things, most sachems leaned toward Hunkerism and scorned the Barnburners' lack of reverence for party traditions. But the amazing fluidity of the city's political scene, the lack of any discernible trend, made the Council's task of choosing the eventual winner extremely difficult. For the time being, then, the Society did nothing.[87]

Upstate, conditions were similarly complicated. Both factions hoped that the national party would intervene and settle the question, but many astute observers of the passing scene doubted that outsiders could unravel the chaotic pattern of state politics. William Marcy, the symbol of New York Hunkerism, observed that "things appear to be worsening in the state of N. Y. The division is widening & the disposition to break asunder becoming more confirmed. From a transcient [*sic*] passion it is widening into an enduring affliction." John Van Buren more than fulfilled Marcy's gloomy prophesy. "Prince John" wrote to a friend, "I shall pursue the course which I deem best calculated to ensure the freedom in the territories now free & to publish a list of names who came into power by accident but will go out by design." Many Hunkers were equally narrowminded. One wrote Polk: "The proud majority this State once gave has been sacrificed at the footstool of Van Burenism & treason to the Democracy." [88]

Historically, the New York party's reputation for fragmenting, then healing, was part of American political folklore. But the Barnburner-Hunker schism defied all precedents. Mordecai Noah knew this well enough: "Mr. Clay used to say, that the democracy of New York always quarrelled fiercely until they got to the threshold of the presidential election, and then they made friends and closed ranks. We apprehend, however, that the pitcher has gone once too often to the well." [89]

In this maelstrom of hatred, emotionalism, and selfishness, party unity was impossible. When the Hall's mayoralty nominating convention opened, near-anarchy reigned. Through twelve fruitless ballots, the delegates failed to name a candidate. Finally, on the thirteenth, the weary Tammanyites selected former mayor William Havemeyer, currently a Barnburner delegate to the Baltimore Convention. Wisely, the Van Burenites hoped to use their foothold in the organization to maximum advantage by downplaying national issues and running solely on local concerns such as reform and municipal fiscal responsibility. By so doing, Noah observed, the Barnburners negated any excuse for Hunker opposition, and forced them to swallow Havemeyer "and all his sugar-pans." The Conservatives were not bluffed; cooperation was impossible. "The greatest possible confusion prevailed," the *Herald* reported, "and the crowd when called upon to adjourn to the house of Mr. Havemeyer and congratulate him, cried out, 'd——n Havemeyer, we'll go the whig before him.' " [90]

The Hunkers carried this spirit into the campaign. Outside of the race for mayor, they opposed Barnburners in all the ward elections. Almost nightly, bands of hotheaded partisans roved through the precincts extolling the particular qualifications of their champions. Yet the embittered combatants were setting an invisible but dangerous precedent. A conflict which sprang out of an effort to control Tammany was now being reduced to a battle that might destroy it. All was confusion. "Do not be surprised if we are defeated," Hunker Fernando Wood wrote. "There is a strong opposition to our nominee for Mayor —He is one of the most bitter of Barnburners who thinks there is no other man in the country but Mr. V. Buren." [91]

Havemeyer won. But the Hunkers achieved startling victories in the aldermanic races and dominated the new Corporation. More hazardous to Barnburner hopes, the Hunkers gained control over Tammany's Naturalization Committee. With these political missiles exploding around them, then, the shattered Radicals faced a gloomy future.[92]

Like most professionals, Martin Van Buren held bunglers in contempt. So far, the Barnburners had fallen into that category. Passing the winter in New York City at Julian's Hotel, near his son John's law office, he grew increasingly restive. Whether he meant to or not, Van Buren dropped his cryptic air as his friends floundered.

Well aware that defensive politicians lose, Van Buren advised the Radicals' board of strategy to carry their case directly to the electorate and, through them, to the convention. Early in February he gave Samuel Tilden a rough draft of a far-ranging manifesto that outlined the Barnburners' substantive differences with the Hunkers. After Tilden and John Van Buren applied needed literary polish, along with some added paragraphs for clarification, their allies in the legislature adopted it as their official policy address to the voters.

What emerged was a major restatement of Jeffersonian principles in an expansionist world. Starting with John Van Buren's succinct resumé of recent state politics, the manifesto passed on to Martin Van Buren's exposition. The Wilmot Proviso, he claimed, was sound party doctrine, deeply rooted in Jefferson's Northwest Ordinance of 1787. Calling attention to the Founding Fathers' apathy towards slavery, he cited a lengthy list of court precedents to back his argument that Congress indeed had the power to exclude slavery from new territories. For the slaveowners' case, he said, "we are satisfied, and we believe that the judgment of impartial posterity will decide, that if the Democracy of the North have erred at all, it has never been in not going sufficiently far to sustain their fellow-citizens of the South." [93]

Tilden's short section came next. Briefly, he summarized the current state of New York politics. Martin Van Buren ended the address on an upswing. Free labor and slave labor could not coexist, he contended. "Where labor is to a considerable extent committed to slaves, to labor becomes a badge of inferiority." The future of the United States rested on free-soilism, open to immigrant and native white yeoman farmers. The great agrarian promise of the American West was too precious a heritage for time-serving expediency. The Baltimore Convention thus faced a momentous choice: the free-soilism of enlightened Jeffersonianism, or the suffocating narrowness implicit in slavery. To do justice to party principles, then, the delegates had but one live option: the "cause of freedom" that the Barnburners exemplified.[94]

For all his militancy, Martin Van Buren never considered himself a presidential candidate. He did not seek the office, nor did he want it. But his denials weakened the Barnburners, for without a national standard-bearer they lacked a rallying point. In fact, the public examined the Barnburners more closely for their party sins than their Jeffersonian virtues. This situation upset John Van Buren. Galled at the bitterness of men like James Gordon Bennett, who excoriated the Radicals in practically every edition, Prince John wanted to strike out and throttle his enemies. He felt that his father should enter the race "as the choice of the Democracy of this state," and that if the convention rebuffed him, the Barnburners should then bolt the party and form an independent ticket.[95]

Martin Van Buren administered parental reproof. The Barnburners needed caution, he counseled, in order to avoid the charge that revenge, not principles, motivated them. Yet the years had not dulled his political acuity. Masterminding Radical tactics, he wrote his son that if the convention did not accept the delegation on equal footing with all the other state delegations, they should stage a walkout and justify the move by "placing this rejection distinctly upon the ground of opposition to the extension of Slavery to the free territories." That done, the Barnburners should blackball the national ticket and select a presidential candidate solely to run in New York. If, on the other hand, the convention did admit the Barnburners on their own terms, they should support firm Jacksonians for the presidency—men such as Thomas Hart Benton of Missouri. But, if the delegates nominated an unsuitable man, party regularity demanded that the Barnburners carry their load, with the qualification that they would not be responsible for the results.[96]

Meanwhile, the Hunkers prepared their own strategy. By cultivating Lewis Cass of Michigan, the leading preconvention favorite, and stressing their ties to the Administration, they planned to force the disgruntled Radicals either to accept the party's will or face ignominious defeat.[97]

Baltimore thronged with many diverse types of people—as if there was the realization that, for the first time, a Democratic convention was coming to grips with a question, the extensionism of slavery, that was to become the pivot of American political history for almost the next two decades. Noah took his place among them. "We never knew Baltimore to be more hot and crowded than it was; we never saw a convention composed of more distinguished men; and we never saw hotels so dreadfully crowded; or more mint juleps consumed, more cigars smoked, or more money lost at brag. We had in our chamber seven beds full of awful snorers. Many of the sleepers came in about two in the morning, and talked politics."

In this atmosphere the delegates deliberated the New York Democracy's fate. The drama was actually settled far in advance of the first session when the Credentials Committee, by a vote of 15 to 14, adopted a resolution that requested each New York faction to pledge its loyalty to the as yet unnamed ticket, no matter what it might be. The Barn-burners refused. "The delegates of the democracy of New York," Churchill Cambreleng said, "must be admitted to the Baltimore convention unconditionally or not at all." In marked contrast, the Hunkers accepted the Committee's terms.

When the chairman opened the question for floor debate, Senator Daniel Dickinson, speaking for the Hunkers, and John Smith, an upstate Barnburner, engaged in a violent shouting match that underlined the difficult choice the delegates faced. If they did not accept the Barnburners on full terms, they would bolt the party; if the delegates did accept them, the party would be tacitly accepting the Wilmot Proviso. On the other hand, the Hunkers were loyal Democrats and it would be poor politics to punish them for their obedience to President Polk's Administration. Stymied, the uncomfortable delegates took the easy way out. In a futile bid to restore party harmony, they proposed that the convention accept both New York delegations on equal terms. The Barnburners withdrew at once, and returned home to an uncertain public.[98]

## ✄ **10** ✄

# Division, Reunion, and the
# Tammany Society

FOR THE embattled New York Democracy, the election of 1848 revolved around the problem of organization. For the insurgent Barnburners in particular, it was a time for a change in the game, played
with different rules. The Van Burenites, the *Herald* clearly saw, "must
. . . assume a bold front, adopt a new course, and hoist their standard
anew." [1]

The Barnburners were prepared to do just this. After publishing a
pamphlet that explained the reasoning behind their bolt, they called for
a special convention to nominate a presidential candidate to run solely
in New York State. Their plans were detailed. To coordinate activities,
they established a five-man central committee, located in Albany, and
formed a correspondence committee. Next, they organized the Jeffersonian Free League in the city, on a ward-to-ward basis, as an extra-
organizational pressure group to establish their legitimacy and counter
the Hunkers' control of the Corporation. But while launching their
efforts, the Radicals left two matters of the highest priority undeter-
mined: control of Tammany Hall, and a suitable presidential candidate.

As practical politicians, the Barnburners understood that without
the Hall's formidable ability to turn out the voters, free-soilism would
fail. The Hunkers also realized this, and called on the General Committee to schedule an immediate special meeting to ratify the Lewis
Cass national ticket. Ordinarily, Van Burenite Chairman Robert Maclay
could have delayed the call. But unmindful of the need for haste, he
took a side-trip to Washington and arrived home the day after the
Hunkers had issued their demand. "This knocks in the head, our proposed meeting for tomorrow night," Benjamin Butler, the acting Barn-

burner state chairman, complained, "or any other public meeting here. After this disgraceful submission to the General Committee, and the surrender of Tammany Hall, it would not be possible to bring together people enough to give any weight or influence to the meeting." [2]

Other politicians, who knew the local scene far better than Butler, however, realized that Tammany Hall was too precious a prize to forfeit without a fight. They decided, then, to have an independent rally. On June 6, several thousand New Yorkers, some Hunkers included, heard Cambreleng, Butler, and John Van Buren assail the Cass ticket and endorse the Wilmot Proviso. The Hunkers stormed back. They imported a group of national leaders led by Cass, Sam Houston, and Thomas Hart Benton, who pleaded with the Barnburners to remain in the party and reform it from within rather than indirectly electing a Whig as president.[3]

Few Barnburners paid attention. Instead, they traveled the road that led toward a third party. But almost at once they hit a roadblock. Martin Van Buren, the only man capable of dramatizing their cause, refused to accept a nomination. City Radicals would not take his no for an answer. On June 16, on behalf of the Jeffersonian Free League, a group of insurgent Tammanyites pressed him to throw his hat into the ring.

His reply was a study in evasion. Eloquently, he pictured his happy retirement—but then made a subtle change in emphasis. "It is not in my nature to decline a compliance with any request which such men are capable of making," he added in his tortured prose, "except for reasons of the strongest character, which they themselves will on further consideration approve." Although his eager supplicants could interpret his Delphian statement in several ways, however, his party needed him and he could not refuse. "I do not see anything in the constitution which enables you to forbid our voting for you," Prince John wrote in closing the matter.[4]

Even so, the Barnburners grimly faced up to Van Buren's heavy political liabilities. In order to avoid any charge that they were interested in revenge, they nominated him on an orthodox platform of Democratic principles, excepting two points: the Wilmot Proviso and a plank calling for a Homestead Act. In regard to slavery, they once again denied any abolitionist leanings; nor did they attempt to reconcile morality and free-soilism. Rather, by making the campaign a question of free versus slave labor, they cleared Van Buren, or so they hoped, from Hunker vilification.[5]

The Hunkers wasted little time in shattering Barnburner illusions.

As an indication of their mood, Dickinson wrote Cass that "I know his [Van Buren's] vengeful appetite had eaten up his good sense. I did not suppose however that it has also abandoned the great leading feature of his character—low cunning, but this is gone too, and he is left like an old lecher with all his hurts, but destitute of power." More to the point, the Hunkers called on both Polk and Collector Lawrence to eliminate the Barnburners from all appointive jobs. Even the *Democratic Review*, a long-time supporter, turned on Van Buren. The Zachary Taylor-oriented *Herald* had the last word. Editor Bennett, who had been nursing a grudge against Van Buren for thirteen years, roasted him as "a cold-blooded, ambitious, revengeful and dishonest man." [6]

When all these recriminations were sorted out, one fact emerged. Van Buren, like DeWitt Clinton in 1812, was an apostate. The General Committee, however, could not solve the paradox. To some men, the preservation of the local party, as Van Buren had advocated in 1812, outweighed all other considerations. Others stressed that Cass' contention that the people actually living in the disputed territories should determine slavery's fate was pure Jeffersonian. Still others admired Van Buren's courage, or felt that free-soilism made both practical and ideological sense. At the July meeting, then, the real issue in full Committee—whether or not to support Van Buren—raised uncomfortable questions. The Hall had no answer: eighteen men were pro-Cass, two favored Van Buren, but five refused to vote and twenty-five were absent. Nevertheless, the Hunkers blithely assumed that they had Tammany in tow and used the General Committee's prestige to demand that Mayor Havemeyer fire all Barnburners from municipal employ.

Yet the Hunkers did not control the organization. As in 1824, 1827, and 1838, there was really no "Tammany Hall," but only various splinter groups, each with partial legitimacy. While the Hunkers were momentarily in command and removed Maclay as chairman, the Van Burenites formed a second General Committee to represent the city's "uncontaminated Democracy." Under these conditions, the Tammany Society became the critical element for both sides.[7]

But the sachems were baffled, and out of their bafflement grew frustration. Their difficulty stemmed from the Barnburners' growing rebellion aimed at orthodox party traditions. In August, their insurgency had spilled out into a national movement, the Free Soil party, based on a new Northern-Western coalition, pledged to the idea that true freedom rested on Jeffersonian principles. Among its leaders were ordinarily stalwart Democrats, abolitionists of the Gerrit Smith type, and young idealists who were just coming of age politically. Once more the party nominated Van Buren over his somewhat passive objections.

That done, city Van Buren Tammanyites scrapped the Jeffersonian Free League, built the Jeffersonian Free Soil League on its foundation, captured the Hall's Young Men's General Committee, and, bursting with excitement, challenged the Hunkers to try and break up their first mass meeting. The bravado paid off. The Hunkers' chosen instrument for disrupting the rally was Mike Walsh's Spartan Club. But the Free Soilers hired their own bully boys, met the Club fist for fist, and drove it from the field.[8]

The situation called for boldness, but the Council of Sachems met it with hedging. As events took shape, the sachems reasoned that because they could not stem the tide of battle, their best idea would be to drift with it until they saw which faction was the strongest. Proper timing was essential—but the formation of the Free Soil party radically restructured the sachems' options. Unlike its earlier choices, the Council could not distinguish which side had a greater degree of legitimacy. Divining the impossibility of choosing between them, the sachems sought the easy way out. The Council, by a vote of 9 to 7, with 8 absentees, refused a Hunker request for exclusive use of the Long Room. But at the same time, the Council rejected a Free-Soiler application to meet in the Wigwam "on the ground that their general political character was different from the general political character of the Democratic General Committee." In effect, the Tammany Society remained neutral.

Both factions were understandably furious. John Cisco, who had replaced Maclay as chairman of the original General Committee, attacked his fellow sachems as men who had "forfeited all claims to the confidence of the democratic party of the State and the Union." Conversely, the *Evening Post*, while taunting the Hunker sachems, realized that the Council had indirectly boosted the Free Soilers' prestige by not making any selection and treating them as Democratic equals. In this vein, Bryant wrote: the Barnburners "are the strong and great party which elected Mr. Havemeyer . . . , and the society of Tammany would have justly incurred the public condemnation if they had done otherwise than to recognize it as the true democratic party of New York." [9]

By September, the Free Soil party had peaked and began to lose momentum. The city Clay Whigs under lawyer Daniel Ullman, on whom the Barnburners had counted for help, instead reluctantly supported Zachary Taylor and his running mate, Millard Fillmore of Buffalo. Then, when Benjamin Butler actively joined the Free Soil party's

"Campaign for Freedom," President Polk removed him from office. The Hunkers immediately flooded the White House with demands for a thorough housecleaning.

Paradoxically, such vindictiveness temporarily halted the dwindling of the Free Soilers' fortunes. Although Collector Lawrence was anxious to take vigorous action against "any violent partisan opposed to Cass," he was a proud and independent man who resented the Hunkers' overbearing impertinence. The upshot of the affair was that while he did make some token dismissals, he fired far more Hunkers. Before the Free Soilers could enjoy their reprieve, the death of Naval Officer Michael Hoffman deprived them of one of their ablest leaders. His replacement, C. S. Bogardus, a John Tyler–Hunker Democrat, levied a tax on clerks, and used his patronage to dismiss as many Free Soilers as possible.[10]

The Hunkers encountered similar difficulties. The General Committee's bureaucracy was Van Burenite, and the Hunkers had simply not developed an upper echelon group of comparable ability. Their future leaders were still in basic training. As one disgruntled Hunker reminisced a year later, in 1848 "[we were] as a flock of sheep without a shepherd—and at that, most literally surrounded by a pack of wolves —the doctrine of Regular Nominations having been thrown to the winds—there seemed nothing to rally one—and no opinion, no voice potential to lead, to rally, or to command." [11]

By November both Democratic parties publicly expected to win, but privately were caught in a nightmarish predicament. Each was so intent on defeating the other that the Whigs slipped ahead of both. Zachary Taylor carried the city with 55 percent of the total votes cast, Cass gained 36 percent, while Martin Van Buren limped badly with only 9 percent. Tammany Hall, counting both factions, lost its entire congressional ticket to the Whigs, and only one Van Burenite, David Dudley Field, made a respectable showing. More embarrassing, they elected just one local municipal candidate. Upstate, the Free Soilers ran slightly better but not well enough: Taylor carried the state; John Dix lost the gubernatorial election. From any angle, the Barnburners had suffered a deep and humiliating rout.[12]

In spite of fading dreams, the Van Burenites refused to face reality. "We have laid the foundation of a mighty party," the *Post* boasted lamely, "with a great principle for its basis." The reasons behind the Free Soilers' defeat, the Barnburners lamented, lay with President Polk's local appointees. Bryant insisted that vengeful Administration Hunkers forced three to five thousand Tammanyites, who worked in the Custom

House, Post Office, Marshal's Office, and the Navy Yard to make the choice between voting for Cass or forfeiting their jobs.[13]

Despite the editor's brave attempt to make the best of free-soilism's loss, Taylor's election carried its own obvious imperatives. Locked out of federal patronage and in danger of losing control over the city, both Tammany factions needed each other. The question now became how a compromise could be effected without either losing face. James Buchanan, Polk's secretary of state, attempted to remedy the situation, but his efforts failed. Only local politicos, using local issues, could restore peace in the New York Democratic party.

The possibility of a reunion was much closer than campaign hyperbole might have led many unsophisticated voters to suspect. Although the Free Soilers and the Cass Hunkers claimed to represent divergent views on slavery extensionism, their basic Jeffersonianism differed only in rhetoric, not substance. Although the Barnburners sincerely championed the Wilmot Proviso, Cass's doctrine of squatter sovereignty, in practical terms, eminently served the same end. As a result, Jabez Hammond, now a Free Soiler, pointed out to Horatio Seymour that very little save personal hurts hindered party reunion. Moreover, many pragmatic men like Azariah Flagg realized that neither faction was wholly wrong, nor wholly right.[14]

Many other Democrats, however, were not so sure that a party conciliation was desirable. Upstate extremists on the left and right wanted to destroy each other for a variety of reasons. Edwin Croswell, for one, felt that the party could not survive unless it dropped its agrarian preoccupations. Senator Dickinson, who had completely absorbed the Regency's shibboleths, assumed that the party should purge the Barnburners because of their disregard for traditional party usages. Preston King, and others like him, argued that the Democracy should reorder its priorities and take a forthright stand on slavery. The same idea held true in the city. Many Hunkers, confident that they controlled Tammany Hall, were convinced that they thus possessed the local organization's "power of sympathy, old associations, and numbers." Consequently, John Dix noted that the Hunkers felt they had a further advantage because the party which dominated the Hall "has always so decided a predominance in numbers that all minor divisions are either swallowed up or presented to the public under the aspect of secession." In the other camp, many Barnburners, like Bryant, were unwilling to accept an accommodation unless the party paid Free Soil its proper due.[15]

One more local problem existed. Standing on the threshold of party leadership, a youthful, ambitious group of expedient politicians paused briefly before grasping for the reins of power. More concerned with winning office than maintaining party principles, they considered thorny questions like municipal reform or slavery extensionism as vehicles for their own ends. The Free Soil insurgency had fired their imagination; the Democracy's defeat merely whetted their appetite. "That there may be, and will be, an entire reorganization of the Democratic party," Mordecai Noah wisely predicted, "is certain; but it will be under different men than those who have hitherto controlled its destinies." [16]

Fernando Wood was such a man. In an era of flamboyant politicians he was by far the most flamboyant. Not a neutral character by temperament and training, his contemporaries either blindly adored him or despised everything about him—objectivity was impossible. If Wood, as a politician, epitomized the critical difference within Tammany, he also personified the Hall's growing malaise. All of his training came in the innocent years when public issues did not stir private convictions to the point where emotionalism and violence blinded rationality. Extremists may have sunk into despair over one cause or another, but the rank and file stolidly lived their lives as they always had—leaving the political cockpit to those who cared. It was in this atmosphere that Wood grew into partisan maturity. Other men went through the same conditioning, yet their chemistry, those vital forces that ascribe one man to greatness and another to mediocrity, did not make them all things to all men. In many ways Wood, then, was unique. But as no other man, he typified the Hall's failure to grasp the need for constructive leadership on both the reform and slavery issues.

Wood had all the personal gifts any man needed. He was tall, elegant, intelligent, and, up to a point, extremely fortunate. Underneath this imposing facade, however, lurked many temperamental flaws. Wood used men as others used horses: to get him somewhere fast, no matter how killing the pace. By the mid-1850s, by dint of hardheaded business sense and downright chicanery, he was worth approximately $250,000. Money could take him a long way. Perhaps too clever and too protean for his own good, the fires of ambition consumed his whole being. One dream animated his life. With all the verve and ardor he could muster, he schemed to play a major role in national politics, far beyond that of any other Tammanyite. His willingness to plot tirelessly, his great resources of will, energy, and money, his agonizing and sweating over each vote, had its roots in his desire to be important— even President of the United States. Wood played for high stakes—and damned anyone who stood in his way. For better or worse, Tammany Hall would not find a day of peace until he was laid to rest.

In early 1849, much of this still lay in the future. Like many of his contemporaries, Wood stood on the edge of power. Essentially, except for John Van Buren, who led a vocal if impotent group, the New York Democracy was an army without a general. The Free Soil revolt had discredited Martin Van Buren and the old Regency; Croswell was in financial difficulty; Horatio Seymour lacked a statewide reputation; and Daniel Dickinson was distracted by his Senate duties. To create party fusion, the Democracy needed a rare man, one capable of combining artful diplomacy with sound political brokerage techniques. City Hunkers, acting under the leadership of Tammanyite committeeman Henry Western, felt that William Marcy was that man. At first Marcy held back. But, on reflection, he did cast about for an expedient to save the party. The man who united the New York Democracy, he reasoned, had a better than even chance of winning the national party's presidential nomination in 1852.[17]

By the spring of 1849, an uneasy lull prevailed in the city Democracy. Both factions seemed ready for a coalition, but hesitated to make the first move, afraid that the other would interpret it as a sign of weakness. To bridge the gap between them and create the impression of a willingness for compromise, pragmatic Tammany leaders sought a mayoral candidate with a foot in each camp. Myndert Van Schaick fitted the bill. A wealthy merchant on good terms with the Van Burenites, he had nevertheless supported Cass. By using a ruse, then, the Barnburners selected Van Schaick in their convention, thus forcing the Hunkers to second their move, and Tammany Hall ran one ticket in the spring election.

These maneuvers created party peace—of a sort. Jolted by the presidential campaign, Tammany could not get out the vote. Caleb Woodhull, a prominent Whig lawyer who later lost favor because of some shady deals in the sale of ferryboat franchises, swamped Van Schaick by gaining 55.1 percent of the total votes cast. On the face of things, the Hall had not yet fused on its lowest levels. The *Herald*, however, felt that a new era was just around the corner: "At the late charter election, organization was the great difficulty, and not the mere abstraction of free soil." [18]

On the defensive, still divided, defeated, and without patronage, the local party faced even a greater challenge when the Whig-controlled legislature made a long overdue revision of the city charter. Honest reformers viewed the document as a dramatic breakthrough for restoring municipal morality, while most Tammanyites visualized it as an attempt to destroy their party. Both were wrong. The 1849 charter turned out to be a clever synthesis that kept some traditional methods while thoroughly revamping others. Its most radical provision had to do with the aldermen's ability to thwart the mayor. The new charter explicitly denied council members any executive powers through the committee system. In its place, the legislature formed nine new departments, with definite duties and prerogatives clearly stated. To further cut down temptation, the Whigs inserted a clause specifying that no member of the municipal government "shall be directly or indirectly interested in any contract, work or business, or the sale of any article, the expense, price or consideration of which is paid from the city treasury." [19]

Whether the Whig legislators had acted from a sincere desire to create a high standard of municipal morality or to help entrench their local party in power was beside the point. The real significance for Tammanyites lay in the fact that the Democracy had lost control over city politics. The new charter, in sum, carried its own demands for party amalgamation.

By May, the groundswell for reunion had become so insistent that state-level chieftains laid aside their war paint. On May 18, Hunker legislators issued a conciliatory, moderate public address, and called for a convention to meet in Rome, one week before the Barnburners scheduled their own for the same city. A deal was in the making. "By taking the initiative," Edwin Croswell explained, "we give the matter the right shape at the outset, with the best chance to hold it there." [20]

Things were different in the city. Although it was too late for the Hunkers to stem the tide, a small group of them—led by Daniel Sickles, a swaggering, impetuous but able lawyer, and Mike Walsh, who once again found a cause—refused to elect delegates for their own state convention. "It pains me to realize that almost every movement of our party is thus ever tangled by the knaves or the fools of our own party," Henry Western moaned. At the Hunker General Committee's formal meeting, Western attempted to change Sickles' policy, but lost in a showdown vote. Refusing to accept the decision as final, Western worked through the Young Men's Committee, and the city Hunkers' Marcy wing selected a full delegation, pledged "to unite with the democracy of the whole country in defending the glorious standard of the national democratic party." [21]

Similarly, many ultra-Barnburners of the William Cullen Bryant and Preston King school felt the proposed reconciliation had grave drawbacks. Above anything, these men kept their free-soil ammunition handy in case they had to fire another salvo. Predictably, their hesitancy added credence to the Sickles Hunker's position. Prosper Wetmore complained: "I can see nothing good in the tone of the Evening Post & other papers of that stamp that bodes any good for this new conciliatory movement." [22]

Even so, state party leaders pushed forward without reflecting on the marked lack of concert in Tammany Hall. Calling on a firm spirit of intraparty amity, they held a round-robin series of meetings in Rome, and finally agreed to meet in a joint convention to be held in Syracuse. At the subsequent gathering, the party formed a united slate for the fall election. The Barnburners deserved much credit, for, despite heated objections from King and Bryant, they accepted (in theory) Cass's squatter sovereignty. Then, too, John Van Buren appeased the Hunkers by agreeing that the federal government had no right to interfere with slavery where it currently existed. In turn, the Hunkers accepted his position that "Congress has power over Slavery in the District of Columbia, but not in the States; that Congress has power, also in the Territories, and ought to exercise the same to prevent the establishment of Slavery in them." [23]

The Syracuse Convention's formula was a judgment on the past; a judgment that stressed that party victory was more vital than intramural squabbling. But some city Hunkers were far from pleased. Grouchy Mordecai Noah wrote: "So, then, we are to have the Van Buren dynasty, after their Benedict Arnold movement, again saddled on the party." Following the example of Daniel Dickinson, who also rejected the formula, these men conjured up a list of grievances, some valid, some specious, and then rejected their Marcyite brethren's efforts at compromise by agreeing to split local offices with the Barnburners—provided the ratio was five to one in their favor.[24]

Anticipating trouble, Marcy's supporters (chiefly Henry Western and Lorenzo Shepard) worked through both General Committees, and tried to force a loyalty oath based on the Syracuse formula on all

Tammanyites. At first all went well. Sickles made a surprisingly graceful speech at the party's joint convention, and nominations followed
without incident. That done, Hunker John McKeon, whom Polk had
named United States attorney in Butler's place, made another conciliatory address. It was time to forget past differences, McKeon said.
Although he admitted that he disliked some of the candidates, "all
personal disappointments and personal griefs" had to be laid "on the
altar of the democratic party." To the sound of thunderous applause,
a most amazing convention ended.[25]

Briefly, Tammanyites paused in astonishment; then lightning struck.
On second thought, Sickles, goaded by Mike Walsh, refused to support
the ticket unless the General Committee placed more Hunkers on the
ballot. "We *condemn* the *Union*," Noah explained, "not the men." But
the committeemen decided to see fusion through no matter what the
consequences and curtly rejected the demand. The Sickles Hunkers
struck back in a paid advertisement in the *New York Herald*: "No
compromise with Traitors and the results of next Tuesday's election
will sound the death-knell of barnburnerism, and leave the political
skeletons of infamous advisers hanging gibbeted in chains, as a warning
to all future malefactors and traitors." [26]

The ultra-Hunkers undid months of careful Democratic politicking.
The Whigs retained control over the new Corporation and swept all
city, county, and state offices. They further added to their victory by
winning twelve out of sixteen assembly seats. Marcy was beside himself
with fury. The irrational Hunkers, he fumed, "sacrificed some barnburners but more genuine democrats. . . . In their game, if successful,
they could win but little; and they lost for themselves much in reputation, and almost everything for their friends." [27]


The furor raised over California's request for statehood compounded the Hall's misery. The slavery extension issue once again
became the burning political topic of the day, and, in Congress, politicians sought desperately for some means to compromise differences.
But in the city, Tammanyites manipulated the question and its emotional byproduct—threats of secession—as political devices to gain
control over the city Democracy's apparatus.

Trouble erupted when the Hunker General Committee sponsored a
meeting to discuss the means for setting a compromise in motion. Once
again, Daniel Sickles stirred up a hornet's nest, this time joined by
Henry Western, who had changed sides. Instead of exhibiting any

willingness to forego past bitterness, Sickles beat down a Marcyite minority group led by Lorenzo Shepard, and only invited to the rally "all the Democratic Republican Electors of this City, who are opposed to the Wilmot Proviso, and the friends of the Union." [28]

Meantime, in an odd sort of way, John Van Buren had gained immense personal leverage. In May 1849, the famous English tragedian, William Macready, arrived in the city and crossed professional swords with Edwin Forrest, the great American Shakespearean actor, who had drawn poor notices during his recent British tour. On returning home, he had blasted his British critics not only for being unable to appreciate talent, but for being galloping anti-Americans. All this fueled the city Irish-Americans' Anglophobia. Under Isaiah Rynders' instigation, the Irish exploded in a bloody riot and turned Astor Place into a no man's land. When the trouble ended, over a dozen men were dead and the police arrested Rynders for inciting the riot. When his trial reached the docket in January of 1850, John Van Buren acted as his attorney and won a brilliant acquittal.

In his own flamboyant way, Rynders showed his gratitude at the Sickles-sponsored meeting. Using a time-honored Tammany stratagem, Rynders' Empire Club arrived in force early in the evening and physically controlled the Long Room. "Under the renowned Captain Rynders," Noah reported sarcastically, hoodlums "tossed the Hon. Dan Sickles over the banisters," and "tore the lapels of counsellor [James T.] Brady's smart blue-frock coat." Then, after passing several pro-Unionist resolutions, the aroused men authorized the formation of another General Committee, over which Fernando Wood soon established control.[29]

This rupture, for all its brutal force, had been imminent for some time. Ever since Sickles had rejected the Syracuse formula, factional lines had become more subjective. Thus, the terms "Barnburners" and "Hunkers" lacked meaning, except as political epithets. Now, on one side were the former Free Soilers, who coalesced with the Marcy–Horatio Seymour followers commanded by Shepard and Elijah Purdy, and commonly called "Softs." Although John Van Buren and Fernando Wood nominally belonged here, each was actually more of a faction unto himself. A second group, the Sickles-Hunker nexus, now labeled the "Hards," rallied around the Henry Western General Committee in the city and Senator Dickinson upstate. Confusing the alignments even more, a third unorganized section huddled around John McKeon, who professed loyalty toward Dickinson but was more interested in trade-and-barter politicking. Above all, one factor set the pattern of hostility —personal ambition.[30]

For the next two months the rival General Committees strove to dramatize their legitimacy. Both piously backed the compromising efforts in Congress, and joined in the various merchant-sponsored Unionist rallies. But behind the scenes they waged a bitter battle, with Tammany Hall the prize. Even so, the Western Committee worked at cross-purposes. While Sickles pleaded for friendship and justice for the South, Hard Mordecai Noah grumbled: "What has the slavery question to do in the general Committee? What right has the general Committee to keep that flag flying? Who cares whether the general Committee is or is not opposed to the extension of slavery?" [31]

By April, the sudden multiplication of the city's Democratic centers of power confounded the entire party's hopes of winning the mayoral and gubernatorial contests. As a remedy, several prominent Tammany-ites, uncommitted to either side, pleaded for an accommodation through the Syracuse formula. The Wood Committee agreed, but the Hards shouted their defiance.[32]

In this impasse, the feuding committees realized that only the Council of Sachems had the prestige to resolve the problem. But while the sachems knew their duty, they had no idea of how to respond. As in 1848, there was nothing un-Democratic or immoral in the Jeffersonian creed of either faction; both contained faithful ward workers, and, above all, the rank and file were confused. If left to themselves, the Council would have preferred no decision to a wrong decision.

Such procrastination was impossible. In order to force the Society to act, both sides, determined to win the new Council election, marshalled support, and even brought in some Whig brothers whose active membership had lapsed. "We advise the proprietors to keep an eye to the gas cocks," the cynical *Herald* warned, "and to remove the mirrors." Two tickets appeared when balloting began. One, headed by Elijah Purdy and Isaac Fowler, represented the Softs; the other, topped by former mayor Mickle and Mordecai Noah, was Hard. When balloting neared completion and the Softs seemed on their way to a narrow victory, the Hards attempted to stuff the ballot boxes. The inspectors discovered three more Hard ballots in a previously emptied box, but the Softs refused to count them. Purdy, the new grand sachem, took physical control of the Society's symbols of authority and announced that the meeting was over. The Hards lashed back. "There are more than ten thousand firm democratic votes in this city which will always be cast against such a corrupt coalition, no matter who the sachems may be in old Tammany," Noah bawled. The less emotionally involved

*Herald,* however, understood the vast psychological consequences implicit in Purdy's victory for the Softs:

> The Sachems hold great power. If they are *united,* they can unite the sections of the democracy, and prevent any party from meeting in the hall, but such as they endorse and consider the regular Democracy. . . . Although the general committee, elected by the 18 wards, appears to be the power that regulates the democracy, yet it is not so. "There is a power behind the throne, greater than the throne itself," and that power is the Sachems of Old Tammany.[33]

Before Purdy could move, however, the old Council, which distrusted his impartiality, finally acted. For the sake of fairness, it recommended that the grand sachem should forbid both committees use of the Wigwam and call for the election of an entirely new organization. Purdy, speaking for the Softs, agreed. Whatever other political involvements he assumed, Purdy knew he simply did not have enough votes to thwart the old Council's suggestion without seriously impairing the Society's prestige. Using reform as their rationale, then, the Purdy sachems authorized a city-wide canvass for ninety-four delegates from each electoral district "to reorganize the democracy on a new plan corresponding with the advance of the population." [34]

The Council's decision shocked both sides. Each expected the sachems to judge regularity, not to seek some middle ground. After much agonizing, the Western Committee refused to accept the plan. Wood possessed more imagination. He agreed to cooperate, loftily explaining that such a move "would protect the best interests of the Country at home, and its honor and character abroad." During the special election, individual Hards cast ballots on their own, but the Western Committee's boycott prevented a real test of strength. Not too surprisingly, then, the Woodites dominated the forthcoming convention.[35]

Meantime, the sachems still sought to maintain their centrist position. Playing on a theme of "Union and Harmony," the Society dedicated a public dinner to sectional peace and formed a special committee, made up of men from both factions, to invite a variety of prominent national leaders. Even so, the festival only symbolized the party's malaise. Despite Marcy's clarion call that the "union is in danger and it is the solemn duty of all to come forth in its defence," Senator Dickinson refused to place party peace over his distaste for the Softs. There were compelling reasons behind Dickinson's stance. The debate in Congress had projected him into a commanding position among the party's hierarchy, and he began to prepare himself for a shot at the presidency. Then, too, he was the only New Yorker capable of resuscitating Martin Van Buren's old Albany-Richmond axis. As things stood, then, the Softs understood that the senator's growing reputation gave the Hards tremendous leverage for control of the local apparatus.[36]

At the end of June, uneasy delegates arrived in the Long Room for their first meeting. With Lorenzo Shepard in the chair, the secretary called the roll. Only forty-six men were present, two more than a quorum. Quickly, Wood introduced a series of resolutions that closely echoed the old Barnburner line—except for a section that roundly endorsed popular sovereignty, the new term politicians used for Cass's original idea. Wood had acted shrewdly. By giving a little to each side, he hoped that the Hards and Softs could share a common program without tearing it to bits. When he finished, Hard John Cochrane, nephew of Gerrit Smith and a popular, flamboyant man, presented counter-resolutions that called for union based on principles, not expediency. Few delegates missed his intent. Using a euphemism all understood, Cochrane dramatized the Hards' strategy of purge and rule. Even before he had finished, the Softs squirmed in their seats and yelled for points of order. But nothing availed. Aware that they were outnumbered, four Hards had quietly slipped out of the building, thus killing the quorum. At this point, Shepard had no alternative but to adjourn.[37]

At the next meeting, four nights later, the Hards' tactics came into focus. Because the Softs held a working majority, not a quorum, some Hards stayed away in order to create a permanent stalemate. But the Softs were just as resourceful. They changed the convention's ground rules, based the quorum on the number of men in actual attendance, not total membership, and went to work. They passed resolutions in favor of a nationalistic Congressional Compromise, accepted Wood's ideas, and defeated Cochrane's last-minute effort to commit the meeting against the moribund Wilmot Proviso. Satisfied, they adjourned for two weeks.[38]

In the interim, conditions had changed rapidly outside the city. President Zachary Taylor had died. His successor, Millard Fillmore, had been at odds with Thurlow Weed for a number of years and local Democrats expected a monumental power struggle between them for control of the Whig party. If this situation took place, Edwin Croswell forecast that the Democrats, "if we are wise in our State, & in other States," could win the next presidency. In New York, the Van Buren

Softs held a separate convention and decided to meet in Syracuse with the Marcyites at the regular meeting and form a united ticket.[39]

In the city, the Hards' continued inflexibility remained a towering obstacle. During July, the special convention had continued to meet, but fewer and fewer men attended. Finally, realizing the futility of going on, the delegates authorized the election—under the Council's strict supervision—of a new General Committee for the remainder of the year. Concurrently, they adopted a resolution sponsored by Cochrane to forbid both the Wood and Western groups from using the Wigwam.

Party moderates now called on the rank and file to custom-tailor a temperate General Committee and state convention delegation. But circumstances made it almost impossible for Tammanyites to stitch together such a pattern. In each ward, the defiant Wood and Western groups launched bitter primary campaigns, selected full convention slates, and called on the new General Committee, which Hard Edward West headed, to decide regularity. In September, the day of reckoning came. West's Committee, with a slight Hard majority, chose a delegation predominantly loyal to Western, but eased tension by certifying such prominent Softs as Rynders, Shepard, Purdy, and John Van Buren.[40]

Compared with the critical convention of the year before, the meeting passed off in relative calm. Recognizing that the Congressional Compromise of 1850 was an umbrella wide enough to shelter all factional elements because it tacitly accepted the Jeffersonian idea of home rule, party leaders such as Marcy and Seymour made it part of the Democracy's political credo and ultimately nominated Seymour for governor on that basis. Even so, both the Softs and Hards found much to exasperate them. The Preston King Softs objected when the delegates endorsed the Fugitive Slave Law, which was part of the Compromise, and bolted from the meeting. The Hards were equally unhappy when the delegates refused to endorse Dickinson's senatorial reelection bid, which the coming legislature would decide.

When the city Hards returned home, they announced that they refused to cooperate with "corrupt recusants," and called on the West Committee for a ruling. In a one-sided reply, the Committee passed a resolution that lauded Dickinson, and, by a vote of 16 to 10, with 31 absentees, tabled a Soft attempt to endorse Seymour. Again, the Council of Sachems acted. Purdy officially notified West that his group could not meet in the Wigwam unless it unequivocally backed Seymour. Reluctantly, West fell into line. At the next meeting, four more Softs attended, several Hards switched sides, and this time, 20–10, the Committee reconsidered the resolution and endorsed Seymour. Yet the refusal of the ten Hards to swallow their disappointment was a warning sign.[41]

Though Tammany's ranks were thinning at an alarming rate, Fernando Wood actively courted the party's nomination for mayor. At the city convention, the ward delegates named him over heated Hard objections. The *Herald* and the newly christened *Irish-American* were elated at his candidacy. Both portrayed him as a reformist-minded businessman, who could weave harmony among all true Democrats. Noah, speaking for the Hards, disagreed, and predicted that many Hards would either vote for the Whig nominee or not at all. The difficulty, he explained, had nothing to do with Wood personally, but hinged on his notorious role in advocating "the union of Hunkers and Barnburners." [42]

By now, events had tangled every traditional political thread into an unravelable mess. As Croswell had hoped, the Whigs split into two warring groups but finally nominated a common candidate, Washington Hunt, for governor. In the city, a normally Whig group of merchants, prodded along by a strong Unionist feeling, held a huge rally at Castle Garden, and threatened to confuse the issue even more by endorsing candidates from both parties. The Van Burenites were just as mettlesome. There were some Hards running for office, Martin Van Buren wrote, whom his friends could not support. The party, he wrote, should drive "the rotters into merited obscurity." [43]

The Democracy's lack of direction turned the Hall into a rudderless ark. Under such conditions, the Whigs piled up impressive citywide gains, easily defeated Wood, won thirteen out of sixteen assembly seats, elected three out of four congressmen, and held Seymour's percentage of the popular vote to 50.3 percent. As a result, Hunt squeaked to victory by less than 1 percent of the total state ballots.

Political pundits had a field day explaining the Democracy's defeat. Wood lost, the *Herald* claimed, because of his henchmen's "rowdy character." Noah laid the blame squarely on Wood's handling of the Western Committee. Upstate, although Seymour was personally satisfied with the Van Burenites' "fidelity," William Marcy detected treason. In his diary he wrote that they were cheaters and ingrates.[44] Daniel Dickinson was the real loser because the Whigs now controlled the legislature and selected Hamilton Fish for the United States Senate. Blind to his own supporters' role in his defeat, Dickinson, in both his private letters and public declarations, blamed the Softs for his failure to be reelected. As a result, for the next seven years he refused to sanction any concessions that might restore party peace.

Within the city Democracy, the strife-torn sachems yearned for a permanent factional armistice because five years of internal warfare threatened to turn the city into a permanent Whig stronghold. A glance at the mayoralty returns since Andrew Mickle's victory in 1846 confirmed the wisdom of peace and conciliation.

VOTES BY PERCENTAGE FOR MAYOR, 1846–1850

| Year | Democrats | Whigs | Others |
|------|-----------|-------|--------|
| 1846 | 47.2 | 32.9 | 19.9 |
| 1847 | 46.5 | 48.4 | 5.1 |
| 1848 | 50.8 | 48.1 | 1.1 |
| 1849 | 44.9 | 55.1 | — |
| 1850 | 43.9 | 56.1 | — |

The problem was more easily diagnosed than cured. Yet in a breathtaking reversal of form, the Hards unexpectedly cooperated with the Softs and followed the Council's moderate course. Both factions agreed to make the Compromise of 1850 official party policy, and, as a symbol of a new era of fellowship, jointly invited John Van Buren, the stormy epitome of factional differences, to the New Orleans Ball. Then, when the Whig legislature skirted the state constitution by passing the "Nine Million Bill" to enlarge the canal system, local Tammanyites from both groups held a protest meeting and called the bill "a palpable and shameless violation" of the law.[45]

The Society's peace crusade gained momentum with each passing day. The new Council of Sachems was a study in moderation and devotion to the Compromise. Even Noah was pleased. These "men may differ," he applauded, "but all are united in favor of the Union." Picking up the pace, the sachems turned Independence Day into a festival that celebrated a party peace free from prior issues. The meeting was all that the Society had envisioned. At the start, Grand Sachem Daniel Delevan read excerpts from letters sent by prominent Democrats who were unable, or unwilling, to attend. Two were especially important. Both Daniel Dickinson and John Van Buren agreed that party unity was an absolute necessity, though they were hazy on specifics. Then the keynote speaker told the wildly cheering brethren "that there was room in Tammany Hall for every Democrat." [46]

When all the rhetoric ended, one major question remained. Why, in the face of two years of dogged opposition, had Tammany Hards smoked the peace pipe? On the surface, the answer seemed self-apparent: the spoils were now in Whig hands. But on a deeper level, the Hards had a more sophisticated purpose in mind. Marcy's broker politics, they reasoned, irritated extremists on both the left and the right. If so, he could never make the New York Democracy his personal creature. The door was open for other presidential candidates, then, if they played a shrewd waiting game. For the next year, therefore, city politics entered a new stage: the search for a winning standard-bearer.

The Hards boomed Lewis Cass and, if he faltered, Daniel Dickinson was available. In March 1851, Cass made a whirlwind tour of the city, and the Union-minded sachems, goaded by Mike Walsh, installed the aged senator as an honorary brave. Just the same, the Hards knew that some Tammanyites, particularly the Marcyites and Van Burenites, would not back Cass on any terms. As a result, the Hards went underground. Patiently, as the months dragged by, they mouthed meaningless party harmony clichés, supported the Council's unity efforts, and hoped for something to turn up.

The Van Burenites pushed their own plans. But unfortunately, one by one, their candidates fell from contention. Thomas Hart Benton was determined to consolidate his Missouri power base and write his memoirs. Once he retired, New England Free Soilers pushed Supreme Court Judge Levi Woodbury of New Hampshire, a former member of Jackson's cabinet, until he suddenly died in September. Bereft of possible candidates, the Van Burenites finally settled on William O. Butler of Kentucky, a slaveowner who favored the Wilmot Proviso.[47]

Concurrently, William Marcy launched a full-scale effort aimed at becoming New York's favorite son. His plan operated on a massive front. In late 1851 and early 1852, he personally wrote to every important Democrat in the state and sought to establish firm camaraderie with them. Nonetheless, he was painfully aware that he could not win unless he had a united party at his back. At first, things went well. The Hards were in a cooperative mood because it suited their long-range plans. Then, in the fall, Marcyites dominated the state convention, including the newly formed state committee, and again kept the party from fragmenting. Only the Van Burenites proved hard to handle. By demanding that the party adopt anti–Fugitive Slave Law resolutions, they unfortunately forced Marcy into making the first of several tactical blunders.[48]

In the city, Tammany Hall's moderation bolstered Marcy's hopes. The General Committee, under joint Hard and Soft auspices, formally ratified the state ticket in a mass harmony meeting. One by one, Rynders, Purdy, Shepard, and Cochrane mounted the rostrum and publicly made their peace. But it was Daniel Sickles who stunned the crowd. It was high time to bury animosities, he shouted. "There has been a return of good sense, and all sections are now found uniformly patriotic and devoted to sound Democratic principles." [49]

The brunt of the campaign fell upon the General Committee, and it performed its job well. Campaigning on Whig mistakes, the Hall placed reconciliation above petty jealousies. Tammany even handled the Union Committee with ease when these businessmen toyed with the idea of forming an independent third ticket based on the Compromise of 1850. Instead of attacking them, the Hall used the *Herald*'s friendly columns to chide them gently as sincere men who had "gradually dwindled down into the small dimensions of a Wall-Street political humbug." [50]

Violence and the abuse of the democratic process characterized election day. Snow fell early in the morning, and by afternoon the temperature had dropped below freezing. Waiting impatiently for the returns, many clubhouse toughs eased the effects of the sudden cold wave with intemperate drinking. Just before the polls closed, they drunkenly smashed and stole ballot boxes in several doubtful precincts. Their efforts were as unnecessary as they were stupid. Tammany Hall, the city's majority party if united, wrested control from the Whigs in all county offices, won two-thirds of the Corporation, all judicial offices, and nine out of sixteen assembly seats. Marcy glowed with elation. To Ohio Congressman William Campbell, he scrawled excitedly: "With an acceptable candidate, I regard N.Y. as sure a state as Pennsylvania." [51]

Although Marcy had no way of realizing it, the fall election marked the end of his bid to become president. In a way, he had anticipated trouble but misread its source. Despite John Van Buren's pledge to Marcy that he meant "to acquiesce in the movement in your favor though not be responsible for it," Marcy did not trust the Van Burenites. But the secretive Hards were his real enemies, and they finally found their long-awaited opening in Senator Douglas' premature presidential candidacy. By using him as a bugaboo, they frightened Marcy into thinking that the young Westerner had firm support among local Democrats.[52]

The plot began with the Young America movement. During and after the debate over the Compromise of 1850, the great giants of American political life had either died or retired. Those who remained of their generation in the Democratic party were honorable but secondary leaders, who nevertheless lusted for the presidency. In their places a new generation of jingoistic politicos, bursting with slogans of Manifest Destiny and aggressive Americanism, jostled with these "Old Fogies" for party control. Impatient with what is called self-serving, superannuated old men, Young America made Stephen Douglas its hero and boomed him for the presidency.

At first glance, Douglas had impressive backing in the city. During May 1851, he made a tumultuous swing through the state, and in September the Tammany Society made him an honorary brave. Then, in October, a group of Hards, led by George Sanders, the *Democratic Review*'s new editor, and George Law, a shipping magnate who hoped that Douglas' drive to annex Cuba would increase business, sponsored a joint rally at the Wigwam to start the senator's formal campaign. Together with its friends in the Young Men's Committee, Young America seemed a fresh, vital force in city politics.

Appearances were highly deceptive. Outside of Congressman Emmanuel Hart, a highly undisciplined Tammanyite, no prominent local Democrat backed Douglas. Young America did not control any organizational machinery, nor any official party newspaper. Even so, Marcy ran scared. In November he made a fateful decision. During the fall election, the Hards, especially Daniel Sickles, had impressed him with their spirit of teamwork. Tammany's overwhelming comeback bore mute testimony to their goodwill. So, when Sickles broached a plan to stall the Douglas bandwagon, Marcy listened with gathering respect. According to Sickles, the Hards did not intend to support Cass because the effort would fragment the party and help Douglas. With Cass out of the picture, then, Sickles proposed that the only way Marcy could maintain his favorite-son status was to lend his name to a movement aimed at stopping Douglas. Since he already feared Douglas and distrusted Van Burenites, while having no reason to doubt Sickles' sincerity, Marcy agreed.

The Hards' plot now took shape. Exuding good fellowship, they pledged to select Marcy delegates during the forthcoming district elections. But once chosen, they really planned to stay with Cass, and, if he stumbled, switch to Dickinson. Yet all their plans hinged on the method the Marcy-dominated state Central Committee used to name these delegates: a traditional state convention that the Van Burenites favored, or a Hard-endorsed district plan. Here, Marcy made another false step. Heedless of warnings from Seymour and Shepard that Sickles was untrustworthy, Marcy opted for the district plan.[53]

For a man of Marcy's august reputation and years as a practicing politician, it was almost implausible to think that a novice like Sickles could hoodwink him. Yet on reflection, Marcy was not as naive as he might appear. 1851 had been a year of peace in Tammany Hall because the Hards had accepted the Council of Sachems' armistice. Marcy would have needed superhuman powers to detect any duplicity. As for the ultra–Van Burenite Softs, their refusal to accept the Fugitive Slave Law made them anathema to large sections of the national party. By renouncing them, Marcy proved his rigid orthodoxy on the Compromise of 1850. Then, too, "Magyar Mania" seemed another ingredient in local politics. In December 1851, Louis Kossuth, the Hungarian revolutionary and demigod in Young America's pantheon, arrived in the city just as the Democracy held its district elections. Marcy reasoned that the hurly-burly over the Hungarian was a device to boom Douglas.

By the first week of December, however, certain oddities in Hard behavior brought the first glimmer of doubt to Marcy's mind. To an Ohio friend he wrote that it seemed that Cass's friends, in league with Young America, were making "wonderful & *extraordinary* efforts in the City of N.Y. to organise a force to carry some of the districts in that City." To his old friend James Wadsworth of Geneseo, Marcy was even more blunt: "my *hunker friends*—those who should be *my friends* by going for Cass-delegates mean to favor the cause of Douglas." [54]

Although Marcy had an inkling, he still did not realize the depth of the Hards' deception. Even his Tammanyite supporters, while suspicious, never assumed a more devious plot was afoot. For example, General J. Addison Thomas, his local campaign manager, was completely in the dark. In letter after letter, Thomas described Douglas as the real enemy, not Cass or Dickinson. "I regret to say that I believe now," Thomas wrote in a typical vein, "that *Sickles, Croswell* & Co are doing all they can to secure Douglas delegates." [55]

On December 17, when the Hall held its district election, the Hards came out in the open. "It is a remarkable fact that recently all the Douglas men have come out for Cass!!" Thomas yelped as soon as he saw the partial returns. The next day, he knew the awful truth: "There was been a complete turning around of the Douglas men. They have all come out for Cass." Perhaps the episode's crowning irony lay in the fact that John Van Buren split with his allies and led a splinter group into Marcy's camp. "The game seems to be a changeable one," a visibly shaken Marcy wrote. "The drop of every card alters the game." [56]

When Tammany's convention met, his worst fears materialized. Despite intense pressure exerted by Shepard, Seymour, and Thomas, the delegates selected a predominantly pro-Cass group. Upstate, Marcy fared better but not as well as he expected. In April, when the party named delegates at large, he made a slight comeback—but it was not enough.

The web of deception that the Hards had woven also ensnared the Tammany Softs. By the time they sensed trouble, they could do little. In the December primary elections, the Hards gained control over the vital General Committee, and, in January, chose as chairman Augustus Schell, an upright, wealthy lawyer. Only the Tammany Society remained an unknown in Hard plans.[57]

Despite the Hards' devious tactics, New York did not represent the national Democratic party. At the convention, the leading contenders neutralized each other and allowed a comparative unknown, Franklin Pierce of New Hampshire, to win. The news of his selection shocked many New Yorkers, yet his greatest political asset—factional neutrality —seemed just the medicine the party needed. As a symbol of this mood, John Dix wrote him that "your nomination has relieved us from an immensity of embarrassment in this State, and I know not whether to congratulate you or ourselves the most." Judge Aaron Vanderpoel added: "The party here [New York City] is united, and the State of New York will again wheel at the democratic line." Perhaps so—but then again, perhaps not.[58]

Meantime, the sachems braced for trouble. In particular, they resented the shabby way in which the Hards had treated Marcy. His long, dedicated public service, they felt, entitled him to far more consideration than Sickles had shown. But Purdy and his close associate, Daniel Delevan, could only brood in silence. Several pressing local problems, coming on top of Pierce's nomination, made party unity an absolute necessity.

First, Tammany had to grapple with the temperance question. In 1851, after Maine passed a law prohibiting the sale of alcoholic beverages, the crusade spread to the city. Up to this point, temperance had been largely a religious concern and had not fared well. By January 1852, New York City had 4,133 licensed taverns and 775 unlicensed drinking spots (which were usually havens for criminals), and 4,360 of these were open on Sunday. Partly by design, partly by attitude, Horace Greeley's *New York Tribune,* which embraced one fad after another, unconditionally backed the temperance movement and helped transform the effort by organizing a prohibitionist party in the city. "This thing of temperance is ripe for political action," the *Herald* noted. "It is getting tired of moral suasion, and is coming to the ballot boxes." The Democrats feared such agitation from the start. While they recognized the problem's social dimensions, they also knew that the temperance movement hid a deeper xenophobic feeling because most such crusades associated drunkenness with foreigners. Then, too, the heart of Tammany's ward organizations often rested with influential tavern owners such as rollicking Thomas Dunlap, owner of the notorious Pewter Mug. For the moment, then, the Hall adopted a cautious policy of watchful waiting.[59]

The Corporation's inner corruption further heightened the sachems' difficulties. The 1849 Charter had proved a sad hoax on reform. Unscrupulous men on both sides of the political fence made and lost fortunes while aldermen lined their pockets with bribes. When the Democrats took over in 1852, disgusted reformers expected further scandals. The Common Council, nicknamed "The Forty Thieves," confirmed these fears. Among its members was young Alderman William Marcy Tweed, who was carefully taking notes for the future.

The sachems were not alarmed at the breakdown of municipal morality. Corruption was so pervasive that many of them, including Purdy, were implicated. But the Council did fear that a combination of reformism, prohibitionism, and nativism might stir political emotions passively shared by other New Yorkers, somewhat as the 1843 American Republicans had done. Under these conditions, then, the Council favored "union, harmony, and concert of action," even though such a course favored the Hards.[60]

This policy did not mean that the Softs were inactive. Like Matthew Davis before him, Elijah Purdy and his main ally, Daniel Delevan, secretly used the Tammany Society to establish a reliable power base. They did so by stepping up the recruitment program. From 1848 to 1850, the Society had only initiated 24 new members. But in 1851 and 1852, the years in which Purdy first gained control over the Society's machinery, it enrolled 142 brothers. A tactic so tricky and so expedient, however, hinged on disarming the suspicious Hards. The measure of Purdy's covertness lay in his willingness to initiate several of their prominent leaders—Schell, Cochrane, Robert Morris, and Edward West —while balancing them off with staunch Softs such as John Purser,

Nelson Waterbury, George Meserve, and Samuel Tilden. But the largest group of these braves were Irishmen who resented the nativism
that the Hards had difficulty concealing. It was on these people that
Purdy depended.

Although Purdy devoted an immense amount of time to Tammany's
political machinery, he lacked the drive to attempt boss rule. A highly
respectable businessman, Purdy, a contemporary wrote, "never courted
public station, being content to make others great rather than seek
place for himself." Happy to remain a comparatively obscure figure,
he sought to rule through others. The first person he selected was
Lorenzo Shepard, who was just nearing his political maturity.[61]

# ~ 11 ~

# Political Chaos and the Tammany Society

DURING the 1852 presidential campaign, city Democrats worked hard for the national ticket. In each ward, under John Cochrane's direction, Pierce's boosters formed auxiliary units called Democratic Union Clubs, and centralized them under a General Union Committee and Young Men's Union Committee. Then the Tammany Society tidied up other matters. It made the election's theme "Union! Strength! Harmony!" and held a splendid Fourth of July festival to underscore the party's hard-won unity.[1]

But while the Democracy's actions were highly successful by traditional standards, true peace was still illusive on local politics. Almost as soon as the convention ended, the Dickinson-men and Marcyites began to carp at each other about their respective roles in the campaign and fought over the best means to distribute electioneering funds. Above that, the two groups split over Horatio Seymour's bid for governor. Part of the difficulty lay with the Hamlet-like Seymour. Before the nomination, he shunned the honor; afterwards, he proved too introspective to supply leadership. Then, too, the Hards viewed him as a potential rival against Dickinson and hardly exerted themselves. "This result will not however materially affect our Electoral Ticket," Augustus Schell assured Pierce. His managers were not so confident. If the state ticket failed, they thought, the other might also go down the drain. As a result, Nathaniel Upsham, Pierce's campaign coordinator, personally saw Dickinson and, using subtle pressure, forced the Hards to back Seymour.[2]

Problems abounded, too, among the ultra–Free Soilers. Unable to swallow Pierce, a group of antiextensionists coalesced with the moribund Liberty party and backed Senator John P. Hale of New Hampshire for the presidency. Their efforts failed. The majority of New York Free Soilers thought Pierce a good choice—good for the country, good for the party. From Lindenwald, Martin Van Buren told Pierce that despite the insurgents, he would carry the state with a comfortable majority.[3]

In a sense, Van Buren was correct. Although the Hards and Softs were prisoners of their own propaganda, both hungered for spoils. As the campaign gained momentum, the desire to elect Pierce did stifle factionalism and helped create a superficial sense of party unity. Even so, this harmony concealed major unresolved problems in Tammany Hall. Locally, both factions continued to wrangle bitterly over city matters but, unlike the situation upstate, the Softs precipitated a fresh round of intraparty brawling.

By midsummer, many impatient Softs began to doubt that the Purdy-Delevan-Shepard strategy would work. In order to prevent a complete loss of morale, several of them took matters into their own hands. On Friday, July 16, they made their move. Two weeks earlier, Henry Clay had died. Partly as a mark of respect, partly as a device to absorb some Union Committee Whigs who disliked General Winfield Scott, their party's presidential nominee, the General Committee as well as the Democratic-dominated Common Council planned a memorial funeral. Making arrangements, however, had proved quite slow. Many committeemen were out of town because of the heat; others considered the "obeisance" a waste of time; and Schell twice postponed meetings for lack of a quorum. Finally, on July 16, thirty-three committeemen gathered in the Wigwam for a discussion. A quick glance around the room gave the Softs new inspiration because for once they were in the majority. Through bitter experience they knew that organization, not rhetoric, swayed voters. In order to reach them and neutralize the Hards' stranglehold over the General Committee, the Softs proposed a novel idea. For the next primary canvass, they suggested that each ward committee, rather than the General Committee, should name election inspectors. The few Hards present immediately objected because the old system guaranteed them control over all party functions. They were voted down, 23–10.

The Hards did not hesitate. Schell quickly called another meeting, and his men passed a counter-resolution that called for the election of delegates under the old system for the forthcoming state convention. By now, the exchange between the two groups threatened the national ticket and the Council of Sachems intervened. Sharply disagreeing with the method the Soft rebels had used because it had compromised Purdy's efforts, the sachems suggested that Schell form a subcommittee to study the matter.

At the next meeting, the subcommittee stirred up more problems than it solved. Hoping to strike a balance, it proposed that the parent Committee name three ward inspectors in the customary manner, but that local ward groups, if they disagreed, could drop two of these men and substitute their own. Meantime, an unruly crowd milled around the meeting room. Without warning, several toughs broke the door down. "They threatened personal harm to Mr. Sickles," the *Herald* noted, "but did not touch him as they understood he was armed with a revolver and a dagger." In the confusion, chairman Thomas Barr, a Hard, abruptly ended the meeting.

Once more the Council of Sachems entered the picture. It called on Barr to hold another discussion, but he refused. There was no time to appoint new inspectors, he insisted, because the state convention could not wait. The issue, unfortunately, was out in the streets, in the hands of professional thugs who fought for hire, not political ideals.

The city had witnessed many a free-for-all, but few surpassed the "riots and bloodshed" among the feuding Tammanyites. Fighting gangs roamed through the polling areas; intimidation and fraud were commonplaces. In some precincts there were more votes than voters; in others, bully boys brazenly stole ballot boxes and scattered the returns before the inspectors could begin the count. Some men were so badly beaten that they required hospitalization. But when all the hubbub ended, the Hards had won. Their inspectors had simply stolen the election.

The convention compounded the Tammany Softs' misery. In a direct slap at them, the delegates accepted the Schell Hards and called on all Democrats to make a supreme effort to throw the Whigs out of office. In a loose way, therefore, the convention settled two major local problems. First, in fully admitting the Tammany Hards, the state party went on record, if only tacitly, in favor of the old primary inspector system. Second, the Softs' failure enhanced Purdy's strategy. Most practical Tammany Softs now accepted as truth the idea that their only chance for salvation lay with the Society.[4]

In the hectic days that followed, relative peace reigned in Tammany Hall. The nominating convention passed off quietly, although many Softs had mixed feelings about the slate. Hard John McKeon, who felt that the choice of Jacob Westervelt (a prominent merchant) for mayor would strengthen the ticket, shared none of their doubts. To Pierce he wrote: "I thought at one time there was a danger of disruption of the party but the danger has passed away and we are likely to do very well." [5]

For all their outward accord, however, the Softs' solidarity with the Hards was extremely shaky. On election eve, some sullen Marcyites who resented Sickles printed spurious tickets which supported the regular state and national candidates but left blank spaces for local races where the voters could write in their own choices. One of the printers informed Sickles just before the ballots were mailed, and the General Committee impounded the material at the Broadway post office. John Van Buren, who was stumping upstate and in New England for Pierce, disowned the effort. Calling the local ticket the best he had seen in years, Van Buren urged all Tammanyites to support the party.

Laboring under these strains, the local Democracy still swamped the Whigs. Pierce and Westervelt won easily. Even more, the Hall gained all twelve city executive and judicial slots, elected six congressmen, including Mike Walsh and young William Tweed, and gave Seymour the healthy plurality he needed to become governor.

In the euphoria of victory and anticipating a huge patronage windfall, Tammanyites, Softs and Hards alike, shunted aside their differences. At the Young Men's Democratic Union Club's invitation, the local Democracy held a gaudy victory celebration in the Long Room. Speakers ranging from Horatio Seymour and John Van Buren to several ward workers lauded the Hall for its yeoman work. But more than any other man, Augustus Schell revealed the true spirit of local politics. After praising Tammany for being "true to herself," he balked at the opportunity to endorse any further party harmony. The meeting, as it turned out, proved to be the peak of Tammany's superficial unity. From then on, the flow of events carried the party downhill.[6]

The Softs began the new era of party chaos by making control over the new General Committee the first item on their list of priorities. They arrived early at the old Committee's last formal meeting in December and organized the meeting. Lorenzo Shepard offered a resolution to hold the primaries as usual but added a fresh suggestion: each ward committee should appoint all three inspectors. Bedlam ensued. The Hunkers gradually rounded up their late arrivals and reorganized the gathering, and Schell, who replaced temporary chairman William Kennedy, called on Sickles who introduced a substitute plan. He called for an immediate election, under the outgoing General Committee's direction, and then read a prepared list of approved inspectors for each ward. The Softs fought back with a motion "to strike out the inspectors named by Mr. Sickles and substitute others in their stead." The Hards defeated the question.

Suddenly, a group of rowdies led by John Austin, " a somewhat notorious character," who "had been amusing themselves with playing 'Father Simon,' as it is called, until they had become mad by drink," the *New York Times* noted, swarmed into the small committee room. When they refused to leave, Schell ordered the sergeant at arms to call the police. Quickly sobered, Austin and his gang attempted to move out, but a "crush of men with their hats off and their sleeves tucked up" hurled them back into the room. At once, an unbelievable melee erupted. One of the rioters hit Schell over the head and cut his scalp "down to the temple." Now in full retreat, the Hards fought their way out, retired to the Astor Hotel, and issued a call for immediate Committee elections.[7]

Restraint was impossible. Among scenes that pitted muscle against muscle, the Softs won in several wards, others went Hard, and four wards remained contested. According to tradition, the outgoing Committee had the right to decide which candidates had won, which automatically meant that the Hards would still dominate the Hall. At this point, the Softs sprang their trap. On the night that the Hards planned to organize the new General Committee, the Council of Sachems ordered the old Committee to select only those winning candidates in the contested elections who had run under the plan that Shepard had proposed. The Hards refused. When the sachems opened the doors, both groups rushed into the Long Room, seated themselves at opposite ends, organized for the coming year, and awaited the Council's ruling. There were now two General Committees, each claiming total legitimacy, formed on hallowed party ground. Once again, the sachems had to decide regularity. But this time, unlike 1848 and 1850, they were ready to assert their authority.

On January 19, the Council met amid great confusion. After both sides had presented briefs, the sachems, in order to create an impression of fairness, adjourned for the evening. The next night, the Purdy Soft sachems nailed the trap shut. By a strict factional vote, they ruled that the Soft General Committee, headed by Daniel Delevan, "shall occupy Tammany Hall to the exclusion of *all* other political Committees whatever." After making the decision, the Council invited the Hards to accept the verdict in good grace, and invited them as fellow Democrats, not deposed committeemen, to yet another meeting to discuss the terms of a party reunion.[8]

The Hards showed no willingness to accommodate themselves to the sachems' ruling. Thomas Barr, the chairman of the supposedly defunct Hard Committee, wasted little time in staking out his position:

> The democrats of the City of New York have never in any manner or by any act, vested in this Society, the right to prescribe the rules for their government, in matters of political organization, and it is easy to see why the society has not been, and cannot be entrusted with any such power, since neither political opinions nor political action have ever been made a qualification for admission or a ground of exclusion from membership.[9]

Unlike the Adams National Republicans and the ultra–Bank Democrats, then, the Hards scorned all precedents and resolutely defied the Tammany Society.

On January 27, they tested their independent position by scheduling a meeting in the Wigwam. But when they arrived, Browne and Howard, the building's lessees, locked the doors. The Hards' failure precipitated another round of spirited wrangling, and they again questioned the Council's right to bar any group from using the Long Room. The sachems had anticipated such a move, and answered back with a two-pronged explanation. Legally, they established the fact that Howard, in 1842, had made a binding contract not to let or lease the building to any group "whose general principles do not appear to him to be in accordance with the general political principles of the Democratic Republican General Committee of the city of New York, of which Elijah Purdy is at present chairman." Above that, the sachems emphasized that in the final analysis, the Tammany Society was morally responsible for maintaining party order and stability

> if there should be any time a doubt arising in his [Howard's] mind or that of his assigns, or in the mind of the Grand Sachem of the Tammany Society for the time being, in ascertaining the political character of any political party that should be desirous of obtaining admission to Tammany Hall for the purpose of holding a political meeting, then either might give notice in writing to the Father of the Council of the Tammany Society, in which event it was the duty of the Father of the Council to assemble the Grand Council, who would determine in the matter and whose decision should be final, conclusive and binding.[10]

On February 10, in remarkly plain language, Barr published a long, emotional, position paper. The crux of the issue, he wrote, was a simple "question of usurpation." The powers that the sachems had appropriated belonged to "the people themselves, delegated only to their General Committee, not to the Council of Sachems." In a final thrust, he announced that the Tammany Society was strictly a fraternal, charitable order. Nothing in its charter, constitution, or bylaws made it a political organization. Furthermore, "the Democrats of New York have never in any manner or by any act, vested in the society the right to prescribe the rules for their government in matters of political organization." [11]

In rebuttal, the sachems recited a lesson in party history. They demonstrated that by every traditional measure, "the power to determine absolutely as to the occupancy of the Hall for political purposes is vested in the Grand Council of the Tammany Society." As for Barr's charge that the Society had overstepped its role, the sachems left no doubt where they stood: "It would be as reasonable to assert at noonday, in the face of the sun, that the orb does not emit light, as to deny that the Tammany Society is not a political organization. Indeed, its political fame is too extended to need mention, much less proof of its existence." [12]

In all this welter of defiance, tangled semantics, and protestations of purity, political muscle settled the issue. On February 12, when the Hards attempted to inspire a popular uprising against the Purdy Soft sachems, the braves overwhelmingly supported the Council's decision. Driven from the Long Room, lacking any of the customary symbols of power, the frustrated Hards were still defiant. In the face of all traditions and party usages, they kept the Barr Committee in operation, and symbolized their insurgency by seeking funds to build a new, "pure" Wigwam. [13]

Each side played one more act at the Society's annual election for a fresh Council. The Softs planned with elaborate care. Before polling began, they prepared the ticket, hired thugs to keep a reasonable amount of order, and personally called on all reliable brothers to urge them to vote. These moves proved unnecessary. The Hards boycotted the election, and, except for a few dissenters, the Softs confirmed their hegemony over the Tammany Society. Under these conditions, then, Purdy's strategy had apparently worked. But only the future could tell how well. [14]

The Tammany Society, at long last, had established its identity. Ever since the Federalist defection in 1795, the Society had been a dual organization—social and political—and uncomfortable with both aspects. But in challenging the whole basis of party organization, the Council had clarified the Society's political character and settled its proper functional role. While the Society still continued its fraternal mumbo jumbo, the Council had confirmed its status as the mainspring in the Democratic machine. As Purdy reasoned, the Society was both an arbitrator and a policy-maker.

Meantime, President Franklin Pierce prepared his patronage policy. A sensitive politician, he was deeply aware of the groundswell in favor of sectional peace and moderation based on the Compromise of 1850. As President, he planned to polarize American politics by making the Democracy a sound, conservative, nationalistic force that would pre-empt the middle of the road and force extremists into narrow isolation. To do so, he intended to forget the past and make loyalty to his formula of moderation the test of Democratic regularity.

He picked his appointees with this idea in mind. Although, as he confessed to John Dix, he had "great embarrassments in disposing of the prominent offices in New York," he named Hards Daniel Dickinson as collector, Charles O'Conor as district attorney, Conrad Swackhammer as naval agent, and John Hillyer as marshal; Softs John Dix to the Sub-Treasury, Isaac Fowler (one of Purdy's close associates) as postmaster, Herman Redfield (a strong Marcyite) as naval officer, and John Cochrane as surveyor.[15]

The President's policy was a reasonable if cautious one. But few New Yorkers were in a reasonable mood. The Van Buren Softs resented Dix's assignment because they felt he deserved a more important post. The Hards were just as unreasonable. Unable to see beyond their personal ends, they chose to interpret the President's moderation as a covert attempt to establish Soft supremacy. As a sign of this irrationality, Dickinson rejected the collectorship as beneath his dignity. Still, Pierce would not let them become martyrs and selected Green Bronson (an elderly, bitter Hard, once one of Martin Van Buren's colleagues) in Dickinson's slot. Only the Marcy-Seymour Softs lacked any reason for complaint because in addition to choice local offices, Pierce had made Marcy secretary of state. But with Bronson as collector, even they felt uneasy.

Pierce was wise enough to know that the Custom House patronage was crucial if he expected his plans to work. Hoping to control the spoils, he instructed Bronson to appoint all Democrats who passed the Administration's loyalty test. With over 700 jobs at his disposal, however, Bronson ignored the President. By July of 1852, it was evident that the collector was laying the groundwork for a massive power grab at the coming state convention. Only Postmaster Fowler prevented a complete Soft rout.[16]

Yet in a larger sense, despite professional politicians' total commitment to spoils, the assumption that the lure of "public plunder" would keep the party intact, and the all-pervasiveness of the extensionism issue, the city Democracy's real problems lay fundamentally in its inability to adjust, solve, or even face a multitude of local needs implicit in urban growth. The slavery question might have been real to many men such as Preston King and William Cullen Bryant, but for most Tammany leaders it was a fake question, a cover that hid other pressing needs.

But as municipal government worsened, the Hall could no longer enjoy the luxury of make-believe. While party leaders kept their eyes on Governor Seymour's problem over canal extension and others bemoaned the fact that the Hards gained control over the state committee, thus almost guaranteeing the end of any semblance of intraparty harmony, a special New York City Grand Jury quietly prepared a report destined totally to disrupt local politics. When finally published, the report was a damning indictment of both political parties, including all their warring factions. The investigation pointed out that the "city fathers" had solicited and received huge bribes from contractors, particularly from railroad interests in connection with rights of way. Other disclosures showed that corruption permeated methods used to win paving contracts, sewer extensions, police jobs and promotions, street lighting, and a variety of other municipal functions. The Corporation often overrode the mayor's veto and, ignoring the lowest bidder, extorted money from inferior contractors who could not, or would not, fulfill their obligations. As the capstone of their venality, the aldermen even used the official mourning period that observed Henry Clay's death to overcharge the city for crepe paper.

Under these conditions, most outraged New Yorkers felt that only a third party of dedicated, honest reformers could cleanse the city. From such a feeling, Peter Cooper, an influential ironmonger and full-time humanitarian, helped launch the Civic Reform party. As its first act, the reformers petitioned the legislature to once again amend the charter.

If the Grand Jury's disclosures induced the need for honest civic stewardship, most legislators also felt that it compelled immediate action and honored the Civic Reform party's memorial. They kept the aldermanic system intact, but made the term two years on a staggered elective system. To make the Corporation more responsive to urban needs, the legislature abolished the Board of Assistant Aldermen and replaced it with a much more decentralized organization, the Board of Councilmen, whose sixty members were elected for one year from districts rather than the larger wards. Only they had the power to initiate appropriation bills. Other amendments to the bill drastically limited the aldermen's prerogatives. All contracts had to be made through sealed bids; leases of city property would go to the highest bidder. To discourage monopolies in public transportation and cut down the temptation for bribery, all leases were to expire after a ten-year period when the aldermen had to reopen bids. In order to override the mayor's veto, both houses needed a two-thirds vote; and no expenditure could be authorized for extralegal functions, such as Clay's funeral, without a positive vote by three-quarters of all Corporation members. Furthermore, the aldermen could no longer serve as judges on the court of oyer and terminer or on the courts of general or special sessions, even though they still could act as magistrates in the police stations and release prisoners on that basis. Finally, in an attempt to make the police department less political, the mayor, recorder, and city judge formed a board of commissioners who ran operations.[17]

In early June, city voters held a special election on the altered city charter. With reform in the air, the battling Democrats treated the changes as nonpartisan. Under the auspices of the Young Men's Democratic Club, Hards and Softs alike formed a common front. As an indication of Tammany's cynicism, Isaiah Rynders, a first-rate corruptionist himself, told the party faithful "to vote for the amendments until we can get something better." On June 8, by a ratio of over ten to one, city voters agreed. Even so, the reformers had accomplished little; the real test would come when they sought to implement these changes.[18]

During the next few months the split between the Hards and Softs became formal. Each held separate state conventions, organized full-scale parties, nominated independent tickets, and immobilized Pierce's harmony policy. In a hopeful vein, Governor Seymour welcomed these developments. With the President's aid, he wrote, "in one year from this time we will have a stronger party in this State than we have ever had since the time of General Jackson." [19]

But Pierce's appointees in the city had other ideas. In reply to Daniel Delevan's invitation to attend Tammany's ratification meeting of the Softs' state ticket, Collector Bronson sneered: "I cannot approve of nominations brought about by fraud and violence. Those who induce convicts and bullies into our conventions for the purpose of controlling events, must not expect that their proceedings will be sanctioned by me, whatever course may be pursued by others." [20]

Bronson's bravado aside, the Hards' local position was unstable because they had not neutralized the Tammany Society's dictum that they were antiorganization Democrats. In fighting the Softs on such treacherous ground, the Hards provoked another flurry of dissent against the sachems. They imported Daniel Dickinson down from Binghamton. Speaking in City Park, he readily agreed with the Barr Committee to "shun the building which is profaned by the tread of the infidel. The people respect the faith, 'principles and men.' They have no respect for 'brick and mortar.'" After he finished, Barr ended any chance for a local compromise. "We . . . from this time forward commence a campaign against . . . the Tammany Society—a secret, self-elected and irresponsible body of men who have dared to usurp the right of determining who shall and who shall not meet in Tammany Hall." Then, as their final gesture of defiance, the Hards organized the Stuyvesant Institute Democracy, named after their new meeting room, and formed Young Men's Democratic National Clubs to emphasize their allegiance towards the Compromise of 1850. All that remained was to convince President Pierce of their orthodoxy.[21]

The President was furious. But when he attempted to discipline the Hards through Secretary of the Treasury James Guthrie, the collector's immediate superior, Bronson at first denied his authority, then added that in appointments "confided to my discretion" the President's moderate policy did not necessarily apply. Bronson's audacity quickly boomeranged. Pierce demanded and received his resignation, and appointed Herman Redfield in his place. At once, the Hards sputtered with anger. By removing Bronson, they shouted, the Administration had interfered in local matters, punished its true allies, and actually formed an "unholy alliance" with men "friendly only to disorganization, agitation and violence." [22]

The Softs viewed Redfield as a godsend. As John Van Buren told Marcy, it was time for a new policy that would show "that bolters may all go out & that union Democrats are to come in." Yet Redfield, intent on following the President's will, only compounded the party's chaos. On taking over, he discovered that Bronson had appointed roughly three Hards for every Soft. For the sake of fairness, he felt it only just to give the Softs the major share of new patronage. Yet, he complained to Marcy, the competition for jobs was fierce. One weigher's slot had over a hundred applicants. As a result, Redfield moved with caution, only removing "Judge Bronson's more obnoxious appointments." The upshot was that the new collector ended by not satisfying anyone.[23]

In the interim, the fall elections had taken place. In the city, the voters, totally disenchanted with both major parties, awarded the Civic Reform party a mandate by giving it control over the Corporation. Upstate, the Whigs capitalized on the Hard-Soft split, the temperance question, and the canal controversy to increase their hold over the legislature.

Most striking of all was the Hards' dazzling surge of popularity, both upstate and in the city. Locally, they sent Francis Cutting and Mike Walsh to Congress, elected thirty men to the Common Council, and out-polled the Softs on the state ticket. With that, the Hards' central state committee, aided by Barr, attempted to restructure the entire political situation. The Democracy's problems, they claimed, began in 1849 when Marcy and Seymour formed a "piebald coalition of unabated animosities and political contradictions" that had subsequently ruined the party. In the city, the only way true Democrats could save the party was for the Tammany Society to disown the Softs' sachems. Nationally, the party ought to cashier Pierce, and organize for the next presidential race.[24]

At this critical juncture, the Softs suddenly reflected all the tensions that had been building up for months. While some observers, like Edward West, Stephen Douglas' strongest local supporter, expected an "extermination of one or the other of the parties," Fernando Wood felt that the Hards had made their point. In the city's roller-coaster politics they were clearly on top, he reasoned. But without Tammany Hall and the Tammany Society they could only punish the party, not rule it. Under these conditions, Wood visualized himself as the one man who could unite the local Democracy. What he needed was a sacrificial lamb. Luckily, one was at hand—John Van Buren.[25]

Taking his cue from the Barr Committee, Wood opened his attack on the old Barnburner Softs through the jittery Marcyites. Four years of ambiguity on free-soilism, he lectured the secretary, had caused the Democracy irreparable harm. John Van Buren was at fault. His continued role in Tammany Hall prevented fusion because the Hards hated him, while his constant abuse of "Shepard & myself" discouraged party workers. The local Democracy, Wood rumbled on, was sound considering the fact that it had never accepted free-soilism. In order to save the party, then, the Marcy Softs had to retire Prince John "from the front ranks, or our circle will be daily growing smaller." That done, the Marcyites should fuse with the nationalistic Hards.[26]

In a way, Wood made sense. The differences between the Marcyites and the Hards, he knew, were personal, not doctrinaire. Both were national Democrats, firmly attached to the Compromise of 1850. If both wanted to amalgamate without losing credibility, they could do so by purging Van Buren.

The Hards were not interested. If anything, they hoped to play off Wood against Van Buren and to profit by their rivalry. As a result, the city Democrats continued on their separate paths, organized new General Committees at the end of the year, and seemed as far apart as ever. In the impasse, Wood turned toward the Tammany Society, and pleaded with the sachems to seek party peace by holding out "an open hand to every Democrat." Again the Hards refused, and made matters worse when Representative Cutting tried to launch a congressional investigation of Bronson's ouster. In exasperation, Prosper Wetmore wrote, "It is perfectly idle to coax these men back into Tammany Hall. There is but one sensible course to be pursued let them alone." [27]

The passage of Stephen Douglas' Kansas-Nebraska bill, and particularly the section that repealed the Missouri Compromise, disrupted the course of city politics even more. At first, both General Committees waited until public opinion formed before acting. But while uncertainty made prudence a virtue, the Marcyite Softs, particularly Lorenzo Shepard, the new chairman of the General Committee, were too closely linked with the Administration for such equivocation. "You will thus perceive that I have a wolf by the Ears," he wrote Marcy. "I am tired of holding on and afraid to let go." [28]

Instead of supplying leadership, Marcy was lost. Certain that any move would automatically shatter the already uneasy Soft coalition, he pleaded unsuccessfully with the President not to make the bill Administration policy. When that failed, Marcy prepared his resignation. But his local supporters dissuaded him, fearing that his abdication would undermine their position with the national party. Much against his better judgment, therefore, Marcy stayed in the cabinet and, by extension, the public identified both him and the Softs as proslavery.

Upstate, the bill completed the process of Democratic disintegration. The Hards, while they sympathized with the bill in principle, could not openly back it without at the same time endorsing the Administration and lost the opportunity to establish any moral consistency on the basis of their Jeffersonian traditions. The Softs were in the worst shape because many former Free Soilers supported the anti-extensionist "Appeal of the Independent Democrats," and moved toward open rebellion. James P. Jones, a Monticello Soft, typified this mood. To Marcy he wrote: "We consider the Missouri Compromise as *sacred* as the Ordi-

nance of 1787, and that if one can be set aside the other may be also."
Horatio Seymour was just as upset. The bill, he wrote, was unnecessary because it was "very odious in this State." [29]

Similar pressures rocked the city Democracy. Federal officeholders
like Cochrane endorsed the bill with few qualms; the Schell Hards
desperately searched for some plausible formula to support it; while
Shepard agonized over finding some consensus policy. Of all Tammany
politicos, however, John Van Buren was the most beleaguered, because
while the bill supported the Jeffersonian principles inherent in popular
sovereignty, he, like James Jones, considered it an elaborate trick that
might lead to the extension of slavery north of the Ohio River. Worse,
his old Free Soil connections demanded that he take a stand and be
counted among the rebels. As his only way out, he adopted the weak
strategy of saying nothing about the bill while demanding that the
Softs' General Committee reendorse the Compromise of 1820.

But Shepard had no intention of aiding Prince John. With some help
from Fernando Wood's followers, the General Committee passed three
carefully worded resolutions: one that praised the Compromise of 1850,
a second that confirmed the Hall's commitment towards popular sovereignty, and a third that lauded Pierce's conduct in the presidency.
That done, the committeemen rejected Van Buren's attempt to endorse
the Missouri Compromise specifically.[30]

Paradoxically, the same forces that were destroying the party upstate were bringing Tammanyites closer together. In particular, Shepard
and Augustus Schell recognized that their similar views on the Kansas-
Nebraska issue could fuse city national Democrats into a fresh, stronger
Tammany Hall. They set to work at once. Schell sent a "deputation" to
Shepard "to propose a union," and he, in return, "made arrangements"
so that the Hards would "abandon their organization, come into ours
and recognize the Tammany Committees." Collector Redfield proved
helpful in the effort. Convinced that the time for quibbling had passed,
he began appointing national Democrats, Hards and Softs alike.[31]

But the negotiations between Shepard and Schell failed. Despite
overwhelming evidence that they agreed on all doctrinal points, they
could not convince a group of hidebound Hards to forget the past.
Blindly, these men commanded the Marcyites to denounce the President as a sign of good faith. This Shepard could not do as long as Marcy
sat in the cabinet. In another way, the breakdown in brokerage politics
symbolized the toll that the slavery extensionism issue was taking among
Tammanyites. Traditional party principles were now irrelevant, because
all the contenders considered themselves the bearers of legitimate Jef-

fersonianism. As a result, no one doubted the morality of any act because all considered themselves morally pure.[32]

Only Fernando Wood remained unconvinced that the party would not fuse around the Kansas-Nebraska question. Certain facts stimulated his instincts. Shepard, while he still headed the General Committee, had begun to lose power because Purdy no longer considered him capable of putting together a winning combination. Thus, if Wood could form an alliance with Purdy, the General Committee and the Tammany Society, by default, would be open for conquest. Then, too, John Van Buren helped when he scheduled an anti–Kansas-Nebraska meeting and the only men in attendance were Whigs and malcontent Democrats.[33]

With these ideas in mind, Wood planned again to make Prince John the catalyst for bringing the local Democracy together. The Softs' pro–Kansas-Nebraska meeting gave Wood his opportunity. Several days before the rally, the Committee's subsection on arrangements, normally chaired by John Cochrane, met to form an agenda. But with Cochrane out of town on official business, Wood took his place, and drew up a series of resolutions aimed against Van Buren in particular and the rebel Democrats in general. Once the rally began, Wood then planned to pack the Long Room with his toughs who would prevent Shepard's supporters from speaking and thus endorse the resolves. As the upshot. Wood thought he could create the impression that the Van Burenites were the only local element opposed to the Administration. That done, the Hards would have no excuse to scorn an accommodation.

Wood's idea was full of audacity but everything went wrong with it. At the eleventh hour, Cochrane came home, learned of the plot, reconvened the subcommittee, and deposed Wood. When the full rally organized, Purdy, "the old warhorse of the Democracy," took the chair and announced that the Hall believed in "the right of self-government which is the essence of Democracy." Redfield, O'Conor, Rynders, and Shepard reemphasized the same Jeffersonian principle. And, to spite Wood, the Committee selected him to read those sections of the resolutions that praised the Administration, approved the bill, but said nothing about the Van Buren people.[34]

If Wood still doubted his hard-earned wisdom, the course of events during the next few months again proved the point. At the end of May, Stephen Douglas visited the city at Purdy's invitation. The Marcy Softs and the Young Men's Democratic Union Club gave him a tumultuous welcome, and the Tammany Society again welcomed him as an honorary brave. But the Hards, ignoring Schell's pleas, refused to attend any of these meetings because of the Council's sponsorship of Douglas.[35]

Upstate, both the Hards and Softs split into warring camps by June. One group of Dickinson Hards, led by Congressman John Wheeler, was anti–Kansas-Nebraska, anti-Administration, anti-Marcy. In opposition were the Augustus Schell–Mike Walsh Hards—anti-Administration, pro-Kansas, pro-Marcy. Predictably among the Softs, the Marcyites led by Shepard and Cochrane, were pro-Administration, pro–Kansas-Nebraska. The Van Buren Softs followed no set pattern. Through the plain logic of his position, Prince John favored the Administration, not the Kansas-Nebraska bill. But, unable to be fully consistent because of his father, he did not join many former Free Soilers who became members of the new Republican party.

The temperance question compounded the mess. In April, prodded along by Senator Myron Clark, the legislature passed a stringent prohibition bill aimed at curbing the sale and use of alcohol and beer. When the proposed "Maine Law" reached his desk, Governor Seymour used his veto. But the nativists and politicians-on-the-make who swelled the temperance crusade's ranks purposely heightened emotionalism for their own ends and would not let the question die. By June, they had formed the American or Know-Nothing party. But as with the American Republicans, the new nativist menace faced two ways. One section, composed of sincere but stubborn bigots, frankly despised all foreigners. But of more importance, conservative, nationalistic Whigs —men like Daniel Ullman, Millard Fillmore, and James Brooks—captured this legacy of hate and used it as a counter to anti–slavery extensionism. Thus, while the temperance question was allied with nativism, not all prohibitionists were nativists.[36]

As the Know-Nothing party's doctrines spread throughout the country, city Democrats initially approached the movement without a well-conceived program. In July, partly as a reflex action, Shepard's General Committee announced that "we utterly repudiate any attempt to proscribe any of our fellow citizens, whether foreign or native, on account of the religious beliefs they might entertain." Despite such pronouncements, many Tammanyites flirted seriously with nativism. After a brief courtship, the Marcyites and Van Burenites backed off as organized groups and defended the immigrants, both Irish and German. On the other hand, the Hards, who had a long heritage of xenophobia, reserved judgment until they saw how the issue developed. Even so, because the Know-Nothing party was a semipatriotic group whose secrecy cut across factional lines, some Tammanyites clandestinely joined local cells and played both sides of the issue.[37]

By September, all the parties upstate were about as solid as a dividing amoeba. The Democrats nominated separate gubernatorial slates; Seymour for the Softs, Bronson for the Hards. The Whigs also split. The Sewardites named Myron Clark, while the Fillmore nationalists joined with the Know-Nothings and selected former Clayite Daniel Ullman. Now, a semblance of order evolved. The Temperance Convention, the Free Democrats, and the Anti-Nebraska Democrats tabled their past differences, found a common denominator in anti-slavery extensionism, and backed Clark.[38]

Similar problems haunted the city Democracy. In July, the Tammany Society, had made another effort at peace but the move reopened two older sources of rancor. The Council dedicated its Independence Day festival to *"Union, Strength, Victory. Regrets for the Past to be Buried in Exertions for the Future."* Shepard delivered the main address, but Cochrane drew the most applause when he toasted the President: "Let no treacherous hand be raised against him." In spite of these words, the Dickinson Hards redoubled their efforts to get the legislature to revoke the Society's charter as a charitable order, while the Free Democrats and the Anti–Nebraska Democrats held aloof and tried to revive the spirit of the 1848 Free Soil "Campaign for Freedom"[39]

In the gubernatorial election, then, the Marcyite Softs, realizing that the extensionism issue was too hot to handle, made Seymour's opposition to prohibitionism and nativism their campaign planks. But the Hards would not let them off the hook. At a Shepard General Committee rally, a group of rowdy Hards kept up an insistent clamor against the ticket. Somewhat lamely, Sachem Robert Kelly, a future General Committee chairman, apologized to Seymour: "The crowd at the meeting was made up in due proportion of rank & file, whose presence is the best indication of a large vote on election day. An audience of mere respectability in T.H. is a failure." [40]

Undaunted, the Shepard Softs tried again. In one ward rally after another, they hammered home the point that Clark, Bronson, and Ullman were the candidates of "all the *isms* of the day," and bypassed the regular organization by forming Seymour Clubs and Liquor Dealers' Associations on a city-wide basis. To prevent future disruptions at their gatherings, they campaigned as Seymour-men, not Tammanyites or Marcyites. Even so, the battlefield lay not in organizations but in men's minds.[41]

For Fernando Wood, the Democracy's drive towards self-destruction was not entirely without redeeming features. First, he watched with unconcealed glee the nativist movement's growth. Ever since 1849 he had assiduously cultivated the Irish, contributed substantial sums to their relief agencies, and generally catered to their interests. By publicly opposing the Know-Nothings and the prohibitionists, then, he cemented his power base among the credulous immigrants. Above that, Shepard had alienated the Administration when Pierce refused to appoint him district attorney when Charles O'Conor resigned. As a result, Shepard was vulnerable as Tammany's titular leader. But above all else, the Civic Reform party had failed. Confronted by the same evils that haunted the regular organizations, the amateurish reformers lacked the technical skills necessary for the art of ruling and quickly alienated their well-wishers. But in their failure, Wood realized that the Civic Reformers had left a huge political vacuum because they had not solved the problem of corruption that permeated municipal life.

With these facts in mind, Wood sought and gained the Shepard Softs' mayoralty nomination largely because other contenders felt that no Democrat could win. Then Wood gave New Yorkers an insight into his peculiar bent for political trickery. Determined to run on a united ticket, he captured the Hards' convention by packing the room with his hired thugs who then intimidated the startled delegates into selecting him rather than two of their more likely men, James Libby or Augustus Schell. Temporarily overpowered, bulky William Tweed and Thomas Barr reacted defiantly. As Barr put it: "Mr. Wood doesn't belong to this organization, and the votes which have been cast for him are, therefore, not in order in this convention." Yet Barr could not deny the simple fact that Wood did have the Hards' nomination. As their only way out then, the Hards bolted their own apparatus and became insurgents by running Schell as an independent.[42]

At this point, Wood showed his political genius. Events during the past spring and summer had indicated several major trends. First, the Democracy could not come to terms with extensionism and the Hards and Softs would never fuse as long as that issue was the critical difference between them. Yet, in the city another equally vexatious problem —reform—could with proper handling divert attention from extensionism and become the means to establish party unity. Moreover, with Shepard in disgrace and John Van Buren touring Europe with his father, Tammany lacked any leader who could supply direction to machine politics.

The party's reward, then, for a man who could neutralize the Kansas-Nebraska bill's enormous impact upon local politics would be immense. The way to do so was obvious to Wood. The reformers had nominated Wilson Hunt, a political chameleon, who had been by turns a Free Soiler, a Hard, then a Civic party man. Since Hunt proved to be an indifferent campaigner, running on a loosely structured platform, Wood stole his thunder. Pledging to bring honest government back into City Hall, Wood labeled himself a liberal reformer and kept up a constant harangue against corruption in municipal life.

Two could play the same game. Still smarting from Wood's attacks, Schell withdrew, threw his support behind Hunt, called for a "wise and just" temperance policy, and disposed of both the Know-Nothings and the Tammany Society in one sharp thrust: "We are opposed to all secret societies," Schell said, "as hostile to the genius of republican institutions, and recognize no distinctions among fellow citizens, arising from birth, sect or creed." [43]

Suddenly, just as all the pieces fell into place, Wood's personal machine stalled. Several nativists filed affidavits that charged him with being a Know-Nothing and actively courting the anti-Catholic vote. Wood emphatically denied the accusations. It would be ludicrous for him to be a nativist, he claimed, because everyone knew his standing among the immigrants. The damage to his reputation was impossible to assess. Although the Softs and the *Irish-American* dismissed the charges as so much mudslinging, Wood's protestations of innocence left many voters unconvinced.

By election day, tension had become routine. If anything, the returns symbolized the disruption of the city's two-party system.

COMPARISON OF PERCENTAGE VOTE CAST FOR EACH
CANDIDATE FOR MAYOR AND GOVERNOR, 1854 [44]

| *Softs* | | *Hards* | | *Sewardites* | | *Know-Nothings* | |
|---|---|---|---|---|---|---|---|
| Wood | Seymour | Small | Bronson | Herrick | Clark | Barker | Ullman |
| 33.5 | 44.3 | 25.8 | 8.6 | 9.6 | 20.6 | 31 | 26.5 |

For the next few weeks, politicians mulled over exactly what had happened. Three results were apparent: New York City lacked a clear majority party, Fernando Wood was the new mayor, and Seymour lost to Myron Clark by a hair's breadth. Gradually other facts grew visible. The nativists ran surprisingly well and their potential for mischief knew no bounds—provided they could maintain their cohesion. The Sewardites, in contrast (even with Clark's victory), held off from becoming Republicans only in order to guarantee "Little Bill's" Senate reelection. The Democrats faced a bleak future. The Marcyites and

Dickinsonites were as far apart as ever. In the gubernatorial race, many Hards had voted for either Ullman or Clark to punish Seymour, not to prove that they held the balance of power within the Democracy. Only Fernando Wood emerged unscathed. Running against a divided field, he had established his vote-getting potential. With the right combination of luck and politicking, he could make Tammany Hall his own personal creature.[45]

It was as a "man of honor, a friend of labor and industry, and a protector of the poor" that Fernando Wood described himself in his inaugural address. "My mind & time is so completely occupied with municipal affairs," he wrote Marcy, "that politics is almost forgotten." In the next weeks, Wood made good on his promises and transformed himself into the "Model Mayor." Calling for business-like municipal financial accounting, he offered an innovative program to solve some of the city's urban ills: reform in the police department, city home rule, separation of election day for local and state contests, the establishment of a complaint book for the little people, and taxes on city-licensed franchises. "People said he was to be the rowdy's man, the rum Mayor, the blackguard's friend, and many other things," wrote an admiring *New York Herald*. "What a blunder was here." [46]

But Wood the reformer could not live down his reputation as Wood the politico, and several other would-be leaders, particularly Naval Officer John Cochrane, did not trust him. A strong, unscrupulous person such as Wood, Cochrane reasoned, who could inspire immense emotional admiration among groups as diverse as the city immigrants and upper-class merchants, might consolidate power as no Tammany politician had even done. But Cochrane knew that Wood's position at this point was impregnable. To counter the mayor then, Cochrane sought an issue or series of issues that might thwart Wood while uniting the party.

Luckily for Cochrane, the pendulum of factional sentiment now began swinging toward reconciliation and he correctly sensed the direction of public opinion. Shepard favored reunion because he still recognized that, save for Dickinson's position, no real difference existed in principles between the Hards and Softs; the John Van Burenites, few in number, hoped to counter the Kansas-Nebraska bill's impact; Young America felt fusion would enhance Stephen Douglas' presidential ambitions; and the pro–James Buchanan Hards, led by Daniel Sickles who had just returned to the city after a stint in the London legation, assumed that a united party would guarantee the Pennsylvanian's nomination.

It was in this spirit of rallying a disunited party that Cochrane helped reorganize the Union Club movement, and formed a central committee with himself as president. Similar efforts had failed, but Cochrane proposed a fresh start. The new Club, he said, was not based on "insecure and hollow" agreements made by rival factional leaders. Instead, the Union movement emanated from an untainted generation of young men, determined to work "upwards from the masses to the leaders." [47]

By January, the seeds Cochrane planted reached early bloom. Meeting in the Wigwam, the Central Democratic Union Club held its first statewide convention, organized New York on a county-by-county basis, called for a "strict construction of the federal Constitution," and welcomed all national Democrats as members. The Tammany Society also helped. With Purdy's blessing, the sachems dedicated their New Orleans Ball to "Union and the Constitution." To make the message clearer, one toaster invited all those who were "estranged from Tammany Hall" to come home and share in the Democratic party's brotherhood.[48]

By February, however, blight threatened the Unionist's growth. The Hards and Softs retained separate General Committees and gave no hint of reconciliation. Then, too, Postmaster Fowler proved obdurate. When he and Cochrane visited Washington to see if Pierce and Marcy would influence Collector Redfield to appoint only Unionists, it quickly became apparent that Fowler was more interested in self-promotion than party fusion or neutralizing Wood. When Cochrane returned home, a deeper hazard materialized. Redfield, urged by the Administration, tried to capture the movement. Such an alliance, Cochrane knew, would be the kiss of death because the Hards would interpret it as an effort to renominate Pierce. So Cochrane had to steer a perilous course between his duties as a federal officeholder and his ambitions as a local politician.

One issue, the annexation of Cuba, held promise for Cochrane as the means to separate fusion—as strictly a local matter that local politicians would solve—from President Pierce's discredited Administration. The *Herald* noted that of all the issues confronting the parties, only Cuba was "an open question" that might "reorganize *en masse* . . . the routed and scattered democratic party." Quick to seize the opening, the Unionists pressed for immediate annexation. The Tammany Society and the Young Men's Democratic Club joined the cry: "Honor requires it; justice pleads for it; the people demand it." Even John Van Buren, now home, added his voice to the growing chorus.[49]

Extensionism's euphoria soon paled before the chronic personal nature of city politics. The Shepardites could not fully support annexation because Marcy opposed it; John Van Buren's miniscule following, on reflection, drew back because proslavery forces favored the move; the Dickinson Hards assumed that Young America backed Cuban annexation to boom Douglas; all this left Cochrane with an issue that was coming apart at the seams.

Still, he was willing to bruise personal feelings if he could jolt some sense of order into the party. But the attitude of the Softs' General Committee made the demise of the Cuban question only a matter of time. Under Robert Kelly's direction, the Hall claimed that the Monroe Doctrine justified annexation. Yet, in the same resolutions, Tammany also criticized prohibitionism and nativism. Frustrated, the Unionists tried to make annexation stand by itself. They failed. Now that the Hall refused to draw a distinction among all three questions, the Union Club regretfully once more began a search for a noncontroversial issue above factionalism. For the moment, they called for party harmony based on the Constitution and opposition to all "isms" that invaded private citizens' personal rights.[50]

By any reckoning, Fernando Wood's first few months in office were a resounding success, although not everything went smoothly. First, trouble brewed in Albany. In April 1855, Governor Clark and his Dry supporters fulfilled their campaign promises and passed a temperance law, based largely upon Maine's model prohibition statute. Under its provisions, the act forbade the sale of any intoxicating liquors and outlined harsh punishments for any public official who hindered its implementation.

The prohibition law cramped Wood's new political style. To enforce it would alienate his Irish and German supporters; to flaunt it would tarnish his reformist halo. Yet undeterred, he approached his dilemma with characteristic skulduggery. When the bill passed, he promised compliance, no matter "the personal consequences." At the same time, he found a convenient escape hatch because the legislators had not been clear on the exact methods of enforcement. Along with Republican District Attorney A. Oakey Hall, Wood stifled the law through indirection. Further, he confided to several sympathetic aldermen that the law was as ridiculous as it was unconstitutional. All in all, his double-faced solution paid off. Despite the loss of a few reformers, Wood solidified his immigrant base, and the foundation of his support was broader because of temperance than it had ever been before. In March 1856, the state court of appeals capped his triumph when it nullified the law.[51]

The mayor was less fortunate with the affair of the *Joseph Walker*, a cargo ship loaded with valuable goods which had sunk at her city pier. In the letting of salvage contracts, it soon appeared that Wood had not awarded the contract to the lowest bidder and might have accepted a bribe. Again, he eased out of a difficult situation. A special investigatory committee found no evidence of his purported dishonesty, and he offered to reimburse the city personally for any revenue lost.[52]

Only the Tammany Society sounded a sour note. In April, over the mayor's covert objections, it elected Lorenzo Shepard as grand sachem. Shepard, intent on rebuilding his prestige, immediately laid plans to convert the Society into a firm Marcyite bastion. To his chief, Shepard wrote that "my design is to draw a large body of your friends, that is men who care more for your interests than they do for a few dollars or a small office, into the Tammany Society so as to hold in check the Van Buren and Hard influence if they should misbehave." Mayor Wood had other ideas. Since he needed the Society to consolidate power, Shepard's intentions presented a formidable challenge. Quietly, Wood mended his fences among the braves, and patiently awaited his chance. Then, too, Elijah Purdy could not accept Shepard's efforts, because he too had other ideas for the Society.[53]


Meantime, the Unionists experimented with fresh party cement. During May, Henry A. Wise, the Democratic nominee for governor of Virginia, scored a spectacular victory over the Know-Nothings, and became a national party hero because he was the first Democrat to halt the nativists' steamroller. This feeling was especially strong in New York City, where the Unionists now sought to use antinativism to tie the Hards and Softs together. At first, all went well. As a Southerner, Wise fulfilled Dickinson's specifications, while John Van Buren hoped the issue would cool the heat that the Kansas-Nebraska bill generated. On May 30, Tammany held a victory celebration in Wise's honor and, for the first time in three years, the Hards and Softs laid aside all differences and held a common rally.

This harmonious spirit evaporated just as it had always done. At the end of June when Robert Hunter of Virginia, Wise's ally, visited the city to guage presidential prospects, both factions held separate meetings. Resting on dead center, the Tammany Society's Independence

Day celebration bore witness to the Democracy's estrangement. Hardly mentioning the Administration, Shepard and the other speakers vilified intolerance and nativism. Yet none of them coped with the vital question of party reunion. Only one man—Fernando Wood—was ready to do so. Yet his ultimate purpose scarcely fit into the Democracy's overall aims.[54]

In the interim, the controversy set off by Stephen Douglas' Kansas-Nebraska bill came to a boil. The Administration was determined to use Kansas as a testing ground to prove that popular sovereignty worked. Opposed was the infant Republican party, with an equally strong will of its own, out to demonstrate that popular sovereignty only brought anarchy and bloodshed. As a result, antiextensionism became the new cutting edge of all political alignments. The question split the Know-Nothings into three feuding internal groups, created havoc among the John Van Burenites, and gave Thurlow Weed an excuse to merge the old "Conscience Whigs" with the Republicans.

On the sidelines, attentive Democrats felt that the situation was tailored to their best interests. Seymour spoke for many of them when he told Marcy that in "agitating" the slavery issue Weed, Seward, and Horace Greeley certainly "got up a strong cry about that subject, but they may be compelled to push it so far as to create a re-action." Such optimism was premature at best. Since the Republican party was elastic enough to win the support of businessmen, Henry Clay Whigs, and western farmers as well as antiextensionists and abolitionists, Seymour's hope rested on a united Democracy.[55]

Yet, as the party's two state conventions proved, this situation was not possible. At the Hards' meeting, Dickinson's followers rejected fusion. Not all Hards agreed, however. Daniel Sickles, the leader of a new splinter group, the "Half Shells," urged some sort of reconciliation as a means to advance James Buchanan's candidacy. But he failed. As one upstater observed, "he'd rather steal sheep than fuse with the Softs." Then, in a further rebuke to Sickles, the delegates named a full slate of men for the national convention, headed by Bronson, nominally unpledged, but clearly committed to Dickinson. Sadly, Marcy concluded that the Hards "appear to be determined to prevent the union of the Dem. party & I fear that they will have sufficient success to accomplish their object." [56]

In the city, Shepard prepared for the Softs' rally with his usual care. Assuming that "every thing in New York is now unsettled & feverish," he felt that the delegates should downplay all topics likely to cause dissension, campaign purely on local issues, and seek common ground with the Hards. John Van Buren recoiled from such trimming. The convention, he urged, had to "censure the administration for repealing the Missouri Compromise & throwing the great States of Ohio, Penn. & New York into the hands of the Whigs almost hopelessly." [57]

At the meeting, the Marcyites, who dominated the state Central Committee, sought to mollify all Democratic groups. Bowing to the fusionists, the delegates called for immediate reunion. The Marcyites received resolutions that condemned nativism and prohibitionism. To lure the Hards, the convention endorsed popular sovereignty. As for Van Buren, the delegates agreed (over Shepard's objections) that the state Democracy, while it still adhered to all "compromises of the Constitution" and would continue to defend states' rights, deemed "this an appropriate occasion to declare and repeat their fixed hostility to the extension of Slavery in territories now free." Then the convention selected their own national convention delegates, and picked a moderate state ticket representing all factions. Seemingly, the question of war or peace now lay with the Hards.[58]

But the upstate Hards held aloof. They warned "all true national men" to avoid "abolitionists, time-servers and free soilers." The Unionists were equally blind because they called for fusion based on Governor Wise's presidential candidacy and popular sovereignty, and ignored the Softs' efforts. Shepard played the same game. Although the Softs' General Committee supported the slate, it rejected the spirit of the Wilmot Proviso inherent in the convention's condemnation of extensionism. Only one ray of hope filtered through the gloom. City Half Shells, Seymour wrote Marcy, were "very indignant at Dickinson's friends for stealing the delegates" to the national convention. "They threaten a third ticket." [59]

The Stuyvesant Institute Democracy had no intention of surrendering to the Sickles Half Shells. Moreover, its determination hardened when Mayor Wood, who had admired Buchanan ever since their days together in Congress, slowly moved toward Sickles' position. Under these conditions, the Hards prudently avoided an open primary election for their nominating convention and hand-picked the delegates. The reason that prompted the move, they blandly told the *Herald*, was to prevent Tammany's "short boys, shoulder hitters, tide waiters, post office chiffoniers, and other riff raff" from stealing nominations, much as their mentor, Fernando Wood, had done the year before.[60]

The Half Shells bridled at these charges but could do little. When Sickles demanded that the delegates at the city Hards' convention pay attention to political reality, the Dickinsonites replied that political reality was a relative question, not an imperative. But Sickles was far from satisfied. Along with Emmanuel Hart and Robert Dillion, he opened negotiations with Robert Kelly's General Committee. Since both groups, Sickles told him, "did not originate in any differences upon principle," fusion made sense.[61]

Sickles and Kelly at once plunged into the delicate task of forming a union slate. Even Seymour helped when he made a major policy address at the Wigwam that praised local conciliation efforts. But although the speech drew immense acclaim throughout the nation and made him Marcy's spiritual, if not physical, successor as New York's favorite son, little material good resulted. Worse, Collector Redfield stampeded Shepard and Cochrane when he insisted that Tammany had to back the Administration and instructed Custom House toughs to steal the local nominations. Without thinking of the consequences, the Hall formed a compromise ticket without consulting Sickles.

The Half Shells were furious but they did not panic. At the end of October, they named a mixed slate, slightly more Hard than Soft, nominated Sickles for the state senate, and anxiously awaited Tammany's reaction. Just at this point, John W. Forney, the editor of Pierce's official party newspaper, the *Washington Union,* arrived in the city, and seconded the Half Shells' efforts. Through his mediation, the state Central Committees of both factions met with Sickles in a final effort to iron out an agreement. They failed because the Dickinsonites refused to budge. Yet even Forney was not disinterested. Despite his close association with the President, Forney, like many other Democrats, was ready to dump Pierce in favor of Buchanan. The editor's trip, then, was no accident. Both he and Sickles were playing a similar fusion game for their own ends.[62]

The election taught the Democrats a lesson. Locally, wherever united, they soared to victory; wherever split, the Know-Nothing won. Upstate, the same sorry spectacle held true with only a slight variation. The Democrats ran poorly, the Republicans were on the upswing, while the nativist thrust held less power than in the city. Even so, the returns were so depressing that neither Tammany Hall nor Stuyvesant Institute held any post-election celebrations.

The most obvious fact that emerged from the Democratic debacle was the sharp decrease in the number of voters who even bothered to cast ballots. Over 230,000 fewer men had voted than in the last gubernatorial race. This defection hurt the Democrats more than its two foes. For even though the Softs had roughly doubled the Hards' statewide totals, together they amassed less than Seymour's 1854 tally. Here was the true lesson of 1855: only through fusion could the Democracy survive. But again, neither the Softs nor the Hards could find common ground for an accommodation. Instead, both looked over the field for a suitable presidential contender and prepared elaborate briefs which each intended to present at the national convention to prove that only their side truly represented the Democracy of New York.[63]

The Tammany Society boldly acted as a peacemaker. The sachems, steering clear of polemics, used the New Orleans Ball as the means to propose a reconciliation based on traditional party values. "The doors of Tammany," Grand Sachem Lorenzo Shepard stressed, "have ever been open to those who love their country and to those oppressed from every clime." The Hards curtly rejected the peace offer. At their rival dance, held in the Metropolitan Hotel, they too called for the party to uphold "ancient usages," but showed little other inclination toward fusion.[64]

The two social affairs, so close in reality, prompted the Democratic Union Club into another flurry of activity. But everything went wrong. Although Shepard and Cochrane voiced the need for complete Democratic concordance before the convention in order to increase the state's bargaining power, Fernando Wood immediately took charge of the actual details. Stressing that an organization divided against itself was a political absurdity, he pledged "everything towards bringing about and perfecting a harmonious union and consolidation of the democratic party." For the time being, however, his efforts dashed the Unionists' hopes. Instead of glorifying fusion, which would have enhanced Wood's prestige in an election year, they now behaved as if they were attending a wake. "You know the Party," the pugnacious Isaiah Rynders fretted to Marcy. "They were never true to any man or principle, and I take it for granted they will act with their usual consistency." [65]


Off in Cleveland, Ohio, recovering from a throat operation, Senator Stephen Douglas still dreamed of winning the party's nomination. In the last two years, much of the contempt originally aimed at him had been shifted to President Pierce. As things stood, Douglas retained a somewhat battered reputation and the admiration, if not the open support, of a sizable section of party workers.

But with increasing uneasiness, he watched the efforts for Buchanan in New York gain momentum. Under Sickles' leadership, the "Buchananeers" had organized Keystone Clubs in each ward and were preparing a gigantic welcoming ceremony for the ambassador's return from London. Douglas' ultimate success, then, rested on deflating the Buchanan boom before his supporters actively launched the Pennsylvanian's campaign. In order to do so, Douglas had to fuse the Hards and Softs with some subtle plan without awakening suspicion.[66]

In late February, Douglasite David T. Disney, a former Ohio congressman who had supported Cass in 1852, arrived in the city. Quickly, he closeted himself with Edward West, a Stuyvesant Institute Hard, who nonetheless supported Douglas. Between them, they matured a plot short on ethics but long on nerve. First, they planned to open secret talks with the Millard Fillmore Know-Nothings and win their aid. If that failed, Disney hoped to finesse the feuding Tammanyites into a harmony front through deception.

Predictably, the first plan fell flat. The Know-Nothings' nomination of Fillmore for president, Disney wrote, "will be a positive loss to us." He then put his second plan into operation. As a diversionary tactic, he posed as a doughface supporter of President Pierce out to test the Administration's local footing. At the outset, all went well. "Now there is no *principle* in controversy between the softs & hards," he reported, "but much personal feelings." In order to cope with this situation, he avoided any specifics and disarmingly suggested to local leaders of both factions that the only way New York could "restore herself in the old position at the head of the republic and have the control for her politics" was to agree on a common candidate, who had a real chance of winning, before the convention met.[67]

Far too clever to advance Douglas' name, Disney held a round robin of separate meetings with Schell, Sickles, and other city chieftains. One by one they disqualified the leading contenders until the name of Douglas suddenly stood out. Schell, with nothing to gain by temporizing, promised his aid—provided Douglas gave Dickinson some exact assurances "*where and what* he is to be." This Disney could not do without alienating the Marcy Softs. But the Ohioan had unsuspected depths of subtlety. Back he went to Shepard and suggested that if the Softs came out openly for Douglas "on the ground that [he] so fully illustrates the principles which both sides now recognise," their move would prove them "to be sincere in their declaration of principles." Disney then tried the same line on the Hards. Yet while the Softs showed signs of relenting, the Dickinsonites wanted firm commitments. In desperation, Disney wrote Douglas to send a "Southern man of standing" to sway Dickinson. But Douglas, ill and feverish after a relapse, failed to respond. "You may rely upon it that Buchanan *has* made such strength that every effort is needed to beat him," Disney pleaded again to Douglas. But in the end nothing worked, and Disney left for home without accomplishing a thing. The balky New York dissidents simply would not, or could not, divorce personal animus from national politics.[68]

As Douglas' trial run collapsed, the Buchanan forces spurted ahead. Exuberant over the reception in the wards, the Keystone Clubs, through Sickles, artfully placated the Stuyvesant Institute Democracy on a number of sensitive points, and dangled before them a bait that Disney lacked: a positive hint of exclusive patronage. By the time Buchanan disembarked in the city, his candidacy had picked up an impressive list of backers. As Fernando Wood put it at the Half Shells' welcoming dinner, the nation would "never be unmindful of, or indifferent to, the return that is due to those who distinguish themselves." Equally impressive, the *Herald*, which had correctly picked the winning presidential candidate in every election since 1836, threw its massive support behind Sickles' efforts.[69]

By May, the Softs contrastingly lacked both candidates and a sense of purpose. Dean Richmond, leader of the "New Albany Regency"— a group of upstate railroad and business entrepreneurs including Erastus Corning and his lawyer, John V. L. Pruyn—favored Douglas. The Custom House group in the city favored Buchanan, although Collector Redfield intended to back Pierce for a few ballots as a sign of good faith. As for the Van Burenites, they renounced any compromise with slavery extensionism. "The fair fertile prairies of the West," the *Voice of the Radical Democracy of New York* declared, shall never "be made to echo to the lash of the overseer's whip or the clank of the Lordman's fetter." Elated, some Republicans invited Martin Van Buren to become one of their convention delegates.[70]

When the convention met, the Softs found themselves outgeneraled. Their first sign of trouble came when the Credentials Committee decided that it was "unable to discover any differences of principles" between the New Yorkers, and adopted a report which suggested that the state's vote be evenly split between the two factions. In an open floor debate, the delegates approved the plan, 137–123.

When nominations began, the Softs cast their eighteen votes first for Pierce, later for Douglas. But when the senator became convinced that he could not win and withdrew, the Softs were caught in a vulnerable position. Although Richmond belatedly swung behind Buchanan, the move came after Buchanan's tally had reached the necessary two-thirds. Richmond's painful experience exhilarated the Dickinson Hards, who had backed Buchanan all the way, and they braced for a massive purge of the Softs. Buchanan had other plans. Certain that he could not carry the state without Soft aid, he ordered the Hards to cooperate with the Marcyites and form a common front.[71]

As an outsider and his party's standard-bearer, Buchanan's decree worked political wonders. Tammany Hall and Stuyvesant Institute co-sponsored a union rally on City Park's neutral grounds. Among the speakers were Shepard, Wood, John Van Buren, Sickles, and even Stephen Douglas. Alderman Thomas Barr ended the evening when he announced that "the democracy of New York with one heart and one voice respond to and ratify the nomination." [72]

During the next few days, hardly an hour passed without a fresh sign of cooperation. Marcy called on all his friends to support Buchanan, Redfield's appointees fell into lockstep, Martin Van Buren sent his fatherly blessings, and the Tammany Society rumbled its approval. Its Fourth of July invitations read: "It is the duty of every citizen to forget past differences, and render cheerful aid to all who are acting in defense of the Constitution and the principles of the Declaration."

By mid-July, Buchanan's dictum took on the permanence of party doctrine. Most New York Democrats, excluding some former Barn-burners who had not yet become Republicans, found amalgamation sentiment obligatory, and factional sniping generally ceased. In the city, as a harmony gesture, the Softs selected Wood's clerk, Wilson Small, as the new General Committee chairman in the place of the deceased Robert Kelly, and delegated Lorenzo Shepard to sound out the Hards about a permanent armistice.[73]

Meantime, Fernando Wood, through a process that he had never intended, hastened the Democracy's fusion. In April, he had attempted to wield his prestige as an original Buchanan-backer to capture the Tammany Society. When that failed, he bided his time until the state party held an amalgamated convention. There, he and Sickles claimed that Buchanan could not carry the state without Wood as the gubernatorial candidate. The delegates were unimpressed. Instead, they named Richmond's close friend Amasa Parker, set up a common Central Committee, and from the city named as presidential electors Tammany-ite Softs John Cochrane and William Kennedy, Tammanyite Hard William Tweed, Woodite Alexander Ming, Jr., and Half Shell Daniel Sickles.[74]

The same fear of falling under the mayor's dictatorial influence quickened the reunion process in the city. By early August, Shepard's discreet diplomacy paid off when the Hards and Softs formed a united

General Committee of 132 men—chaired by Shepard, not Wilson Small—including such men as Tweed, Purdy, Fowler, Sickles, Kennedy, Cochrane, and Peter B. Sweeny, a hard-driving lawyer soon to become notorious. Only through trickery did Wood gain a spot. To dramatize the new era of sweetness and light, both Young Men's General Committees met together in the Wigwam and with a hired band playing appropriate marching music, trekked to Stuyvesant Institute, where, along with the Young Men's Union Club, they ceremoniously escorted the defunct Hard General Committee back to the Long Room.[75]

The political complexion of Shepard's Committee, coupled with the Tammany Society's open hostility, placed Wood at the crossroads of his career. Temperamentally incapable of defensive action, he decided to fight back by placing himself above the organization and slowly began to lay the groundwork for an independent machine based on his personal magnetism, not his status as a faithful party worker. In the campaign Wood waged, the lines of battle were subjective rather than partisan. Tammany Hall did not split into Hard and Soft factions as in the past; instead, Wood generated a new alignment. The Softs and Unionists, led by Shepard, Purdy, Fowler, Cochrane, and Sweeny, joined the Augustus Schell Hards in an attempt to block the mayor's renomination. "Honest John" Kelly, one of the city's Irish leaders and a future party boss, and Half Shell Daniel Sickles allied themselves with Wood. Even so, the lines that separated the two groups were extremely fluid. Men shifted loyalty with ease as the art of expediency reached its apotheosis.

Almost at once, the anti-Woodites ran into difficulty when nearly a hundred stiffly upright businessmen pleaded with him in an open letter to stand again for office and, feigning surprise, Wood agreed. Cynics pounced on the request and charged that Wood had either bribed or coerced the men by threatening to raise their taxes. But there were powerful reasons for Wood's popularity. He was pro-Southern at a time when city merchants coveted Southern trade, public-spirited citizens still considered him a reformer, and the Irish treated him practically as a folk hero. In summing up his appeal, the *Herald* concluded that "Fernando Wood, who with all his short comings, has proved that he has the energy and the will to govern the city, and reform abuses." [76]

The mayor's next move again proved his cunning. Receiving word that the General Committee meant to censure him for his purported flirtation with the nativists, he packed the Long Room with his hired thugs. Not only did these toughs intimidate the committeemen into dropping the motion, but they helped ram through a primary election system which gave Wood full control over naming inspectors and ballot counters.

The primary bore the stamp of Wood's peculiar genius. His henchmen instructed some voters, barred others, stole ballot boxes, and used every illegal trick imaginable to win the contest. As a result, not only had Wood rebuilt his personal juggernaut, but he also now had the apparent power to make himself the full master of Tammany Hall. His foes were aware of the danger. Crying fraud, they revolted before the nominating convention opened, bolted the organization, held a rump meeting on the Wigwam's first floor, and named tavern owner James Libby for mayor on a platform that charged Wood with having broken down "established usages and subverted the party." [77]

Even so, the Libbyites carried a tremendous burden. Despite endorsements by such diverse interests as the Marcyites, the Union Clubs, and the Young Men's Democratic Club, Wood campaigned as a regular Tammanyite, with all the party's legitimacy behind him. Thus, in a year when party harmony had become a Democratic fetish, he gained enormous leverage by belaboring his opponents as disorganizers bent on destroying Buchanan's conciliation formula. Wood's argument was so persuasive that William Tweed, who had little reason to like Wood, loyally supported the regular ticket.[78]

Fate struck the Libbyites an even worse blow. Without any warning, Lorenzo Shepard died. Only thirty-six, he was the only local leader outside of John Van Buren, whose influence was on the wane, who could match Wood's shrewdness, drive, and personal magnetism. Other potential challengers—men such as Cochrane, Sickles, Fowler, John McKeon, and Tweed—were either too young, too second-rate, or too controversial. In its obituary, the Herald underscored the immense political consequences inherent in Shepard's death. His demise "has created an entirely new phase in city politics, and gives Mayor Wood the vantage ground and position. The late Mr. Shepard was a man of ability, and was the head and front of the opposition against the Mayor." [79]

Once they recovered from shock, the General Committee selected Postmaster Isaac Fowler, a firm anti-Woodite, as the new chairman. Even this move disrupted the Libbyite coalition. Fowler and William Kennedy, a hard-driving sachem whom Shepard had been grooming for leadership both in Tammany Hall and in the Tammany Society, were personal enemies, while Collector Redfield and Naval Officer Cochrane resented the postmaster's poaching in federal patronage matters. To make matters worse, Peter Sweeny's harsh position paper de-nouncing the primary system, coupled with an extensive attack on the corruption rife in the mayor's office, had little real impact. For above anything else, Wood controlled Tammany Hall's apparatus and linked his reelection with James Buchanan's best interests.[80]

Other factors aided Wood. Besides Libby, Isaac Barker represented the Know-Nothings; Judge James Whiting, an undistinguished lawyer who had few reformist credentials, ran for the Civic party; and An-thony Bleeker, an anti-Seward, anti-Fillmore Whig, tried to spark some life into his moribund party. Yet, in the end, Wood won. He gained 44.5 percent of the total mayoralty vote, while Barker received 32.2 percent, Bleeker had 12.3 percent, and Libby and Whiting, with 6.2 percent and 4.6 percent, respectively, trailed badly.

As a whole, the Democracy scored an impressive victory. It elected eleven assemblymen, to the Republicans' five, while the Know-Nothings were shut out. The Common Council for the first time in several years was Democratic. John Cochrane and Daniel Sickles won congressional seats. James Buchanan carried the city with 53 percent of the total votes cast. The only sour note was that Parker lost the gubernatorial race to John King, Rufus' son, and the state went for the Republican presidential nominee, John C. Frémont.

The Libbyites had the least reason for cheering. Wood was now a giant among pygmies. He had completely smashed his foes, outmaneu-vered the Marcyites, dominated Tammany Hall, and stood on the verge of making the local Democracy his personal property. Only two things could stop him: President-elect James Buchanan, and the Tammany Society.[81]

# ∽ 12 ∾

# The Tammany Society and Mozart Hall

HARDLY HAD James Buchanan savored the achievement of his life's dream than the incessant rumble from New Yorkers about patronage matters turned his pleasant reveries into a nightmare. In typical thrusts, Amasa Parker, Samuel Beardsley, and Patrick Lynch, the *Irish-American*'s editor, chorused agreement that the party was still sick and needed careful doctoring to restore its vitality. Wood, on the other hand, ignored the problem—perhaps, because he was at its center. "My own election I know will be gratifying to you," he happily wrote Buchanan. "The disaffection in the party towards me succeeded in polling less than 5,000 votes out of 80,000, and my majority is signal & tryumphant [*sic*]." [1]

But the President-elect, a witness of many New York brawls and knowing that patronage was the key to political security, patiently tolerated the strident letters that flooded his desk and kept his own counsel, gradually showing a bent for personal brokerage leadership. Conscious of the mistakes Polk and Pierce had made, Buchanan planned to create a new era of harmony by appealing to the conservative nature of American political life and ending "the agitation of the Slavery question at the North" while destroying "sectional parties." [2]

Mayor Wood had other ideas. Acquiring an impressive forum when he purchased the bankrupt *New York Daily News*, he gained another formidable ally in James Gordon Bennett. On this basis, regarding himself as the real head of Tammany Hall, Wood demanded that no one receive a local federal job without his prior approval. Buchanan held his temper. Assuring the mayor of his good will, the President-elect refused any commitment. [3]

While the mayor busied himself with spoils, his foes launched their counterattack under the Tammany Society's protective sponsorship. First, in late November, the sachems foiled Wood's bid to name Wilson Small as grand sachem, instead selecting Daniel Delevan, a thorough anti-Woodite. Next, the Society initiated thirty-eight braves, none of them the mayor's followers. If anything, however, these moves increased his determination to neutralize the sachems.

Wood began with the General Committee. At the December primary election, he stationed bully boys at each polling place. Since anyone who professed to be a Democrat could vote, the Woodites stuffed the ballot boxes and illegally barred anyone they could not trust. At the January organizational meeting, then, the mayor's henchmen held a working majority despite contested seats in seven wards, and named Wilson Small as the chairman. To Buchanan, Wood gloated that "the General Committee of the city for 1857 was completed last night at Tammany Hall without the slightest acrimony or lack of harmony." [4]

The mayor's use of power did not deter his foes. Purdy and Fowler boycotted the Small Committee, and formed a second one with John Savage, a minor functionary, as the figurehead chairman. Wood expected this gambit, positive that the Council of Sachems would intervene, citing its 1842 lease much as it had done three years earlier. Anticipating the move, Wood bribed Howard, the lessee, and the Small Committee met in the Wigwam as the regular, authoritative voice of the city Democracy. Such a step cut into the Society's very meaning. Without hesitation, the anti-Wood sachems voted to dissolve both General Committees and called for new elections—but to end Wood's strong-arm tactics they also proposed a semiregistry law. "The Grand Council believe that the proper basis for the organization of the party is the enrollment of the active and undoubted Democracy of each Election District into a permanent association for the district, and the holding of primary elections by the district association." [5]

Wood foresaw the Council's action but he had badly underestimated the sachems' resourcefulness. If the majority of sachems, led by Purdy and Fowler, reformed the primary system, Wood knew that he could never weld the city Democracy into a single disciplined machine. His main concern, therefore, was to block the sachems by denying the theory that the lease gave the Council the right to judge regularity. Like Barr before him, Wood claimed that the Society had appropriated a power held only by the rank and file. Moreover, the lessee, not the Council, held the building at his absolute disposal. Under his reasoning, the Small Committee alone could exclude all potential rivals from the Wigwam as antiorganizational Tammanyites.

Wood's manifesto provoked a flurry of counter-moves. Rather than debate the Small Committee's legality, the Council's majority translated its efforts into a reformist dimension that made Mayor Wood's seem rather selfish by comparison:

> This double claim to the occupancy of Tammany Hall is but one of the many indications of the disorganized and unhealthy condition of the Democratic Party in this City. It cannot be denied that it is rent by divisions and paralyzed by wrongs fatal to its integrity, harmony and success. The causes of this deplorable state of things are obvious. Usurpations and frauds have been accomplished and tolerated till the strength of the party is shattered, and its members have ceased to feel confidence in each other.

The inevitable corollary of this situation, the sachems concluded, was to reform the primary system. Anything less would destroy the Hall, and prevent the rank and file from acting as the Democracy's real decision-makers.[6]

On a second but coordinate front, Purdy and Fowler hired four respectable lawyers, unconnected with either side, to study the original lease. They quickly found for the sachems. While admitting that the Council's call for a new election "was not a right especially recognized by the lease," the four men agreed that party traditions, hallowed by "the acquiescence of the Democracy of the city," had established the need for a "common arbiter," acting for the party's general interest, to determine "the claims of conflicting organizations." As for the lessee, he had no voice in these matters: "he can neither require nor object to its exercise; he must simply obey the final decision which the Council of Sachems shall pronounce." With that, the sachems ordered Howard not to allow any meetings in the Wigwam unless "the regular officers of the Society" concurred, "and in accordance with the laws and usages of the said Society." Thus, once again, Purdy's insight and tenacity bore impressive results.[7]

Even so, political machines run on patronage and voter identification, not traditionalism or reverence to such ephemeral clichés as "party usages." The sachems, both sides understood, were no stronger in the long run than the interests they were protecting. As a result, Wood's need to control federal spoils became imperative.

When news of city appointments finally became public, President

Buchanan, like Pierce before him, selected men because of the interests they represented, not because of talent or fitness for high office. For the vital collector's spot, he named Augustus Schell. Emmanuel Hart, a Douglasite, became surveyor of the port. Marcyite Fowler retained the post office. Isaiah Rynders, an anti-Woodite, received the United States marshal's job, a rather unfit selection considering his questionable probity. George Sanders, once Young America's spokesman, who had later joined Sickles, succeeded John Cochrane. In minor federal offices, Buchanan left the incumbents undisturbed, including Marcyite John Cisco in the Sub-Treasury and John McKeon as district attorney.

The President's policy was as well-intentioned as it was ineffective, for in diffusing power, Buchanan squandered his opportunity to exert party discipline. Rival Tammany leaders, without a firm hand from Washington, could ignore Administration harmony directives and use the President's own selections to determine the outcome of their internal power struggle.[8]

Only Fernando Wood was satisfied. Making a shrewd guess, he had been cultivating Schell for several months, and by April the two formed a working alliance. In return for the mayor's pledge to support Dickinson in 1860, Schell agreed to give Wood's henchmen preferential spoils treatment. There were other compelling reasons for the collector's quick assent. He personally disliked Sickles, and saw in Wood the instrument for revenge. Then, too, Schell's Hard friends had been antiorganization Democrats since 1853. They now frankly gambled that with Wood's aid they could dominate the Hall and reassert their claims on the state party. In the long run, President Buchanan supplied Wood with a second chance to become master of the local Democracy.[9]

After officially disbanding both General Committees, the Tammany Society laid the ground rules for a new election. To thwart Wood's strong-arm tactics, the sachems authorized voting by all legal Democrats in each ward, supervised by three inspectors, the defunct Small and Savage Committees to choose one apiece, the other to be chosen by the Council. Wilson Small objected. Heaping scorn on the sachems, he belligerently held his independent course.

All this preceded Buchanan's official announcement of his New York appointees. When Wood saw the drift of the selections, he immediately held a secret meeting with Sachem John Kelly, one of the minority Woodites, and they worked out a fresh approach. Under the guise of accepting Buchanan's party harmony formula, Kelly proposed to his fellow sachems that the Council adopt the principle of popular sovereignty to settle the dispute by creating a city-wide convention, formed by five men from each ward—four named by the local committeemen from the Small and Savage groups respectively, one by the Council, to act as a temporary General Committee until a final, fusion General Union Committee emerged. The sachems agreed.

This awkward display of unity scarcely lasted a week. Collector Schell, working closely with City Hall, hung out a sign on the Custom House that none but Woodites and Dickinson Hards need apply. The mayor's intent became even clearer when the interim General Committee took shape. Trading on his grasp over federal spoils, he reneged on his deal with Kelly, charged that the Committee was rife with corruption, revived the Small group, and met at the Chinese Museum to plot further strategy.

The mayor's first priority was the coming elections for a new Council, and he prepared a ticket that largely consisted of his henchmen. Seldom had the Tammany Society convened in an atmosphere so charged with political static. But Purdy and Fowler were also ready. Emulating Wood, they packed the building with professional brawlers, and locked the Long Room's doors. After six hours of violent debate that left the braves with frayed nerves, they picked an anti-Wood ticket headed by Isaac Fowler.

Never had Wood so badly lost the initiative. While some of the Small Committee, dubbed the "Mandarins," still boycotted the special convention, the remaining delegates commissioned ward leaders to copy the names of all bona fide Democrats from the poll lists. Only these men could vote. Then, the convention called a special election using this formula and created the Union General Committee, chaired by anti-Woodite Sachem Edward Cooper, which legally represented Tammany Hall. Yet the Small Committee still refused to dissolve and sought a conference meeting with the new group to settle outstanding differences. But when Small demanded that the Cooper Committee abolish the primary system in exchange for a fusion state convention delegation, the Unionists refused and selected their own group. The Woodites followed suit. And, to add a farcical note, the Savage Committee, which had reanimated itself for self-protection, devised yet a third slate of delegates.[10]

While Tammany Democrats carried on their internecine warfare, the Republican-dominated legislature used reformism as a means for increasing its local position. By 1857, the city had simply shed its old skin and emerged as a complex creature that few men understood. With an increase of over a quarter of a million in population in less than a decade, the multiplication and urgency of the city's chronic urban ills grew to endemic proportions. For all his faults, Wood recognized the need for change, and called for another charter revision that would establish responsibility and end the diffusion of executive power through a strong mayor–weak council system loosely paralleling the federal model.

Other reformers agreed in substance but not as to technique. "We need a vigorous government," the crusading *New York Times* acknowledged, "and vigorous men to administer it." Yet the same men who wanted municipal regeneration feared Wood's demagoguery, and the legislature thus produced a new charter that was marked more by political than reformist considerations. The Republicans reduced the sizes of both the Boards of Aldermen and Councilmen, but replaced most of their prerogatives with a county, bipartisan, twelve-man Board of Supervisors that by fiat would always consist of six Democrats and six Republicans. All the legislation and ordinances passed by the Board were made subject to the mayor's veto, but this could be overridden by a simple majority. To further twist authority, the solons created an entirely new police force, the Metropolitans, run by five commissioners to be appointed by the governor with senate approval, and having the mayors of New York City and Brooklyn as ex-officio members. Only one of Wood's proposals went through: the formation of executive departments, appointed by the mayor with the aldermen's consent.

In placing the city government at the mercy of the state legislature, the Republicans scored a partisan victory over reform. But in their selfish inversion of priorities they blundered badly. By deciding that political necessity outweighed all other considerations, they compartmentalized responsibility so narrowly that no legal instrument of government could rule. Only by working outside the system, or subverting it, could effective government take place. When government fragmented, the day of the political boss was at hand.[11]

After absorbing two stiff setbacks at the Society's hand, Mayor Wood could not allow the Republicans to finesse him. Raising the banners of home rule, he challenged the Metropolitan Police Law's constitutionality and asked the state court of appeals for a ruling. In the meantime, Governor King appointed five commissioners, all Republicans, and the police force began operations. Again, the mayor moved. Claiming that he still retained the power to authorize a night watch, similar to the system used before 1845, he created the Bureau of Day and Night Watch or Municipal Police.

Wood's ploy proved a costly blunder. During May and part of June, the city functioned with a dual police force. Trouble erupted on June 16 when Daniel Conover, whom Governor King had appointed street commissioner, attempted to take office. Once more, Wood charged that the Republicans had infringed on the city's sovereignty, refused to accept Conover, and instructed Municipal Police Chief George Matsell to bar him from the building. But when Conover obtained a warrant for Wood's arrest and attempted to serve it through Metropolitan Captain George Walling, a general free-for-all among the rival police began. Only the intervention of the Seventh Regiment, which happened to be marching on Broadway in transit to Boston, ended the battle. At last, the Metropolitans served Wood with the warrant, and, for good measure, charged him with inciting a riot.[12]

Wood's problems became more acute when the court of appeals ruled for the legislature and ordered the mayor to disband the Municipals. On reading the report, he followed the court's directive, promised to seek some means to repeal the act, and took his place on the Board of Commissioners. His words, however, were cold comfort for the jobless Municipals. On July 4, taking their cues from these difficulties, two rival gangs, the Dead Rabbits and Bowery Boys, began a riot that engulfed the city in disorder. Barely hiding their approval, the Municipals egged on the bloody conflict, and took great delight in the Metropolitans' inability to restore order.

Up to this point, Wood's behavior had provoked little cynicism among the voters. In fact, he gained political capital by defending the city's right of home rule. But the riots sent a wave of emotionalism and resentment surging through the city that washed away his reformist image. Even the most credulous do-gooder was now convinced that he would stop at nothing to advance his career. In short, Wood, the "Model Mayor," had become Wood, the criminal's friend.[13]

Despite his plummeting prestige, Wood still remained the leading city Democrat. In order to fully mobilize public pressure against him, Tammanyites once more turned toward Buchanan. But the President, who wanted party peace, refused to take sides, and dispatched two mediators, Samuel Latham Mitchill Barlow, a shrewd railroad businessman, and Henry Wickoff, a minority party busybody. The effort was a failure because of two points on which the rival Tammanyites could not agree: Schell's and Wood's control of federal patronage, and the Society's recognition of Cooper's Union Committee.

Buchanan's failure at reorganizing the local party lay in his inability to decide whether Sickles or Wood should become the Administration's favorite. As a result, each man felt that the President favored him alone. Neither man, therefore, seriously considered any accommodation. On one side, Wood and Schell feverishly plunged into building their party, while, on the other, Sickles and Purdy broadened their base through the Tammany Society and the Union Committee. Even so, Wood's grasp over the Custom House's spoils slowly tipped the balance. In desperation, Sickles pleaded with the President for action. *"Fowler, Hart, and Rynders did all that was possible,"* he wrote, "in conjunction with me to reconcile matters." But nothing more could be done unless Buchanan helped destroy "the complete subjugation of Mr. Schell to the control of Wood." But the President still held back.[14]

While Buchanan continued to make inaction a virtue, the anti-Woodites shifted their attack and tried to discredit the mayor with the state Democracy. If the convention denied the Small delegates their seats, Wood's prestige would correspondingly diminish. But the up-staters refused. Instead, they accepted Wood's contention that they could only select candidates, not judge regularity. As a result, the credentials committee proposed a compromise: the convention would admit both the Small and Union Committee delegates, which included some of the Savage group, and they would evenly split the number of New York City votes between them. Wood wasted no time in accepting, since the arrangement fitted his needs. Sickles and Purdy, sensing that they could expect little more, bowed to the inevitable and now tried to make the best of a poor situation.

In this fashion, by trying to sweep factionalism under the rug, the convention set out on its business and nominated a full ticket of minor state officials that included Woodite Sachem Gideon Tucker for secretary of state. But on the last day, Honest John Kelly disrupted the uneasy peace. With Wood's masterly hand doing the manipulating, Kelly offered an amendment to the Committee on Resolutions' final report: "It appears to this Convention that although there are distinct organizations of the Democratic party in the City of New York, there is no material differences of principle. Therefore, Resolved—That both join together to form unbroken ties." Sickles was aghast. Any such statement, he shouted, would merely encourage insurgents because the Tammany Society had already settled the matter. In the confusion that followed, the chairman ruled Honest John out of order, and a voice vote ended the meeting *sine die.* Thus, in many ways, Wood's foes were fortunate to be able to board the New York Central for home with their apparatus intact—though with little else.[15]

The convention's failure to judge regularity wreaked havoc on the

Hall's strategy. Left stranded, the Cooper Committee could not discipline the Woodites with any assurances of success. To make matters bleaker, the convention, in spite of Wood's notorious disregard for law and order, named him a state committeeman—although the delegates softened the blow somewhat by also selecting his bitter enemy, Peter Sweeny.

Wood's next move left Tammany more distressed. The legislature, in meddling with local matters, had altered the city charter, cut Wood's term in half, and ordered a new canvass for the following December. Blithely assuming that the recently formed Democratic primary system would name anti-Woodites, Purdy and Sickles underestimated the mayor's daring. By fraud, theft, and downright violence, his henchmen named friendly delegates and easily renominated him. At once, Wood thanked the convention for its endorsement. Ordinarily, he said in his disarming manner, he would never have thought of running again because the mayoralty's heavy burden had worn him out. But he could not ignore his moral debt to the people, both to defend them against the "Black Republican" abolitionists who ran the state legislature and to establish firmly the principle of home rule. Anything less, he implied, was cowardice.[16]

Tammany's leadership elite faced a conundrum. The Cooper Committee could not oppose Wood openly until after the November canvass without endangering the state ticket. However, it also knew that Wood would claim any Democratic victory as his vindication. As a result, Purdy, Sickles, and Fowler quietly supported the ticket; but at the same time they covertly hunted for a different mayoralty candidate. The election, then, was the calm before the storm. The Democrats won easily, and Tucker became secretary of state. With these preliminaries over, Tammany poised for attack. But before it could move, Wood again undercut its position.


In late summer of 1857, the economy throughout the North fell on hard times. In adjusting to changing conditions, startled businessmen and bankers found themselves caught in a short-lived but vicious recession. Misery enshrouded the city, especially among the poorer classes, who taxed the resources of local relief agencies. As unemployment spurted and employers cut losses by cutting wages, immigrants and unskilled workingmen suffered the most. To the exasperation of many politicians, Wood came forward with a bold plan. He recommended that the city hire the unemployed as construction laborers for Central Park and provide food and coal, at cost, for the needy. No matter his motives, the mayor's humanitarianism refurbished his image. Gone were the bitter memories of the Municipal Police fiasco; Wood had transformed himself into the defender of the downtrodden, immigrants and natives alike.[17]

Tammany Hall's opposition remained solid. As painful as the experience might be, Tammanyites, Civic Reformers, and even a smattering of Know-Nothings coalesced behind Daniel Tiemann, a Soft alderman, as their candidate. Echoing the respectable William Havemeyer's strictures against Wood's "improvidence, prodigality and jobbing," such diverse political personalities as John McKeon and John Van Buren agreed with the *New York Times* on one thing: Tiemann must win. Sickles told Buchanan: "The opposition vote will be entirely concentrated upon Tiemann, and he will be supported by thousands of Democrats. There is a very strong desire among the best men in our party to get rid of Wood, as Mayor, provided a better Democrat and a more reliable man can be got in his place." [18]

Few men under such attack rivaled Wood's instinct for survival. Anything, legal or illegal, was legitimate as far as he was concerned, just so long as he won. To overcome his foes, Wood ridiculed Tiemann's nativist backers, and worked the naturalization mill full blast. "Over 200 new citizens," the *Irish-American* noted with approval, "have been naturalised since the present canvass commenced; and of these it is not too much to say he [Wood] will receive the support of ninety-nine out of every hundred." John Cochrane added his support. Pointing out the embarrassing fact that Wood was the Democracy's only legal candidate, Cochrane asserted that "Fernando Wood is the regular nominee of Tammany Hall, and must be supported as such." Ending the campaign on a high note, one Woodite became so excited that he called the mayor's foes "a heterogeneous conglomeration of Abolitionists, Fourierites, Kansas-shriekers, Know-Nothings, Shoulder-hitters, Women's Rights Advocates, Infidels, and Atheists." Here, the defense rested.[19]

Tiemann won. The overly cautious *Times* immediately warned that "the result is not, in any sense, or to any extent, a party triumph." These sobering words fell on deaf ears. The exultant Tiemann quickly dashed off a letter to President Buchanan assuring him that with Administration aid "we shall soon see the day, when the Democratic party will be a tower of strength." Even the normally undemonstrative Augustus Belmont, currently bankrolling the Dean Richmond Softs, wrote Louisiana Senator John Slidell that "Wood is a d——d man, & no action of the Executive can galvanize him into political life again." [20]

But, like the proverbial cat, Wood had more than one political life. He began a new phase in city politics by becoming the first local politician to support President Buchanan's demand that all loyal Democrats back his stand on admitting Kansas to the Union under the proslavery Lecompton Constitution, even though it had been adopted through fraud and deceit.

Wood then translated his psychological triumph into practical terms. In the December primary elections, under the Association system, he gave the Hall another lesson in the art of the unexpected. When the partial returns trickled in, all evidence indicated that his supporters held a working majority. At the first organizational meeting, under the pretense of reestablishing the sanctity of regular nominations no matter who the candidate, his supporters disciplined two of Mayor Tiemann's more vigorous Tammany spokesmen, Daniel Sickles and C. Godfrey Gunther, the darling of the German Democrats. Both men had intended to resign as committeemen in any case, for personal reasons. But the Woodites craved revenge and expelled them for not supporting Tammany's regular nominee, Fernando Wood, in the past mayoralty election. When all the returns were counted, the story was far different. At the next meeting, in a scene of confusion marred by rioting and the wounding of a bystander, the anti-Woodites gained control, reinstated both men, and selected Peter Sweeny as chairman.[21]

Wood breathed fire. Refusing any compromise, he called the Association System a mockery of the democratic process, arrogantly sponsored another election under the old primary method, and formed his own General Committee with Small again as chairman. But once again, the Council of Sachems blasted his insurgency. William D. Kennedy, the Father of the Council, directed Charles Brown, the new lessee, to bar all but the Sweeny Committee from using the Wigwam.[22]

Kennedy's move forced Wood into making a fateful decision, a decision destined to alter the course of his entire career. Far from holding the Tammany Society in contempt, he regarded it as the mainspring of local power. Certainly, every time that he had woven a web of intrigue that looked promising, the Council had thwarted him. At stake was not only his pride but also his standing as the single most important Democratic politician in the city. Only one achievement could shift the balance and restore his role as the party's center of gravity—winning full control over the Council of Sachems at the Society's annual April election.

Before acting, Wood went to Washington on a fence-mending mission. That done, he moved to Richmond where he sounded out Governor Wise as a possible dark horse presidential candidate. By April, Wood was home, primed for his confrontation with the Society. Setting the stage for the forthcoming struggle, he appointed a special five-man commission, headed by Small, to prepare a statement which "shall fully and more distinctly set forth the true issues in the contest, by which the members of the Tammany Society may be better enabled to vote understandingly upon the tickets to be presented for their suffrages." [23]

The anti-Woodites were also busy. "Postmaster Fowler presided . . . at the regular monthly meeting of the Tammany Society," the watchful *Times* reported. "After the usual routine business and new members were initiated, the Order adjourned and in good order." Here was the main thrust of Purdy's counterattack: the enrollment of new braves. Taking poetic revenge in stuffing the Society's ballot boxes, as Wood had done in the primary election, the sachems systematically increased their voting potential. Wood's only chance lay in extorting the support of a few uncommitted brethren. To make the stakes even higher, Secretary of the Treasury Howell Cobb, Schell's immediate superior, promised to throw all his support behind whichever faction won. [24]

Wood's campaign revolved about his opponents' refusal to honor "regular nominations" during the mayoralty contest. Posing as a defender of traditional party "usages," he stressed the idea that the braves had to decide if the techniques of direct, popular rule still governed Tammany Hall, or whether a degenerate "cabal-dictated party nominations." As he phrased the alternatives: "We present a ticket leaving to the people a right to settle and determine questions for themselves and pertinent to their own interests." [25]

Until the last moment, the perpetually optimistic Wood felt that he would win. But he had miscalculated. Purdy, besides stepping up the initiation program, corralled many inactive braves. "Members who had not voted before for years came to the Old Wigwam in carriages to deposit their votes," a reporter attested. "The infirm and superannuated members were brought out in carriages, a long line of which filled the streets in front of the Hall." John Dix, long a strong man in local politics, was among these men. After casting his first ballot in twenty-eight years of brotherhood, he explained to Buchanan that "I have no doubt the vote at Tammany Hall last night was influenced, to a considerable extent, by the apprehension that the defeated ticket, if it had succeeded, would have been a weapon in the hands of a selfish man." [26]

The defeat, and the political debacle that it indicated, placed Wood at the crossroads of his career. His first impulse was to justify his actions. But on reflection, his experience with the Council of Sachems convinced him that it made little sense to remain with the Hall as the loyal opposition. His only possible path now led toward a third-party force that would replace Tammany as the true Democracy of New York City. It would be a personal party, a Fernando Wood party; one based on his money, political cunning, control over Custom House patronage, and his promises of future victories. As his supporters, Wood counted on frustrated local interests: immigrants, Negrophobes, disgruntled reformers, displaced nativists, the poor, and politicians on the make—men such as A. Oakey Hall, who felt the traditional organizations stifled their ambitions.

Such party-building took time. First, Wood had to convince the state and national leadership that he was a true Democrat while his foes were traitors. Next, he needed to establish the idea that the sachems pursued him on a personal vendetta that was unconnected to issues or principles. Finally, since an outright bolt against the sacrosanct Tammany Society and Hall might acquire a tinge of heresy, he needed allies among other Democratic "out" groups. For the next few months this requirement remained unfilled. A group of Custom House appointees (some with Schell's approval, some not), longing for a louder voice in party affairs, formed the People's General Committee. While these men indeed sympathized with Wood and his apparatus, Mozart Hall, they made it plain that they preferred to go their own way.[27]

Inevitably, the participants in this battle for survival would not implement their strategy within the accepted rules of the game but in back alleys and on the streets. As these amoral politicos inflamed suspicions and matter-of-factly stirred violent emotions, they searched for issues with mass appeal. Although some New Yorkers resented the South's agrarian, low-tariff leadership in national affairs, the question of slavery extensionism dominated the political spotlight. Painful as the case might have been, the issue became a stratagem, adopted through sheer expediency, to define Democratic loyalty. Both Mozart and Tammany Halls used traditional principles as their rationales, and, in a limited sense, each represented a legitimate strain. Even so, reason and responsibility went out the window as the mad drive for office and patronage stifled moderation—and symptomatically paralleled the ferment evolving into civil war.

In the White House, a frustrated but impotent Buchanan fumed as Wood and Schell seized the spoils for their own ends. Precious government jobs, the President saw, accelerated the progress that Wood made in dismantling the Democratic party and undoing Administration policy. But while Buchanan now considered the collector a bitter disappointment, the Administration could ill afford to make him a martyr, as Pierce did for Greene Bronson, by a peremptory removal. The uncertain President, then, despite Cobb's hard prodding, hesitated and did not act. "I regret as much as you do," the baffled Cobb wrote, "that Mr. Schell yields to the influences around him; but if he persists in that course he cannot be sustained. The simple question is whether your policy or that of Fernando Wood . . . is to be carried out." [28]

Less obvious for the moment, city Democrats were deeply involved in a guessing game to find a suitable candidate for 1860. Since Tammany assumed that Wood favored Buchanan, the Sweeny General Committee endorsed Stephen Douglas, despite its unhappiness with his Freeport Doctrine of "unfriendly legislation" which denied the Dred Scott decision's applicability. Tammany's move confounded Wood. Aware that Buchanan's age precluded a second term, the astute Wood looked elsewhere and finally settled on Governor Wise. But Wise cautiously hinted that only Douglas could control the party's centrifugal forces, and expressed a willingness to step aside, provided the conditions were right. Now, it was Wood's turn to equivocate. Since he could not openly aid Douglas without being swallowed by Tammany Hall, Wood paid the President the necessary lip service, and covertly helped finance the senator's reelection campaign against Abraham Lincoln.[29]

During this jockeying, Grand Sachem Fowler, confident that Tammany had permanently blunted Wood's career, attempted to drive a wedge between him and his supporters by welcoming them back into the party as individuals rather than as representatives of any one group. The Society's peace offering encouraged Wood to plot as never before. At the August State Committee meeting, still working through regular channels, he accepted Dean Richmond's directive to begin harmony talks with Tammany. Out of the subsequent deliberations a deal emerged. Tammany would support Honest John Kelly for sheriff; Wood would not field an independent delegation for the fall convention.[30]

But with almost arrogant disdain, Wood, along with Schell and Dickinson, secretly planned to doublecross Tammany. First, the People's General Committee would fuse with the Woodites and form an anti-Tammany delegation. The plot had a deeper skein, however. Mozart would not challenge one Tammany delegate, Gideon Tucker, one of Wood's presumably former henchmen, who now supported Douglas. Next, at the state convention, the Dickinsonites would pack and organize the meeting, elect their own chairman, who would then appoint the supposedly neutral Tucker, the only city delegate "with an uncontested seat," as the chairman of the "Committee on Contested Seats." Once installed, Tucker would admit the Woodites. In exchange, Wood promised not to aid the state ticket if it proved anti-Dickinson. "Such a course," the *Times* commented, "would seem to give the verdict of New-York against Buchanan, and (it was thought) would aid Mr. Dickinson with reference to the succession." [31]

The plan might have worked had not the watchful *Times* exposed the deception. With that, Fowler and Sweeny took great care in electing safe delegates by the Democratic Association system. Now that his foes had flushed him into the open, Wood wrote Buchanan a curious letter, half challenging, half pleading. In it, after reminding the President of their long friendship, Wood suggested that if perhaps he appointed him governor of the Nebraska territory, "my absence from the scene of tumult [might] restore peace." [32]

Somewhat startled, Buchanan shrugged off his suggestion. "Such is the condition of the Democratic party in the city of New York," he wryly noted, "that to appoint to a high office any one of the distinguished leaders attached to the one or the other division would only render confusion worse confounded." Taking the mild rebuke in stride, the effervescent Wood indicated his willingness to settle for a lesser prize: Buchanan's active intervention on his behalf in city politics.[33]

Tammanyites also badgered Buchanan. Isaac Fowler sought the President's confidence by assuring him that the Association System's delegation destroyed the "great inducement to dissension & management" that Wood had counted on to embarrass the Administration. Sickles was equally assertive. He chided the by now weary President that unless he disciplined the collector, Schell would make a shambles of the city Democracy. In Washington, the President nodded at these complimentary pieces of advice but still did nothing.[34]

The state Democratic Convention ended Wood's drift. In a scene of pandemonium, the delegates recognized Tammany as the regular city party. Mozart Hall at once bolted the convention, and angrily threatened to boycott the state ticket. When he arrived home, Wood made one last effort to enlist the President's aid. After warning Buchanan that Tammany supported Stephen Douglas, whom the President now despised, Wood announced that his party would proceed with or without Administration aid. Buchanan's patience finally snapped. He reprimanded Wood in clear terms, and said that Sickles would get White House support in the future. It was an idle threat. Since the President made no move for Schell's removal, Mozart Hall still controlled local patronage.[35]

Hardly had Wood digested these words when his natural resiliency in the face of disaster met another severe test. Intent on lifting the cover hiding some of Wood's chicanery, Albert Ramsey, a *New York Herald* correspondent, who doubled as Fowler's aid, left for Washington with some incriminating evidence designed to take advantage of the President's paranoia against Douglas. After days of waiting, Ramsey finally saw the President and gleefully told him that "Fernando furnished the 39,000$" that Douglas had mysteriously raised to finance his race against Lincoln. Thus, despite the fact that Tammany's inclination for Douglas was well known in Washington, Fowler further isolated Wood from the President.[36]

But Tammany could not so easily dismiss Wood. Mozart Hall made a respectable showing in the fall election and succeeded in electing Barr and Cochrane to Congress. In December, Wood shored up his ward committees, avoided a showdown with the Sweeny General Committee in the regular Tammany contests, and reorganized his political ties with the People's Committee. By February 1859, the Woodites and People's Committee formally merged. As their justification, they charged that Tammany "was a rotten trunk which it is necessary to cure or lop off." Wood further undercut his foes by organizing Mozart Hall on the Association model, and welcomed all Democrats who "recognized no political superiors." Wood, then, came forward again as a reformer, out to "purify" Tammany's "folly and wickedness," and he constantly emphasized that Mozart was a buffer against those men whose "official conduct and acts" were "hourly receiving the denunciation of the whole community." [37]

Control over the Custom House rapidly crystallized as the focal point of local partisanship. In December, spurred and goaded by the Administration, eighteen prominent New Yorkers, including Schell, Wood, Sickles, and Fowler, signed an agreement that all city federal officeholders would funnel patronage through Tammany. As soon as Mozart Hall took shape, Schell reneged. Back to Washington trekked Fowler and Sickles, intent on the collector's dismissal. Again, Buchanan refused. Unmoved, if not relieved by the President's tacit surrender, Schell reduced Tammany's share of the spoils to a trickle, then a drop.[38]

Unwittingly, Secretary Cobb, who disliked Wood, hurt Tammany even more by inopportunely pushing a retrenchment program. In the past, the collector had rented a series of warehouses to store imported goods until bonds upon them were paid. Since thieves occasionally pilfered the goods, the collector hired extra men as guards. Before long, the collector's right to select these men became a juicy patronage plum, and Tammany, from its earliest days, supplied the watchmen. Here Cobb miscalculated. Believing the system highly inefficient, he tried to have private contractors do the job. Tammanyites recoiled in horror. They could ill afford to lose such a lush handout that Schell had barely disturbed. Finally, under mounting pressure exerted by the Tammany Society and Sickles, Cobb temporarily rescinded the order. Even so, the specter haunted Tammany for the next few months.

One morning in late February of 1859, Tammanyites awoke to some more bad news. Fiery Daniel Sickles, who was quite willing to overlook his own peccadillos, could not do the same for those of his neglected young wife. Acting on an anonymous tip he shot and killed her lover, Philip Barton Key, on a quiet street in Washington. Sickles' timing—at least his political timing—could not have come at a worse juncture. For the next two years, he became a shadow in city politics, just at a period when Tammany lacked another direct pipeline to the President.[39]

By midsummer, the same basic flaws in New York politics that left Democratic politicking to the whims and discretion of individuals now again compounded the party's woes. The difficulty evolved out of the search for Buchanan's successor. Strange, often contradictory alliances became the order of the day. Even though he had led the state Hards and gained a reputation as a Southern sympathizer, Dickinson secretly made a deal with Richmond, a known moderate, that in exchange for his aid in the state convention, Richmond would back his presidential bid. Yet the bargain meant little to the New Regency because it favored Douglas, and under the unit rule Richmond controlled New York's vote. Tammany still favored Douglas, but could not do so openly because of Wood's menacing figure and the need to keep Buchanan happy. As for Wood, no one knew where he stood. In the public mind, he created the powerful impression that he was pro-Southern because of his support of Governor Wise. But, on the other hand, he still covertly flirted with Douglas. Perhaps the *Herald* understood Wood best. Wood, it noted, "has two strings to his bow and his position as a messenger and manager is strong." [40]

In a larger sense, New York's basic problem lay less in finding a suitable candidate than in lacking a home-bred, dark horse favorite son. Only one man, Horatio Seymour, could fill the bill, but he rejected the whole idea. To John Pruyn he confided that he was "tired of public life" and longed for "retirement." Any ambitions "he once had," Pruyn noted in his diary, "has he says passed away. . . . He does not wish or desire the Presidency could he have it—and he would by every means avoid it." [41]

Just before the state convention met, Secretary Cobb put his retrenchment program into operation, and the firm of Mather, Craig, McIntyre & Bixby took over the Custom House's warehousing functions. Immediately, over two hundred and seventy wardheelers, mostly Tammanyites, lost their jobs.

Wood turned the situation to his own advantage. First, he announced his candidacy for the December mayoralty race. Then, using the same tactics that had made him a power in the city, Wood brought a gang of professional brawlers with him to the convention. Once in Syracuse, with these men backing his every move, Wood and his anti-Richmond friends forced the other delegates from the hall, and established an independent identity. They nominated a state ticket and formed a separate state Central Committee, which then ordered the election of national delegates by the district plan. That done, they adjourned until the following February, when their state convention would name delegates at large and hopefully coalesce behind a winning presidential candidate. [42]

The out-muscled Richmond delegates fought back. In the late afternoon they returned to the hall and set to work, while Wood's men caroused in the local bars. With Dickinson firmly in tow, the skeleton convention formed a state ticket, and named a national convention delegation that consisted of Richmond moderates, anti-Wood Tammanyites, Seymour Softs, and Dickinson Hards. At the same time, Richmond completely gulled the credulous Dickinson. By confirming the unit rule, even though fifteen of the thirty-five delegates favored Dickinson, Richmond had the edge to play broker politics if Douglas' candidacy faltered. [43]

While the blight of disintegration spread over the party, a group of city Democratic businessmen, deeply concerned about losing Southern trade, took a hand. Led by August Belmont, William B. Astor, Myndert Van Schaick, and William Havemeyer, these men formed the Democratic Vigilant Association, and refused to contribute any money to either Tammany or Mozart Halls unless some sanity returned. The mere fact that the Association's members commanded a net worth of $20 million should have sobered local politicos. But its chief influence was more psychological than practical, and its major effect upon city politics was basically negative. Since the Association's leaders were more sympathetic to Tammany and Douglas than Mozart, Wood's supporters labeled it "a kid glove, scented, silk stocking, poodle-headed, degenerate aristocracy." In the long run, Mozart's emphasis on class distinctions increased Wood's following among the city's poor, especially those men still suffering from the aftermath of the Panic of 1857.[44]

Despite this, Mozart Hall fared poorly in the state contests. Tammany elected all its senatorial candidates and ten out of thirteen assemblymen, and out-polled Mozart 25,625 to 7,933. Nonetheless, the small turnout of voters diminished Tammany's showing because less than half the possible electorate cast ballots. If anything, the election proved that Mozart Hall was a one-man operation that would rise or fall more upon Wood's popularity than its own merits.[45]

The mayoralty contest was the real test of Wood's vote-pulling power. In a conscious effort to capture the Association, Tammany nominated a very unwilling Havemeyer. The move held grave drawbacks. Havemeyer, a friend of Richmond and Erastus Corning, had been a Barnburner and people incorrectly considered him anti-Southern. Mozart, which of course ran Wood, began a calculated effort to identify his election with Southern interests, particularly among Havemeyer's mercantile associates who were intimately tied, economically and politically, with the South. The Republicans named George Opdyke, a wealthy importer, who was also backed by the remnant of Daniel Ullman's Know-Nothing party. And to make the picture more indistinct, many Republicans, as well as Greeley's *Tribune*, talked of "swelling Wood's vote" in order to further disrupt the Democracy.[46]

As the campaign neared its riotous end, Mozart absorbed two punishing blows. First, the influential *Herald*, although it endorsed Wood, set the voters straight on the slavery question. "There is no party issue involved in the municipal election," it stoutly maintained, "no question of North and South." Second, Collector Schell, under Dickinson's urging, deserted Mozart, and placed the Custom House at Tammany's disposal.[47]

To the astonishment of many people, Mozart Hall scored a huge political upset. In the mayoralty race, Wood gained 38.2 percent of the total, to Havemeyer's 34.6 percent, while Opdyke limped along with

27.4 percent. In the local municipal contests, Wood's coattails proved equally potent as his followers won a working majority among the councilmen and elected eleven school commissioners. All in all, Mozart won local offices that Tammany had long considered its private property.[48]

Without pausing to sift the evidence, commentators read their own prejudices into the returns. For the *Herald*, in a reversal of its earlier statement, Wood's success "was a rebuke to anti-slavery agitation in its duplicated shape, as represented by Havemeyer and Opdyke." Tammany, Bennett gloated, lost because it stood too close to the "Negro worshippers" and had thus suffered a "deathblow." In Republican eyes, the election confirmed Wood's mastery over the local Democracy. Unless upstate Democrats did something "to restore their prestige," Greeley mused, "they will have to get on their knees to Wood to obtain admission to the Convention for even one-half of their delegates." To the Administration, which aside from Schell's turnabout had little at stake in the controversy, Wood's victory meant nothing.[49]

Yet in terms of the future, Tammany Hall was in a calamitous position. Perhaps Samuel Tilden, who vented his spleen to the permanently retired Martin Van Buren, understood the situation best. Blaming Tammany's defeat on Wood's control "of the lower stratum of the Irish, combined with special interests, and at the last moment the aid of jobbing Republicans," Tilden sadly concluded that political moderation was now a luxury the Democracy could no longer afford. Douglasite George Sanders agreed. "The centre must be immediately strengthened," he wrote the senator, "or we may be wrecked." As for Wood, the sweetness of victory soon turned sour. His wife died in childbirth, leaving him to raise several motherless children.[50]

The excitement that Wood generated in launching Mozart Hall, coupled with his stirring mayoralty victory, temporarily obscured the rise of an equally brilliant politician, William Marcy Tweed. After his congressional term expired in 1854, Tweed came home to partial eclipse. He seemed a jolly, convivial fellow; a wardheeler, no better or worse than his close neighbor, Isaiah Rynders. But Tweed possessed political genius; all he needed was direction. Elijah Purdy supplied the need. Under his paternal wing, the young Tweed began to move into the Hall's leadership elite. In 1857 he became a Union General Committee member, and, in the following year, the leader of his Seventh Ward.

By 1859 he climbed into complete Democratic respectability when the Tammany Society initiated him with Purdy's blessing.[51]

Tweed's activities as a supervisor marked him as a coming man. Although the Board was supposedly nonpartisan, Tweed soon mastered it. This became apparent when upstate Republican legislators modernized the little-used 1840 Registry Law; first by extending its provisions statewide, then by setting up a Board of Registry, consisting of three inspectors for each city election district appointed by the supervisors. Implicit in their thinking was the idea that Republican Board members would name at least half the inspectors, thus eliminating the Democracy's main source of illegal voters. Under Tweed's guidance, the reverse took place. Before the Board set the date for naming inspectors, he bribed Peter Voorhis, the weakest link in the Republican chain, to stay away. Without serious opposition, the Democratic supervisors named Tammany inspectors who closed their eyes when party hacks herded unqualified voters through the polls.[52]

But Tweed was more than a cheap political gamester. A brilliant student of practical politicking, he was a man of action and imagination, and possessed an unparalleled ability to absorb and store away facts. From Wood, Sickles, and Fowler he learned that the rank and file respected a winner, no matter the means; from Bronson and Schell, that patronage could provide an umbrella over local politicos that protected the organization's interests no matter what the feelings of the President or governor; and from Purdy, who recognized in Tweed the man he had always looked for, he gained an appreciation of the Tammany Society's pivotal role in city partisanship.

Even so, Tweed surpassed them all. He translated Wood's welfare program into a methodical formalization of municipal graft. Moreover, while patronage was a fine means of buying support, he understood that party hacks wanted respectability just as much. He used established institutions to accomplish this. Tammany Hall, he felt, could break Wood's grasp over ambitious politicians and the immigrant bloc by opening avenues for advancement, while the Tammany Society, by welcoming Irish and Germans, could confer prestige on the larger ethnic groupings as a whole. Beyond these, Tweed's experience as a municipal legislator convinced him that in a decentralized city such as New York, a united political machine could supply connecting links between powerless, but important, interest groups.[53]

Above all, however, Tweed realized that the Democracy was the city's majority party—if it could find some means to purge Fernando Wood without damaging the machine's vital cogs. A close rereading of the previous decade's *total* Democratic vote proved Tweed correct:

TOTAL DEMOCRATIC VOTE FOR MAYOR, 1850–1859

| Year | % Democratic | % Other |
|------|------|------|
| 1850 | 43.9 | 56.2 |
| 1852 | 57.4 | 42.6 |
| 1854 | 59.3 | 40.7 |
| 1856 | 51.7 | 48.3 |
| 1857 | 48.7 | 51.3* |
| 1859 | 72.6 | 27.4 |

*Tiemann

By 1859, then, the local Democracy was ripe for a vigorous leader, the "Boss," who could save Tammany Hall by coming up with an exciting vote-getting program that could neutralize Wood without alienating his followers. But, at this point, Tweed hardly fitted that description. Still on the rise, he took his place with Purdy, Fowler, and William A. Kennedy as merely one steward of Tammany's somewhat tarnished glory.

The year 1860 was year of crisis. Blithely ignoring the explosive potential of the issues they were toying with, local Democrats were "effete, mercenary, and selfish," the *Herald* noted. For better or worse, in the city, state, and nation, politicians were irrevocably committed to divergent positions on the slavery extension issue, thus limiting any chance for compromise.[54]

By the time the Democrats met in Charleston for their national convention, all hope for moderation was forlorn. Tammany and Richmond favored Douglas; Mozart Hall created the powerful impression that it was pro-Southern by backing John C. Breckenridge, Buchanan's favorite; and Dickinson kept up his futile quest for the presidency. But, in the end, all failed. Even though the Credentials Committee admitted only Richmond's group, the delegates could not agree either on a platform or a candidate and adjourned in confusion.[55]

Momentarily, Stephen Douglas seemed the real loser because the ease with which the Republicans nominated Abraham Lincoln forced many New Yorkers to reassess the senator's candidacy. Samuel Barlow spoke for many Democrats when he pleaded with Erastus Corning to drum some sense into Richmond. "We may nominate but cannot elect Douglas & his nomination will in my judgment put an end to the Democratic party," Barlow cautioned. In Washington, with an ear tuned to these grumblings, Buchanan now took a hand. Tammany Hall suddenly discovered what pressure really meant. The President's agents fanned out through the state and city, and called on New York's sense of pride to replace Douglas with Seymour. Others worked on the New York Central Railroad junto, and suggested that Kentuckian James Guthrie would make a fine replacement if Seymour declined.[56]

The Administration's eleventh-hour attack galvanized the Douglasites into counter-action. But while they hastily dispatched agents to plead the senator's case with Richmond, their worries were ill founded. Seymour felt "no responsibility to the administration," and scorned all overtures. Above that, Richmond was convinced that none of the other possible candidates would carry the state. Among Tammanyites, the Douglas-men met an equally heartwarming response. As John Cochrane put it at a mass rally, "we are throughout for Douglas, first and last, beginning and ending with him." Throwing up his hands in disgust, Gideon Tucker growled to Buchanan: "If your Excellency really had as many friends proportionally in Tammany Hall as you have outside, some striking public movement would have been effected long ere this." [57]

Despite Tammany's apparent sincerity, it had a very compelling reason for not displeasing either Douglas or Richmond. Postmaster Isaac Fowler, chairman of the General Committee, grand sachem of the Tammany Society, a man privy to the party's deepest secrets, suddenly left the city—a fugitive to Cuba, pursued by government agents for an alleged defalcation of $155,000. Part of the reason for Fowler's crime lay in his penchant for high living; part in bankrolling party hacks against Wood's lavish handouts. But these reasons were beside the point. His flight, coupled with the determination of Buchananite John Dix, the new postmaster, to root out all corruption, made it essential that Tammany have time to regroup. Under these conditions, it could not afford to alienate the possible next president, Stephen Douglas, nor his chief local patronage agent, Dean Richmond.[58]

Impelled by their illogical positions, most Democrats believed that a reunion might be possible, but their conception of what the means should be proved painfully ambiguous. Unable to find middle ground, the generally pro-Northern Baltimore Convention nominated Douglas; while their pro-Southern brethren, with Administration aid, selected Breckenridge. One more party entered the lists. The old, conservative nucleus of Know-Nothings, now called the Constitutional Union party, named moderate John Bell of Tennessee. Paralleling the 1848 free-soil revolt, then, the Democrats on the national level failed to find a common denominator. Bitterness, not forgiveness, was the order of the day. For a tormented Daniel Dickinson, even his full lexicon of invective lacked sufficient epithets. The Douglasites, he sputtered to Buchanan, "for perfidy, treachery, falsehood, want of democratic principles & pure & unalloyed political rascality generally [are] beyond anything an honorable mind can conceive of." [59]

Such splenetic reaction purged the soul, but other less emotionally involved local Democrats came to a different realization. As Isaiah Rynders lectured the President: "I have come to the conclusion that we cannot under the present circumstances Elect a Democrat by the people although we could do it with but one candidate." Yet while many leaders agreed, their mutual suspicions made a political horse trade seem unlikely. Dean Richmond favored "concession and compromise"; Buchananite Samuel Butterfield would concur only if Douglas dropped out; Collector Schell, on Administration orders, felt he "must sustain [the] feeling that prevails for Buchanan"; while in contrast, Seymour "trusted" that Breckenridge would "not suffer" the extreme folly of running an electoral ticket in New York." [60]

Boldly, Fernando Wood knifed through the web of suspicion. In despair after the Charleston convention delegates had not admitted his faction, Wood felt the national party's split gave him a second chance to be a major leader. With this in mind, he made a hurried trip to Washington for interviews with Buchanan, Douglas, and Breckenridge. On his return, he published an open letter to the state Democracy that warned that unless the party agreed on a fusion or joint-ballot ticket in those individual states where either Douglas or Breckenridge had the best chance of winning, Lincoln and "the Black Republicans" would prevail. Under such conditions, he ended, "why not let Douglas have the state [New York]?" [61]

In light of his career, however, Wood lacked the necessary nonpartisan aura for so delicate an operation. His support came from August Belmont, the national committee chairman. On July 15, meeting in New York City at the house of Watts Sherman, Corning's close business associate, Belmont laid the law down to two separate but coordinate groups. To the politicos—Wood, Purdy, Cochrane, and Richmond—Belmont stressed fusion. From the financiers—William B. Astor, Sherman, and William Duncan—Belmont demanded some workable plan for raising operating funds. Initially, while these men made no binding commitments, they did produce, Sherman told Corning "much *good feeling* & opened the door to greater good hereafter." [62]

Events in the days that followed belied Sherman's optimism. Tammany saw no logic in fusion because it would guarantee Wood's return to grace. Dickinson and Schell pursued their own ends. The Constitutional Unionists split. One section, supporter of Daniel Ullman, merged with the Republicans; the second, allied with Washington Hunt, accepted the wisdom of fusion with the Democrats but were skeptical of the means.

The balance shifted by August, because of economic and political pressures. Gathering at Belmont's house, the leaders of the Democratic Vigilant Association formed a fresh group, the Volunteer Democratic Association, and demanded that all parties seek a real accommodation or face a complete loss of funds. Then, at the state convention, oblivious to the Tammany Society's howls of rage, Richmond admitted both Mozart and Tammany Halls on equal footing, shunted aside the thorny question of regularity, and formed a subcommittee consisting of Mozart's Ben Wood (Fernando's brother), Tammany's William Kennedy, and the Regency's F. L. Laflin to negotiate with Hunt, Schell, and Dickinson. Although the forces of inertia—particularly among the Breckenridge supporters—were impressive, the merchants mobilized sufficient public pressure to make the politicians finally pay heed. By the end of August, a special fifteen-man committee ironed out an agreement, and split the state's electoral vote: Douglas with eighteen, ten for Bell, seven to Breckenridge.[63]

The statewide agreement encountered stiff resistance in the city. The major question local politicians faced involved the meaning and intent of fusion: How far should it go; what did it basically mean? For Tammany, determined to throttle Wood, it meant cooperation only so far as it involved saving the state from Lincoln; nothing more. For Schell and Dickinson, it meant seizing a share of municipal offices disproportionate to their voting strength. For Wood, as the *Herald* announced, it meant that Mozart Hall had gained tremendous prestige "as the centre of conservatism. It was the original nucleus of nationality in this city, and is now a great party." [64]

Wood's new-found importance in helping to create the joint ballot, then, became Tammany's agony. In their enthusiasm about the Union fusion ticket, city merchants magnified Mozart's role and made the mayor their hero. Wood made the most of the leverage. Relentlessly pushing his advantage, he unleashed a hardhitting campaign that devastated Tammany's ward structures and increased Mozart's claim that it was the only legitimate local party.

As a result, the contest for power within the Democracy became unseemly and bitter. Although party lines held firm on the national ticket, Mozart, Tammany, and the Irregulars, a group of foot-loose Democrats led by John McKeon, could not agree on common candidates and ran separate slates. During the last week before the election, Dean Richmond, George Sanders, and Horatio Seymour all tried in vain to shake some sanity into the squabbling Democrats. In a way, they need not have bothered. Although the Republicans scored some gains locally, the fusion ticket carried the city with 65 percent of the total. Upstate and nationally, however, the trend was to Lincoln and the Republicans, thus helping to create the secessionist crisis in the South.[65]

With the nation teetering on the brink of disintegration, city Democrats ignored the need for self-restraint, and, if anything, increased the volume of their mutual recriminations. Speaking for Wood, the *Daily News* argued that Democratic traitors had beaten the party, not Lincoln's inherent strength. "As soon as the excitement of the campaign is over," the paper warned, "the traitors may be sure they will be punished and drummed out with little hope of mercy or reprieve." Tammany fielded the barbed criticism with aplomb, and retorted that Wood's manipulation of pro-Southern feeling was the root cause of the party's malaise. In despair, moderates on all sides called for "compromise, concession and conciliation," and demanded that the Democracy show the same reasonableness it had exhibited during the stormy days that preceded the Compromise of 1850. Strangely, Daniel Dickinson, who epitomized the entire problem, doubted that the system could respond. To Thomas Olcott he wrote: *"political parties*, in the old sense of the term, are to exist *no more in this country*. The trouble is first now, that we are in transit from where old organizations left off to where the popular sense should begin." For once, Dickinson was correct.[66]

# ⤙ 13 ⤚

# The Civil War, the Tammany Society, and Tweed's Consolidation

IN THE PERIOD between Lincoln's election and the Confederate firing on Fort Sumter, New Yorkers viewed secession with mixed emotions. In particular, Tammany and Mozart Halls underwent several changes in attitudes before coming to terms with the new political situation.

Wood's first reaction was one of silence, even though his official newspaper, the *Daily News*, disparaged South Carolina's secession "as the leap of the suicide, not the mark of the hero." Several considerations prompted Wood's hesitancy. Even though a burgeoning economic recession gripped the city because Southern merchants repudiated their debts, he still feared a premature move might disenchant local mercantile interests. Moreover, his emotional ties with the South were deep and abiding. Then, too, public opinion had not yet hardened. Next, he feared that the Republican legislature might again undercut his executive powers. But above all else, he felt that the Confederacy was a passing stage of Southern grievances and that the seceded states would voluntarily come back into the Union—provided the Republicans did not antagonize them.

After weighing all these considerations, Mayor Wood advanced an extraordinary proposal in his annual message. He suggested that because the federal government could not hold the Union together, New York should become a free city after peacefully withdrawing from the Union. In such a manner, the city could "preserve a continuance of uninterrupted intercourse with every section." [1]

The proposal met a cool response. Although Wood's idea appealed to some merchants, they believed that different leaders could maintain stability through less radical means. Bennett gave the plan some support but reserved judgment until Buchanan exhausted all alternative options. Both Tammany and the *Irish-American,* one of Wood's staunchest supporters, scorned the mayor. Horace Greeley had the last word. "Fernando Wood," the *Tribune* jibed, "evidently wants to be a traitor; it is the lack of courage that makes him content with being a blackguard." [2]

Mired in the same quandary as Wood, Tammany saw the fact of secession emerge—but had no understanding of what it meant to the organization. Some braves, such as Virginia-born Isaiah Rynders, had dual loyalties. Others, like John Cisco in the Custom House, complained about the "stagnation of business" but offered no practical remedies. After weeks of indecision, the General Committee came up with an unexpected plan, totally divergent from anything proposed in years of spread-eagle oratory. If the new Confederate states left the Union in a quiet, willing, orderly way, after serious deliberations, the Hall felt that the Union should let them depart in "peace—sorrowfully, but not in anger." The main editorial in Tammany's official newspaper, the *New York Leader,* edited by Sachem John Clancy, stated, "let us, therefore, have no coercion, no civil war." Despite these near-traitorous words, Tammany Hall assumed that secession would fail because of its belief that the Confederates could not survive economically without Northern trade and credit. Once Jefferson Davis realized this, once the passage of time laid a healing balm over sectional wounds, a new and greater United States would come forth.[3]

At the party's state convention, called by Richmond and other national Douglas Democrats to find some middle way in the crisis, Tammany could see no distinction between its own local partisan needs and the nation's ultimate survival. Only when he realized that the majority of delegates had no patience to again discuss which Hall actually represented the city Democracy did Purdy accept Richmond's insistence that both Tammany and Mozart should come into the convention on equal footing. But although the delegates formed an eight-man special committee to correspond with other national conservatives on ways to avoid war, most New Yorkers still lacked any understanding of what means to employ. Basically, these men were politicians seeking political solutions of a crisis that the political system had created yet could not solve. Above all, they were anticoercionists; men who could not accept the idea that war was inevitable. Surely, they felt, men of good will would save the day.[4]

By late March and early April, Tammany's attitude had undergone a massive change. Finally recognizing the depth of the national crisis, the Hall proposed a solution which might preserve the Union and still placate the secessionists. The new Confederate constitution, the *Leader* suggested, provided a sensible framework for "a readjustment of our National system and the reconstruction of the Union." A compromise was yet possible, the paper insisted, if the United States would amend its Constitution on that basis.[5]

The Hall's efforts convinced few people. The Republicans rejected the idea because the Confederate Constitution legitimatized slavery extension and specifically banned all government efforts to stimulate or protect business interests. Mayor Wood still did not take any position on secession other than lecturing President-elect Lincoln to seek reunion based on "peaceful and conciliatory means, aided by the wisdom of Almighty God." As for Mozart, it continued to treat secession as a partisan hobbyhorse, mouthed slogans of "reconciliation and harmony," and vilified the Republicans for making all compromises "hollow subterfuges." As a result, Samuel Barlow told James Watson Webb (whose newspaper verged on final dissolution) that if war came, "New York will be in the hands of what you call *a mob*." [6]

The attack on Fort Sumter changed the political game, but not its rules. In the first surge of patriotism, Tammany and the New Regency momentarily forgot party lines and joined the Republicans to form a solid front against the Confederacy. The General Committee and the Tammany Society formed a regiment, Grand Sachem William Kennedy volunteered to become its commanding officer, and they all dedicated themselves to fight for "democratic institutions and constitutional liberties." [7]

By contrast, Mozart Hall briefly lost its way. "Let not the perfidious Administration invoke the sacred names of the Union and the Constitution, in the hope of cheating fools in the support of the unholy war which it has begun," the *Daily News* countered. But Wood read public opinion better than his editor, Gideon Tucker. Directly taking issue with his own newspaper, Wood issued a proclamation that all citizens must obey the law, support the public peace, preserve order, and protect property. But the patriots were not satisfied. "How can there be peace between loyal citizens and traitors," Greeley scoffed. Tammany also refused to let Wood off the hook. Mayor Wood, the *Leader* goaded, "stands solitary and alone among the Municipal chiefs of the North as having taken sides with the conspirators against the Union." The upshot of the strategy split between Wood and the *Daily News* restored Tammany's prestige and identified it firmly in the public mind as being prowar. The *Herald* typified this mood when it lauded the General Committee for its "readiness to cast off the shackles of the past, in view of the dangers which menace the Union." [8]

Once he realized his mistake, Wood made his peace with public opinion. In a brief speech at the city's first Union rally, he urged "every man, whatever had been his sympathies to make one great phalanx in this controversy, to proceed to conquer a peace. I am with you in this contest. We know no party now." Then, to solidify his position, he became an ex-officio member of the Union Defense Committee. Finally, through this committee, Mozart Hall raised its own regiment, subsequently called the 40th New York Volunteers. By July 4, the recruits entrained for Washington.[9]

Despite Mozart's belated support of the war, however, Wood maintained his cool detachment. His main problem was one of approach. As a politician, he treated the war as a political question in which loyalty to self outweighed loyalty to the Union. Skilled at taking divergent positions on the same issue, he waited to see which question—war or antiwar—could gain him the maximum leverage. As a result, he gave the war effort the necessary lip service—even to the extent of writing Lincoln, with suitable publicity, that he was ready to serve in "any military capacity consistent with my position as Mayor of New York." His real purpose did not escape George Templeton Strong, one of his severest critics. "The cunning scoundrel sees which way the cat is jumping," Strong wrote in his diary, "and puts himself right on the record in a vague general way, giving the least offence to his allies on the Southern Democracy." [10]

Yet neither was Tammany Hall all that it seemed. Its leaders objected to the Union Defense Committee's propensity for blurring party lines and treating the war as an end in itself. Purdy agreed that Tammany should team with the Unionists, but saw no connection between patriotism and politics, as did Daniel Dickinson, who used the Committee's bipartisanship to cooperate with Lincoln. Despite the Unionists' pleas for unity in thought and deed, Tammany followed its own needs. Any "further distractions and divisions in our ranks will permanently destroy our prestige and power as the controlling party of this great city," the *Leader* explained. We "must unite on Democratic principles —preserve the Union—but Tammany must be the head." [11]

For New York City Democrats, then, love of country could not stem the political tides that swept through the party. If politics moved the nation toward secession, partisanship and internal factionalism did not ebb once the Civil war actually started. By the summer of 1861,

the same professionals and small-minded men who had been instrumental in aiding and abetting the crisis formulated the basic question
of the Civil War locally—how much allegiance should they give to
Administration war efforts?

Under the sense of panic and shame that New Yorkers felt because
of General Irvin McDowell's defeat at the first battle of Manassas, the
Democrats prepared for their fall convention. Many Tammanyites were
even more disturbed emotionally when news reached the city that
Colonel William Kennedy was one of the battle's first victims. As a
result, many Democrats rediscovered their constitutional scruples and
began to assail President Lincoln's high-handed use of arbitrary arrests
and abrogation of civil rights. Fully aroused, party leaders advanced
other doubts. Many suspected that the Republicans were deliberately
manipulating the war as a partisan trick to solidify their power. Still
others feared the Administration might free the slaves as a wartime
expedient to please the abolitionists. Dean Richmond bore the weight
of such party suspicions. Wavering erratically as he sought to master
the rising peace movement within the Democracy, he rejected Republican suggestions for a joint prowar ticket, although he did leave the
door open for future negotiations. Tammany backed him. Democratic
policy, the *Leader* stated, "must deny the right of Secession, but . . .
allow no infraction of the Constitutional liberties guaranteed to every
state and section." [12]

As a statement of policy, editor Clancy was correct. But at the convention, Tammany's delegation, led by Purdy, failed to consider the
possibility of a change in the circumstances on which the idea was
predicated. For although the delegates admitted Tammany Hall as the
only legitimate Democratic organization in the city, they only did so
after Peter Sweeny hastily prepared and circulated a memorandum
which characterized Tammany's battle with Mozart as a question of
war or treason. To admit Mozart, according to Sweeny's reasoning,
was synonymous with criticizing the effort to save the Union. Yet the
compulsions of politics also made it imperative that the Democracy
rebuke the Administration for its shoddy war record. The upshot was
the famous "Ninth Resolution" favored by the Peace Democrats, a
resolution that belabored Lincoln as a quasi-dictator and full-time failure. But at the same time, the party also resolved that the conflict should
continue "until the struggle is ended by the triumph of the Constitution
and laws, and the restoration of the Union." [13]

Since the Democracy, in attempting to please everyone, ended only in spreading more confusion, the Unionists turned the ambivalence into a case for supporting Administration war plans. Within days, a fairly loose alliance of prowar groups, who called themselves the People's party, fused with the Republicans on a Unionist slate and headed their ticket with Daniel Dickinson for secretary of state. In a way, the move excused men such as Bronson, Croswell, John Cochrane, and Dickinson from their checkered past. By placing nation above party, these men added some consistency to their previous behavior, and most of them ultimately moved toward the Republican party's conservative wing where they remained once the war ended.[14]

Back in the city, the Democrats were totally distracted. Mozart Hall, with Wood strategically silent, backed the Ninth Resolution, and, under Tucker's direction, called on all honest citizens to aid "in the restoration of harmony and quiet to our distracted and desolated land. The issue is between a useless and destructive war and a prosperous and enduring peace." In Tammany, divided councils prevailed. Some pragmatists such as Tweed, who eyed the party's nomination for sheriff, wanted to damp the organization's martial spirit. Others, led by Clancy, let their emotions rule. Using Kennedy as its martyr, the *Leader* announced that "Tammany Hall will support no candidates who are not of a loyalty as unimpeached and stainless as her own." [15]

For the moment, Tammany's war hawks flew high on the state elections. The Purdy-led General Committee repudiated the Ninth Resolution, adopted a strong war policy, and pledged itself "to the earnest and resistless prosecution of the war, until the rebellion is utterly suppressed." Even if Purdy's effort won few friends among the fence-sitters, there was profit in Tammany's political strategy, especially when contrasted with that of Horatio Seymour, whose constitutional quibblings against the war sounded more and more pro-Confederate.[16]

But in the city elections, Tammany's prowar spirit hinged on Fernando Wood's actions. Since the lines of political battle were so imprecisely drawn, Wood continued to straddle the issue, allowed his brother Ben and Gideon Tucker to move into the vanguard of the peace movement, and schemed to be reelected. Yet he could not do so without Tammany's aid because of a burgeoning reform movement. By themselves, the reformers posed no danger. But in October, four major groups—the Fifth Avenue Committee, the St. Nicholas Committee, the German League, and the Tax-Payers Committee—linked with the Republicans on a Unionist, reformist slate. The move proved a tactical blunder because it drew the Democrats together. Both Halls charged that the Unionist movement was an elaborate hoax and agreed that the Democracy could not survive unless it fused.

Even so, Tammany was trapped by its own words. After the state convention, it had exacted a pledge from each candidate that he favored the war. Anything less, Tammanyites knew, would destroy the electorate's faith on the local level. But hidden from view, leaders of the General Committee locked in a massive power struggle that revolved over whether it should follow Tweed's practical approach or Clancy's adamant position. In the end, Tweed won. Both Halls cooperated, but only on an informal level, and selected independent slates although they substantially agreed on a number of common nominees. As to three vital offices, however—those of mayor, district attorney, and sheriff—confusion reigned.

The office of sheriff, as in Mordecai Noah's day, was a politician's dream because, aside from the normal graft, the sheriff shared in all fees his office collected. Moreover, the spoils at his disposal guaranteed a highly strategic power base. Tweed coveted these opportunities and gained Tammany's nomination; Mozart named James Lynch, an Irish favorite. The *Leader*, however, felt that Tweed had overmatched himself "against the popular Lynch." [17]

Well aware of the odds, Tweed, though quiet on his own war record, attacked Lynch (who had volunteered in the Army for three months) for having demanded his discharge just before the Battle of Bull Run. But Tweed's tactics backfired. Wood, playing deeply on the sentiments of the gullible Irish, strongly defended Lynch, not so much on his actual record as a soldier, but on the idea that "he belongs to a race which never produced a coward." An attack on him, therefore, was a sign of xenophobia, not patriotism. As Wood hammered away at these points, Lynch gained support. In a key move, the *Irish-American*, which Tweed had been cultivating, endorsed Lynch.

In the district attorney contest, two equally controversial candidates appeared. Running on a combined Mozart-Republican slate was Abraham Oakey Hall, the "Elegant Oakey," a political turncoat who had been a Whig, Know-Nothing, Republican, and Woodite. The incumbent, Sachem Nelson J. Waterbury, a highly capable lawyer and a man just emerging as Purdy's and Tweed's chief rival in the Society, represented Tammany.[18]

The mayoralty race generated the most interest. The problem here rested on the fact that Wood's foes wanted to defeat him, but could not agree on a common standard-bearer. As William Havemeyer worried, "if each of the opposing parties places its own Candidate in the field, he [Wood] will have an easy victory." In order to stop Wood, Tammany again exhibited an ability to make neat distinctions between its words and its deeds. In a conscious effort to capture the Unionists, the General Committee invited "all honest men who are against Wood" to discuss plans. Encouraged by the turnout, Purdy then appointed a Committee of Conference to see if the Unionists and Republicans would unite "upon some gentlemen whose position and interest would guarantee, to the combination, an easy victory." But in the end, Tammany's greed made compromise impossible. It felt that because the city was overwhelmingly Democratic, "such candidate should be selected from the Democratic party." The Unionists rejected Purdy's overtures and, along with the Tax-Payers Committee and the Rent-Payers Association, nominated wealthy Republican George Opdyke on a reformist slate. The chagrined Tammanyites selected an equally upright citizen, fur merchant C. Godfrey Gunther, who had impressive backing among the city's German citizens.

Originally, Wood had planned to campaign on local issues. But his enemies anticipated the move, and forced him to alter tactics. Republican Hiram Ketchum charged that Wood had openly bartered Mozart's judicial nomination for $500 to the highest bidder, while at the same time secretly promising Tammany that he would not name a candidate in exchange for a joint mayoralty ticket. Equally unnerving, District Attorney Waterbury began an investigation of other Republican charges that Wood had awarded city franchises without competitive bidding.

Now that Opdyke's supporters had preempted reform, Wood abandoned his plans to conduct a vigorous, high-level, locally orientated campaign, and made Lincoln's handling of the war the chief election issue. The mayor's move was a major switch in tactics, for as late as November 2 he had pledged the Administration his support. But now that he was fighting for his political survival, Wood could no longer live in two worlds. In another way, however, he had no choice. Tammany was too closely associated with the war issue for him to adopt that position; while Mozart Hall, through his brother and Tucker, rarely let up on its incessant peace calls.

On November 27, Wood made an all-out appeal for the peace vote when he delivered a ringing anti-Administration speech at the Volks Garten, a popular meeting hall for German Democrats. As long as the Republicans were in power, he shouted, neither the Constitution nor the institutions of free government were safe. Above that, he reviled the Administration for needlessly prolonging the war in order to emancipate the slaves.

Yet Wood had lost none of his cunning. Still hoping to keep his feet in both camps, Wood, on the same day that he gave the Volks Garten speech, wrote Secretary of State William Seward a fawning letter that praised Lincoln's efforts, and promised to sustain all efforts that led to a constitutionally sound "restoration of peace."

For once Wood's political cynicism skewered him. Totally oblivious to the emotions involved, he could not understand that the public took the war seriously and demanded consistency. Where New Yorkers could once forgive his drive for personal advancement, they could no longer accept his methods. Quite simply, they felt that saving the Union was far too worthy a cause for such cheap gamesmanship. As a result of the Volks Garten address and the controversy he created, then, Wood was literally dragooned into a position that he was not fully ready to adopt. True, by instinct and inclination, he probably would have settled down as a Peace Democrat anyway. But it was equally possible for him to become a War Democrat if he thought that position had greater vote appeal. That door was now closed. As the *Leader* summed up the situation: "Fernando Wood is heart and soul with the armed traitors of the South." [20]

By and large, the course and content of New York City politics was now set for the next three years. Tammany became the chief local Democratic proponent of the war, sometimes less enthused about its stance than at other times, but nonetheless content with its position. Contrarily, Fernando Wood drifted with the Peace Democrats and flirted with disloyalty as his situation became more precarious. These maneuverings, in a larger sense, were no different from the power struggle that had been ripping the Democracy apart for the last fourteen years. Thus, the Civil War, as far as Tammany and Mozart were concerned, was a political as well as a military question, whose final answer was as intimately linked to the fortunes of the Union Army as to the success of the Democratic party.

The mayoralty contest approached its climax. As a politician, Wood knew that he still had a chance until the last vote was dropped in the ballot box. What he needed was some popular issue with deep vote-getting appeal to remove the onus of his Volks Garten speech. He nearly found it in the *Trent* Affair.

Captain Charles Wilkes, a native New Yorker, with impeccable ties to the New Albany Regency, had created a storm of controversy when his men boarded the British mail packet, the *Trent*, and removed two Confederate diplomats bound for duty in Europe. Although the Administration deprecated Wilkes' disregard for neutral rights, many Americans treated the captain as an authentic war hero.

While Lincoln searched for some face-saving gesture, Wood sought to transfer some of Wilkes' glitter onto his own tarnished image. Two days after his speech, Wood wrote to Caleb Cushing, the eminent Massachusetts lawyer, for a legal opinion that would justify the seizure. Wood then planned to sponsor a public rally to dramatize Mozart's prowar spirit. Cushing, however, smelled trouble. No stranger to city politics and aware of Wood's gamy reputation, he delayed an answer until the mayoralty canvass ended.[21]

Left stranded, Wood fell back on his by now traditional rough tactics. His foes answered in kind. With so much at stake, corruption, fraud, bribery, and premature naturalizations reached epic proportions. The situation became more critical after the polls closed when the counters held up the returns in three wards that were all Republican strongholds. But, in the end, Opdyke squeaked to victory.

MAYORALTY ELECTION, 1861

| | Totals | Percentage |
| --- | --- | --- |
| Opdyke | 25,380 | 34.3 |
| Gunther | 24,767 | 33.3 |
| Wood | 24,167 | 32.4 |

The closeness of these returns did not form a mandate concerning the war. Lynch, in beating Tweed, nearly doubled his vote, but Waterbury lost a close race to Hall. But one trend was clear. Wood was out of power and Mozart Hall no longer commanded the city's tremendous patronage. Under these happy conditions, Clancy called for party reunion—on Tammany's terms—and predicted that "with the Waterloo defeat and downfall of Fernando, our troubles cease, and those who have been led away from the ancient standards of the true faith are 'coming in' and resurrecting their places in the ranks of our party." [22]

When the Hall formed its new General Committee, Purdy implemented the suggestion. The time was ripe, he suggested, for a "thorough union of the Democracy" without "regard to past divisions." But before

either he or Tweed could repair the Hall's old rifts, they faced an
entirely new challenge from within their own maturing organization.

1862 was the critical year in Tweed's rise to power. Still a force on
the Board of Supervisors, he was nonetheless still only one of several
contenders for the spot as Tammany's "Boss." With Purdy's aid, he
had temporarily overshadowed most of his personal rivals. But, ironically, with Wood's downfall, a new and volcanic power struggle
began within the General Committee. Its motive force came from one
man, Henry W. Genet, in whose chromosomes rested the incompatible
genes of two noted ancestors: the erratic Citizen Genêt and "The Old
Sachem," George Clinton.

Behind artfully contrived diletantism, "Prince Hal" flexed supple
political muscles. First elected as an alderman in 1857, he had steadily
risen in the ranks and became Board president four years later. In the
same year, through a political horse trade, he gained a dual Mozart-
Tammany nomination for county clerk and won easily. Once in office,
he, along with Shepard Knapp, Thomas Byrnes, George Lynch, Harry
Vandewater of the Street Department, the Croton Water Department's
Thomas Tappan, and Commissioner of Jurors Ulysses D. French, built
up a powerful "combination" whose sole criterion for appointment
rested on party workers' rejections of both Halls.

In January 1862, Genet launched his bid for power over Tammany
by taking advantage of twelve contested ward elections for seats on
the new General Committee. Since representation on the Committee
was allotted among the wards on a equal basis, not in proportion to the
number of registered Democrats, whoever dominated a few key "rotten
boroughs" almost invariably ruled the organization. It was in these
wards that the combination, in collusion with State Senator Richard
Connolly, State Committeeman William Miner, and Sachem Joseph
Develin, exerted maximum leverage. The upshot was, the *Leader* complained, that Genet's men virtually decided the vote on the contested
seats, "and were becoming substantially the hubs upon which all the
political wheels of the Tammany machine revolved." [23]

Tweed framed his tactics in the *Leader*. Posing as a reformer, he,
Peter Sweeny, Thomas Barr (Sweeny's uncle), and Nelson Waterbury,
demanded that the wards elect "live men" with real "constituencies at
their back," not those "who make a business out of politics." If Tammany were to survive, it had to revamp its entire ward structure. Thus,
only through a thorough reapportionment, responsive to public control

and opinion could the rank and file save the General Committee from mass corruption.

Genet was unimpressed. When Tweed and Purdy made the contested seats in Byrnes' ward a test case and offered a substitute who "would give real strength" to Tammany, the combination demanded and received traditional party formulas. This meant that Purdy's Democratic Association System, based on a legal delegate having a certificate of election signed by three inspectors, would settle the question. Savoring the irony of the situation, then, the combination turned the Association idea against its founder, and forced the Committee to adopt in each ward the "uniform rule" of admitting only the men with signed certificates.[24]

Genet next moved to capture the Tammany Society. In a way, the Society was ripe for a political buccaneer. In a bewildering two-year period, the Council of Sachems had lost the scandal-ridden Isaac Fowler; William Kennedy had fallen on the field at Manassas; James Connor, long a stabilizing force among the sachems, quietly died; while Elijah Purdy, "The Old Warhorse," tired and in poor health, panted for his second wind. In the resultant power vacuum, two groups poised for a monumental fight: Genet's ring against the young braves led by Tweed, whom Purdy had been grooming for the past eight years.

Tweed, pulling wires from behind the scenes, portrayed the April Council election as the Society's major opportunity to save the party "from disgrace." In Clancy's words, "Whatever doubts may have existed in the past, in reference to the action of the Society in contributing to reforms, there can be no doubt or hesitation now." Pledging itself to "the redemption and union of the party," the Committee on Nominations—Tweed, Judge Matthew Brennan, and Recorder John Hoffman —judiciously wove the old with the new, and finally presented an impressive list of candidates. Tweed was even more careful to avoid any parallel with the old Hard-Soft factional disagreements. Through Purdy, he secured the endorsements of Daniel Delevan, Thomas Barr, Wilson Small, and Augustus Schell.

On election night, Tweed rounded out his efforts by hiring professional toughs, most of whom he recruited from the volunteer firemen's ranks, to maintain order. Amidst the noise and confusion, Tweed held a towering position. Confident that his forces would dominate the new Council, he insisted that the braves select Joseph Develin, one of Genet's close aides, who had recently broken with the combination. Taken aback, some of the brethren balked but soon assented. Tweed's compassion, however, had a purely practical side. Unlike some men who personalized politics—DeWitt Clinton or Fernando Wood, for examples—Tweed, like Martin Van Buren before him, perceived that today's enemy was perhaps tomorrow's friend.

With the Tammany Society safely tucked away, Tweed gained tremendous prestige with which to structure party policy favorable to his interests. But while he realized that he had withstood the combination's move to control Tammany's fount of legitimacy, there was no sign that Genet was willing to surrender. The next test would come in the fall municipal contests. Then, too, new Grand Sachem Nelson Waterbury, on whom Tweed relied to carry out his directives, soon proved to have ambitions of his own. Tweed was not as safe as he thought.[25]

During this jockeying, the cracks in the state Democracy's facade widened to reveal gaping holes. Out of power on the local, state, and national levels for the first time as far back as most living politicians could recall, the party lacked any coherent program to restore its hegemony. With their imaginations and nerves atrophied, party leaders seemed devoid of hope.

Luckily for the Democracy, help came from without. The Republicans were beset by a number of problems they could not solve. Besides a split between the dogmatic Greeley-men and the more pragmatic followers of Thurlow Weed, Republican Speaker of the Assembly Henry Raymond, owner of the New York Times, could not discipline the balky Unionists, who resented the party's pro-business orientation. Above that, the Republicans' inability to handle the emancipation question gave the Democrats the issue they needed. Consistent with past performances, local Democrats remained obtuse about slavery's moral dimensions and shared the same wide-ranging white-supremacy attitudes typical of most Northerners. At one extreme, Union Democrats declared that they were fighting secession, not slavery; at the other, the Peace Democrats played on immigrant fears that emancipation would cheapen an already glutted labor pool and drive wages down to a bare subsistence level; in the middle, War Democrats and constitutionalists such as Horatio Seymour and John Pruyn doubted that Lincoln had the power to erase legal contracts or invalidate the rights and obligations inherent in property ownership. Still others, nominally Democrats, adopted a frank racist line. James Gordon Bennett's Negrophobia was notorious throughout the nation, while hate-mongering sheets like the New York Caucasian stated bluntly "that this government was made on the WHITE basis, by WHITE MEN, for the benefit of WHITE MEN and their POSTERITY FOREVER." [26]

At the same time, Fernando Wood still hoped to accomplish the feat of being on good terms with the Peace Democrats, the War Democrats, and the Administration. In January 1862, he wrote Lincoln a long, obsequious letter in praise of the Union war effort. A month later, Wood sounded the same theme in a public address, reversed his Volks Garten speech, and called on all Americans to maintain national unity even if it meant further bloodshed. Horace Greeley drew back in disgust, and he accused Wood of secretly organizing and contributing funds to a movement that proposed to negotiate peace with the Confederates. At once, Wood wrote Lincoln that "the ultra radical abolitionists of this state persistently represent me as hostile to your administration, and as in sympathy with the states in rebellion against the government. I sincerely hope there [*sic*] allegations (false in every respect) will have no influence upon your generous mind." [27]

Since Lincoln, who did not yet dominate the Republicans, sought allies from as many sources as possible from within and without the party, Wood's efforts partially fitted Administration needs. Even so, the President was unsure of exactly what game the New Yorker was playing and made no commitments. Left dangling, then, Wood was forced to turn his attention to a different but equally knotty problem.

As a reaction due to his loss of the mayoralty, several of Wood's key ward chairmen revolted against his one-man operation of Mozart Hall and threatened to displace him. Although Wood managed to retain control through one of his underlings, Benjamin Ray, the crisis of confidence was not over. The growing anti-Wood clique in Mozart Hall was frankly skeptical of his ability to cope with the mounting pressures of local politics.

Wood's problem stemmed from his handling of the sensitive street commissioner's slot during his tenure as mayor the year before. Since the incumbent commissioner had an immense amount of patronage at his disposal, Wood eyed the position for one of his supporters. Yet a stalemate developed because the replacement needed the Board of Supervisors' approval. At that point, Genet concocted a plan as bold as it was ingenious. As the means to secure a dual endorsement from both Halls in the county clerk's race, he tied his candidacy to the vexatious impasse. First, he picked an uncontroversial young man, Shepard Knapp, the son of a prominent Tammany chieftain, as a compromise appointee. Then Genet secured Tammany's clerk nomination by promising the delegates that Knapp "would give them *carte blanche* in the distribution of the patronage." Genet played the same game with Wood. In return for his support, Genet secretly assured the mayor that Knapp would give Mozart the bulk of the spoils. The plot worked. Wood selected Knapp, the Board concurred, and Genet ran on a single ticket.

Once in office, however, Knapp and Genet followed their own interests. Knapp, the *Leader* reported, "sneeringly dismissed without any, even the slightest consideration for the deal," all requests Wood made, and steadily built up Genet's personal machine. "Caught Knapping" by the "adroit and unscrupulous" combination, Wood now suffered a fate no politician ever relished—people laughed at him behind his back.[28]

The task that confronted Wood at this point was formidable. But again his incredible luck, this time in the form of General Robert Hunter's premature emancipation order, gave Wood an opportunity to use the resentment all sections of the Democratic party held in common against abolitionism to reestablish his sovereignty over Mozart, and return to the party's good graces without explicitly taking any stand on the war. Working through William Prime, editor of the *Journal of Commerce*, he sponsored a mass meeting of conservatives against those radicals whose "attempted innovation" posed a clear danger "to our liberties," and signaled "the commencement of an irresponsible military despotism." [29]

Strange things occurred in the next few weeks. Most local party leaders pragmatically decided that the Democracy could not survive without patronage. Using their defense of the Constitution and opposition to emancipation as catalysts, they dropped all mention of the actual nature of the war, and agreed to seek out new avenues for Democratic cooperation. The Tammany Society followed the same lines. When the time came for toasts at the Independence Day celebration, Elijah Purdy had something for everyone. For the War Democrats, he promised that Tammany would fight "for the suppression of the rebellion and the supremacy of the law"; to please the Peace Democrats, he used their slogan of restoring "the Union as it was, and maintaining the Constitution as it is." And for all Democrats, he continued, if Lincoln prosecuted the war "for the dishonest purpose of emancipating the negroes of the South, he cannot expect the support of Democrats." Tammany's General Committee placed its seal on these efforts. Besides offering a few pious disclaimers that the Union ought to be preserved, Purdy introduced a resolution, which the Genet-men routinely sent to their Committee on Organization, "to ascertain what 'honorable means' a Union could be effected between Tammany Hall and the outside organizations." [30]

In September, when Lincoln finally issued the Emancipation Proclamation, the dissident Democrats had their final excuse for an intraparty accommodation. Tammany deplored the decree as "the bankrupt death-rattle of a discredited Administration," while the Peace Democrat *New York World,* snarled that Lincoln was "fully adrift on the current of radical fanaticism." [31]

On the surface, then, full party unity was merely a matter of time and circumstance. Yet when party leaders shelved the practical problem of making the city Democracy predominantly prowar or propeace, they overlooked two hazards that could undo all their calculations: Henry Genet's soaring ambitions, and Fernando Wood's abrasive record as a maverick.

Genet viewed himself rather than emancipation as the vehicle for fusion. Although deeply shocked by the Tammany Society's rebuff, he had turned its actions into a badge of honor, especially among the Mozart Democracy who shared his animus toward the sachems. Then, when Wood ran into trouble over the Knapp affair, Genet decided to widen the gap that separated Wood and the rebellious Mozarters. With this is mind, Genet and Richard Connolly opened negotiations to turn Wood "neck and heels out of his political house and home." [32]

Using his control over the General Committee's subgroup, the Committee on Organization, as his opening point, Genet suggested to his counterparts that both Tammany and Mozart should hold a common primary to elect a single state convention delegation. Mozart accepted, despite Tammany's determination to nominate Seymour for governor, a post that Wood coveted. For the first time in many years, the city Democracy began a state campaign as participants, not an issue.

The state convention contrasted starkly with the virile displays of partisanship that had marred previous meetings. For the unknowing or naive, a new day had really dawned. As a symbol of peace, Wood and Purdy walked arm in arm down the aisle to their seats. As expected, the unwilling Seymour, who had been previously nominated by the moribund Constitutional Unionists, was selected for governor by a unanimous vote. But his acceptance speech started the campaign off on the wrong foot when he opened a states' rights attack on the Administration that created the incorrect impression that he was a rabid Peace Democrat. Coupled with his endorsement by several fellow-traveling, pro-Confederate newspapers in other Northern states, he laid himself open to Horace Greeley's harsh editorials. By contrasting Republican nominee General James Wadsworth (a former Barnburner and impeccable on the war issue) with Seymour, the powerful but nearsighted

Greeley concluded that Seymour's election "would be hailed with exultation beyond the lines of the Union Army." [33]


Although Genet had engineered the Tammany-Mozart accord, party peace in the state convention constituted only a minor point in his full blueprint for a new political engine. Of far more importance, he now put finishing touches on his plan to dominate the local government through the city comptroller and the counsel to the corporation. Of the two, the comptroller's office was the more lucrative prize. Elected for a four-year term, the slot was a spoilsman's dream. Clancy felt that "it is the most powerful office in the State next to that of Governor—locally and in point of patronage far greater." The reason for the editor's belief lay in the fact that the comptroller exercised complete autonomy over "subordinate departments, bureaux, clerkships, and offices of every description," all of which he could sell to the highest bidder, or award to faithful party workers on a sliding scale for services rendered. But above everything else, the comptroller had full supervision "over all the city's financial concerns." Whoever dominated the office had a powerful club, not only over the municipality but both political parties as well.[34]

Since Genet had no intention of giving up his current jobs, every would-be candidate sought his endorsement. Gradually two major applicants, Francis Boole and Richard Connolly, and one minor one, Police Justice Michael Connolly (no relative), outdistanced their nearest rivals.

Supervisor Boole soon withdrew. The year before, he had avidly courted Tammany's nomination for county clerk but dropped out when Genet promised to support him for comptroller at the next canvass. For the next few months, Boole waited in vain for some sign that Genet meant to fulfill the bargain. When Genet proved evasive, Boole at last realized that he had been duped, and joined forces with his fellow supervisors, Tweed and Purdy, against the combination. The move had far-reaching consequences, Clancy noted, for Boole carried with him "all the solid and substantial members of the Board," while Genet was forced "to recruit from the outside."

Boole's defection elated Richard Connolly. Earlier, he and Genet had drawn up the necessary details for party fusion. In doing so, however, he had incurred Tweed's wrath for ignoring "fairness and decency." Arriving home from the convention, he took his place on the Committee on Organization and soon immersed himself in the delicate barter with Mozart preliminary to forming a single municipal ticket. Just then, Connolly received a jolt when Mozart balked at accepting him for comptroller but readily endorsed Boole.[35]

Much to Connolly's astonishment, Genet bowed before Mozart's objections, and made no effort to change its mind. As the *Leader* analyzed the brusque dismissal, the combination had simply used him "for their own purposes" to draw him "away from his friends and proving that he was unworthy of them, and [after] securing him within their clutches," to nominate "another man of their own." Furious, Connolly bolted to Tweed, but met with little sympathy. Connolly, Clancy explained, was "now seeking to make terms with his old 'friends'—but 'friends' and foes alike turn their backs on him."

Connolly, however, still remained a pivotal member on the subcommittee; thus Genet could not completely alienate him. Under these conditions, he informed reporters that Connolly remained his personal choice, although most politicians now conceded "that no candidate nominated in that interest can be elected." [36]

Nonetheless, Genet had begun to write his own political obituary. In duping Connolly and Boole, Prince Hal commited the darkest sin in the politicos' handbook. When he refused to make his word his bond, when he scoffed at firm commitments, he forfeited massive public trust. As a result, only a fool would put faith in him in the future. And most Tammanyites were not fools.

Despite Genet's disgrace, his foes still faced a critical situation because the combination dominated the Committee on Organization. But the opposition lacked firm direction; Tweed's and Purdy's tactics, as a whole, were merely instinctive reactions to the combination's initiatives. Yet the more Genet followed his own dreams, the more he thrust Tweed and Wood together. Paradoxically, Prince Hal indeed acted as a catalyst for party fusion—but in a way that he never intended.

By the first week of October, Tweed and Wood formed a mutual defense pact. But neither man entered the agreement blindly. Both were leaders by nature and instinct, jealous of their prerogatives, and neither would accept divided authority for long. Knowing this, many cynics doubted that Tweed, Purdy, and Wood could share an organization without tearing it into bits. Events proved the skeptics temporarily incorrect.

The *Leader* took to the offensive first and aroused popular indignation against the combination for its shabby record in the Knapp affair and the Boole-Connolly fiasco. On the strength of these disclosures, Clancy then demanded that Tammany break some long-standing party customs. As Sweeny put it, the General Committee had to abolish the outmoded ward system and replace it with a new formula based on the number of actual Democratic voters in each district. Furthermore, the Committee on Organization had outlived its usefulness. In its place, Sweeny recommended an interim group, headed by Tweed, to make a "just and equitable union" with Mozart for the November elections.[37]

Since Sweeny's proposal was the first order of business at the General Committee's regular meeting, each side prepared for battle. Genet brought along underlings from the street department, Wood's plug-uglies took their stations on the Wigwam's ground floor, while Tweed and Purdy packed the corridors around the Long Room with hardened roughnecks recruited from the city's many volunteer fire clubs.

Genet rested his defense on more than brute force. Appealing to the Committee's sense of continuity, he argued that Tammany's entire justification for party leadership rested on long traditions. To change them, he said, would destroy the party. But words could not stop Tweed's momentum. The delegates dissolved the Committee on Organization and authorized Tweed to begin negotiations with Mozart.

After a few days of wheeling and dealing, Wood and Tweed split the ticket to their own satisfaction. Of more importance, at a later meeting Tammany gained the coveted comptroller's nomination; Mozart, that of corporation counsel. With this deal, William Marcy Tweed emerged from the shadows as Tammany's real strong man. Taking the opportunity to eulogize Tweed after the General Committee renominated him for supervisor, Clancy gushed: "He is a live man, in the most vigorous sense—energetic, industrious, courageous and indefatigable. His vitality is felt in every movement with which he is connected, and he is withal a true man in the highest degree. . . . He never turned his back on a friend or a foe." [38]

One last task remained. The General Committee had to mobilize the voters and make sure that public opinion understood the reasons for the accommodation. Clancy did the job with commendable guile. The "movement for union," he told the faithful, was dictated "by its movers from high convictions of patriotism and party unity." As for the embarrassing fact that Fernando and Ben Wood, both Peace Democrats, were running as regulars for Congress, Clancy explained: "We believe that both Woods are earnestly and honestly opposed to the damnable and destroying heresies of Abolitionists, and in favor of maintaining the Union at every hazard and every sacrifice." Despite such tortuous ratiocinations, however, the editor's words were needless. Party workers simply wanted victory, no matter the means.[39]

Even so, an unforeseen complication in the Eighth Congressional District, where Nelson Waterbury was Tammany's nominal candidate, caused trouble. Unhappy that Tweed had rebuffed his efforts to become comptroller, Waterbury had accepted the lesser prize. But in the rapidly shifting panorama of city politics, he became the chief victim of Tweed's deal with Wood. In order to complete an earlier bargain Genet had struck with the old Constitutional Unionists, Tweed and Wood forced Waterbury to drop out of the race, although they eased his withdrawal with the promise of some future office. Publicly, Waterbury took his dismissal with apparent good will. But among his close friends, he raged against Tweed's interference. The upshot was that Tweed had created an enemy sure to use the Council of Sachems against him.[40]

The Democrats' determination to win depressed even the normally ebullient Horace Greeley. "We shall be beaten worse than I at first calculated, though not so much (I think) as in 1860," he wrote Gerrit Smith. Greeley was correct. Almost effortlessly, Seymour carried the city by 31,347 votes, the brothers Wood were elected to Congress, and the combined Tammany-Mozart slate won easily. "The returns of the city are overwhelming our cause," distraught John Cochrane, now a devoted Republican, wrote Lincoln. Explaining the reasons for this situation, Cochrane continued, some voters were "adverse to the proclamation," others "by some uncertain, indefinable reason that all was not right." Hence, "they have been asking for a head to smash. They thought they saw one, and they smashed Wadsworth."

Even so, men like Cochrane, Daniel Dickinson, and David Dudley Field all felt that in the long run "the Democrats could end with no victory at all." The reason behind their assumption, they assured Lincoln, lay in the idea that public opinion favored a speedy end of the war—but not if it split the Union. The Democrats had won because the electorate was frustrated, not because they had an alternative to Administration policy.[41]

In many ways, these men were correct. Seymour's election intensified the running feud between those Democrats who wanted a negotiated peace and others who felt the Union ought to be preserved at all costs. If prudence during the campaign dictated evasion, then victory bred reaction. The Democracy had clearly indicated that it was New York's majority party—as long as it was united. But cooperation could not last; the ambitions and hatreds that had split the party in the past were still alive, and a postponement of the showdown between the two Democratic wings could no longer be avoided. Again, and with greater urgency, the question arose: which would be the dominant faction within the Democracy, and what shape, what issue, would it adopt? Only the most naive politico could lose sight of the fact that, just as on the battlefield, only one winner could emerge, only one faction could survive.

William Tweed wasted little time in worrying about the deep-seated problem of war or peace. Instead, he plunged ahead for the kill against the moribund combination. That done, he next planned to change the city's whole political climate by fully consolidating Tammany's mechanism under his total control, with himself, not public opinion, as the party's chief policy-maker.

Tweed's long-range hopes hinged on the December municipal elections. At first, all went according to plan. Wood continued to fulfill his part of the bargain; Tammany selected Tweed's close associate, Matthew T. Brennan, for comptroller; Wood named John Develin, once a Genet supporter, for corporation counsel. Then, the delegates accepted the prearranged formula for the remaining offices.

Nonetheless, trouble erupted among several disappointed claimants. Richard Connolly, with unexpected aid from Purdy and Emmanuel Hart, reminded the party of his past yeoman work, particularly in having convinced the Constitutional Unionists to back Seymour, and pleaded with the committeemen for an open primary where the rank and file could clear his name. But when Tweed refused, Connolly joined forces with another office-seeker, Police Justice Michael Connolly, and, against Hart's and Purdy's advice, ran as a "stump candidate."

In contrast, Francis Boole, who also desired the nomination, proved remarkably pliable by showing that he could get along with the new order of things. In an open letter, which Clancy published, Boole wrote that Tammany's main function was winning, not catering to personal ambitions. "Political death is the only fate due to political traitors," he concluded. Tweed appreciated these words. In Boole he recognized a man like himself: a political realist with a talent for opportunism. Such a person could go far in city politics.

Once the party published the fusion ticket, the Democracy showed that past divisions had not dulled its organizational genius. Precinct captains drilled voters, the *Leader* papered the war-or-peace issue with ambiguities, and party orators, led by John Van Buren and James T. Brady, harangued the faithful at a series of well-synchronized ward meetings that culminated in a monster rally at Cooper Union. Under these conditions, the ticket won easily. At last, Tweed neared the prize that had eluded Wood for so long: full mastery over Tammany Hall.[42]

Because of his own pride, Congressman-elect Fernando Wood badly underestimated William Tweed's seminal political genius. In January 1863, Wood certainly would have scoffed at any suggestion that in eight months Tweed could oust all his rivals from power and become the Hall's first autocrat, "the Boss." Wood's fundamental error lay in his approach to the party's political imperatives. As part of their fall armistice, Mozart and Tammany ironed out an organizational concordance which they kept secret until after the election. On December 13, 1862, Clancy published the terms. First, both Halls would elect separate General Committees, but made a gentlemen's agreement that, at the proper time, they would merge into a single group. Next, Tweed accepted Wood's long-held desire to dump the Association System. Furthermore, Tweed promised to modernize the ward committees with a decentralized structure over which the General Committee would "exercise nothing more than supervisory power." Finally, as his major concession, Tweed pledged to abandon the old Wigwam and replace it with a new building "in which the union of the organization is to be inaugurated." [43]

For all his reputation as a political seer, Wood was singularly inept at divining Tweed's real intentions. Positive he could handle the ponderous supervisor, Wood overlooked the fact that each point in their agreement actually strengthened his rival's over-all position. Tweed wanted to diffuse authority in the wards in order to undercut potential challengers, but at the same time he intended to centralize authority in himself through a fresh shift in party management. True, the Tammany Society had physically outgrown the old Wigwam, but Tweed had no intention of emasculating the Council of Sachems' authority. Finally, in erasing the Association System, Tweed had a new formula in mind that would give him more leverage.

In paying attention to Tweed's fiction, then, Wood missed his real substance. Further backing for Tweed's bet was the fact that with Wood in Washington, Tammany would have a clear local field. Without Wood's commanding presence on a day-to-day basis, Tweed reasoned that Mozart's fragmentation was only a matter of time. Whatever he openly promised, therefore, was meaningless in the real world of politics.

Tweed's plans were precise and efficient. First, he replaced the ailing Elijah Purdy as General Committee chairman. Then, in an ironic move,

Tweed used Wood to wreck the Tammany-Mozart accord. He did so by getting Wood to help him convince Mayor Opdyke to select a relative moderate, State Senator Charles Cornell, for street commissioner. Cornell, the *Leader* enthused, was a good choice; a man who was acceptable to all sides, blessed with the "integrity" and "necessary executive ability to faithfully administer the responsible duties of the position." But once the mayor swore him in, Cornell abruptly changed the ground rules. Pleading that his duties in Albany demanded all his attention, he named Tweed as deputy commissioner—with complete charge of hirings and firings.

Tweed quickly exploited the position. In the space of one month, he sliced all of Genet's and Wood's underlings off the city payroll and replaced them with "reliable" men. Under his leadership, Clancy promised, the "guillotine" could "be relied on to do all the work laid out for it." Even more, Tweed, with the aid of his obliging fellow supervisors, quadrupled the department's appropriations and doubled its employees without any noticeable improvement in services.[44]

Uninspiring as his title might have been, Tweed neared full control over local government. By dominating the comptrollership, the street department, the Board of Supervisors, and, through them, the city and county government, he brought a new sense of physical vitality and order into the chaotic nature of local partisanship. Only the mayoralty eluded his grasp.

Nor was it a surprise when he gained power over the Tammany Society. Weeks before the braves voted for the new Council, Tweed and Purdy prepared a ticket that bore little family resemblance to the old leadership elite. As the *Leader* put it, many of the antiquated sachems no longer deserved respect because "they have grown fat and sleek. The young braves have borne this for many years—they will bear it no longer and intend to see no concession is made to them, to win their right to recognition in a fair and manly encounter." [45]

Even so, Tweed handled Grand Sachem Nelson Waterbury with caution because Seymour had appointed him adjutant general, an office that Waterbury used to become the chief state patronage agent in the city. Distressed, Tweed wrote Seymour: "We ask from you a fair consideration *of and on all* matters pertaining to our City as our organization must be duly recognized to preserve our strength." When the governor remained silent, Tweed changed tactics. He showed his disdain for both men, endorsed Purdy for grand sachem, and ousted Waterbury in the resultant showdown. Moreover, the new sachems were all Tweed's willing followers. Only Richard Connolly's election marred his triumph.[46]

During the next few months, Purdy acted as grand sachem but Tweed pulled the strings. Finally, in August, both men grew weary of the charade. Purdy, Clancy noted, called a special Society meeting, "without any previous caucus or private consultation to control its deliberations." After some time-wasting discussion, mainly tributes to Tweed's "energetic and indefatigable" leadership, the braves elected him the new grand sachem without a "single dissenting vote." [47]

At last, Tweed had solved and mastered Matthew Davis' equation. In dominating the General Committee, the municipal government (excepting the mayoralty), the county government, and the Tammany Society, the rank and file recognized him for what he really was: a master of his chosen profession. True, his control rested on an imperfect foundation. The Republicans still ran City Hall, Waterbury had Seymour's ear, the New Regency drifted with uncertainty, and, most menacingly, Fernando Wood had emerged in Congress as a leading Peace Democrat. Before Tweed fully "bossed" Tammany Hall, then, he had to come to terms with public opinion on the war question. A false step might undo all his careful calculations.

While Tweed concentrated on parochial issues, Fernando Wood launched a bid to become one of the Democracy's national leaders. He did so by riding the waves of defeatism that washed through the Union in the winter of 1862 and the spring of 1863. Convinced that the Administration could not maintain itself militarily—and, perhaps, politically—Wood thrust himself into the peace movement's vanguard by suggestively querying President Lincoln as to whether or not "the time has now arrived when other methods than brute fighting may not accomplish what military force has failed to do." In reply, the President expressed grave doubts about the proposal. The plan could not work, he told the scheming Wood, because the Confederacy knew Union terms. But Wood was not satisfied. "I feel that military operations so bloody and exhausting as ours must sooner or later be suspended," he answered. If anything, however, Lincoln's determination to press forward made the Peace Democrats loom larger in Wood's thinking.[48]

Since caution and circumspection were not part of Wood's temperament, he now attempted to use the Administration's freshly wrought Draft Law to garner support among conservative Democrats who supported the war but disliked Lincoln's disregard for the Constitution. Moreover, the section that exempted a draftee if he could buy a substitute or pay a $300 commutation fee distressed the poor. Mozart Hall made the most of such emotions. At a series of rallies, Wood flayed the

Republicans, charged the War Democrats with being crypto-abolition-
ists because they supported Lincoln, and proposed that the Administration hold a national referendum on whether or not to continue "the
war or recognize the independence of the South." [49]

As a hint of things ahead, however, Wood's normal constituency
showed a streak of unsuspected rebellion. From the battlefield, the
Mozart Regiment repudiated "any claims of Fernando Wood's to our
sympathy, our obligations or our support," while the prowar *Herald*,
long Wood's ally, indirectly criticized him by calling brother Ben a
blackguard who aided "the cause of the rebellion and disunion, and the
cause of sedition and insurrection in the North." [50]

While Fernando Wood's oratory rang through the city, Tammanyite War Democrats hit bottom in their determination to hold the Union
together by force. In January, Clancy began a steady attack on Lincoln's conduct of the war, his disregard for the Constitution, the Republican tendency to interpret legitimate dissent as synonymous with
disloyalty, the Draft Law, and the National Banking Act. The Republicans aimed both pieces of legislation, he raged, "at making the President
the sole controller of the sword and the purse." [51]

What Clancy failed to mention in his editorials was what made
Tammany War Democrats so frustrated. Essentially lacking any consistent policy, these men wavered between the conflicting advice of
politicos such as August Belmont, who wanted to rally the party
through the conservative Society for the Diffusion of Political Knowledge, and others like State Senator William Bogart, who felt that
Republican mistakes would alienate the people. To make things more
uncertain, some former Democrats—men like James T. Brady, John
Van Buren, William Cullen Bryant, and David Dudley Field—organized
a local branch of the Loyal Union League, an organization dedicated
to eradicating old partisan lines and saving the Union as an end in itself.
The idea caught fire as the Peace Democrats became more vocal. By
May, the League held a state convention, adopted a program similar to
the Union party, and stirred a fresh ingredient into the witches' brew
that was New York politics. Then, to top the Democracy's complica-
tions, General Ambrose Burnside made a patently absurd arrest of
Clement L. Vallandingham, the leader of the midwestern Peace Democrats.

It was under these somber conditions that the State Committee met.
Few members, however, joined the Peace Democrat stampede. Instead,
Richmond took away with one hand what he gave with the other. He
did criticize Lincoln for tacitly backing the arrest, but at the same time

censured the Peace-men for their rampant defeatism, and reemphasized the Committee's determination to preserve the Union.[52]

In a larger way, the Vallandingham incident served as a catharsis for local War Democrats. Faced with a question they could not avoid, they chose war. The attitude of Ohio Democrats from Vallandingham's home state also helped. Congressman "Sunset" Cox, who hoped to boom General George McClellan for the presidency, told Manton Marble, the new editor of the *New York World*, not to confuse public indignation with political support of Vallandingham's views. Tammany Hall also ended its months of flirtation with the Peace wing. At its regular July meeting, the General Committee reiterated its prowar stand. The only sort of peace the North would accept, it stressed, was "upon the basis of a preservation of the Union and of the Government established by the Constitution." Simultaneously, Clancy denounced Wood and warned the party against "the Rebel sympathisers, who, under the plea of Peace, are only seeking to give aid and comfort to the enemy." [53]

Even though the War Democrats had made their decision, the Draft Law's unpopularity, coupled with Secretary of War Edwin Stanton's refusal to lower the state's quota in proportion to the excess of men who had volunteered before the act passed, turned public opinion against them. Furthermore, the *Freemen's Journal*, the *New York World*, and especially the *Daily News* unleashed a torrent of ill-judged invective calculated to win public support. Almost daily, they played on the same themes. The war was a poor man's fight, fought to emancipate the slaves, who, in turn, would increase the labor pool and depress wages. Above that, they emphasized that "the genuine Democracy will support the Peace Platform because that platform is founded upon Democratic principles." [54]

By early July, just before the draft commenced, the situation became so explosive that Mayor Opdyke asked Seymour to set aside some state militia to quell a riot if one started. The governor, however, felt Opdyke was overreacting and did nothing. Making the problem more critical, the Federal Government detailed almost the entire state militia to help the Union Army blunt Robert E. Lee's thrust into Pennsylvania. Now the city was practically defenseless, unable to maintain law and order if major trouble erupted.

Two events, coming within days of each other, underscored the Democracy's lack of equilibrium. On Independence Day, Elijah Purdy, still Tammany's grand sachem, reaffirmed that the organization fought the war to maintain "one Union, one Constitution, and one government on the American Continent." In marked contrast, Seymour, after turning down Purdy's invitation to address the Society, spoke at the Academy of Music and warned the party that defense of the Union was secondary to the defense of the Constitution. Unfortunately, he added an ill-timed aside: "Remember this—that the bloody and treasonable and revolutionary doctrine of public necessity can be proclaimed by a mob as well as a government." In the future, men did not recall the speech's main part, but took these few words out of context and assumed that the governor condoned violent demonstrations against conscriptions. The words haunted him for the rest of his life.[55]

What then followed was totally unexpected. Seriously underestimating the emotions involved, the Peace Democrats never anticipated that their words would set off an antidraft riot that would hold the city in a bloody grip for three days, create an orgy of pillage, and kill scores of citizens. In a city long conditioned to riots, with a police force wise in the ways of handling mob frenzy, people reacted with impotent disbelief at the outburst of hate. At long last, the fury abated, ended by the arrival of the Seventh Regiment, fresh from Gettysburg, and the announcement that Stanton had temporarily suspended the draft.

Each faction viewed the riot in partisan terms. On the Republican side, both Greeley and Stanton charged that Governor Seymour had actually ignited the situation through his constitutional quibblings and secretly approved of the rioters' actions. Both Tammany and Mozart analyzed the trouble in a similar manner. If anyone was to blame, they claimed, it was the draft officials who had not fully kept in touch with the police department.[56]

Nonetheless, the Irish bore the brunt of national shame. Almost reflexively, outsiders blamed the Irish for the riot, and Horace Greeley, who had never forgiven Archbishop John Hughes for supporting the Thurlow Weed Republicans in internal party squabbles, further insinuated that he condoned the mob's action. The insulted *Irish-American* reacted angrily. Nativism, not patriotism nor partisanship, it cried, was behind Greeley's words. The city had contributed more than its quota of volunteers, most of whom were Irish, the paper pointed out in justification. But in a larger sense, such charges forced the Irish to become even more patriotic than before in order to refute them. Thus, as never before, even though they despised the Emancipation Proclamation, the Irish could not support the Peace Democrats and, by extension, Fernando Wood.[57]

The riots marked the nadir of the Peace Democrats' influence in the city, then, and became the turning point in the Mozart-Tammany struggle. In the riot's sobering aftermath, Wood clearly perceived that he had gambled and lost on the wrong issue. Tammany, in contrast, gained immeasurable prestige and increased its position at Wood's expense. As a result, while Wood still retained impressive credentials as a national party leader, he forfeited massive local leverage—especially among the Irish. Furthermore, Tammany's stock increased when compared to Seymour and Richmond. As the *Leader* crowed, "Tammany Hall is the center of conservatism and patriotism in the North and the natural rallying point for all Democrats." Tweed, in short (through luck, not foresight), had identified Tammany with an overwhelmingly popular issue—provided he could control it.[58]

Tweed tested his new-won strength by challenging the New Regency and Governor Seymour on two key issues. First, he opened a veiled attack on the governor's authority by criticizing Adjutant General Nelson Waterbury's interference in local politics. Second, Clancy demanded that Richmond bar Wood from attending the state convention.

Suddenly, despite the War Democrat ground swell, Tweed stopped hammering away at Wood. The reason behind the halt lay in the formation of an entirely new force in city politics. After the riot, an odd collection of anti-Wood Peace Democrats, reform-minded businessmen, independent Irishmen, and disappointed office-seekers coalesced around John McKeon's leadership. With this inter- and intra-party fusion, the McKeonites demanded that the state party give them sole local recognition at the coming convention.

Tweed, Purdy, Boole, and Cornell—a "combination equal to Scott, Grant, McClellan and Rosecrans," Clancy wrote—met privately to discuss tactics. After weighing the priorities, they showed an uncommon degree of flexibility by freezing the McKeonites out through a division of delegates with Mozart. When the convention adopted the formula, the McKeonites, bristling with wrath, vowed in no uncertain terms to revenge themselves in local contests.[59]

When the united delegation returned home, it found the situation much less to its liking. Mozart Hall rejected Wood's compromise, refused to support the state ticket, and moved toward the McKeonites. But Tweed refused to accept the bait. Again, seemingly due to McKeonite pressure, the General Committee piously mouthed a few war slogans—but used abolitionism as a bugaboo to propose a joint local slate with Wood's supporters in Mozart. The move split Mozart into two groups. One followed Wood and formed a joint ticket with Tammany; the other fused with the McKeonites. The *Herald* immediately blasted all concerned because they treated the problem "of war for the Union or peace at the price of dissolution, as if it was an irrelevancy." But what the paper did not know was that Tweed's equivocation had accomplished two major goals: splitting Mozart, and determining the consequent probability of winning the December mayoralty contest.[60]

Meantime, Clancy worked out an explanation that would appease the War Democrats yet stay within the agreement's bounds. Far from selling out, he wrote, Tammany had patriotically cooperated with Mozart in order to save the Democracy from certain defeat at the hands of the Republicans and the Loyalty League. As for Mozart's peace posture, Clancy blandly claimed that in each Hall "there is an ardent love for the Union; but the difference is as to the mode of bringing about the same result."

The results of the fall elections tested Tweed's patience and ability to ignore the screams of unhappy War Democrats. The McKeonites, with anti-Wood support from Mozart Hall, made a strong showing; upstate, the Republicans scored impressive gains, and elected John Cochrane as attorney general. The moral here, as far as Bennett was concerned, was for Tammany "to keep upon the war platform sure and simple." [61]

Tweed did not panic. His major concern was to achieve a final consolidation of power by dominating the mayoralty, and he had sacrificed the state ticket in order to do so. In a way, prospects looked bright. The Republicans, after failing to coax General John Dix into the race, settled on a poor choice, Weedite Orson Blunt, a man Greeley had helped defeat for Congress two years before. The McKeonites nominated wealthy Peace Democrat C. Godfrey Gunther, a former Tammany standard-bearer, who carried the onus of being a loser. In contrast, Tammany ran Francis Boole, who had recently gained immense public approval by reforming some obnoxious slaughterhouse practices and making popular changes in the city's methods of garbage collection. A War Democrat, Boole won the *Herald*'s endorsement; but, of far more importance, Wood used his remaining prestige to force Mozart to back him as part of the October bargain. This, after all, had been Tweed's secret aim.[62]

On the surface of things, Tammany expected an easy victory. It anticipated a strong Republican cross-over vote for its prowar candidate, and assumed that its union with Mozart would draw many Peace Democrats from the McKeonites. Moreover, George Barnard, one of Tweed's henchmen, used a subtle blend of bandwagon psychology and blackmail on the *World*'s Manton Marble. "I have seen Boole," Barnard wrote. "He will give you at once the printing if he is elected, which he will be. Be good enough to give him a first rate notice tomorrow. It will pay. I am satisfied he will be elected & keep faith. So let us make a virtue of necessity & go in strong for him." [63]

Barnard read signs that did not exist. Tweed's cynicism touched off a wave of revulsion throughout the city that chiefly benefited Gunther. Above that, the majority of Irish and Germans, stung by the riot's lingering reactions, bolted party traces in search of new leaders. It came as no major surprise, then, when Gunther won with 40.9 percent of the total votes cast, to Boole's 31.7 percent and Blunt's 27.4 percent. [64]

The more James Gordon Bennett pondered the mayoralty results, the more he concluded that the election had "used up" the Republicans, smashed the New Regency, "and, with Tammany and Mozart repudiated, not one of these factions has any moral strength." Hard-bitten Tammanyites viewed the situation another way. Boole's defeat, they reasoned, was an object lesson in political consistency. Tweed, in retrospect, realized that the Hall was too closely tied with the War Democrats to associate with Wood and the Peace wing. The General Committee now deduced that victory lay not in compromise but in stressing the war issue to the exclusion of all other items. Even more, Tweed saw that Mozart's aid was a heavy liability. As a result, he reshuffled his imperatives and carefully laid out fresh strategy: close, active association with the War Democrats, and an all-out effort to beat Wood, both as a man and as a symbol, when he ran for reelection. [65]

Before grappling with the Peace Democrats, Tweed completed his reorganization of Tammany Hall. First, the old General Committee, accepting his directive that it could determine the number of ward representatives, increased the next Committee's membership to 150, reapportioned the wards, and helped select many new men, Clancy noted approvingly, "calculated to strengthen" the machine. Next, posing as a radical, egalitarian reformer, Tweed decentralized the entire nomination process, a sore spot since at least Clintonian times. Under his new "democratic system," each ward committee selected the legislative, municipal, and Board of Education tickets. The parent Committee merely drafted party platforms and directed "the mode of nominating candidates for county offices." [66]

It soon became apparent, however, that these moves masked a deeper purpose on Tweed's part. By enlarging the Committee, he made it too unwieldly for decision-making. The upshot was that Tweed, through control over a few vital subcommittees, minimized the danger that rivals, like Genet's combination, could rise to power by the domination of one branch of government. Above that, in designating ward quotas, he made service on local committees dependent on good behavior, and, with this subtle type of party discipline, still dictated whom the machine would nominate. Moreover, by not disturbing the Tammany Society, Tweed kept a tight grip over the party's operational core.

All such fragmentation of authority, despite the appearance of being inimical to boss rule, actually typified urban life. When Tweed altered Tammany's tightly knit apparatus, he actually modernized the machine to meet new conditions. Boss rule in New York City, then, was more than the traditional picture of machine politics. In his own way, Tweed, the cynical reformer, culminated years of dogged opposition against Tammany's customary "usages," its closed system of managed primaries, hand-picked candidates, and lockstep politicking. In its place, he substituted an equally stylized apparatus—but one which gave the electorate a sense of involvement in managing public affairs. Somewhat as in the caucus controversy in 1823, his change in party management seemed a response to the popular will. In this way, Tweed followed the mainstream of Tammany's Jeffersonianism and kept traditional party principles alive.

Meantime, the Peace Democrats tried to regain their popularity by increasing the tempo of their politicking. By conjuring up grievances against "Stantonian despotism" and Lincoln's failure at "negotiations, reconciliation and peace," they gave the electorate the impression of great vitality. Consequently, as the uncertain Democrats went to Albany for the state convention to name delegates for the national convention, no one, including Dean Richmond, quite knew how to handle the question. As far as the city was concerned, the delegates had to further decide which group, the Peace Democrats of Mozart Hall and the McKeonites, or Tammany's War Democrats, represented the local party. To make the situation more tense, the General Committee rejected any temporizing, "attended with dishonor and disgrace" that would "virtually surrender the cause of the Union." [67]

Although forewarned, the Credentials Committee showed the New Regency's political bankruptcy by formulating a weak compromise. It suggested that the three contenders equally split the city's delegation without a clear statement that would define either principles or issues. Both Mozart and the McKeonites accepted; Tammany balked. But when the issue reached the floor, Purdy and Tweed discovered that the party as a whole would not alter the report. At once, Tammanyites bolted the convention and went home. "Tammany Hall stands for this war until the rebellion is overthrown," Clancy explained, "and the authority of the federal government vindicated." [68]

The remaining delegates then selected men for the national convention, ironed out procedures—particularly the unit rule which again allowed Richmond to cast all the state's votes—and finally adjourned without taking a stand on either issues or candidates. The only positive thing that the New Regency accomplished was to guarantee that in the future, city voters should name delegates for state conventions in their assembly districts, not through competing Halls. Never again would the entire party have to settle regularity. In the long run, however, the decision actually invigorated boss rule. Any future leader who firmly controlled his districts through loyal captains could send delegations without fear that a minority group might challenge him. Thus, in preventing a repetition of the virulent partisanship that had seared the Democracy during the old Hard-Soft brawls, Richmond unwittingly opened the door to the stifling conformity that future Tammany bosses would impose. [69]

Once the convention ended, the General Committee's propaganda mills began to spin out an explanation for its insurgency. Each ward group published resolutions praising the bolters, Tweed sponsored a prowar rally, and Clancy blared that Tammany "had resolved never again to be forced into any such degrading alliance" with traitorous Peace Democrats. On a secondary front, Tweed, as General Committee chairman, formed a special subcommittee consisting of himself, Eli Hart, and George Purser, to consider the problem, and ordered Peter Sweeny to prepare a preliminary position paper. In it, Sweeny wrote that the delegation had bolted the convention because "the *status* of Tammany, as a powerful local organization, was not recognized by the managers of the Convention." Worse, the Peace wing dominated the gathering and favored a dishonorable end to hostilities. If the Hall had dignified this treasonable act, Sweeny continued, Tammany would be disgraced forever. Time was ripe, he ended, for a change in "rulers" so that the people could name the next president from among "practical military statesmen." [70]

Sweeny and Tweed had not tailored the document for publication, but merely as a starting point for discussion within Tammany's inner circle. But when someone leaked the document to Greeley, Tweed sent Bennett a second copy. Yet as things worked out, the "manifesto" proved a valuable trial balloon. The subcommittee's report turned out to be something less effective than the original document. Claiming that the party's overriding need was to separate legitimate dissent from disloyalty, the report called for preserving the Union by "a thorough and perfect organization of national democrats, based on a generous and patriotic surrender of personal preferences, interests and opinion." Until that time, the Hall's major role was to pursue military victory.[71]

Even though the document was hardly exciting, the entire episode accomplished three major purposes. It placed Tammany's bolt in the very best light, disparaged the Peace Democrats and linked them irrevocably with the hated Confederacy, and became both an apology and a weather vane. Although Tweed had not consciously intended it, the manifesto created the framework within which the rank and file could make a choice. But at the same time, he limited the options. Thus, in helping to clarify public opinion, Tweed could then use it as his justification for action. The public would eventually tell the machine when to move, but Tweed had already set the direction.

As Tweed succeeded in modernizing the machine, his foes sought to undercut his authority by gaining control over the Tammany Society. In April, a group of his personal enemies—including Waterbury, Mayor Gunther, Richard Connolly, and old Fitzwilliam Byrdsall, now a leading figure in the Anti-Abolitionist States Rights Association—met secretly and assembled their own slate for the Council election. Unknown to them, however, Connolly had finally made his peace with Tweed and acted as an informer. With his aid, Tweed moved with smooth skill. Invoking the spirit that animated the "manifesto," he structured the election as a test between the War and Peace Democrats by heading his ticket, "The Union and the Constitution." Waterbury swallowed Tweed's bait, and needlessly called his slate, "Peace, Re-Union and Reform." Given this choice, the braves gave Tweed a thumping victory and confirmed his absolute control over the Tammany Society.[72]

In a secondary sense, Tweed scored an important psychological victory. On the defensive locally, the Peace Democrats needed to dominate the Society in order to dramatize their legitimacy and continuity with past party traditions. When Tweed denied them these symbols, they lost immense moral prestige and forfeited any remaining chance of winning rank-and-file support.


By the end of July it was clear that in New York City the War Democrats were in the process of forming a fresh coalition based on antagonism toward Lincoln, support of the war (but under different leaders), and General George C. McClellan's presidential candidacy.

Tweed was particularly active. As early as October of 1863, his supporters had organized ward clubs for the general and hoped that their strategy of supporting him before the convention would earn them special favors when he became president. For the next few months, aided by Dean Richmond, Manton Marble, Samuel Barlow, and August Belmont, Tammany began a crash operation to coordinate activity with other McClellan backers throughout the nation in order to create a national ground swell.[73]

The national Peace Democrats, although they were as vocal as ever, were on the wane. Encouraged by President Lincoln, they sponsored a futile, if not ridiculous, meeting with some Confederates at Niagara Falls. Activities of this sort cushioned public reaction to General Grant's failure to capture Richmond and end the war. Similar problems hounded them in the city. Ironically, even the Administration's suppression of the normally pro–Peace Democrat *New York World* for printing a bogus proclamation hardly interrupted their massive decline in popularity. On the contrary, Marble had already decided that any candidate "who runs for the Presidency on an open Peace platform . . . is doomed to an utter rout at the polls," and placed McClellan's name high on the *World*'s masthead when the paper began publishing again.[74]

Fernando Wood's difficulties followed the same course. In late July, he completely lost control of Mozart. Perhaps disgruntled by his intemperate Copperhead activities, perhaps disturbed by the lack of patronage, Mozart shattered into small squabbling factions, each claiming to represent the organization. On August 5, the revolution reached its zenith. Pausing only momentarily to publicize their independence, a group of insurgents drummed their erstwhile leader out of Mozart, began moving toward the McKeonites, and left him without a local power base.[75]

The setback sharpened Wood's combative spirit. As he had done so effectively in the past, Wood reached into his political bag of tricks. But this time he found it empty. President Lincoln, who had strung him along, offered no help. Above that, Dean Richmond scorned Wood and planned to limit his activities at the convention. As a forecast of things ahead, John Pruyn noted in his diary that "Mr R. [Richmond] complained in very sharp terms of the course of Governor Seymour, . . . Mr. Vallandingham, Mr. Wood & others who had pressed for peace & this merely broke up the party—That they wanted a peace party only to drive a bargain, and make terms for office & power in the future." [76]

For a brief moment in August, as the Union Army continued to falter, Wood made a partial comeback. Meeting in Syracuse to plot strategy for the convention, the Peace Democrats pictured a dire future unless the national Democracy accepted a peace platform. Such a formula, Wood predicted, would elect a Democratic president, who would then issue "an armistice and [sponsor] a convention of all the States to consider and reconcile the differences existing between them." [77]

All these maneuverings placed Tammany Hall in an ideal position. Under no circumstances could either Wood or the McKeonites support McClellan's candidacy without forfeiting massive credibility. Tweed, Purdy, and Sweeny underscored the point just before leaving for Chicago as unofficial but interested observers. In a press release, they claimed that only McClellan's nomination could "restore hope and confidence to the country" by giving the "people their own chosen leaders." [78]

For a moment at the convention, the Peace Democrats, for all their obvious liabilities, seemed to have control over the party. Despite the opposition of the War Democrats, they practically wrote the entire platform, including the famous Second Resolution which condemned the war as a complete failure and virtually acknowledged the Confederacy's right to exist.

But the Peace Democrats lost their momentum when nominations began because they lacked anyone who could compete with the general. After trying to scare up a nominee, *any* nominee, they settled on two Seymours—Thomas of Connecticut and Horatio of New York. Here, Wood made an eleventh-hour move, and groomed Horatio Seymour as a dark-horse candidate in order to create the impression that the governor had bolted the New Regency. If he could accomplish this, Wood hoped that Richmond might offer him the fall gubernatorial nomination as a rebuke to Seymour. The plot failed; McClellan won on the first ballot. Then, in a weak move to straddle the fence, the delegates named George Pendleton, a well-known Ohio Copperhead, for vice president.[79]

While letters of congratulation poured into his office, McClellan pondered the platform. The Second Resolution bothered his conscience, and for over a week he delayed writing a formal acceptance letter. Meantime, everyone was ready with advice. "Throw the Chicago Platform overboard," one Tammanyite cried. Seek to avoid insulting the Peace wing, Barlow counseled. Totally distracted, the general let his emotions rule. After shifting positions with alarming uncertainty, he finally rejected the Second Resolution.[80]

At this critical juncture, the rattled Peace Democrats held a conference in the city to discuss the future. But even though the *Daily News* clique and the McKeonites hotly assailed McClellan for rejecting the peace plank, smoldering local animosities prevented full, or even partial, cooperation. John McKeon disliked McClellan's decision but was more enraged at Fernando Wood. Wood, he snarled, "pledged me his support, and then came out at public meetings against me, and set his secret service people at work to accomplish my defeat." In reply, Wood made another of his dazzling twists. Bowing to public opinion, he openly endorsed McClellan, thereby breaking with brother Ben over the *News'* stubborn refusal to back the national ticket. The split delighted Samuel Barlow, now the general's campaign manager. "Ben Wood's opposition here helps rather than hurts us," he wrote gleefully.[81]

In contrast, Tammany Hall rode the crest of public approval. As soon as the convention made its choice, the sachems called a mass meeting in the general's honor and held a spectacular illumination at the Wigwam. The *Herald* reported these moves with superlatives: "Whether upon national or party grounds Tammany is the only representative of the democracy of New York. . . . She stands for the Union, for the war and for McClellan, while the speculating, bargaining, copperhead concerns are for dis-union, for peace on the rebels' terms, for whoever will buy them, and against McClellan." [82]

Aware that Bennett spoke for many New Yorkers, Clancy capitalized on the feeling and demanded that the state convention, which still labored under the old delegate system, admit only Tammany. "It speaks not with the voice of any one man, or set of men," he averred, "but hallowed by its tradition, it speaks with the responsible voice of the past as well as of the future." When deliberations opened, the Hall's triumph became complete. From Richmond's standpoint, the power vacuum that Fernando Wood had created, welcome though it was, could not have been more poorly timed. No less than six different city delegations were present, and each asked for exclusive admittance and recognition. The excitement culminated in a bitter battle within the Credentials Committee. Cautious politician that he was, Richmond overlooked the realities of city politics and proposed that the Committee award Tammany nine seats; the McKeonites, Wood's Old Mozart, and the New Mozart, two each; and Gunther's German Democrats, one. Upon hearing the news, all withdrew but Tammany. Tweed's persistence, luck, and tact paid off even more when Wood, powerless for the first time in over a decade, walked out of the building, sped on his way by hisses and groans. To Clancy, it meant that "this is a great triumph. It is success achieved after many years of sore and trying struggles." [83]

The party's apparent prowar policy, however, was highly deceptive. Having taken the purge in the city, the delegates resorted to less drastic medicine for the fall campaign. With more weakness than courage they lauded the Copperheads for defending constitutional liberties, the War Democrats for their devotion to the Union, and then shouted down Seymour's objections to renominate him.

The national campaign began inauspiciously for the Democrats. With much of its once robust prewar organization now anemic, party leaders desperately searched for the proper tonic. Yet mounting problems hindered them: long-time sources of campaign funds went dry, Peace and Union Democrats played coy, and McClellan himself proved an enigmatic candidate. Nonetheless, Marble and Barlow made maximum use of the medicines at hand. With Belmont's aid, they formed a national Central Executive Campaign Committee that included such stalwart Tammanyites as John Kelly, William Tweed, and John Hoffman, the future mayor and governor. Furthermore, they wooed the Peace Democrats and conservatives through the Society for the Diffusion of Political Knowledge.[84]

In the city, Tweed shaped the party in McClellan's image. As organized groups, both the McKeonites and the Old Mozart Hall, now led by Gideon Tucker, were too tainted by their Copperhead efforts to have a direct impact on the election and they quietly lapsed into temporary retirement. Even the Irish, whose loyalty to McKeon and Fernando Wood had transformed them into major political figures, deserted them. Some outside observers, however, still underestimated Tweed and feared Fernando Wood's amazing recuperative powers. As one upstater worried, "Wood means mischief & he is trying to use the *Leader* and Tammany (through Sweeny) for his own purposes." Yet Tweed knew what he was doing. Men like Wood were indeed supporting the national ticket, but not on their own terms. Only by accepting Tweed's will could they find "a most cordial and substantial recognition" in Tammany Hall.[85]

For every dissident Democrat who slunk back into the Hall, however, there were many others who cherished their independence and mocked Tweed. They quickly made it clear that whatever Tammany's posture on the war, they preferred to elect a Republican than elevate one of Tweed's captive candidates. Thus, in six congressional city districts, twenty-one men, each claiming to be some sort of Democrat, ran for office. For discipline, Clancy wielded the Hall's popular prowar credentials. Again and again the *Leader* reminded the party that Tammany was "the only organization which specifically represents General McClellan." [86]

As for Wood, his position had so degenerated that he was forced to run without any formal backing. Even worse, he nominally election-eered for McClellan in New England and the Midwest, but somehow mustered the gall to reassure Lincoln that "I have faithfully executed the enterprize undertaken in Indiana, Pennsylvania, & Ohio. . . . *The States are safe*—My Success has been beyond expectations." Where Wood really stood, then, was so problematical that when he ran for reelection, Bennett, his one-time admirer, growled, "Fernando Wood is the nominee of Fernando Wood. Fernando Wood is patrolling the district, making speeches for Fernando Wood." [87]

Gripped by self-deception, some of McClellan's supporters pre-dicted a smashing victory in New York State. They were partially correct. The general did carry the city, but not the state nor the nation. Tammany, however, all but disarmed its opponents. It elected its entire congressional slate, and "on the County ticket she loses but one warrior." To make victory even sweeter, Wood went down to resounding defeat and lost his House seat.[88]

In such flamboyant fashion, Tammany proved itself the master of New York City and confirmed William Marcy Tweed as its first "Boss." Putting things in proper perspective, the *Herald* spoke for many New Yorkers when it editorialized: "Tammany Hall is the only regular democratic organization of this city. She has stood firmly by the Union and repudiated the peace men. Had the democracy of the country followed her noble example McClellan might have been elected. As it is, Tammany now triumphs amid the general wreck." The exuberant Clancy gushed a similar judgment. "The brethren who are outside should now come in from the cold and rain, and find shelter beneath the old Wigwam." [89]

In the city, Wood resigned himself to defeat, and after futilely seeking some sort of recognition from Lincoln for services rendered, went on an extended tour of Europe when his term in Congress ended. Just before leaving, however, he gave a *New York Tribune* reporter a dock-side interview in which he summed up the style, the rhythm, the meaning of Tammanyism: "It is folly to persist in the application of impractical doctrines instead of accepting those which inevitable fate has forced upon us." [90]

# ⌣ **14** ⌣

# Epilogue: Tammanyism

IN THE OPENING PAGES, the question posed was: What were the ingredients, the motives, the causes behind Tammany Hall's amazing success and longevity? Part of the answer lies in the fact that Tammanyites were masters of nuts-and-bolts politicking—the art of building and running a political machine.

To Tammanyites, organization was stability; stability was organization. Beginning in 1801, party leaders abandoned the informal electioneering committees which had functioned in the previous decade, and began to use a popularly elected three-man ward committee system which represented, in turn, the rank and file in each electoral district. Charged with coordinating policy between the precincts and party headquarters, these committees operated as clearinghouses for problems that arose in their limited jurisdictions. The combined ward committees formed the General Democratic Republican Committee, which had sweeping powers to call meetings, synthesize arrangements for elections, and articulate policy-making. Over a period of time, the Committee reapportioned its membership as the city grew—but not its basic functions. Popularly called Tammany Hall, the committee selected a chairman from within its own ranks, and, because party regulars considered it a continuing body, the governing council gradually centralized authority in itself.[1]

Theoretically, the ward committees, as John L. O'Sullivan explained, "constitute the organization through which our local Democracy act for the support of our measures and principles." In practice, the Hall adopted a more cold-blooded, undemocratic stance. Making a fetish out of party unity, the General Committee believed in bickering behind closed doors, then publicly presenting closed, well-drilled ranks instructed through party newspapers. The Committee settled any tensions that erupted between contenders for office in a similar fashion. That done, the Committee drafted a campaign platform that so blurred all internal differences that an outsider would never have suspected trouble. Once the slate appeared, all dissension halted. These party usages, a Tammanyite emphasized, were "principles of the Democratic party— [they are] to concentrate opinion—to unite individual and general interests, and to act in a body to ensure success." [2]

Behind all of Tammany's egalitarian pretensions, then, a relatively small group of men met in private caucus and set policy. In defending the system, the Hall always insisted that the caucus, rather than being a closed system, was an instrument of majoritarian rule needed by the unorganized masses to frustrate a moneyed and landed aristocracy. Further, the General Committee negotiated with all potential trouble-makers and refused to excommunicate any faction which could deliver votes—as long as that faction did not repel more votes than it could deliver.

As the electorate grew, Tammany altered its tactics. Because of the People's party, the Hall opened party management, scrapped the caucus, and catered to a variety of new interest groups. Nonetheless, Tammany kept the caucus system alive in other ways. Until Boss Tweed's advent, the Hall never adequately solved the contradictions implicit in the use of both a centralized system that guaranteed continuity and a decentralized one that involved a credible degree of rank-and-file participation in decision-making. Despite the difficulty, the lure of public spoils often kept disgruntled voters in line. On one occasion, when an internal Tammany split evoked a disruptive feud, an annoyed Martin Van Buren asked: "When will the . . . party be made sensible of the indispensible necessity of nominating none but true and tried men, so that when they succeed they gain something?" [3]

Beyond such naked coercion, the machine's basic discipline, the idea of "party usages," emanated from the rank and file's belief that the apparatus had a life of its own, a life that transcended individual ambitions. Moreover, in making the Hall synonymous with democracy, Tammanyites felt that certain techniques were sacred forms of political behavior that would guarantee the effectiveness of popular government. Under these circumstances, party discipline became the means toward the achievement of two great ends: preservation of the party, and establishing majoritarian rule. Silas Wright wasted few words on this score: "Tell them they are safe if they face the enemy, but the first men we see *step to the rear, we cut down.*" Such a feeling, Adamsite Joseph Blunt observed, made Tammany's "partisans active & zealous.

They each in his sphere have a special object in view & labour as if they were labouring for themselves."⁴

The General Committee had several auxiliary arms. The Correspondence Committee, a Tammany Society offshoot, kept in contact with other chapters and organized festivals. The Committee on Charity aided indigents through the machine's private, but artful, welfare system. The Naturalization Committee ploughed similar fertile ground. Through the Young Men's General Committee, the Hall cultivated a certain amount of self-examination and groomed its future leaders. The Committee on Organization (until 1864) arranged agendas, held General Committee elections yearly, and counted the vote. As a result, this subgroup gained immense authority. It could originate policy, discipline insurgents, and direct campaigns. Anyone who could control it for his own purposes could logically dominate the entire party.⁵

Another part of Tammany's organizational durability rested on its close working agreement with Martin Van Buren and his upstate Albany Regency. A cool, analytical master of broker politics, Van Buren prided himself on understanding his fellow politicos: "who they were, what they were, what they wanted, and what were their width, breadth, depth and the water each drew." Despite his awesome reputation, however, Van Buren only helped to manage Tammany Hall; he rarely succeeded in becoming its master. Very simply, because of the state's urban-rural split, Tammany faced different problems than the Albany Regency and often responded to pressures that the upstaters could see but not appreciate. Until 1845, both acted as countervailing checks on each other, and used their diversity to seek an equilibrium of interests.⁶

By 1863, Tammany's organization table reached full maturity. In each of the city's 220 electoral districts, the *Leader* noted, "there are representatives delegated by Tammany Hall—captains, lieutenants, and corporals—to organize, discipline and to look after the interests of the district votes." Such a structured organization, which divided responsibility into well-defined zones with a strong chain of command from the General Committee to the precincts, suggests a certain bureaucratization that might have strangled individual initiative and stifled the machine's innovative powers. This did not happen. Since the organization served as a substitute for the municipal government, performing a variety of roles in the process, the Hall concerned itself with everyday problems which were all geared to make the city a better place for people to live in. Moreover, because a series of revolving leadership cliques ran Tammany, most party members had a fair chance to rise in the organization. Under these conditions, ordinary citizens did not become alienated from the thrust of politics, and the Hall evolved a working form of democracy out of the mundane quest for office.[7]

The Tammany Society was the keystone of the organization. It served as a sign of respectability for party workers, a link with the past, the keeper of pure party traditions, the formulator of party myths that rewrote the Hall's history to create the impression that its rise to power was synonymous with the continuous improvement of the human condition in a democratic, humanitarian, egalitarian society —and, above all, the final authority in judging regularity. Going far beyond its original purpose, the Tammany Society, by Tweed's day, had become the mainspring of the local Democratic machine.

Tammany's second approach to building its machine lay in the use of its ability to turn its organizational structure into an emotional, vote-getting program that forced city voters to identify their aspirations with the party's best interests. In so doing, the General Committee sponged up support from all layers of city life.

The immigrant bloc was the most critical. Beginning in the 1790s, the organization catered to "adopted citizens" and sought to win their voting loyalty. By undertaking services that other public agencies could not or would not perform, the Hall ultimately became the major force in city politics. Despite the familiarity of this story, there was nothing inevitable about the process. Like other Americans, many Tammanyites were emotionally nativist but swallowed their xenophobia as long as the bulk of these immigrants were Protestant. The upshot of this hypocrisy was that the more sensitive newcomers sought an alternative to the Hall and generally supported DeWitt Clinton. With his passing, Tammany became his heir. But in the 1840s, as a new wave of Roman Catholic immigrants replaced the older Protestant groups, the Hall's xenophobia resurfaced. Consequently, until the School Controversy forced Tammany to face the problem squarely, it placed a higher premium on subservience than on equality.[8]

The Hall's approach to the city's unprecedented urban problems closely paralleled its handling of the immigrants. As the municipality grew into an organism few men understood, Tammany undertook a multitude of roles to humanize the situation. It gave voters a direct access to power, acted as a relief and welfare agency, built sewers, piped water, constructed mass transit systems, paved the streets, ran the school system, helped construct homes; in short, it became an indispensable agency in making New York City a fit place in which to live, to flourish, to raise a family. In return, the Hall expected a small price for its services: the vote of each individual citizen.

The Hall's recruitment program took other forms. Tammany used the bizarre city fire department as a highly valuable means of attracting young, active men who were often leaders in their wards. The Hall flattered these fire-eaters despite the department's nativistic tendencies, sponsored its own units, and often held dances to honor heroic firemen, occasionally running them for office. In many cases, prominent Tammanyites, notably William Tweed and Honest John Kelly, got their political starts through these units.[9]

The police department proved equally attractive. Even though many greedy Tammanyites hungered to use the department as a means to institutionalize graft, the machine had a more sophisticated purpose in mind. It wanted the policemen's votes and influence. Just as important, the police helped the Hall cultivate the immigrants by providing them with jobs and aid when they got in trouble with the law.[10]

Tammany's control over the police became most critical during elections since electoral frauds were a fact of political life. Besides herding unnaturalized aliens to the polls, politicians of all persuasions freed prisoners on election day, levied assessments against municipal employees, and expected the collector of the port, who generally had over seven hundred men working for him, to gather tribute from them to grease party machinery. Both the Hall and its foes also resorted to using "ghost" voters—men who voted in the names of dead electors. In 1828, that High-Minded Federalist turned Tammanyite, Gulian Verplanck, noted the haunting effect a certain Mr. Herbert had on the election: "It is not only true that Mr. H. voted for the whole Jackson ticket in the 5th ward, but did it *twice* running, and then observed that he was now going over to Hoboken, but to-morrow would vote in the first ward, for all the Jackson ticket except Alderman Cebra, whom he could not swallow." [11]

Saloon-keepers also helped Tammany keep its virility and broad appeal. Often important figures in their electoral districts, bartenders watched local needs, and usually converted their neighborhood hangouts into political annexes. Fernando Wood, for example, began his career in such a way. Equally vital, these men contacted repeaters ("sluggers") during a doubtful contest. On more than one occasion, when it appeared that the Hall might lose a key precinct, bartenders dispatched the waiting toughs to steal ballot boxes, intimidate counters, and sometimes set the polling booths afire. Such tactics often turned certain defeats into sweeping victories.[12]

Another source of potential allies rested in the city's business community. Like the immigrants, most commercial and maritime interests supported DeWitt Clinton. After his death, the business community flowed into either the Jacksonian or Whig parties depending on individual preferences. The Bank War and the resultant panic, however, convinced many city businessmen that Tammany was untrustworthy. By the 1840s, as fiscal problems and slavery extensionism became the cutting edges of new coalitions, the Hall forfeited more business allies who later became either Know-Nothings or Republicans. Even so, while these men scorned the state and national Democracy, they remained on good terms with Tammany and often contributed to the machine's campaign war chest. They did so purely for self-protection. They realized that if they angered the General Committee, the Democratic-controlled Common Council could raise taxes or limit them in other ways.

A real source of strength was the Hall's local orientation. The primacy of "local feelings," the idea that local interests prevailed over state or national needs, prompted several influential New Yorkers to vacate substantial national offices. Tammany operated along similar lines. With its service preoccupation, the Hall catered to the electorate's concerns, generally to the exclusion of national problems. Tammany, in short, took on the coloration of local congeries of interest and thus became the creature of its own rank and file.[13]

Tammany's localism had a negative side, for it limited the organization's role in party affairs outside of the state. During times of crisis, when Tammanyites should have acted for the general good, they could not climb above their self-imposed provincialism. On the eve of the Civil War, James Gordon Bennett complained that while the nation hung on the edge of "revolution," most Tammanyites were "absorbed in mere local squabbles . . . about who shall represent this or that grogshop ward, and who shall get the largest share of the plunder." In reply, the Hall had an answer formed years before: "The democratic party of this state acts on their own principles and from their own principles. They owe but a small portion of gratitude to the folks at a distance, but that portion they will be just enough to give." Another Tammanyite expressed this attitude more simply: "No man should have power in this state if that power is to be swayed by the authorities in Washington." [14]

Tammany's final asset lay in its ability to appeal to man's worst side. Aware that the city contained a society based on marked class distinctions, the Hall in some elections deliberately widened the gulf of misunderstanding between rich and poor, native-born Protestants and Roman Catholic immigrants for its own uses. If these methods failed, Tammany held other unsavory tactics in reserve: vast patronage, particularly that wielded by the collector; public and private bribery; and preferential municipal financial policies. By giving all influential or potential power blocs a stake in the Hall's continued success, leaders bought forgiveness, smothered dissent, and acted as caretakers over pressing urban problems. Even so, boodle-mongering was a touchy business. The danger always existed that reformers, such as the Civic Reform party or the American Republicans, could stimulate enough mass indignation to destroy the machine.[15]

The General Committee's entire political foundation, continually strengthened by innovations, explains *how* Tammany was successful, not *why*. As noted earlier, the Hall's political techniques—recruitment, organization, persuasion, public spoils, argument, manipulation, compromise, maneuver—were familiar gimmicks to all city politicians. Something else existed. In its most compelling sense, Tammanyism meant more than just a party of skilled political mechanics and gifted technicians. It was a political philosophy that the majority of city voters found congenial. And it was this philosophy that provided the crucial reason for Tammany Hall's mastery over New York City.

Tammanyism as a political philosophy began in the 1790s when the bits and pieces of the Republican-Interest began to fuse around the electorate's generally unarticulated democratic beliefs, later becoming Thomas Jefferson's Republican party. The process, however, was neither simple nor predictable. Local Federalists, despite their wish to create an ordered, structured, elitist society, had inherited a network of interstate ties and a democratic reputation as a carry-over from their successful ratification struggles. In order to combat them, the Republican-Interest politicos found their inspiration in Lockean idealism which became the basis for a coherent value system, grounded on highly acceptable ideals, that ultimately evolved into a plausible political philosophy.

The America that the Republican-Interest postulated was a land free of all aristocratic influences; a land where progress and human improvement were possible; a land where the national government was man's servant, not his master. In practical terms, the people were sovereign and fully capable of self-government. The popular will, then, became the ultimate judge of any elected official. In 1795, a letter to the *New York Journal* claimed that "talent and virtue, not birth and riches, should entitle a man to the suffrages of free men." Similarly, another writer maintained that legislators should be "friends to the equal rights of the citizens, or in other words, enemies to the Aristocratic distinction." Thus, the voters, by using the political system in a wise manner, could raise the nation to democratic heights that they could hardly have attained otherwise. As one Interest editorial put it: "The political controversy in this country is not a SPECULATIVE QUESTION, but depends upon the result of benefits arising to the United States AS A GOVERNMENT." [16]

Despite the Interest's faith in man, however, New Yorkers realized that injustice abounded and the people had not yet moved toward a state of democratic perfection. In answer, the Interest claimed that man was not at fault but instead blamed corrupt aristocratic institutions. But the people, through self-criticism, could achieve progress if they followed the bold new departures implicit in recent American experience. "May the flame of freedom," one Tammany brave proposed, "which was kindled in 1776, soon extend its rays through the universe." In this context, logic dictated that "the real principles of the constitution and the original intentions of the Revolution" formed the dynamics of social change. [17]

The same approach applied to man himself, particularly his relationship to the character of government and its sources of authority. The Interest's perfectionist hopes rested on an amalgam of five *a priori* principles: first, natural law was self-evident; second, all men deserved equal rights; third, absolute power implied corruption; fourth, majority rule should control the basic instruments of government; fifth, public opinion formed "the foundations of our liberties, and constitute the only solid ground of dogma." On these specific principles that would improve mankind's social, political, moral, and economic conditions, the Interest stressed the conclusion that political leaders should not seek to impose their will on the electorate, but rather to help the people decide wisely for themselves. [18]

In order to implement these principles, the Interest advocated certain techniques that promised success. The humanitarian object of government, it felt, was to improve all institutions by ending slavery, ameliorating the penal code, abolishing imprisonment for debt, liberalizing mechanics' laws, and protecting freedom of the press. On even a more practical level, the Interest called for frugality in public expenditures, low taxes, a small standing army and navy, a limited tariff schedule, free public education, and a banking system based on specie and sound credit.

For all their faith in moral progress, Interest politicians acknowledged that one of democracy's major faults was its tendency to place power in the hands of elected officials who, if left unrestricted, might centralize authority in themselves. To protect the nation from human frailty, then, the Interest interpreted government as restraint. The cornerstone of this idea was the notion that all power should be as decentralized as possible. A moral political system further should demand strict construction of the Constitution, and hedge temptation with swift rotation in office.[19]

By the logic of its position, the Interest's political ideas were essentially negative without being obstructionist. Taking a cue from the Bill of Rights, the Interest was more concerned with what the government could not do than in what it could do. What the Interest demanded was not radical leveling, as some of its detractors charged, but the Utilitarian idea of maximizing the most happiness for the most people through the framework of the popular will, social justice, and individual freedom.

By the end of the 1790s, the loosely knit Republican-Interest systematically evolved into a precise, structured political apparatus. The newly organized Republicans developed formal tactics for turning out the voters, subsidized a series of short-lived newspapers, encouraged discussions of the issues, and electioneered with gusto. For example, in the 1796 congressional canvass, young William P. Van Ness described typical campaign strategy: "Committees were appointed in each ward to further his [Edward Livingston's] election; to do which they were aroused to take a list of all the Elector's names in their respective wards, and then to go to them and remove their objections if they had any to Mr. Livingston. The Committees are to meet every other evening till the Election commences." When Chancellor Robert R Livingston ran for governor two years later, the same intimate procedure, modified by new conditions, again proved useful. Self-appointed nominating committees picked thirty-six men from the wards to form a general committee which they charged with the responsibility of bringing out the vote, sponsoring rallies, and coordinating action with upstate Republicans. Even in the famous 1800 New York City assembly election, Aaron Burr used similar methods.[20]

These tactics were productive but they lacked consistency. Although attendance at party meetings proved gratifying, the Interest recognized the need for a larger scale of operation; the need to capture explosive issues, and mold them symbolically into attractive programs. Up to this point, the Federalists showed the same drive. As effective campaign techniques, the use of democratic slogans and appeals to public opinion were common practices that neither side monopolized. But the events of the 1790s, particularly foreign policy questions, shook New Yorkers' faith in Federalist leadership. Slowly boxed in, Federalist tendencies toward establishing an integrated, elitist society became more pronounced. As a result, they surrendered their democratic pretensions, while the Republicans became more credible.

Perhaps through self-deception, perhaps through sincerity, perhaps through sheer cynical political necessity, city Republicans—and generations of Tammanyites after them—sensed the popularity implicit in these ideals and used infinite finesse to make them the party doctrine to lead an awakening electorate. But again, what these Republicans truly believed was less important than how they acted. Whether out of sincerity or gamesmanship, they convinced the public that their party stood for a political ideology in which the government derived its will from the people, and where public opinion limited what that government could or could not do.

By so doing, the party moved from the realm of self-interest to the realm of morality. Before, in opposing Federalism, the Republicans trapped themselves in a jungle of pure expediency. As any essentially "out" faction must do, they politicked on pure negativism. Whatever Federalists proposed, Republicans opposed. But political expediency that lacked any rationale except the lust for office was highly inconsistent and unstable. Such conditions were intolerable. In a democratic system where the public had a wide-ranging faith in the mechanics of popular sovereignty, a party needed a shared moral code, a conviction that in any given election there was more at stake than mere time-serving programs or men. If voters assumed that caprice, not basic principles, formed the standards of political conduct, that party could never reconcile freedom with order, liberty with morality. To maintain credibility and loyalty, a party had to act as if it was the agency for implementing a belief system that ordinary citizens found compatible.

In consciously adapting to the coloration of the city's democratic values, the Republicans displayed the first rule of winning in politics—they convinced voters that public opinion guided party policy. Cynics called this style naked opportunism; some felt it was a way to conduct the government by seeking the lowest common denominator—but it worked. Speaking the phraseology of the people and insisting that they were basically right and basically rational, the Republicans uncovered a tremendous lever in the art of popular appeal and helped usher in a major revolution in city politics.

By 1801, the local apparatus had established the main thrust of Tammany Hall's subsequent political philosophy. As events demonstrated, the Hall's principles were ameliorative and humanitarian, and could only work by persuasion, by practice in the real world of experience. While elitists grumbled that professional politicians "will face about at the call of interest and sacrifice [public] rights for a piece of bread," Republicans paid strict heed to public opinion. In doing so, the party qualified the options for self-rule. Politics and political parties, instead of being hazardous for the young nation, as the Founding Fathers and the Great Virginians assumed, were a blessing in disguise. As Mordecai Noah noted, "Our party strife is by no means dangerous or obnoxious—it is governed certainly, on our parts, by a cordial attachment to the freedom and safety of the Country; and if our old principles were to be surrendered, party, in a new, and probably a worse shape, may spring up." [21]

By 1809, when the Tammany Society made its name synonymous with the New York County Republican organization, party leaders had already carefully garnered a public image of immaculate Lockean-Jeffersonianism. Under the tutelage of such hardheaded politicos as Tunis Wortman and Stephen Allen, the Hall's philosophy reached the point of a coherent textbook approach to practical politicking. So pervasive was this attitude that when party mavericks such as Aaron Burr and DeWitt Clinton broke with Presidents Jefferson and Madison, respectively, they insisted that they were purer Jeffersonians than the Virginians.

In any given election, Tammany emblazoned its war banners with the democratic slogan, "Measures not Men." Used in this sense, the Hall rejected dogmatism's straightjacket in favor of a flexible program in tune with the popular will. By making public opinion the framework within which they carried on political action, Tammanyites could be totally inconsistent on issues. Rather than rigidly commit itself to a preconceived plan with no allowances for changing realities, the Hall pledged a general approach, broad enough to encompass all the interests and demands of its constituents. An effective party chieftain, therefore, was essentially a broker, deeply aware of the popular temper. Matthew Davis maintained that "the life of a politician is a perpetual warfare with everything bordering on tranquility and repose." By becoming orientated to issues and public opinion, the Hall solved the major problem in any political ideology: how to be inconsistent on day-to-day politics while being consistent on principles.[22]

As a secondary rule, the Hall consciously avoided going into detail on exactly how its principles were involved in any given contest. Rather, it relied on euphemisms, those ambiguous clichés that everyone understood but no one could define. Tammany did not use these bromides to drug the public. Its game was to avoid commitments on principles, beyond coming to terms with public opinion, since conceivably a situation might arise from which it could not easily extricate itself. The braves, therefore, thought of themselves as doers: men more interested in live possibilities than in dead causes.

From the decline of Federalism until the 1820s when universal, white manhood suffrage became the rule, New York politics often degenerated into personality struggles and created the impression that political principles were either nonexistent or unimportant. The reason for this situation lay with both the national Republican party's leadership and the peculiarities of localized internal Republican schisms. The Great Virginians who ruled the party until 1825 felt that with the demise of the High Federalists the danger of monarchism had ended. Assuming that a broad national interest existed independent of parties, then, Jefferson, Madison, Monroe, and even John Quincy Adams, felt that continued factional bitterness would impede the nation's development. With this in mind they played consensus politics, sought to isolate any remaining monarchists, and hoped to amalgamate all factions into one great party. Under these conditions, when the New York party split, each faction could form shifting alliances with another, or even with the miniscule Federalist party, and still plausibly claim that they operated within the various Administrations' fusion boundaries. As a consequence, since most voters considered themselves Republicans, the electorate generally measured a candidate more on what he did than what he believed.[23]

Even so, Tammanyites had already exhibited their unique ability to submerge their differences without compromising principles. Again— call it practicality, pragmatism, or plain opportunism—the Hall had stumbled on the technique for legitimately insisting that novelty and fluctuation determined public policy. The acid test of the Hall's political morality lay in the premise that each issue and its solution were proximate approaches to the continuous problem of making public policy responsive to the popular will. In 1819, for example, Henry

Meigs explained how the Hall suddenly supported Clinton's Erie Canal after four years of dogged opposition: "Governments answer their end when they put no obstacle in the way of Individual exertion. No Government can contain Science enough to direct. And never did. Government first knows what is wanted by the people and then acts. . . . Sit still, say the People to the Government, see *which way* we wish to proceed & *direct us otherwise at your peril.*" [24]

Like any growing political organization, the Hall's program was plagued with ambiguities, problems, and inconsistencies. Because of these, Tammany's foes castigated it as an immoral gang of unscrupulous politicos bent on deluding the public and accumulating power as an end in itself. Such criticism missed the point. Tammanyites drew a sharp distinction between principles as universals and tactics as temporary political guides. As the game of politics unfolded, principles circumscribed and regulated the Hall's politicking—but these same principles did not rigidly define the action. Principles formed the rules of the game, but the techniques, the programs for implementing them, had to be reconstructed continually according to change.

Thus, the Hall acted on the assumption that politics was the art of the possible. It constantly sought out new issues and utilized them according to their popularity with the voters. Moreover, if it was not identified with a successful issue, it had to somehow adopt that issue. By necessity, Tammany formed no mandate, no prepackaged plan to hand-tailor reality to fit into neat bundles. Rather, it appropriated ideas and issues already in existence. The public created the issues; Tammanyites used them. Time and time again, the Hall engineered bewildering policy shifts seemingly without cause. But it did carry an internal consistency in all its gyrations. A good issue brought votes; a bad issue repelled votes. In the final analysis, then, expediency became a technique; and principles became the determinant of expediency—as long as both fitted into the Hall's democratic Lockean-Jeffersonian framework.

It would be a naive oversimplification, however, to suggest that Tammany's political theories and practices worked perfectly. The Hall's major structural weakness was that it could not lead. In frequently yielding to the darker side of human nature in order to gain votes, Tammany was no better or worse than the often irrational characteristics of public opinion. Then, too, the Hall's reliance on popular will ignored man's capacity for self-delusion and selfishness. By accepting the public's wishes as the appropriate fuel to run the machine, the organization overlooked the vital question of what ends justify what means under what circumstances. Even more, ambitious demagogues, using the proper levers, could manipulate public opinion so that the rank and file lacked proper guides to distinguish between sham and reality. Beyond that, the danger always existed that an aggressive minority who simply made the most noise could hold the entire organization captive.

Equally troublesome, Tammany could efficiently turn out voters any time it wished. But however brilliant its electioneering, the Hall's legislative programs were usually unimaginative pieces of flummery. So long as it played each new issue by ear, the General Committee sponsored a relatively passive program, bordering on conservatism, until the public forced it to act. Even this situation was perilous. Tammany enjoyed massive stability if the public substantially agreed on "measures not men." But if no consensus existed, if many shrill voices cried for attention, Tammany's pragmatism boomeranged: responsibility diffused, many power centers grappled for the advantage, and self-perpetuating elites worked for their own greater glory.

Just as politically indefensible was the rank and file's tendency to leave the machine's day-to-day affairs in the hands of a professional cadre which often put its own desires first and conflicted with, rather than supplemented, the community's larger interests. Over a period of time, these professionals came to consider office-holding practically their sovereign right, and used their position to make graft a way of life. Yet such corruption did have some beneficial side effects on the apparatus as a whole. Internal reformers often used the corruption issue, as Boss Tweed did, to prevent other political parties from profiting by Tammany's mistakes, and to create the impression that the Hall had the ability for self-criticism and self-rejuvenation. In such ways, corruption worked as a safety valve, brought fresh leaders into the organization, and prevented the machine's older leadership cliques from becoming unresponsive bureaucracies. Furthermore, when the Hall acted in such a manner, many New Yorkers were willing to tolerate a degree of Tammany's corruption as their price for having the organization help them adjust to the city's bewildering urban problems.

Other tensions compromised the Hall's efficiency. Although Tammany revered Jefferson as both a man and a symbol, it did not swallow his political theories intact. Moreover, as politics became increasingly institutionalized after the 1820s, many men who lacked a coherent, articulated political philosophy joined the Hall, and made it appear that all of Tammany's programs were subordinate to two overriding aims: preservation of the party, and promotion of selfish individuals.

Yet despite such drawbacks, the Hall's democratic rhetoric—reenforced by the Tammany Society, which hardened the party's Jeffersonian past into the form of a myth—developed a compelling force of its own. The same factors that limited the Hall's efficiency became the catalysts for producing consistent policies and transforming them into action. As the machine evolved, the logic and imperatives of supporting certain types of issues coalesced around the Hall and fabricated a predictable internal program. On key issues, habits, myths, symbols, and ideology preserved the party, maintained stability, and gave Tammany its distinctive form and style.

One larger problem remains. If Tammany Hall was as unprincipled as political mythology suggests, then its expediency should have enabled the machine to avoid splitting over certain issues. But the reverse situation occurred. On several occasions when the public forced the Hall to choose between expediency and principle, the organization underwent volcanic internal upheavals.

Tammany's first ideological test came during the Jacksonian period when the Loco Focos tested the Hall's sincerity. The thorny question the Locos posed was whether the machine's political creed was purely expedient rhetoric devoid of meaning, or had substance based on the principle of equal rights. After much agonizing, the Hall's response clearly fitted into its over-all philosophy. Despite the realization that many of their commercial-minded allies disagreed, party leaders knew that the Locos' main article of faith—equality for all—strengthened, reinforced, and modernized traditional party principles.

The Locos' conception of Jeffersonianism, however, unleashed forces party chieftains never anticipated. By the 1840s, what had begun as a difference of opinion over the party's economic ambiguities mushroomed into a monumental explosion when slavery extensionism became the political crucible. Here, the Hall faltered because its political philosophy lacked solidity and suddenly became the rationale for all sides. One faction, friendly to the South, felt that party principles sanctioned the idea of home rule embodied in the doctrine of popular sovereignty. A second, huddled around Martin Van Buren, also taking its cue from Jeffersonianism, believed that the nation's future rested with a free, propertied, white yeoman farmer class, who would eventually settle the western public domain. A third group, the small but vocal abolitionists, were also Jeffersonians; they derived ethical support from the Declaration of Independence, and opposed slavery on moral grounds.

In the next decade, one additional factor caused this latent antagonism to burst the bonds of political propriety. A new generation of men to whom expediency was paramount, typified by Fernando Wood and totally amoral on slavery, perverted the entire meaning of party principles by seeking to manipulate public opinion through brute force. Personality clashes, not principles, spoils-mongering, not Jacksonian equalitarianism, splintered the party's foundations. Urged on by selfish, low-caliber men, several Tammany factions split off, created new grounds for controversy, and set the stage for more shifts in party loyalties.

In a desperate effort to ward off almost inevitable disaster, a fresh leadership elite, headed by Tweed, slowly centralized authority and set up an orderly mechanism for implementing public opinion. Paradoxically, in terms of his subsequent career, Tweed grasped control as a reformer, and once again Tammany's political creed smoothed his path.

By 1864, the electorate had become frankly disillusioned with the sanctity of public opinion. During the previous decade, the voice of the people had indeed spoken. But it was a muffled, often foreign, and jumbled sound that ultimately created confusion. Beyond that, when men of Wood's ilk manipulated the popular temper, they cast doubt on Tammanyism's basic premise: the voters' ability to set intelligent public policy.

Tweed suggested that the people were being served badly by their political system, and recommended certain changes, chiefly the decentralizing of the nominating process, that gave the impression of great public participation in decision-making. In reality, however, these moves barely disturbed the machine's basic functions. When his rivals protested, Tweed artfully claimed that he was only revitalizing the machine after years of abuse.

In terms of Tammanyism, Tweed brought it up to date. Since public opinion had proved too dangerous and too complex a guide, he made the "Boss" not only the functional substitute for the old leadership clique, but also the determinant of public policy. There were multiple causes for Tweed's action. In a city that had roughly doubled its population during the preceding decade, the old homogeneous way of life had scattered into the hurly-burly that epitomized mid-nineteenth-century urbanism. The changes were irrevocable. The political process had thus become less of a game and more of a science as a new host of problems clamored for attention. In dealing with the situation, Tweed showed great skill at welding conflicting groups into a unit for political power and modernized party traditions. First, the Hall expanded its paternalism, played a variety of roles as a welfare agency, and sought an equilibrium of interests. Second, the Boss, using his precinct captains at shock troops, cleverly molded public opinion—and then appealed to it as his justification for action. Third, Tweed superseded the General Committee's functions. He made himself the party's chief disciplinarian and tied the voters to himself or his henchmen through personal obligations.

Even so, Tweed's approach, no matter how innovative, ultimately ended in failure. When he altered the party's conventional techniques, he actually tinkered with the machine's cogs, not its design. The Hall modernized under his leadership because conditions had changed. Expediency had become an extension of principle; and principle became an extension of expediency. While the Hall still maintained its community orientation, picking up massive vote-getting appeal along the way, neither Tweed nor his successors really eliminated Tammany's greatest flaw—its inability to shape progressive rule.

# ABBREVIATIONS

| | |
|---|---|
| *AHR* | *American Historical Review* |
| *AHAR* | *Annual Reports of the American Historical Association* |
| BHS | Buffalo Historical Society |
| *BHSP* | *Buffalo Historical Society Publications* |
| CU | Columbia University |
| HSP | Historical Society of Pennsylvania |
| *JAH* | *Journal of American History* |
| LC | Library of Congress |
| MHS | Massachusetts Historical Society |
| *MVHR* | *Mississippi Valley Historical Review* |
| NYHS | New-York Historical Society |
| *NYHSQ* | *New-York Historical Society Quarterly* |
| *NYH* | *New York History* |
| NYPL | New York Public Library |
| NYSL | New York State Library |
| OSHS | Ohio State Historical Society |
| *PSQ* | *Political Science Quarterly* |
| SU | Syracuse University Library |
| UR | University of Virginia Library |
| *WMQ* | *William and Mary Quarterly* |

# BIBLIOGRAPHICAL ESSAY

THE PURPOSE of this bibliographical essay is threefold. First, to acquaint the reader with the sources used in this study. Second, to evaluate these sources. Third, to give the reader an insight into my methods and conclusions.

## GENERAL INTRODUCTION

The primary source for studying the Tammany Society and Tammany Hall is the remarkable Edwin Kilroe Collection located at Columbia University. It contains articles, books, pamphlets, broadsides, Tammany Society minutes, membership lists, and other memorabilia. A limited number of Tammany Society minutes and some correspondence can also be found in the New York Public Library.

The literature on Tammany Hall is impressive in quantity but not necessarily in quality. The most authoritative of these studies is Gustavus Myers, *The History of Tammany Hall* (New York: Boni & Liveright, 1917). Less satisfactory is Morris Werner, *Tammany Hall* (New York: Doubleday, Doran & Company, 1928). Alfred Connable and Edward Silberfarb in their *Tigers of Tammany: Nine Men Who Ran New York* (New York: Holt, Rinehart & Winston, 1967) update Myers and Warner but leave much to be desired in their treatment of the early Tammany Hall. Books which are uncritical and more indicative of their authors' state of mind than descriptive of actual events are: William H. Allen, *Al Smith's Tammany Hall* (New York: Institute for Public Service, 1928); Euphemia Vale Blake, *History of the Tammany Society From Its Organization to the Present Time, 1901* (New York: Souvenir Publishing Company, 1901); Edwin Kilroe, Abraham Kaplan, and Joseph Johnson, *The Story of Tammany: A Patriotic History* (New York: 1924); William Gover, *The Tammany Hall Democracy of the City of New York* (New York: 1875); and James E. Finnegan, *Tammany at Bay* (New York: Dodd, Mead & Company, 1933). Two recent studies that offer a wealth of insights into the mature Tammany are: Seymour Mendelbaum, *Boss Tweed's New York* (New York: John Wiley & Sons, 1965); and Alexander Callow, Jr., *The Tweed Ring* (New York: Oxford University Press, 1966). In addition, readers should consult

**383**

Denis Tilden Lynch, *Boss Tweed, The Story of a Grim Generation* (New York: Boni & Liveright, 1927). Other biographies of later Tammany "Bosses" are: J. Fairfax McLaughlin, *The Life and Times of John Kelly* (New York: The American News Company, 1885), and Lothrop Stoddard, *Master of Manhattan: The Life of Richard Croker* (New York: Longmans, Green, 1931). Besides these books a variety of "Muckraking" magazines published many articles about Tammany. As a sampling, readers should consult: *The Fortnightly Review, McClure's Magazine, Review of Reviews, Munsey's Magazine, Colliers, The Arena,* and *Twentieth Century*. In the same class is Lincoln Steffens, *The Shame of the Cities* (New York: Sagamore Press, 1948 reprint).

Any student of Tammany Hall should also use the many volumes, located in the New York City Municipal Archives, that detail the day-by-day activities of the city government. Here one can find the documents and proceedings of the Board of Aldermen, Board of Assistant Aldermen, the Board of Councilmen, the Board of Supervisors, and the minutes of the Common Council. Some of these are in printed form. Other useful sources for municipal government can be found in the various *Manuals of the Corporations* edited by Daniel Valentine and John Hardy. The 1870 volume contains an excellent summary of voting statistics. An equally vital source for information on elections is the *Civil List and Constitutional History of the Colony and State of New York* (Albany: 1879).

### GENERAL HISTORIES

There are a number of state histories which are very useful tools to understand the nature of both New York City and New York State politics. Far and away the best source is Jabez Hammond, *The History of Political Parties in the State of New York* (Albany: Van Benthuysen, 1842). John Jenkins, who wrote in the same period, published three studies which are useful in spots but must be used with care: *History of Political Parties in State of New York* (Auburn: Alden & Markham, 1846); *The Lives of the Governors of the State of New York* (Auburn: Derby & Miller, 1851); and *The Life of Silas Wright* (Auburn: J. M. Alden, 1850). The best comprehensive history of New York is the ten-volume work edited by Alexander Flick, *The History of the State of New York*, 10 vols. (New York: I. J. Friedman, 1962 reprint). DeAlva S. Alexander, *A Political History of the State of New York*, 4 vols. (New York: H. Holt & Company, 1906–1923) is an ambitious work which recent scholarship has corrected in many places. For constitutional history, two studies are valuable: Alfred Street, *The Council of Revision of the State of New York* (Albany: W. Gould, 1859), and Charles Z. Lincoln, *The Constitutional History of New York*, 5 vols. (Rochester: Lawyers Co-operative Publishing Company, 1906). An unexcelled chronology of New York City history can be found in the monumental effort of I.N.P. Stokes, *The Iconography of Manhattan Island, 1498–1909, Compiled from Original Sources and Illustrated by Photo-Intaglio Reproduction of Important Maps, Plans, Views and Documents,* 6 vols. (New York: R.H. Dodd, 1915–1928). Susan Lyman's *The Story of New York: An Informal History of the City* (New York: Crown Publishers, 1964) is just that. The basic one-volume history of New York is the scholarly and authoritative joint work by David Ellis, James Frost, Harold Syrett, and Harry J. Carman, *A History of New York State* (Ithaca: Cornell University Press, 1967). The New-York Historical Society has published much source material that is relevant to local politics: *Collections: First Series,* I–V (1809–1830); Second Series, I–V (1841–1859); *Proceedings,* I–VI (1843–1849); and *Publication Fund Series* (1868–). In addition, its *Quarterly* contains many useful articles. The New York State Historical Association, which began publishing its *Proceedings* in 1901, added much substance to the study of local politics with its *Quarterly Journal* (1919) and *New York History* (1933–). Three indispensable guides for locating material in New York City are: *A Guide to the Principal Sources for Early American History (1600–1800) in the City of New York,* ed. by E.B. Greene and Richard Morris (New York: Columbia University Press, 1953); and Harry Carman and Arthur Thompson, *A Guide to the Principal Sources for American Civilization, 1800–1900, in the City of New York: Manuscripts* (1960), *Printed Material* (1962), (New York: Columbia University Press, 1960 and 1962).

Foreword

On the subject of urbanism in the colonial period, I have used Carl Bridenbaugh, *Cities in The Wilderness* (New York: Alfred A. Knopf, 1938) and his *Cities in Revolt* (New York: Alfred A. Knopf, 1955). Richard Wade's *The Urban Frontier, 1790–1830* (Cambridge: Harvard University Press, 1957) and Constance McLaughlin Green's *American Cities in the Growth of the Nation* (New York: Harper & Row, 1965), are praiseworthy discussions. Older but still valuable is Arthur Schlesinger, *The Rise of the City, 1878–1898* (New York: Macmillan, 1933). In dealing with New York City, I have relied upon Sidney Pomerantz, *New York—An American City, 1783–1803: A Study of Urban Life* (New York: Columbia University Press, 1938). For the effect of urban change on traditional politics and social patterns another invaluable source is Dixon Ryan Fox, *The Decline of Aristocracy in the Politics of New York, 1801–1840* (New York: Columbia University Press, 1919). Helpful along the same lines, although both have their own axes to grind, are two diaries: Philip Hone, *The Diary of Philip Hone,* edited by Bayard Tuckerman, 2 vols. (New York: Dodd, Mead &

Company, 1910), and George Templeton Strong, *The Diary of George Templeton Strong*, edited by Allan Nevins and Milton Thomas, 4 vols. (New York: Macmillan, 1952). For the impact of immigration, see Robert Ernst, *Immigrant Life in New York City, 1825–1863* (New York: I.J. Friedman, 1965 reprint). James Richardson, *New York Police: Colonial Times to 1901* (New York: Oxford University Press, 1970) is the definitive work on the subject. Older studies which can be used are: Augustine Costello, *Our Police Protectors* (New York: A.E. Costello, 1885); John Gerard, *London and New York: Their Crimes and Police* (New York: 1853); Joel Headley, *The Great Riots of New York, 1812 to 1873* (New York: E.B. Treat, 1873); Charles Loring Brace, *The Dangerous Classes of New York* (New York: Wynkoop & Hallenback, 1872), and George Walling, *Recollections of a New York Chief of Police* (New York: Caxton, 1887). Other aspects of crime are covered in Jeremy Felt, *Hostages of Fortune: Child Labor Reform in New York State* (Syracuse: Syracuse University Press, 1965), and Robert S. Pickett, *House of Refuge: Origins of Juvenile Reform in New York State, 1815–1857* (Syracuse: Syracuse University Press, 1969). David Schneider, *The History of Public Welfare in New York State, 1609–1866* (Chicago: University of Chicago Press, 1938) is a detailed and informed treatment of a neglected chapter of local history. For the fire department, I have used *Citizens Committee of Safety* (New York: 1840); Augustine E. Costello, *Our Firemen* (New York: A.E. Costello, 1887); and Lowell Limpus, *History of the New York Fire Department* (New York: E.P. Dutton & Company, 1940).

Several studies that deal with the development of urban political machines are available. James Bryce, *The American Commonwealth* (London and New York: Macmillan and Company, 1889), although not at all favorable to Tammany, provides an interesting view of the mature machine. Moisei Ostrogorski, *Democracy and the Origin of Political Parties* (New York: Macmillan, 1902) is an invaluable piece of work, particularly his chapters on practical machine politics. William L. Riordan, *Plunkitt of Tammany Hall* (New York: McClure, Phillips, and Company, 1905) is both amusing and instructive. Matthew Breen, *Thirty Years of New York Politics Up-to-Date* (New York: 1899), is an insiders' view of Tammany. Samuel Orth, *The Boss and the Machine* (New Haven: Yale University Press, 1919) is rather superficial. For city machines and immigrants see Nathan Glazer and Daniel P. Moynihan, *Beyond the Melting Pot* (Cambridge: Massachusetts Institute of Technology Press, 1963). In dealing with the functional theory of political behavior, three works are outstanding: Robert Merton, *Social Theory and Social Structure* (New York: Free Press, 1957); Edward C. Banfield and James Q. Watson, *City Politics* (New York: Alfred A. Knopf, 1966); and Edward Costikyan, *Behind Closed Doors* (New York: Harcourt, Brace & World, Inc., 1967). The series on urban history, published by the Oxford University Press, contains several monographs on political machines in other cities.

CHAPTERS 1, 2, AND 3 (1787–1815)

General works relating to the development of the first party system are: Noble E. Cunningham, Jr., *The Jefferson Republicans: The Formation of Party Organization, 1789–1801* (Chapel Hill: University of North Carolina Press, 1957) and his *The Jeffersonian Republicans in Power: Party Operations, 1801–1809* (Chapel Hill: University of North Carolina Press, 1963); William Chambers, *Political Parties in a New Nation* (New York: Oxford University Press, 1963); and Roy Nichols, *The Invention of the American Political Parties* (New York: Macmillan, 1967). The best book on local politics in the 1790s is Alfred Young, *The Democratic Republicans of New York: Their Origins, 1763–1797* (Chapel Hill: University of North Carolina Press, 1967). Eugene Link, *Democratic-Republican Societies, 1790–1800* (New York: Columbia University Press, 1942), discusses the development of the "self-created society" issue. For the relationship between politics and banking, Joseph Davis, *Essays in the Earlier History of American Corporations*, 2 vols. (Cambridge: Harvard University Press, 1917), and Bray Hammond, *Banks and Politics in America from the Revolution to the Civil War* (Princeton: Princeton University Press, 1957), are excellent. For the War of 1812, see Roger H. Brown, *The Republic in Peril: 1812* (New York: Columbia University Press, 1964). Alvin Kass, *Politics in New York State, 1800–1830* (Syracuse: Syracuse University Press, 1965) develops an interesting thesis, which I do not fully accept.

Other informative studies that throw light on the era's politics are the many biographies about prominent New Yorkers. For the Livingstons, I have used George C. Dangerfield, *Chancellor Robert R. Livingston of New York, 1746–1813* (New York: Harcourt & Brace, 1965); William B. Hatcher, *Edward Livingston* (Baton Rouge: Louisiana State University Press, 1940); the eulogistical Edward B. Livingston, *The Livingstons of Livingston Manor* (New York: The Knickerbocker Press, 1910); and Charles H. Hunt, *Life of Edward Livingston* (New York: D. Appleton and Company, 1864). The Clintonians are represented by E. Wilder Spaulding, *His Excellency George Clinton* (New York: Macmillan, 1938) which is disappointing on national politics; Howard Lee McBain, *Dewitt Clinton and the Origin of the Spoils System in New York* (New York: Columbia University Press, 1907), is an indispensable source because many letters that McBain cites were destroyed in the New York State Library fire of 1911; and the superficial Dorothie Bobbie, *DeWitt Clinton* (New York: Minton, Balch & Company, 1933). DeWitt Clinton still awaits a definitive biography. Until one appears, readers will have to relie on David Hosack, *Memoir of DeWitt Clinton* (New

York: J. Seymour, 1829), William L. Campbell, *Life and Writings of De-Witt Clinton* (New York: Baker & Scribner, 1849), and Edward Fitzpatrick, *The Educational Views and Influence of DeWitt Clinton* (New York: Columbia University Press, 1911). For Aaron Burr, I have used: Nathan Schachner, *Aaron Burr, A Biography* (New York: Frederick A. Stokes Company, 1937), and Herbert Parmet and Marie Hecht, *Aaron Burr: Portrait of an Ambitious Man* (New York: Macmillan, 1967). Both are fine studies, but each accepts uncritically Burr's domination of Tammany, a view that I do not feel is true. Ray W. Irwin, *Daniel P. Tompkins* (New York: New-York Historical Society, 1968) fills a void although it does not cover fully Tammany's relationship with the governor. For the Federalist side of the story, I have consulted: Frank Monaghan, *John Jay: Defender of Liberty* (Indianapolis: Bobbs-Merrill, 1935); Allan McLane Hamilton, *The Intimate Life of Alexander Hamilton* (New York: Charles Scribner's Sons, 1910); Robert Ernst, *Rufus King, American Federalist* (Chapel Hill: University of North Carolina Press, 1968); and David H. Fischer, *The Revolution of American Conservatism* (New York: Harper & Row, 1965).

The printed works of prominent politicians have also been useful. Henry Adams, *The Writings of Albert Gallatin*, 3 vols. (Philadelphia: J.B. Lippincott & Company, 1879) contains interesting material on New York patronage problems. Julian Boyd's *The Papers of Thomas Jefferson* (Princeton: Princeton University Press, 1950-) does not yet reach the end of the 1790's. I supplemented this collection with the older, if somewhat inaccurate, A.A. Liscomb and A.L. Bergh, *The Monticello or Memorial Edition of the Writings of Thomas Jefferson*, 20 vols. (Washington: Thomas Jefferson Memorial Association, 1903). Matthew Davis, *Memoirs of Aaron Burr with Miscellaneous Selections from his Correspondence*, 2 vols. (New York: Harper & Bros., 1836-1837), was more notable for what it did not include. Thomas Earle and Charles C. Congden, *Annals of the General Committee of Mechanics and Tradesmen of the City of New York, 1785-1880* (New York: The Society, 1882), is useful for its membership lists. Jared Sparks, *The Life of Gouverneur Morris with Selections from His Correspondence and Miscellaneous Papers*, 3 vols. (Boston: Gray & Bowen, 1832); Harry Warfel, *Letters of Noah Webster* (New York: Macmillan, 1936); the incomplete Harold Syrett et al., *The Papers of Alexander Hamilton* (New York: Columbia University Press, 1961-), and the older Henry Cabot Lodge, *The Works of Alexander Hamilton*, 12 vols. (New York: G.P. Putnam's Sons, 1904) view local politics from a Federalist angle. Herbert Johnson, *Correspondence and Public Papers of John Jay*, 4 vols. (New York: G.P. Putnam's Sons, 1890-1893) is disappointing as is William Kent, *Memoirs and Letters of James Kent. LL.D. and Late Chancellor of the States of New York* (Boston: Little, Brown and Company, 1898). By far, the best printed collection is Charles King, *The Life and Correspondence of Rufus King*, 6 vols. (New York: G.P. Putnam's Sons, 1894-1900).

I found several reminiscences valuable. Isaac Q. Leake, *Memoirs of the Life and Times of General John Lamb* (Albany: Joel Munsell, 1850) is good for Antifederalist activity. Winslow Watson, *Men and Times of the Revolution: Memoirs of Elkanah Watson* (New York: Dana & Company, 1856) contains material on the canal projects. *The Burghers of New York and the Freemen of New York City* (New York: The New-York Historical Society, 1885) is a valuable source for the study of city voters and changes in the electoral laws. Catherine Van Rensselaer, *A Legacy of Historical Gleanings*, 2 vols. (Albany: Joel Munsell, 1875) contains letters otherwise not available. John F. Francis, *New York During the last Half Century* (New York, Trow, 1857) gives a view of early city life, as does Charles Haswell, *Reminiscences of an Octogenarian of the City of New York* (New York: Harper & Bros., 1896) for a later period, Mordecai Meyers, *Reminiscences, 1780–1814* (Washington: Crane Company, 1900) is a slim volume that must be used with care.

Outside of Edwin Kilroe, *Saint Tammany and the Origins of the Society of Tammany or Columbian Order in New York City* (New York: Columbia University Press, 1913), I have relied partially on articles in historical journals for the Tammany Society's activities. Peter Paulson, "The Tammany Society and the Jeffersonian Movement in New York City," *NYH*, 34 (1953), 72–84, extends Kilroe, but needs added work on occupational breakdowns of Tammany Society members. Edward de Lancey, "Columbian Celebration of 1792," *Magazine of American History*, 29 (January 1893), 1–18, provides a detailed account of a Tammany festival. Lloyd Haberly, "The American Museum from Baker to Barnum," *NYHSQ*, 43 (July 1959), 273–88; Robert and Dale McClung, "Tammany's Remarkable Gardiner Baker," *NYHSQ*, 43 (April 1959), 143–70, and Walter Whitehall, "John Pintard's Antiquarian Society," *NYHSQ*, 45 (October 1961), 346–64, have interesting materials on this aspect of the Society's early endeavors. William Miller, "A Note on the Early History of the Tammany Society," *NYH*, 20 (1939), 463–76, contains several articles from the *New York Journal* on the Tammany Tontine's waterworks. For further explanations, readers should use the pamphlet, *Plan of the New York Tammanial Society* (New York: 1792). Beatrice Reubens, "Burr, Hamilton and the Manhattan Company," *PSQ*, 72 (1957), 578–607, and 73 (1958), 100–24, adds details to this phase of Burr's career. Marshall Smelser, "The Federalist Period as an Age of Passion," *American Quarterly*, 10 (1958), 391–419, is excellent for the ideological nature of the 1790's. Frederick Stevens, "New York in the Society of Cincinnati," *NYH*, 25 (1944), 18–34, is a rich source of information. For the Tammany Society in other states, I have consulted William Utter, "Saint Tammany in Ohio: A Study in Frontier Politics," *MVHR*, 15 (1928), 321–40, and Samuel Williams, "Tammany Society in Ohio," *Ohio Archeological and Historical Quarterly*, 12 (1913), 349–70.

Other articles were helpful for the general politics of the era. Harry

Ammon, "The Genet Mission and the Development of American Political Parties," *JAH*, 52 (March 1966), 725–41, is quite good. William Apgar, "New York's Contributions to the War Effort of 1812," *NYHSQ*, 29 (October 1945), 203–12, is a brief survey. Whitefield Bell, Jr., "The Federal Procession of 1788," *NYHSQ*, 46 (January 1962), 5–40, gives an indication of the Federalist strength at the start of the 1790s. Nobel E. Cunningham, Jr., "John Beckley: An Early Party Manager," *WMQ*, 13 (1956), 40–52, sheds light on an obscure but important figure. J. Hampden Dougherty, "Constitutions of New York," *PSQ*, 3 (September 1888), 489–519; Hugh Flick, "The Council of Appointment," *NYH*, 15 (1934), 253–77; J.M. Gitterman, "The Council of Appointment in New York," *PSQ*, 7 (March 1892), 80–115; and Frank Goodnow, "The Charter of New York City," *PSQ*, 17 (March 1902), 1–23, are convenient accounts. Meryle Evans, "Knickerbocker Hotels and Restaurants, 1800–1850," *NYHSQ*, 36 (October 1952), 377–408, has some information on another side of Tammany Hall. David H. Fischer, "The Myth of the Essex Junto," *WMQ*, 21 (April 1964), 191–235, does a good job in demolishing that myth. Galliard Hunt, "Office-Seeking during Jefferson's Administration," *AHR*, 3 (1898), 270–91, is excellent for Burr's patronage problems. Beatrice Hyslop, "American Press Reports of the French Revolution, 1789–1794," *NYHSQ*, 42 (October 1958), 329–48, is fine for an understanding of Tammany's Gallomania. Ray Irwin, "Governor Tompkins and the Embargo, 1807–1809," *NYH*, 22 (1941), 309–20, is interesting for Tompkins' initial break with the Clintonians. William Miller, "The Democratic Societies and the Whiskey Insurrection," *Pennsylvania Magazine of History and Biography*, 63 (April 1939), contains material on the "self-created society" question. Harry Ammon, "James Monroe and the Election of 1808 in Virginia," *WMQ*, 20 (January 1963), 33–66; Samuel E. Morison, "The First Nominating Convention, 1808," *AHR*, 17 (July 1912), 744–63; and Moisei Ostrogorski, "The Rise and Fall of the Nominating Caucus," *AHR*, 4 (1899–1900), 253–83, are significant for early political techniques.

The manuscript materials on early New York City are quite rich. The Stephen Allen Papers (NYHS) have some interesting letters, but his memoirs are most valuable. The Ethan Allen Brown Papers (OSHS) contain a few important letters from his city friends about the impact of the Embargo and Clinton's 1812 presidential campaign. The Burr Papers are scattered in the Library of Congress, New-York Historical Society, New York Public Library, and New York State Library. In general, they are not useful. The DeWitt Clinton Papers, located in the New-York Historical Society, the New York Public Library, and the New York State Library, are fragmentary but useful for different phases of his career. The main collection in the Columbia University Library is a gold mine of information. The George Clinton Papers and the Daniel Tompkins Papers, both in the New York State Library, were largely destroyed in the 1911 fire. But the material in the Tompkins Papers that remains, particularly for the period 1810–1815, is vital to explain his final break with the Clintonians. Some George Clinton letters survive in the Edmund Genêt Papers (NYHS), but they give a distorted picture of Clinton as a complaining hypochondriac. For banking, particularly in 1791–1792, the Andrew Craigie Papers (American Antiquarian Society) are good. In a later period, the William Edgar Papers (NYPL) are invaluable for the activities of the Manhattan Company under Burr and Clinton. For the Federalists, the Ebenezer Foote Papers (NYSL, LC) and the Alexander Hamilton Papers (LC) provide fine insights. The Horatio Gates Papers (NYHS) have some Burr letters, as do the John Lamb Papers in the same library. The James Madison Appointment Papers in the National Archives have several letters that detail the Clintonian patronage fall and the rising prominence of Tammanyites and Governor Tompkins. The Wilson Cary Nicholas Papers (LC, UVA) have material on the opposition to the Alien and Sedition Acts, and George Clinton's 1808 bid for the presidency. The Samuel Osgood Papers (NYHS) has one interesting letter about the banking situation in 1812. The John Smith Papers (NYHS) adds Clintonian material as does the Van Cortland–Van Wyck Papers in the New York Public Library and the New-York Historical Society. The Mathias Tallmadge Papers (NYHS) compliments these two. The Melancton Smith Papers, the Morgan Lewis Papers (both in the NYSL), and the Smith Thompson Papers (LC) were all disappointing.

Beyond any doubt, eight collections provided me with the most information on local politics. The Livingston Family Papers (NYHS) are rich on almost all aspects of Republican activity. The Albert Gallatin Papers are another major source. The Rokeby Collection contains important Ambrose Spencer–John Armstrong letters. The collections of three presidents, Thomas Jefferson, James Madison, and James Monroe (LC) were the focal points for many letters from New York politicians. Two smaller collections, the Van Ness Family Papers (NYPL and NYHS) and the Matthew Davis Papers (NYHS) are absolutely vital for the Burrites. I am extremely grateful for them.

Because city newspapers, at least until the 1840s, were not independent forums or news-gathering agencies to enlighten the public but party organs, subsidized or controlled by various political organizations, they are vital sources for appreciation of how the Republicans and Tammany Hall operated. In them, a researcher can locate notices of meetings, party goals, attitudes on public issues, and propaganda that set the party line. If a reader is not careful, however, he might become a latter-day polemicist because of the mendacity of his material. For that reason, I have attempted to balance my study by using newspapers that represented all New York City factions.

For the 1790s, Thomas Greenleaf's *New York Journal and Patriotic Register* is very helpful as both a sounding board for ideas and a means of reading Republican opinion. Through a careful study, one can also see the development of party machinery. Several short-lived Republican papers are good for the same reasons. The *Columbian Gazetteer* (1793-1794) covers the Genêt Affair; the *Evening Post* (1795) has excellent material on the Federalist defection from Tammany; and the *Time Piece* (1797-1798) is informative on the XYZ Affair and the Alien and Sedition Acts. For the Federalist side of the story, I consulted the *Daily Advertiser* (1789-1795) and the *Commercial Advertiser* (1799-1800).

In the first decade of the nineteenth century, the *American Citizen* (1800-1810), edited by James Cheetham, is a prime example of political polemics. After Cheetham broke with the Clintonians, DeWitt Clinton established a new organ, the *Columbian* (1809-1819). The *Morning Chronicle* (1803-1806) presents the Burrite side of the story, and its successor, the *Public Advertiser* (1807-1812) has much information about the Tammany Society's new role in politics. In 1813, Tammany formed a new print, the *National Advocate* (1813-1828), which was quite influential until the Adamsites secured its control in 1827. For the Federalists, I used the *Evening Post* (1801-1829), not to be confused with the earlier one. Ably edited by William Coleman, the paper is particularly valuable in the period from 1801 to 1804 on the Burrite-Federalist flirtation, and later as an anti-Clintonian sheet, with occasional lapses, until Coleman's death.

For more information on journalism and politics see: Charles Levermore, "Rise of Metropolitan Journalism," *AHR*, 6 (April 1901), 446-64; Frederick Hudson, *Journalism in the United States* (New York: Harper & Bros., 1873); Frank L. Mott, *American Journalism: A History of Newspapers in the United States* (New York: Macmillan, 1953); and Milton Hamilton, *The Country Printer New York State, 1785-1830* (New York: Columbia University Press, 1936). Louis Fox, *New York Newspapers, 1820-1850: A Bibliography* (Chicago: University of Chicago Press, 1928) is essential as a check list. For pertinent biographies, James Gordon Bennett is presented in Isaac Pray, *Memoirs of A Journalist* (New York: Stringer & Townsend, 1855) and in Oliver Carlson, *The Man Who Made News* (New York: Duel, Sloan and Pearce, 1942); Isaac Goldberg, *Major Mordecai Noah* (Philadelphia: The Jewish Publication Society of America, 1936) offers a somewhat limited study of that controversial man; and James L. Crouthamel, *James Watson Webb: A Biography* (Middletown: Wesleyan University Press, 1969) is a sound and scholarly work. At present, James Cheetham lacks a biographer.

Political pamphlets served the same function as newspapers. James Cheetham was a master at this type of propaganda, and his works form a vital part of Tammany's history: *A Letter to a Friend on the Conduct of the Adherents to Mr. Burr* (1803); *A Reply to Aristides* (1804); *A View of the Political Conduct of Aaron Burr* (1802); *An Impartial Inquiry into Certain Parts of the Conduct of Governor Lewis* (1806); *Nine Letters on the Subject of Aaron's Political Defection* (1803); *Peace or War? Or Thoughts on our Affairs with England* (1807); *Remarks on the "Mer-*

*chants" Bank* (1804). Matthew Davis answered for the Burrites: *The Letters of Marcus* (1806); *The Plot Discovered* (1807); and the *Letters of Marcus and Philo Cato* (1810). Other anti-Clintonian works are: William Rose, *A Narrative of the Dyde Supper* (1810); William P. Van Ness [Aristides], *An Examination on the Various Charges Against Aaron Burr* (1803); John Wood, *A Full Exposition of the Clintonian Faction* (1802); and Gulian Verplanck, *A Fable for Statesmen . . . by Abimelech Coody* (1815). On Burr and Hamilton, see William Coleman, *A Collection of the Facts and Documents Relating to the Death of Major General Alexander Hamilton* (1804).

The Tammany Society published many "Long Talks" in pamphlet form. In them, one can see the Society's Americanism, Lockean idealism, and myth-making that the mature Tammany Hall used as a basis for Tammanyism. A brief list would include: Samuel Berrian, *An Oration Delivered before the Tammany Society or Columbian Order, July 4, 1811;* John B. Johnson, *An Oration on Union Delivered in the Dutch Reformed Church of New York, May 4, 1794, the Anniversary of the Tammany Society;* Samuel Miller, *A Sermon Preached in New York City, July 4, 1793 at the Request of the Tammany Society or Columbian Order;* Samuel Latham Mitchill, *The Life, Exploits and Precepts of Tammany, the Famous Indian Chief, Being the Anniversary Oration before the Tammany Society . . . May 12, 1795;* John Rodman, *An Oration Delivered before the Tammany Society or Columbian Order, July 4, 1813.* The best one of these efforts is Matthew Davis, *An Oration, delivered in St. Paul's Church on the Fourth of July, 1800 . . . before the Tammany Society.* All these pamphlets are in the Kilroe Collection.

## CHAPTERS 4 AND 5 (1815–1830)

A great deal of the material already cited is relevant to the post-1815 period. For the development of the Democratic party, five studies are vital: Robert Remini, *Martin Van Buren and the Making of the Democratic Party* (New York: Columbia University Press, 1959) and his *The Election of Andrew Jackson* (Philadelphia: J.B. Lippincott Co., 1963); Charles McCarthy, "The Anti-Mason Party," *AHAR*, (Washington, D.C.: Government Printing Office, 1902); Michael Wallace, "Changing Concepts of Party in the United States: New York, 1815–1830," *AHR*, 74 (1968), 453–91; and Richard McCormick, *The Second American Party System* (Chapel Hill: University of North Carolina Press, 1966). Lee Benson, *The Concept of Jacksonian Democracy: New York as a Test Case* (Princeton: Princeton University Press, 1961) I found stimulating but not valid in some assumptions.

As general background material I used: George Dangerfield, *The Awakening of American Nationalism, 1815–1828* (New York: Harper & Row, 1965); Glover Moore, *The Missouri Controversy* (Lexington: University of Kentucky Press, 1953); Robert July, *The Essential New Yorker: Gulian Crommelin Verplanck* (Durham: Duke University Press, 1951); Shaw Livermore, Jr., *The Twilight of Federalism, 1815–1830* (Princeton: Princeton University Press, 1962); James Parton, *Life of Andrew Jackson*, 2 vols. (New York: Mason, 1861); and Samuel Bemis, *John Quincy Adams and the Union* (New York: Alfred A. Knopf, 1956). Chilton Williamson, *American Suffrage: From Property to Democracy, 1760–1860* (Princeton: Princeton University Press, 1960) was a fine companion to Nathaniel Carter and William L. Stone, *Reports of the Proceedings and Debates of the Convention of 1821* (Albany: E. & E. Hosford, 1821). For the Panic of 1819, I consulted Murray Rothbard, *The Panic of 1819* (New York: Columbia University Press, 1962), and Samuel Rezneck, "The Depression of 1819–1822, A Social History," *AHR*, 38 (1933), 23–47. The literature on the Erie Canal is impressive in scope. I have relied on three studies in addition to the material already cited on Clinton: "The Holland Land Company and Construction in Western New York," *Buffalo Historical Society Publications* (1919); Ronald Shaw, *Erie Water West: A History of the Erie Canal, 1792–1854* (Lexington: University of Kentucky Press, 1965); and Tactitus [DeWitt Clinton] *Canal Politics of the State of New York* (New York: 1822). Charles Rammelkamp, "The Campaign of 1824 in New York," *AHAR* (Washington, D.C.: Government Printing Office, 1905), 177–201, is dated on the rise of Jacksonian Democracy. For Calhoun, see Thomas Hay, "John C. Calhoun and the Presidential Election of 1824," *North Carolina Historical Review*, 12 (1935), 20–45, and his "Calhoun Letters on the Campaign of 1824," *AHR*, 40 (October 1934, January 1935), 92–96, 287–300.

The published memoirs and letters for this period are not as rich as for the preceding era. Everett S. Brown, *The Missouri Compromises and Presidential Politics, 1820–1825* (St. Louis: Missouri Historical Society, 1926) is excellent. In order to understand John Quincy Adams, his diary is indispensable: Charles Francis Adams, Jr., *Memoirs of John Quincy Adams: Comprising Part of His Diary from 1795 to 1848*, 12 vols. (Philadelphia: J.B. Lippincott Co., 1877). For opinions of an informed Clintonian, see Dorothy C. Barck, *Letters from John Pintard to his Daughter, Eliza Noel Pintard Davidson, 1816–1833*, 4 vols. (New York: New-York Historical Society, 1940–1941). There are several good DeWitt Clinton letters in John Bigelow, "DeWitt Clinton as a Politician," *Harper's New Monthly Magazine*, 50 (1874–1875), 409–17, 556–71. James F. Hopkins, *The Papers of Henry Clay*, 3 vols. (Lexington: University of Kentucky Press, 1963–) are good but must be supplemented with the Clay Papers in the Library of Congress and the transcripts in the Ohio State Historical Society.

Since Martin Van Buren was the key figure in local politics during this period, no study of Tammany Hall can ignore him. In addition to the works by Robert Remini already cited, readers should use his: "The Albany Regency," *NYH*, 39 (1958), 341–55; "Martin Van Buren and the Tariff of

Abominations," *AHR*, 63 (July 1958), 903–17; and "New York and the Presidential Election of 1816," *NYH*, 31 (1950), 308–24. For Van Buren's own attitudes, see: Martin Van Buren, *Inquiry into the Origin and Course of Political Parties in the United States*, edited by Abraham and Smith Thompson Van Buren (New York: Hurd & Houghton, 1867), and Martin Van Buren, *The Autobiography of Martin Van Buren*, edited by John C. Fitz-Patrick, *AHAR* (Washington, D.C.: Government Printing Office, 1920). Max Mintz, "Political Ideas of Martin Van Buren," *NYH*, 30 (1949), 422–45, is a brilliant piece of work. Above all else, I found the Martin Van Buren Papers in the Library of Congress an indispensable source for New York politics in the period 1810–1862. The Van Buren Papers in the New York State Library have some material not in the Library of Congress.

Other Regency leaders and foot soldiers wrote each other at length about local, state, and national issues. Their letters, plus many from Tammanyites, help to put the Hall's history in perspective. Among these vital collections are those of: John Dix (CU); Azariah Flagg (NYPL), particularly the Silas Wright letters; William Marcy (LC), which rival Van Buren's in scope and importance; and the Silas Wright Papers (NYPL). The Henry Meigs Papers (NYHS), though few in number, provides great help in the meaning of Tammanyism. For the Adamsites, the John Quincy Adams Papers (MHS) and the John W. Taylor Papers (NYHS) are excellent. Smaller collections with relevant material are: William Crawford Papers (LC); the Granger Family Papers (LC); the Holley Family Papers (NYSL); the John O'Connor Papers (University of Michigan), which contains several key letters from Matthew Davis; the Peter Porter Papers (BHS) has many Clay letters not in the Library of Congress; the John Randolph Papers (University of Virginia); and the Gulian Verplanck Papers (NYHS). The Thurlow Weed Papers (NYSL) and the Albert Tracy Papers (NYSL) are good for studying the disillusionment of local Adamsites and the rise of the Anti-Mason party. For Jackson, I found that his papers in the Library of Congress supplemented John S. Bassett, *The Correspondence of Andrew Jackson*, 4 vols. (Washington, D.C.: Carnegie Institute, 1926–1935).

Newspapers again formed the main thrust of my study. The Regency's *Albany Argus*, which I used throughout my manuscript, was vital for party directives, at least until Edwin Croswell, its editor, split with Van Buren in the 1840s. For Tammany, the major journals were: Noah's *New York National Advocate* (1825–1826), *New York Patriot* (1823–1824), *The New York Enquirer* (1826–1829), the *New York Courier and Enquirer* (1829–1830), and the *National Advocate* (1815–1827). For the Clintonians I used: *The Columbian* (1815–1819), and *The Statesman* (1823–1824). The High-Minded Federalists turned Adamsites had the *New York American* (1819–1829) and the *National Advocate* (1827–1829). The *Evening Post*, under Coleman (1815–1829), is difficult to categorize although it was generally Democratic. The DeWitt Clinton Newspaper Collection in the New York

State Library has copies of some newspapers that are unavailable elsewhere. Among them were such pro-Irish papers as *The Exile* (1817), *The Emerald* (1826), and the *Truth Teller* (1825–1827).

The use of political pamphlets declined in the post-1815 period. Some that are pertinent are: DeWitt Clinton and Pierre van Wyck: *The Martling Men* (1819); Charles Haines, *An Appeal to the People of New York on the Expediency of Abolishing the Council of Appointment* (1819); Mordecai Noah's *An Oration Delivered Before the Tammany Society, July 4, 1817*, and his *A Statement of Facts Relating to the Conduct of Henry Eckford Esq., as Connected with the NATIONAL ADVOCATE* (1824), John Woodward, *Address of the Tammany Society to Its Absent Members* (1819); and Archibald McIntyre, *A Letter to His Excellency, Daniel D. Tompkins* (1819).

<h3 style="text-align:center">CHAPTERS 6 AND 7 (1830–1838)</h3>

Perhaps no comparable period of New York history has been more thoroughly studied in recent years. On the banking question's general background, in addition to Bray Hammond's study, I have consulted: Ralph Catterall, *The Second Bank of the United States* (Chicago: University of Chicago Press, 1903); Thomas P. Govan, *Nicholas Biddle: Nationalist and Public Banker, 1786–1849* (Chicago: University of Chicago Press, 1959); David McKinley, *The Independent Treasury of the United States* (Washington, D.C.: Government Printing Office, 1910); Henry W. Lanier, *A Century of Banking in New York: 1822–1922* (New York: Gillis Press, 1922); Reginald McGrane, *The Panic of 1837* (Chicago: University of Chicago Press, 1924); Fritz Redlick, *The Molding of American Banking, Men and Ideas* (New York: Hafner Publishing Co., 1951); Robert Remini, *Andrew Jackson and the Bank War* (New York: W.W. Norton & Company, 1967); Don Sowers, *The Financial History of New York State from 1789 to 1912* (New York: Columbia University Press, 1914); Peter Temin, *The Jacksonian Economy* (New York: W.W. Norton & Company, 1969); John Van Fenstermaker, *The Development of American Commercial Banking, 1782–1837* (Kent: Kent State University Press, 1967); and Jean Wilburn, *Biddle's Bank: The Crucial Years* (New York: Columbia University Press, 1967). Arthur Schlesinger's *The Age of Jackson* (Boston: Little, Brown and Company, 1950) is a comprehensive study of the entire era.

Several articles contributed to an understanding of banks and politics, particularly the discerning ones of Frank O. Gatell: "Spoils of the Bank War: Political Bias in the Selection of Pet Banks," *AHR*, 60 (October 1964), 33–59; "Sober Second Thoughts on Van Buren, the Albany Regency, and the Wall Street Conspiracy," *JAH*, 53 (June 1966), 19–32; and "Money and Party in Jacksonian America: A Quantitative Look at New York's Men of Quality," *PSQ*, 82 (June 1967), 235–52. Bray Hammond, though generally pro-Bank, adds balance: "Jackson, Biddle, and the Bank of the United

States," *Journal of Economic History*, 6 (1947), 1–23, and "Free Banks and Corporations: The New York Free Banking Act of 1838," *Journal of Political Economy*, 46 (1936), 184–209. Others with important information are: Jacob Meerman, "The Climax of the Bank War: Biddle's Contraction, 1833–1834," *Journal of Political Economy*, 62 (August 1963), 278–388; Samuel Rezneck, "The Social History of An American Depression, 1837–1843," *AHR*, 40 (1935), 622–87; and Ivor Spencer, "William S. Marcy Goes Conservative," *MVHR*, 31 (1944), 205–24. Edward Pessen, "The Wealthiest New Yorkers of the Jacksonian Era: A New List," *NYHSQ*, (April 1970), 145–72, updates two earlier pamphlets that are basic for a study of wealth and political allegiance: Moses Yale Beach, *Wealth and Biography of the Wealthy Citizens of New York . . . with the Sums Appended to Each Name* (New York: 1845) and Reuben Vose, *The Rich Men of New York* (New York: 1861).

Contemporary materials are also useful. James Hamilton, *Reminiscences of Men and Events* (New York: Charles Scribner's Sons, 1869) is good for Jackson's Bank War and conservative reaction. Amos Kendall's *Autobiography*, edited by William Stickney (Boston: Lee & Shepard, 1872), presents a pro-Jackson view. James Gordon Bennett's diary (NYPL) only covers part of 1831, but has good material on the attitude of pro-Bank forces in upstate New York. William Mackenzie, *The Lives and Opinions of Benjamin Franklin Butler and Jesse Hoyt* (Boston: Cook & Company, 1845) has many illegally printed Van Burenite letters that are unavailable elsewhere. Theodore Sedwick, Jr., put together many of Leggett's editorials in *A Collection of the Political Writings of William Leggett* (New York: Taylor & Dodd, 1840). *The Proceedings of a Meeting of Whig Young Men of the City of New York* (New York: 1834) is good for the beginnings of the local Whig Party. Reginald McGrane, *The Correspondence of Nicholas Biddle* (Boston: J.S. Canner & Company, 1919) is highly selective and limited in its usefulness. Joseph A. Scoville, *The Old Merchants of New York*, 4 vols. (New York: Thomas R. Knox and Company, 1885) contains short biographies of prominent New Yorkers.

In addition to the Van Buren, Marcy, and Flagg Papers, I found the Nicholas Biddle Papers (LC) vital. The Thomas Olcott Papers (CU) are indispensable for the attitudes of the Albany business community. The *Evening Post* (1830–1838), edited by William Cullen Bryant and Leggett, and then Leggett's *Plaindealer* (1837) are basic sources for the Hall's activities. The *New York Herald* (1834–1838) is fairly impartial. The *Courier and Enquirer* (1830–1838) presents a unique view of the transformation of pro-Bank Jacksonians into Whigs. James Brooks' New York *Daily Express* (1837–1838) is a firm Whig Papers. The *New-York Times* (1834–1838) not to be confused with the later paper of the same name, was a vehicle for pro-Jackson conservatives.

Historians have treated the rise of the Working Men's party and the

Loco Focos with an outpouring of studies. For general background, the following are excellent: Edward Pessen, "The Working Men's Party Revisited," *Labor History* 4 (Fall 1963), 203–26; Walter Hugins, *Jacksonian Democracy and the Working Class* (Stanford: Stanford University Press, 1960); and Frank T. Carleton, "The Working Men's Party of New York City, 1829–1831," *PSQ*, 22 (September, 1907), 401–15. For a discussion of the workies' intellectual views see: William Trimble, "The Social Philosophy of the Loco Focos," *American Journal of Sociology*, 26 (1921), 705–15; and Carl Degner, "The Locofocos: Urban 'Agrarians,' " *Journal of Economic History*, 16 (September 1956), 322–33. Lee Benson accepts the idea of Seymour Savetsky's "The New York Working Men's Party" (Unpublished Master of Arts thesis, Columbia University, 1948), that the 1829 workie revolt stemmed from Tammany's factionalism. In a way, the Hall was indifferent to the workies, for example: *A Brief Investigation of the Causes Which Created the Late Controversy on the Election of Mayor* (New York: 1830). But as I see the situation, the workies had legitimate labor grievances brought on by local bankers' efforts to fight the Safety Fund. Furthermore, the workies were manipulated by Clay's forces. I feel that even though he has his own axe to grind, Philip Foner, *History of the Labor Movement in the United States* (New York: International Publishers, 1947), and Joseph Rayback, *A History of American Labor* (New York: Free Press, 1966) are closer to the truth.

For the Loco Focos themselves, Fitzwilliam Byrdsall, *The History of the Loco-Focos or Equal Rights Party* (New York: Clement & Packard, 1842), and the *Report and Constitution or Plan or Organization of the Democratic Party in Favor of Equal Rights and opposed to ALL Monopolies by Legislation* (New York: 1836) are basic. For pertinent biographies on key figures, see: William Watterman, *Frances Wright* (New York: Columbia University Press, 1924); Edward Pessen, "Thomas Skidmore, Agrarian Reformer in the Early Labor Movement," *NYH*, 25 (July 1954), 280–96; and Richard Hofstadter, "William Leggett: Spokesman of Jacksonian Democracy," *PSQ*, 58 (1943), 581–94. Edward Pessen, *Most Uncommon Jacksonians* (Albany: State University of New York Press, 1967) is profitable for information on figures such as Skidmore, Slamm, and men of their ilk. Leland W. Meyers, *The Life and Times of Colonel Richard M. Johnson* (New York: Columbia University Press, 1932) adds material on the workies' hero. Ivor Spencer, *The Victor and the Spoils: A Life of William Marcy* (Providence: Brown University Press, 1959) has several fine chapters on Marcy's problems as a governor. Douglas T. Miller, *Jacksonian Aristocracy: Class and Democracy in New York, 1830–1860* (New York: Oxford University Press, 1967) supplements the contemporary Francis Grund, *Aristocracy In America* (New York: Harper & Row, 1959 reprint) on the class assumptions that the workies resented.

Additionally, several articles on the rise and decline of Loco Focoism as a political force are available. Leo Hershkowitz presents the definitive connection between nativism and Loco Focoism in his "The Native American Democratic Association of New York City, 1835–1836," *NYHSQ*, 46 (January 1962), 41–60, and "The Loco-Foco Party of New York: Its Origins and Career, 1835–1837," *NYHSQ*, 46 (July 1962), 305–29. William Trimble, "Diverging Tendencies in New York Democracy in the Period of the Locofocos," *AHR*, 24 (April 1919), 396–421, is the single best source for Democratic factionalism, Tammany's problems, and understanding of how the Equal Rights party set the stage for the problems of the 1840s. Glyndon Van Dusen's "Thurlow Weed and the Seventh Ward Bank Scandal," *NYH*, 26 (1945), 4–18, is illuminating on the greed exhibited by the legislature.

The workies left a clear imprint of their attitudes and activities in the newspapers that they spawned: *Free Enquirer* (1830), the *Working Man's Advocate*, with its various changes in title (1829–1837), *The Man*, (1834–1835), *The Democrat* (1836), and the *New Era* (1837–1841). For the nativists I used *Courier and Enquirer* (1834–1836), Noah's *Evening Star* (1835–1838), *Spirit of '76* (1835), *New York American* (1835), and the *American Citizen* (1835). Samuel Morse's pamphlet, *Foreign Conspiracy against the Liberties of the United States* (New York: Leavitt, Lord & Company, 1835) is good for the nativist mentality. For traditional Whig views, see Horace Greeley's *The New Yorker* (1835–1841), *Daily Express* (1837–1838), and the maverick *Courier and Enquirer*. The *Evening Post* (1830–1838) is a balance against the *New-York Times* (1834–1837).

In addition to the manuscripts already mentioned, particularly the Marcy and Van Buren Papers, smaller ones had some illuminating letters: Luther Braddish Papers (NYSL), the William Seward Papers (NYSL), and one Byrdsall letter to Curtis in the New-York Historical Society.

CHAPTER 9 (1838–1842)

The most comprehensive study of the school crisis is in Vincent Lannie, *Public Money and Parochial Education* (Cleveland: Case Western Reserve University Press, 1969). Edward M. Connors, *Church-State Relationships in Education in the State of New York* (Washington: Catholic University of America Press, 1951) and John Pratt, *Religion, Politics, and Diversity: the Church-State Theme in New York History* (Ithaca: Cornell University Press, 1967) are excellent background surveys. For my discussion, I have also used several articles: Henry Hald, "The Catholic School Debate of 1840," *Catholic World*, 136 (1932), 38–44; Joseph J. McCadden, "Bishop Hughes Versus the Public School Society of New York," *Catholic Historical Review*, 50 (1964), 13–34; John W. Pratt, "Governor Seward and the New York City School Controversy, 1840–1842," *NYH*, 42 (1961), 351–64; and Glyndon Van Dusen, "Seward and the School Question Reconsidered," *JAH*, 52 (1965), 313–19. John Garraty, "Silas Wright and the

Election of 1840 in New York," *NYH*, 28 (1947), 288–303, is a good summary of Democratic politics.

For contemporary materials, Seward is represented in *The Works of William Seward*, edited by George E. Baker, 3 vols. (New York: J.S. Redfield, 1853). For Bishop Hughes, see: John R.S. Hassard, *Life of the Most Reverend John Hughes, D.D.* (New York: D. Appleton & Company, 1866), and Lawrence Kehoe's *Complete Works of the Most Reverend John Hughes, D.D.* (New York: American News Company, 1865). Two histories of the New York City school system are vital: William O. Bourne, *History of the Public School Society of the City of New York* (New York: William Wood and Company, 1870); and Thomas Boese, *Public Education in the City of New York* (New York: Harper & Bros., 1869). Stephen Allen's Memoirs in the New-York Historical Society gives a good insight into Democratic xenophobia. Six pamphlets are good. For the school question, *Debate Before the Common Council on the Catholic Petition, Respecting the Common School Fund, and the Public School System of Education in the City of New York* (New York: 1840); for Whig frauds in the 1840 election, James Glentworth, *A Statement of the Frauds on the Election Franchise in the City of New York* (New York: 1840); and for pro- and anti-Irish views, Mike Walsh, *Sketches of the Speeches and Writings of Michael Walsh* (New York: 1843); *The Only Genuine and Authenticated Report of Morgue More O'Molahan's Dream on the School Question* (New York: 1841); Barney O'Democrat [?], *The Irish Office-Hunter* (New York: 1838), and William Stoddard, *The Royal Decree of Scanderoon* (New York: 1869).

There are two basic books on American nativism: Louis Scisco, *Political Nativism in New York State* (New York: Columbia University Press, 1901), and Ray C. Billington, *The Protestant Crusade 1800–1860* (New York: Macmillan, 1938). Several studies on the Irish are useful: Stephen Byrne, *Irish Emigration to the United States* (New York: Catholic Publishing Society, 1873); Jonathan Greenleaf, *A History of the Churches of All Denominations in the City of New York* (New York: E. French; Portland, Hyde, Lord & Duren, 1842); John F. Maguire, *The Irish In America* (New York: D. & J. Sadlier & Company, 1887); and James R. Bayley, *A Brief Account of the Catholic Church on the Island of New York* (New York: E. Dunigan & Brother, 1853). The best of these books is William Shannon, *The American Irish* (New York: Macmillan, 1963). For a general view of immigration, see Jesse Chickering, *Immigration into the United States* (Boston: Charles C. Little and James Brown, 1848).

The major sources for the school controversy and the Whigs are in the William Seward Papers and the Thurlow Weed Papers in the University of Rochester. The Van Buren Papers contain information on general politics, but little on the school question. The *Evening Post* (1838–1842), the *Albany Argus* (1840–1842), the *New Era* (1838–1841), and the *New York*

*Herald* (1838–1842) cover Tammany's side of the story. The *Truth Teller* (1840–1842) is good for an anti-Seward Irish viewpoint. For the Whigs, I used the *Daily Express* (1838–1842), *The New Yorker* (1838–1841), and Webb's *Courier and Enquirer* (1838–1842). The *New York Observer* (1840–1842) gives the Protestant, pro-Public School Society attitude.

## CHAPTERS 10, 11, AND 12 (1843–1852)

As general background for the unrest of this period, I suggest: Herbert Donovan, *The Barnburners* (New York: New York University Press, 1925); Alexander Flick, *Samuel Tilden: A Study in Political Sagacity* (New York: Dodd, Mead & Company, 1939); John Garraty, *Silas Wright* (New York: Columbia University Press, 1949); Philip Foner, *Business and Slavery* (Chapel Hill: University of North Carolina Press, 1941); Florence Gibson, *The Attitudes of New York Irish Towards National Affairs, 1848–1898* (New York: Columbia University Press, 1954); Ransom Gillet, *The Life and Times of Silas Wright*, 2 vols. (Albany: Joel Munsell, 1874); Charles B. Going, *David Wilmot, Free Soiler* (New York: D. Appleton & Company, 1924); Holman Hamilton, *Prologue to Conflict: The Crisis and Compromise of 1850* (New York: W.W. Norton & Company, 1966); Ralph Harlow, *Gerrit Smith* (New York: H. Holt and Company, 1939); Dennis Lynch, *An Epoch and a Man: Martin Van Buren and his Times* (New York: Liveright, 1929); Eugene McCormac, *James K. Polk: A Political Biography* (Berkeley: University of California Press, 1922); Charles McCoy, *Polk and the Presidency* (Austin: University of Texas Press, 1960); James Paul, *Rift in the Democracy* (Philadelphia: University of Pennsylvania Press, 1951); Stewart Mitchell, *Horatio Seymour of New York* (Cambridge: Harvard University Press, 1938); Champlain Morrison, *Democratic Politics and Sectionalism* (Chapel Hill: University of North Carolina Press, 1967); Roy F. Nichols, *Franklin Pierce* (Philadelphia: University of Pennsylvania Press, 1931); Roy F. Nichols, *The Democratic Machine, 1850–1854* (New York: Columbia University Press, 1924); Robert Rayback, *Millard Fillmore* (Buffalo: H. Stewart and Company, 1959); Glyndon Van Dusen, *William H. Seward* (New York: Oxford University Press, 1967); Charles Sellers, *James K. Polk: Continentalist, 1843–1846* (Princeton: Princeton University Press, 1967); Helen Zahler, *Eastern Workingmen and National Land Policy, 1829–1862* (New York: Columbia University Press, 1942); and David Ellis, *Landlords and Farmers in the Hudson-Mohawk Region, 1750–1850* (Ithaca: Cornell University Press, 1946).

Robert Ernst, "Economic Nativism in New York State During the 1840s" *NYH*, 29 (1948), 170–86, and Ira Leonard, "The Rise and Fall of the American Republican Party in New York City, 1843–1845," *NYHSQ*, 50 (April 1966), 151–92, are excellent on xenophobia. Two pamphlets cover the same topic: *Proceedings of a Meeting in Favor of Municipal Reform,*

*22 March 1844* (New York: 1844), and *The Declaration of Principles of the Native American Convention* (New York: 1845). On Polk's patronage policy, see Norman Graebner, "James K. Polk: A Study in Federal Patronage," *MVHR*, 38 (1952), 613–32, and Barrett Learned, "The Sequence of Appointments to Polk's Original Cabinet: A Study in Chronology, 1844–1845," *AHR*, 30 (October 1924), 76–81. Matthew A. Fitzsimmons's "Calhoun's Bid for the Presidency, 1841–1844," *MVHR*, 38 (June 1951), 39–60, is excellent on internal Tammany politics. For the Free Soilers, four articles are vital: John D.P. Fuller, "The Slavery Question and the Movement to Acquire Mexico," *MVHR*, 21 (1934), 31–48; Julian Platt, "John L. O'Sullivan and Manifest Destiny," *NYH*, 14 (July 1933), 213–34; Joseph Rayback, "Martin Van Buren's Desire for Revenge in the Campaign of 1848," *MVHR*, 40 (1954), 707–16; and Eric Foner, "Racial Assumptions of the New York Free Soilers," *NYH*, 46 (October 1965), 311–29. Dixon Ryan Fox's "The Negro Vote in Old New York," *PSQ*, 32 (1917), 252–75, helps clarify the Hall's attitude. Sheldon Harris, "John Louis O'Sullivan and the Election of 1844 in New York," *NYH*, 41 (July 1960), 149–68; and Hershel Parker, "Gansevoort Melville's Role in the Campaign of 1844," *NYHSQ*, 49 (April 1965), 143–74, are interesting sidelights. Merle Curti, "Young America," *AHR*, 32 (October 1926), 34–55; and Herbert Johnson, "Magyar-Mania in New York City: Louis Kossuth and American Politics," *NYHSQ*, 48 (July 1964), 237–50, provide some additional background on Marcy's 1852 presidential bid.

Horace Greeley, *Recollections of a Busy Life* (New York: J.B. Ford & Company, 1868) helps to explain some of his positions. For Thurlow Weed see his *Autobiography*, edited by Harriet A. Weed (Boston: Houghton, Mifflin Company, 1883) and Glyndon Van Dusen, *Thurlow Weed: The Wizard of the Lobby* (Boston: Little, Brown and Company, 1947). James Polk's *Diary*, edited by Milo Quaife, 4 vols. (Chicago: A.C. McClung & Company, 1910) reveals the President's thoughts on New York politics. Thomas Marshall, "Diary and Memoranda of William L. Marcy," *AHR*, 12 (1919), 444–62, has some pertinent material. *The Speeches, Correspondence, Etc. Of the Late Daniel S. Dickinson*, edited by John Dickinson, 2 vols. (New York: G.P. Putnam & Sons, 1867), contains little of the fire that made Dickinson such a controversial figure. *The Letters and Literary Memorials of Samuel J. Tilden*, edited by John Bigelow, 2 vols. (New York: Harper & Bros., 1885) has Martin Van Buren's statement of free soil principles.

Three pamphlets cover the political ferment that spawned the Van Burenite walkout at the 1848 national convention: *The Syracuse Convention, Its Spurious Origin & Oppressive & Anti-Republican Action* (Albany: 1847); the *Herkimer Convention: The Voice of the People!* (New York: 1847); and the *New York State Convention Held at the Capitol, January 26 & January 27, 1848* (Albany: 1848).

The Van Buren and Marcy papers are basic for Barnburner and Hunker views, respectively. The James Polk Papers (LC) reveal much of what was taking place among New York Democrats. For nativism, see the James Harper Papers (NYHS). The Edmund Burke Papers (LC) and the Lewis Cass Papers (the University of Michigan) contain a few Dickinson letters. Edwin Croswell's letter to William Seaver (NYSL) a fellow editor, though few in number, are very good for Hunkerism, while the James Wadsworth (UR), John Dix (CU), and Azariah Flagg (CU) Papers are excellent for the Barnburners. The Fairchild Collection (NYHS) contains many Marcy-Seymour letters. The Gerrit Smith Papers (Syracuse University) has several letters that describe the impact of the Free Soil Party on old-line Abolitionists. The Franklin Pierce Papers, on microfilm, contains important letters written by local politicians in the period from June to November, 1852. The Samuel Tilden Papers (NYPL) has much to offer on local politics in the pre-1848 period.

Newspapers again provide great quantities of historical data on Tammany. The *Evening Post* (1842–1852) and the *Morning News* (1844–1846) are Barnburner and Free Soil organs. The *New York Plebeian* (1843–1845) is a Hunker print. The *New York Herald* (1843–1852) generally remained anti-Van Buren, but I found it the best source for local news and reporting. Not far behind is the Whig *New York Times* (1851–1852). The *New York Tribune* (1841–1852) is firmly Whig. The *Subterranean* (1845–1847) and *Young America* (1847) inherited the Democracy's workie, radical wing. The *Sunday Times and Noah's Weekly Messenger* (1847–1851) is a delight for its political insights and Noah's reminiscences.

CHAPTERS 13 AND 14 (1852–1860)

In a way, the history of Tammany Hall in the 1850s is an extended biography of several flamboyant politicos. Edgcumb Pinchon, *Daniel Sickles, Hero of Gettysburg and Yankee King of Spain* (Garden City: Doubleday and Company, 1945) and William Swanburg, *Sickles the Incredible* (New York: Charles Scribner's Sons, 1956) are colorful but not overly reliable. A Citizen of New York [?], *A Model Mayor—The Life of the Honorable Fernando Wood* (New York: 1855), Abijah Ingraham, *A Biography of Fernando Wood. A History of the Forgeries, Perjuries, & Other Crimes of our "Model" Mayor* (New York: 1856) and Donald McLeod, *Biography of Hon. Fernando Wood, Mayor of the City of New York* (New York: 1856) are to be used with caution, but each, in a way not intended, illustrate how controversial Wood appeared to his contemporaries. Samuel A. Pleasants, *Fernando Wood of New York* (New York: Columbia University Press, 1948) is scholarly but leaves much to be desired, particularly on Wood's relationships to Tammany and the registry system. Dennis Lynch's *Boss Tweed*, though weak on organizational politics, is good on Tweed as a man. William A. Bales, *Tiger in the Streets* (New York: Dodd, Mead and Company, 1962) and Croswell Bowen, *The Elegant Oakey* (New York: Oxford University Press, 1956) are well written but weak on analysis. Purdy, Shepard, and John Van Buren at present lack biographies.

In addition to Billington and Scisco, two books evoke the spirit of the Know-Nothing party: An American [?], *The Sons of the Sires* (Philadelphia: Lippincott, Grambo and Company, 1855), and Thomas Whitney, *A Defense of the American Policy* (New York: DeWitt and Davenport, 1856). Thomas Curran, "Seward and the Know-Nothings," *NYHSQ*, 41 (April, 1967), 141–59, explains the local Republican party's birth pains.

The softening of institutionalized political parties is covered in the following works: Gibson, *Attitudes of New York Irish;* Jeter Isely, *Horace Greeley and the Republican Party* (Princeton: Princeton University Press, 1947); James Klein, *President James Buchanan* (University Park: Pennsylvania State University Press, 1962); Leon Litwack, *North of Slavery* (Chicago: University of Chicago Press, 1961); George Fort Milton, *The Eve of Conflict: Stephen Douglas and the Needless War* (Boston and New York: Houghton Mifflin Company, 1934); and Roy F. Nichols, *The Disruption of American Democracy* (New York: Macmillan, 1948).

Several articles are useful: Philip Auchampaugh, "The Buchanan-Douglas Feud," *Journal of Illinois State History,* 25 (1946), 5–48; William Hartman, "The New York City Custom House: Seat of Spoils Politics," *NYH*, 34 (1953), 149–53; John Krout, "The Maine Law in New York Politics," *NYH*, 34 (1936), 260–72; Samuel Rezneck, "Influence of Depression Upon American Opinion, 1857–1859," *Journal of Economic History,* 2 (1942), 1–24; James Richardson, "Mayor Fernando Wood and the New York Police Force," *NYHSQ*, 40 (1966), 5–40; and Sidney Webster, "Mr. Marcy, the Cuban Question and the Ostend Manifesto," *PSQ*, 8 (March 1893), 1–32.

Several pamphlets and contemporary documents contain fascinating information. Bartholomew Purdy, *Affidavits before the Recorder Relative to Abuses in the City Government* (New York: 1854) is the best source for understanding the nature of municipal frauds and the Civic Reform party's rise to prominence. *Voice of the Radical Democracy of New York* (New York: 1856) is a ringing declaration of principles on the anti-slavery extensionism issue. By judiciously mixing the *New York Hards and Softs— Which is the True Democracy* (New York: 1856) and *The Softs, The True Democracy of the State of New York* (New York: 1856), one can get a clear picture of Tammany's factionalism. Two pamphlets are vital for understanding of the Tammany Society and its political importance: *Address of the Grand Council of the Tammany Society or Columbian Order Upon the Subject of Their Decision Relative to the Political Use of Tammany Hall* (New York: 1853), and *Statement of the Majority of the Grand Council of the Tammany Society or Columbian Order* (New York: 1857).

Despite such a wealth of material, it is necessary to turn almost exclusively to newspapers and manuscripts to find out about the full nature of local politics. Again, for the reporting of facts, the *New York Herald* (1852–1860) is superb. Then, too, the *New York Times* (1852–1860), although it became firmly Republican, is reliable. The Democratic *Daily News* (1855–1860) is strongly anti-Wood, as is the Republican *New York Tribune* (1852–1860). The *Irish-American* (1852–1860) is Democratic and pro-Wood. The *Volunteer* (1854) is a Tammany campaign newspaper, pro-Wood and pro-Seymour.

The James Buchanan Papers (LC, HSP, and Dickinson College) contain many important letters from Tammanyites. The Erastus Corning Papers (Albany Institute) are good for the new leaders of the upstate Democracy, as are John V.L. Pruyn's diaries in the New York State Library. The Stephen Douglas Papers (University of Chicago) are excellent on local politics. The Fairchild Collection, the Horatio Seymour Papers (NYHS, NYSL), and the Marcy Papers are also invaluable, particularly for the Lorenzo Shepard letters. Several Albert Ramsey letters in the New-York Historical Society are good for Isaac Fowler's manipulation of President Buchanan's dislike of Stephen Douglas. For the nativists, the Daniel Ullman Papers (NYHS) are strong for the Clayite, nationalist Whig transformation into anti-Seward, anti-Weed Know-Nothings. Fernando Wood's letters, like Burr's, are scattered in the New York State Library, the New York Public Library, and the New-York Historical Society. But the material in these collections is limited and generally disappointing.

## CHAPTER 15 (1860–1865)

Two basic books on the Civil War and its local political impact are: Frederick Phisterer, *New York in the War of the Rebellion, 1861–1865* (Albany: J.B. Lyon and Company, 1912), and Sidney Brummer, *Political History of New York During the Period of the Civil War* (New York: Columbia University Press, 1911). For books already cited, Foner's *Business and Slavery* and Gibson, *Attitudes of New York Irish* are judicious. On the draft question and the Emancipation issue, see: Eugene Murdock, *Patriotism, Limited, 1862–1865* (Kent: Kent State University Press, 1967); William Lofton, "Northern Labor and the Negro During the Civil War," *Journal of Negro History*, 34 (1949), 251–53; Albon Man, Jr., "Labor Competition and the New York Draft Riots of 1863," *Journal of Negro History*, 36 (1951), 375–405; David Barnes, *The Draft Riots in New York, July 1863* (New York: Baker and Godwin, 1863); James McCague, *The Second Rebellion: The Story of the New York City Draft Riots of 1863* (New York: Dial Press, 1968); Strong, *Diary;* and Mitchell, *Seymour.* For the Peace Democrats and Wood, I used: Edward Kirkland, *The Peacemakers of 1864* (New York: Macmillan, 1927); Gray Wood, *The Hidden Civil War: The Story of the Copperheads* (New York: Alfred A. Knopf, 1964 reprint);

Frank Klement, *The Copperheads in the Middle West* (Chicago: University of Chicago Press, 1960); and William Zornow's "McClellan and Seymour in the Chicago Convention," *Journal of the Illinois State Historical Society* 43 (1950), 282–95, and "Clement L. Vallandingham and the Democratic Party in 1864," *Historical and Philosophic Society of Ohio*, 29 (January 1961), 21–37. Noah Brooks, *Washington D.C. in Lincoln's Time* (New York: Collier, 1962 reprint) has several important insights on Wood's role. For another view, see *The Copperhead Catechism—For the Instruction of Such Politicians as are of Tender Years* (New York: 1864). For the 1864 election, see David Lindsey, *"Sunset" Cox: Irrepressible Democrat* (Detroit: Wayne State University Press, 1959); Charles Wilson, "McClellan's Changing Views on the Peace Plank of 1864," *AHR*, 38 (1933), 498–505; and Charles Murphy, "Samuel J. Tilden and the Civil War," *The South Atlantic Quarterly* 23 (1934), 261–71. For Republican politics and the Unionist movement, see: James D. Rawley, *Edwin D. Morgan, 1811–1888* (New York: Columbia University Press, 1955); John Stevens, *The Union Defense Committee of the City of New York* (New York: The Committee, 1885); William Zornow, *Lincoln and the Party Divided* (Norman: The University of Oklahoma Press, 1954); and Henry Pearson, *James S. Wadsworth of Geneseo* (New York: Charles Scribner's Sons, 1913). Basil Lee, *Discontent in New York City 1861–1865* (Washington, D.C.: Catholic University Press, 1943) is a general survey with excellent newspaper material.

Articles that should be consulted are: Milledge Bonham, "New York and the Election of 1860," *NYH*, 15 (April 1934), 124–32; Thomas Bonner, "Horace Greeley and the Secessionist Movement," *MVHR*, 38 (1951), 425–44; Bray Hammond, "The North's Empty Purse, 1861–1862," *AHR*, 62 (1961), 1–18; James Heslin " 'Peaceful Compromise' in New York City, 1860–1861," *NYHSQ*, 44 (October 1960), 349–62; John Pritchett, Francis Katzman, and Howard Dillon, "The Union Defense Committee of the City of New York during the Civil War," *NYHSQ*, 30 (July 1948), 142–60; and Frank Severance, "The Peace Conference at Niagara Falls in 1864," *BHSP*, 18 (1914), 79–84.

For some of Tammany's activities, see: *Documents Relative to the Withdrawal of Nelson J. Waterbury from the Canvass in the Eighth Congressional District* (New York: 1862); *Official Proceedings of the Democratic Republican Nominating Convention of Tammany Hall and the Joint Committee of Mozart and Tammany Halls, November 21, 1862* (New York: 1862); *Tammany Society or Columbian Order, Annual Celebration, July 4, 1863.*

The Erastus Corning Papers and the Stephen Douglas Papers have excellent material on the 1860 campaign. For the political nature of the war from a conservative standpoint, use: Corning Papers, Pruyn's diaries, the Seymour Papers, and the Fairchild Collection. The Dix Papers and the Wadsworth Papers are good for the Unionists. The Robert Lincoln Papers

(LC) have several interesting letters from local Democrats such as Wood and Cochrane. The Manton Marble and George McClellan Papers, both in the Library of Congress, have excellent material on the 1864 campaign and local politics in general. The Caleb Cushing Papers (LC) has some material on Wood, the Trent Affair, and the 1861 mayoralty election.

The *New York Herald*, the *New York Tribune*, and the *New York Times*, all for 1860–1865, though preoccupied by the war, have vital information on local politics. Wood's *Daily News* (1860–1864), though it did not publish in 1862, is a sound source for the Peace Democrats. The *Journal of Commerce* (1860–1863) and the *Irish-American* (1860–1865) were conservative in politics. The *New York World* (1862–1865), normally for the Peace Democrats, has much to say about Tammany and the war. Above all else, the *New York Leader* (1860–1865) was my major source for Tammany and Tweed. No study of local politics in this period can be made without its full use.

# NOTES TO CHAPTERS

## 1. THE EARLY TAMMANY SOCIETY

1. Samuel L. Mitchill, *The Life, Exploits and Precepts of Tammany: the Famous Indian Chief . . . Being the Anniversary Oration Pronounced before the Tammany Society . . . May 12, 1795* (New York, 1795); Edwin Kilroe, *Saint Tammany and the Origin of the Society of Tammany or Columbian Order in the City of New York* (New York: Columbia University Press, 1913), 1–110.

2. Journal and Rules of the Council of Sachems of St. Tammany's Society, 1789–1795, Minutes of Tammany Society or Columbian Order, 1791–1795, 1799–1801, Edwin Kilroe Collection, CU; Minutes of the Committee of Amusement of the Tammany Society, 1791–1795, NYPL.

3. *New York Journal*, August 3, 10, 17, 1790; May 14, 1791, October 17, 1792, May 22, 1799; Edward de Lancey, "Columbian Celebration of 1792," *Magazine of American History*, 29 (January 1893), 1–18.

4. *Evening Post*, July 1, 1813; *National Advocate*, October 9, 1813; Minutes of the Tammany Society or Columbian Order, 1815–1845, May 26, 1815, October 21, 1816, NYPL.

5. *New York Journal*, June 1, 1790; Samuel Berrian, *An Oration Delivered before the Tammany Society or Columbian Order, July 4, 1811* (New York: 1811), 21; The Secret Constitution of the Society of Tammany or Columbian Order in the City of New York, August 9, 1813, Kilroe Collection; *National Advocate*, December 15, 1814; Kilroe, *Tammany*, 128.

6. Marinus Willett to DeWitt Clinton, March 11, 1790, DeWitt Clinton Papers, CU; Minutes of the Tammany Society or Columbian Order, October 31, 1791, NYPL; *New York Journal*, May 22, 1799; *American Citizen*, June 4, 1806.

7. Pintard to Jeremy Belknap, October 11, 1790, cited in Kilroe, *Tammany*, 135–36; *New York Journal*, May 14, 1791; "Bye-Laws of the Society of Tammany or Columbian Order in the City of New York, May 4, 1804," *Tammaniana of Edwin Kilroe* (New York: 1934), 144–45, Kilroe Collection. This typescript is a valuable source for early Tammany Society constitutions and miscellaneous information.

8. *New York Journal*, September 3, 1789; "Foreword, A Brother of 1776 and One of Surviving Founders." Constitution of the Tammany Society or Columbian Order, November 10, 1817, Kilroe Collection.

9. *New York Journal*, May 12, 1792; *Evening Post*, January 19, 1795; Frederick R. Stevens, "New York in the Society of the Cincinnati," *NYH*, 25 (1944), 18–34.

10. Pintard to Walter Livingston, January 18, September 1, 1792, Livingston Papers, NYHS; Elias Boudinot to Hamilton, May 23, 1796, Hamilton Papers, LC;

*Evening Post*, February 18, 1808; Matthew L. Davis to Henry Clay, July 13, 1837, Henry Clay Transcripts, OSHS; Walter M. Whitehill, "John Pintard's Antiquarian Society," *NYHSQ*, 45 (October 1961), 346–64.

11. Josiah Odgen Hoffman to Horatio Gates, May 7, 1792, Gates Papers, NYHS; *New York Journal*, May 19, 1792; William Pitt Smith, "An Oration Before the Tammany Society, May 12, 1790," *New York Magazine*, 1 (1790), 294.

12. Receipts and Expenditures of Tammany Society or Columbian Order, 1789–1795, Kilroe Collection; Tammany Membership Lists, *Tammaniana of Edwin Kilroe* (New York: 1924), 3–202, Kilroe Collection. This typescript contains a list of all Tammany Society members, a year by year listing of the Council of Sachems, and the membership of the Tammany Tontine.

13. James Cheetham, *Political Equality and the Corporation of New York* (New York: 1800); J. Hampden Dougherty, "Constitutions of New York," *PSQ*, 3 (September 1888), 489–519; J. M. Gitterman, "The Council of Appointment in New York," *ibid.*, 80–95.

14. *New York Journal*, July 24, 1788; James Hughes to John Smith, February 27, 1789, John Smith Papers, NYHS; Whitefield Bell, Jr., "The Federal Procession of 1788," *NYHSQ*, 46 (January 1962), 4–40; Alfred Young, *The Democratic Republicans of New York: Their Origins, 1763–1797* (Chapel Hill: University of North Carolina Press, 1967), 3–105.

15. *New York Journal*, March 19, April 9, 23, 27, 30, 1789, April 18, 1790; John Armstrong to Gates, October 4, 1789, Gates Papers; David Gelston to John Smith, April 17, 21, 1970, Smith Papers.

16. Tammany Membership Lists, *Tammaniana of Edwin Kilroe*, 3–202.

17. *New York Journal*, July 20, 1790, March 30, April 4, 1791; Robert R Livingston to Morgan Lewis, January 27, 1791, Livingston Papers; George Clinton to James Monroe, February 16, 1791, Monroe Papers, LC; Herbert Parmet and Marie Hecht, *Aaron Burr: Portrait of an Ambitious Man* (New York: Macmillan Company, 1967), 59–67.

18. *Daily Advertiser*, July 23, 1791; *New York Journal*, August 10, 13, October 5, 1791; Joseph Davis, *Essays in the Earlier History of American Corporations* (Cambridge: Harvard University Press, 1917), 1: 370–409. For more information see the letters of Seth Johnson to Andrew Craigie, December 1791–March 1792, Craigie Papers, American Antiquarian Society.

19. *New York Journal*, February 11, 1792, cited by William Miller, "A Note on the Early History of the Tammany Society of New York," *NYH*, 30 (1939), 463–67.

20. *Plan of the New-York Tammanial Tontine Association* (New York: 1792).

21. *New York Journal*, February 24, 29, June 27, 1792; Alfred Young, "The Mechanics and the Jeffersonians: New York, 1789–1801," *Labor History*, 5 (1964), 221–55.

22. *New York Journal*, February 15, 25, March 31, April 11, 14, 18, 1792; Jabez Hammond, *The History of Political Parties in the State of New York* (Albany: Van Benthuysen, 1842), 1: 62–68; Frank Monaghan, *John Jay: Defender of Liberty* (New York and Indianapolis, 1935), 325–41.

23. Rufus King to Gouverneur Morris, September 1, 1792, *The Life and Correspondence of Rufus King*, ed. by Charles R. King (New York: G.P. Putnam's Sons, 1894–1900), 1: 425; James Cheetham, *Nine Letters on the Subject of Aaron Burr* (New York: 1803), 9–16; George Dangerfield, *Chancellor Robert R. Livingston of New York* (New York: Harcourt, Brace and Company, 1960), 256–64.

24. Jonathan Havens to Smith, June 18, 1792, Smith Papers; Robert R Livingston to Edward Livingston, June 19, July 20, October 1, 1792, Livingston Papers; Jefferson to Madison, June 29, 1792, Madison Papers, LC; Monroe to Jefferson, July 17, 1792, Monroe Papers, LC.

25. *New York Journal,* March 14, 17, 21, 28, April 4, 1792; Josiah Ogden Hoffman to Ebenezer Foote, April 29, 1792, Foote Papers, LC; Broadside, "To the Free Electors in the State of New York" (New York: 1792); Tammany Membership Lists, *Tammaniana of Edwin Kilroe,* 3–202.

26. *New York Journal,* July 7, 1792; William Pitt Smith, *Observations on Conventions Made in a Tammanical Debate* (New York: 1793). See also Burr to Monroe, September 10, 1792, Monroe Papers; Melancton Smith and David Gelston to Pierpont Edwards, August 20, 1792, Melancton Smith Papers, NYSL.

27. *New York Journal,* September 3, 24, 1789; Beatrice Hyslop, "American Press Reports of the French Revolution, 1789–1794," *NYH,* 42 (October 1958), 329–48.

28. *New York Journal,* May 14, July 13, 17, September 3, December 26, 1792.

29. *Ibid.,* December 29, 1792.

30. *Ibid.,* October 2, 1792, March 20, 30, April 6, May 15, 1793.

31. John Armstrong to Gates, January 12, 1793, Gates Papers; Edward Livingston to Robert R Livingston, May 15, 1793, Livingston Papers.

32. *New York Journal,* June 12, 15, 19, 1793.

33. *Ibid.,* July 20, August 3, 1793.

34. *Daily Advertiser,* August 14, 1793; Robert R Livingston to Edward Livingston August 15, 1793, Livingston Papers; *Columbian Gazetteer,* September 23, October 14, November 25, 1793; Schuyler to Hamilton, December 15, 1793, Hamilton Papers; Harry Ammon, "The Genet Mission and the Development of American Political Parties," *JAH,* 52 (March 1966), 725–41.

35. Pierre Van Cortland to David Gelston, January 30, 1794, Van Cortland–Van Wyck Papers, NYPL; *New York Journal,* February 15, 19, March 22, 1794; *Columbian Gazetteer,* February 27, April 17, June 9, 1794; William Miller, "First Fruits of Republican Organization: Political Aspects of the Congressional Election of 1794," *Pennsylvania Magazine of History and Biography,* 63 (1939), 118–43.

36. *New York Journal,* May 31, 1794; Eugene Link, *Democratic-Republican Societies, 1790–1800* (New York: Columbia University Press, 1942; Young, *Democratic Republicans,* 392–412.

37. *New York Journal,* March 8, May 14, 1794; *Columbian Gazetteer,* July 7, 1794.

38. *New York Journal,* March 12, 15, 1794; Edward Livingston to DeWitt Clinton, March 30, 1794, Clinton Papers, CU; Peter Schuyler to Walter Livingston, March 30, 1794, Livingston Papers.

39. Robert R Livingston to Edward Livingston, April 18, 1794, *ibid.;* New York *Journal,* April 20, May 14, June 2, July 5, 7, 1794; Burr to Monroe, May 30, 1794, Monroe Papers.

40. *New York Journal,* January 10, 14, 17, February 15, 18, 1795; *Evening Post,* January 19, 21, 26, February 4, 1795; *Daily Advertiser,* January 22, 1795; Leland Baldwin, *Whiskey Rebels* (Pittsburgh: University of Pittsburgh Press, 1939), 259–71.

41. *Evening Post,* January 30, 1795; *Daily Advertiser,* January 31, February 9, 10, 28, 1795; List of Sachems, 1789–1924, *Tammaniana of Edwin Kilroe,* 212.

42. *New York Journal,* February 4, 8, 18, 1795.

43. *Ibid.,* February 4, 25, 1795; *Daily Advertiser,* February 9, 25, 31, 1795.

44. *New York Journal,* February 28, April 8, July 8, 1795; March 6, 1799; *Evening Post,* June 2, 1795; *Time Piece,* June 29, August 6, 1798. For more on the Keteltas Affair, see Young, *Democratic-Republicans,* 468–95.

45. James Dawson to Madison, November 28, December 12, 1799, Madison Papers; Tammany Membership Lists, *Tammaniana of Edwin Kilroe,* 3–202. The list extends that of Peter Paulson, "The Tammany Society and the Jeffersonian Movement in New York City," *NYH,* 34 (1953), 72–84.

46. *New York Journal,* July 6, November 30, 1799, January 8, 1800.

47. *American Citizen,* May 16, July 5, November 28, 1800, February 25, May 16, July 5, 7, 1801; Matthew Davis, *An Oration, delivered in St. Paul's Church, on the Fourth of July, 1800, Before the . . . Tammany Society or Columbian Order and Other Associations* (New York: 1800); William Boyd to DeWitt Clinton, May, 1801, Clinton Papers; List of the Council of Sachems, *Tammaniana of Edwin Kilroe,* 210; Mordecai Meyers, *Reminiscences, 1780 to 1814* (Washington, D.C.: Crane Publishing Company, 1900), 11–12; Gustavus Myers, *The History of Tammany Hall* (New York: Boni & Liveright, 1917), 11–15.

Part of the folklore surrounding Tammany Hall's role in the 1800 election sprang from a confusion of terms on one hand, and an incorrect assumption by Gustavus Myers, Tammany's best historian, on the other.

In 1900 the descendants of Major Mordecai Meyers, a minor figure in Burr's Little Band, published the major's short *Reminiscences.* In it, Meyers recalled Burr's frenetic 1800 campaigning, and supposedly recalled a dialogue in which Burr said to "keep up frequent meetings at Tammany Hall until the election." Subsequent historians, then, suggest that the Tammany Hall the major mentioned was the mature Tammany Hall so familiar to most people. Major Meyers was wrong; perhaps not in memory, but certainly in facts. The Tammany Hall he cites was not a political entity; it was merely the Tammany Society's temporary wigwam. Throughout the 1790s scattered references in newspapers and pamphlets refer to Tammany Hall, but they denoted a building, not a political party.

Gustavus Myers made a similar mistake. Citing a speech made by Matthew Davis in 1809 [see page 39] as proof, Myers concluded that Burr indirectly manipulated the machine that was Tammany Hall and was responsible for its victory. Myers was only partially correct. Burr indeed had spearheaded Republican strategy in the local assembly election and deserved full credit for the party's success, but he did not direct Tammany Hall since it simply did not exist in any political sense.

48. *American Citizen,* November 30, December 8, 23, 1801; Davis to Albert Gallatin, December 21, 1801, Gallatin Papers, NYHS.

49. *Evening Post,* December 18, 1801; Tammany Membership Lists, List of the Council of Sachems, *Tammaniana of Edwin Kilroe,* 3–202, 210–12; Myers, *Tammany Hall,* 15–16; Nathan Schachner, *Aaron Burr, A Biography* (New York: Frederick A. Stokes, 1937), 175.

50. *American Citizen,* May 29, 31, June 3, 1802; *Evening Post,* June 4, 8, 1802; *Morning Chronicle,* October 1, 14, 1802.

51. *American Citizen,* May 16, 1803, February 3, 1804.

52. Samuel Mitchill to Madison, May 3, 1804, Madison Papers; *American Citizen,* May 7, 1804; John Armstrong to Ambrose Spencer, June 4, 1804, Rokeby Collection, NYHS; Theodorus Bailey to Thomas Jefferson, June 9, 1804, Jefferson Papers, LC; Broadside, "To the Republican Electors of the State of New York" (New York: 1804), NYSL; Broadside, "New York, Address, 1804" (New York: 1804),

NYPL; Tammany Membership List, List of the Council of Sachems, *Tammaniana of Edwin Kilroe,* 3–202, 214. The broadsides contain the names of men who acted as a central committee or ward representatives for the respective candidates.

53. *American Citizen,* May 14, 1804, July 6, 9, 1805.

54. *Ibid.,* June 11, 1806; Tammany Membership Lists, List of the Council of Sachems, *Tammaniana of Edwin Kilroe,* 213–16, 277–359.

55. Elbridge Gerry to Madison, July 5, 1807, Madison Papers; Macon to Gallatin, July 12, 1807, Gallatin Papers; Jefferson to Armstrong, July 17, 1807, Jefferson to Duane, July 20, 1807, Jefferson Papers.

56. *American Citizen,* July 1, 3, 8, 27, 1807; *Evening Post,* July 2, 1807; George Clinton to Jefferson, July 9, 1807, Armstrong to Jefferson, October 1, 1807, Jefferson Papers.

57. *Public Advertiser,* July 7, 8, 11, 12, 21, 1807.

## 2. THE BIRTH OF TAMMANY HALL

1. George Clinton to DeWitt Clinton, June 17, 1807, Clinton Papers; *Evening Post,* November 28, 1807. See also Henry Remsen to Edgar, July 9, 1808, Edgar Papers.

2. *American Citizen,* November 25, December 1, 2, 3, 4, 12, 24, 28, 29, 31, 1807, January 2, 6, 7, 11, 15, 18, 23, 1808; *Public Advertiser,* December 3, 4, 12, 28, 1807; George Clinton to Pierre Van Cortland, Jr., December 12, 1807, Van Cortland Papers; James Cheetham, *Peace or War? Or Thoughts on Our Affairs with England* (New York: 1807).

3. George Clinton to DeWitt Clinton, January 7, 1808, Clinton Papers; Robert R. Livingston to Madison, January 7, 8, 1808, Morgan Lewis to Madison, January 9, 1808, Madison Papers; Davis to William P. Van Ness, February 3, 1808, Matthew Davis Papers, NYHS.

4. *Public Advertiser,* January 1, 8, 19, February 1, 1808; *American Citizen,* January 13, 20, 1808; Granger to Jefferson, January 18, 1808, Jefferson Papers.

5. George Clinton to DeWitt Clinton, February 13, 18, 26, 1808, Clinton Papers; DeWitt Clinton to John Smith, February 20, 1808, Smith Papers; *American Citizen,* March 10, 1808; Jefferson to Thomas Mann Randolph, June 28, William Plumer to Jefferson, July 22, 1808, Jefferson Papers; *Evening Post,* October 12, 14, 1808; William Pope to Madison, November 9, 1808, Madison Papers; M. Ostrogorski, "The Rise and Fall of the Nominating Caucus," *AHR,* 5 (1899–1900), 253–83.

6. Francis Bloodgood to Matthias Tallmadge, February 2, 1808, Matthias Tallmadge Papers, NYHS; William Keteltas to Jefferson, March 31, 1808, Jefferson Papers; Martin Van Buren to DeWitt Clinton, April 16, 30, 1808, Clinton Papers; James Main to Madison, April 18, May 11, James Jay to Madison, May 11, Davis to Madison, May 16, Morgan Lewis to Madison, May 16, 1808, Madison Papers; *Public Advertiser,* May 30, 31, 1808.

7. *American Citizen,* September 1, 6, 13, 15, 17, 22, 1808; *Evening Post,* September 16, 1808; *Public Advertiser,* September 8, 11, 17, 18, 1808.

8. *Columbian Gazetteer,* March 31, 1794; *Public Advertiser,* February 18, 21, 1808; *Evening Post,* February 18, 19, 1808; *American Citizen,* February 20, March 18, 1808.

9. *Ibid.,* March 28, April 12, May 4, 1808; Tammany Society or Columbian

Order, *Wallabout Committee Account of Interment of Remains of American Patriots* (New York: 1864).

10. *Public Advertiser*, July 5, 16, September 10, 1808; Davis to William P. Van Ness, August 1808, Davis Papers.

11. David Thomas to Jefferson, October 20, 1808, Jefferson Papers; *Public Advertiser*, October 22, December 10, 1808.

12. Morgan Lewis to Madison, December 29, 1808, Madison Papers; Mumford to Edgar, December 12, 1808, Edgar Papers; *Public Advertiser*, January 14, 17, 18, 28, 31, 1809; Morgan Lewis to Foote, January 29, 1809, Foote Papers, NYSL.

13. *American Citizen*, February 1, 14, 1809.

14. *Public Advertiser*, January 30, February 9, 11, 22, 1809; *Evening Post*, February 6, 23, 1809; Henry Dearborn to Tompkins, February 9, 1809, Tompkins, NYSL; *American Citizen*, March 1, 1809.

15. *Public Advertiser*, March 6, 8, 15, 18, 21, 25, 1809; *American Citizen*, March 13, 14, 15, 21, 25, 1809; *Evening Post*, April 1, 1809.

16. *American Citizen*, April 1, 7, 8, 13, 20, 25, May 11, 1809; *Evening Post*, April 2, 1809; Cheetham to DeWitt Clinton, April 4, 1809, Clinton Papers.

17. *Evening Post*, April 21, May 2, July 5, 1809; J.H. Tiffanis to Tompkins, April 24, 1809, Tompkins Papers; *Public Advertiser*, July 11, 1809.

18. Robert Macomb to Pierre Van Cortland, Jr., May, 1809, Van Cortland Papers; *Public Advertiser*, May 17, July 6, 1809; *American Citizen*, July 6, 1809.

19. *Ibid.*, July 18, 1809; *Public Advertiser*, July 22, 1809.

20. *Ibid.*, July 24, August 2, 1809; *American Citizen*, July 31, September 30, October 3, 1809; John Irving to William P. Van Ness, August 18, 1809, Van Ness Papers, NYHS.

21. *Public Advertiser*, September 12, 26, October 27, November 6, 10, 11, 21, 28, 29, 1809; *New York Columbian*, November 10, 25, 28, December 1, 1809; Elisha Williams to Foote, March 23, 1809, Foote Papers, NYSL.

22. Davis to William P. Van Ness, January 1, 2, February 10, 1810, Davis Papers; William Crawford to James Hamilton, January 8, 1810, Crawford Papers; LC; *Columbian*, January 26, February 15, March 16, April 26, 1810; DeWitt Clinton to Remsen, February 4, 1810, Clinton Papers; *American Citizen*, May 1, 1810; Madison to Jefferson, May 7, 1810, Madison Papers; Macomb to Tompkins, December 10, 1810, Tompkins Papers.

23. *Columbian*, August 13, September 6, October 12, November 21, 22, 24, 1810; Holt to Jefferson, October 25, 1810, Jefferson Papers; *Public Advertiser*, November 10, 1810; List of Holders of Stock for Building Tammany Hall, 1809–1819, *Tammaniana of Edwin Kilroe*, 467.

24. Davis to William P. Van Ness, February 13, 1810, Davis Papers; *Public Advertiser*, January 6, 1811; Spencer to Armstrong, January 18, 1811, Rokeby Collection; David Durham to Tompkins, January 24, 1811, Tompkins Papers; DeWitt Clinton to Peter Porter, February 4, 1811, Porter Papers, BHS; Jonas Humbert to Madison, July 8, 1811, Madison Papers.

25. *Public Advertiser*, January 7, 24, 28, 1811; DeWitt Clinton to Remsen, March 22, 1811, Clinton Papers, NYPL; Joseph Howland to Edgar, March 24, 1811, Edgar Papers; Walter Bowne to DeWitt Clinton, March 26, 1811, Clinton Papers, CU.

26. DeWitt Clinton to Remsen, March 16, 1811, Clinton Papers, NYPL; *Public Advertiser*, March 30, 1811; DeWitt Clinton to Edgar, April 2, 1811, Edgar Papers.

27. Davis to William P. Van Ness, June 3, December 26, 1811, Davis Papers.

28. *Public Advertiser,* February 4, 5, 9, 11, 28, March 4, 5, 15, 23, 30, 1811; *Columbian,* March 2, 16, 1811; Macomb to Tompkins March 4, 24, 1811, Tompkins Papers.

29. Foote to William P. Van Ness, April 1, 1811, Van Ness Papers; *Columbian,* April 6, 1811; DeWitt Clinton to Porter, April 10, 1811, Porter Papers.

30. *Public Advertiser,* April 13, 15, 23, 25, 26, 1811; *Columbian,* April 26, 1811.

31. *Public Advertiser,* May 4, 7, June 10, 1811; Morgan Lewis to Madison, May 12, 1811, Madison Papers.

32. Thomas Butler to DeWitt Clinton, March 12, 1808, Thomas Eddy to DeWitt Clinton, April 2, 1824, Clinton Papers; *Public Advertiser,* July 11, 16, December 12, 17, 1811; William Paulding to Tompkins, December 18, 1811, Tompkins Papers; Ronald Shaw, *Erie Water West* (Lexington: University of Kentucky Press, 1966), 22–55.

33. Davis to William P. Van Ness, January 8, 1811, Davis Papers; *Public Advertiser,* July 6, August 16, 1811; *Columbian,* July 12, 1811.

34. Gallatin to Davis, March 15, Tompkins to Gallatin, March 21, Davis to Gallatin, July 21, 1811, Gallatin Papers; *Columbian,* October 23, November 1, 18, 25, 27, 1811.

35. Mumford to George Clinton, January 1, 1812, George Clinton Papers, NYSL; *Columbian,* March 9, 1812.

36. *Public Advertiser,* July 24, August 27, 1811; William Paulding to Tompkins, January 16, 1812, Tompkins Papers; *Evening Post,* February 27, 1812; Dearborn to Jefferson, March 10, 1812, Jefferson Papers.

37. Davis to Gallatin, April 1, 1812, Gallatin Papers; *Public Advertiser,* May 15, 1812; *Evening Post,* July 29, 1812; Stephen Allen to Jesse Hoyt, November 28, 1832, *Lives and Opinions of Benjamin Franklin Butler and Jesse Hoyt,* ed. by William Mackenzie (Boston: Cook & Company, 1845), 70.

38. Davis to William P. Van Ness, January 23, 29, February 5, 15, 1812, Davis Papers; *Evening Post,* January 31, 1812; Macomb to Tompkins, February 1, Francis Cooper to Tompkins, February 3, 1812, Tompkins Papers; Bray Hammond, *Banks and Politics in America from the Revolution to the Civil War* (Princeton: Princeton University Press, 1957), 161–64.

39. Davis to William P. Van Ness, January 27, 1812, Davis Papers; *Columbian,* March 18, 1812; Hammond, *Political Parties,* 1: 306.

40. Samuel Osgood to [?], February 22, 1812, Osgood Papers, NYHS; *Columbian,* April 10, 1812; Don C. Sowers, *The Financial History of New York State, from 1789 to 1912* (New York: Columbia University Press, 1914), 48–49.

41. Beal Lewis to Tompkins, February 9, Macomb to Tompkins, March 31, April 4, William Irving to Tompkins, April 1, 1812, Tompkins Papers; Davis to Gallatin, April 1, 1812, Gallatin Papers; *Evening Post,* April 1, 1812.

42. Elam Tilden to Tompkins, April 6, Sylvanus Miller to Tompkins, April 30, 1812, Tompkins Papers; Ambrose Spencer to Armstrong, April 9, 29, 1812, Rokeby Collection; Edmund Genêt to George W. Clinton, April 12, 1812, Edmund Genêt Papers, NYHS; *Public Advertiser,* August 30, 1812.

43. Tallmadge to Pierre Van Cortland, Jr., April 9, 1812, Van Cortland Papers; Martin Van Buren to James Hamilton, December 28, 1828, cited by James Hamilton, *Reminiscences of Men and Events* (New York: Charles Scribner & Company, 1869), 81.

44. *Evening Post,* January 14, 23, February 2, 6, March 9, 10, 1812; DeWitt Clinton to Pierre Van Cortland, Jr., January 21, 1812, Van Cortland Papers;

Marinus Willett to Madison, January 26, Jacob Barker to Madison, February 24, 1812, Madison Papers; Robert Macomb to Edgar, January 28, 1812, Edgar Papers; *Columbian,* February 26, 1812.

45. DeWitt Clinton to Pierre Van Cortland, Jr., January 31, April 7, 1812, Van Cortland Papers; George Clinton to John Craemer, February 10, George Clinton to George W. Clinton, February 16, 1812, George Clinton Papers; *Columbian,* March 11, 17, 21, 28, April 23, 24, 1812; *Evening Post,* April 18, 19, 1812.

46. *Columbian,* April 28, 1812; *Evening Post,* April 30, May 4, 1812; Davis to Gallatin, May 1, 1812, Gallatin Papers.

47. Peter Schenck to Mitchill, May 2, John Haff to Mitchill, May 5, John Bingham to Mitchill, May 5, Adrian Hegeman to Mitchill, May 7, Mitchill to Madison, May 10, 1812, Madison Appointment Papers, National Archives.

48. *Columbian,* May 21, 22, 1812; Armstrong to Spencer, May 23, 1812, Rokeby Collection; Maturin Livingston to Gallatin, May 30, 1812, Gallatin Papers.

49. *Evening Post,* June 22, 23, 27, 1812; *Columbian,* June 24, June 3, 1812; *Public Advertiser,* June 25, 26, July 8, 1812; Robert Macomb to Tompkins, June 25, 1812, Tompkins Papers.

50. William Keteltas to Madison, September 2, 1812, Madison Papers; *Evening Post,* September 3, 1812; Joseph Gardner Swift, *The Memoirs of General Joseph Gardner Swift, LL.D., U.S.A.,* ed. by Ellery Harrison (Worcester: F.S. Blanchard & Co, 1890), 113.

51. King to Gore, September 19, 1812, *King's Writings,* 5: 276–80; *Public Advertiser,* September 19, 24, 30, October 16, 1812; *Columbian,* September 24, 1812; *Evening Post,* October 14, 1812; Pierre Van Wyck to Ethan Brown, September 17, 1812, Brown Papers; Duane to Jefferson, September 20, 1812, Jefferson Papers.

52. John Smith to Gallatin, October 6, Robert Tillotson to Gallatin, November 9, Morgan Lewis to Gallatin, November 10, 1812, Gallatin Papers; *Public Advertiser,* October 13, 16, 20, November 12, 13, 17, 1812; Spencer to Armstrong, December 22, 1812, Rokeby Collection.

53. Davis to William P. Van Ness, November 26, 1812, Davis Papers; Davis to Daniel Parker, September 20, 1814, Davis to George Strong, January 19, 1822, Gratz Collection, PHS; Davis to Matthew Carey, November 30, 1819, Edward Carey Gardiner Collection, PHS; *National Advocate,* May 16, 1826.

54. Maturin Livingston to Gallatin, January 8, 1813, Gallatin Papers; Spencer to Monroe, May 10, Haff to Monroe, May 22, 1813, Ferguson to Madison, January 22, Tompkins to Monroe, May 7, 1814, Clinton to Monroe, June 29, Tompkins to Dallas, July 8, Brockholst Livingston to Madison, July 15, 1816, Madison Appointment Papers; Tompkins to Meigs, April 25, July 9, Madison to Tompkins, July 9, 1814, Tompkins Papers; George White to DeWitt Clinton, June 29, 1818, Clinton Papers.

55. *Columbian,* January 6, 9, 16, February 8, 1813; *National Advocate,* January 8, 13, 15, 28, February 8, 1813; Jacob Barker to Benjamin Thompson, January 18, 1813, Miscellaneous Papers, NYHS; Hammond, *Political Parties,* 1: 343–45; Van Buren, *Autobiography,* 47–48.

56. *Columbian,* March 5, 26, April 20, May 3, 1813; *National Advocate,* March 6, 10, 22, May 1, 3, 1813; Spencer to Armstrong, March 31, 1813, Rokeby Collection; *Evening Post,* April 21, 1813.

57. Spencer to Armstrong, May 4, 1813, Rokeby Collection.

58. *National Advocate,* November 13, 1813; Madison to Tompkins, September 8,

October 14, 1814, Madison Papers; Tompkins to Porter, January 6, 1815, Porter Papers; Davis to William P. Van Ness, January 17, 1815, Davis Papers; Orville Holley to Luther Holley, February 15, 1815, Holley Family Papers, NYSL; Minutes of the Tammany Society, May 12, 1815, NYPL; John Ward, *Andrew Jackson: Symbol of An Age* (New York: Oxford University Press, 1955).

59. *National Advocate*, November 24, 1814, January 11, 1815; Minutes of the Tammany Society, July 3, 1815, NYPL; Gulian Verplanck, *A Fable for Statesmen and Politicians of All Parties and Descriptions, by Abimelech Coody, Esq., Formerly Ladies Shoemaker* (New York: 1814).

60. *National Advocate*, January 11, February 28, 1815; Spencer to Armstrong, January 17, 1815, Rokeby Collection; Davis to William P. Van Ness, February 18, 1815, Davis Papers; James Emott to King, February 19, 1815, *King's Writings*, 5: 573; Ruggles Hubbard to DeWitt Clinton, March 3, 8, 1815, Clinton Papers; Hugh Flick, "The Council of Appointment," *NYH*, 15 (1934), 274–75.

61. Naturalized Citizens of Irish Birth to Clinton, March 16, New York Common Council to Clinton, March 20, Rodney to Clinton, April 22, 1815, Clinton Papers; *National Advocate*, March 28, 1815.

### 3. THE SPIRIT OF TAMMANYISM

1. William W. Van Ness to Solomon Van Rensselaer, October 17, 1815, cited by Catherine Van Rensselaer Bonney, *A Legacy of Historical Gleanings* (Albany: Joel Munsell, 1875), 1: 326; Cadwallader Colden to Clinton, December 15, 1815, Ellicott to Clinton, January 18, 1816, William Darby to Clinton, January 23, 1822, Clinton Papers; Tactitus [DeWitt Clinton], *Canal Policy of the State of New York* (New York: 1822); David Hosack, *Memoir of DeWitt Clinton* (New York: J. Seymour, 1829), 406–18.

2. MacNeven to Clinton, March 11, Clinton to Ellicott, April 4, Clinton to Hammond, April 19, 1816, Clinton Papers; Porter to Monroe, March 25, 1816, Monroe Papers; Spencer to Armstrong, April 2, 1816, Rokeby Collection.

3. *National Advocate*, April 18, 1816; *Evening Post*, April 19, 26, 1816; Hosack, *Memoir*, 436–37; Van Buren, *Autobiography*, 84.

4. James Geddes to Clinton, April 24, 1816, Clinton Papers; *National Advocate*, May 4, 1816; Broadside, "The Grand Canal Defeated by a Democratic Senate," (New York: 1816) NYPL.

5. *National Advocate*, June 9, 1816; Charles Ferris, *An Oration Delivered before the Tammany Society or Columbian Order . . . in the City of New York* (New York: 1816).

6. Van Buren to Porter, February 5, 1817, Porter Papers; Porter to Van Buren, February 13, Robert Swartwout to Van Buren, February 20, Samuel Betts to Van Buren, February 26, Enos Throop to Van Buren, March 15, 1817, Van Buren Papers.

7. *National Advocate*, March 4, April 18, 1817; Van Buren, Notes on the Canal, April 15, 1817, Van Buren Papers; Van Buren to James Hamilton, December 20, 1828, *Reminiscences*, 63; *Sunday Times and Noah's Weekly Messenger*, September 30, 1849; Van Buren to [?], July 20, 1859, Herbert and Dorothy Metzger Papers, Cornell University.

8. Peter Irving to Van Buren, March 7, 1817, Van Buren Papers; *Columbian*, April 22, 1817; *Evening Post*, April 26, 1817; William Graham to William P. Van

Ness, April 28, 1817, Van Ness Papers, NYPL. Graham, a participant in the riot, gives an excellent account.

9. John Rodman, *An Oration Delivered Before the Tammany Society or Columbian Order, July 4, 1813* (New York: 1813); *National Advocate*, April 24, 1815; MacNeven to Clinton, February 27, 1816, Clinton Papers.

10. *Columbian*, February 11, 17, March 4, 1817; *Evening Post*, March 14, 1817.

11. John C. Spencer to Albert Tracy, March 13, 1817, Albert Tracy Papers, NYSL; *National Advocate*, April 26, 27, May 3, 23, 1817; *Evening Post*, May 2, 1817; Henry Meigs to Josiah Meigs, May 2, 1817, Meigs Papers, NYHS.

12. *National Advocate*, June 7, July 1, 10, 31, August 14, 17, 18, 1817.

13. Minutes of the Tammany Society or Columbian Order, July 4, 1817, NYPL; *National Advocate*, July 7, 1817; Mordecai Noah, *An Oration delivered to the Tammany Society or Columbian Order, July 4, 1817* (New York: 1817).

14. *National Advocate*, August 20, November 17, December 24, 1817.

15. Crawford to Gallatin, April 23, 1817, Gallatin Papers; Clinton to Pintard, August 7, 1817, Clinton Papers, NYHS; Clinton to Isaac Briggs, September 8, Clinton to Jonas Humbert, September 20, Crawford to Clinton, November 24, Clinton to King, December 13, 1817, Willett to Clinton, February 3, 1818, Clinton Papers; John King to Rufus King, January 8, 1818, *King's Writings*, 6: 102; Van Buren to Gorham Worth, April 27, 1818, Van Buren Papers; Van Buren, *Autobiography*, 124.

16. *National Advocate*, March 20, 1818.

17. *Columbian*, April 20, 28, 1818; *National Advocate*, April 21, 22, May 11, 1818; *Evening Post*, May 6, 1818; Myron Holley to Clinton, May 19, Clinton to Thomas O'Connor, June 26, 1818, Clinton Papers.

18. *National Advocate*, June 29, 1818.

19. *Evening Post*, January 7, 1819; *National Advocate*, January 12, 1819.

20. Clinton to Joseph Ellicott, February 23, 1819, "The Holland Land Company and Construction in Western New York," *Buffalo Historical Society Publications*, 23 (1919) 1: 41–42; Tactitus [DeWitt Clinton], *Canal Politics of the State of New York* (New York: 1822).

21. Ambrose Spencer to Albert Tracy, January 24, 1819, Tracy Papers; *Evening Post*, March 1, 1819; *National Advocate*, March 10, 1819; *Columbian*, March 14, 1819; Hammond, *Political Parties*, 1: 488–89.

22. John Spencer to Albert Tracy, May 28, 1818, Tracy Papers; Shaw Livermore, Jr., *The Twilight of Federalism, 1815–1830* (Princeton: Princeton University Press, 1962), 62–79.

23. James Hamilton to Van Buren, December 31, 1818, Van Buren Papers; Henry Meigs to Josiah Meigs, January 8, 1819, Meigs Papers; James King to Rufus King, January 14, 1819, *King's Writings*, 6: 192–193; Charles Dudley to Morris Miller, December 11, 1819, Miscellaneous Papers, NYSL.

24. Smith Thompson to Van Buren, January 23, 1819, Van Buren Papers; John King to Rufus King, January 28, 1819, *King's Writings*, 6: 199; *National Advocate*, February 11, 1819; Ambrose Spencer to Armstrong, February 14, 1819, Rokeby Collection.

25. John King to Rufus King, February 22, 1819, *King's Writings*, 6: 216; *Evening Post*, March 3, 15, 25, April 2, 9, 1819; *Columbian*, March 15, 18, 1819.

26. *National Advocate*, March 29, 1819; *Evening Post*, March 29, 1819, May 10, 1831; Hammond, *Political Parties*, 1: 496–97; Van Buren, *Autobiography*, 91. For more on Henry Seymour's extracurricular canal activities see Steward Mitchell,

*Horatio Seymour of New York* (Cambridge: Harvard University Press, 1938), 9–21.

27. *National Advocate*, April 9, 1819.

28. Charles Dudley to Morris Miller, April 8, 1819, Miscellaneous Papers, NYSL; *National Advocate*, April 9, 15, 20, 21, 1819; Broadside, "Meeting held at Tammany Hall, April 22, 1819" (New York: 1819), Kilroe Collection.

29. *National Advocate*, March 16, 23, April 23, November 12, 1819; Van Buren to Worth, April 22, 1819, Van Buren Papers.

30. DeWitt Clinton and Pierre Van Wyck, *The Martling Men* (New York: 1819), 21.

31. Henry Meigs to Josiah Meigs, May 2, 1819, Meigs Papers.

32. *New York American*, March 3, 1819; William W. Van Ness to Solomon Van Rensselaer, July 14, 1819, *Historical Gleanings*, 1: 337.

33. Gulian Verplanck to John Quincy Adams, December 22, 1819 (material from the Adams Papers are from the microfilm edition, by permission of the Massachusetts Historical Society); Johnston Verplanck to Van Buren, December 25, 1819, Van Buren Papers; John Randolph to Harmanus Bleecker, January 20, 1820, Randolph Papers, UVA; Gulian Verplanck, *The State Triumvirate* (New York: 1819); Robert July, *The Essential New Yorker: Gulian Crommelin Verplanck* (Durham: Duke University Press, 1951), 60–69.

34. *National Advocate*, July 29, November 2, 3, 29, 1819, February 18, 1820; Tompkins to Archibald McIntyre, August 5, Van Buren to Noah, December 19, 1819, James Hamilton to Van Buren, January 18, Van Buren to Smith Thompson, January 19, 1820, Van Buren Papers; Archibald McIntyre, *A Letter to his Excellency, Daniel D. Tompkins* (Albany: 1819); Hammond, *Political Parties*, 1: 520–22; Van Buren, *Autobiography*, 95–96.

35. *National Advocate*, November 29, 1819; Van Buren to Noah, December 17, 1819, Van Buren Papers.

36. James Tallmadge to Taylor, April 4, 1819, John Taylor Papers, NYHS; Van Buren to Noah, December 17, 1819, Van Buren to George Tibbetts, January 9, 1820, Van Buren Papers; William W. Van Ness to Solomon Van Rensselaer, January 18, 1820, *Historical Gleanings*, 1: 341. For a different interpretation see Glover Moore, *The Missouri Controversy* (Lexington: University of Kentucky Press, 1953), 54–178.

37. *National Advocate*, January 25, February 10, 16, 20, 23, 1820.

38. Rufus King to Van Buren, March 25, 1820, Van Buren Papers; *Evening Post*, April 22, 26, May 1, 1820; Broadside, "An Address to the Independent Federal Electors of the State of New-York on the Subject of the Election of a Governor and Lieutenant Governor, April 14, 1820" (New York: 1820), NYSL; Van Buren *Autobiography*, 105.

39. Betts to Van Buren, January 31, Van Buren to Madison, March 15, Madison to Van Buren, March 27, Van Buren to Worth, June 1, 1820, Van Buren Papers; *National Advocate*, May 1, 3, June 2, 1820.

40. John W. Taylor to John Taylor, May 3, 1820, Taylor Papers; Samuel Rezneck, "The Depression of 1819, A Social History," *AHR*, 39 (October 1933), 28–37; Chilton Williamson, *American Suffrage from Property to Democracy, 1760–1860* (Princeton: Princeton University Press, 1960), 195–207; Murray Rothbard, *The Panic of 1819* (New York: Columbia University Press, 1962), 21–22, 34, 143–47.

41. *Evening Post*, March 2, 1818; *National Advocate*, May 24, 1819; Charles

Haines, *An Appeal to the People of the State of New York on the Expediency of Abolishing the Council of Appointment* (New York: 1819), 29–31.

42. Charles Haines to Clinton, May 24, 1820, Clinton Papers; *National Advocate*, July 7, 28, 31, August 19, 24, September 1, 14, October 7, December 21, 1820.

43. *Ibid.*, November 8, 11, 14, 1820; Clinton to Henry Post, November 19, 1820, "DeWitt Clinton as a Politician," John Bigelow, ed., *Harper's New Monthly Magazine*, 50 (1875), 413.

44. Clinton to Solomon Van Rensselaer, November 22, 1820, *Historical Gleanings*, 1: 355; *New York American*, November 23, 1820; Clinton to Post, November 25, 1820, *Harper's New Monthly Magazine*, 414.

45. Nathaniel Carter to Tracy, November 24, 1820, Tracy Papers; Meigs to Van Buren, November 26, 1820, Van Buren Papers; Alfred Street, *The Council of Revision of the State of New York* (Albany: W. Gould, 1859), 391.

46. *National Advocate*, December 2, 8, 14, 20, 21, 1820.

47. *Ibid.*, February 20, March 1, 20, April 23, 25, May 1, 9, July 3, 10, 1821.

48. Van Buren to King, January 14, 1821, *King's Writings*, 6: 375–76; *National Advocate*, August 6, 8, 9, 11, 1821.

49. Van Buren to John King, October 21, 1821, Van Buren Papers; Nathaniel Carter and William L. Stone, *Reports of the Proceedings and Debates of the Convention of 1821* (Albany: E. & E. Hosford, 1821), 48–71, 137–56, 219–61, 367–76; Leon Litwack, *North of Slavery* (Chicago: University of Chicago Press, 1961), 82–83.

50. Ulshoeffer to Van Buren, September 21, 1821, Van Buren Papers; Rufus King to Charles King, October 20, 1821, *King's Writings*, 6: 414; Carter and Stone, *Reports*, 297–383; Dixon Ryan Fox, *The Decline of Aristocracy in the Politics of New York, 1801–1840* (New York: Columbia University Press, 1919), 82–83.

51. Peter A. Jay to John Jay, October 10, 1821, *Jay's Writings*, 4: 452–53; Rufus King to Charles King, October 15, 1821, *King's Writings*, 6: 417; Edward Shepard, *Martin Van Buren* (Boston and New York: Houghton Mifflin Company, 1888), 79–87.

52. Ambrose Spencer to Tracy, May 28, 1821, Tracy Papers; Pintard to Mrs. Davidson, August 6, 1821, *Letters of John Pintard to his Daughter, Eliza Noel Pintard Davidson, 1816–1833*, Dorothy C. Barck, ed. (New York: New-York Historical Society, 1940), 2: 69.

53. *National Advocate*, November 1, December 22, 1821, January 15, 1822; James Geddes to Taylor, January 8, 1822, Taylor Papers; Hammond, *Political Parties*, 2: 94.

54. Gideon Granger to Clinton. April 4, 1822, Clinton Papers; *New York American*, April 18, 1822; *Evening Post*, April 20, 1822.

## 4. THE CHALLENGE OF JACKSONIAN DEMOCRACY

1. *Columbian*, March 28, 1819; *National Advocate*, April 30, 1822; Michael Wallace, "Changing Concepts of Party in the United States: New York, 1815–1828," *AHR*, 74 (1968), 453–91.

2. *Evening Post*, May 6, 1822.

3. Clarkson Crolius to John Quincy Adams, November 29, 1819, Adams Papers; *Evening Post*, January 25, 1825; John Lester to Joseph Hopkins, May, 1845, C. S.

Bogardus to Cornelius Van Ness, May 15, 1845, James Polk Papers, LC; *New York Herald*, April 17, 1850; *Address of the Grand Council of the Tammany Society or Columbian Order upon the Subject of their Recent Decision Relative to the Political Use of Tammany Hall* (New York: 1853); *Republican Campaign Book* (New York: 1901); Myers, *Tammany Hall*, 49–50.

4. John Randolph to Harmanus Bleecker, December 29, 1821, Randolph Papers; Henry Meigs to Josiah Meigs, January 13, 1822, Meigs Papers; *National Advocate* June 8, 1822; Robert Remini, *Martin Van Buren and the Making of the Democratic Party* (New York: Columbia University Press, 1959), 4–29.

5. Michael Ulshoeffer to Van Buren, January 12, 27, 1822, Van Buren Papers; *National Advocate*, May 9, June 10, 19, 1822; Peter Porter to Henry Clay, September 30, 1822, *The Papers of Henry Clay*, James F. Hopkins, ed. (Lexington: University of Kentucky Press, 1963), 3: 364–65.

6. *New York American*, August 19, 1822, April 8, 1823; *National Advocate*, September 22, 1822; James Brown to Gallatin, December 10, 1823, Gallatin Papers.

7. Ulshoeffer to Van Buren, January 22, Rufus King to Van Buren, January 22, 1822, Van Buren Papers; *National Advocate*, October 9, November 3, 8, 1822; *Evening Post*, October 31, November 3, 1822; *New York American*, November 5, 6, 1822. Chronically short of cash, Noah needed the office because the sheriff shared in certain fines collected.

8. Noah to Van Buren, November 12, 1822, Van Buren Papers. Wendover won by a vote of 3,826 to 2,493.

9. James O. Morse to Adams, December 8, 1822, January 26, July 24, 1823, Adams Papers; *National Advocate*, June 3, 1822, August 2, 1823; Alexander Hamilton to Taylor, January 25, 1823, Taylor Papers.

10. Calhoun to Porter, April 13, 1823, Porter Papers; *National Advocate*, June 18, 22, 27, 1823; *New York Patriot*, August 28, 29, October 3, 1823; Thomas R. Hay, "John C. Calhoun and the Presidential Election of 1824," *The North Carolina Historical Review*, 13 (April 1937), 32.

12. John King to Van Buren, February 23, 1823, Van Buren Papers.

13. Henry Shaw to Clay, April 4, 1822, *Clay's Papers* 3: 185, Josiah Johnston to Clay, August 30, 1824, *ibid.*, 3: 822; Rufus King to John King, January, 1823, *King's Writings*, 6: 495; Calhoun to Joseph Swift, May 10, 1823, "John C. Calhoun and the Presidential Election of 1824," Thomas Hay, ed., *AHR*, 40 (1834), 87; *National Advocate*, August 23, 1823; Livermore, *Twilight of Federalism*, 151–54.

14. Clinton to Cadwallader C. Colden, January 2, 1823, Clinton Papers; Clinton to Stephen Van Rensselaer, January 23, 1823, Miscellaneous Papers, NYSL.

15. Jackson to Donelson, August 6, 1822, Jackson Papers, LC; *National Advocate*, July 15, 1823; Calhoun to Swift, August 24, 1823, "Calhoun's Letters," *AHR*, 40: 90; *National Advocate*, July 15, 1823; Clinton to Post, March 4, 1824, "Clinton as a Politician," *Harper's New Monthly Magazine*, 50: 568; John Quincy Adams, *Memoirs of John Quincy Adams: Comprising Portions of His Diary from 1795 to 1848*, Charles F. Adams, ed. (Philadelphia: J. B. Lippincott & Company, 1877), 6: 302–16.

16. Jackson to Clinton, March 9, 1819, August 31, 1823, Clinton Papers; Calhoun to Swift, December 3, 1823, "Calhoun's Letters," *AHR*, 40: 388; Clinton to Gideon Granger, January 25, 1824, Granger Family Papers, LC; *New York Enquirer*, May 1, 1829.

17. William Rochester to Clay, November 1, 1823, *Clay's Papers*, 3: 511, Jack-

son to Donelson, January 14, 1824, Jackson Papers; Van Buren, *Autobiography*, 223; Livermore, *Twilight of Federalism*, 158–60.

18. Erastus Root to Van Buren, January 3, 1823, Van Buren Papers; Samuel Gouverneur to Monroe, April 12, 1823, Monroe Papers; *National Advocate*, August 5, 23, September 6, 23, 25, October 3, 19, 1823; *New York American*, August 30, 1823; *New York Statesman*, September 11, 20, 1823; *New York Patriot*, September 11, 1823. Van Buren introduced a similar bill in the United States Senate.

19. Clinton to Granger, August 23, 1823, Granger Family Papers; Orville Holley to Luther Holley, September 14, 1823, Holley Papers; *Evening Post*, October 4, 5, 1823; *New York American*, October 8, 1823.

20. *New York American for the Country*, October 23, 1823; *Evening Post*, October 28, 1923.

21. *National Advocate*, October 28, 30, November 3, 4, 6, 12, 1823; *New York Patriot*, November 8, 1823; John Fellows to William Lee, November 11, 1823, Adams Papers.

22. Noah to Monroe, June 23, 1823, Monroe Papers; *National Advocate*, November 12, 13, 1823; Azariah Flagg to Van Buren, November 12, 1823, Van Buren Papers.

23. Marcy to Van Buren, January 11, 1824, *ibid.*; *New York Patriot*, January 24, 1824; *National Advocate*, February 14, 1824; *New York Statesman*, February 15, 1824.

24. *New York American*, January 30, 1824; William A. Tompkins to Flagg, January 30, 1824, Flagg Papers, NYPL; Stephen Allen to Churchill Cambreleng, February 14, 1824, Stephen Allen Papers, NYHS.

25. *National Advocate*, February 21, April 5, 1824; Clinton to James Kent, March 17, 1824, Clinton Papers; Wright to Flagg, August 20, 1827, Flagg Papers; John Jenkins, *Life of Silas Wright* (Auburn: J.M. Alden, 1850), 34–36.

26. Wheaton to Adams, March 31, 1824, Adams Papers; *Evening Post*, April 6, 1824; C.H. Rammelkamp, "The Election of 1824 in New York," *Annual Report of the American Historical Association* (Washington, D.C.: Government Printing Office, 1905), 174–78.

27. Marcy to Van Buren, January 11, 1824, Van Buren Papers; *National Advocate*, April 20, 1824; Van Buren, *Autobiography*, 143–44.

28. Pintard to Clinton, April 15, Citizens of Village of Geneva to Clinton, May 1, 1824, Clinton Papers; *Evening Post*, April 20, 21, 1824; Rufus King to Charles King, April 21, 1824, *King's Writings*, 6: 567–68.

29. Charles King to Adams, March 31, John Fellows to William Lee, April 5, Daniel Brent to Adams, April 17, 1824, Adams Papers; *Evening Post*, April 9, 1824; *New York Patriot*, April 9, 20, 1824.

30. John Sterling to Adams, May 22, 1824, Adams Papers; William Rochester to Clay, May 29, 1824, *Clay's Papers*, 3: 769–71; Livermore, *Twilight of Federalism*, 161–69.

31. *New York Patriot*, May 6, 1824; *New York Leader*, January 10, 1863.

32. *Evening Post*, April 10, 1824; Minutes of the Grand Council of Sachems, May 27, 1824, NYPL.

33. *New York Patriot*, September 11, 1824; *Evening Post*, October 25, 27, 1824.

34. Clinton to Astor, May 25, Clinton to John Easton, July 1, 1824, Clinton

Papers; Blunt to Adams, July 15, 29, August 4, 6, Thomas Hertell to Adams, July 31, Wheaton to Adams, August 9, Tallmadge to Adams, August 22, 1824, Adams Papers; *National Advocate*, July 20, 21, 24, August 14, 1824; *New York American*, August 4, 12, 13, 1824; *Evening Post*, August 11, 14, 1824; Clinton to Tracy, August 10, 1824, Tracy Papers.

35. *Evening Post*, August 31, September 4, 1824; Tobias Watkins to Adams, September 4, 6, 1824, Adams Papers; *National Advocate*, September 6, 1824; Mordecai Noah, *A Statement of Facts Relating to the Conduct of Henry Eckford, Esq. as connected with the NATIONAL ADVOCATE* (New York: 1824).

36. *Evening Post*, September 24, 1824; Blunt to Adams, October 2, 1824, Adams Papers; Samuel Southard to Smith Thompson, November 2, 1824, Smith Thompson Papers, LC.

37. *New York American*, September 25, October 4, 6, 7, 1824; Tallmadge to Adams, October 17, Adams to Tallmadge, October 21, 1824, Adams Papers; Broadside, "Address to the People" (New York: 1824), NYSL.

38. *National Advocate*, October 7, 28, 1824; James Hamilton to Van Buren, October 7, 1824, Van Buren Papers; Blunt to Adams, October 10, 1824, Adams Papers; *Evening Post*, November 6, 1824.

39. Tallmadge to Adams, October 28, November 11, 14, Blunt to Adams, November 8, 11, 13, Wheaton to Adams, November 16, 1824, Adams Papers; Matthew Davis to John O'Connor, November 2, 3, 1824, O'Connor Papers; John Dix to Taylor, November 3, 1824, Taylor Papers.

40. Broadside, "Meeting at the Tontine Coffee House, August 13, 1824" (New York: 1824), NYPL; Blunt to Adams, November 26, 1824, Adams Papers; *Evening Post*, November 30, 1824; Clinton to Stephen Van Rensselaer, December 11, 1824, Clinton Papers; James Hamilton to Van Buren, December 12, 1824, Van Buren Papers; Van Buren, *Autobiography*, 152.

41. *National Advocate*, December 12, 14, 24, 1824.

42. Worth to Brown, January 22, 1825, Brown Papers; *Evening Post*, February 12, March 14, 1825; *New York National Advocate*, March 2, 4, 1825; *Albany Argus*, March 12, 1825; *National Advocate*, March 12, 1825; Van Buren to Butler, December 25, 1825, Van Buren Papers; Van Buren, *Autobiography*, 197.

43. Hammond, *Political Parties*, 2: 86–87, 115, 139.

44. Adams to Crawford, February 10, Crawford to Adams, February 11, 1825, Adams Papers; Thurlow Weed to Tracy, February 24, 1825, Tracy Papers; Tallmadge to Weed, September 3, 1825, Weed Papers, NYSL; *New York American*, September 17, 1825.

45. William Plumer to Adams, July 8, 1824, Adams to Clinton, February 18, Clinton to Adams, February 25, 1825, Adams Papers; Clay to Porter, November 29, 1825, Porter Papers; Adams, *Diary*, 6: 493.

46. Wheaton to Adams, January 13, Clay to Adams, March 8, Blunt to Adams, April 7, John Duer to Adams, June 8, 1825, Adams Papers; Samuel Flagg Bemis, *John Quincy Adams and the Union* (New York: Alfred A. Knopf, 1956), 138.

47. Duer to Adams, August 20, Wheaton to Adams, August 22, John Fiske to Adams, August 27, Clinton to Adams, August 20, Algernon Sidney [?] to Adams, September 3, 1825, Tallmadge to Adams, January 21, February 3, Adams to Tallmadge, January 31, 1826, Adams Papers; Tallmadge to Taylor, February 23, 1826, Taylor Papers.

48. Hammond, *Political Parties*, 2: 181; Wright to Minet Jenison, December 9, 1824, cited by Ransom Gillet, *The Life and Times of Silas Wright* (Albany: Joel Munsell, 1874), 1: 84.

49. James Mallory to Flagg, July 19, 1825, Flagg Papers; Remini, *Van Buren*, 96–97.

50. *New York National Advocate*, March 8, April 11, May 2, 4, July 13, October 29, 1825.

51. Spencer to Tracy, November 21, 1824, Tracy Papers; *New York National Advocate*, March 4, July 6, 1825.

52. Jesse Hoyt to Verplanck, March 7, 1825, Verplanck Papers, NYHS; Benjamin Waterhouse to Adams, July 4, 1825, Adams Papers.

53. Clinton to Swift, March 12, 1825, Clinton Papers; *New York National Advocate* March 24, 1825; Blunt to Adams, March 26, Swift to Adams, March 29, 1825, Adams Papers; Swift, *Memoirs*, 201.

54. *New York National Advocate*, September 8, 28, 1825; *National Advocate*, September 10, 17, 1825; *Evening Post*, September 14, October 29, 1825.

55. *New York American*, October 17, 1825; Blunt to Adams, October 29, 1825, Adams Papers; *National Advocate*, November 2, 14, 1825; *Evening Post*, November 12, 1825; *New York National Advocate*, November 29, 1825.

56. Wright to Flagg, November 20, 1825, Flagg Papers; Edward Livingston to Van Buren, November 30, Van Buren to Livingston, December 7, 1825, Van Buren Papers; James Campbell to Verplanck, December 13, 1825, Verplanck Papers; Clinton to Atwater, December 25, 1825, Clinton Papers.

57. Campbell to Verplanck, February 25, Rudolph Bunner to Verplanck, March 5, 1826, Verplanck Papers; Erastus Root to Van Buren, April 2, Edwin Croswell to Van Buren, April 3, 1826, Van Buren Papers; Wright to Van Buren, April 4, 1826, *Lives and Opinions*, 204.

58. *New York National Advocate*, March 3, 14, 31, 1826; Weed to Tracy, April 10, 1826, Tracy Papers; Tallmadge to Adams, April 16, Mower to Adams, June 8, 1826, Adams Papers; Mower to Taylor, May 5, June 15, Taylor to Tallmadge, May 10, 1826, Taylor Papers; *New York Enquirer*, November 30, 1826; Remini, *Van Buren*, 120–21.

59. Clinton to Atwater, May 23, 1826, Clinton Papers; Jesse Hoyt to Van Buren, June 11, 1826, Van Buren Papers; Weed to Francis Granger, July 5, 1826, Granger Family Papers.

60. *New York Enquirer*, July 6, August 2, 9, 1826; *National Advocate*, July 8, August 30, 1826; Michael Hoffman to Marcy, July 31, August 14, 1826, Marcy Papers, LC.

61. Rochester to Tracy, June 4, 1826, Tracy Papers; Van Buren to Thomas Ritchie, January 13, 1827, Van Buren Papers; Van Buren, *Autobiography*, 161–64; Remini, *Van Buren*, 120–22.

62. *New York Enquirer*, October 21, 1826; Van Buren to Cambreleng, November 3, William Bouck to Van Buren, November 17, 1826, Van Buren Papers; *Evening Post*, November 11, 1826; Clinton to Hector Craig, November 15, 1826, Clinton Papers; Bunner to Verplanck, November 20, 1826, Verplanck Papers; Adams, *Diary*, 7: 184–85.

63. *New York Enquirer*, October 9, 30, 1826; *Evening Post*, October 18, 19, 30, 1826; *National Advocate*, October 31, November 1, 4, 1826; *New York American*, November 14, 1826, September 17, 1827.

64. *National Advocate,* November 26, 30, December 4, 5, 1826. James Gordon Bennett was the author of these attacks.

65. *New York Enquirer,* November 30, November 1, 4, 11, 1826; *National Advocate,* December 14, 1826; *Albany Argus,* December 14, 20, 1826; Van Buren to Hamilton, December 20, 1826, *Reminiscences,* 63.

66. Van Buren to Nicholas, November 1826, Van Buren to Ritchie, January 13, 1827, Cornelius Van Ness to Van Buren, February 22, 1827, Van Buren Papers; Ritchie to Jackson, January 28, James Hamilton to Jackson, February 16, 1827, Jackson Papers; *New York Enquirer,* March 2, 1827; *National Advocate,* April 2, 1827; Remini, *Van Buren,* 124–26.

### 5. TAMMANY AND THE NEW POLITICS

1. Tallmadge to Weed, February 5, 1827, Weed Papers; *New York American,* February 8, 1827; Blunt to Adams, September 11, 1827, Adams Papers.

2. Hammond to Adams, September 11, Taylor to Adams, September 13, Charles King to Adams, December 22, 1826, Adams to Blunt, March 20, 1827, *ibid.; New York Herald,* May 2, 1853.

3. *Evening Post,* November 14, 1826, March 27, April 24, 1827; *New York Enquirer,* March 28, 1827; Van Buren to Cambreleng, July 4, October 23, Van Buren to Jackson, September 14, 1827, Van Buren Papers.

4. *Evening Post,* November 16, 28, 1826, February 8, 14, 19, 26, March 19, June 28, July 31, September 12, 1827; *New York American,* February 20, 26, 27, July 16, 1827; *New York Enquirer,* February 28, July 20, 24, 30, August 5, September 5, 15, 1827; Marcy to Van Buren, June 25, 1827, Van Buren Papers; Robert Remini, *The Election of Andrew Jackson* (Philadelphia: J.B. Lippincott, 1963), 145–48.

5. Clay to Porter, May 13, 1827, Porter Papers; *National Advocate,* May 18, 24, June 13, 18, 1827; *New York Enquirer,* June 25, 1827.

6. *National Advocate,* May 12, July 7, September 28, 29, October 2, 1827; *New York Enquirer,* May 15, July 7, August 4, September 28, 29, 1827; *New York American,* September 29, 30, 1827.

7. *Evening Post,* October 2, 6, 1827; *National Advocate,* October 4, 6, 8, 1827; *New York American,* October 7, 1827; *New York Enquirer,* October 7, 8, 1827.

8. *National Advocate,* October 10, 1827.

9. Rochester to Clay, October 9, 1827, Clay Papers; *New York Enquirer,* October 17, 20, 1827; *New York American,* October 18, 20, 1827.

10. Van Buren to Cambreleng, October 22, 23, 1827, Van Buren Papers; *National Advocate,* November 1, 1827; *Evening Post,* November 3, 1827.

11. *New York Enquirer,* November 6, 1827; *Evening Post,* November 6, 1827; *National Advocate,* November 9, 28, 1827.

12. *New York Enquirer,* November 7, 8, 9, 14, 1827, April 4, 7, 9, 1828; *Evening Post,* January 11, 1838; Minutes of the Grand Council of Sachems, January 18, 1844, NYPL.

13. *National Advocate,* November 8, 1827; Blunt to Adams, November 14, Meigs to Adams, November 24, 1827, Adams Papers; Charles Benton to Flagg, December 2, 1827, Flagg Papers; Tallmadge to Tracy, December 26, 1827, Tracy Papers; Adams, *Diary,* 7: 344.

14. *National Advocate,* January 24, 1824, April 1, 14, May 23, 1828; *New York*

*Enquirer,* February 13, May 1, 4, 1828; *New York American,* April 21, May 5, 1828.

15. *Evening Post,* May 5, 1828; *New York Enquirer,* May 5, 8, 1828.

16. *New York American,* March 11, 14, 27, 1828; *New York Enquirer,* March 28, May 23, 1828.

17. Noah to Clinton, November 27, 1827, Clinton Papers; *National Advocate,* January 28, 1828; Campbell to Hoyt, February 22, 1828, *Lives and Opinions,* 203; Charles Clinton to DeWitt Clinton, Jr., February 27, 1828, Clinton Papers, NYSL; DeGrand to Adams, March 16, 1828, Adams Papers; Daniel Webster to Jeremiah Mason, March 20, 1828, *The Letters of Daniel Webster,* Charles H. Van Tyne, ed. (New York: McClure, Phillips & Company, 1902), 137.

18. *New York Enquirer,* February 16, October 21, November 3, 1828; Atwater to Jackson, February 29, 1828, *Correspondence of Andrew Jackson,* John Bassett, ed. (Washington, D.C.: Carnegie Institute, 1926), 1: 394; Hammond to Taylor, April 14, 1828, Taylor Papers; John Andrew Graham to Jackson, May 24, 1828, Jackson Papers; Hammond to Adams, October 29, 1828, Adams Papers.

19. Wright to Flagg, February 18, 1828, Flagg Papers; *New York Enquirer,* June 3, August 14, 16, November 9, 1828.

20. Broadside, "Meeting in Tammany Hall, December 4, 1827" (New York: 1827), Jackson Papers; *Evening Post,* January 4, 5, 9, 10, 11, 1828; *National Advocate,* January 31, 1828; *New York Enquirer,* June 25, 1828; Remini, *Election of Jackson,* 51–120.

21. *Report of the State Convention Held at the Capitol in the City of Albany to Select Candidates for President & Vice President of the United States of America* (New York: 1828), 35; *Address of the Republican General Committee of Young Men of the City of New York, Friendly to the Election of Andrew Jackson* (New York: 1828), 35.

22. *New York Enquirer,* April 7, July 17, 1828; Swift to Jackson, April 8, 1828, *Jackson's Letters,* 3: 397–98; *National Advocate,* April 17, July 1, 1828; *New York American,* June 7, August 18, 1828; *Evening Post,* October 3, 1828; Livermore, *Twilight of Federalism,* 216–61.

23. *National Advocate,* June 5, August 28, September 23, 27, 1828; *New York American,* September 26, 1828; *New York Enquirer,* September 27, 1828; *Sunday Times and Noah's Weekly Messenger,* March 17, April 7, 1850.

24. Monroe to Adams, September 10, December 1, George Sullivan to Adams, September 19, 1828, Adams Papers; *New York American,* September 17, 1828.

25. *Evening Post,* October 11, 15, 21, 1828; *National Advocate,* October 13, 1828; *New York Enquirer,* October 13, 18, 21, 1828.

26. James Thomas to Adams, July 18, 1828, Adams Papers; *National Advocate,* October 1, 21, 28, 1828; *New York American,* October 24, 27, November 4, 1828; *Evening Post,* October 25, 27, 1828.

27. *National Advocate,* October 30, 31, 1828; *New York Enquirer,* November 3, 1828; Charles Levermore, "Rise of Metropolitan Journalism," *AHR,* 6 (April 1901), 453–56.

28. *Evening Post,* October 30, 1828; *New York Courier,* November 4, 8, 1828; *New York American,* November 7, 1828.

29. Blunt to Adams, November 6, Charles Francis Adams to Louisa C. Adams, November 8, 1828, Adams Papers; Van Buren to Hoyt, November 8, 1828, *Lives and Opinions,* 204; *Evening Post,* November 10, 11, 12, 1828, January 14, 1829; *New York Enquirer,* November 11, December 18, 20, 1828.

30. *National Advocate*, November 15, 22, 1828; *New York Enquirer*, January 2, 3, 7, 14, 1829; Van Buren to John Spencer, July 4, 1829, Van Buren Papers, NYSL; Van Buren, *Autobiography*, 220–23.

31. Van Buren to James Hamilton, February 21, 1829, *Reminiscences*, 94; Van Buren, *Autobiography*, 230–33, 242–43.

32. *New York Enquirer*, November 8, December 8, 30, 1828; *National Advocate*, November 24, 1828; *New York American*, January 12, 1829; Coddington to Hoyt, February 13, 16, 1829, *Lives and Opinions*, 208; Van Buren, *Autobiography*, 262.

33. Coddington to Hoyt, March 29, 1829, *Lives and Opinions*, 213–14; Van Buren to Hoyt, April 13, 1829, *ibid.*, 216; Van Buren to Cambreleng and Bowne, April 20, Van Buren to Cambreleng, April 23, Van Buren to Jackson, April 23, 1829, Van Buren Papers; Van Buren, *Autobiography*, 263–69.

34. Swartwout to Hoyt, March 14, 1829, *Lives and Opinions*, 50; Cambreleng to Van Buren, April 28, 1829, Van Buren Papers; *Evening Post*, May 1, 14, 1829; *New York Enquirer*, May 1, 8, 1829.

35. Forman to Van Buren, January 24, 1829, Van Buren Papers; Hammond *Political Parties*, 2: 294–99.

36. James Gordon Bennett to Nicholas Biddle, April 13, 1829, Biddle Papers, LC; Hammond, *Political Parties*, 2: 249–52; Barry Beyer, "The Chenango Canal and the Campaign for its Construction," *NYH*, 38 (July 1957), 257–62.

37. *New York Enquirer*, August 23, 1828; Van Buren to Cambreleng, February 1, 1829, May 10, 1835, Van Buren Papers; Bennett to Biddle, April 2, 1829, Biddle Papers.

38. Hammond, *Political Parties*, 2: 299–300; Fritz Redlick, *The Molding of American Banking, Men and Ideas* (New York: Hafner Publishing Company, 1951), 88–95.

39. Bennett to Biddle, April 2, 21, Roswell Colt to Biddle, May 2, 14, Robert Lenox to Biddle, June 2, 1829, Biddle Papers; *Evening Post*, April 3, 13, 1829; Flagg to Van Buren, May 6, 1829, Van Buren Papers.

40. *Evening Post*, April 4, 12, 22, 30, May 5, 1829; Biddle to I. Lawrence, May 19, June 9, Biddle to Lenox, May 28, June 4, Biddle to Charles Davis, June 9, 13, Charles Davis to Biddle, June 19, 1829, Biddle to Albert Tracy, February 3, March 30, 1830, Biddle Papers.

41. Charles Davis to Biddle, January 15, Bennett to Biddle, April 9, May 30, 1830, *ibid.*

42. Colt to Biddle, January 7, 1829, Biddle to Cambreleng, May 12, 14, Biddle to Lenox, June 4, 1829, Biddle to Samuel Smith, April 22, 1830, *ibid.*

43. Biddle to Bennett, April 9, October 14, 1829, *ibid.*, Thomas Govan, *Nicholas Biddle, Nationalist and Public Banker* (Chicago: University of Chicago Press, 1959), 147–48.

44. Biddle to Spencer, August 10, Biddle to Porter, September 25, Bennett to Biddle, October 17, November 9, Biddle to Bowne, November 16, 17, December 4, 1829, April 26, 1830, Lenox to Biddle, December 3, Biddle to Lenox, December 4, Biddle to John Lawrence, December 4, 1829, Biddle Papers.

45. *Courier and Enquirer*, May 26, 1829, September 6, 1833; Bennett to Hoyt, June 7, 11, July 20, 1829, *Lives and Opinions*, 91–92; *Evening Post*, October 15, 1829; Isaac Pray, *Memoirs of a Journalist* (New York: Stringer and Townsend, 1855), 71–150.

46. *New York Enquirer*, January 19, February 9, 1829; *Evening Post*, May–November, 1829, April 8, 9, 12, 1830.

47. Daniel Valentine, *Manual of the Corporation of the City of New York for the Years 1842 and 1843* (New York: 1843), 19–24; *Proceedings of the Board of Aldermen* (New York: 1843), 25: 78–81; *New York Plebeian*, May 4, 16, 18, 29, 1843.

48. William Lawrence to Clay, August 31, Porter to Clay, October 2, 1829, Clay Papers.

49. Walter Hugins, *Jacksonian Democracy and the Working Class* (Stanford: Stanford University Press, 1960), 219–24.

50. Frank T. Carleton, "The Working Men's Party of New York City: 1829–1831," *PSQ*, 22 (1907), 401–403; Edward Pessen, "The Working Men's Party Revisited," *Labor History*, IV (Fall 1963), 208–10.

51. *Evening Post*, October 31, November 2, 3, 5, 1829; *Courier and Enquirer*, October 31, November 2, 3, 1829.

52. *Evening Post*, November 10, 14, 1829; *Courier and Enquirer*, November 29, 1829; Carleton, "The Working Men's Party," *PSQ*, 22: 404.

53. *Courier and Enquirer*, November 26, 1829; *Evening Post*, December 2, 6, 1829; Philip Foner, *History of the Labor Movement in the United States* (New York: International Publishers, 1947), 133; Hugins, *Jacksonian Democracy*, 16–17.

54. *Working Man's Advocate*, January 16, February 17, 29, March 6, April 3, 10, 24, May 29, June 19, 30, 1830; Porter to Clay, May 25, 1830, Clay Papers.

55. *Working Man's Advocate*, June 16, 19, 30, 1830.

56. *Evening Post*, December 15, 1829, January 20, 25, 30, 1830; Clay to Porter, June 13, 1830, Clay Papers; *Working Man's Advocate*, July 8, 1830; *Report of the Select Committee on the petition of sundry Master Builders and others, of the City of New York* (New York: 1830).

57. *Evening Post*, December 30, 1829, January 8, 19, 27, June 22, July 15, 16, 17, 18, 1830; *Working Man's Advocate*, July 17, 21, August 5, 1830; *A Brief Investigation of the Causes which Created the Late Controversy on the Election of Mayor* (New York: 1830), 3. Although the *Working Man's Advocate* changed its title several times, I have used one consistent title to avoid confusion.

58. Clay to Porter, June 13, John Lawrence to Clay, August 21, William Lawrence to Clay, October 30, 1830, Clay Papers; *Working Man's Advocate*, September 11, October 1, 1830; *Evening Post*, October 6, 16, 20, 29, 30, 1830.

59. John Dix to Flagg, September 10, 1830, Flagg Papers; Bennett to Biddle, September 11, 1830, Biddle Papers; *Evening Post*, September 13, 1830; Cambreleng to Van Buren, October 23, 1830, Van Buren Papers.

60. *Evening Post*, October 26, November 4, 1830.

61. Cambreleng to Van Buren, October 11, 1830, Van Buren Papers; Pintard to Mrs. Davidson, November 3, 1830, *Pintard's Letters*, 3: 184–85; *Evening Post*, November 8, 10, 1830, January 4, 13, February 25, 1831.

62. Bennett to Biddle, November 10, 1830, Biddle Papers; Clay to Porter, November 21, 1830, Porter Papers; Hammond to Taylor, December 22, 1830, Taylor Papers.

63. William B. Lawrence to Clay, November 29, 1830; for more on Matthew Davis, see Clay to Porter, November 22, 1829, Clay Papers.

64. William Ireland *et al.*, Circular National Republican General Committee, January 11, 1831, James Lawrence to Clay, February 11, March 29, July 13, Clay to Porter, May 14, 1831, *ibid.*

65. *Working Man's Advocate*, November 13, 1830.

6. THE BANK WAR

1. *Evening Post,* December 9, 14, 1829; Hamilton, *Reminiscences,* 149–51; Robert Remini, *Andrew Jackson and the Bank War* (New York: W.W. Norton & Company, 1967), 15–66.

2. *Courier and Enquirer,* November 30, December 7, 11, 15, 21, 1829, April 9, 1830; Campbell White to Biddle, December 9, 1829, Biddle Papers; *Evening Post,* December 16, 1829, May 14, 1830.

3. Biddle to Bowne, May 1, Biddle to Charles A. Davis, May 19, 1830, Biddle Papers.

4. Verplanck to Gallatin, May 27, 1830, Gallatin Papers; John Targee *et al.* to Van Buren, July 1830, Van Buren Papers; Rochester to Biddle, July 21, 1830, Biddle Papers; Hammond, *Political Parties,* 2: 327.

5. Biddle to Bennett, September 15, Bennett to Biddle, September 25, October 22, Webb to Biddle, October 19, 1830, Biddle Papers; Hammond, *Political Parties,* 2: 366–82.

6. Biddle to Robinson, December 20, 1830, Biddle to Burrows, January 25, Biddle to William Lawrence, February 8, Burrows to Biddle, February 8, 1831, Biddle Papers; Ralph Catterall, *The Second Bank of the United States* (Chicago: University of Chicago Press, 1903), 205.

7. Burrows to Biddle, February 9, 17, 19, March 7, 11, Lawrence to Biddle, February 10, Tracy to Biddle, February 21, Charles Livingston to Burrows, March 12, 1831, Biddle Papers; Frank O. Gatell, "Sober Second Thoughts on Van Buren, the Albany Regency, and the Wall Street Conspiracy," *JAH,* 53 (June 1966), 19–32.

8. Biddle to Tracy, February 17, Biddle to Ingersoll, February 21, Biddle to Robinson, February 28, March 3, 5, 18, Lawrence to Biddle, March 14, Robinson to Biddle, March 23, 1831, Biddle Papers; Hammond, *Banks and Politics,* 351–58.

9. *Evening Post,* March 18, 21, 31, April 2, 6, 8, 9, 12, 1831; *Courier and Enquirer,* March 21, April 10, 14, 16 1831; Burrows to Biddle April 15, 16, 18, 19, Lawrence to Biddle, April 16, Bloodgood to Biddle, April 18, 1831, Biddle Papers.

10. *Niles Register,* April 16, 1831, 114, 1831; *Evening Post,* April 18, 1831; Jean Wilburn, *Biddle's Bank: The Crucial Years* (New York: Columbia University Press, 1967), 20–30.

11. *Evening Post,* April 6, 8, 9, 1831; *Working Man's Advocate,* April 7, 1831.

12. Webb to Van Buren, December 19, 1829, February 6, 1831, Van Buren Papers; Burrows to Biddle, March 7, 8, 22, 1831, Biddle Papers, James Gordon Bennett, Diary, June 22, 1831; NYPL; Govan, *Biddle,* 152–58.

13. Biddle to Burrows, April 14, May 4, November 27, Verplanck to Biddle April 28, Burrows to Biddle, May 2, 3, 14, 25, October 5, November 19, 25, Biddle to Webb, November 13, Webb to Biddle, November 17, 25, 1831, Biddle Papers; James L. Crouthamel, *James Watson Webb: A Biography* (Middletown: Wesleyan University Press, 1969), 34–42.

14. Robinson to Biddle, November 12, Biddle to Swartwout, December 11, Biddle to Webb, December 29, 1831, January 4, 5, 1832, Webb to Biddle, January 4, Burrows to Biddle, January 11, 1832, Biddle Papers; Jackson to Van Buren, December 6, 17, 1831, Van Buren to Jackson, January 13, 1832, Van Buren Papers; Remini, *Bank War,* 73–74.

15. Biddle to Rochester, January 16, Biddle to I. Lawrence, January 23, 28, Devereaux to Biddle, January 28, Ingersoll to Biddle, January 31, February 2, 1832, Biddle Papers.

16. William Astor to Biddle, January 17, Webb to Biddle, January 19, Lenox to Biddle, February 4, 1832, *ibid.; Evening Post*, January 21, 29, 31, February 3, 9, 18, 20, March 19, 1832.

17. *Courier and Enquirer*, March 3, 6, 7, 22, 1832; Webb to Biddle, March 6, 1832, Biddle Papers.

18. Biddle to Burrows, March 11, Webb to Biddle, March 15, 18, 20, Burrows to Biddle, March 19, 1832, *ibid.; Debates in Congress* (22nd Congress, 1st Session), Appendix 37; Govan, *Biddle*, 181–92.

19. Cambreleng to Hoyt, March 15, 1832, *Lives and Opinions*, 101–102; *Courier and Enquirer*, April 26, 1832.

20. *Working Man's Advocate*, December 18, 29, 1830, February 9, 11, April 2, November 5, December 17, 1831; January 6, 18, February 18, March 13, 16, 31, April 3, 1832.

21. *Ibid.*, May 31, June 1, 2, 8, 9, 16, 21, 30, July 12, 19, September 19, 22, 1832.

22. Porter to Clay, January 9, March 10, Stoddard to Clay, March 10, 1832, Clay Papers; I. Lawrence to Biddle, February 10, 1832, Biddle Papers; Cambreleng to Hoyt, February 5, 1832, *Lives and Opinions*, 231; *Courier and Enquirer*, March 13, 14, 19, 26, April 7, 10, 11, 1832.

23. Burrows to Biddle, March 26, May 3, Webb to Biddle, April 2, Noah to Clayton, April 9, Gales to Biddle, April 22, Biddle to Watmough, April 30, Biddle to Webb, May 1, 1832, Biddle Papers; Webb to Gallatin, April 14, 15, 1832, Gallatin Papers; Catterall, *Second Bank*, 228–32.

24. *Debates in Congress* (22nd Congress, 1st Session), Appendix 33–73. The *Courier and Enquirer*'s total indebtedness to the Bank amounted to $52,975, a figure which included the three loans, interest on them, and Burrows' commission.

25. *Evening Post*, April 11, 20, May 2, 4, June 10, 1832.

26. *Courier and Enquirer*, May 12, 19, 1832; *Evening Post*, May 15, 19, 1832.

27. *Courier and Enquirer*, April 12, May 3, 7, 9, 14, 25, 1832; Webb to Biddle, May 8, 9, Cambreleng to Biddle, May 8, Burrows to Biddle, May 16, 1832, Biddle Papers.

28. *Evening Post*, July 5, 30, August 16, 30, 1832.

29. Biddle to Webb, July 9, 13, 17, Webb to Biddle, July 16, August 1, 14, Biddle to Clay, August 14, 1832, Biddle Papers.

30. *Courier and Enquirer*, August 22, 23, 24, 27, September 8, 16, 1832; *Evening Post*, August 23, September 18, 1832; Webb to Biddle, August 24, 1832, Biddle Papers.

31. *Courier and Enquirer*, September 8, 11, 13, 19, 20, 24, 27, October 22, 1832; Webb to Biddle, September 10, 30, 1832, Biddle Papers.

32. Cornelius Lawrence to Biddle, June 26, Burrows to Biddle, June 19, Buckner to Biddle, September 29, Biddle to I. Lawrence, November 8, Biddle to Rathbone, November 9, 1832, *ibid.*

33. *Evening Post*, September 17, 22, 27, October 3, 12, 18, 24, 25, 29, 31, 1832; *Courier and Enquirer*, October 27, 30, 1832; Barker to Biddle, November 6, 1832, Biddle Papers; July, *Verplanck*, 176–79.

34. *Evening Post*, October 29, 30, 1832.

35. *Ibid.*, October 3, 4, 14, November 3, 1832.

36. Matthew Davis to Weed, June 17, September 23, 1832, Weed Papers, UR; Davis to Hiram Ketchum, August 6, 28, 1832, Gratz Collection; Bennett to Biddle, November 9, 1832, Biddle Papers; *Courier and Enquirer*, November 9, 13, 24, 1832; *Evening Post*, November 16, 22, 30, 1832.

37. *Courier and Enquirer*, November 23, 26, 29, December 1, 6, 7, 10, 13, 1832, March 9, September 6, 1833; Noah to [?], March 27, Webb to Biddle, June 26, Matthew Davis to Colt, July 17, Bennett to Biddle, December 1, 16, 1833, Biddle Papers; *Evening Star*, November 8, 1833; Hoyt to Van Buren, December 19, 1833, Van Buren Papers.

38. Allen to Jesse Hoyt, November 28, 1832, *Lives and Opinions*, 70.

39. *Working Man's Advocate*, December 14, 1832, January 7, 1833; Clay to Porter, January 5, 1833, Clay Papers; Biddle to Swartwout, March 27, 1833, Biddle Papers.

40. *Working Man's Advocate*, December 20, 26, 1832, January 23, February 13, 26, 1833; July, *Verplanck*, 148–57.

41. *Evening Post*, November 29, December 12, 17, 1832, January 2, 4, 12, February 28, March 14, 30, 1833; Cambreleng to Van Buren, December 5, 1832, Van Buren Papers; William Lawrence to Clay, January 8, 1833, Clay Papers; *Courier and Enquirer*, March 25, 1833.

42. Jackson to the Members of the Cabinet, March 19, 1833, *Jackson's Letters*, 5: 33; Remini, *Bank War*, 109–15.

43. Clay to Biddle, February 16, 1833, Clay Papers.

44. *Evening Post*, May 13, 25, 31, June 8, 13, 1833.

45. *Working Man's Advocate*, January 11, 19, February 8, April 27, 1833; *Evening Post*, May 3, June 19, 1833; *Courier and Enquirer*, June 15, 19, 1833.

46. Charles Stebbins to Van Buren, April 17, 1833, Van Buren Papers; *Evening Post*, May 28, 1833.

47. *Courier and Enquirer*, May 23, 1833; *Evening Post*, May 23, 26, June 28, July 10, 1833; Glyndon Van Dusen, "Thurlow Weed and the Seventh Ward Bank Scandal," *NYH*, 26 (January 1945), 8–9.

48. *Evening Post*, July 31, August 6, 1833; *Courier and Enquirer*, August 7, September 2, 24, 26, 27, October 1, 1833; Kendall to Gallatin, August 7, 1833, Gallatin Papers; Charles Davis to Biddle, August 9, 1833, Biddle Papers.

49. *Evening Post*, October 3, 1833; Frank O. Gatell, "Spoils of the Bank War: Political Bias in the Selection of Pet Banks," *AHR*, 60 (October 1964), 35–60.

50. Govan, *Biddle*, 236–37; Jacob Meerman, "The Climax of the Bank War: Biddle's Contraction, 1833–1834," *Journal of Political Economy*, 61 (August 1963), 378–88.

51. Matthew Davis to Colt, December 14, 1833, Biddle Papers.

52. Swartwout to Biddle, December 8, 31, 1833, *ibid.*

53. Webb to Biddle, September 22, Alexander Hamilton to Biddle, September 26, Adams to Biddle, November 12, Charles Davis to Biddle, December 7, 1833, *ibid.*; James A. Hamilton to Van Buren, December 30, 1833, Van Buren Papers.

54. *Evening Post*, April 1, 1833.

55. *Courier and Enquirer*, February 12, 28, March 8, 21, April 9, July 13, 14, 1833; *Evening Post*, March 19, 30, April 3, 10, 12, August 31, 1833; Biddle to Webb, July 9, 1833, Biddle Papers.

56. *Working Man's Advocate*, January 5, February 8, April 6, August 10, 1833; Bennett to Biddle, September 17, 1833, Biddle Papers; Bennett to Van Buren, Sep-

tember 25, 27, 1833, Van Buren Papers; *Evening Post*, October 3, 1833; *Evening Star*, October 9, 18, 1833.

57. *Courier and Enquirer*, October 8, 9, November 2, 1833; *Evening Star*, October 23, 1833.

58. *Evening Post*, October 9, 18, 23, November 2, 4, 5, 6, 1833; Colt to Biddle, October 9, Bennett to Biddle, October 14, 1833, Biddle Papers; *Courier and Enquirer*, October 14, 24, 26, November 8, 1833.

59. Charles Davis to Biddle, November 2, 1833, Biddle Papers.

60. *Courier and Enquirer*, November 1, 8, 11, 1833; *Evening Post*, November 11, December 21, 1833; Dudley Selden to Gallatin, December 22, 1833, Gallatin Papers; Robinson to Biddle, January 21, Stilwell to Biddle, January 27, 1834, Biddle Papers.

61. *Working Man's Advocate*, December 6, 21, 1833; Taylor to Swift, January 14, 1834, Taylor Papers; *Courier and Enquirer*, January 22, 23, February 26, March 3, 8, 13, 15, 22, 24, 27, 29, 1834; Webb to Van Buren, January 22, 1834, Van Buren Papers; Verplanck to Biddle, March 24, 1834, Biddle Papers.

62. Lenox to Biddle, January 10, Charles Davis to Biddle, January 13, 27, Stilwell to Biddle, February 10, 1834, *ibid.*; Van Schaick to Van Buren, January 31, 1834, Van Buren Papers; Philip Hone, *The Diary of Philip Hone, 1828-1851*, Bayard Tuckerman, ed. (New York: Dodd, Mead, and Company, 1910), 1: 84.

63. Gideon Lee to Van Buren, January 6, Bunner to Van Buren, January 15, James Hamilton to Van Buren, January 18, James Van Alen to Van Buren, January 27, Hoyt to Van Buren, January 29, 1834, Van Buren Papers; *Evening Post*, January 10, 14, 1834; Cornelius Lawrence to Hoyt, January 26, 1834, *Lives and Opinions*, 102.

64. Charles Davis to Biddle, January 20, 22, Robinson to Biddle, January 25, Colt to Biddle, January 25, February 20, 1834, Biddle Papers; *Evening Star*, January 23, 24, 25, 1834; James King to Van Buren, March 14, 1834, Van Buren Papers; Van Buren, *Autobiography*, 720-31.

65. *Courier and Enquirer*, January 30, 31, February 3, *Evening Post*, February 1, 1834; Charles Davis to Biddle, February 1, 8, 11, 1834, Biddle Papers; Throop to Van Buren, February 1, Hoyt to Van Buren, February 4, Eldad Holmes to Van Buren, February 7, 1834, Van Buren Papers.

66. *Courier and Enquirer*, January 17, 1834; Butler to Hoyt, February 24, 1834, *Lives and Opinions*, 171.

67. N.P. Tallmadge to Olcott, December 13, 1833, Butler to Olcott, February 1, March 10, 1834, Olcott Papers, CU; Wright to Erastus Corning, December 27, 1833, Corning Papers, Albany Institute; Van Buren to Thomas Suffern, January 15, Martin Van Buren to John Van Buren, February 10, 1834, Van Buren to Cambreleng, May 10, 1835, Van Buren Papers; Wright to Flagg, March 25, 1834, Flagg Papers; Webb to Biddle, March 27, 1834, Biddle Papers; Ivor Spencer, "William L. Marcy Goes Conservative," *MVHR*, 31 (September 1944), 211-14.

68. Clay to Biddle, February 2, Rathbone to Biddle, February 5, 1834, Biddle Papers; Butler to Olcott, February 8, 1834, Olcott Papers; Govan, *Biddle*, 254.

69. *Courier and Enquirer*, February 10, 11, 12, 14, 1834; *Evening Post*, February 10, 13, 1834; Charles Davis to Biddle, February 11, 12, Stilwell to Biddle, February 13, Webb to Biddle, February 14, 18, 1834, Biddle Papers; Hone, *Diary*, 1: 92.

70. *Courier and Enquirer*, February 25, March 3, 12, 1834; Webb to Biddle, February 26, Charles Davis to Biddle, March 11, 1834, Biddle Papers; Stebbins to

Van Buren, March 1, Throop to Van Buren, March 2, 1834, Van Buren Papers; *The Man*, March 8, 18, 1834.

71. *Evening Post*, March 11, 13, 15, 20, 28, April 3, 4, 5, 1834; *The Man*, March 15, 24, April 1, 4, 7, 1834; *Courier and Enquirer* April 3, 8, 11, 1834; Broadside, "Democratic Party, Fifth Ward, April 7, 1834," (New York: 1834), NYPL.

72. Bennett to Biddle, April 4, 1834, Biddle Papers.

73. *Working Man's Advocate*, February 15, 1834; Matthew Davis to William Seward, March 28, 1834, Seward Papers, UR; *The Man*, April 4, 7, 1834.

74. *Proceedings of a Meeting of Whig Young Men of the City of New York* (New York: 1834), 8–9; *Proceedings of the Board of Assistant Aldermen* (New York: 1839), Document 18: 26; Hone, *Diary*, 1: 100.

75. *Courier and Enquirer*, April 11, 12, 14, May 12, 17, 1834; *Working Man's Advocate*, April 12, 1834; *Evening Post*, April 12, 15, May 16, 1834.

76. *The Man*, April 14, June 5, 17, 1834; Saul Alley to Van Buren, April 17, 1834, Van Buren Papers; *Working Man's Advocate*, May 17, June 14, 1834.

77. Gideon Lee to Van Buren, January 6, Paulding to Van Buren, December 6, 1834, Van Buren Papers; *The Man*, April 1, May 12, July 9, 22, 1834; Butler to Olcott, June 19, 1834, Olcott Papers; *Evening Post*, July 8, 1834.

### 7. THE LOCO FOCO REVOLT

1. *Working Man's Advocate*, August 22, September 3, 10, October 24, 1834; *The Man*, October 9, 1834; *Evening Post*, October 8, 16, 18, 1834.

2. John Windt *et al.* to Marcy, October 6, Marcy to Windt *et al.*, October 11, 1834, Marcy Papers; *Evening Post*, October 25, 27, 30, 31, 1834.

3. Richard Blatchford to Biddle, October 10, Charles Davis to Biddle, October 13, 1834, Biddle Papers; *Evening Post*, November 7, 8, 16, 1834; *Courier and Enquirer*, November 8, 16, 1834; Jackson to Samuel Swartwout, November 10, 1834, James Kent Papers, LC.

4. Charles Davis to Biddle, November 6, Blatchford to Biddle, November 7, Webb to Biddle, November 7, 1834, Biddle Papers.

5. *New-York Times*, November 15, 17, December 17, 24, 1834, January 10, 1835; *Evening Post*, November 17, 20, 29, December 17, 19, 22, 24, 1834; George D. Strong to Van Buren, December 23, Gideon Lee to Van Buren, December 25, Theodore Sedgwick, Jr., to Van Buren, December 27, 1834, Van Buren Papers.

6. Parke Wendell to Van Buren, November 13, 1834, John Van Buren to Martin Van Buren, January 14, Paulding to Van Buren, January 19, Barnabas Bates to Van Buren, February 11, 1835, *ibid.*; *The Man*, January 7, 1835.

7. *Evening Post*, January 16, 19, 22, 1835; *The Man*, March 2, 3, 1835; Wright to Van Buren, May 22, 1835, Van Buren Papers; *Working Man's Advocate*, June 13, 1835.

8. Butler to Olcott, March 2, May 22, 1835, Olcott Papers; Hone, *Diary*, 1: 131–36.

9. *Working Man's Advocate*, January 3, April 11, 18, 1835; *The Man*, February 9, 19, 21, March 19, 25, April 3, 1835; *The Democrat*, March 18, 1835; James Kent to Moses Kent, April 3, 1835, *Memoirs And Letters of James Kent, L.L.D. Late Chancellor of the State of New York* (Boston: Little, Brown and Company, 1898),

218; Leo Hershkowitz, "The Loco Foco Party of New York: Its Origins and Career, 1835–1837," *NYHSQ*, 46 (July 1962), 314–15.

10. *Evening Post*, April 2, 4, 13, 15, 20, 1835; *Working Man's Advocate*, April 18, 1835.

11. *New-York Times*, May 13, 1835; Cambreleng to Van Buren, June 23, 1835, Van Buren Papers; *The American Citizen*, August 3, 1835; *Courier and Enquirer*, June 7, 1835; Louis Scisco, *Political Nativism in New York* (New York: Columbia University Press, 1901), 23–30.

12. *Courier and Enquirer*, March 19, April 3, 14, May 27, June 5, 19, 23, 27, July 7, 13, 1835; *Evening Post*, April 3, 8, June 10, 1835; *Evening Star*, April 3, 8, May 26, June 5, 8, 9, 11, 1835; *New-York Times*, April 18, May 10, June 10, 1835; *Spirit of '76*, July 2, 1835.

13. *Evening Star*, June 24, 26, July 2, 13, August 26, 1835; *Courier and Enquirer*, June 26, 30, July 1, 7, 13, August 8, 1835.

14. *Spirit of '76*, September 16, 1835; *Evening Star*, September 18, October 9, 31, 1835; *Courier and Enquirer*, October 30, November 2, 3, 1835; Leo Hershkowitz, "The Native American Democratic Association in New York City, 1835–1836," *NYHSQ*, 46 (January 1962), 51–54.

15. *Courier and Enquirer*, May 10, June 3, July 22, 24, August 3, 1835; *New-York Times*, June 2, 23, 1835; *Evening Post*, June 26, July 2, 13, October 19, 1835; Gilbert Barnes, *The Anti-Slavery Impulse, 1830–1834* (New York: Appleton-Century, 1933), 17–28, 47–48.

16. *Evening Post*, August 8, 12, 14, 15, 20, 22, 27, 29, 1835.

17. *Courier and Enquirer*, August 25, 27, September 5, 7, 8, 15, 18, 1835; *Evening Post*, August 26, September 3, 4, 17, 18, 21, 1835; *New-York Times*, August 28, September 8, 12, 1835.

18. *Evening Post*, September 9, 15, 26, 28, 29, 1835.

19. *Courier and Enquirer*, September 22, November 3, 1835; *Evening Post*, September 23, 27, October 7, 9, 10, 1835; *New-York Times*, October 1, 2, 1835.

20. *Ibid.*, September 22, October 3, 6, 9, 1835.

21. *Evening Post*, October 5, 6, 22, 28, 29, 1835; *Working Man's Advocate*, October 10, 17, 24, 1835; *New-York Times*, October 14, 1835; Leo Hershkowitz, "Loco Foco Party," *NYHSQ*, 320–21.

22. *New-York Times*, November 2, 1835; *Working Man's Advocate*, November 7, 1835; Fitzwilliam Byrdsall, *The History of the Loco-Foco or Equal Rights Party* (New York: Clement and Packard, 1842), 23–27.

23. *New-York Times*, November 2, 3, 1835; *New York Herald*, November 4, 1835; Cambreleng to Van Buren, November 5, 1835, Van Buren Papers.

24. *Evening Post*, October 29, November 2, 3, 4, 5, 1835; *Courier and Enquirer*, November 6, 7, 1835.

25. *Working Man's Advocate*, November 21, 1835; Marcy to Wetmore, December 15, 1835, Marcy Papers; *The Democrat*, February 14; *The New Era*, February 20, 1836.

26. *Evening Post*, November 7, 21, 1835, May 20, 1836; *The Democrat*, March 10, 1836; *Report and Constitution or Plan of Organization of the Democratic Party in Favor of Equal Rights and Opposed to ALL Monopolies by Legislation* (New York: 1836), 6–7; Hugins, *Jacksonian Democracy*, 40–41.

27. *The Democrat*, March 9, 21, October 8, 1836.

28. *Ibid.*, February 14, March 18, 1836; Byrdsall, *Loco-Foco Party*, 34, 35, 39, 43.

29. *The Democrat*, April 11, 1836.

30. Byrdsall, *Loco-Foco Party*, 15–17; "Radicalism," *The United States Magazine and Democratic Review*, 3 (October 1838), 99–111; William Trimble, "The Social Philosophy of the Loco-Foco Democracy," *The American Journal of Sociology*, 26 (May 1921), 705–21; Hugins, *Jacksonian Democracy*, 51–128; Edward Pessen, *Most Uncommon Jacksonians* (Albany: State University of New York Press, 1967).

31. *Courier and Enquirer*, December 12, 17, 18, 19, 20, 22, 1835, January 27, February 22, October 4, 1836; Flagg to Van Buren, May 27, 1836, Van Buren Papers; Alexander Wall, Jr., "The Great Fire of 1835," *NYHSQ*, 20 (January 1936), 3–22.

32. *The Democrat*, March 16, April 7, 11, 20, 1836; *New Era*, March 28, 1836; *Evening Post*, April 8, 9, 14, May 5, 23, 1836; *New Yorker*, May 25, 28, June 25, 1836.

33. *Courier and Enquirer*, March 14, 15, 17, April 14, 15, 16, 1836; Samuel Beardsley to Van Buren, April 17, Cambreleng to Van Buren, April 24, Edgar Davis to Van Buren, May 28, Dix to Van Buren, June 7, 1836, Van Buren Papers; *The Democrat*, April 25, 27, 1836; *New Yorker*, June 4, 1836; *New-York Times*, July 19, 1836.

34. Hammond to Gerrit Smith, January 23, 1836, Gerrit Smith Papers, Syracuse University; Van Buren to Junis Amis *et al.*, March 6, Democratic Committee of the City and County of New York in favor of Equal Rights . . . to Van Buren, July 1, 1836, Van Buren Papers; *The Democrat*, August 4, October 19, 1836; Byrdsall, *Loco-Foco Party*, 57.

35. Riker to Van Buren, August 29, Jameson Summers to Van Buren, August 20, 1836, Van Buren Papers; Marcy to Wetmore, July 20, October 6, 1836, Marcy Papers; *Evening Post*, November 7, 1836.

36. *The Democrat*, October 8, 1836; Byrdsall, *Loco-Foco Party*, 68.

37. *Evening Post*, September 24, 1836.

38. *Evening Star*, October 4, 5, 6, 1836; *Courier and Enquirer*, October 14, 26, 27, November 1, 1836; *Daily Express*, November 1, 4, 1836.

39. *New Yorker*, November 12, 19, 1836; *Evening Post*, November 13, 15, 1836; *Daily Express*, November 15, 1836.

40. *New Yorker*, November 12, 1836; *The Democrat*, November 26, 1836.

41. Cambreleng to Flagg, November 21, 1836, Flagg Papers; Flagg to Hoyt, December 4, 1836, *Lives and Opinions*, 175–76.

42. *New Era*, February 14, 18, 20, 1837; Gorham Worth to Van Buren, March 12, Nathaniel Tallmadge to Van Buren, March 15, Cornelius Lawrence to Van Buren, March 18, 1837, Van Buren Papers; Arthur Schlesinger, Jr., *The Age of Jackson* (Boston: Little, Brown and Company, 1950), 176–221; Peter Temin, *The Jacksonian Economy* (New York: W.W. Norton & Company, 1969).

43. Mann to Van Buren, March 23, 1837, Van Buren Papers.

44. Wright to Flagg, January 9, 18, 1837, Flagg Papers; Wright to Van Buren, January 11, Throop to Van Buren, January 28, 1837, Van Buren Papers.

45. Marcy to Wetmore, January 16, February 12, April 4, May 18, June 11, 16, 1837, Marcy Papers; Ivor Spencer, *The Victor and the Spoils: A Life of William L. Marcy* (Providence: Brown University Press, 1959), 82–96.

46. *New-York Times*, March 16, 20, April 6, 7, 1837; *New Era*, March 20, April 5, 7, 14, 1837; *Evening Post*, April 1, 4, 1837; Granger to Weed, April 18, 1837, Granger Papers.

47. *New-York Times*, April 15, 1837; *Evening Post*, April 16, 1837; *New Era*, April 17, 1837; Davis to Weed, April 20, 1837, Weed Papers; *New Yorker*, April 22, 1837; Davis to Clay, July 13, 1837, Clay Papers.

48. Cambreleng to Van Buren, April 8, Flagg to Van Buren, April 10, Van Buren to Jackson, April 20, 1837, Van Buren Papers.

49. John McClure to Van Buren, April 26, "A Real Friend" to Van Buren, May 1, New York Committee of Fifty to Van Buren, May 3, Cambreleng to Van Buren, May 6, William Price to Van Buren, May 20, Van Buren to Jackson, May 23, 1837, *ibid.*; Stephen Allen to Flagg, May 15, June 4, 1837, Flagg Papers; Marcy to Wetmore, July 12, 20, August 18, 1837, Marcy Papers.

50. Throop to Van Buren, May 10, Marcy to Van Buren, May 25, Wright to Van Buren, June 4, 1837, Van Buren Papers; *Evening Post*, May 25, June 9, 1837.

51. Bates to Van Buren, May 25, Cambreleng to Van Buren, May 30, June 14, 1837, Van Buren Papers.

52. *Evening Post*, May 23, June 7, 9, 14, 1837; *Plaindealer*, June 6, 24, 28, 1837; Byrdsall, *Loco-Foco Party*, 151.

53. Tallmadge to Croswell, June, 1837, cited in *New Yorker*, June 17, 1837; Lee to Van Buren, August 14, 1837, Van Buren Papers.

54. Cambreleng to Van Buren, July 20, August 2, Flagg to Van Buren, August 11, 1837, *ibid.*

55. *Evening Post*, August 21, 25, 31, 1837; Cambreleng to Flagg, August 21, 1837, Flagg Papers; *New Era*, August 23, 28, September 2, 1837.

56. Silas Wright to Flagg, September 5, 1837, Flagg Papers; Marcy to Wetmore, September 10, 1837, Marcy Papers; Martin Van Buren, *Inquiry into the Origin and Course of Political Parties in the United States*, Abraham and Smith Thompson Van Buren, eds. (New York: Hurd and Houghton, 1867), 231, 422–23.

57. *Evening Post*, September 5, 8, 1837; Byrdsall, *Loco-Foco Party*, 162.

58. *New-York Times*, September 8, 11, 1837; *Evening Post*, September 8, 9, 1837; Marcy to Van Buren, September 18, 1837, Van Buren Papers.

59. *Evening Post*, September 16, 22, 1837.

60. Throop to Van Buren, September 16, Van Schaick to Van Buren, September 23, 1837, Van Buren Papers; *New-York Times*, September 23, 1837; *Evening Post*, September 26, 1837; *New Era*, September 27, 1837.

61. McClure to Van Buren, September 27, 1837, Van Buren Papers; *Evening Post*, September 28, 1837; *New Yorker*, September 30, 1837.

62. Byrdsall to Curtis, September 29, 1837, Miscellaneous Papers, NYHS.

63. *Evening Post*, September 29, 1837; *Courier and Enquirer*, October 3, 1837; *New-York Times*, October 10, 17, 1837; Gallatin to Flagg, October 10, 1837, Flagg Papers; *Evening Post* October 12, 17, 1837; John Van Buren to Martin Van Buren, October 15, Martin Van Buren to Jackson, October 17, 1837, Van Buren Papers.

64. *New Era*, October 25, 1837; Byrdsall, *Loco-Foco Party*, 173–78.

65. Marcy to Wetmore, October 25, November 6, 9, 1837, Marcy Papers; *Evening Post*, October 31, November 3, 9, 10; *Courier and Enquirer*, November 11, 12, 13, 1837. The term "slam bangism" was used by conservatives as a play on Levi Slamm's name. Slamm, a leading Loco Foco, was a printer and editor among other

things, and his intemperate attacks on the conservatives made him a symbol (in their eyes) of all radical ideas.

66. Parke Wendell to Van Buren, November 13, Marcy to Van Buren, December 8, 1837, Van Buren Papers.

67. Vanderpoel to Van Buren, November 14, Cambreleng to Van Buren, November 15, 18, 1837, *ibid.*

68. "New York City *vs.* New York State," *Democratic Review*, 6 (December 1839), 500–506; Hammond, *Political Parties*, 2: 503; William Trimble, "Diverging Tendencies in the New York Democracy in the Period of the Loco Focos," *AHR*, 24 (April 1919), 396–21.

69. Preston King to Flagg, November 21, 1837, Flagg Papers; *New Era*, November 29, 1837.

70. *Evening Post*, June 4, 1835, January 3, 1838; *New-York Times*, November 20, 1837; Cambreleng to Van Buren, November 27, 1837, Van Buren Papers; *New York Herald*, January 1, 3, 1838; *Daily Express*, January 1, 1838; Marcy to Wetmore, January 22, 30, Worth to Marcy, March 20, 1838, Marcy Papers.

71. *Evening Post*, January 10, 13, March 9, 1838; *New York Herald*, January 10, 1838; *Daily Express*, January 10, 14, 1838.

72. Clay to Porter, November 24, December 5, 1837, Clay Papers; *Daily Express*, February 6, 8, 10, March 2, 3, 7, 9, 13, April 6, 7, 1838; John Dix to Van Buren, February 12, Elam Tilden to Van Buren, February 22, 1838, Van Buren Papers.

73. Evening Post, March 2, 28, April 3, 7, 14, 18, 1838; *A Voice from Old Tammany! Meeting of the People* (New York: 1838).

74. *Evening Post*, April 7, 1838; John McClure to Van Buren, April 12, 1838, Van Buren Papers.

75. Marcy to Wetmore, March 26, April 12, 1838, Marcy Papers.

76. *Evening Post*, April 19, 1838; Jackson to Van Buren, May 1, Theron Rudd to Van Buren, May 24, Jabez Hammond to Van Buren, May 26, Croswell to Van Buren, June 3, 1838, Van Buren Papers.

## 8. THE PIVOTAL YEARS: TAMMANY, NATIVISM, AND THE SCHOOL CRISIS

1. Weed to Luther Braddish, November 23, 1837, Braddish Papers, NYSL.

2. *Daily Express*, June 15, 1838.

3. *Evening Post*, June 24, August 22, 1837, April 14, 1838; *Plaindealer*, July 22, 1837; *Daily Express*, February 27, March 3, 7, April 6, 9, 26, May 30, 1838; *New Yorker*, April 14, 1838; *Evening Star*, August 8, 1838; *Truth Teller*, August 11, 1838; Barney O'Democrat [?], *The Irish Office-Hunter* (New York: 1838).

4. *Daily Express*, May 23, July 11, September 22, November 2, 1838; *Courier and Enquirer*, June 28, July 16, August 3, 16, 22, November 14, 1838.

5. Croswell to Van Buren, May 11, October 18, Van Buren to Kendall, August 6, Van Buren to Flagg, October 18, 1838, Van Buren Papers.

6. *New Era*, June 6, 8, 16, 28, August 7, 1838; *Daily Express*, September 6, October 8, 1838; *Evening Post*, September 29, October 31, 1838; Marcy to Wetmore, October 19, 1838, Marcy Papers.

7. *Evening Post*, October 16, 22, 1838; *New Era*, November 2, 3, 1838; Hoyt to Van Buren, November 4, 1838, Van Buren Papers.

8. *Daily Express*, October 9, November 3, 1838; *Truth Teller*, November 3, 1838.

9. *Courier and Enquirer*, November 10, 12, 1838; N.P. Tallmadge to Seward, November 11, 1838, Seward Papers, NYSL; Weed to Braddish, November 12, 1838, Braddish Papers; George Barstow to Tracy, December 5, 1838, Tracy Papers.

10. Flagg to Van Buren, November 9, Cambreleng to Van Buren, November 12, Dix to Van Buren, November 15, 1838, Van Buren Papers; *Evening Post*, November 14, 15, December 7, 21, 1838.

11. Cambreleng to Van Buren, November 12, 1838, Van Buren Papers; *Courier and Enquirer*, December 13, 14, 15, 16, 21, 1838, March 4, 15, 1839; *Daily Express*, March 14, 1839; "Defalcations," *Democratic Review*, 5 (May 1839), 468–86; Leo Hershkowitz, " 'The Land of Promise': Samuel Swartwout and Land Speculation in Texas, 1830–1838," *NYHSQ*, 48 (October 1964), 307–25.

12. *Courier and Enquirer*, January 16, 24, March 15, 1839; *Daily Express*, January 21, 26, March 8, 11, 14, 1839.

13. *Evening Post*, March 18, 19, 23, 27, 28, 29, April 4, 5, 1839.

14. *Daily Express*, January 12, 31, 1839; *Evening Post*, January 31, March 13, 1839; *Courier and Enquirer*, April 9, 10, 18, 1839; *Proceedings of the Board of Assistant Aldermen* (New York: 1839), Documents 8 and 18.

15. *Evening Star*, April 12, 1839; *Daily Express*, April 12, 14, 18, 1839; *Courier and Enquirer*, April 12, 13, 17, 19, 20, 1839; Butler to Van Buren, April 12, 1839, Van Buren Papers.

16. *Daily Express*, January 3, April 13, 24, 1839; *Evening Post*, April 16, 24, 1839; *Courier and Enquirer*, April 24, 1839; Flagg to Van Buren, April 30, 1839, Van Buren Papers.

17. *Daily Express*, April 7, May 14, 1839; *Courier and Enquirer*, May 3, 9, 1839.

18. Seward to Thomas Tallmadge, June 30, 1839, Van Buren Papers; Davis to Weed, July 17, 1839, Weed Papers, UR; *Daily Express*, September 20, October 9, 23, 1839; Broadside, "Circular, October 1, 1839" (Albany: 1839), Flagg Papers.

19. *Evening Post*, October 2, 4, 6, 21, 24, 30, 31, November 2, 1839; John Edmonds to Van Buren, November 12, Dix to Van Buren, November 19, 1839, Van Buren Papers; Marcy to Wetmore, January 7, 1840, Marcy Papers.

20. *Daily Express*, November 4, 5, 6, 9, 1839; *Courier and Enquirer*, November 11, 1839; "New York City vs. New York State," *Democratic Review*, 6 (December 1839), 504; Hone, *Diary*, 2: 19–20, 45–47.

21. Glyndon Van Dusen, *Thurlow Weed: Wizard of the Lobby* (Boston: Little, Brown and Company, 1947), 91.

22. William O. Bourne, *History of the Public School Society of the City of New York* (New York: William Wood, 1870), 4–26; Glyndon Van Dusen, "Seward and the School Controversy Reconsidered," *JAH*, 52 (September 1965), 313–19.

23. Thomas Boese, *Public Education in the City of New York* (New York: Harper & Bros., 1869), 110.

24. *Courier and Enquirer*, January 3, 6, 7, 9, 11, 1840.

25. *Evening Post*, January 9, 23, February 24, 1840; *Albany Argus*, January 23, 1840; *Truth Teller*, February 18, 1840.

26. *Albany Argus*, February 18, 1840; *Documents of the Board of Aldermen* (New York: 1840), 7: 39–50.

27. *Evening Post*, February 23, March 14, 1840; Flagg to Van Buren, April 30, 1840, Van Buren Papers.

28. James Kelley to Seward, March 5, Richard Blatchford to Seward, March 25, Philip Hone to Seward, March 29, 1840, Seward Papers, UR; *New Era*, March 24, 1840; *New Yorker*, March 28, 1840; Horace Greeley, *Recollections of a Busy Life* (New York: Ford, 1868), 313.

29. *Evening Post*, April 1, 1840.

30. Jacob Harvey to Seward, February 15, 1840; Seward Papers; *Evening Post*, February 29, 1840; *New York Herald*, February 29, 1840; John Pratt, "Governor Seward and the New York City School Controversy, 1840–1842," *NYH*, 43 (October 1961), 355.

31. Flagg to Van Buren, March 7, 1840, Van Buren Papers; Blatchford to the Very Reverend John Power, March 11, Westervelt to Seward, March 18, Seward to Westervelt, March 25, 1840, Seward Papers.

32. *New York Herald*, March 16, 1840; *Evening Post*, April 1, 1840; Robert Minturn to Seward, April 8, Westervelt to Seward, April 18, 1840, Seward Papers; Stephen Allen to Wright, July 4, 1840, Van Buren Papers; Allen, *Memoirs*, 191.

33. *Evening Post*, April 3, 11, 15, 17, May 3, 18, 28, 1840; *New Era*, April 9, 1840; Blatchford to Seward, April 11, 1840, Seward Papers.

34. Robert Minturn to Seward, April 10, 1840, *ibid.*; *The Important and Interesting Debate on the Claims of the Catholics for a Portion of the Common School Fund* (New York: 1840); Bourne, *Public School Society*, 318–20.

35. T.D. James to Van Buren, August 8, John J. Bedient to Van Buren, October 22, Flagg to Van Buren, November 15, 1840, Van Buren Papers; John Edmonds to Flagg, October 18, 1840, Flagg Papers; Van Buren to Bancroft, November 20, 1840, "Van Buren–Bancroft Correspondence," *Massachusetts Historical Society Publication*, 42 (1909), 388; James Glentworth, *A Statement of the Frauds on the Election Franchise in the City of New York* (New York: 1840).

36. Flagg to Tracy, August 16, 1840, Tracy Papers; *Truth Teller*, September 1, 1840; *Evening Post*, September 1, 2, 3, 4, 1840; *Albany Argus*, September 17, 1840.

37. *Albany Argus*, September 21, 1840; Greeley to Seward, September 30, 1840, Seward Papers; *Evening Post*, October 7, 1840.

38. *New York Herald*, November 2, 6, 1840; *Evening Post*, November 6, 1840; Simeon Draper to Seward, November 7, 1840, Seward Papers; *New York Observer*, January 16, 1841.

39. Morgan to Seward, January 10, 1841, Seward Papers; *Evening Post*, January 11, 20, 1841.

40. *Albany Argus*, January 9, February 17, March 17, 22, 24, 1841. The *Evening Post* published a similar series.

41. *Evening Post*, March 22, 1841; Bourne, *History of Public Schools*, 350–53.

42. Minturn to Seward, April 26, 1841, Seward Papers; *Evening Post*, April 28, 30, 1841; *New Yorker*, May 8, 1841.

43. Bishop Hughes to Seward, May 11, Seward to Bishop Hughes, May 13, 1841, Seward Papers; Ray Billington, *The Protestant Crusade, 1800–1860* (New York: Macmillan, 1938), 146–50; Edward M. Connors, *Church-State Relations in Education in the State of New York* (Washington, D.C.: Catholic University Press, 1951), 16–20.

44. *Evening Post*, May 29, 1841.

45. Birdsall to Seward, June 28, Verplanck to Seward, July 1, Harvey to Seward, July 1, 1841, Seward Papers.

46. *Albany Argus,* June 6, 1841; Minturn to Seward, June 27, 1841, Seward Papers; *Evening Post,* July 14, 1841; *New Era,* September 19, 1841.

47. Nagle to Seward, October 25, 1841, Seward Papers; Scisco, *Political Nativism,* 34–35.

48. *Evening Post,* October 26, 29, 1841; Nagle to Seward, October 28, 1841, Seward Papers; *New York Herald,* October 28, 29, 31, November 1, 1841; J.R.G. Hassard, *Life of the Most Reverend John Hughes* (New York: D. Appleton & Company, 1866), 244–45, 279.

49. *Evening Post,* October 30, 31, November 1, 1841.

50. Nagle to Seward, October 31, Greeley to Seward, November 1, 1841, Seward Papers.

51. *New York Herald,* November 5, 1841; *Evening Post,* November 8, 23, 1841; John F. Adriance to Weed, November 5, 1841, Weed Papers.

52. Bishop Hughes to Seward, November 8, Seward to Bishop Hughes, November 10, Nagle to Seward, November 15, 22, Blatchford to Seward, November 21, 1841, Seward Papers.

53. *New York Herald,* November 12, 17, 1841; *Evening Post,* November 13, 18, 19, 1841.

54. Bishop Hughes to Seward, November 29, 1841, Seward Papers; *New York Herald,* December 16, 1841; *Evening Post,* December 18, 1841.

55. Greeley to Seward, January 7, Bishop Hughes to Seward, January 10, 1842, Seward Papers; *New York Observer,* February 26, 1842.

56. *Evening Post,* January 15, February 10, 1842; *New York Observer,* February 5, 1842.

57. *Albany Argus,* January 31, 1842; *Evening Post,* February 11, 1842; *New York Herald,* February 12, 1842.

58. Bishop Hughes to Seward, January 20, 1842, Seward Papers; *Albany Argus,* February 15, 21, 1842; *New York Observer,* February 26, 1842.

59. *Evening Post,* March 2, 17, 27, April 12, 1842; Harvey to Seward, March 9, 1842, Seward Papers; *Truth Teller,* April 2, 1842; *New York Observer,* April 9, 1842; Bourne, *History of Public Schools,* 521–25.

60. *New York Observer,* July 30, 1842; Hassard, *Hughes,* 250–52; John Francis Maguire, *The Irish in America* (New York: D. & J. Sadlier & Company, 1887), 434–37; Billington, *Protestant Crusade,* 154–55.

61. *New York Herald,* April 13, 14, 16, 1842; *Truth Teller,* April 16, 1842; Harvey to Seward, May 5, 1842, Seward Papers; Broadside, "Facts and Reasoning on Church Government" (New York: 1843), NYPL.

## 9. THE POLITICS OF FLUX

1. *Evening Post,* March 22, 25, 26, November 11, 14, 23, 1842; Croswell to Tracy, October 26, 1842, Tracy Papers; Marcy to Van Buren, February 4, 1843, Van Buren Papers; Herbert Donovan, *The Barnburners* (New York: New York University Press, 1925), 20–33.

2. Matthew Fitzsimmons, "Calhoun's Bid for the Presidency, 1841–1844," *MVHR,* 28 (June 1951), 39–60; Schlesinger, *The Age of Jackson,* 406–408.

3. Fernando Wood to Van Buren, January 29, February 20, Parke Wendell to Van Buren, March 10, Wright to Van Buren, June 19, October 2, Thomas Carr to Van Buren, July 15, August 14, 1843, Van Buren Papers; *New York Herald*, September 8, 1843; Clay to Porter, September 17, 1843, Clay Papers.

4. Carr to Van Buren, September 15, 1843, Van Buren Papers.

5. Vanderpoel to Van Buren, October 26, Marcy to Van Buren, November 1, Hoyt to Van Buren, November 9, Wright to Van Buren, December 6, 1843, *ibid.;* Van Buren to James Wadsworth, December 6, 1843, Wadsworth Papers, UR; *New York Plebeian*, January 2, 5, 1844.

6. Ritchie to Van Buren, March 20, Alexander Gordon to Van Buren, March 28, Salmon Chase to Van Buren, March 30, Butler to Van Buren, April 6, Jabez Hammond to Van Buren, April 7, 1844, Van Buren Papers; Spencer to Olcott, March 23, 1844. Olcott Papers.

7. Wright to Van Buren, April 8, Cave Johnson to Van Buren, April 20, Van Buren to Hammet, April 20, 1844, Van Buren Papers.

8. Preston King to Flagg, May 7, 1844, Flagg Papers.

9. *New York Plebeian*, April 20, 26, 29, 30, May 8, 16, 20, 1844; Edmonds to Van Buren, April 30, Tilden to Van Buren, May 4, Carr to Van Buren, May 15, 1844, Van Buren Papers.

10. Flagg to Butler, May 17, Vanderpoel to Van Buren, May 22, O'Sullivan to Van Buren, May 29, Butler to Van Buren, May 31, 1844, Van Buren Papers; Daniel Dickinson to Mrs. Dickinson, May 22, 1844, *Speeches, Correspondence, Etc. of the Late Daniel D. Dickinson* (New York: G.P. Putnam & Sons, 1867), 2: 369.

11. *New York Plebeian*, May 20, 25, 31, June 5, 1844; Melville *et al.* to Van Buren, June 1, 1844, Van Buren Papers; Wood to Polk, June 1, Vanderpoel to Polk, June 4, 1844, Polk Papers, LC; Hershel Parker "Gansevoort Melville's Role in the Campaign of 1844," *NYHSQ*, 49 (April 1965), 154–55.

12. S.S. Southwick to Polk, June 4, John McKeon to Polk, June 5, 1844, Polk Papers.

13. Bouck to Polk, June 3, Croswell to Polk, June 6, 1844, *ibid.*

14. Wright to Polk, June 2, Polk to Wright, June 12, 1844, *ibid.*

15. Wright to Van Buren, June 2, Cambreleng to Van Buren, June 8, 1844, Van Buren Papers; Van Buren to Wadsworth, June 8, 1844, Wadsworth Papers; Slamm to Polk, June 27, Wood to Polk, July 19, 1844, Polk Papers; *New York Plebeian*, July 26, 1844.

16. *Ibid.*, August 8, 16, 1844; Myers, *Tammany Hall*, 134; Ira Leonard, "The Rise and Fall of the American Republican Party in New York City, 1843–1845," *NYHSQ*, 50 (April 1966), 153–62.

17. Hoyt to Van Buren, November 9, 1843, Van Buren Papers; *New York Plebeian*, November 10; *New York Citizen and American Republican*, November 23, 1843, February 17, 24, 1844; Scisco, *Political Nativism*, 40–46.

18. Vanderpoel to Van Buren, February 5, 1844, Van Buren Papers; Thomas McElrath to James Harper, March 25, 1844, James Harper Papers, NYHS; Joseph Harper, *The House of Harper* (New York: Harper & Bros., 1912), 37–45.

19. *New York Plebeian*, January 18, February 1, March 3, 11, 28, April 1, 4, 9, 1844; Carr to Van Buren, April 3, 1844, Van Buren Papers; James Richardson, "The Struggle to Establish a London-Style Police Force for New City," *NYHSQ*, 49 (April 1965), 186–87.

20. *New York Plebeian*, April 9, 1844; *New York Tribune*, April 12, 1844.

21. *Working Man's Advocate*, April 20, 1844; Joshua Hilton to Harper, April 23, 1844, Harper Papers; Elijah Purdy to Polk, July 16, 1844, Polk Papers; Hassard, *Bishop Hughes*, 276–78; Scisco, *Political Nativism*, 46–48.

22. *New York Plebeian*, July 1, 17, 22, August 2, 17, 20, 1844; John Tyler to [?], July 17, 1844, Tyler Papers, LC; Donelson to Polk, July 29, 1844, Polk Papers.

23. *New York Plebeian*, July 9, 1844; *New York Morning News*, September 12, 17, 22, 1844.

24. John L. O'Sullivan to Polk, July 8, 1844, Polk Papers; Sheldon Harris, "John Louis O'Sullivan and the Election of 1844 in New York," *NYH*, 41 (July 1960), 278–95.

25. Wood to Polk, July 11, Wadsworth to Polk, July 29, Henry Riel to Polk, August 8, 1844, Polk Papers; Wright to Dix, July 18, August 6, 1844, Dix Papers; Wright to Edmund Burke, August 8, 1844, Burke Papers, LC; *New York Plebeian*, July 27, August 12, 20, 1844; John Garraty, *Silas Wright* (New York: Columbia University Press, 1947), 295–302.

26. Gallup to Polk, September 5, Moore to Polk, September 10, Coddington to Polk, September 11, 1844, Polk Papers; *Morning News*, September 6, 1844; *New York Herald*, September 17, 1844.

27. Bouck to Polk, September 7, Marcy to Polk, September 11, Purdy to Polk, October 21, Wood to Polk, November 4, 1844, Polk Papers; Wright to Dickinson, October 9, 1844, *Dickinson's Letters*, 2: 371; Wright to Horatio Seymour, October 28, 1844, Fairchild Collection, NYHS; Circular Letter of William Cullen Bryant to Albert Tracy, July, 1844, Tracy Papers; Donovan, *Barnburners*, 85–86.

28. *New York Plebeian*, July 18, 1844; *Evening Post*, August 20, 1844; Amasa Parker to Polk, August 17, Vanderpoel to Polk, August 27, Gillet to Polk, August 27, 1844, Polk Papers.

29. Flagg to Tracy, October 25, 1844, Tracy Papers; Glyndon Van Dusen, *The Life of Henry Clay* (Boston: Little, Brown and Company, 1937), 358–78.

30. McKeon to Polk, October 23, 29, November 4, Melville to Polk, October 26, 29, 1844, Polk Papers; *New York Plebeian*, November 6, 1844.

31. Wood to Polk, October 31, Alexander Jones to Polk, November 2, Melville to Polk, November 4, 1844, Polk Papers; *Morning News*, November 2, 1844; *The Subterranean*, November 4, 1844.

32. Wood to Polk, November 5, 1844, Polk Papers.

33. *Morning News*, November 9, 1844; *Niles Register*, November 23, December 7, 1844, 67: 181, 211.

34. Butler to Polk, November 12, Bouck to Polk, November 15, Polk to Butler, November 25, 1844, Polk Papers; *Morning News*, November 20, December 18, 1844.

35. Croswell to Polk, November 30, 1844, Polk Papers.

36. Walker to Purdy, July 19, 1845, *ibid.*; Norman Graebner, "James K. Polk: A Study in Federal Patronage," *MVHR*, 38 (1952), 613–32.

37. Wood to Robert Hunter, November 20, 1844, Hunter-Garnett, Papers, UVA; Van Buren to Polk, January 4, 1845, Van Buren Papers; Seymour to Polk, February 6, Croswell to Polk, February 18, Marcy to Polk, February 24, Van Buren to Polk, February 27, O'Sullivan to Polk, March 2, Kemble to Polk, March 2, 1845, Polk Papers.

38. Smith Van Buren to Martin Van Buren, March 4, Polk to Van Buren, March 4, 1845, Van Buren Papers.

39. Wright to Tracy, March 15, 1845, Tracy Papers; Flagg to Van Buren, May 16, Cambreleng to Van Buren, May 16, 1845, Van Buren to Butler, November 17, 1846, Van Buren Papers; F.F. Marbury to Tilden, February 23, 1846, Tilden Papers, NYPL.

40. *Albany Argus,* March 12, 1845; Marcy to Benton, March 24, 1845, Marcy Papers, NYSL.

41. Butler to Dix, March 8, Flagg to Kemble, March 10, Polk to Butler, March 14, Vanderpoel to Polk, March 22, King to Polk, April 2, 1845, Polk Papers; *Morning News,* March 21, 1845; Paulding to Van Buren, May 8, 1845, Van Buren Papers.

42. *Evening Post,* December 2, 26, 1844; *New York Plebeian,* December 8, 1844, January 6, 1845; *Morning News,* November 19, December 28, 31, 1844, February 1, 2, 1845; Julius Pratt, "John L. O'Sullivan and Manifest Destiny," *NYH,* 14 (July 1933), 213–34.

43. Purdy to Tilden, January 14, 1845, Tilden Papers; *New York Plebeian,* January 15, 1845; Edward Collins *et al.* to the Council of Sachems, January 15, 1845, Minutes of the Tammany Society, NYPL.

44. *New York Plebeian,* January 16, 1845; C.S. Bogardus to Cornelius Van Ness, May 15, 1845, Polk Papers; *New York Herald,* April 22, 1851; Membership Lists, *Tammaniana of Edwin Kilroe,* 3–202.

45. James Connor to Polk, May 10, 1845, Polk Papers.

46. Purdy to Tilden, January 17, 1845, Tilden Papers; *Morning News,* January 23, February 13, 1845; *New York Plebeian,* January 24, 28, 30, 1845; David Dudley Field to Dix, January 27, 1845, Dix Papers.

47. Van Ness to Polk, January 17, March 17, 1845, Polk Papers; *Morning News,* March 12, 13, 21, April 3, 7, 1845.

48. Van Ness to Polk, April 4, Alexander Jones to Polk, April 4, 9, Vaché to Bogardus, April 6, 1845, Polk Papers.

49. S.S. Southwick to Polk, April 8, 1845, Polk Papers; *Morning News,* April 9, 10, 11, 1845; *Courier and Enquirer,* April 14, 1845.

50. Billington, *Protestant Crusade,* 262–81; Leonard, "American Republican Party," *NYHSQ,* 50: 185–91.

51. Purdy to Polk, March 29, Butler to Polk, April 8, O'Sullivan to Polk, April 12, 14, Van Ness to Polk, April 15, James Towle to Polk, April 16, 22, Wood to Polk, May 29, 1845, Polk Papers.

52. Society of Tammany to Polk, May 9, 27, John L. Graham to Polk, May 23, James Connor to Polk, May 29, 1845, *ibid.*

53. Lester to Joseph Hopkins, June, 1845, Connor to Polk, June 5, 1845, *ibid.*

54. Polk to Hoffman, June 2, Polk to Lawrence, June 3, Lawrence to Polk, June 7, 1845, *ibid.;* O'Sullivan to Tilden, June 3, 1845, Tilden Papers.

55. *Morning News,* June 9, August 27, 1845.

56. Polk to Wright, July 4, August 4, Wright to Polk, July 12, 21, 1845, Polk Papers; Wood to Lawrence, July 5, 1845, Wood Papers; NYPL; *The Subterranean,* September 5, 1845.

57. Marcy to Seymour, February 22, 1845, Fairchild Collection.

58. *Morning News,* April 12, 19, 24, 26, May 14, 22, 27, 1845; *New York Plebeian,* April 29, 1845; Van Buren to Dix, October 2, 1845, Dix Papers.

59. *Morning News,* July 4, 16, August 28, 1845; *Albany Argus,* August 18, 1845;

O'Sullivan to Polk, September 21, McKeon to Polk, October 23, 1845, Polk Papers; Van Buren to Dix, October 24, 1845; Dix Papers.

60. *Morning News*, October 4, 25, 30, 1845; McKeon to Polk, October 30, 1845, Polk Papers; *Young America*, November 1, 1845; *The Subterranean*, November 8, 1845.

61. *Morning News*, November 5, 7, 8, 10, 13, 21, 1845; White to Polk, November 10, 1845, Polk Papers.

62. Andrew Corrigan to Tilden, January 9, Isaac Fowler to Tilden, January 26, John Kellog to Tilden, January 26, 1845, Tilden Papers; Gardiner to Julia Gardiner Tyler, April 17, 1845, Tyler Papers.

63. *Morning News*, December 2, 3, 4, 13, 18, 25, 1845; Resolutions of the Democratic Republican Young Men's Committee, December 3, 1845, McKeon to Tilden, December 5, 1845, Polk Papers.

64. *Morning News*, October 14, November 22, 1845, January 13, 1846; J. Hampden Dougherty, "The Constitutions of the State of New York," *PSQ*, 3 (1888), 506–11.

65. *Morning News*, February 25, March 7, 1846; *Young America*, February 28, 1846.

66. Havemeyer to Tilden, February 10, 1846, Tilden Papers; *Morning News*, March–August, 1846.

67. *New York Herald*, April 2, 10, 13, May 4, 1846; *Morning News*, May 16, 19, 21, 1846; Cambreleng to Van Buren, May 16, 1846, Van Buren Papers; Dickinson to Polk, June 17, 1846, Polk Papers.

68. *New York Tribune*, July 9, 1846; *Morning News*, July 13, 15, 1846; D.B. Taylor to Polk, July 27, John Grogan to Dix, September 2, 1846, Polk Papers; *New York Express*, August 31, 1846.

68. James K. Polk, *Diary of James K. Polk*, Milo Quaife, ed. (Chicago: McClurg, 1910), 2: 458–59.

70. Bouck to Seymour, March 21, 1846, Seymour Papers, NYHS; *Morning News*, July 31, August 6, 8, 12, 29, September 3, 1846; Seymour to Marcy, October 17, 1846, Fairchild Collection.

71. Fowler to Tilden, July 25, August 14, Nelson Waterbury to Tilden, August 10, 1846, Tilden Papers; Croswell to Seaver, August 15, 1846, Croswell Papers, NYSL; James Lee to Polk, October 31, 1846, Polk Papers; *Evening Post*, January 15, 1847.

72. Wright to Dix, November 2, Van Buren to Dix, November 21, 1846, Dix Papers; Jacob Gould to Polk, November 6, E.A. Maynard to Polk, November 9, 1846, Polk Papers; Wright to Van Buren, November 10, Cambreleng to Van Buren, November 3, 1846, Van Buren Papers; Garraty, *Wright*, 374–75.

73. Hoffman to Flagg, November 6, 1846, Flagg Papers; John D.P. Fuller, "The Slavery Question and the Movement to Acquire Mexico," *MVHR*, 21 (1934), 31–48.

74. *Sunday Times and Noah's Weekly Messenger*, January 7, May 20, September 2, 1849, January 6, April 7, 1850; Franklin Hough, *Statistics of Population of the City and County of New York* (New York: New York Printing Company, 1866), 240; Helene Zahler, *Eastern Workingmen and National Land Policy, 1829–1862* (New York: Columbia University Press, 1941); Eric Foner, "Racial Attitudes of the New York Free Soilers," *NYH*, 46 (October 1965), 311–29.

75. Wright to Dix, January 19, 1847, Dix Papers.

76. Gardiner to Julia Gardiner Tyler, January 2, 1847, Tyler Papers; *Evening Post*, January 6, 8, 10, 11, 25, 1847; Dix to Tilden, January 20, 1847, Tilden Papers; Purdy to Polk, February 16, 1847, Polk Papers; *Sunday Times and Noah's Weekly Messenger*, February 17, 28, 1847; Minutes of the Tammany Society or Columbian Order, February 27, 1847, NYPL; Chaplain Morrison, *Democratic Politics and Sectionalism* (Chapel Hill: University of North Carolina Press, 1967), 21–92.

77. *New York Herald*, February 17, 19, March 3, April 5, 1847; *Evening Post*, February 19, 27, March 1, 24, April 9, 12, 17, 24, 1847; *New York Express*, April 12, 16, 1847.

78. *Sunday Times and Noah's Weekly Messenger*, April 18, May 16, 23, 1847; *Evening Post*, April 26, 1847; *New York Herald*, April 28, May 16, 1847.

79. John Van Buren to Wadsworth, April 25, June 26, 28, 1847, Wadsworth Papers; *Evening Post*, August 5, 13, 17, 24, 1847; William Cassidy to Tilden, September 14, 1847, Tilden Papers.

80. Croswell to Seaver, August 30, 1847, Croswell Papers; Minutes of the Society of Tammany, August 31, 1847, 103–104, NYPL; Simeon Bloodgood to Caleb Cushing, September 20, 1847, Caleb Cushing Papers, LC; Wilmot to Martin Van Buren, September 25, 1847, Van Buren Papers.

81. *Evening Post*, September 17, September 17, October 6, 1847; *New York Herald*, September 18, October 6, 7, November 1, 1847; King to Flagg, October 15, 1847, Flagg Papers; *The Syracuse Convention—Its Spurious Organization & Oppressive & Anti-Republican Action* (Albany: 1847); *The Herkimer Convention, The Voice of New York!* (New York: 1847).

82. *Sunday Times and Noah's Weekly Messenger*, October 17, 1847.

83. *Evening Post*, October 29, 31, November 3, 5, 20, 1847.

84. John Van Buren to Wadsworth, November 8, 1847, Wadsworth Papers; John Van Buren to Martin Van Buren, November 13, 1847, Van Buren Papers; King to Dix, November 13, Flagg to Dix, November 13, 22, 1847, Dix Papers.

85. Croswell to Seaver, December 19, 1847, Croswell Papers.

86. *New York Herald*, January 4, 17, 21, 30, 1848; *Evening Post*, January 14, 24, 31, 1848; Dix to Flagg, February 3, 1848, Flagg Papers, CU; *New York State Convention held at the Capitol, January 26 and January 27, 1848* (Albany: 1848).

87. *New York Herald*, January 31, 1848; *Evening Post*, February 16, 1848.

88. Marcy to Wetmore, January 28, 1848, Marcy Papers; Albert Gallup to Polk, February 19, 1848, Polk Papers; John Van Buren to William Collins, May 15, 1848, Miscellaneous Papers, NYSL.

89. *Sunday Times and Noah's Weekly Messenger*, January 30, 1848.

90. *New York Herald*, March 13, 28, 29, 1848; *Evening Post*, March 20, 22, 23, 31, 1848; *Sunday Times and Noah's Weekly Messenger*, April 2, 1848.

91. Wood to I.O. Birney, March 29, 1848, Miscellaneous Papers, NYSL.

92. *Evening Post*, April 12, 13, 1848.

93. Martin Van Buren, "Address of the Democratic Members of the Legislature of the State of New York," *The Writings and Speeches of Samuel J. Tilden*, John Bigelow, ed. (New York: Harper & Bros., 1885), 2: 563; Alexander Flick, *Samuel J. Tilden* (New York: Dodd, Mead & Co., 1939), 82–83.

94. Martin Van Buren, "Address," *Tilden's Works*, 2: 569, 572, 573

95. John Van Buren to Martin Van Buren, April 30, 1848, Van Buren Papers.

96. Martin Van Buren to John Van Buren, May 3, 1848, *ibid.* See also Joseph Rayback, "Martin Van Buren's Desire for Revenge in the Campaign of 1848," *MVHR*, 40 (March 1954), 710–15.

97. *New York Herald*, May 6, 18, 1848; Walker to Polk, May 22, 1848, Polk Papers.

98. *New York Herald*, May 24, 27, 29, 1848; *Evening Post*, May 27, 29, June 3, 1848; *Sunday Times and Noah's Weekly Messenger*, May 28, 1848.


10. DIVISION, REUNION, AND THE TAMMANY SOCIETY

1. *New York Herald*, May 26, 1848.

2. *Evening Post*, May 26, June 7, 8, July 23, August 5, 8, 14, 1848; Butler to Van Buren, May 31, 1848, Van Buren Papers; Marcy to Wetmore, June 29, 1848, Marcy Papers.

3. *New York Herald*, June 4, 7, 11, 1848.

4. Samuel Waterbury to Van Buren, June 16, Van Buren to Waterbury, June 20, John Van Buren to Martin Van Buren, June 26, 1848, Van Buren Papers.

5. *Evening Post*, June 23, 28, 1848; *Proceedings of the Utica Convention for the Nomination of President and Vice-President of the United States* (Albany: 1848).

6. Marcy to Wetmore, June 10, July 10, 1848, Marcy Papers; Croswell to Seymour, June 24, 1848, Fairchild Collection; Dickinson to Polk, July 8, 1848, Polk Papers; Dickinson to Lewis Cass, July 10, 1848, Cass Papers, Clements Library; *Democratic Review*, 23 (July 1848), 6–12; *New York Herald*, July 8, 1848.

7. Flagg to Dix, July 2, Butts to Dix, July 10, 1848, Dix Papers; Gideon Welles to Flagg, July 4, 1848, Flagg Papers, CU; *New York Herald*, July 1, 1848, January 19, 23, 1853; *Sunday Times and Noah's Weekly Messenger*, July 2, 1848.

8. Van Buren to Butler, August 2, 1848, Van Buren Papers; Van Buren to Wadsworth, August 2, 1848, Wadsworth Papers; *Evening Post*, August 9, 11, 12, 23, 26, 1848; *Sunday Times and Noah's Weekly Messenger*, August 20, 1848; Marcy to Wetmore, August 20, 1848, Marcy Papers; *New York Herald*, August 27, 1848.

9. *Evening Post*, September 1, 1848; *New York Herald*, January 21, 1853.

10. J. Addison Thomas to Polk, August 24, Cargill to Polk, September 25, McKeon to Polk, September 29; Wood to Polk, September 29, Bogardus to Polk, October 7, 1848, Polk Papers; *Evening Post*, September 13, 18, 26, October 12, 15, 1848; Butler to Van Buren, October 3, 1848, Van Buren Papers. Bogardus was an unpopular man among Democratic workingmen. When an assistant to Collector Van Ness, he had introduced some mechanical innovations that displaced many laborers on the docks.

11. Henry Western to Marcy 10, 1849, Marcy Papers. In his analogy, Western was making a play on the word "sheperd," which really stood for Lorenzo Shepard, the emerging leader among city Marcyites.

12. Purdy to Polk, October 18, 1848, Polk Papers; *Evening Post*, September 28, 29, October 22, 25, 27, 30, November 6, 8, 1848; Marcy to Cass, October 26, 1848, Cass Papers; *New York Tribune*, November 24, 1848.

13. *Evening Post*, November 8, 22, 1848.

14. Hammond to Seymour, November 22, 1848, Fairchild Collection; *Sunday Times and Noah's Weekly Messenger*, February 13, 1849; Flagg to Van Buren, July 9, 1849, Van Buren Papers; Polk, *Diary*, 4: 228, 243; Frank Woodford, *Lewis*

*Cass, The Last Jeffersonian* (New Brunswick: Rutgers University Press, 1950). "Squatter sovereignty," which Stephen Douglas later called "popular sovereignty," proposed that the actual settlers should decide for themselves whether or not they wanted to establish slavery in their territory.

15. Byrdsall to Marcy, April 7, 1849, Fairchild Collection; Dix to Van Buren, June 9, 1849, Van Buren Papers; Croswell to Seaver, July 21, 1849, Croswell Papers; *New York Herald*, August 29, 1849.

16. *Sunday Times and Noah's Weekly Messenger*, August 19, 1849.

17. Charles Noble to Seymour, March 21, 1849, Fairchild Collection; Henry Western to Marcy, April 28, May 10, Marcy to Wetmore, May 31, 1849, Marcy Papers.

18. *New York Herald*, February 13, April 4, May 1, 1849; *Evening Post*, March 15, 17, 31, April 12, 1849; *Sunday Times and Noah's Weekly Messenger*, April 8, 1849.

19. Marcy to Wetmore, February 25, 1849, Marcy Papers; Lewis Birdsall to Stephen Douglas, March 18, 1849, Douglas Papers, University of Chicago; Matthew Davis to Seward, March 23, 26, 1849, Seward Papers; *The Manual of the Corporation of the City of New York* (New York: 1852), 34–36.

20. *New York Herald*, April 18, May 19, 22, 1849; *Evening Post*, May 24, 1849; Croswell to Seaver, June 28, 1849, Croswell Papers.

21. *New York Herald*, June 30, July 4, August 1, 13, 1849; *Evening Post*, July 2, 1849; Cass to Marcy, July 23, Western to Marcy, July 31, August 2, 1849, Marcy Papers.

22. Marcy to Wetmore, July 23, Wetmore to Marcy, July 24, 1849, *ibid.*

23. *New York Herald*, July 14, 18, 27, August 13, 18, September 13, 15, 1849; Croswell to Seaver, August 25, 1849, Croswell Papers; *Evening Post*, September 14, 15, 18, 1849; Marcy to Wetmore, October 23, 1849, Marcy Papers; *Official Proceedings of the State Convention Held at Rome*, August 15, 16 & 17, 1849 (Albany: 1849).

24. *Sunday Times and Noah's Weekly Messenger*, September 16, 23, October 7, 1849; Dickinson to Marcy, September 23, 1849, Marcy Papers; *New York Herald*, September 23, 1849.

25. *New York Tribune*, October 24, 1849; *New York Herald*, October 29, 30, 1849.

26. *Evening Post*, October 31, 1849; *New York Herald*, November 1, 1849; *Sunday Times and Noah's Weekly Messenger*, November 4, 1849.

27. *Evening Post*, November 7, 9, 11, 1849; Marcy to Wetmore, November 13, 1849, Marcy Papers.

28. *Evening Post*, January 4, 22, 1850; Dickinson to Marcy, January 29, Shepard to Marcy, February 2, 1850, Marcy Papers; *Sunday Times and Noah's Weekly Messenger*, February 10, 1850; *New York Herald*, February 12, 16, 1850.

29. *New York Tribune*, May 7, 10, 12, 1849; *New York Herald*, January 11, 17, February 11, 17, 1850; *Evening Post*, February 17, 20, 21, 1850; *Sunday Times and Noah's Weekly Messenger*, February 24, April 7, 1850.

30. Shepard to Marcy, February 20, 1849, Marcy Papers; *New York Herald*, March 11, 1850.

31. *Evening Post*, January 26, 1850; *New York Herald*, February 23, 26, March 3, 14, April 1, 3, 1850; *Sunday Times and Noah's Weekly Messenger*, February 3, 24, March 17, 1850; Marcy to Wetmore, March 1, 1850, Marcy Papers; Philip

Foner, *Business and Slavery* (Chapel Hill: University of North Carolina Press, 1941), 20–30.

32. Shepard to Marcy, April 5, Western to Marcy, April 11, 1850, Marcy Papers; *Evening Post*, April 5, 7, 10, 1850; *Sunday Times and Noah's Weekly Messenger*, April 14, 1850.

33. *New York Herald*, April 16, 17, 1850; *Sunday Times and Noah's Weekly Messenger*, April 21, 1850; Myers, *Tammany Hall*, 146–47.

34. *New York Herald*, April 29, May 1, 6, 7, 1850; *Evening Post*, May 7, 1850.

35. *New York Herald*, May 10, 20, 21, 23, 1850.

36. Cutting *et al.* to Marcy, May 7, Marcy to Cutting *et al.*, May 10, Schell to Marcy, June 7, Marcy to Schell, June 17, 1850, Marcy Papers; Edward West to Douglas, May 11, 1850, Douglas Papers; *New York Herald*, May 13, June 18, 1850; *Sunday Times and Noah's Weekly Messenger*, June 16, 1850.

37. *New York Herald*, May 24, June 22, 1850.

38. *Ibid.*, June 27, 1850.

39. Flagg to Wadsworth, March 8, 1850, Wadsworth Papers; Dix to Flagg, July 27, 1850, Flagg Papers; Croswell to Seymour, July 28, 1850, Fairchild Collection; Marcy to Seymour, July 28, 1850, Marcy Papers; Robert Rayback, *Millard Fillmore* (Buffalo: Henry Steward, Incorporated, 1959), 238–53.

40. *New York Herald*, July 16, 18, 22, August 1, 15, 24, 28, September 4, 10, 11, 1850; *Sunday Times and Noah's Weekly Messenger*, August 25, September 1, 1850.

41. *New York Herald*, September 13, 14, 27, 29, 1850; Gillet to Douglas, September 15, 1850, Douglas Papers; *Sunday Times and Noah's Weekly Messenger*, September 15, 22, 29, October 13, 1850; *Irish-American*, October 5, 1850.

42. *New York Herald*, October 8, 12, 13, 1850; *Sunday Times and Noah's Weekly Messenger*, October 20, 1850; *Irish-American*, October 26, 1850.

43. Van Buren to Worth, October 30, 1850, Van Buren Papers; Foner, *Business and Slavery*, 34–54.

44. *New York Herald*, November 6, 7, 12, 14, 18, 1850; *Sunday Times and Noah's Weekly Messenger*, November 10, 1850; *Manual of the Corporation*, 732; Thomas Marshall, "Diary and Memoranda of William L. Marcy," *AHR*, 24 (April 1919), 451.

45. John Van Buren to Martin Van Buren, January 20, 1851, Van Buren Papers; Simeon Jewett to Marcy, May 7, Wetmore to Marcy, June 4, 1851, Marcy Papers; Croswell to Seaver, June 19, 1851, Croswell Papers; *New York Herald*, July 22, 1851; Shaw, *Erie Water West*, 362–73.

46. *Sunday Times and Noah's Weekly Messenger*, April 27, 1851; Delevan to Bennett, June 18, cited by *New York Herald*, July 5, 6, 1851; Storms to Marcy, June 11, 1851, Marcy Papers.

47. *New York Herald*, March 15, 1851; *Sunday Times and Noah's Weekly Messenger*, March 16, 1851; Byrdsall to Buchanan, December 1, 18, 1851, Buchanan Papers, HSP; Roy Nichols, *The Democratic Machine, 1850–1854* (New York: Columbia University Press, 1923), 79–86.

48. Bouck to Seymour, July 30, 1851, Fairchild Collection; *Evening Post*, August 4, 1851; Seymour to Marcy, August 7, Jewett to Marcy, August 11, 1851, Marcy Papers; *New York Herald*, September 10–15, 1851; *New York Times*, September 20, 1851.

49. *Sunday Times and Noah's Weekly Messenger*, September 14, 21, October 5, 1851; Marcy to Wetmore, September 15, 18, Wetmore to Marcy, September 26, Buchanan to Marcy, September 30, 1851, Marcy Papers.

50. *New York Herald,* October 30, 31, 1851.
51. *Ibid.,* November 5, 1851; *New York Times,* November 6, 1851; *New York Tribune,* November 7, 8, 1851; Marcy to Buchanan, November 10, Marcy to Campbell, November 10, 1851, Marcy Papers.
52. Shepard to Marcy, December 5, 1851, *ibid.*
53. *New York Herald,* October 22, 1851; Thomas to Marcy, November 6, Seymour to Marcy, November 11, 20, Shepard to Marcy, November 26, Wetmore to Marcy, November 28, Marcy to Wetmore, November 29, Marcy to Beardsley, December 10, 1851, Marcy Papers; Marcy to Seymour, December 12, 1851, Fairchild Collection; Merle Curti, "Young America," *AHR,* 32 (October 1926), 34–55.
54. Marcy to Campbell, December 6, Beardsley to Marcy, December 9, Croswell to Marcy, December 10, 1851, Marcy Papers; Marcy to Wadsworth, December 8, 1851, Wadsworth Papers; Herbert Johnson, "Magyar-Mania in New York City," *NYHSQ,* 43 (July 1964), 237–49.
55. Thomas to Marcy, December 2, 8, 12, 1851, Marcy Papers.
56. Shepard to Marcy, December 17, 27, 29, Thomas to Marcy, December 18, 19, Marcy to Wetmore, December 23, 1851, Marcy to Thomas, January 12, John Van Buren to Pratt, February 13, 1852, *ibid.*
57. Shepard to Marcy, January 13, Marcy to Wetmore, January 17, February 2, Marcy to Tilden, April 2, 1852, *ibid.;* Marcy to Seymour, January 16, 1852, Fairchild Collection; *New York Herald,* January 15, April 6, 9, 10, 1852.
58. Pruyn to Marcy, June 2, 3, Wetmore to Marcy, June 17, 1852, Marcy Papers; Dix to Pierce, June 5, Marcy to Pierce, June 5, Vanderpoel to Pierce, June 8, Dickinson to Pierce, June 9, Dunlop to Pierce, June 24, 1852, Pierce Papers, LC; *Sunday Times and Noah's Weekly Messenger,* June 13, 1852; Nichols, *Democratic Machine,* 129–62.
59. *New York Herald,* January 27, 30, February 1, 1852; *Sunday Times and Noah's Weekly Messenger,* March 14, 1852; Greeley, *Recollections,* 99–100.
60. Thomas to Marcy, January 9, May 28, 1852, Marcy Papers; *New York Herald.* April 9, 1852; Byrdsdall to Buchanan, May 18, 23, 1852, Buchanan Papers; Dennis Lynch, *Boss Tweed; The Story of a Grim Generation* (New York: Boni & Liveright, 1927), 67–74.
61. *New York Leader,* April 17, 1862, August 23, December 19, 1863; *New York Times,* January 9, 1866; Tammany Membership Lists, *Tammaniana of Edwin Kilroe,* 3–202.

## 11. POLITICAL CHAOS AND THE TAMMANY SOCIETY

1. Tammany Society to Van Buren, June 14, Van Buren to Tammany Society, July 1, 1852, Van Buren Papers; *New York Herald,* June 14, July 5, 1852.
2. Marcy to Pierce, July 12, Auburn Birdsall to Pierce, September 28, Schell to Pierce, September 28, McKeon to Pierce, October 1, Upsham to Pierce, October 25, 1852, Pierce Papers; Thomas to Marcy, July 19, 29, 31, August 14, 1852, Marcy Papers; Buchanan to Sickles, October 25, 1852, Buchanan Papers, Dickinson College.
3. Salmon Chase to Van Buren, June 27, 1852, Van Buren Papers; King to Flagg, August 16, 1852, Flagg Papers, CU; Van Buren to Pierce, October 18, 1852, Pierce Papers.
4. *New York Herald,* August 20, 24, 25, 26, 27, 28, September 1, 3, 8, 11, 12, 13, 14, 30, 1852; *Report of the Committee of Arrangements of the Common Council*

*of New York of the Obsequies in Memory of the Honorable Henry Clay* (New York: 1852).

5. McKeon to Pierce, October 1, 1852, Pierce Papers.

6. *Irish-American,* October 2, 15, 1852; *New York Times,* October 28, November 8, 16, 1852; *New York Herald,* October 29, 31, November 2, 18, 1852; Seymour to Flagg, November 4, 1852, Flagg Papers, CU.

7. *New York Times,* December 4, 1852.

8. *New York Herald,* December 4, 5, 10, 14, 25, 1852, January 9, 10, 15, 20, 22, 1853; *New York Times,* January 21, 1853.

9. *New York Herald,* January 21, 22, 27, 1853.

10. *Ibid.,* February 10, 1853.

11. *Ibid.,* January 29, February 3, 4, 10, 1853.

12. *Address of the Grand Council of Tammany Society Upon the Subject of their Recent Decision Relative to the Political Use of Tammany Hall* (New York: 1853), 3, 12.

13. *New York Times,* January 22, 1853; *New York Herald,* February 11, 13, July 5, 21, 1853; Myers, *Tammany Hall,* 164–65.

14. *New York Herald,* April 19, 1853.

15. Pierce to Dix, March 28, 1853, Dix Papers; John Van Buren to Isaac Fowler, March 21, 1853, *Tilden's Letters,* 1: 99–101; *New York Herald,* March 30, 1853; Roy Nichols, *Franklin Pierce* (Philadelphia: University of Pennsylvania Press, 1931), 232–38.

16. *New York Herald,* April 12, May 17, June 3, July 21, 1853; Thomas to Marcy, April 19, Tilden to Marcy, June 21, Cochrane to Marcy, June 23, 1853, Marcy Papers; Marcy to Dix, June 12, 1853, Dix Papers; Fowler to Pierce, August 15, 1853, Tilden Papers.

17. *New York Herald,* March 3, 1853; *Evening Post,* March 3, 4, 8, 1853; Myers, *Tammany Hall,* 167–71; I.N.P. Stokes, *Iconography of Manhattan Island, 1498–1909* (New York: R.H. Dodd, 1915–1928), 5: 1848–49.

18. *New York Times,* June 5, 7, 8, 1853.

19. Marcy to Tilden, August, 1853, Tilden Papers; *New York Herald,* September 2, 3, 6, 9, 10, 13, 14, 1853; Seymour to Marcy, November 5, 1853, Marcy Papers.

20. *New York Herald,* September 24, 1853.

21. *Ibid.,* September 22, 27, October 7, 1853; *New York Times,* September 29, 1853.

22. *New York Herald,* October 14, 17, 22, 26, 28, 1853; Marcy to Tilden, October 16, 1853, Tilden Papers; Wetmore to Marcy, November 2, 1853, Marcy Papers.

23. Purdy to Marcy, October 26, Tilden to Marcy, October 27, John Van Buren to Marcy, October 29, Wood to Marcy, November 28, Seymour to Marcy, December 7, Redfield to Marcy, December 10, 14, 1853, February 2, 27, 1854, *ibid.;* Redfield to Douglas, December 9, 1853, Douglas Papers.

24. *New York Herald,* October 14, 16, November 1, 3, 13, 24, 1853; Seymour to Marcy, November 13, 24, 1853, Marcy Papers; James Cooley, *Speech of the Hon. James E. Cooley, Before the Democracy of Syracuse in Mass Meeting Assembled* (Syracuse: 1853).

25. Edward West to Douglas, November 15, 1853, Douglas Papers; Stryker to Marcy, November 24, 1853, Marcy Papers; *New York Herald,* December 16, 1853.

26. Wood to Marcy, November 24, 1853, Marcy Papers.

27. *New York Herald,* January 6, 9, 10, 19, 26, 1854; Wetmore to Marcy, January 11, 1854; Nichols, *Pierce,* 317.

28. *New York Herald,* January 7, 10, 26, 1854; Shepard to Marcy, January 18, 24, 1854, Marcy Papers.

29. Croswell to Douglas, February 1, 1854, Douglas Papers; Jones to Marcy, February 7, Seymour to Marcy, February 21, 27, 1854, Marcy Papers; Blair to Dix, March 9, 1854, Dix Papers; Spencer, *Marcy,* 274–82.

30. *New York Herald,* January 30, February 1, 2, 27, 28, 1854; Shepard to Marcy, February 7, Cochrane to Marcy, February 9, Cochrane to Pierce, February 9, John Van Buren to Marcy, February 12, 1854, Marcy Papers.

31. *New York Herald,* February 4, 8, 13, 14, 1854; Redfield to Douglas, February 27, 1854, Douglas Papers; Redfield to Marcy, March 18, 1854, Marcy Papers.

32. Shepard to Marcy, March 4, 6, 1854, *ibid.*

33. John Van Buren to Marcy, March 8, 1854, *ibid.; New York Herald,* March 10, 12, 14, 16, 18, 1854.

34. Cochrane to Marcy, March 18, 1854, Marcy Papers.

35. Purdy to Douglas, March 9, 1854, Douglas Papers; *New York Herald,* May 24, June 5, 7, 8, 11, 16, 17, 30, 1854.

36. Flagg to Seymour, March 10, 1854, Seymour Papers; *New York Herald,* March 26, April 1, 10; *New York Tribune,* April 2, 1854; Seymour to Marcy, May 25, 1854, Marcy Papers; Scisco, *Political Nativism,* 62–107; Rayback, *Fillmore,* 375–93.

37. *Irish-American,* June 3, July 1, 1854; Darius Perrin to Daniel Ullman, September 21, 1854, Ullman Papers, NYHS; *New York Times,* October 10, 1854.

38. Cutting to Marcy, August 8, Seymour to Marcy, September 9, 18, 1854, Marcy Papers; *New York Herald,* August 13, 30, September 7, 8, 23, 28, 1854; John J. Taylor to Seymour, August 30, Garvin, Richmond, and Cassidy to Seymour, September 7, 1854, Seymour Papers, NYSL; Mitchell, *Seymour,* 160–64; John Krout, "The Maine Law in New York Politics," *NYH,* 34 (1936), 260–72.

39. *New York Herald,* March 28, July 1, 5, August 2, 1854.

40. Robert Kelly to Seymour, October 7, 1854, Seymour Papers.

41. *The Volunteer,* October 13, 1854; *New York Herald,* October 14, 22, November 3, 1854.

42. *Irish-American,* October 26, 1850, September 2, 30, October 28, 1854; Shepard to Marcy, June 21, 28, July 6, 9, 10, Purdy to Marcy, July 6, Wood to Marcy, July 12, 1854, Marcy Papers; *New York Herald,* October 10, 1854.

43. *Ibid.,* October 27, November 2, 3, 13, 1854; *The Volunteer,* October 30, 1854; *Evening Post,* November 2, 1854; *Irish-American,* November 4, 1854.

44. *New York Times,* November 1, 9, 1854; *Irish-American,* November 4, 1854; Abijah Ingraham, *A Biography of Fernando Wood, a History of the Forgeries, Perjuries, and other Crimes of Our "Model" Mayor* (New York: 1856), 21–22; *Manual of the Corporation,* 734.

45. *New York Herald,* November 8, 19, December 12, 20, 1854, January 25, March 31, 1855; Alexander Mann to Ullmann, November 16, 1854, Ullman Papers; Butler to Van Buren, December 2, 1854, Van Buren Papers; John Kelly to Marcy, May 31, Seymour to Marcy, June 21, 1855, Marcy Papers.

46. *New York Times,* January 2, 12, February 26, March 6, 1855; Wood to Marcy, March 20, 1855, Marcy Papers; *New York Herald,* March 31, 1855; George Templeton Strong, *The Diary of George Templeton Strong,* Allan Nevins and Milton Thomas, eds. (New York: Macmillan, 1952), 2: 211.

47. *New York Herald,* November 16, December 4, 16, 18, 1854, January 1, 1855.

48. *Ibid.,* January 9, 20, 1855.

49. *Ibid.*, March 3, 7, 8, 14, 21, April 4, 1855; Sidney Webster, "Mr. Marcy, the Cuba Question and the Ostend Manifesto," *PSQ,* 8 (March 1893), 1–32; Nichols, *Pierce,* 326–71.

50. Robert Morris to Marcy, April 14, Shepard to Marcy, April 14, 20, 1855; Marcy Papers; *New York Herald,* April 20, 1855.

51. *New York Tribune,* November 21, 1854; *New York Times,* April 17, 1855; *New York Daily News,* April 30, 1855; Wood to Chief of Police, June 25, 1855, cited by Donald MacLeod, *A Biography of Fernando Wood* (New York: 1856); T.R. Whitney, *A Defense of American Policy* (New York: DeWitt & Davenport, 1856), 388; Lynch, *Boss Tweed,* 128–37.

52. *Irish-American,* May 22, 1855; *New York Tribune,* August 4, 1855; Samuel Pleasants, *Fernando Wood of New York* (New York: Columbia University Press, 1948), 56–57.

53. Shepard to Marcy, May 12, 23, 29, 1855, Marcy Papers.

54. *New York Herald,* May 29, 30, June 1, 5, 23, 27, 28, July 2, 8, 12, 13, 15, 16, 29, August 16, 1855; *Daily News,* August 22, 1855; Dickinson to Edmund Burke, September 2, 1855, Burke Papers, LC; John S. Wise, *The End of an Era* (Boston and New York: Houghton Mifflin Company, 1899), 54–57.

55. Raymer to Ullman, January 22, March 4, Sargeant to Ullman, March 18, 1855, Ullman Papers; Seymour to Marcy, July 31, 1855, Marcy Papers; Thomas Curran, "Seward and the Know-Nothings," *NYHSQ,* 41 (April 1967), 141–69.

56. *New York Herald,* August 3, 5, 15, 17, 18, 24, 1855; Marcy to Seymour, August 24, 1855, Fairchild Collection; Marcy to Buchanan, September 2, 1855, Marcy Papers.

57. Shepard to Marcy, August 9, Seymour to Marcy, September 8, John Van Buren to Marcy, September 20, 1855, *ibid.*

58. *New York Herald,* August 28, 31, September 1, 2, 3, 1855.

59. *Ibid.*, September 3, 7, 1855; Shepard to Marcy, September 8, Seymour to Marcy, September 9, 1855, Marcy Papers.

60. *New York Herald,* September 14, 20, 21, 28, 30, 1855; *New York Times,* September 20, 26, 1855; *Daily News,* September 30, 1855.

61. *New York Herald,* September 22, 27, 29, October 1, 2, 1855.

62. Seymour to Marcy, September 26, October 5, November 9, Parker to Marcy, November 10, 1855, Marcy Papers; *New York Herald,* September 29, October 1, 3, 5, 6, 8, 9, 11, 16, 16, 18, 19, 22, 23, 26, 31, 1855; Loomis to Seymour, October 11, 1855, Seymour Papers, NYSL; Seymour to Tilden, October 11, 1855, Tilden Papers.

63. *New York Herald,* November 7, 11, 12, December 6, 1855, January 3, 11, 1856; Bloodgood to Marcy, November 17, Seymour to Marcy, November 27, Redfield to Marcy, November 27, Dickie to Marcy, December 24, 1855, Marcy Papers; H.H. Van Dyke to Van Buren, December 21, 1855, January 14, 1856, Van Buren Papers; *New York Times,* January 9, 10, 11, 12, 14, 1856; *New York Hards and Softs—Which is the True Democracy* (New York: 1856); *The Softs, The True Democracy of the State of New York* (New York: 1856).

64. *New York Herald,* January 6, 9, 1856.

65. *Ibid.*, January 30, 1856; Rynders to Marcy, April 18, 1856, Marcy Papers.

66. Marcy to Seymour, February 25, 1855, Fairchild Collection; *New York Herald,* February 2, 20, 1856; West to Douglas, February 15, 1856, Douglas Papers.

67. *New York Herald*, February 27, 28, 1856; Disney to Douglas, February 26, 28, 1856, Douglas Papers.

68. Disney to Douglas, March [March 1, 2, 3, 4, 5, 7,] 1856, *ibid.*

69. Singleton to Douglas, March 5, Dillaye to Douglas, March 22, West to Douglas, April 8, 1856, *ibid.; New York Herald*, April 19, 24, 1856; *New York Times*, April 25, 1856.

70. Morgan to Van Buren, May 14, Tilden to Van Buren, May 15, 1856; Van Buren Papers; West to Douglas, May 10, Richard Connolly to Douglas, May 22, 1856, Douglas Papers; *New York Herald*, May 18, 1856; *Voice of the Radical Democracy of New York* (New York: 1856).

71. John Pruyn, Diary, June 1–6, 1856, NYSL; *New York Herald*, June 1–8, 1856; Disney to Douglas, June 7, 1856, Douglas Papers; Roy Nichols, *Disruption of American Democracy* (New York: Macmillan, 1948), 16–17.

72. Byrdsall to Buchanan, June 7, Dix to Buchanan, June 13, 1856, Buchanan Papers, HSP; *New York Herald*, June 8, 12, 13, 1856; *Irish-American*, June 21, 1856.

73. *New York Herald*, May 22, June 22, July 3, 6, 9, 1856; Delevan to Seymour, May 6, 1855, Seymour Papers, NYSL; Marcy to Savage, June 10, 1856, Marcy Papers; Tammany Society or Columbian Order, *Invitation to Fourth of July Celebration at Tammany Hall, 1856,* Tammany Society Papers, NYPL.

74. Wood to Seymour, July 24, Seymour to Furlong, September 1, 1856, Seymour Papers, NYSL; *New York Herald*, July 10, 17, August 11, 1856; *Daily News*, August 11, 1856.

75. *New York Herald*, August 3, 6, 1856.

76. *New York Times*, September 3, 4, October 16, 1856; *Irish-American*, September 6, October 25, 1856; *New York Herald*, November 2, 1856.

77. *Ibid.*, September 6, 9, 12, 16, 17, 1856; *New York Times*, September 16, 1856; *Daily News*, September 18, 1856.

78. *New York Herald*, September 18, 27, October 14, 1856.

79. *Ibid.*, September 20, 1856.

80. *New York Times*, October 8, 23, 1856; *New York Herald*, October 8, 9, 20, 1856; Lynch, *Boss Tweed*, 156–60.

81. *New York Herald*, November 5, 11, 15, 22, December 2, 1856; *Manual of the Corporation*, 734.

## 12. THE TAMMANY SOCIETY AND MOZART HALL

1. Parker to Buchanan, November 6, Beardsley to Buchanan, November 7, Wood to Buchanan, November 8, Lynch to Buchanan, November 11, 1856, Buchanan Papers.

2. Dix to Buchanan, November 24, 1856, Dix Papers; Sickles to Buchanan, November 25, 1856, Buchanan Papers; Buchanan to John Y. Mason, December 29, 1856; *The Works of James Buchanan*, John B. Moore, ed. (Philadelphia: J.B. Lippincott Company, 1911), 10: 100; Philip Klein, *President James Buchanan* (University Park: Pennsylvania State University Press, 1962), 261–72.

3. Wood to Buchanan, November 28, December 26, Buchanan to Wood, December 1, Bennett to Buchanan, December 23, 1856, Buchanan Papers; Butterfield to Arnold Harris, December 22, 1856, Douglas Papers.

4. *New York Times*, November 24, 27, 1856, January 2, 3, 5, 8, 1857; *New York Herald*, November 24, 1856; Wood to Buchanan, January 8, 1857, Buchanan Papers.

5. *Statement of the Majority of the Grand Council of the Tammany Society or Columbian Order* (New York: 1857), 12–13, 14.

6. *Ibid.*, 4–5; *New York Times*, February 21, 23, 1857.

7. *Statement*, 22; *New York Times*, March 3, 1857.

8. *New York Herald*, January 10, March 20, 23, 24, 1857; Redfield to Corning, January 9, 1857, Corning Papers; Sickles to Buchanan, January 26, Seymour to Buchanan, January 26, Dickinson to Buchanan, March 5, 1857, Buchanan Papers; *New York Times*, March 24, 1857; Marshall, "Marcy's Diary," *AHR*, 24 (July 1919), 646–47.

9. *New York Times*, March 26, April 16, August 1, 2, December 18, 1857; Wickoff to Buchanan, March 27, April 22, 1857, Buchanan Papers; Wood to Schell, June 1, 1857, Miscellaneous Papers. NYHS.

10. *New York Herald*, April 18, 20, 21, 1857; *New York Times*, May 5, September 8, 9, 10, 1857.

11. *Ibid.*, November 29, December 11, 16, 1856, January 6, 8, 15, February 19, March 18, 1857; *Daily News*, January 8, 15, February 20, March 16, 1857; James Parton, "The Government of New York," *North American Review*, (October 1866), 414–65.

12. *New York Times*, April 16, 18, May 18, 19, 20, 23, June 15, 17, 20, 1857; George Walling, *Recollections of a New York Chief of Police* (New York: Caxton, 1887), 26–33; James Richardson, "Mayor Fernando Wood and the New York Police Force," *NYHSQ*, 40 (January 1966), 26–33.

13. *New York Times*, July 4, 5, 6, 12, August 14, 1857; *New York Herald*, August 4, 5, 1857; Charles Loring Brace, *The Dangerous Classes of New York* (New York: Wynkoop & Hallenbeck, 1872), 27–30.

14. Barlow to Buchanan, July 18, Wickoff to Buchanan, July 22, August 6, Sanders to Buchanan, July 26, Fowler to Buchanan, August 17, Sickles to Buchanan, September 8, 1857, Buchanan Papers.

15. *New York Times*, September 1, 2, 4, 8, 11, 12, 13, 14, 1857.

16. *New York Herald*, October 16, 22, November 24, 1857.

17. *Irish-American*, November 14, 1857; Samuel Rezneck, "Influence of Depression Upon American Public Opinion, 1857–1859," *Journal of Economic History*, 2 (1942), 1–24; Strong, *Diary*, 2: 369–70.

18. *New York Herald*, October 31, November 4, 6, 9, 1857; *New York Times*, November 14, 16, 21, 25, 28, 29, December 1, 1857; Sickles to Buchanan, November 20, 1857, Buchanan Papers.

19. *Irish-American*, November 21, 1857; *New York Times*, November 24, 1857; *New York Herald*, November 24, 1857.

20. *New York Times*, December 2, 1857; Tiemann to Buchanan, December 8, Belmont to Slidell, December 8, 1857, Buchanan Papers. Tiemann gained 51.3 percent of the total votes cast. On a ward-by-ward basis, he carried twelve out of twenty-two. Wood, however, ran strongest wherever Irish immigrants lived.

21. *New York Herald*, December 4, 5, 17, 18, 19, 24, 1857; *New York Times*, December 4, 1857, January 7, 8, 1858; Corning to Dix, January 20, 1858, Dix Papers; Nichols, *Disruption*, 125–81.

22. *New York Herald*, January 2, 7, 8, 11, 12, 1858.

23. Albert Ramsey to Buchanan, February 11, 1858, Buchanan Papers; *Irish-American*, March 6, 20; *New York Times*, April 2, 1858; Wood to Wise, June 28, 1858, Wood Papers, NYPL.

24. *New York Times*, April 8, 13, 1858; Tammany Membership List, *Tammaniana of Edwin Kilroe*, 3–202.

25. *New York Herald*, April 2, 8, 1858; *New York Times*, April 9, 14, 18, 19, 1858.

26. *Ibid.*, April 20, 1858; Dix to Buchanan, April 20, 1858, Buchanan Papers.

27. *Daily News*, April 24, 1858; *New York Times*, May 10, 1858; *New York Herald*, June 15, 1858, March 3, 1859.

28. *New York Times*, June 8, 15, 19, 23, 1858; *Irish-American*, June 15, 1858; *New York Herald*, June 23, 1858; Sickles to Buchanan, July 9, Cobb to Buchanan, August 4, 6, 1858, Buchanan Papers.

29. Douglas to Wise, November 7, 1858, *The Letters of Stephen Douglas*, Robert W. Johannsen, ed. (Urbana: University of Illinois Press, 1961), 429; Douglas to Wood, October 3, 1859, *ibid.*, 477.

30. *New York Times*, June 8, July 13, 19, 29, August 5, 26, September 1, 2, 1858; *New York Herald*, July 7, 1858; Sickles to Buchanan, August 5, 1858, Buchanan Papers; *Daily News*, August 28, 1858.

31. *New York Times*, September 2, 7, 8, 16, 1858; Fowler to Corning, September 7, 1858, Corning Papers; Fowler to Buchanan, September 8, 1858, Buchanan Papers.

32. Wood to Buchanan, September 8, 1858, *ibid.*

33. Buchanan to Wood, September 9, Wood to Buchanan, September 10, 1858, *ibid.*

34. Fowler to Buchanan, September 8, Sickles to Buchanan, September 8, 1858, *ibid.*

35. *Daily News*, September 16, 1858; *New York Herald*, September 16, 17, 1858; Wood to Buchanan, September 27, October 8, 10, 15. John Kelly to Buchanan, October 12, Buchanan to Wood, October 15, Sickles to Buchanan, October 31, 1858, Buchanan Papers.

36. Ramsey to Fowler, November 6, 10, 1858, Miscellaneous Papers, NYHS.

37. *Daily News*, November 2, 5, 18, 1858; *New York Times*, November 10, 1858, January 3, 5, 6, 8, 9, 1859; Ramsey to Fowler, December 5, 1858, Miscellaneous Papers, NYHS; Dickinson to Buchanan, December 8, 1858, Buchanan Papers; *New York Herald*, December 27, 28, 29, 31, 1858, February 12, 15, 19, March 3, 20, 30, April 2, 4, 1859.

38. Schell, Fowler, *et al.* to Buchanan, December 17, 1858, Buchanan Papers; *New York Herald*, January 14, 25, 28, 31, February 10, March 1, 1859.

39. *New York Times*, January 28, 29, 31, February 28, 1859; *New York Herald*, March 15, 1859; Nichols, *Disruption*, 260; William Swanburg, *Sickles the Incredible* (New York: Charles Scribner's Sons, 1956), 36–67.

40. *New York Herald*, May 12, 15, June 2, 3, 4, 16, 20, July 1, 24, 1859; Dyer to Douglas, June 5, Connolly to Douglas, August 19, Wilson Hunt to Douglas, October 6, Wood to Douglas, September 30, 1859, February 16, 1860, Douglas Papers.

41. Pruyn, Diary, December 6, 1859; Seymour to Pruyn, January 10, 1859, Seymour Papers, NYSL.

42. *New York Herald*, July 30, August 2, 4, September 1–16, 1859; *Daily News*, August 9, 11, September 1, 2, 1859; Dyer to Douglas, August 6, Sanders to Douglas,

September 13, 1859, Douglas Papers; Dickinson to Burke, January 26, 1860, Burke Papers; *Proceedings of the Democratic State Convention held at Syracuse, September 14 & 15, 1859* (Albany: 1859).

43. *Daily News,* September 9, 16, 1859; *New York Times,* September 15, 18, 1859.

44. *New York Herald,* September 26, 28, October 10, 13, 14, 19, 28, 30, 1859; Charles Havens to Douglas, October 13, MacMaster to Douglas, October 30, 1859, Douglas Papers; Cagger to Corning, November 1, 1859, Corning Papers.

45. *New York Herald,* November 4, 7, 9, 14, 1859; Croswell to Corning, November 14, 1859, Corning Papers.

46. *Daily News,* November 3, 26, 30, 1859; Cassidy to Tilden, November 22, 1859, Tilden Papers; *Irish-American,* November 26, 1859; Anderson to Douglas, December 4, 1859, Douglas Papers.

47. *New York Herald,* November 22, 26, 28, December 4, 1859; *Daily News,* November 29, 1859; Wood to Tilden, December 1, 1859, Tilden Papers; Wood to [?], December 1, 1859, Wood Papers, NYHS.

48. *New York Times,* December 6, 7, 8, 1859.

49. *New York Herald,* December 7, 8, 9, 1859; *New York Tribune,* December 15, 1859; Dix to Buchanan, December 7, 1859, Buchanan Papers.

50. *New York Herald,* December 10, 1859; Tilden to Van Buren, December 25, 1859, *Tilden's Letters,* 1: 126–27; Sanders to Douglas, December 28, 1859, Douglas Papers.

51. *New York Herald,* July 22, 1857; *New York Times,* January 9, 1858; Tammany Membership List, *Tammaniana of Edwin Kilroe,* 3–202.

52. *New York Herald,* March 5, 7, April 15, November 2, 10, 1859; *Report of the Special Committee of the Board of Aldermen Appointed to Investigate the "Ring" Frauds, Together with the Testimony Elicited During the Investigation* (New York: n.d.), Kilroe Collection; Alexander Callow, Jr., *The Tweed Ring* (New York: Oxford University Press, 1966), 24–26.

53. John W. Pratt, "Boss Tweed's Public Welfare Program," *NYHSQ,* 45 (October 1961), 396–413; Seymour Mandelbaum, *Boss Tweed's New York* (New York: John Wiley & Sons, 1965).

54. *New York Herald,* February 1, 1860; Dickinson to Buchanan, June 30, 1860, Buchanan Papers.

55. Murat Halstead, *Political Conventions of 1860* (Columbus: 1860), 1–100; Nichols, *Disruption,* 288–320.

56. Richardson to Douglas, May 13, 14, 17, Sanders to Douglas, May 19, 25, 1860, Douglas Papers; *New York Herald,* May 17, 1860; Barlow to Corning, May 19, 1860, Corning Papers; Guthrie to Tilden, May 21, 1860, Tilden Papers.

57. Seymour to Barlow, May 15, 1860, Fairchild Collection; Cagger to Douglas, May 18, Sanders to Douglas, May 20, Cutting to Douglas, June 11, 1860, Douglas Papers; Tucker to Buchanan, May 25, 1860, Buchanan Papers.

58. Fowler to Develin, April 5, 1860, Weed Papers; *Journal of Commerce,* May 18, 1860; *New York Herald,* May 11, 16, 19, 1860; Croswell to Corning, May 19, 1860, Corning Papers.

59. *Journal of Commerce,* June 4, 14, 28, 1860; Seymour to Barlow, June 8, 1860, Fairchild Collection; *New York Herald,* June 13, 17, 20, 21, 22, 23, 27, 1860; Dickinson to Buchanan, June 30, 1860, Buchanan Papers.

60. Schell to Corning, June 28, Butterworth to Corning, June 30, Kemble to

Corning, July 6, 1860, Corning Papers; Rynders to Buchanan, June 30, 1860, Buchanan Papers; Seymour to Barlow, July 26, 1860, Fairchild Collection.

61. *New York Herald*, June 28, 29, July 7, 1860; *Irish-American*, June 30, 1860; Tucker to Douglas, June 29, 1860, Douglas Papers.

62. Ward to Douglas, June 23, Belmont to Douglas, July 28, Taylor to Douglas, July 29, 1860, *ibid.; New York Herald*, July 15, 1860; Sherman to Corning, July 17, 1860, Corning Papers.

63. *New York Herald*, July 2–October 5, 1860; Belmont to Corning, August 1, 1860, Corning Papers; Preston King to Ullman, August 13, 1860, Ullman Papers; Milledge Bonham, Jr., "New York and the Election of 1860," *NYH*, 15 (April 1934), 124–43; Foner, *Business and Slavery*, 169–77.

64. *New York Herald*, September 26, October 4, 1860; Cassidy to Tilden, October, 1860, Tilden Papers; Watts Sherman to Corning, October 27, 1860, Corning Papers.

65. *New York Herald*, October 3, 9, 14, 21, 22, 24, 25, 30, 31, 1860; Sanders to Douglas, October 18, 1860, Douglas Papers; *Daily News*, October 21, 1860; Cagger to Tilden, October 24, 1860, Tilden Papers.

66. *Daily News*, November 9, 1860; *New York Herald*, November 10, 16, 2, 21, 1860, January 6, 1861; Dickinson to Olcott, November 17, 1860, Olcott Papers; *Irish-American*, December 15, 1860; Cochrane to Tilden, December 20, 1860, Tilden Papers.

## 13. THE CIVIL WAR, THE TAMMANY SOCIETY, AND TWEED'S CONSOLIDATION

1. *New York Herald*, December 7, 1860, January 2, 6, 1861; *Daily News*, December 15, 20, 1860; Kemble to Corning, December 29, 1860, Corning Papers; Bray Hammond, "The North's Empty Purse, 1861–1862," *AHR*, 67 (October 1961), 1–18.

2. *New York Herald*, January 8, 9, 1861; *New York Tribune*, January 8, 1861; *New York Leader*, January 12, 1861; *Irish-American*, January 19, 1861; James Heslin, "'Peaceful Compromise' in New York City, 1860–1861," *NYHSQ*, 44 (October 1961), 349–62.

3. John Cisco to Dix, February 2, 1861, Dix Papers; *New York Leader*, February 12, March 30, 1861.

4. *New York Herald*, January 25, 29, 30, 1861; *New York Leader*, January 26, 1861; *Proceedings of the Democratic State Convention* (Albany: 1861).

5. *New York Leader*, March 30, April 6, 1861.

6. *New York Herald*, January 25, February 16, 21, 1861; *Irish-American*, February 26, 1861; *Daily News*, March 21, April 1, 1861; Webb to Lincoln, April 11, 1861, Lincoln Papers, LC.

7. Democratic Republican General Committee to Lincoln, April 26, Hardy to Lincoln, April 30, 1861, *ibid.; New York Leader*, April 24, May 4, 11, 1861.

8. *Daily News*, April 15, 16, 1861; *New York Tribune*, April 16, 1861; *New York Leader*, April 26, 1861; *New York Herald*, April 28, 1861.

9. *Ibid.*, April 21, 1861; Broadside, "Union Defense Committee of the City of New York" (New York: 1861), NYSL; *New York Leader*, May 25, 1861.

10. Wood to Lincoln, April 29, 1861, Lincoln Papers; Strong, *Diary*, 3: 121. The letter also appeared in the *Irish-American*, May 2, 1861.

11. *New York Leader,* June 15, 29, 1861; John Austin Stevens, *The Union Defense Committee of the City of New York* (New York: Published by the Committee, 1885), 1–38.

12. *New York Leader,* July 20, August 10, 24, 1861; *Journal of Commerce,* August 1, 1861; *Daily News,* September 3, 1861; Stanton to Dix, August 14, 1861, Dix Papers; Weed to Lincoln, August 18, 1861, Lincoln Papers; Sidney Brummer, *Political History of New York State During the Period of the Civil War* (New York: Columbia University Press, 1911), 154–59.

13. *Daily News,* August 20, 1861; *New York Herald,* August 30, September 6, 8, 1861; Sidney Webster to Cushing, September 2, 10, 22, Brooks to Cushing, September 25, 1861, Cushing Papers; *New York Leader,* September 2, 28, 1861.

14. *New York Herald,* September 10, 11, 12, 16, 1861; Brummer, *History,* 166–70.

15. *Daily News,* September 11, 1861; *New York Leader,* September 14, October 5, 1861; Webster to Cushing, September 22, 1861, Cushing Papers.

16. *New York Herald,* October 4, November 5, 1861; *Utica Morning Herald,* November 3, 1861, *Chicago Times,* November 19, 1861, Seymour Scrapbooks, NYSL.

17. *New York Times,* October 9, 11, 15, 17, 18, 20, 23, 26, 28, 30, November 2, 1861; *New York Leader,* October 12, 26, November 2, 1861.

18. *New York Herald,* October 23, 24, 27, November 7, 1861; *Irish-American,* October 26, 1861; Lynch, *Boss Tweed,* 236; Croswell Bowen, *The Elegant Oakey* (New York: Oxford University Press, 1956), 28–38.

19. Havemeyer to Dix, November 8, 23, 1861, Dix Papers; *New York Leader,* November 9, 16, 23, 1861; *New York Herald,* November 17, 26, 1861.

20. *New York Times,* November 2, 1861; *New York Herald,* November 16, 1861; *New York Tribune,* November 25, 28, 1861; Wood to Seward, November 27, Frederick Seward to Wood, November 29, 1861, Wood Papers, NYPL; *New York Leader,* November 30, 1861.

21. Wood to Cushing, November 29, Cushing to Wood, December 6, Seymour to Cushing, December 6, 1861, Cushing Papers; Pruyn, Diary, December 20, 1861.

22. *New York Leader,* November 23, December 14, 1861; *New York Herald,* December 8, 1861, Hardy, *Manual of the Corporation,* 737.

23. *New York Leader,* December 28, 1861, March 22, October 2, 1862.

24. *Ibid.,* January 4, 25, February 22, March 29, April 5, 1862.

25. *Ibid.,* February 13, March 22, 29, April 19, 23, 1862; *New York Times,* April 18, 22, 1862.

26. *New York Caucasian,* January 18, 1862; Henry J. Raymond to Wadsworth, February 9, 1862, Wadsworth Papers; *New York Leader,* April 19, 1862; Pruyn, Diary, January 3, 1863; Harry Carmen and Reinhard Luthin, *Lincoln and the Patronage* (Gloucester: Peter Smith, 1964), 11–139.

27. Wood to Lincoln, January 15, August 20, 1862, Lincoln Papers.

28. *New York Leader,* January 18, July 26, 1862; *New York Herald,* January 25, 1862.

29. *Irish-American,* May 24, 1862; *New York Leader,* June 21, 1862; *Weekly Journal of Commerce,* June 26, 1862.

30. *New York Herald,* June 22, July 2, 1862; *Weekly Journal of Commerce,* July 3, 1862; *New York Leader,* July 3, 26, 1862; *Tammany Society or Columbian Order, Annual Celebration, July 4, 1862* (New York: 1862).

31. *New York Leader,* August 30, 1862; *New York World,* September 24, 1862.

32. *New York Leader,* July 26, 1862.

33. R.J. Stevens to Connolly, January 20, 1862, Seymour Papers; *New York Herald*, July 11, 17, September 2, October 11, 1862; *New York Leader*, August 9, September 13, 1862; *New York World*, September 11, 1862; *New York Tribune*, September 15, 16, 1862; Wadsworth to Greeley, September 14, Raymond to Wadsworth, October 4, 1862, Wadsworth Papers; Belmont to Marble, October 2, 1862, Marble Papers, LC.

34. *New York Leader*, June 28, 1862.

35. *Ibid.*, June 21, August 9, 23, 30, September 6, 13, 1862.

36. *Ibid.*, September 20, 27, 1862.

37. Wood to Lincoln, September 12, 1862, Lincoln Papers; *New York Leader*, October 4, 18, November 15, 1862.

38. *New York Herald*, October 3, 1862; *New York Leader*, October 4, 11, 1862; *New York Times*, October 7, 11, 1862; *New York Tribune*, October 9, 1862; *Official Proceedings of the Democratic Republican Nominating Convention of Tammany Hall . . . and the Joint Committee of Mozart and Tammany Halls . . . November 21, 1862* (New York: 1862).

39. *Weekly Journal of Commerce*, October 15, 21, 1862; *New York Leader*, October 18, 1862; *Irish-American*, November 1, 1862.

40. *New York Leader*, October 25, November 1, 1862; *Documents Relative to the Withdrawal of Nelson J. Waterbury from the Canvass in the Eighth Congressional District* (New York: 1862).

41. Greeley to Smith, October 21, 1862, Smith Papers; Cochrane to Lincoln, October 26, November 5, Field to Lincoln, November 8, Dickinson to Lincoln, November 9, 1862, Lincoln Papers; Seymour to Marble, November 11, 1862, Marble Papers.

42. *New York Leader*, November 2, 15, 22, 29, December 6, 1862; William McMurray to Marble, November 14, 1862, Marble Papers; *New York Tribune*, November 30, 1862.

43. *New York Leader*, December 13, 1862.

44. *Ibid.*, December 6, 27, 1862, January 3, 10, 17, 24, 1863; Charles Wingate, "An Episode in Municipal Government," *North American Review*, (October 1874), 387–88.

45. *New York Leader*, April 18, 1863.

46. Tweed to Seymour, January 4, 1863, Fairchild Collection; *New York Leader*, May 18, 1863.

47. *Ibid.*, August 8, 1863.

48. Wood to Lincoln, December 8, December 17, 1862, February 6, 1863; Lincoln to Wood, December 12, 1863.

49. A. Oakey Hall to Thurlow Weed, December 31, 1862, Weed Papers; *New York World*, January 3, 5, 7, 25, 1863; *New York Tribune*, April 9, 25, 1863; Eugene Murdock, *Patriotism Limited, 1862–1865* (Kent: Kent State University Press, 1967), 1–42.

50. *Irish-American*, April 11, 1863; *New York Herald*, April 20, 1863; *New York World*, May 8, 1863.

51. *New York Leader*, January 10, 31 February 7, 18, 1863.

52. Belmont to Tilden, January 24, 1863, Tilden Papers; Bogert to Marble, February 16, Vallandingham to Marble, February 21, May 12, 15, 21, Cox to Marble, March 11, 1863, Marble Papers; *New York Leader*, April 4, 11, 18, May 6, 16, 1863; *New York Herald*, May 26, 28, June 1, 1863; Brummer, *History*, 290–320.

53. Cox to Marble, June 1, 1863, Marble Papers; *New York Leader*, June 6, 1863.

54. *New York Herald*, January 8, April 20, April 25, 1863; *New York World*, March 12, April 20, 25, 1863; Seymour to Stanton, March 28, 1863, Seymour Papers, NYSL; *Daily News*, June 25, July 8, 11, 13, 1863; Williston Lofton, "Northern Labor and the Negro During the Civil War," *Journal of Negro History*, 34 (1949), 251-73.

55. *New York Leader*, June 13, 30, July 4, 1863; Purdy to Seymour, June 26, Opdyke to Seymour, June 30, 1863, Seymour Papers, NYSL; *New York Tribune*, July 6, 1863; *Society of Tammany or Columbian Order Celebration at Tammany Hall on Saturday, July 4, 1863* (New York: 1863).

56. *Daily News*, July 13, 1863; *New York Tribune*, July 16, 1863; *New York Herald*, July 16, 1863; Porter to Marble, July 16, 1863, Marble Papers; Stanton to Edwin Morgan, July 17, 1863, Seymour Papers, NYHS; Seymour to Tilden, August 6, 1863, Tilden Papers.

57. *New York Tribune*, July 18, 1863; *Irish-American*, July 18, 25, August 23, 1863; *New York Herald*, July 24, 1863.

58. *New York Leader*, August 1, 1863.

59. Seymour to Dix, August 7, 1863, Dix Papers; Kemble to Corning, August 29, 1863, Corning Papers; *New York Leader*, August 29, September 12, 19, 1863; *New York Herald*, September 8, 9, 10, 1863.

60. *Daily News*, September 24, 1863; *New York Herald*, October 8, 28, 1863; *New York Leader*, October 3, 10, 1863.

61. *Ibid.*, October 17, 1863; *New York Herald*, October 25, 26, 28, November 2, 8, 1863; *New York World*, October 26, 28, November 8, 1863.

62. *New York Leader*, September 12, November 21, 1863; Charles Halpine to Dix, October 20, November [?], Stanton to Dix, November 9, 1863, Dix Papers; *New York Times*, November 12, 16, 1863.

63. Barnard to Marble, November 18, 1863, Marble Papers.

64. *Irish-American*, December 2, 1863; *New York Times*, December 3, 6, 1863; Hardy, *Manual of the Corporation*, 736.

65. *New York Herald*, December 16, 1863; *New York Leader*, January 2, 1864.

66. *Ibid.*, January 2, 9, 1864.

67. *New York Herald*, January 5, 10, 23, 27, 1864; *New York Leader*, January 16, 23, February 20, 27, 1864; Pruyn to Marble, January 16, 1864, Marble Papers; Pruyn to McClellan, January 24, 1864, McClellan Papers, LC.

68. *New York Herald*, February 25, 1864; *New York Leader*, March 5, 1864.

69. *New York World*, February 26, 1864; *New York Herald*, February 26, 27, March 1, 1864; Brummer, *History*, 371-74.

70. *New York Herald*, February 29, March 13, 18, 1864; *New York Tribune*, February 29, March 4, 14, 1864; *New York Leader*, March 12, 19, 1864.

71. *Ibid.*, March 19, 26, 1864; *New York Herald*, March 23, April 20, 1864.

72. *New York Leader*, April 23, 30, 1864.

73. Seymour to McClellan, April 11, 1863, Barlow to McClellan, June 14, Cox to McClellan, August 4, 1864, McClellan Papers; *New York Leader*, June 4, 1864; Pruyn to Marble, June 15, Richmond to Marble, June 16, Barlow to Marble, August 9, 1864, Marble Papers; Delevan to Corning, July 16, 1864, Corning Papers; *New York Herald*, August 5, 6, 7, 1864.

74. Marble to James Wall, March 30, Cox to Marble, August 9, 1864, Marble Papers; Frank Severance, "The Peace Conference at Niagara Falls in 1864," *BHSP*, 18 (1914), 79-84.

75. *New York Herald,* July 29, 31, August 2, 6, 7, 1864; *New York Leader,* July 30, August 4, 1864.

76. Wood to Lincoln, April 29, 1864, Lincoln Papers; Pruyn, Diary, August 8, 1864; *New York Herald,* August 19, 1864.

77. *Ibid.,* August 19, 21, 22, 1864.

78. Cox to Marble, August 7, 1864, Marble Papers; *New York Herald,* July 23, August 9, 18, 19, 21, 25, 27, 29, 1864; *New York World,* July 27, August 5, 6, 26, 27, 1864; William Zornow, *Lincoln and the Party Divided* (Norman: University of Oklahoma Press, 1954), 126–28.

79. William Zornow, "McClellan and Seymour in the Chicago Convention," *Journal of the Illinois Historical Society,* 43 (1950), 288; William Zornow, "Clement L. Vallandingham and the Democratic Party in 1864," *Historical and Philosophical Society of Ohio,* 29 (January 1961), 21–37.

80. Delevan to McClellan, September 1, Belmont to McClellan, September 3, Barlow to McClellan, September 3, 1864, McClellan Papers; Charles R. Wilson, "McClellan's Changing View of the Peace Plank of 1864," *AHR,* 38 (April 1933), 498–505.

81. *New York Leader,* September 3, 1864; *Daily News,* September 9, 12, 15, 1864; Barlow to McClellan, September 12, 14, 1864, McClellan Papers; *New York Herald,* September 15, 1864.

82. *Ibid.,* September 1, 2, 3, 5, 11, 13, 1864.

83. *New York Leader,* September 10, 17, 1864; *New York Herald,* September 14, 1864.

84. Seymour to Belmont, September 26, McClellan to Barlow, September 27, Plan of the Democratic Committee for October, 1864, Douglas Taylor to Marble, October 5, 1864, Marble Papers; Zornow, *Party Divided,* 162–78.

85. Cassidy to Marble, October, 1864, Marble Papers; Barlow to McClellan, October, 1864, McClellan Papers; *New York Leader,* October 19, 24, 1864.

86. *New York World,* October 4, 1864; *New York Leader,* October 6, 1864; *Irish-American,* October 8, 23, 1864; *New York Herald,* October 19, 24, 1864.

87. Wood to Lincoln, October 6, 1864, Lincoln Papers; *New York Herald,* November 6, 1864.

88. Albert Ramsey to McClellan, October 18, November 7, Prime to McClellan, October 20, Seymour to McClellan, October 23, 1864, McClellan Papers; *New York Herald,* October 15, November 7, 8, 10, 14, 1864; *New York Leader,* November 12, 1864.

89. *New York Herald,* November 10, 1864; *New York Leader,* November 12, 1864.

90. Wood to Lincoln, November 18, December 4, 1864, Lincoln Papers; *New York Tribune,* February 1, 1865.

## 14. EPILOGUE: TAMMANYISM

1. Matthew Breen, *Thirty Years of New York Politics Up-to-Date* (New York: Published by the author, 1899), 38–43.

2. *New York National Advocate,* September 8, 1825; *The Democrat,* September 5, 1836; *Morning News,* December 23, 1845; Allen, *Memoirs,* 100.

3. Martin Van Buren to Jesse Hoyt, February 1, 1829, *Lives and Opinions,* 206.

4. Silas Wright to Azariah Flagg, January 26, 1826, Flagg Papers; Joseph Blunt to John Quincy Adams, November 14, 1827, Adams Papers.

5. *New York Leader*, August 9, 1862.

6. Robert Morris to James Polk, April 18, 1845, Polk Papers; *Sunday Times and Noah's Weekly Messenger*, March 17, 1850.

7. J. Addison Thomas to William Marcy, October 31, 1851, Marcy Papers; *New York Leader*, February 14, 1862.

8. Samuel Osgood to Albert Gallatin, October 28, 1802, Gallatin Papers; *New York Columbian*, April 27, 1817; *Truth Teller*, December 24, 1825; *New York Emerald*, July 21, 1826, DeWitt Clinton Newspaper Collection, NYSL; *Evening Post*, April 15, 1840; Mike Walsh, *Speeches and Sketches*, 12–23; Daniel Thompson, *Politics In a Democracy* (New York: Longmans, Green & Company, 1893), 92–107.

9. *Citizens Committee of Safety* (New York: 1840), 18–24; Augustine E. Costello, *Our Firemen* (New York: A.E. Costello, 1887), 505–667; Alvin Harlow, *Old Bowery Days* (New York: D. Appleton & Company, 1931), 204; Lowell Limpus, *History of the New York Fire Department* (New York: E.P. Dutton & Company, 1940), 161–65.

10. John Gerard, *London and New York: Their Crimes and Police* (New York: 1853); Ingraham, *Wood*, 30; *Documents of the New York State Assembly* (Albany: 1858), Document 4: 80; James Richardson, *The New York Police: Colonial Times to 1901* (New York: Oxford University Press, 1970).

11. *New York Enquirer*, April 27, 1827; Verplanck to Jesse Hoyt, December 27, 1828, *Lives and Opinions*, 206; Cornelius Van Ness to Alexander Vaché, April 4, 1845, Polk Papers; *Documents of the Board of Aldermen* (New York: 1847), Document 2: 29.

12. *Proceedings and Documents of the Assistant Board of Aldermen* (New York: 1842), Document 7; *Documents of the Board of Aldermen* (New York: 1848), Document 8; Callow, *Boss Tweed*, 104–105.

13. Silas Wright to Flagg, August 29, 1827, Flagg Papers; Adams, *Diary*, 7: 404; Hammond, *Political Parties*, 2: 79–80; Alvin Kass, *Politics in New York State: 1800–1830* (Syracuse: Syracuse University Press, 1965), 55–73.

14. *New York Enquirer*, November 23, 1826; *National Advocate*, February 3, 1827; *New York Herald*, January 6, 1861.

15. *Ibid.*, January 8, March 23, 1855; Mandelbaum, *Tweed's New York*.

16. *New York Journal*, April 9, 1791, April 4, 1795, October 21, 1797.

17. *Ibid.*, July 13, 1791; *Columbian Gazetteer*, June 9, 1794.

18. *New York Journal*, March 19, 1792, May 31, 1794, December 6, 1794; *Columbian Gazetteer*, April 17, 1794; *Evening Post*, November 26, 1794; *Time Piece*, April 12, August 11, 1797.

19. *New York Journal*, March 17, 1792.

20. William P. Van Ness to P.V. Van Ness, December 16, 1796, Van Ness Papers, NYPL; *New York Journal*, April 2, 1798.

21. *Commercial Advertiser*, April 19, 1800; *New York National Advocate*, March 8, 1825.

22. Matthew Davis to William P. Van Ness, February 11, 1807, Davis Papers.

23. James Parton, *Life of Andrew Jackson* (New York: Mason, 1861), 3: 122–28.

24. Henry Meigs to Jonathan Meigs, May 2, 1819, Meigs Papers.

# INDEX

Abolitionism, and Leggett, 163–165; and Tammany, 231–33; and Wood, 312. *See also* Slavery

Adams, John Quincy, presidential candidate, 80–92; patronage policy, 93–95; nonpartisanship, 102; and Tammany Society, 104–107; and Anti-Masons, 107; and Anti-Auctioneers, 112–13; defeated, 114–15; Clayton Committee, 138; mentioned, 220

Adamsites. *See* John Quincy Adams, and Joseph Blunt

*Albany Argus*, 64, 69, 193, 198, 205, 227. *See also* Edwin Croswell

Albany Regency, 6, 50, 116–18, 153, 159–60, 209–10, 231–33, 366. *See also* Martin Van Buren

Allen, Stephen, joins Tammany Society, 51; and Van Buren, 61; and reform, 70; supports Crawford, 85, favors Bank, 138, 142; attacks Bank, 142; changes, 143; moderate, 178, 179; and Public School Society, 192; and Tammanyism, 374

Alley, Saul, Bank director, 119; and Morehead Resolution, 131

American Institute. *See* Anti-Auction party

American-Republican party, origin, 214–16; defeat, 224

Anti-Auction party, origin, 108; and 1828 election, 112–14

Anti-Mason party, origin, 102–103; and Weed, 103; and Adams, 107; and Clay, 126; and 1832 election, 142; and Whigs, 158

Anti-Rent movement, 227

"Aristides." *See* William P. Van Ness

Armstrong, John, and Spencer, 47; failure, 53; and Clinton, 56

Astor Place Riots, 253

Atwater, Caleb, 109

Bailey, Benjamin, 61, 97, 105, 120

Bailey, Theodorus, 44, 111

Bank Democrats, origins, 142; and local banks, 146; and new banks, 152; speculations, 159–60; and Equal Rights party, 158–66; and Specie Circular, 173–74; and Van Buren, 177–79; and Tammany Society, 182–83

Bank of America, and legislature, 41; and Clinton, 46; and Tompkins, 46; bill passes, 47

Bank of the Manhattan Company, 26, 41

Barker, Isaac, 299

Barker, Jacob, on Clinton, 52

Barker, James, 285

Barlow, Samuel Latham Mitchill, 306, 321, 328, 359

Barnard, George, on Boole, 354

Barnburners, origins, 209; and Polk, 213; and patronage, 221–22; and Texas, 222–23; and Mexico, 227; and reform, 228; and war, 229; and Wright, 230–31; and slavery, 231–33; and Wilmot Proviso, 233, 235; Herkimer Convention, 235–36; Baltimore Convention, 240–41; forms ticket, 242–43; Free Soil party, 244–45; conciliation with Hunkers, 250–51; and Hards and Softs, 253. *See also* Tammany Hall, and Martin Van Buren

Barnum, David, 45

Barr, Thomas J., 269, 273, 277, 284, 301, 337

Bates, Barnabas, on Equal Rights party, 176, 179

Belmont, August, 309, 317, 323, 359

Bennett, James Gordon, and Biddle, 119; joins *Courier and Enquirer*, 120; attacks Bank, 128; resigns, 140; on 1834 election, 155; forms *New York Herald*, 166; on school reform, 195; and Hunkers, 234; backs Wood, 258; on Union businessmen, 261; on temperance, 265; and Cuba, 287; and Half Shells, 297; supports Wood, 300, 318, 319; on 1860 politicians, 321; and free city, 326; criticizes Tammany, 354; and Manifesto, 357; and McClellan, 361–62; lauds Tammany, 362

Benton, Thomas Hart, 240, 242

Biddle, Nicholas, and Safety Fund, 118; and New York politics, 118–19; feels threatened, 129–30; and Burrows, 130–33; and first Burrows loan, 131–32; and loan to Noah and Webb, 133; and Clayton Committee, 138; and 1832 election, 141; contraction, 147–48; and Union Committee, 154

Blunt, Joseph, and patronage, 94, 102; and Tammany Society, 104–107; false strategy, 107; and Anti-Auction party, 108; and Tammany Hall, 366

Bogardus, Charles L., 246

Bogart, William, 350

Boole, Francis, and Genet, 342–43; and Tweed, 346, 353; runs for mayor, 354–55

Bouck, William, 209, 210, 213, 218

Bowery Boys, 208, 306

Bowne, Walter, 63, 112, 115, 119, 124, 146

Brady, James T., 217, 253, 350

Breckenridge, John C., 321–24

Brennan, Matthew, 337, 346

Bronson, Greene, 274, 277, 285, 313, 331

Broome, John L., 42

Brownell, J. Sherman, 233–34

Bryant, William Cullen, edits *Evening Post*, 129; on recharter, 135; on Ver-

planck, 141; on Equal Rights party, 166; and moderates, 176; attacks Hughes, 200; and expansionism, 218, 227; on war, 229; and Wilmot Proviso, 233; and Free Soil, 234; and fusion, 250; and Softs, 274; and Loyalty League, 350

Buchanan, James, and New York politics, 247; and Half Shells, 295–97; as a candidate, 299; local patronage, 300, 303; and Sickles, 306–307; and Wood, 314–15; backs Schell, 322; and 1860 campaign, 322–24

Bucktails, 63. *See also* Tammany Hall, and Martin Van Buren, *passim*

Bureau of Day and Night Watch (Municipal Police), 305–306

Burr, Aaron, 1; and Republican-Interest, 16; relation to Tammany, 26, 39, 412; and Tontine, 26–27; and Davis, 36. *See also* Matthew Davis, *passim*

Burr Conspiracy, 36

Burrites. *See* Aaron Burr and Matthew Davis, *passim*

Burrows, Silas, characteristics, 119; Biddle's lobbyist, 130, bribery charges, 31; and *Courier and Enquirer* loan, 133–34; Clayton Committee and disgrace, 138

Butler, Benjamin F., and Olcott, 153; on electoral frauds, 190; and Wright, 220; and Polk, 222; and Tammany Hall, 242, 243; resigns, 245–46

Byrdsall, Fitzwilliam, objects to fusion, 179; and Calhoun, 210; and Tammany Society, 358

Calhoun, John C., and 1824 candidacy, 80–83, 88; and Jacksonian coalition, 107; and Tammany Hall, 210–11; mentioned, 216

"A Calm Observer," 23

Cambreleng, Churchill, C., and Anti-Auction party, 112–13; on Swartwout, 115; special Bank agent, 119; on Clayton Committee, 135, 138, 139; on abolitionism, 164; on Equal Rights party, 171, 177; and electoral reforms,

188; at Baltimore Convention, 241; on Van Buren's candidacy, 243

Cass, Lewis, nominated, 240; on extensionism, 244; and Hards, 260; and Tammany Society, 262; and Marcy, 263

Chamber of Commerce (New York City), and Anglo-French War, 29; and Biddle, 135

Cheetham, James, joins Tammany Society, 25; and 1800 election, 26; attacks Burr, 28; and George Clinton, 32; attacks Madison, 32–33; and 1808 election, 32–36; censure of, 37–38; dropped by DeWitt Clinton, 38; mentioned, 143

Cincinnati, Order of, and Tammany Society, 11

Cisco, James J., 245, 327

Civic Reform party, formed, 275; wins Corporation, 278; decline, 284–85

Clancy, John. See New York Leader

Clark, Aaron, becomes mayor, 174; nativism, 184–85; reelected, 187; defeated, 189

Clay, Henry, and Tammany, 81; and Clinton, 87–88; and 1824 legislature, 91–92; and 1828 election, 115; seeks allies, 121; and Working Men's party, 123–24; and Davis, 126; and 1832 election, 142–43; and 1844 election, 219; and Ullman, 245; death, 268

Clayton Committee, 135, 138

Clinton, DeWitt; joins Tammany Society, 14; Long Talk, 26; and foreign policy, 30–34; and 1808 election, 32–36; and Whig Clubs, 37–38; and banking, 41; Grand Canal, 42, 43; splits with Spencer, 46–47; and 1812 election, 48–50; break with Van Buren 52; retains mayoralty, 52; conduct during war, 53; loss of mayoralty, 54–55; sponsors Erie Canal, 56–59; joins with Spencer, 57; and immigrants, 59–60; becomes governor, 59–61; split on canal policy, 62–63; and Federalists, 63; and Martling-Men, 66–67; and Missouri controversy, 68; and constitutional reforms, 71–73;

retires, 74; supports Jackson, 82–83; removal, 86–87; becomes governor, 89–90; and Van Buren, 96–99; backs Jackson, 108; dies, 109; mentioned, 150, 195, 240

Clinton, George, and Constitution, 13–14; and Tammany Society, 16–17; on Cheetham, 32; and 1808 election, 32–36; death, 46–47

Clinton, George, Jr., 25, 37

Cobb, Howell, 311, 313, 316

Cochrane, John, and West Committee, 256–57; and Pierce, 267, 270, 274; opposes Wood, 280–81; and Cuba, 286–87; supports Wood, 298, 309; becomes a Republican, 331; on 1862 election, 345

Coddington, Jonathan, 115, 215, 225

Coleman, William. See New York Evening Post

Conant, Samuel, 104

Congressional Caucus, 33, 47–48, 56, 85

Conner, James, 225, 237

Connolly, Richard, and Henry Genet, 336; and Mozart Hall, 341; breaks with Genet, 341–43; runs as an independent, 347; makes peace with Tweed, 358

Constitution, state (1777), 3–5, 12–13, 70–73

Constitution, state (1822), 70–73, 228–29

Constitution, state (1846), 228–29

Constitutional Union party, 322, 324

"Coody, Abimelech." See Gulian Verplanck

Cooper, Edward, 304, 308

Cooper, Peter, 275

Copperheads (Peace Democrats), 350–63

Corning, Erastus, 249–51, 295, 321

Council of Appointment, 12, 40, 42, 52, 54, 64, 73

Council of Revision, 12, 71, 72

Council of Sachems. See Tammany Society

Crawford, William, and local patronage, 61; election of 1824, 78–90; favors Adams, 107

Crolius, Clarkson, Jr., 123

Croswell, Edwin, dispute with Noah, 100; on Loco Focoism, 184; school reform, 198, joins Hunkers, 209; to Polk, 220; and patronage, 221; on Wright's death, 235; on progress, 247; on fusion, 250; and Whig split, 258; and Republicans, 331

Curtis, Edward, 172, 179

Cushing, Caleb, 335

Davis, Charles, 151, 159

Davis, Matthew L., and self-created societies, 22–24; joins Tammany, 25; and 1800 election, 26; "A Son of Tammany," 28; Burrites infiltrate Tammany Society, 31; dominates Tammany Society, 35–36; joins with Clinton, 38–40, 40–41; and Tompkins, 43–44; and birth of Tammany Hall, 45; and banks, 45; war profiteering, 49; and Clinton's removal, 54; and High Federalists, 69; and Clay, 81; supports Adams, 107; and Working Men's party, 122, 125; and Clayites, 126; and 1832 election, 142; "A Spy in Washington," 143; and Whigs, 150; and 1836 election, 175; and Whigs, 223, on political life, 374–75

"Dead Rabbits," 208, 306

Debt, Imprisonment for, 10, 122, 124, 126, 137, 371

Delevan, Daniel, 265, 269, 270

The Democrat (New York), 172

Democratic party, origins, 93, 95; Jacksonian coalition, 107. See also Tammany Hall, and Martin Van Buren

Democratic-Republican General Committee. See Tammany Hall

Democratic Review, 6, 244

Democratic Society, background and ideology, 20; and Tammany Society, 21–23; and "Jacobin" Conspiracy, 22

Democratic Vigilant Association, 317–18

Denman, William, 193

Denniston, David, 25

Depression of 1792, 16

Depression of 1819, 70

Depression of 1837, 173–84

Depression of 1857, 317

Dickinson, Daniel, background, 209; and Baltimore Convention, 241; on Van Buren, 244; on fusion, 247; and national stature, 253–56; loss of senate seat, 257; anger, 258–59; and Pierce, 274; and Tammany Society, 277; on Half Shells, 291–92; joins with Richmond, 314–15; on Douglas, 323; to Olcott, 325; joins Republicans, 329; runs for secretary of state, 331

Disney, David, 294–95

Dix, John A., and Loco Focoism, 170; and Marcy, 188; and Wright, 217; defeat in 1848, 246; on Tammany Hall, 247; and Pierce, 264, 274; on Wood, 311; declines to run for mayor, 354

Douglas, Stephen, premature presidential bid, 262; and Kansas-Nebraska bill, 279; and Tammany, 281; seeks 1856 nomination, 293–95; and Wood, 313; and 1860 election, 322–24

Draft Riot, 352

Duane, William, 50

Duer, William, 16

Dyde Affair, 39

Eckford, Henry, 89

Edgar, William, 40

Electioneering practices. See Electoral fraud, Municipal reform, Tammany Hall, and Tammany Society

Electoral fraud, 59, 84, 107, 167, 186, 188, 202, 219, 261, 269, 270–71, 285, 298, 300, 305, 308, 368

Electoral regulations. See Electoral fraud, Municipal reform, Tammany Hall, and Tammany Society

Ellicott, Joseph, 63

Embargo of 1807, 30–33

Emmett, Thomas Addis, 54, 58

Empire Club. See Mike Walsh

Equal Rights party, origins, 158–60; formed, 165–66; program, 167–68; and 1836 election, 171–72; and Van Buren, 177; fuses with Tammany Hall, 179–81; and nativism, 216; and 1846 state constitution, 228–29

Erie Canal. *See* DeWitt Clinton, Mordecai Noah, Tammany Hall, and Martin Van Buren
Ethnic group conflict. *See* Nativism
Evans, George, 123, 124, 154, 157, 158, 159

Fairlie, James, 105
Federalist party, early strength, 13–14; attacks Tammany, 22–24; New Federalists, 37–38; and 1812 election, 50; and Clinton, 52; resurgence, 52–53; aftermath of Hartford Convention, 53–54; and Governor Clinton, 63–64; High Federalists, 69; and Jackson, 83, 87, 107; patronage problems, 113; Tammanyism, 372–73. *See also New York Evening Post,* and Rufus King
Ferguson, John, as naval officer, 51; becomes mayor, 54
Ferris, Charles, 166
Fillmore, Millard, 219, 245, 257
Fish, Preserved, 177
Flagg, Azariah, and Jacksonian Democracy, 95; and Bank Democrats, 169, 175; and electoral reform, 190; and Power, 195; and Barnburners, 209, 235, 236
Flour Riot, 173
Forrest, Edwin, 253
Fowler, Isaac, postmaster, 274; and Cuba, 287; and Wood, 298; grand sachem, 310–11; and defalcation, 322
Free Soil party, formed, 244–45; defeated, 247. *See also,* Barnburners, Hards, Hunkers, Softs, Tammany Hall, and Martin Van Buren
Frémont, John C., 299
French Revolution, 18–22
Freneau, Philip, 25

Gallatin, Albert, 43
Gangs, youth, 4, 208, 306
Gardiner, Addison, 217, 231, 233
Gelston, David, 14
Genêt, Edmond, 20
Genet, Henry W., combination, 336; and 1862 Council election, 337–38;
and Knapp, 339–40; and Tammany Hall, 341–43; and Tammany Society, 346
Glentworth Affair, 197
Gouverneur, Samuel, appointed postmaster, 111; attacks Leggett, 164
Granger, Francis, 114, 117, 125, 140, 171
Greenleaf, Thomas, on French Revolution, 11; on Bank bill, 14–15; joins Tammany Society, 14; and "Tammany," 17; Gallomania, 18–24; mentioned, 75
Greeley, Horace, and *New Yorker,* 162; on illegal voters, 186; and Mexican War, 229; and temperance, 265; on Wood in 1859, 318; on free city, 327; on Wood, 328; on Seymour, 341; to Smith, 345; and Manifesto, 357
Greenwich Savings Bank, 146
Gunther, C. Godfrey, 354–55

Haff, John P., 48, 51
Half Shells, 290–92. *See also* Dickinson, Hards, and Sickles
Hall, A. Oakey, 288, 312, 332
Hamilton, Alexander, 3, 20
Hamilton, James, 64
Hammond, Jabez, 63, 126, 247
Hammond, Judah, 180, 182, 186
Hards, formed, 253–54; primary system, 268–69; back reform, 276; and Bronson, 274–75; and Redfield, 277; attacks Tammany Society, 272–73, 278; and Kansas-Nebraska bill, 278–80; in 1854 election, 282–86; and Sickles, 290–92; and Douglas, 293–95; at 1856 convention, 295–96; and Wood, 297. *See also* Fernando Wood, and Tammany Hall
Harper, James, 215, 216
Harrisburg Convention, 104
Hart, Emanuel, 210, 262, 292, 303, 357
Hart, Ephraim, 63–64
Hartford Convention, 53–54
Hauterive, Citizen, 19
Havemeyer, William, 224, 238, 317, 318, 333
Hegeman, Adrian, 48
Hibernian Provident Society, 65

High Federalists. *See* Federalist party, Rufus King, Tammany Hall, and Martin Van Buren

Hoffman, John T., 337, 362

Hoffman, Josiah Ogden, 17

Hoffman, Michael, 209, 222, 246

Holmes, Eldad, 61

Holt, Charles. *See New York Columbian*

Hone, Philip, 152, 154, 194

House of Refuge, 195

Houston, Samuel, 243

Hoyt, Jesse, 152, 171, 183

Hughes, Bishop John, and Webb, 162; supports Seward, 197–200; Carroll Hall movement, 201–203; house attacked, 207; Draft Riot and Greeley, 362

Hunkers, origin, 209; and Polk, 213; and patronage, 221–23; and Mexico, 227; and reform, 228; and war, 229; and Wright's death, 230–31; and Wilmot Proviso, 233, 235; and 1847 election, 233; Syracuse Convention, 235; on Van Buren and Free Soilers, 243–44; and Tammany Society, 244–45; fusion, 250–51; and Hards and Softs, 253. *See also* Edwin Croswell, Mordecai Noah, Tammany Hall, John Van Buren, and Martin Van Buren

Hunt, Washington, 258

Hunt, Wilson, 285

Immigrants. *See* DeWitt Clinton, Electoral fraud, Nativism, Tammany Hall, and Tammany Society

Independent Democrats. *See* Whig party

Irving, Peter, 51

Irving, William, 51

Jackson, Andrew, Battle of New Orleans, 53; and election, 83–90; and Adams, 94; rise of Jacksonian Democracy, 101; and tariff, 103; and 1828 election, 107–11; local patronage, 115–16; attacks Bank, 128; veto message, 140; election of 1832, 141–43; removals, 144; Loco Focos, 158; and Depression of 1837, 173; and Van Buren, 174; on fusion, 184; and Texas, 211

Jay, John, 16, 22

Jay Treaty, 25

Jeffersonian Free League, 243, 245

Jeffersonian Free Soil League, 245

Jefferson, Thomas, 26, 66–71; 105, 280, 377. *See also* Tammany Hall, Tammany Society, Tammanyism, and Martin Van Buren

Johnson, Richard, 137, 149, 160

Kansas-Nebraska bill, 278–80

Kelly, "Honest" John, and Irish, 297; supports Wood, 303–304; at Syracuse Convention, 313; and Tweed, 362; and Tammany Society, 368

Kelly, Robert, 283, 292, 296

Kendall, Amos, leaks message, 128; special agent, 146–47; and Leggett, 164

Kennedy, William, 310, 321, 330, 331

Ketchum, Hiram, 200, 333

Keteltas, William, 25

King, Charles, forms *New York American*, 67; and High Federalists, 69; supports Adams, 79; attacks Noah, 79; rejects Clinton, 82, 89, 90; and People's party, 97; and tariff, 103; and Conant, 104; and Adams' reelection, 111–12; and Bank, 131

King, John, 81, 84, 305

King, Preston, on Loco Focoism, 181; and Wilmot Proviso, 223; and slavery, 247; and fusion, 251; rejects Fugitive Slave Law, 257; and Republicans, 275

King, Rufus, on Republican-Interest, 16; and 1812 election, 50; dislikes Clinton, 63; rejects Tompkins, 68; and Missouri Controversy, 69; and High Federalists, 69; reelected, 70; and Adams, 83, 94, 107. *See also* Federalist party, and Martin Van Buren

Knapp, Shepard, 339–40

Knower, Benjamin, 117, 118, 135, 136, 147. *See also* William Marcy, and Thomas Olcott

Know-Nothing party, 284–85, 289, 292, 299. *See also* Nativism.

Lawrence, Cornelius, and Biddle, 141; congressman, 142; and removals, 147; favors third national bank, 152; runs for mayor, 153–56; veto of registry bill, 162; reelected, 169; appointed collector, 226; and Barnburners, 246

Lawrence, John, 119

Lee, Gideon, 153, 172, 186

Leggett, William, joins *Evening Post*, 129; attacks Webb, 148–49; on reform, 157, 158, 159; on abolition, 163–65; ill-health, 166; forms *Plaindealer*, 176. *See also* Equal Rights party, and Tammany Hall

Lewis, Morgan, 29, 32, 108

Libby, James, 298

Lincoln, Abraham, 315, 328, 330, 339, 345, 363

Little Band. *See* Aaron Burr, and Matthew Davis

Livingston, Brockholst, 14

Livingston, Charles, 130, 131, 134, 142, 151, 162, 169

Livingston, Edward, 372

Livingston, Maturin, 59

Livingston, Robert R, 16, 29, 33, 372

Loco Foco party. *See* Equal Rights party

Lynch, James, 332, 335

Maclay, Robert, 242, 245

Maclay, William, 199, 205–207, 220

Macomb, Robert, 46

Macready, William, 253

Madison, James, opposed by Cheetham, 32–33; election of 1808, 34–35; and Tompkins, 43; decline in popularity, 44–45; and War of 1812, 48–50; election of 1812, 50; changes patronage policy, 51

Main, James, 75

*The Man* (New York), 155, 156

Mann, Abijah, 173

Marble, Manton, and Barnard, 354; and McClellan, 359; and Central Executive Committee, 362

Marcy, William, 68, 140; runs for governor, 141; reelected, 159; conservatism, 174–75; on fusion, 178; on

Bank Democrats, 183; loss to Seward, 187; and Hunkers, 209; and Polk, 222; on Wright, 226–27, 230; on split, 237; repairs party, 249–52; distrusts Van Burenites, 258; bid for presidency, 260–61; duped, 261–64; and Pierce, 274; and Wood, 278; and Kansas-Nebraska bill

Martling, Abraham (tavern owner), 30; opposes Clinton, 34

Martlingism, origin, 34; and banking, 41–42; and Tammany Society, 38–40; merges into Tammany Hall, 44

Martling-Men. *See* Martlingism

McClellan, George, and Tweed, 358; nominated for presidency, 360; rejects peace plank, 361; defeated, 362–63

McElrath, Thomas, 215

McKeon Democrats, formed 353; at 1863 convention, 353; nominate Gunther, 354–55; and McClellan, 360; and Tammany Hall, 361–62

McKeon, John, and Irish, 186; and Polk, 213; and Barnburners, 227; political independent, 253; district attorney, 303; supports Tiemann, 309; reasserts independence, 325. *See also* McKeon Democrats

Meigs, Henry, 66–67, 71, 375–76

Melville, Gansevoort, and Van Buren, 212–13; on naturalization, 219

Metropolitan Police Force, 305–306

Mickel, Andrew, 230, 254

Ming, Alexander, Jr., 165, 169

Ming, Alexander, Sr., 123

Missouri Crisis, 68–70. *See also* DeWitt Clinton, Mordecai Noah, Rufus King, and Martin Van Buren

Mitchill, Samuel Latham, 37, 48

Monroe, James, and 1808 election, 33; as President, 77; and 1824 election, 85

Mooney, William, 11, 28

Moore, Eli, 158, 186

Morehead Resolution, 130, 132

*Morning Courier and New York Enquirer*, 395

Morris, Gouverneur, 42, 43

Morris, Robert, 120, 214, 215, 265

Morse, Samuel F. B., 169

Mozart Hall. *See* Tammany Hall, and Fernando Wood

Mozart Regiment, 329, 350

Mumford, John, 132

Municipal reform, 120–21, 190, 213–20, 228, 234, 250, 262, 265, 275, 276, 284–85, 305–306, 320

Nagle, David, 201, 203

*The National Advocate* (New York), 51, 58, 60–62, 64–65, 89–90, 99–100, 104, 109, 111, 122. *See also* Noah, and Wheaton

National Republican party, formed, 93; organization, 127; and Whigs, 150. *See also* Adams, Clay, Tammany Hall, and Webb

Native American Democratic Association, 161–63, 185

*Native American Independent Press* (New York), 163

Nativism, and Tammany Society, 9–10, 66, 367, 369–70; and Webb and Noah, 161–63; and Clark, 185, 187; and school issue, 193–207; pivotal year, 202; American Republican party, 214–16, 224; and temperance, 265, 282; and Hards, 266; and Know-Nothings, 282–83; and Draft Riots, 352

New Albany Regency. *See* Dean Richmond

*New Era* (New York), 175, 182, 186, 200

*New York American*, formation, 67; supports Adams, 80–92; and DeWitt Clinton, 97. *See also* Charles King

*New York Columbian*, edited by Holt, 39; and Martlingism, 44; and election of 1812, 50; and War of 1812, 52; and Irish, 56–57

*New York Columbian Gazetteer*, 35

*New York Daily Advertiser*, 23, 24

*New York Daily Express*, 175, 189

*New York Daily News*, 300, 328, 351

*New York Enquirer*, 99, 100, 110, 133. *See also* Mordecai Noah

*New York Evening Post* (1795), 23–26

*New York Evening Post*, edited by Coleman, 28; and Tammany Society, 35; opposes caucus, 77–80; and Adams, 81; and Clinton, 87; on free trade, 103; on Working Men's party, 125; and Bryant and Leggett, 128–29; on Verplanck, 141; abolitionism, 163–65; on Equal Rights party, 166; on school reform, 193, 195, 198, 204; and Texas, 218; and extensionism, 222, 229; and Barnburners, 234; on Tammany Society, 245; and Free Soil party, 247

*New York Herald*. *See* James Gordon Bennett

*New York Irish-American*, 258, 300, 309, 327, 357. *See also* Fernando Wood

*New York Journal and Patriotic Register*. *See* Thomas Greenleaf

*New York Journal of Commerce*, 340

*New York Leader*, on secession, 327–29; criticizes Wood, 329; patriotism, 329; on War Democrats, 330; on Peace Democrats, 334; calls for fusion, 335–36; on Genet, 336–38; fusion with Wood, 343–44; loss of election, 350; and Manifesto, 357–58; and state convention, 361–63; Tweed's triumph, 363; on organization, 366

*New York Morning Courier*, 113, 120

*New York Morning News*, 217, 219, 224, 227, 229, 230

*New York National Advocate*, 96, 98, 99. *See also* Noah

*New York Observer*, 205

*New York Patriot*, 80, 85

*New York Plaindealer*, 176

*New York Public Advertiser*, 36–37, 39–40, 44

*New-York Times*, 159, 163–65, 166, 174

*New York Times*, 309, 314

*New York Tribune*. *See* Horace Greeley

*New York World*. *See* Manton Marble

*New Yorker*. *See* Horace Greeley

Ninth Resolution, 330

Noah, Mordecai, characteristics, 58; opposes Erie, 58–60; nativism, 60; shifts on Erie, 62; rejects King, 64; supports

Erie, 65–66; and Missouri, 68–70; constitutional reform, 70–74; loses sheriff job, 79; and Adams, 80; and Jackson, 82; and Yates, 86; plots against Clinton, 86–87; dismissed, 89–90; on political parties, 95; support for Jackson, 96; forms *Enquirer*, 99; and Croswell, 99–100; on Anti-Masons, 103; on Clinton's death, 110; and Webb, 113; loss, 114; on 1828 campaign, 112–14; fuses with Webb, 120; attacks Bank, 128; loan, 132–34; bribery, 136, 138; nativism, 161–63; as Whig, 223; forms *Sunday Times and Noah's Weekly Messenger*, 223; on party split, 238; on party reunion, 248, 252; and Tammany Society, 254–55; on reconciliation, 259; on parties, 374
Nullification crisis, 132, 145

O'Conor, Charles, 182, 274, 281, 284
Olcott, Thomas, 117, 118, 135, 147, 325
Opdyke, George, 318, 333, 335, 348, 351
O'Sullivan, John L., and school reform, 198, 204–206; editor, 222; on nativism, 224; on extensionism, 229; and organization, 364
Owen, Robert Dale, 122, 123

Paulding, William K., 155
People's party, formed, 84–86; and Clinton, 87–90; importance, 92–93; demise, 97
Pewter Mug Democrats, 122–23
Pierce, Franklin, 264, 267–68, 274–77, 279, 295
Pintard, John, 10, 72–73, 110
Polk, James, nominated, 212–13; local patronage, 221–23, 225–26; and Wright, 227; and extensionism, 229; local popularity, 230; and Hunkers, 231
Population (New York City), 3, 75–76, 232, 365
Porter, Peter, 60, 124
Power, Reverend John, 195
Price, William, Tammany moderate, 178; defalcation, 188
Proclamation of Neutrality, 19

Pruyn, John V. L., and fusion, 249–51; favors Douglas, 295; on Seymour, 317; Peace Democrat, 338; on Wood, 359
Public School Society, 192, 193, 195, 205–207
Purdy, Elijah, 184, 189; and 1844 election, 217; and Polk, 221, 222; and Texas, 222–23; and Tammany Society's potential, 225–26; party reorganization, 253–54; use of Tammany Society, 272–73; and Douglas, 281; and Shepard, 289; against Wood, 301–303; and Tweed, 320; and secession, 327; and Peace Democrats, 331; and reunion, 335–36; and emancipation, 340–41; replaced by Tweed, 347; and war, 351–52
Purser, George, 357

Ramsey, Albert, 315
Redfield, Herman, 277, 287, 298
Registry Law, 193–94, 320
Republican-Interest, origins, 13–16; 1792 election, 16–17; and Tammany Society, 16; and French Revolution, 17–20; and Democratic Society, 21; and national party, 24; and Tammanyism, 371–74
Republican party, origins, 279–82, 285; and Kansas, 290; increases strength, 292; and 1856 election, 299; and reform, 305, 308; and Wood, 318–19; and Lincoln, 321; and secession, 325, 328; Union Defense League, 329; and Opdyke, 334–35; and emancipation, 34; and Cochrane, 345
Restraining Act, 169, 172
Richmond, Dean, and New Albany Regency, 295; and 1856 convention, 295–96; and Wood, 313; tricks Dickinson, 316–17; and fusion, 321–23; and war, 327; uncertainty, 330; and Peace Democrats, 356; and McClellan, 359
Riker, Richard, 170, 183, 186
Rochester, William, 99, 129
Romaine, Benjamin, 30, 60, 105
Root, Erastus, 75, 125

Rynders, Isaiah, founder of Empire Club, 4, 208; and Astor Place Riot, 253; and Softs, 257; and reform, 276, to Marcy, 293; and Buchanan, 303; and secession, 327

Safety Fund, 116–18, 125
Sanford, Nathan, 42
Savage, 301–303, 307
Schell, Augustus, and Tammany Hall, 264; rejects peace, 370; joins Wood, 303, and patronage, 306, 315
Selden, Dudley, 131, 134, 141, 223
Seventh Ward Bank Scandal, 146,
Seward, William, 186–87, 192–95, 196–207, 285, 334
Seymour, Henry, 64
Seymour, Horatio, and Marcy, 227, and Hammond, 247; at Syracuse Convention, 249–51; and Hards and Softs, 253, 254; nominated 257; defeated, 258; renominated and wins, 265, 268; and Kansas-Nebraska bill, 279; loss, 286; on Half Shells, 291; and 1860 campaign, 317, 322; and Peace Democrats, 331, 338; race for governor, 341, 345; and Waterbury, 349; and draft riot, 351–52; and 1864 election, 360
Shepard, Lorenzo, and Marcy, 223; and party fusion, 251; and California, 253; and primary system, 256–57; and Marcy, 261–64; and Purdy, 266; and primary system, 268–71; and Wood, 278; and Kansas-Nebraska bill, 279; and Schell, 280; break with Pierce, 284, 289; grand sachem, 289, and Sickles, 291–92; as peacemaker, 293; premature death, 298
Sickles, Daniel, characteristics of, 251; and fusion, 251–52; and California, 252; and Rynders, 253; dupes Marcy, 261–63; and registry system, 268–70; and Half Shells, 290–92; and Buchanan, 306–307; and Wood, 310; and wife, 316
Skidmore, 122, 123
Slamm, Levi, 178, 180, 212, 218, 436

Slavery, 10, 231–32, 338, 352, 377. See also, Barnburners, Hards, Hunkers, Softs, Tammany Hall, and Tammany Society
Small, Wilson, 296, 297, 301, 303, 304
Smith, Melancton, 14
Snowden, James, 93, 104
Social changes, 2–6, 75–76, 208–209, 296–303, 365, 367, 369–70, 379–80
Society for the Diffusion of Political Knowledge, 350
Softs, formed, 253–54; and Purdy, 268; primary system, 268–69; back reform, 276; and Redfield, 277; and Kansas-Nebraska bill, 279–80; in 1854 campaign, 282–83; and Seymour, 285–86; and Sickles, 290–92; and Douglas, 293–95; at 1856 convention, 295–96; and Wood, 297
"A Son of Tammany," 28
Southwick, Solomon, 41, 47
Spartan Club. See Isaiah Rynders
Spencer, Ambrose, 46–47, 51, 54, 56–58, 73
Spencer, John, 96, 199
Spirit of '76 (New York), 163
Stagg, Peter, 102, 105
Stilwell, Silas, 124, 126, 142, 146, 151, 154
Stop and Tax Law, 209, 227
Strong, George Templeton, 329
Stuyvesant Institute Democracy, 273, 291, 295, 296
Suffrage, 12–13, 70–73, 81, 94, 96, 167–68, 228–29, 374. See also Electoral fraud, Nativism, Tammany Hall, and Tammany Society
Sunday Times and Noah's Weekly Messenger. See Mordecai Noah
Swartwout, John, 51
Swartwout, Robert, 51, 223
Swartwout, Samuel, joins Tammany Society, 51; Pan-American dinner, 96–97; as collector, 115–16; ignores Tammany, 125; on recharter, 134; and Biddle, 148; and fusion, 171; becomes a Whig, 182; and defalcation, 188
Sweeny, Peter B., character, 296; General Committee chairman, 310; and

reform, 336, 344; Manifesto, 357; and Wood, 362

Swift, Joseph, 80, 96, 102

Syracuse Convention (1847), 235; (1850), 249–51; (1851), 257; (1857), 314; (1858), 317

Tallmadge, James, 89, 94–95, 108

Tallmadge, Mathias, 47

Tallmadge, Nathaniel P., 177

Tamanend, 8

Tammany Hall, confusion in terms, 1–2; humanitarianism, 3–4, 10, 29, 37–38, 167–68, 308, 320, 367–68; nominating methods, 14, 16, 33, 47–48, 56, 76–77, 167–68, 296–303, 355, 356, 364–65; origin, 45, discipline (party usages) 45, 75–76, 93, 112–13, 167–68, 288, 320, 364–65; and Tompkins, 46–47; caliber of leadership, 49, 209, 284, 320, 368, 369; and War of 1812, 52–55; and patronage, 53, 115, 167–68, 183, 221–23, 231, 306, 315, 320, 364–66, 370; purges Clinton, 54–55; opposes canal, 57–58; Irish riot, 58–62; and Van Buren, 61; and Bucktails, 63; changes on canal, 65–66; and Meigs, 66–67; and Tompkins, 67–69; and High Federalists, 69; and reform, 70–74; organizational changes, 75–77, 208–209, 296–303, 369–70, 372; use of newspapers, 75; and Crawford, 79–90; and People's party, 84–93; and Democracy, 93–95; and reform, 97; and Jackson, 98; and Jeffersonianism, 100–101; and tariff, 103; and Adamsites, 107; and Clinton merger, 109; anti-auction movement, 111–13; and 1828 election, 114; Safety Fund, 117–19; new charter, 120–21; workie revolt, 122–27; and Bank War, 128–37; and Webb, 141; and 1832 election, 142; nullification, 144–45; Bank Democrats, 148–49; and Whigs, 150–56; and Equal Rights party, 158–62; and nativists, 162–63; and Leggett, 163–65; and merger with Loco Focos, 166–85; illegal naturalization, 186, 219; and Marcy, 187; electoral fraud, 191;

school reform, 193–202; critical point, 202; and Calhoun, 210–11; and Texas, 212, 222; nativism, 213–16; and Polk, 216–22; Barnburners and Hunkers, 220, 226–27, 235; and slavery, 231–34; and Barnburners, 237; Free Soil movement, 242–47; and Dix, 247; and Wood, 248; decline, 249–52; and California, 253–54; and Purdy, 255–56; Syracuse formula, 257–58; election abuse, 261; and Sickles, 271–74; Democratic Union Clubs, 267–70; and Softs and Hards, 271–74; and Stuyvesant Institute Democracy, 273, 291, 295, 296; and reform, 275–77; and Redfield, 277; and Shepard, 280; Wood's victory, 283–85; Cuba, 287–88; Know-Nothings, 289; and Half Shells, 291; and Democratic Association System, 296–301; and Buchanan's patronage, 303; legislative interference, 305–306, 366; police riot, 305–306; and Tiemann, 309; and Richmond, 313; and Democratic Vigilants, 317; Tweed's emergence, 319–22; corruption, 320, 377; efficiency, 320, 364, 370, 377; fusion, 321–24; secession, 325–28; patriotism, 329–30; politics of war, 329–30; and Wood, 335; Genet, 336–40; and emancipation, 341; fusion with Wood, 343–44; Tweed's mastery, 346–63; localism, 363; and slavery, 377

Tammany, Saint, 8

Tammany Society, confusion in terms, 1–2; origins, 8–9; as fraternal order, 10–11; class composition, 12, 25, 77, 167–68, 223, 265, 320, 337, 366; and banking, 15–16; and 1792 election, 16–17; and French Revolution, 18–22; and Democratic Society, 21–22; and Jay, 22; self-created society issue, 22–24; decline in membership, 24–25; helps form Republican party, 25; and 1801 election, 26–27; and Burr, 28–29; and Burrites, 30–31; and Martlingism, 43–44; new Wigwam, 45; control of Long Room, 45, 78, 89, 104–107; 169, 182–84, 208, 221–22, 245, 265, 272–73,

Tammany Society (*Continued*)
348, 349, 366, 378; and Clinton, 52;
and High Federalists, 69; decline, 77–
78; rents Long Room, 88; and Jackson, 96; and Adamsites, 104–107, 111,
114; attacks Webb, 139; and banking,
143; greets Jackson, 145; and Johnson,
147; rebuffs Loco Focos, 169; judges
regularity, 182–84; political potential,
208; and Texas, 221–22; and Purdy,
225–26; and Barnburners, 236, 244;
and Free Soil Party, 245; and party
reorganization, 253–57; duped by
Sickles, 261–63; used by Purdy, 265;
and Pierce, 267; and Purdy, 272–73;
finds identity, 274; and Dickinson,
377; and Douglas, 281; and Cuba,
287–88; anti-Wood, 301–20; and
Genet, 337–38; and emancipation, 340–
41; controlled by Tweed, 348, 349,
358; summary of position, 367
Tammany Tontine, 15–16
Tammanyism, 11, 25, 66–67, 167–68, 320,
355–56, 366, 370–80
Tappan brothers, 163
Tariff of 1828, 103–104, 112–14
Tariff of 1846, 230
Taylor, John, 52, 69
Taylor, Zachary, 245, 256
Thomas, J. Addison, 261–64
Throop, Enos, 115, 125, 126, 141, 153,
174
Tiemann, Daniel, 309, 321
Tilden, Samuel, 211, 217, 239, 266, 319
*Time Piece* (New York), 25
Todd, William, 88
Tompkins, Daniel D., and Martlingism,
40–41; prorogues legislature, 45–47;
alliance with Tammany Hall, 46–47;
as war leader, 53–54; becomes vice
president, 56–57; gives up governor-
ship, 67–69; runs for governor, 67–70;
retires, 85
*Trent* Affair, 335
*Truth Teller* (New York), 187, 193, 200
Tucker, Gideon J., 307, 308, 313, 314,
328
Tweed, William Marcy, 209; and Corporation, 265; opposes Wood, 284,

and Libby, 298; early career, 319–21;
runs for sheriff, 331–32, 335; and
Genet, 336–37; and Tammany Society in 1862, 337–38; defeats Genet,
342–44; fuses with Wood, 343; and
*Leader*, 344; deal with Wood, 347;
and street department, 348; and Seymour, 349; becomes grand sachem,
349; and 1863 council election, 353–
54; as reformer, 355–56; and Richmond, 356; and Manifesto, 356–57;
and McClellan, 359; and state convention, 361; on Central Executive
Committee, 362; triumph, 363; and
Tammanyism, 368, 377, 379–80
Tylee, Daniel, 120, 131, 132, 138
Tyler, John, 210, 216, 217, 222

Ullman, Daniel, 245, 282
Ulshoeffer, Michael, 70, 72, 79
Union Defense League, 329
Urbanism, 2–4, 6, 75–76, 208–209, 367–
68, 379–80. *See also* Municipal reform,
and Population

Vallandingham, Clement L., 350–51, 359
Van Beuren, Coertland, 24, 274
Van Buren, John, as speculator, 153;
bitterness, 237; and Martin Van
Buren, 239–40; on Barnburners, 242–
43; accepts Syracuse formula, 251;
and Astor Place Riot, 253; and Hards
and Softs, 253–54; at New Orleans
Ball, 259; and Marcy, 261, 263; and
Pierce, 270; on Redfield, 277; and
Kansas-Nebraska bill, 280; on Cuba,
288; and Wise, 289; and Know-Nothings, 291; aids Tiemann, 309; and
Loyalty League, 350; and McClellan,
361
Van Buren, Martin, 6, 47; and 1812
election, 50; breaks with Clinton, 52;
on canal, 57–58; and Tammany Hall,
61; and Bucktails, 63; and Federalists,
63–64; and Tompkins, 67–69; and
King, 68–70; and reform, 74–76; and
caucus, 78–79; and Crawford, 79–90;
and Adams, 93–94; aligns with Clinton, 96–99; and Jacksonian Democ-

racy, 100; and tariff, 104; on 1827 election, 106; becomes governor, 114; becomes secretary of state, 115; and Jackson's patronage, 115–16; and Safety Fund, 116–18; and Bank, 128; nominated for vice president, 137; opposes new Bank, 153–54; nominated for president, 160; on Leggett, 164; and Equal Rights party, 169–79; tours New York, 190–91; loss of presidency, 197; seeks renomination, 209; on Texas, 211–13; rejected, 212–13; helps Polk, 219; anger, 221; and Barnburners, 238–41; on candidacy, 243, 244–45; defeated, 247; on Hards, 258; endorses Pierce, 268; and Republicans, 295; and Tilden, 319, on organizational politics, 365; and Tammany Hall, 366

Vanderpoel, Aaron, 181, 264

Van Ness, Cornelius, 217, 223–25

Van Ness, William P., as "Aristides," 36; federal judge, 51; rents Long Room, 88; and Jackson, 89–90; dies, 102

Van Schaick, Myndert, 124, 152, 179, 249, 317

Varian, Isaac, 142, 146, 186, 189

Verplanck, Gulian, and Washington Clubs, 35; splits with Clinton, 54; as "Abimelech Coody," 67; and anti-auction movement, 112–13; Bank loan, 119, aids Bank, 131; on Burrows, 133; loss of Tammany Hall's support, 141; and tariff, 145; becomes Whig, 150, runs for mayor, 154–56; on school issue, 200; on electoral fraud, 368

Verplanck, Johnston, 66

Wadsworth, James, 262, 341

Wallabout Celebration, 35

Walsh, Mike, and Spartan Club, 4, 208; and school reform, 201, 203; and gangs, 209; and Calhoun, 210; and Hards, 251, 252, 278

Washington, George, 8, 13, 21, 22, 24, 26, 222

Waterbury, Nelson J., 266, 332, 345, 349, 358

Webb, James Watson, 113; fuses with Noah, 120, and Bank, 128, supports Morehead, 131, Burrows loan, 132–34; on recharter, 135; bribery, 136, 138; dilemma, 138–40; attack on Jackson, 140–42; and nullification, 144; attacks Leggett, 148–49; and Whig party, 150–51; baits Irish, 156; nativism, 161–63, 186; on Equal Rights party, 179; and Barlow, 328

Webster, Daniel, 109

Weed, Thurlow, 91, 94, 103, 146, 185, 201, 257, 285, 290, 338

West, Edward, 257, 258, 265, 278

Western, Henry, 249, 251–54

Westervelt, Harmon, 195

Westervelt, Jacob, 269, 270

Wetmore, Prosper, 174, 178, 251, 278

Wheaton, Henry, 51, 91, 102

Whig Clubs, 37–39

Whig party, formed, 150–52; 1834 mayoralty race, 154–56; new coalition, 185; and nativism, 214–16; and Clay, 219; and 1848 election, 245–46; and Fillmore, 248; and Kansas-Nebraska bill, 280–82; and Republicans, 285, 290

Whiskey Rebellion, 22

White, Campbell, 112

Whiting, James R., 285

Wigwam. *See* Tammany Society

Willcocks, William, 23

Willett, Marinus, 39, 42–43

Wise, Henry, 289, 310, 311, 316

Wood, Benjamin, 324, 331, 361

Wood, Fernando, 216, on 1844 election, 219; on Van Ness, 225; on Van Buren, 238; his character, 248; and Hards and Softs, 254; fusion committee, 256–57; nomination and defeat, 258; purge of John Van Buren, 278; and Kansas-Nebraska bill, 281–82; and reform, 284–85; "model mayor," 285–89; and Tammany Society, 289; backs Buchanan, 291, 299; as peacemaker, 293; allied with Sickles, 297; second term, 299; acquires *Daily News*, 300; and Tammany Hall elections, 301, seeks control over Tammany Society, 301;

Wood, Fernando (*Continued*)
loss, 304; and police, 306; and depression, 308; and Irish, 309; loss to Tiemann, 309; and Lecompton, 310; failure to control Tammany Society, 311–12; forms Mozart Hall, 312; and Douglas, 313; and Buchanan, 314–15; and 1857 convention, 317; and re-election, 318; fusion ticket, 323–24; new status, 325; and secession, 326–28; patriotism, 329; and Peace Democrats, 331, 333; and Seward, 334; *Trent Affair*, 335; and Genet, 339–40; seeks aid from Lincoln, 339; and emancipation, 340–41; deal with Tweed, 347; national links with party Peace Democrats, 349; and draft, 345–53; Mozart Hall splits, 353–54; and Peace Democrat meeting, 359; and national convention, 361; defeated, 363; and slavery, 377

Woodbury, Levi, 260
Woodhull, Caleb, 249
*Working Man's Advocate (New York)*, 123, 137, 144, 149, 156, 158, 165, 166
Working Men's party, origins, 121–23; and Clay, 123–24; failure, 126–27
Wortman, Tunis, 14, 37, 38, 374
Wright, Frances, 122, 123
Wright, Silas, on Clinton, 97, on Safety Fund, 117; on Bank, 131, 137, 153; on Equal Rights movement, 178; and Van Buren's candidacy, 211; rejects vice-presidency, 212; runs for governor, 217–20; declines cabinet post, 221; and Polk, 226; problems as governor, 230; loses election, 230; and slavery, 231–33; and Barnburners, 234; dies, 235; and party discipline, 366

*Young America* (New York), 262